D0214381

ROBBING THE JEWS

Robbing the Jews reveals the mechanisms by which the Nazis and their allies confiscated Jewish property; the book demonstrates the close relationship between robbery and the Holocaust. The spoliation evolved in intensifying steps. The Anschluss and Kristallnacht in 1938 reveal a dynamic tension between pressure from below and state-directed measures. In Western Europe, the economic persecution of the Jews took the form of legal decrees and administrative measures. In Eastern Europe, authoritarian governments adopted the Nazi program that excluded Jews from the economy and seized their property, based on indigenous antisemitism and plans for ethnically homogenous nation-states. In the occupied East, property was collected at the killing sites – the most valuable objects were sent to Berlin, whereas items of lesser value supported the local administration and rewarded collaborators. At several key junctures, robbery acted as a catalyst for genocide, accelerating the progression from pogrom to mass murder.

Martin Dean is an Applied Research Scholar at the United States Holocaust Memorial Museum's Center for Advanced Holocaust Studies in Washington, DC. He received a scholarship in history from Queens' College, Cambridge, in 1980 and was awarded his PhD also at Queens' in 1989. His publications include *Collaboration in the Holocaust: Crimes of the Local Police in Belorussia and Ukraine, 1941–44* (2000); *Austrian Policy during the French Revolutionary Wars, 1796–99* (1993); and numerous articles. He has also worked as a Staff Historian for the Australian Special Investigations Unit and as the Senior Historian for the Metropolitan Police War Crimes Unit in London (1992–97). He has held a DAAD grant and was awarded the Pearl Resnick Post-Doctoral Fellowship by the United States Holocaust Memorial Museum in 1997. He has acted as an expert witness in Nazi war crimes cases in Australia and Germany.

Robbing the Jews

The Confiscation of Jewish Property in the Holocaust, 1933–1945

Martin Dean

*Published in association with the
United States Holocaust Memorial Museum*

UNITED STATES
HOLOCAUST
MEMORIAL MUSEUM

CAMBRIDGE
UNIVERSITY PRESS

CAMBRIDGE UNIVERSITY PRESS

Cambridge, New York, Melbourne, Madrid, Cape Town, Singapore, São Paulo, Delhi

Cambridge University Press
32 Avenue of the Americas, New York, NY 10013-2473, USA

www.cambridge.org
Information on this title: www.cambridge.org/9780521888257

© United States Holocaust Memorial Museum 2008

This publication is in copyright. Subject to statutory exception
and to the provisions of relevant collective licensing agreements,
no reproduction of any part may take place without
the written permission of Cambridge University Press.

First published 2008

Printed in the United States of America

A catalog record for this publication is available from the British Library.

Library of Congress Cataloging in Publication Data

Dean, Martin, 1962–
Robbing the Jews : the confiscation of Jewish property in the Holocaust, 1933–1945 /
Martin Dean.
p.   cm.
Includes bibliographical references and index.
ISBN 978-0-521-88825-7 (hardback)
1. World War, 1939–1945 – Confiscations and contributions.   2. Holocaust, Jewish
(1939–1945) – Economic aspects.   3. Jewish property – Europe.   4. Aryanization.   I. Title.
D810.C8.D43   2008
940.53′18132 – dc22   2008008538

ISBN   978-0-521-88825-7 hardback

The assertions, opinions, and conclusions in this book are those of the author. They do not
necessarily reflect those of the United States Holocaust Memorial Council
or of the United States Holocaust Memorial Museum.

Cambridge University Press has no responsibility for
the persistence or accuracy of URLs for external or
third-party Internet Web sites referred to in this publication
and does not guarantee that any content on such
Web sites is, or will remain, accurate or appropriate.

CONTENTS

v

CONCORDIA UNIVERSITY LIBRARY
PORTLAND, OR 97211

LIST OF PHOTOGRAPHS

ACKNOWLEDGMENTS

Very many persons have supported my extensive research on this book over the past nine years, including archivists, scholars, librarians, colleagues, and administrators. It is not possible to name every one, but I wish to express my thanks here to many of those who have given me some of their most precious possessions – their time, energy, and expertise.

Foremost thanks must go to Paul Shapiro, Director of the Center for Advanced Holocaust Studies at the United States Holocaust Memorial Museum, for assigning me to this research project at the end of the 1990s and gently encouraging its completion along the way. Of my many colleagues in the Center, special thanks must go to Juergen Matthaeus, Wendy Lower, Severin Hochberg, Avinoam Patt, Suzanne Brown-Fleming, Ann Millin, Peter Black, Lisa Yavnai, Patricia Heberer, and many others, for their advice and support on a daily basis. Reference archivists Aaron Kornblum and Michlean Amir have been especially patient and helpful, and I have also benefited enormously from the Museum's outstanding collections of photographs and books. Thanks go also to Benton Arnovitz, Director of Academic Publications, for skillfully steering this project through to completion, and to Michael Gelb for his diligent and incisive editing.

Many archives and other institutions, especially in Germany, have assisted with the research, making available photocopies and granting me in some cases privileged access to specific collections. Among these, particular thanks should go to Klaus Dettmer at the Landesarchiv and Frau Kube of the Oberfinanzdirektion in Berlin, Alfons Kenkmann and his colleagues at the Villa ten Hompel in Münster, Gerd Blumberg of the Zollstelle Münster, Manfred Pohl and the staff of the Historical Archive of Deutsche Bank in Frankfurt, the staff of the Bundesarchiv in Berlin-Lichterfelde, and many other archivists.

I have had the opportunity to present draft versions of parts of several chapters as conference papers or guest lectures during the gestation of the book. For these welcome opportunities to test my ideas, thanks go to Susanne Meinl and the Fritz Bauer Institute; Claus Füllberg-Stolberg at the University of Hannover; Saulius Suziedelis and the organizers of the Annual Holocaust Conference in Millersville, Pennsylvania; the Center for Advanced Holocaust Studies; the Society for European Business History; the Max-Planck Institute for European Legal History, Frankfurt am Main; the Institute for Contemporary History, Munich; and especially Florent Brayard and Marc-Olivier Baruch and their respective institutes in Paris.

Many other scholars, including a series of distinguished Visiting Fellows at the Center for Advanced Holocaust Studies, have influenced and assisted me with my work, both through their own research and in numerous discussions and scholarly exchanges. Again, these individuals are too legion to mention all by name, but my thanks go to Jean Ancel, Götz Aly, Claire Andrieu, Britta Bopf, Richard Breitman, Bernhard Chiari, Jeanne Dingell, Bernward Dörner, Jean-Marc Dreyfus, Wesley Fisher, Wolf Gruner, Christian Gerlach, Peter Hayes, Susanne Heim, Helen Junz, Eric Laureys, Ingo Loose, Bernhard Lorentz, Regula Ludi, Marc Masurovsky, Lynn Nicholas, Ilana Offenberger, Ilaria Pavan, Jonathan Petropoulos, Dieter Pohl, Steven Sage, Kurt Schilde, Tatjana Toensmeyer, Philipp Ther, Bob Waite, James Ward, Susanne Willems, and Dieter Ziegler.

A particular word of appreciation is owed to the late Raul Hilberg, who not only founded the modern field of Holocaust studies but also integrated the role of expropriation directly into his comprehensive analysis of the Holocaust. Needless to say, his seminal work, *The Destruction of the European Jews*, is cited more frequently than any other in this book. In addition to the loss of Raul Hilberg, another severe blow just prior to publication was the sad loss of Gerald Feldman, whose outstanding work in German economic history I have admired since my student days. Gerry always gave me tremendous inspiration and support, as both a friend and a colleague during the research and writing of this monograph.

Very special thanks also go to Ralph Banken, Frank Bajohr, Constantin Goschler, Joe White, and Sarah Harasym for their careful reading of the manuscript, and their useful comments, suggestions, and corrections. Despite all this help, I must remain solely responsible for any mistakes that may have crept into a book of this length and breadth, and I thank in advance you the reader, for your patience and any comments you may wish to offer. Finally, I wish to dedicate this work to my charming daughter Iris, who came into this world shortly after I started this project.

Martin Dean, July 2008

INTRODUCTION

Registration and Confiscation

On April 26, 1938, Field Marshal Hermann Göring ordered the registration of Jewish property in the Third Reich by June 30, 1938. Under the terms of this decree, it was possible for Göring "to secure the deployment of the registered property in accordance with the needs of the German economy."[1] Thus, as the Foreign Office acknowledged internally, by creating an inventory of remaining Jewish property, Göring was preparing the ground for its subsequent systematic confiscation by the state.[2] Victor Klemperer commented in his diary on June 29, 1938, "We spent the morning filling out the forms: Property List of the Jews. . . . What do they want this list for? We have become so used to living in this condition of lost rights and waiting for the next despicable attacks that it hardly disturbs us any more."[3]

In archives throughout Europe, millions of such property registration forms from the Nazi period can be found. A similar process of property registration was repeated for Jews attempting to emigrate, and even for those awaiting deportation and murder. Germany's allies and collaborating states, such as Vichy France, Romania, Bulgaria, Croatia, Slovakia, and Hungary, all introduced similar measures against Jewish property, as did the Nazi authorities in the countries Germany occupied directly. Beginning in the fall of 1941, the arrival of the "list" to be filled out describing their

---

[1] *Reichsgesetzblatt*, 1938, Teil I, pp. 414–16.

[2] See Nuremberg Document NG-3802.

[3] Quoted by *Bundesfinanzminister* Hans Eichel in the foreword to Kurt Schilde, *Bürokratie des Todes: Lebensgeschichten jüdischer Opfer des NS-Regimes im Spiegel von Finanzamtsakten* (Berlin: Metropol, 2002), p. 7.

meager remaining property was a clear indication to the Jews of Berlin of their imminent deportation.[4] Tax officials, bank clerks, and property evalua- tors also prepared detailed inventories as they settled up Jewish accounts and sold off remaining property after the so-called evacuations. If the Holocaust is to be understood as a function of bureaucratic process, this is particularly well illustrated by the perpetrators' exhaustive efforts to register all Jewish property in conjunction with the deportation and murder of the Jews. After the war, another generation of archives was created as a result of the lengthy and imperfect attempts at restitution, predominantly conducted in the West.

These massive Nazi era and postwar archives on Jewish property, much of them rarely used by historians, provided the starting point for my work on this project. The United States Holocaust Memorial Museum's Center for Advanced Holocaust Studies, directed by Paul Shapiro, became aware of this considerable resource for Holocaust research and asked me in the late 1990s to carry out detailed work in some of these emerging archives. The aims of this book are to describe the many mechanisms by which property was confiscated and to assess what the property records can tell us about the events of the Holocaust and the lives of those persecuted by the Nazis.

Essentially, this volume tells the story on three different levels. First, it sheds light on Nazi plans for confiscation and how they were implemented by many and various state organizations. Second, it presents the perspective of Jewish victims, who had to deal with mounting economic persecution on a daily basis as a growing threat to their existence. Third, it reveals the responses and responsibility of low-level perpetrators, Nazi collabora- tors, profiteers, and bystanders, including companies and individuals in the neutral countries, who may have benefited from or become aware of the Holocaust via the vast trail of property left behind.

Legal Means

For many historians, one distinctive aspect of Hitler's seizure of power was the skillful abuse of supposedly legal means to acquire legitimation for his regime. This application of pseudo-legal and bureaucratic methods is also the defining characteristic of the confiscation of Jewish property. In spite of, or partly because of, certain initial excesses of plunder, theft, and "wild Aryanizations," after 1938 the bulk of remaining Jewish property was

---

[4] Marion A. Kaplan, *Between Dignity and Despair: Jewish Life in Nazi Germany* (New York: Oxford University Press, 1998), p. 185; Kurt Schilde, *Bürokratie des Todes*, p. 69.

confiscated by "legal" and bureaucratic means under close state supervision. In particular, the leaders of the Nazi state sought to ensure that the lion's share of the proceeds went to the benefit of the Reich. This, of course, did not prevent widespread corruption, interdepartmental rivalries, and private gain, which, as Frank Bajohr argues, were all inherent in the practice of Nazi rule.[5]

An important distinction has to be made between the transfer of property into "Aryan" hands – that is, the "Aryanization" of the economy – and the confiscation of Jewish property by the state. Generally Aryanization preceded and prepared the way for confiscation, converting various forms of Jewish wealth into bank accounts or investments (at a considerable loss to the owners) that then could be confiscated more easily by the state. Aryanization, especially of businesses, sought to deny the Jews any significant economic influence. Confiscation by the state had the object of ensuring that the German Reich, not private individuals, became the prime beneficiary of Jewish property.

As the complex legal regulations and proceedings concerning postwar restitution demonstrate, the transfer of property was inextricably linked with the concept of "legal title." The Nazi expropriation of Jewish property could be conducted on a grand scale only through the deployment of a wide array of special taxes, punitive measures, and confiscatory decrees that purported to provide legal title to the Reich and other beneficiaries. This process in turn has left in diverse sources a very sizable archival footprint in the form of tax returns, bank accounts, land registers, and claims for unpaid bills. Without a legal guarantee from the state, the market for stolen Jewish property would have remained limited, as would the revenues to be realized. In Western Europe in particular, growing expectations of an Allied victory as the war progressed considerably depressed demand for former Jewish property that might have to be returned if the Germans were defeated.

The term "confiscation," rather than theft, expropriation, or seizure, all of which apply to some degree, has been used here for specific reasons. First, this term directly reflects the legalized, bureaucratic, and state-organized nature of the process. After the deportations, the Nazis used legal artifice to make it appear that they were merely collecting, on behalf of the state, ownerless property left behind. The deliberate euphemism of property "falling" to the Reich was intended to reassure bureaucrats of the legality of their actions. In reflecting the original German language, my intention is not in any way to minimize the criminal nature of the thefts and expropriations,

---

[5] See Frank Bajohr, *Parvenüs und Profiteure: Korruption in der NS-Zeit* (Frankfurt am Main: S. Fischer, 2001).

but rather to reflect on the essential characteristics of this massive program of state-sponsored theft.

This legalistic approach to the problem did, however, have some surprising side effects. Particularly in Western Europe, much confiscated Jewish property was paid into blocked accounts that remained in existence at the liberation, facilitating the process of restitution where there were still claimants to come forward. In the Netherlands, the authorities' postwar return of items to the rightful owners or their representatives was known as "*Rechtsherstel*" or the restoration of legal rights.[6] Similarly, the extensive records created in Germany and elsewhere for the purposes of settling any outstanding debts made it possible to some extent to reconstruct certain details of the process of confiscation, both for restitution and historical purposes.

Archival Sources and Approaches

There are certain key reasons why the issue of Jewish property emerged with such potency during the 1990s. The opening of archives in Eastern Europe following the end of the Cold War, as well as the discovery of major archival collections from Western Europe that ended up in communist hands, made it possible to put together some missing parts of the puzzle.[7] Access to these collections has been supplemented by considerable archival releases in the West. For example, Greg Bradsher and his colleagues at the National Archives made staunch efforts to render the massive documentation related to Holocaust-era assets more accessible to researchers.[8] This effort has been reinforced by the large-scale release of remaining classified Nazi-related files, a process begun under the Clinton administration. Less well known are the

---

[6] The strict insistence on legal procedures also for the restitution of property after the war did, however, slow the process and make it harder for the victims, as the onus was on them to prove their previous ownership. I am grateful to Helen Junz for making this point during a presentation at the United States Holocaust Memorial Museum in February 2004.

[7] For example, in the former Osobyi (Special) Archive in Moscow, extensive collections from not only the Security Police and SD but also from the Reich Economics Ministry were uncovered. Major collections in the East German archives included the War Booty Office (Reichshauptkasse Beutestelle) and Deutsche Bank collections.

[8] See Greg Bradsher (ed.), *Holocaust-Era Assets: A Finding Aid to Records at the National Archives at College Park, Maryland* (Washington, DC: Published for the National Archives and Records Administration by the National Archives Trust Fund Board, 1999).

massive openings of millions of pages of relevant documentation in other archives, such as those of France, Switzerland, and Belgium.[9]

The gradual unlocking of key state financial archives for academic research has empowered historians to conduct more detailed research. Two main types of state documentation are available: first, the detailed contemporary German and collaborator records listing and evaluating the property seized, and second, extensive documentation regarding postwar claims for compensation and restitution. Both sets of files usually are organized according to the names of the victims, requiring painstaking research to piece together the processes of both expropriation and restitution, even on the basis of only a representative sample. Unfortunately, relatively few general files on the administration of the expropriation process have survived.[10] In addition, some private companies have opened their archives for closer academic scrutiny.[11] Despite the progressive opening of the archives, there remain certain types of documentation for which historians still have to wait. For example, most German tax records and also health-related compensation claims generally remain closed to historians, as they are subject to strict privacy laws for up to eighty years after their creation.[12]

The sheer scale of these massive property archives presents a particularly challenging problem. In the time available, I was not able to conduct an exhaustive examination of large collections or even attempt to examine a representative sample. Rather, I studied a few examples that serve to reveal

---

[9] The United States Holocaust Memorial Museum has received a very large collection of microfilm records from the French archives over the past few years, much of it related to Jewish property. Large parts of this documentation were made accessible to historians in France only at the same time that it became accessible at the United States Holocaust Memorial Museum on microfilm; see USHMM, RG-43.023M (Commissariat général aux questions juives: AJ 38, 1940–1947, 443 reels).

[10] For example, in the Landesarchiv and at the Oberfinanzdirektion in Berlin, there are only two surviving *Handakten* (personal copies kept by employees) containing a sample of the flood of internal administrative regulations that governed the implementation of Jewish property confiscation.

[11] The most notable examples include larger German banks and insurance companies, such as the Deutsche Bank, Dresdner Bank, Commerzbank, and Allianz; these commissioned academic studies, as have other firms such as Bertelsmann and Degussa. In Austria, where Oliver Rathkolb has pioneered the opening of company records with other historians such as Dieter Stiefel, the Postsparkasse is one of many organizations to have begun reassessing their corporate history. In Switzerland, the establishment of the Commission of Independent Experts was accompanied by legislation guaranteeing its right of access to relevant private company archives.

[12] Harold James, *The Deutsche Bank and the Nazi Economic War against the Jews* (Cambridge: Cambridge University Press, 2001), p. 8.

the main processes at work. Thus, the analysis has concentrated on grasping the qualitative nature of the confiscation process, leaving most quantitative analysis to the larger research teams, such as those working for the large French, Swiss, and Austrian Historical Commissions, or for the Deutsche Bank, which were better equipped for crunching the numbers from vast collections of individual files.

Much of the archival research for this book was conducted in the recently opened files of the German financial administration, now available in various Berlin archives and other regional centers. In particular, by piecing together the surviving collections from various German regions, I was able to reconstruct a more complete picture of the system than is available from the fragments surviving in any one location.[13] I also conducted considerable archival research on the seizure of Jewish property outside the Reich's borders, especially in collections concerning the occupied territories of the Soviet Union and the Netherlands. Inevitably, however, I relied on the existing but still rapidly expanding secondary literature for much of the international comparative work. I also used written and oral testimonies of survivors, as well as contemporary documents from Jewish victims, to gain an impression of what the loss of property actually meant to those who suffered persecution at the Nazis' hands.

Another important documentary source that has been surprisingly underutilized by historians, especially in more recent years, is the large collection of documents gathered for the Nuremberg trials. These have the advantage of having been extensively indexed, especially those materials relating to the Holocaust. Roughly 30 percent or more of all Holocaust-related documents in this collection deal with matters involving economic discrimination and exploitation.[14]

I derived the methodological approach for this broad survey directly from the nature of the sources used. Whereas historians previously focused mainly on the wording and intention of Nazi laws directed against Jewish property, by using individual case files, more stress here is placed on their implementation by the bureaucracy and their impact on Jewish lives. In addition, bringing together materials from various recently opened archives – documents reflecting the perspectives of perpetrators, victims, and beneficiaries – permits a differentiated analysis of the topic. In particular,

---

[13] For example, surviving Currency Office files from Thuringia, Berlin, and Münster have been examined, as different types of files survived in each case.

[14] See especially the very useful guide by Jacob Robinson and Henry Sachs (eds.), *The Holocaust: The Nuremberg Evidence. Part One: Documents* (Jerusalem: Yad Vashem and YIVO, 1976).

this approach allows documents from diverse sources to "talk to each other," opening up simultaneous analysis from several perspectives.

Historiography

In general terms, the Aryanization of Jewish businesses in Nazi Germany has, at least until recently, attracted more attention than has the seizure of other assets through taxes, forced payments, and confiscation measures. Nonetheless, the focus has been primarily on a few, larger, more spectacular cases[15] or on regional studies limited mainly to the local implementation of Aryanization measures.[16] Recent research also has highlighted the role of the banks in mediating the Aryanization process,[17] as well as the treatment of their own Jewish employees and directors.[18] The emphasis generally has focused more on the organizers and beneficiaries of Aryanization than on the responses of the victims,[19] although some local studies have attempted to document extensively the lives of the victims and their former businesses.[20]

Until the 1990s, most historians treated the issue of property confiscation as an abstruse and largely secondary aspect of the Holocaust. The registers of and revenues from Jewish property were seen as a byproduct of the

---

[15] See, for instance, Raul Hilberg, *Die Vernichtung der europäischen Juden* (Frankfurt am Main: S. Fischer, 1982) vol. I, pp. 120–27; and Martin Friedenberger, "Das Berliner Finanzamt Moabit-West und die Enteignung der Emigranten des Dritten Reichs 1933–1942," *Zeitschrift für Geschichtswissenschaft* 49:8 (2001): 677–94, concerning the Aryanization of the Petschek group. A number of works also examine the Warburg Bank case, usually as part of broader studies of the business.

[16] See, for example, Franz Fichtl et al., *"Bambergs Wirtschaft Judenfrei": Die Verdrängung der jüdischen Geschäftsleute in den Jahren 1933 bis 1939* (Bamberg: Collibri, 1998).

[17] See, for example, the article of Bernhard Lorentz, "Die Commerzbank und die 'Arisierung' im Altreich. Ein Vergleich der Netzwerkstrukturen und Handlungsspielräume von Grossbanken in der NS-Zeit," *Vierteljahrshefte für Zeitgeschichte* 50:2 (April 2002): 237–68.

[18] See, for example, Dieter Ziegler, "Die Verdrängung der Juden aus der Dresdner Bank, 1933–1938," *Vierteljahrshefte für Zeitgeschichte* 47:2 (April 1999): 187–216.

[19] See for example Dirk van Laak, "Die Mitwirkenden bei der 'Arisierung': Dargestellt am Beispiel der rheinisch-westfälischen Industrieregion 1933–1940," in Ursula Büttner (ed.), *Die Deutschen und die Judenverfolgung im Dritten Reich* (Hamburg: Christians, 1992): 231–58.

[20] For example, Barbara Händler-Lachmann, *Vergessene Geschäfte – verlorene Geschichte: Jüdisches Wirtschaftsleben in Marburg und seine Vernichtung im Nationalsozialismus* (Marburg: Hitzeroth, 1992); Alex Brüns-Wüstefeld, *Lohnende Geschäfte: Die "Entjudung der Wirtschaft am Beispiel Göttingens* (Hanover: Fackelträger, 1997).

destruction process that officials diligently collected. It was not expected that these specialized sources could add much to our understanding, as the Holocaust was not seen as having been motivated primarily by material gain. These sources attracted instead the attention of genealogists and local historians attempting to trace the fates of family members or to compile memorial lists. There were, however, a few detail-oriented historians who did not underestimate the role of property confiscation in the destruction process.

Most notable in this respect is the seminal work of the late Raul Hilberg, who defined the removal of property (*Enteignung*) as one of the essential steps common to the development and implementation of the Holocaust throughout Europe.[21] Another key contribution was made by H. G. Adler, who perceived the exhaustive measures of property confiscation and the bureaucratic chicanery involved as integral to the dehumanizing effect of Nazi persecution. Nazi bureaucratic procedures steadily degraded human beings into mere objects of administrative regulation.[22] Helmut Genschel examined the Aryanization of the German economy in terms of direct Nazi pressure as well as legal measures, outlining the main chronology of events in the 1930s.[23] A particularly lucid analysis of the unfolding dynamic of Nazi Aryanization and confiscation measures is provided by the Dutch historian Hans van der Leeuw, who also worked extensively on restitution problems in the postwar decades.[24] Joseph Billig's work on the *Commissariat General des Questions Juives*[25] deserves mention as a rare early monograph on confiscation; the book stressed the centrality of this issue as a key to understanding the complex relationship between Vichy France and Nazi Germany. He thus foreshadowed some of the main arguments of more recent research, especially Professor Wolfgang Seibel's international project, "The Holocaust and Polycracy in Western Europe."[26]

[21] R. Hilberg, *Die Vernichtung der europäischen Juden*, 3 vols.

[22] H. G. Adler, *Der verwaltete Mensch: Studien zur Deportation der Juden aus Deutschland* (Tübingen: J. C. B. Mohr, 1974).

[23] Helmut Genschel, *Die Verdrängung der Juden aus der Wirtschaft im Dritten Reich* (Göttingen: Musterschmidt, 1966).

[24] See especially A. J. van der Leeuw, "Der Griff des Reiches nach dem Judenvermögen," in A. H. Paape (ed.), *Studies over Nederland in oorlogstijd* ('s-Gravenhage: Martinus Nijhoff, 1972): 211–36, first published in *Rechtsprechung zum Wiedergutmachungsrecht* (1970): 383–92.

[25] Joseph Billig, *Le Commissariat Général aux Questions Juives, 1941–1944* (Paris: Editions du Centre, 1953, 1955 and 1960) 3 vols.

[26] Wolfgang Seibel (ed.), *Holocaust und 'Polykratie' in Westeuropa, 1940–1944: Nationale Berichte* (December, 2001).

In the 1980s, Avraham Barkai's work emphasized the effects of Nazi economic persecution on the German Jewish community throughout the 1930s, attempting to reconstruct the Jewish perspective of events.[27] Frank Bajohr presented the first detailed study of local Aryanization, focusing on Hamburg; he stressed the cooperation of various local authorities in the process and the interplay between initiatives from below and national measures.[28] Stefan Mehl's work on the Reich Finance Ministry provides an overview of the involvement of this key institution in the financial aspects of the Holocaust, but does not examine the implementation of anti-Jewish measures.[29] Especially with regard to property confiscation, it is important to contrast the laws with their actual implementation. This process can be accomplished only by an examination of the case files.

In recent years, there has been a flurry of interest in the extensive records of the regional financial administrations. Exhibitions in Düsseldorf and Münster were accompanied by publications incorporating both documents and analysis.[30] Regional projects in Hessen, Hanover, and Munich have combined the registration of archival holdings with their evaluation and presentation to a wider public.[31] The value of such sources for reconstructing something of the fabric of Jewish life at the onset of the Holocaust is demonstrated by the excellent biographical dictionary of Jews from Münster. This work draws extensively on financial documentation and more conventional sources.[32] Michel Hepp edited and published lists of denaturalized persons. This publication also includes introductory essays stressing the

[27] Avraham Barkai, *Vom Boykott zur "Entjudung": Der wirtschaftliche Existenzkampf der Juden im Dritten Reich, 1933–1943* (Frankfurt am Main: Fischer, 1987).

[28] Frank Bajohr, *"Arisierung" in Hamburg*, 2nd ed. (Hamburg: Hans Christians, 1997). Available in translation as *"Aryanisation" in Hamburg: The Economic Exclusion of the Jews and the Confiscation of their Property in Nazi Germany* (New York: Berghahn, 2002).

[29] Stefan Mehl, *Das Reichsfinanzministerium und die Verfolgung der deutschen Juden, 1933–1943* (Berlin, 1990).

[30] Wolfgang Dressen, *Betrifft: "Aktion 3". Deutsche verwerten jüdische Nachbarn: Dokumente zur Arisierung* (Berlin: Aufbau, 1998); Alfons Kenkman and Bernd-A. Rusinek (eds.), *Verfolgung und Verwaltung: Die wirtschaftliche Ausplünderung der Juden und die westfälischen Finanzbehörden* (Münster: Oberfinanzdirektion Münster, 1999).

[31] On Hessen, see Susanne Meinl and Jutta Zwilling, *Legalisierter Raub: Die Ausplünderung der Juden im Nationalsozialismus durch die Reichsfinanzverwaltung in Hessen* (Frankfurt am Main: Campus, 2004).

[32] Gisela Möllendorf and Rita Schlautmann-Overmeyer, *Jüdische Familien in Münster, 1918–1945: Biographisches Lexikon* (Münster: Westphälisches Dampfboot, 1995); another study that draws extensively on financial documentation to help reconstruct the destroyed Jewish community of Berlin is Mario Offenburg (ed.), *Adass Jisroel, Die Jüdische Gemeinde in Berlin (1869–1942): Vernichtet und Vergessen* (Berlin: Museumspädagogischer Dienst, 1986).

hitherto underestimated significance of denaturalization in the development of anti-Jewish policy.[33]

The legal and diplomatic activity that led to numerous international lawsuits and some notable financial settlements in the late 1990s demonstrated clearly that the plundering of Jewish property was a European-wide phenomenon, with ripple effects spreading beyond the continent.[34] More than twenty countries established historical commissions, and many others have prepared official reports and position papers.[35] The present volume seeks to assess the impact of this vast amount of new research and to draw together themes touched on by the various commissions – themes that must be examined in an international perspective.

Thus, one can see that important strands of methodology, archival access, and historiography have been emerging, above all in Germany, for some time. However, it has been the intensified focus on financial issues from the perspective of survivors, combined with historians' more realistic evaluation of the role of practical aspects in the unfolding of the Holocaust, that has brought this constellation of issues to the fore. Since the late 1980s, a number of notable scholars, such as Götz Aly, Susanne Heim, and Hans Safrian, have contributed to the reassessment of practical, material, and bureaucratic factors alongside ideology in the development of the Holocaust.[36] They have been followed by many others, such as Wolf Gruner, who has examined the living conditions, forced labor, and pauperization of German and Austrian

---

[33] Michael Hepp (ed.), *Die Ausbürgerung deutscher Staatsangehöriger 1933–45 nach den im Reichsanzeiger veröffentlichten Listen*, 3 vols. (Munich: Saur, 1985–88).

[34] Among the better accounts of these negotiations are Stuart Eizenstat, *Imperfect Justice: Looted Assets, Slave Labor, and the Unfinished Business of World War II* (New York: Public Affairs, 2003), and John Authers and Richard Wolffe, *Of the Victim's Fortune: Inside the Epic Battle over the Debts of the Holocaust* (New York: HarperCollins, 2002).

[35] Those countries that established historical commissions include Argentina, Austria, Belgium, Brazil, Croatia, Estonia, France, Italy, Latvia, Liechtenstein, Lithuania, Luxemburg, the Netherlands, Norway, Portugal, Spain, Sweden, Switzerland, Turkey and the United States. Official publications on assets-related issues were also published in the United Kingdom, Germany, Canada, Belarus, and Ukraine. See especially J. D. Bindenagel (ed.), *Washington Conference on Holocaust-Era Assets, November 30–December 3, 1998 Proceedings* (Washington, DC: U.S. Government Printing Office, 1999) for the position papers of various countries.

[36] See, for example, Götz Aly and Susanne Heim, *Vordenker der Vernichtung: Auschwitz und die deutschen Pläne für eine europäischer Neuordnung* (Hamburg: Hofmann und Campe, 1991); Götz Aly, *"Endlösung": Völkerverschiebung und der Mord an den europäischen Juden* (Frankfurt am Main: S. Fischer, 1995); and Hans Safrian, *Eichmann und seine Gehilfen* (Frankfurt am Main: Fischer, 1995). More recently, see also Götz Aly, *Hitlers Volksstaat: Raub, Rassenkrieg und nationaler Sozialismus* (Frankfurt am Main: S. Fischer, 2005).

Jews prior to deportation, on the basis of detailed regional sources.[37] This book builds upon my research reflected in conference papers and other essays and combines some of these key methodological and historiographical approaches simultaneously to relate the story on both the micro and the macro levels. Among the aspects of the confiscation process to be examined in some detail are denaturalization, the blocking of accounts, and the practices of states allied to Nazi Germany, all of which have hitherto been largely neglected in the literature.

Questions

In approaching this wide-ranging topic, a number of key questions are posed. How much and what types of Jewish property were seized? What mechanisms were applied and which institutions were involved? What happened to the property and which persons and organizations profited directly from the theft? Is it possible to assess the degree of corruption involved? What was the role of the local population? To what extent did lust for Jewish property act as a motive for the killings? Finally, what does the perspective of the victims add to our understanding of the expropriation process? These questions are addressed using a wide range of the available sources. A careful examination of these issues can tell us more about both the implementation of the Holocaust and the significance of Jewish property within that process.

Comparative Aspects

One reason for the apparent lack of clear direction behind the overall Nazi strategy of confiscation was that it always remained a "work in progress" in the Reich. The Nazi leaders did not develop the fundamental principles and mechanisms of confiscation until 1938, as anti-Jewish policy accelerated rapidly in the wake of the Anschluss of Austria.[38] There was an important

---

[37] Wolf Gruner, *Der geschlossene Arbeitseinsatz deutscher Juden: zur Zwangsarbeit als Element der Verfolgung 1938–1943* (Berlin: Metropol, 1997); Wolf Gruner, *Jewish Forced Labor under the Nazis: Economic Needs and Racial Aims, 1938–1944* (New York: Cambridge University Press, published in association with the United States Memorial Museum, 2006); Wolf Gruner, "Poverty and Persecution: The Reichsvereinigung, the Jewish Population, and Anti-Jewish Policy in the Nazi State, 1939–1945," *Yad Vashem Studies* XXVII (1999): 23–60.

[38] Hans Safrian, *Eichmann und seine Gehilfen*, pp. 46–49; H. Genschel, *Die Verdrängung*, p. 166; Hans Safrian and Hans Witek, *Und keiner war dabei: Dokumente des alltäglichen*

learning process in the development and application of property seizure measures throughout Europe – measures that encompassed laws, institutions, and even the transfer of certain key personnel.[39]

Through a combination of special taxes, the blocking of accounts, and confiscatory decrees, Jews were progressively robbed of their entire private means. In the initial phase, the mechanisms of expropriation were closely linked to the procedures of forced emigration. The regular financial bureaucracy was the main agency concerned with the expropriation of Germany's Jews, in accordance with discriminatory Nazi laws and decrees. The comparative success of the punitive tax and other measures in securing Jewish assets through the regular tax administration calls into question previous interpretations focused more on the role of the Security Police as the agent of financial exploitation. Once the Jews had been banished from their professions, forced out of business, and either driven into exile or deported during the war to forced labor and death in the East, their assets were seized by the financial bureaucracy working together with the Gestapo.

Financial exploitation relied on close cooperation between the executive authority of the Security Police and the technical expertise of the financial administration to accomplish this complex task. Considerable rivalry and friction still remained, however, between the two branches and were especially intense in the occupied eastern territories, where new institutions competed openly for jurisdiction without concern for existing structures and norms.[40]

Victims' Perspectives

It is now no longer tenable to describe Jewish responses to mounting persecution solely in terms of passivity or their alleged failure to act effectively. The detailed analysis of questions relating to emigration and the preservation of property reveals great energy and activism in the way Jewish families tackled the problems they faced, but often there were no easy

---

Antisemitismus in Wien 1938 (Vienna: Picus, 1988), p. 16; A. J. van der Leeuw, "*Der Griff*," pp. 213 and 223; Peter Longerich, *Politik der Vernichtung: Eine Gesamtdarstellung der nationalsozialistischen Judenverfolgung* (Munich: Piper, 1998), pp. 162–65.

[39] For example, the key role of Dr. Hans Fischböck in developing Aryanization and confiscation methods in both the Reich and the German-occupied Netherlands.

[40] See especially Martin Dean, "Seizure of Jewish Property and Inter-Agency Rivalry in the Reich and in the Occupied Soviet Territories," in Wolfgang Seibel and Gerald Feldman (eds.), *Networks of Nazi Persecution: Division-of-Labor in the Holocaust* (New York: Berghahn, 2005), pp. 88–102.

options available. The choices facing Jews have to be assessed in the light of the considerable material and practical impediments to emigration; the necessity for this approach becomes apparent from the analysis of the enormously bureaucratic nature of the emigration process. Amid the mountains of registration forms, tax payments, inventories, and applications, one may catch occasional glimpses of the desperation of those seeking to flee. It is not possible here to reconstruct the full biographies of the many characters encountered, but it is important that their voices be included if we are to keep in mind the direct material and psychological effects on human lives.

Chronology and Interpretations

One major purpose of my work has been to relate the confiscation of Jewish property to other Nazi policies, including the confiscation of property from other groups of persecutees. This in turn has led me to see important linkages between the emigration phase and the deportation phase of German anti-Jewish policy. Many of the mechanisms that were first developed to deal with the property of Jewish emigrants were then merely expanded and modified to apply them to the remaining Jewish population. Blocking bank accounts was a key mechanism that was later extended to occupied countries, especially Poland and the Netherlands. This modality emerged initially from measures taken to prevent Jewish emigrants from transferring funds abroad.

There also emerged similar links between the treatment of the property of Jews who fled before the Nazi invasion and of those who remained. The most extreme case is perhaps Luxembourg, where initial legislation to confiscate the property of absentee Jews was simply extended to all remaining Jews well before the Germans started to deport them. But in almost all of the Nazi-dominated territories, the confiscation of Jewish property manifested similar phases, as partial measures that initially were confined to specific groups of victims and types of property were successively extended to become an encompassing claim to all of it.

Collaboration

In most occupied areas, the Germans relied to a considerable extent on the cooperation of the local administration, institutions, and population.[41] In

---

[41] For France, see Joseph Billig, *Le Commissariat General*, vol. 1, p. 25.

the Netherlands, for instance, German officials expressed repeated concerns about the willingness of Dutch banks to comply fully with German registration and confiscation measures.[42] The main problem facing the authorities' administration of Jewish property almost everywhere, however, was corruption rather than sabotage. Just as the Nazi Party and its members claimed their share of the spoils in the Reich, so collaborationist organizations such as the Norwegian Nazi Party or the Belorussian Self-Help Organization exploited access to Jewish property to reward their followers and distribute patronage.[43]

A key question is the extent to which collaborating regimes initiated confiscation measures themselves. For the French in particular, concerns to defend their own sovereignty with regard to the spoliation of the Jews encouraged them to seize the initiative in order to retain control of the process. In Romania, the government introduced indigenous antisemitic legislation and engaged in plunder largely without direct German prompting. Many of the mechanisms, however, reflected earlier measures in Germany, even though there also were certain unique aspects to the "Romanianization" of the economy.[44] In spite of the belated nature of measures taken in Hungary in 1944, the active participation of the Hungarian administration in the economic expropriation of the Jews reveals some autonomy from the Germans in this sphere.[45]

Beneficiaries

Who were the main beneficiaries of plundered Jewish property, and where did the proceeds go? Despite the widespread incidence of private plunder and corruption, there is no doubt that the seizure of Jewish property in Europe was primarily a state-directed process linked closely to the development of the Holocaust. As Götz Aly and Christian Gerlach argue,

[42] G. Aalders, *Geraubt!*, pp. 315–16.

[43] See *The Reisel/Bruland Report on the Confiscation of Jewish Property in Norway* (part of official Norwegian report 1997: 22) (Oslo, June 1997), p. 19; and Martin Dean, "Die Enteignung 'jüdischen Eigentums' im Reichskommissariat Ostland 1941–1944," in Irmtrud Wojak and Peter Hayes (eds.), *"Arisierung" im Nationalsozialismus: Volksgemeinschaft, Raub und Gedächtnis* (Frankfurt am Main: Campus, 2000), pp. 201–18.

[44] See Jean Ancel, "Seizure of Jewish Property in Romania," in *Confiscation of Jewish Property in Europe, 1933–1945: New Sources and Perspectives*, Symposium Proceedings (Washington, DC: United States Holocaust Memorial Museum, 2003).

[45] For an overview of the measures taken to dispossess Hungarian Jews in 1944, see Gábor Kádár and Zoltán Vági, *Self-Financing Genocide: The Gold Train, the Becher Case, and the Wealth of Hungarian Jews* (Budapest: Central European University Press, 2004).

throughout Europe, Aryanization (that is, the transfer of Jewish property to non-Jewish hands in a broad sense) usually was not a direct transaction between private individuals. Rather, every cooking pot that was taken from a deported Jewish family was first registered and then auctioned by the financial administration. The bulk of the profit thus remained with the state, whereas private individuals were able to purchase scarce consumer goods at a discount.[46]

However, the widespread participation of the local population as beneficiaries from Jewish property served to spread complicity and therefore also acceptance of German measures against the Jews beyond the smaller circle of immediate perpetrators. In this way, the Nazis and their collaborators were able to mobilize society in support of Nazi racial policies to a greater extent than the spread of racial antisemitism alone would have permitted. Thus, the existence of economic antisemitism and widespread opportunism must be incorporated into explanations of the Holocaust that have generally focused primarily on Nazi racial ideology.

Property Confiscation in Comparative Perspective

What can be learned from a comparative perspective of the plunder and confiscation of Jewish property throughout Europe? The recent work of national historical commissions, company historians, and other researchers has greatly increased our knowledge of the complex processes involved in and the archival resources available on property seizure. Going beyond the raw data, it is now appropriate to develop new interpretations and analyses using a broader comparative approach. Both the implementation of spoliation and the extent of indigenous participation may be assessed more effectively in this international context.

An additional question that has remained of significance throughout my research has been the role played by Jewish property in the development of the Holocaust. This issue is constantly reflected in the analysis of specific events and regions, and some key conclusions are summarized in the final chapter. A comparison with other genocides reinforces the growing impression among historians and political scientists that seizure of property acts as an important catalyst in accelerating the downward spiral across the threshold to genocide.

---

[46] See Christian Gerlach and Götz Aly, *Das letzte Kapitel: Der Mord an den ungarischen Juden* (Stuttgart: DVA, 2002), p. 227.

What can the vast collections of documents on Jewish property tell us about the lives of the Jewish victims and their experience of the confiscation process? Detailed property inventories, whether created for the purposes of emigration or listing what remained at the time of deportation, can provide some image of how people lived. For survivors and the relatives of those who died, personal items such as family portraits, photographs, or even furniture provide a link to the past. The extensive records of both confiscation and restitution give us valuable clues as to the otherwise unknown fate of individuals. At the same time, for historians they can also shed new light on previously unexplored aspects of the role played by Jewish property in the European-wide implementation of the "Final Solution."

The Nazis removed much of the remaining Jewish population from Western Europe by deportation, which limited the direct impact of the Holocaust on the non-Jewish population in the West. However, there were many aspects of the disposal of Jewish assets that were not so easy to overlook. As Jacob Presser notes for the Netherlands, even though the deportations were often carefully concealed, few people in the vicinity could fail to observe the furniture vans being loaded up in broad daylight.[47] In the West, many local officials, businesses, and even private citizens came into contact with the Holocaust through the processing of Jewish property. The ripple effect of processing some of the more valuable items, such as gold, jewelry, or securities, even extended to the neutral countries, spreading a degree of complicity throughout Europe.

In Eastern Europe, the stripping of property was linked much more directly to the physical process of destruction. The Nazi confinement of Jews within ghettos was accompanied by the liquidation of their businesses, mobilization for forced labor, and the imposition of onerous tributes. Impoverished Jews had to exchange the clothes off their backs for scraps of food in order to survive a few more days or weeks. The Nazi liquidation of these ghettos developed in many places into a desperate hunt for booty by the non-Jewish neighbors. For some locations, the lists of property collected at the killing sites provide rare and valuable evidence of brutal massacres. In Auschwitz and other factories of death, the Nazis temporarily kept a few Jewish workers alive for the processing of vast quantities of stolen possessions. The enormous piles of shoes preserved at the killing sites, like the many thousands of pages of property reports, form a key part of the remaining physical evidence on how the Holocaust was organized and the role Jews' property played in that process.

---

[47] Jacob Presser, *The Destruction of the Dutch Jews* (New York: E. P. Dutton, 1969), p. 359.

Part I: Economic Persecution inside the Third Reich, 1933–1941

I
THE NAZIS' INITIAL CONFISCATION MEASURES

In July 1933 the Nazi Party leadership enacted a series of laws that enabled them to expropriate the property of their political opponents. These laws targeted both individuals and organizations, such as trade unions, political parties, and Masonic lodges. Exploiting these and other laws, the Nazis

Figure 1.1. German students and Nazi SA plunder the library of the Institute for Sexual Research in Berlin, May 6, 1933. *Source:* USHMM, courtesy of NARA, RG 306-NT-856-D-1. USHMM, WS # 01628 Public Domain.

also steadily intensified the confiscation of Jewish property throughout the 1930s. For example, the Gestapo increasingly applied the July 1933 Law for the Denaturalization of Citizens Living Abroad as a means of confiscating Jewish property. Experience gained from this process and other confiscation measures provided the basis for more comprehensive expropriation during the war. This chapter examines the development of denaturalization and confiscation policy up to 1938, looking especially at how the Nazis increasingly targeted Jews as a group.[1]

The initial Nazi confiscation policies ran parallel to a more general economic persecution of Jews. After the seizure of power in early 1933, the effects of a series of boycotts, discriminatory treatment, and specific legal measures rapidly undermined the position of Jewish businesses, employees, and professionals. Jews were not only excluded from government service, but state and Nazi Party initiatives progressively drove them out of many other trades and professions. Large numbers of Jews emigrated or ran into economic difficulties, so that more than half of all Jewish businesses were sold or liquidated by the summer of 1938.[2] In a number of cases, Party and state officials exerted direct pressure to coerce Jewish entrepreneurs into "selling" their businesses at prices well below market value. However, for several reasons, the government stopped short of full-scale expropriation. Only during the course of 1938 did Hermann Göring develop more comprehensive plans to remove all Jews from the economy in connection with the incorporation of Austria and the *Kristallnacht* pogrom.[3]

The Nazis exploited the overlap between measures taken against political opponents and those directed against the Jews to legitimize and normalize their discriminatory policies. The gradual redirection of certain pre-existing measures to target the Jews and other groups thereby facilitated a progressive radicalization. During their first months in power, the Nazi leadership tried to reassure their conservative allies and the public that the initial violence and excesses would be only temporary. Therefore, they refrained from imposing

---

[1] This chapter is based in part on the author's article entitled "The Development and Implementation of Nazi Denaturalization and Confiscation Policy up to the Eleventh Decree to the Reich Citizenship Law," published in *Holocaust and Genocide Studies*, vol. 16, no. 2 (Fall, 2002): 217–42.

[2] The number of Jewish companies declined by some 60 percent up to 1938. Many went into liquidation as a result of the boycott measures, and others were sold or transferred into "Aryan" ownership, often at knockdown prices due to the pressure exerted on Jewish owners. See Nea Weissberg-Bob and Thomas Irmer, *Heinrich Richard Brinn (1874–1944): Fabrikant – Kunstsammler – Frontkämpfer. Dokumentation einer "Arisierung"* (Berlin: Lichtig, 2002), p. 76.

[3] See Chapter 3.

comprehensive economic measures against the Jews, fearing the negative effects of boycotts overseas and economic disruption at home. As the threat of domestic political opposition receded, the Nazis then exploited their more secure position to intensify the pressure against the Jews and other "ideological enemies." After the introduction of the Nuremberg Laws in 1935, which contributed further to the progressive criminalization of the Jews, persecutory measures included a systematic attack on Jewish property rights, for both ideological and practical reasons.

The Nazi Party Program and Its Implementation

The Nazi Party program of February 1920 included specific items that pointed toward the subsequent "Aryanization" and spoliation of Jewish property.[4] By proposing to deny citizenship to Jews and reserving only to citizens the right to earn a living, the program effectively demanded the exclusion of Jews from economic life and their progressive expulsion from Germany. It also proposed a more general confiscation of "war profits," the prevention of land "speculation," and the confiscation of land for public purposes without compensation. These ideas reflected the strongly anti-capitalist orientation of the Nazi Party at that time. A program clarification issued by Hitler in April 1928, however, specified that confiscation without compensation would be directed primarily against "Jewish land speculation companies." Such statements sought to reassure voters that the Nazi Party would not threaten most private property while also insinuating that Jewish property had been acquired illegally and therefore should be confiscated.[5] As Joseph Goebbels argued in July 1928, the Nazi view was that "the Jew" is "unproductive" and engaged only in trade. "And everything that he trades in, at some time and somewhere he has stolen."[6] This alleged "revenge" motive, reclaiming "ill-gotten gains" taken from the German people, was

[4] USHMM, RG-6.005.02, Office of the U.S. Chief of Counsel for War Crimes, Nuremberg, Germany. Preliminary Briefs of Economics Division, vol. 1, fr. 01378, "The Aryanization of Jewish Property in Germany."

[5] *The Trial of the Major War Criminals Before the International Military Tribunal* (Blue Series) (Nuremberg, 1947), vol. XXVII, pp. 477–81, 1708-PS; Ian Kershaw, *Hitler 1889–1936: Hubris* (London: Penguin, 1998), p. 301; Donald L. Niewyk, *Jews in Weimar Germany* (New Brunswick, NJ: Transaction, 2001), p. 53, also notes that a Nazi statement in 1931 added "the systematic removal of Jews from economic and cultural life" to their program.

[6] Joseph Goebbels, *Der Angriff: Aufsätze aus der Kampfzeit* (Munich: Franz Eher Nachf., 1936), p. 329.

widespread among Nazi Party members in their attitudes toward Jewish property.

At the local level, the Nazis directed their attacks primarily against the large department stores, claiming to represent the interests of a healthy German middle class. In Bamberg, for instance, the Nazi press initiated a vicious personal campaign against the Jewish director of the Tietz department store in 1926. Nazi-led campaigns to buy only from German businesses and to boycott Jewish shops were common as early as the mid-1920s. The Nazi economic program at this time advocated that local authorities should take over large department stores so that their space could be rented out to smaller shopkeepers.[7]

There were historical precedents in Germany for both special taxes applied to the Jews (before their emancipation in the nineteenth century) and the confiscation of property belonging to political opponents.[8] After World War I, the state confiscated the property of the German princes, who in turn looked to the courts for compensation. Following the proposal by the Communists and Socialists for a national referendum on the issue of confiscation of princely property without compensation to be held in June 1926,[9] in April of that year Wilhelm Frick introduced for the Nazis a counter-proposal before the Weimar Parliament: It proposed the "confiscation of the property of 'bank and stock market princes' and other parasites of the German people (*Volk*)." Intended partly as a satire of the referendum proposal, Frick stressed that under the Socialist and Communist joint plan the money to be "stolen" from the princes would benefit only the Jews. The first article of Frick's proposed legislation demanded "the confiscation of all property without compensation from 'Eastern Jews' and their families who came to Germany after 1914." From Frick's rhetoric, it was clear that in the Nazi worldview both finance capital and the Marxist parties were seen as synonymous with Jewish interests.[10] Thus, there were certain

[7] Franz Fichtl, Stephan Link, Herbert May, and Sylvia Schaible, "*Bambergs Wirtschaft Juden-frei*": *Die Verdrängung der jüdischen Geschäftsleute in den Jahren 1933 bis 1939* (Bamberg: Collibri, 1998), pp. 25–26.

[8] Jeanne Dingell, "Property Seizures from Poles and Jews: The Activities of the Haupt-treuhandstelle Ost," in *Confiscation of Jewish Property in Europe, 1933–1945: New Sources and Perspectives* (Washington, DC: United States Holocaust Memorial Museum, 2003): 33–41, here p. 34; Brigitte Scheiger, "Juden in Berlin," in Stefi Jersch–Wenzel and Barbara John (eds.), *Von Einwanderern zu Einheimischen: Hugenotten, Juden, Böhmen, Polen in Berlin* (Berlin: Nicolai, 1990), pp. 153–488, here pp. 185–91.

[9] On the 1926 referendum, see for example, Hagen Schulze, *Weimar Deutschland 1917–1933* (Berlin: Severin & Siedler, 1982), pp. 300–302.

[10] Günter Neliba, *Der Legalist des Unrechtsstaates: Wilhelm Frick. Eine politische Biographie* (Paderborn: Ferdinand Schönigh, 1992), p. 47; Martin Döring, "*Parlamentarischer Arm der*

clear warnings in the 1920s of what to expect later from a Nazi-controlled government.

After he came to power in 1933, Hitler was quick to apply the instrument of confiscation against his main political opponents. Throughout the 1930s, the Nazi Party remained ideologically committed to the implementation of its original program.[11] However, Hitler's first concern was to consolidate his position without scaring off certain conservative allies he still needed temporarily. As one Gestapo official noted in 1935, citing the Führer, the Party's racial program could not be achieved completely all at once, but only in conjunction with the organic construction of the new Reich.[12]

Confiscation of Communist and Socialist Property

The first few months of Nazi rule, up to the summer of 1933, were marked by considerable violence throughout Germany, mainly perpetrated by members of the *Sturmabteilung* (SA), the storm troopers, who were also widely employed as auxiliary policemen. These actions featured brutal beatings and gangster-style killings. Among the main targets of their attacks were political opponents of the new regime and persons against whom local Nazis harbored personal and political grudges. Many Jews were among the initial victims. On July 1, 1933, the Ministry of the Interior recorded that 26,789 persons were being held in "protective custody," the euphemism for the internment of political opponents.[13] As the initial aim was to disband and demolish organized political opposition, these measures included extensive seizures of property.

For example, the Prussian state confiscated the Karl-Liebknecht House of the Communist Party in Berlin on March 12, 1933, and subsequently renamed it the Horst-Wessel House. The authorities in Berlin ordered further confiscations during the following weeks. In the first half of May, the trade unions and the Socialist Party (SPD) witnessed the seizure of

---

Bewegung": die Nationalsozialisten im Reichstag der Weimarer Republik (Düsseldorf: Droste, 2001), p. 152.

[11] See, for example, the public expression of Josef Bürckel Gauleiter in Rheinland-Pfalz on October 3, 1933: "Für uns gibt nichts anderes, als die Erfüllung des Programms, so wie es der Führer will." Cited in Helmut Genschel, *Die Verdrängung der Juden aus der Wirtschaft im Dritten Reich* (Göttingen: Musterschmidt Verlag, 1966), p. 82.

[12] USHMM, RG-11.001M.01, Records of the Reichssicherheitshauptamt, Berlin, reel 5, 500-1-379 Gestapoamt an Preuss. Staatsmin., August 1935 (draft).

[13] Herbert A. Strauss (ed.), *Jewish Immigrants of the Nazi Period in the USA*, vol. 6, *Essays on the History, Persecution, and Emigration of German Jews* (New York: K. G. Saur, 1987), p. 154.

much of their property by the Nazi-controlled state. An official notice was published in the *Völkischer Beobachter* on May 4 announcing that "the measures were not directed against the worker... but rather were to serve the purpose of securing the funds... for the worker."[14] Banks supplied information to support the police actions, in contravention of bank secrecy regulations. It was not until May 26, however, that the Nazis decreed a Law for the Confiscation of Communist Property. As Gerlinde Grahn argues, the Nazis decreed new laws in 1933 with the intention of giving the already ongoing confiscation of property a "legal" basis.[15]

This process of demolishing political opposition was consolidated on July 14, 1933, when the Nazis published further laws banning the formation of political parties and providing for the confiscation of the "property of enemies of the people and the state" ("*Volks- und staatsfeindliche Vermögen*").[16] The police also made efforts to prevent the concealment of funds by the SPD or the transfer of its money abroad. The tax files of organizations linked to the SPD were passed on to the Gestapo.[17] Other early victims of confiscation in the summer of 1933 included the German Society of Free Thinkers and the Society for Sexual Reform (see Figure 1.1).[18]

Confiscation of Publishing Companies and Communal Property

At the postwar Nuremberg trials, Max Amann, the former head of the Reich Press Chamber, admitted that the Nazis' aim had been to eliminate all opposition publications and establish their own monopoly of the press.[19] In

[14] Max Domarus (ed.), *Hitler: Speeches and Proclamations 1932–1945. The Chronicle of a Dictatorship* (Würzburg: Henninger, 1990), vol. 1, p. 317.
[15] Gerlinde Grahn, "Die Enteignung des Vermögens der Arbeiterbewegung und der politischen Emigration 1933 bis 1945," in *1999* no. 3 (1997): 15–16.
[16] *Reichsgesetzblatt*, Teil I (1933), pp. 479–80. "Das Gesetz über die Einziehung volks- und staatsfeindlichen Vermögens" extended the provisions of the law against Communist property to the SPD and other "Marxist" organizations.
[17] Martin Friedenberger, "Die Rolle der Finanzverwaltung bei der Vertreibung, Verfolgung und Vernichtung der deutschen Juden," in Martin Friedenberger, Klaus-Dieter Gössel, and Eberhard Schönknecht (eds.), *Die Reichsfinanzverwaltung im Nationalsozialismus: Darstellung und Dokumente* (Bremen: Edition Temmen, 2002), pp. 10–94, here p. 11.
[18] J. Walk (ed.), *Das Sonderrecht für die Juden im NS-Staat*, 2nd edition (Heidelberg: C. F. Müller, 1996) I 172, 177; Gerlinde Grahn, "Die Enteignung," pp. 16–19. The files regarding many of these early confiscations are located in the former Prussian Secret State Archives in Berlin–Dahlem; see GSPK, Rep. 151, Reg. II G, Prussian Finance Ministry.
[19] IMT (Blue Series), vol. XXXI, pp. 495–97, 3016–PS.

May 1933, the Nazi authorities in Berlin exploited allegations of corruption to seize control of many socialist newspapers. The Nazi Party then took much of the seized property for its own use. Publishing houses owned by Jews (such as Ullstein) or by political parties were seized or sold under duress to the Nazis' own Franz Eher publishing house.[20] The Nazis used the Konzentration AG as a trustee company to consolidate and liquidate SPD property that had been confiscated by the state.[21]

Some Jewish property was among that seized during this first wave of confiscations. In July 1933, the political police in Bavaria ordered that all the buildings of Jewish organizations be searched and all their property and documentation be confiscated. The leadership was also to be arrested if any evidence of activity "hostile to the state" was found. Subsequently only those Jewish organizations that had no political character were permitted to continue operating.[22] In Brandenburg, the authorities ordered the confiscation of a Jewish youth training center in Wolzig on October 30, 1933, accusing members of the teaching staff of antistate activities. The center belonged to the Berlin Jewish community, which protested the confiscation one month later, stressing that it was an apolitical organization. The Jewish community expressed concern that closing the home would hinder its good work of retraining wayward youths, but offered not to use the property for this purpose if it were returned. Nevertheless, these appeals were in vain. The Nazi Party initially made plans to use the building as a training school for the SA, but ultimately it was taken over by the Prussian state for "cultural purposes."[23]

Both the Nazi Party and the state were among the main beneficiaries of these confiscations. At this time, property seized from political opponents was booked to the benefit of the regional state administrations. Often, practical items were seized by the State Police and used directly to assist with the further persecution of their declared "enemies." For instance, the State Police in Prussia maintained a store of typewriters obtained from confiscations, and in November 1933, the concentration camp in Papenburg requested some radio equipment with a loudspeaker from confiscated

---

[20] Harold James, *The Deutsche Bank and the Nazi Economic War Against the Jews* (Cambridge: Cambridge University Press, 2001), pp. 48–49.

[21] GSPK, Rep. 151, Reg. II G, HA IA, 7931.

[22] Johannes Simmert (ed.), "Die nationalsozialistische Judenverfolgung in Rheinland-Pfalz 1933 bis 1945," in *Dokumentation zur Geschichte der jüdischen Bevölkerung in Rheinland-Pfalz und im Saarland von 1800 bis 1945*, vol. 6 (Koblenz: Landesarchivverwaltung Rheinland–Pfalz, 1974), pp. 25–26.

[23] GSPK, Rep. 151, Reg. II G, HA IA, 1501/77.

property.[24] A precedent was thereby set that the implementation of Nazi repressive measures should also contribute toward covering their own cost.

Max Wolf Case

From the perspective of those affected by these confiscations, their patent unfairness and "illegality" were apparent from the start, as shown in the Max Wolf case. Jewish industrialist Max Wolf's companies were seized by the state under the Law for the Confiscation of Communist Property shortly after the Nazis came to power. Wolf had been a member of the SPD from 1923 on and was accused of providing funds for an alleged "communist training center disguised as a philosophical and political academy." He was also accused of employing persons who were active in Marxist parties. His private property was not expropriated, but most of his assets had been invested in his companies.

The companies were managed initially by state-appointed trustees and subsequently sold off to other local businessmen. From his refuge abroad, however, Wolf had the temerity to make a claim for compensation against the Nazis. In response, the head of the local government (the *Regierungspräsident*) in Kassel responded that he had authorized the confiscation as an executive order. As such, he proclaimed that it should not be subjected to judicial review with a view to granting compensation, as it was a purely political matter. Indeed, he described the claim for compensation as an example of "typical Jewish impudence."[25]

In a further complaint addressed to the German consul in Liverpool in 1938, Wolf denied the accusations made against him, maintaining that the organization to which he had contributed was a publicly registered charity that he had supported along with other local charities. Clearly, Wolf stood no chance of regaining his property directly from the Nazi authorities, but the official response to his determination serves to document how brazenly the Nazis justified the expropriation of even minor political opponents, using the laws passed in 1933. In the case of Wolf, it is likely that the local authorities exploited flimsy accusations of political activity to persecute him as a Jew and seize his businesses.

---

[24] GSPK, Rep. 151, Reg. II G, HA IA, 7952, Bücherei Jürgen Kurczynski. On the use of typewriters, books, and other materials in the Nazi early camps see also Fritz Kleine, *Konzentrationslager: Ein Appell an das Gewissen der Welt: Ein Buch der Greuel; die Opfer klagen an* (Karlsbad: Graphia, 1934), pp. 182–83. I am grateful to Joe White for bringing this reference to my attention.

[25] BAL, R 1500 Anh. (Reichsfeststellungsbehörde), 10817, Note of Reg. Präs. Kassel on August 24, 1936.

Pressure from Below Steered from Above, 1933–1935

Most accounts of Jewish economic persecution under the Nazis start with the laws passed from 1933 onward, excluding Jews from the civil service and other professions, and with the boycotts applied against Jewish businesses at this time.[26] These twin examples illustrate how a combination of legal measures from the center and direct pressure at the local level was applied to force Jews out of the German economy. This was, however, a gradual process as the Nazi leadership initially shied away from large-scale direct expropriation. Indeed, there were repeated calls, especially from Germany's economic leaders, but also from within the Party, to limit the "wild boycott" measures, partly due to a fear of international trade reprisals and other adverse effects on economic recovery.[27]

As Frank Bajohr argues, the organized boycott of Jewish businesses and legal and medical practices on April 1, 1933, served as an outlet for channeling the pent-up hatred of Jews among Nazi activists. During the build-up to "Boycott Day," there was considerable violence against Jewish stores. In Emden, for example, on March 28, local Nazis smashed shop windows.[28] On April 1, SA men were stationed in front of Jewish stores, and placards inscribed with "Don't buy from Jews!" were placed in front of shops. There were a wide variety of public responses: although the "boycott" was widely observed, some individual non-Jews also made a point of visiting Jewish businesses out of solidarity, if only to make a token purchase. Hitler called off the boycott within a short period, however, preferring to retain it as a constant threat that could be reinstated later against the Jews.[29]

The next practical step taken against the Jews was their dismissal from the civil service and other public entities, in accordance with paragraph 3 of the Law for the Reestablishment of the Professional Civil Service,

---

[26] See for example *Plunder and Restitution: The U.S. and Holocaust Victims' Assets: Findings and Recommendations of the Presidential Advisory Commission on Holocaust Assets in the United States and Staff Report* (Washington, DC: U.S. Government Printing Office, 2000), pp. SR–14–16.

[27] H. Genschel, *Die Verdrängung*, pp. 78–82; Frank Bajohr, *"Aryanisation" in Hamburg: The Economic Exclusion of the Jews and the Confiscation of Their Property in Nazi Germany* (New York: Berghahn, 2002), p. 25.

[28] Shmuel Spector and Geoffrey Wigoder (eds.), *The Encyclopedia of Jewish Life before and during the Holocaust* (Jerusalem: Yad Vashem, 2001), p. 363.

[29] F. Bajohr, *"Aryanisation" in Hamburg*, pp. 28–34; N. Weissberg–Bob and T. Irmer, *Heinrich Richard Brinn*, pp. 58–59; Elke Fröhlich (ed.), *Die Tagebücher von Joseph Goebbels: Sämtliche Fragmente. Teil I, Aufzeichnungen 1924–1941*. Band 2 1.1.1931–31.12.1936 (Munich: K. G. Saur, 1987), p. 402, entry for April 4, 1933.

decreed on April 7, 1933.[30] Again, this measure sought to control and regulate the dismissals of Jews that had already begun. The law included certain exceptions for Jews appointed to the civil service before World War I or those who had served at the front. Paragraph 4 included provisions for dismissal on the grounds of political activities, and it was applied against both Jews and non-Jews. A majority of those dismissed, however, including many Jews, fell under paragraph 6, which permitted the compulsory retirement of officials if it was necessary for the "simplification" of the administration. Thus, the removal of Jews from the civil service was conducted as part of a wider purge undertaken for political and practical reasons.[31]

An example of how these initial measures were perceived by far-sighted Jews at the time can be seen in this letter written on April 9, 1933, by Georg Solmssen, then spokesman for the managing board of the Deutsche Bank:

> The expulsion of the Jews from the civil service, now enshrined in law, prompts one to ask what further consequences for the private sector will flow from the measures that even the educated sector of the population has accepted almost as a matter of course. I fear we are only at the beginning of a development that is deliberately aimed, in accordance with a well-thought-out plan, at the economic and moral extermination of all members of the Jewish race living in Germany – quite indiscriminately.[32]

Solmssen's expectation that this purge from the civil service would have repercussions for Jews engaged in the private sector was well founded. In the sphere of public contracts, for example, a number of cities had already moved to exclude Jewish tenders at the end of March 1933. In July 1933, the Reich government tried to moderate the effects of these local measures by issuing guidelines that "Aryan" businesses should receive preference only if their bids were otherwise of "equal quality." In practice, however, many regional governments continued excluding Jewish firms from public contracts. Yet, in some instances, Jews continued to be granted contracts, particularly when there was no effective "Aryan" competitor for the business. The complete exclusion of Jews from public contracts was not regulated centrally until 1938.[33]

---

[30] *Reichsgesetzblatt*, I (1933), pp. 175–77, Gesetz zur Wiederherstellung des Berufsbeamtentums. 7. April 1933.

[31] F. Bajohr, *"Aryanisation" in Hamburg*, pp. 58–68.

[32] Georg Solmssen to Urbig, chairman of the supervisory board, April 9, 1933, quoted in H. James, *The Deutsche Bank*, p. 34.

[33] For a more complete analysis of this complex issue, see F. Bajohr, *"Aryanisation" in Hamburg*, pp. 58–68.

There were also many "spontaneous" initiatives by the SA, by the Nazi factory cells (*Nationalsozialistische Betriebszellenorganisationen*) in specific enterprises, and by the Party to drive Jews out of employment.[34] In the wake of the April boycott, for example, the Nazi works' cells pressed for the dismissal of Jewish employees in the Karstadt department store chain and in the Rudolf Mosse publishing company.[35]

Cleansing of Boards and Employees in Banks and Insurance and Industrial Companies

How did German businesses respond to this growing pressure from the governing party to eliminate Jews from positions of influence and employment? Extensive research, conducted recently in the banking and insurance sectors, provides some insights into the responses of commercial enterprises. In the Dresdner Bank, for example, the Law for the Reestablishment of the Professional Civil Service had a significant impact from May 1933 onward, as the company was still under partial state control following government intervention in 1931 to save it from collapse. In June 1933, the Dresdner Bank distributed questionnaires to be completed on the "Aryan background" of its employees and soon afterward began to dismiss some Jews, starting with those seen as least indispensable. It did pay some limited compensation to those dismissed. The number of Jews working as senior employees was halved during the course of 1933, although the rate of dismissal had slowed considerably by late 1934, when very few junior employees remained. By the end of the year, with only two exceptions, all the Jewish members of the board had been forced to resign.

After the introduction of the Nuremberg racial laws in September 1935, a second wave of dismissals removed the remaining Jewish employees and board members of the Dresdner Bank. Thus, although the bank was able to delay the initial economic impact on its activities by retaining some "privileged" Jewish staff, it soon fell into line with the general dismissal of Jewish employees by early 1937, agreed to by all three of Germany's main banks. German historian Dieter Ziegler points to both a degree of latent anti-semitism within the middle class and the acceptance of apparently "legal" measures in explaining the Dresdner Bank's removal of its Jewish directors and employees.[36]

---

[34] Gerald D. Feldman, *Die Allianz und die deutsche Versicherungswirtschaft 1933–1945* (Munich: C. H. Beck, 2001), p. 96.

[35] H. Genschel, *Die Verdrängung*, pp. 73–74.

[36] Dieter Ziegler, "Die Verdrängung der Juden aus der Dresdner Bank 1933–1938," in *Vierteljahreshefte für Zeitgeschichte* 47, no. 2 (April 1999): 187–216.

Although the widespread and progressive exclusion of Jews from employment had begun in 1933, in the insurance industry that process was delayed.
Gerald Feldman demonstrates with respect to Allianz that the company
was not keen to dismiss valuable employees just because they were Jewish
and that it kept some Jewish agents as long as possible – partly to retain
their Jewish customers. Allianz made efforts to continue employing some
Jews as representatives overseas, but this became increasingly difficult in
the face of strict Nazi regulations. Nevertheless, in spite of the existence
of long-term employment contracts, increasing pressure from the Party
resulted in the almost complete exclusion of Jews from the insurance industry by the end of 1938.[37] In the case of I. G. Farben also, some attempts
were made to protect Jewish employees initially, but only insofar as these
efforts did not have any negative consequences for the company.[38] As Peter
Hayes observes, "Most corporations sooner or later abandoned directors
or employees whenever organs of the Party or the regime got around to
insisting on their removal."[39]

Early Examples of Aryanization and Liquidation

In anticipation of further anti-Jewish measures to come, many Jewish businessmen responded to the initial Nazi threats in 1933 by liquidating their
assets in preparation for emigration. The Salomon Bienenstock clothing
business in Münster, for example, was located in a working-class district
where there were frequent confrontations between left- and right-wing
groups, as well as Nazi demonstrations and house searches, which left a
strong impression of immediate personal danger. In addition, the owners
of the building in which the Bienenstocks lived were Party members, and
they stopped their son from playing with Jewish children. Therefore, the
Bienenstock family, which came originally from Galicia, had no illusions
about the implications of Hitler's accession to power and quickly drew the
necessary conclusions. They sold the business and migrated to Palestine
in September 1933, receiving permission to transfer the RM 2,500 they
realized from its sale.[40]

---

[37] G. D. Feldman, *Die Allianz*, pp. 168–75.

[38] Stephan H. Lindner, *Hoechst: Ein I.G. Farben Werk im Dritten Reich* (Munich: C. H. Beck,
2005), pp. 159–90.

[39] Peter Hayes, *Profits and Persecution: German Big Business and the Holocaust* (Washington,
DC: United States Holocaust Memorial Museum, 1998), p. 10.

[40] Gisela Möllenhoff and Rita Schlautmann–Overmeyer (eds.), *Jüdische Familien in Münster,
Teil 2,1: Abhandlungen und Dokumente 1918–1935* (Münster: Westfälisches Dampfboot,
1998), p. 155.

Some Jewish businesses, such as Leo Jordan's men's clothing store in Göttingen, had been severely hit by the economic depression before 1933, so that the Nazi seizure of power was only the last straw. Due to the proximity of several Nazi offices, many clients stayed away, whereas others exploited the antisemitic mood by refusing to pay their debts. On March 28, 1933, the same day that he declared bankruptcy, Leo Jordan was personally manhandled by an angry SA mob in the run-up to the "Boycott Action." A former employee then took over the business for only a nominal sum, but also paid RM 400 toward the Jordans' emigration. With almost no money, Leo Jordan then migrated to Palestine where he had to perform manual labor to make ends meet. Meanwhile, the new "Aryan" owner quickly restored the German business to profitability, advertising official Nazi uniforms for sale in August 1933.[41] In Münster, three Jewish businesses declared bankruptcy during the first twelve months of Nazi rule. Although the precise economic backgrounds of these bankruptcies are not known, the initial boycott measures, and in two cases the sudden flight abroad of a partner, clearly played a role.[42]

Other Jewish businessmen sought to limit their exposure by handing leadership over to "Aryan" partners while hoping to retain their influence behind the scenes. The case of the Berlin Jewish businessman Heinrich Brinn presents an example of how such "voluntary Aryanizations" (under duress) could rapidly go sour. Brinn was the joint owner of a paint manufacturing business that had extensive government contracts. In early March 1933, Brinn learned that the Berlin Public Transport Company[43] would no longer do business with his company because it was viewed as "non-Aryan" so long as he remained a director.[44] Initially, Brinn agreed with his partner that he should formally resign his position as director but retain his 50 percent shareholdings. Things took a nasty twist when the firm's main creditor, the Dresdner Bank, insisted that Brinn's income from the firm he had personally built up should be drastically reduced following his resignation. At the same time, he was refused a position as an overseas sales representative. His former "close friend" and partner exploited Brinn's sudden

---

[41] Alex Brüns–Wüstefeld, *Lohnende Geschäfte: Die "Entjudung der Wirtschaft am Beispiel Göttingens* (Hannover: Fackelträger, 1997), pp. 190–93.

[42] G. Möllenhoff and R. Schlautmann–Overmeyer (eds.), *Jüdische Familien in Münster, Teil 2,1*, pp. 156–59.

[43] Berliner Verkehrsbetriebe Gesellsellschaft (BVG).

[44] On the widespread nature of such local prohibitions on giving contracts to Jewish firms, see Peter Longerich, *Politik der Vernichtung: Eine Gesamtdarstellung der nationalsozialistischen Judenverfolgung* (Munich: Piper, 1998), p. 40.

economic vulnerability to drive him out of the company by "legal means" with only a meager pension, while the business continued to flourish.[45]

In some early cases, considerable state and Party pressure was exercised to force through Aryanization against the wishes of the Jewish owners. In Rosenthal Porzellan AG in Bavaria, for example, hostile members of the board of directors and the supervisory board, who enjoyed close ties to the Nazi Party, pulled some powerful strings to drive out the Jewish founder of the company, Phillip Rosenthal. Not only did they obtain the support of the regional Party leadership in getting the passports of the Rosenthal family confiscated (in an attempt to prevent them from attending the annual general meeting) but an arrest warrant was then also presented at the meeting to ensure that the family gave up any last attempts to retain control. Ultimately, in January 1935, the president of the Upper Franconia Chamber of Industry and Commerce, SS-Hauptsturmführer Erich Köhler, who had been appointed as "commissar" for the Aryanization of the company, imposed on the Rosenthal family a brutal contract that completely removed them from any further influence on the company's direction. After the company's former owner died in 1937, remaining family members managed to emigrate only with a considerable loss of their property.[46]

In Bamberg too, there was a coordinated effort by the local Party organization to drive certain Jewish enterprises out of business. Here the local industry and trade council (*Industrie und Handelsgremium*) was brought under close Nazi control in March 1933 by the head of the Union of Struggle (*Kampfbund*) and Special Commissar, Strömsdörfer, just before the boycott. Then in April, the recently opened Heimann shoe store, owned by a Czech Jew living in Munich, was quickly forced into bankruptcy for falling behind in payments to local craftsmen. The close cooperation of the industry and trade council, under Strömsdörfer's control, with the local authorities forced the closing of the shop and the "securing" of its stocks by the police for the benefit of the creditors. In one local newspaper, the Heimann firm was defamed as a "Jewish swindle company." As in many such cases, the mere threat of arrest or a criminal investigation under the prevailing circumstances

---

[45] N. Weissberg–Bob and T. Irmer, *Heinrich Richard Brinn*, pp. 20–86. Brinn was a convert to the Evangelical Church prior to the Nazi seizure of power, but was treated as a Jew according to Nazi racial definitions.

[46] Jürgen Lillteicher, "Rechtsstaatlichkeit und Verfolgungserfahrung: 'Arisierung' und fiskalische Ausplünderung vor Gericht," in Constantin Goschler and Jürgen Lillteicher (eds.), *Die Rückerstattung jüdischen Eigentums in Deutschland und Österreich nach 1945 und 1989* (Göttingen: Wallstein, 2002), pp. 134–37.

was sufficient to drive the owners abroad, more or less abandoning their investment.[47]

Official and Informal Economic Discrimination

According to the wording of a new law published in October 1934, the tax laws were to be interpreted "in accordance with National Socialist ideology."[48] This wording merely reflected the existing tendency for local officials to implement regulations to the disadvantage of Jewish property owners where possible. Banks, mortgage companies, and other creditors progressively reduced credit ratings of Jewish clients, leading to higher interest rates and even foreclosures.[49] Similar informal discrimination was common in other areas of business and economic life. For example, soon after the Nazi seizure of power, many Jewish owners of real estate encountered difficulties with "Aryan" tenants who unilaterally reduced their rental payments or discontinued them completely, confident that they had little to fear from a German court.[50]

In 1935, the Deutsche Bank sent out a series of circulars that warned against increasing its "credit exposure" to Jewish firms and recommended that full details of businesses in acute danger should be provided to the authorities to reduce the risks involved in these credit relationships. Subsequently banks kept a close eye on the debt positions of Jewish-owned firms, particularly out of a fear that the owners might emigrate without paying off their debts.[51]

Boycott Actions and State Response, 1935

In rural areas such as Hessen-Nassau, a combination of economic measures and even the threat of physical violence caused the Jewish population to become "very nervous and intimidated" by the summer of 1935. Local

---

[47] Franz Fichtl, et al., *"Bambergs Wirtschaft Judenfrei,"* pp. 38–57.

[48] Kurt Schilde, *Bürokratie des Todes: Lebensgeschichten jüdischer Opfer des NS-Regimes im Spiegel von Finanzamtsakten* (Berlin: Metropol, 2002), p. 36.

[49] See Britta Bopf, "Economic Discrimination: The Case of Jewish Real Estate," in *Confiscation of Jewish Property in Europe, 1933–1945: New Sources and Perspectives* (Washington, DC: United States Holocaust Memorial Museum, 2003), pp. 105–26.

[50] See Marion A. Kaplan, *Between Dignity and Despair: Jewish Life in Nazi Germany* (New York: Oxford University Press, 1998), p. 24.

[51] H. James, *The Deutsche Bank*, pp. 53–54.

shops refused to serve Jewish customers, and Jewish tradesmen were unable to make a living, causing many to flee. Even those "Aryans" who wanted to trade with the Jews suffered discrimination and found themselves excluded from public contracts.[52] In the same area, the smashing of windows and even shots fired into houses caused the few remaining Jews to live in fear.[53]

Max Schuss recalls the Nazi boycott measures directed against his parents' shop in Hanau in the mid-1930s: "Young SA-men were posted in front of the shop in the Nürnberger Strasse and they photographed the customers who went in." In 1935, his parents moved the shop to a less exposed location on the second floor to limit the effects of this campaign. However, Max's sister, who had in the meantime inherited the business, was forced to sell the entire stock cheaply and liquidate the business in 1937 due to the continuing pressure of the Nazis.[54]

The public displays of violence that accompanied the boycott movement in 1935, in which Nazi thugs beat up Jews and damaged their property, did meet with some condemnation.[55] At this time, the Nazi leadership was concerned with retaining centralized control over Jewish policy, and in August 1935, Hitler ordered that "isolated actions" against Jews by lower Party organizations should cease.[56] After the anti-Jewish demonstrations in Berlin in the summer of 1935, the mayor, the Central Office of the Gestapo, the State Police, the Police Präsidium, the Gau (regional Party) leadership, and the SA convened a meeting to discuss measures to be taken against the Jewish population. The aim of the meeting was to find ways of undermining the position of Jews in Berlin without resorting to public demonstrations and "isolated actions."

One proposal was to prevent the establishment of new Jewish businesses by refusing to issue new licenses to Jews. In addition, existing regulations regarding construction and health matters were to be applied very stringently against Jewish businesses. For example, all Jewish ice cream vendors

---

[52] USHMM, RG–11.001M.31 (Osobyj Moscow), reel 99, 721–1–98 (Centralverein der Juden in Deutschland), Reports on the conditions of the Jewish population in Hessen–Nassau in August, 1935.

[53] Ibid., reel 139, 721-1-2969, Reports from Sterbfritz (March 7, 1934) and Ortenberg (March 7, 1935).

[54] Monika Ilona Pfeifer, "Entrechtung und Verfolgung," in Evangelischer Arbeitskreis "Christen – Juden" Hanau (eds.), *Hanauer Juden 1933 – 1945* (Hanau: CoCon, 1998), p. 42

[55] I. Kershaw, *Hitler: Hubris*, p. 562.

[56] Johannes Simmert and Hans-Walter Herrmann (eds.), *Die nationalsozialistische Judenverfolgung in Rheinland-Pfalz 1933 bis 1945: Das Schicksal der Juden im Saarland 1920 bis 1945* (Koblenz: Landesarchivverwaltung Rheinland-Pfalz, 1974), pp. 54–55.

would be compelled to install a toilet for customers. Similarly, building-police officials were to examine carefully all properties belonging to Jews to see if any repairs were necessary. In particular, investigators were to determine whether any Jews were benefiting from government contracts.[57]

Draft guidelines for the treatment of the "Jewish Question," drawn up in the Gestapo Central Office in Berlin in August 1935, stressed that "the Jewish Question cannot be solved by the mistreatment of individuals or by damaging their property, but rather it is exclusively the task of the executive offices of the state and the movement."[58] Nonetheless, these guidelines did not result in a lessening of the pressure on the Jews, but rather a shift toward more concerted governmental and Party measures, such as imposing the Nuremberg Laws, tightening currency regulations,[59] and broadening the grounds for denaturalization.

Denaturalization Law and Its Implications

The Law for the Revocation of Naturalization and the Annulment of German Citizenship,[60] published on July 14, 1933, ultimately was to become one of the main legal mechanisms exploited by the Third Reich for comprehensive confiscation of Jewish property by the state. This law authorized both the retraction of citizenship from persons recently naturalized (especially Eastern European Jews) within Germany and the denaturalization of German emigrants (including Jews) who allegedly had violated their loyalty to the Reich or "damaged German interests."[61] The main initial targets for

---

[57] USHMM, RG-11.001M.01, reel 5, 500-1-379, SD Report to Head of Gestapa (Heydrich), July 31, 1935; see also Gestapoamt an Preuss. Staatsmin., August 1935 (draft).

[58] Ibid., reel 5, 500-1-379, Gestapoamt an Pr. Staatsmin., August 1935 (draft). The same document reiterates this point later on: "Nicht der Einzelne, sondern lediglich die vom Staat hierzu berufenen Organe sind befügt, dem Streben staatsfeindlicher Elemente zu begegnen und Schädlinge des Volkskörpers restlos auszurotten."

[59] For details of this aspect of persecution, see Chapter 2.

[60] Gesetz über den Widerruf von Einbürgerungen und die Aberkennung der deutschen Staatsangehörigkeit.

[61] Hans Georg Lehmann, "Acht und Ächtung politischer Gegner im Dritten Reich," in Michael Hepp (ed.), Die Ausbürgerung deutscher Staatsangehöriger 1933–45 nach dem im Reichsanzeiger veröffentlichten Listen 3 vols. (Munich: K. G. Saur, 1985), vol. I, ix–xxiii, here p. xi; see also Diemut Majer, "Fremdvölkische" im Dritten Reich (Boppard am Rhein: Harald Boldt Verlag, 1993), pp. 195–99. This work is also available in English as "Non-Germans" Under the Third Reich (Baltimore: Johns Hopkins University Press in association with the United States Holocaust Memorial Museum, 2003). The law and its implementation decree are published in Schriftenreihe des Bundesamtes zur Regelung offener Vermögensfragen,

denaturalization were prominent left-wing politicians, writers, and artists who had fled Germany during the first months of persecution in 1933, including a number of Jews.

Under the terms of this July 1933 citizenship annulment law, both the temporary impounding of property and the final transfer of its ownership to the state could be decreed.[62] In practice, confiscation generally was applied to all Jews recommended for denaturalization and who were known to own property inside Germany. The confiscation measures were administered by the Tax Office (*Finanzamt*) Moabit-West in Berlin, which ultimately provided much of the institutional expertise for coordinating the confiscation of remaining property from Jewish deportees after the introduction of the Eleventh Decree to the Reich Citizenship Law in November 1941.[63]

The First Denaturalization Cases, 1933–1936

Initially, the German bureaucracy did not envisage the application of denaturalization on a massive scale. Rather, each case was to be decided individually on the basis of documented evidence. The minutes of a conference held at the Interior Ministry in February 1934 indicate that the aim was to concentrate on those emigrants who were actively spreading propaganda against the Nazi regime. The authorities did not intend "to reduce the impact of the denaturalization measures by applying it to unimportant cases."[64] On these grounds, only 136 names were published up until the end of 1935, and a further 155 in 1936, as the instrument of denaturalization was directed primarily against a few well-known political opponents.[65]

Two examples of Jews who were among those initially selected for denaturalization are Arnold Zweig and Albert Einstein. Einstein's name was actually included on the first denaturalization list sent to the Reich and Prussian Interior Ministry on August 9, 1933, by the Gestapa (Gestapo Central Office).[66] At that time, the Foreign Ministry was opposed to Einstein's

---

Heft 6, *Behandlung der vermögensrechtlichen Ansprüche der NS-Verfolgten* (Berlin, 1994), pp. 115–18 (*Reichsgesetzblatt* I [1933], pp. 479–80 and pp. 538–39); see also J. Walk (ed.), *Das Sonderrecht für die Juden im NS-Staat,* 2nd edition (Heidelberg: C. F. Müller, 1996), I-172.

[62] See J. Walk (ed.), *Das Sonderrecht*, I-172.

[63] See Chapters 4 and 6.

[64] PAAA, Inl. II A/B, R 99639, Fiche No. 6257, record of a conference concerning denaturalization at the Interior Ministry on February 9, 1934.

[65] Statistics from M. Hepp (ed.), *Die Ausbürgerung*, vol. I, p. lvii.

[66] PAAA, Inl. II A/B, R 99638, Fiche No. 6251, first list sent to the Interior Ministry on August 9, 1933.

inclusion because of his imposing international reputation. The Gestapa, however, argued that Einstein's position as honorary president of the "International Aid Committee for the Victims of Hitler-Fascism" and other "anti-German" propaganda activities meant that the German government would be sending the wrong message if Einstein were excluded from the first published list.[67]

Representatives of the Interior Ministry, the Gestapa, and the Foreign Ministry who met on August 16, 1933, decided to go ahead with the publication of the first list. They decided to denaturalize the listed German communists and socialists, who included prominent Jews and other leading critics of the regime, to set a clear example. Meeting participants also agreed to prepare detailed internal reports citing the reasons for each proposed denaturalization. Furthermore, in specific cases, they decided to denaturalize close relatives as well. One reason for this measure was to prevent property from escaping confiscation by being transferred to relatives.[68] Einstein's denaturalization was initially postponed because of Foreign Ministry reservations and his own application to renounce his citizenship. However, his name was included on the second denaturalization list, published on March 24, 1934, after the U.S. House of Representatives recommended that he be granted American citizenship.[69]

It was novelist Arnold Zweig's writings that brought him to the Gestapo's attention. In the words of a Gestapo report, "in all his novels he embodied the spiritual level of the passed Marxist years and tried to bring down the precious moral and ethical values of German culture in favor of an alien Jewish proletarian one inspired by class hatred." The Gestapo accused Zweig of defaming the image of German officers by portraying them in his World War I novel, *The Case of Sergeant Grischa*, as inefficient and unjust. He also was said to have attacked the Nazi government in the *Free Press* of Amsterdam and the *Pariser Tageblatt*. The Gestapa recommended his denaturalization on March 13, 1935, and his name was published in the fifth list, on March 3, 1936.[70]

That Zweig was not intimidated by the efforts of the Gestapo is evident from his spirited response to the confiscation of his furniture and extensive library in December 1933. Confronting the Gestapo's claim that they had confiscated the items in accordance with the laws for the Confiscation of

---

[67] Ibid., Foreign Ministry to *Staatssekretär* von Bülow on August 18, 1933.
[68] Ibid., Meeting of the Interior Ministry, Foreign Office, and Gestapa on August 16, 1933.
[69] Einstein did not actually receive U.S. citizenship until October 2, 1940. PAAA, Inl. II A/B, R 99639, no. 6258.
[70] PAAA, Inl. II A/B, R 99647, no. 6302.

Communist Property and the Confiscation of Property of Enemies of the People and the State, Zweig's lawyer replied that "the confiscated items do not belong to a Marxist party but are the private items of Mr. Zweig. Therefore, they cannot be confiscated according to the above-mentioned laws. The apartment furnishings as well as the carpets and rugs certainly do not serve the furtherance of Marxist purposes."[71]

These two early cases are interesting as the Gestapo ordered the expropriation of the subject's property prior to denaturalization on the basis of legal decrees that were designed for the confiscation of the property of the Nazis' political opponents inside Germany.[72] Thus, the motivation for denaturalization was not in principle the seizure of property, but rather to exclude individuals from citizenship because they were opponents of the regime. Nevertheless, the possibility of confiscation was linked to denaturalization from the start, and guidelines were issued for its implementation. The task of securing property in advance of denaturalization fell to the Gestapo, whereas the Finanzamt Moabit-West collected and disposed of this property on behalf of the Reich Finance Minister, after the name of the person being denaturalized was published.[73]

Therefore, all cases of expropriation via denaturalization are well documented, as the names were published in the *Reichsanzeiger* state gazette to inform creditors of the deadline for making claims.[74] It was not a secret policy, but one that was enforced publicly by the tax authorities and even the

---

[71] See GSPK, Rep. 151 (Reg. IIG), HA IA, no. 8074, Arnold Zweig. Zweig ultimately received some compensation for his furniture and library – in 1955; see (OFDB) 3-343/51. Zweig received about DM 40,000, based on an estimate of the replacement value of the items he described. There was some dispute about the value of his original manuscripts, many of which were permanently lost. The law for the confiscation of property of "enemies of the people and the state" is also published in *Schriftenreihe des Bundesamtes zur Regelung offener Vermögensfragen, Heft 6*, pp. 115–16.

[72] As Martin Friedenberger has noted, in some cases this practice created an internal conflict between the Finanzamt (FA) Moabit-Wes, a Reich authority, and the Gestapo, at that time a regional state authority, as under the relevant confiscation decrees confiscated property went to the benefit of the regional state administration (*Länder*); see Martin Friedenberger, "Das Berliner Finanzamt Moabit-West und die Enteignung der Emigranten des Dritten Reichs 1933–1942," in *Zeitschrift für Geschichtswissenschaft* 49, no. 8 (2001): 677–94, here, pp. 678–80.

[73] LAB, A Rep. 092/54564, report of FA Moabit-Wes, December 15, 1938; Stefan Mehl, *Das Reichsfinanzministerium und die Verfolgung der deutschen Juden 1933–1943* (Berlin, 1990), p. 33. The Finanzamt Moabit-West also had to apply for a confiscation declaration (*Verfallserklärung*) individually from the Interior Ministry, which had to be published before the funds were collected; see Martin Friedenberger, "Das Berliner Finanzamt Moabit-West," pp. 680–82.

[74] For the complete lists of published names, see M. Hepp (ed.), *Die Ausbürgerung*, 3 vols.

banks in cooperation with the Gestapo. In the early cases, the Nazi authorities were keen to stress the damage to the German state caused by specific
named subjects of denaturalization. For example, in December 1936, the
Berliner Morgenpost published the names of thirty-nine "parasites," including
details of the allegations made against them. The list included three Jewish
newspaper owners, who were alleged to be in close contact with Jewish
emigrant organizations in Paris and were described as "actively hostile" to
the German state. Others included former members of the SPD and alleged
Marxists and Communists, including a Jewish emigrant to the United States
who had publicly criticized the political situation in Germany.[75]

An early instance in which considerations of property confiscation clearly
played a role was the denaturalization of "J. C.," a Jewish former director
of a large medical insurance office in Berlin. The report prepared by the
Gestapo Central Office in support of its July 8, 1936, denaturalization
proposal illustrates the tendentious logic employed at the time. It cited, for
example, J. C.'s links to the SPD and his alleged acquisition of false health
documents to enable his early retirement, as he allegedly foresaw in 1932
("with typical Jewish instinct") the development of the political situation.
The Gestapo argued that he remained actively hostile toward Germany after
his emigration, since "the anti-German work of the Jews concentrated in
Palestine is generally known," but that he "still received a monthly pension
of RM 737.58 from the German Reich." Therefore, they demanded his
denaturalization "in order to put an end to this unacceptable situation."[76]

The denaturalization of J. C. was not published until April 14, 1937,
by which time the Labor Ministry in Berlin already had decided to withdraw permission for him to receive his pension abroad.[77] Meanwhile, the
Gestapo had broadened its guidelines regulating denaturalization to include

---

[75] NARA, RG-242, T-580, reel 28, *Berliner Morgenpost*, December 4, 1936; list of thirty-nine
names of persons denaturalized with property confiscated.

[76] PAAA, Inl. II A/B, R 99657, no. 6354.

[77] Up until the end of 1934 it was possible for Jewish emigrants to receive their pensions
abroad due to reciprocal agreements Germany had with a number of countries, including France, Poland, and the Netherlands. Those who emigrated after January 1, 1935,
however, no longer received the necessary approval from the currency offices. From the
spring of 1940 the pensions of emigrants living in "enemy states" were withheld under
the "enemy property" regulations, including of course those resident in Palestine. See
Susanne Heim, "Vertreibung, Raub und Umverteilung: Die jüdischen Flüchtlinge aus
Deutschland und die Vermehrung des 'Volksvermögens,'" in *Beiträge zur Nationalsozialistischen Gesundheits- und Sozialpolitik* no. 15, pp. 107–38, here p. 115. As this example
demonstrates, some pensions were also withheld following administrative decisions prior
to 1940.

those persons, especially Jews, who allegedly were causing economic damage to the German Reich. This case, initiated in mid-1936, shows how the Nazi administration gradually broadened the population subject to denaturalization. The Gestapo referred not only to J. C.'s political opposition from abroad but also deployed specific economic arguments.[78] According to postwar restitution files, the transfer to the Reich of J. C.'s remaining domestic property, consisting of a bank account, the repurchase value of a life insurance policy, and the value of insurance rights with the German Labor Front, was not completed until December 1938.[79]

Up to the end of 1936, denaturalization remained primarily a limited measure directed against political opponents who were active abroad. Increased Jewish emigration and intensified "legal" persecution in Germany, however, led to the broadened use of denaturalization to punish Jewish emigrants. New guidelines issued in April 1937 considerably enlarged the target group to include Jews who had infringed Germany's stringent racial and currency laws.

Implementation of New Guidelines for Denaturalizing Jewish Emigrants, 1937–1939

The introduction of the Nuremberg racial laws in September 1935 represented a considerable radicalization of persecution. These laws not only carefully defined who was a Jew but also prohibited marriage and sexual relations between Jews and Germans. They opened the way for additional criminal prosecutions against Jews for "defiling the German race" (*Rassenschande*), and they stimulated further emigration. At the same time, the Nazi regime faced a severe shortage of foreign currency to buy raw materials for its rapidly expanding armaments sector. This shortage was a primary concern of Hermann Göring's Office of the Four-Year Plan, created in 1936. To prevent emigrant Jews from "smuggling capital" out of the country, by 1936, the Gestapo had strengthened its cooperation with the financial administration.[80] Thus by 1937, the increasing criminalization of the Jews under new racial and currency control statutes prepared the ground also for the intensified application of denaturalization proceedings against Jewish emigrants.

---

[78] PAAA, Inl. II A/B, R 99657, No. 6354.

[79] OFDB, 1-6154-56/57. J.C. died in Tel Aviv on October 22, 1941.

[80] See especially the extensive correspondence on this issue from 1936 on in BAL, R 2/5978. This topic is dealt with in more detail in Chapter 2.

Decisive to this development was the distribution of new denaturalization guidelines to regional Gestapo posts in April 1937. Reinhard Heydrich (head of the Gestapa) demanded that reports be prepared on the economic activity of emigrant Jews and on any commercial or tax obligations they had left behind. Precise details were to be provided about any "typically Jewish crimes."[81] He enclosed a decree prepared by Reichsführer-SS Himmler at the end of March, which argued that, regardless of their activities abroad, the behavior of Jews before their emigration had already demonstrated their "hostile attitude to the state and the people." Himmler recommended moving "against this population group with greater severity than before with regard to denaturalization."

Himmler wished to enlarge the "group of enemies of the people" to include those who, although not politically active, had come to notice through "a typically Jewish behavior that was damaging to the German people (Volk)." This category was to include those who infringed upon the currency and tax laws or committed other crimes out of Jewish "avarice," such as fraud, blackmail, or the falsification of documents; Jews guilty of "defiling the German race sexually" (Rassenschande); and those who were members of Marxist parties or supported them financially. He deemed annulment of citizenship appropriate for individuals who had already been convicted of such crimes and who sought to avoid punishment by flight abroad.[82] The linking of financial and "racial" offenses to denaturalization meant that their punishment would be imposed via confiscation.

Several subsequent denaturalization proposals made specific reference to these instructions.[83] Yet, it still took time for this much-increased emphasis on economic crimes to have an impact on denaturalization proposals passed on to the Interior Ministry. According to an analysis of Gestapo files from Düsseldorf, up until 1939, the main sources of denaturalization proceedings against Jews were passport renewal applications received from overseas, rather than investigative initiatives at the local level.[84]

A proposal prepared by the Gestapo in Düsseldorf and dated August 11, 1937, exemplifies how Nazi Germany's new racial laws were applied with regard to denaturalization. "H. A.," a Jewish man who had migrated to the Netherlands in April 1936, had previously been investigated for alleged

---

[81] BAL, R 58/62, Heydrich to Gestapo Offices on April 12, 1937.

[82] Ibid., RFSS (Himmler) to Gestapo Central Office on March 30, 1937; see also H. G. Lehmann, "Acht und Ächtung", pp. XIII–IV.

[83] See, for example, LAB, A Rep. 092/50484, Gestapo Darmstadt to Gestapo Central Office on September 22, 1937.

[84] Holger Berschel, Bürokratie und Terror: Das Judenreferat der Gestapo Düsseldorf 1933–1945 (Essen: Klartext, 2001), pp. 264–70.

"defilement of the race" and currency offenses. The file was subsequently closed for lack of evidence. H. A. was accused of having had sexual relations with "E. K.," a German woman. Both admitted this relationship, but maintained that after the publication of the Nuremberg Laws they wrote each other parting letters, saying they wanted nothing more to do with one another. That these letters were only a deception became evident from the fact that both emigrated in 1936 and were married in London. They then opened a fashion salon together in Amsterdam. The Gestapo concluded that their disrespect for the German blood laws had shown them unworthy of German citizenship. They had not come to the Gestapo's attention for political, espionage, or criminal reasons, and they possessed no property in Germany. The application also proposed the denaturalization of the "German-blooded wife," directly citing Heydrich's circular.[85]

Increasing Economic Motivation for Denaturalizations

The files of Gestapo denaturalization proposals, preserved in the archives in Berlin, include a number of cases that demonstrate how economic motives played an increasing role in denaturalization policy by the late 1930s. Among the detailed Gestapo proposals prepared in 1936 and 1937, mostly dealing with alleged political opponents of the regime, there are several cases based mainly on economic grounds. The case of a family of five Jewish businessmen from Nuremberg, all with the surname "R.," is representative of the emergence of this type of case.

The family owned a paintbrush manufacturing business in Nuremberg and received permission in 1931 to establish a subsidiary plant in Britain for the purpose of boosting German foreign earnings. In response to Nazi economic persecution, members of the family then started to emigrate successively. They used their international business contacts to build up capital in Switzerland, in defiance of Germany's strict currency laws. When the Nazi authorities confiscated the passports of the last two remaining brothers to prevent their emigration, they fled illegally to Czechoslovakia. According to the Gestapo report, in an attempt to regain their confiscated passports, the family "threatened" to close down the factory in Nuremberg.

The Nazi administration's response was to initiate denaturalization proceedings against several members of the family. As the Gestapo recommendation concluded, "In order to thwart the plans of the Jewish brothers 'R.,' the most important aspect is to get hold of their property and thereby

---

[85] PAAA, Inl. II A/B, R 99678, no. 6451, Gestapo Düsseldorf, Denaturalization Proposal against H. A. and his wife on August 11, 1937.

also their business through the denaturalization case." This was particularly urgent, as one of the brothers had applied to become a British subject, which might even forestall the planned confiscation of their property. The Gestapo's denaturalization proposal received direct support from the local Reichsbank office, the Currency Office, the Nuremberg Chamber of Industry and Commerce, the Regional Economic Advisor (*Gauwirtschaftsberater*), and the Customs Investigation Office in Nuremberg. In political terms it was known only that two of the brothers had been members of the "Association for Defense against Antisemitism." In addition to the currency offense charged against one of the brothers, the main motivation for the denaturalization proceedings was the anticipated financial loss to the Reich that would result from the family's emigration and the closure of their business.[86] Given that the family was more or less forced to emigrate by economic and political pressure in Germany, the circular nature of the Gestapo's argumentation is transparent.

German investigations of Jews and resulting prosecutions that were abandoned because the accused had fled abroad might also move the Gestapo to instigate a denaturalization case. Many such cases involved alleged political "crimes," but increasingly they also related to currency or customs offenses. For example, the Jewish man, "A. L.," was recommended for denaturalization in May 1937 on the basis of currency and tax offenses. Allegedly, he had kept an illegal stock of business-related household goods and fled abroad before he could be arrested. All his domestic property was seized in connection with tax debts of RM 43,000. The Gestapo also recommended denaturalization of his immediate family.[87]

In January 1938, the Gestapo Central Office issued further guidelines for denaturalization aimed mainly against Jewish emigrants. Reports proposing Jews for denaturalization were henceforth to be confined to details relating to their political or economic activity, their criminal punishment, and the date of their emigration. Heydrich argued that Jewish emigrants' property relations could not always be established with the necessary degree of certainty, as it was to be expected that they were engaged in "murky" transfers of capital. Therefore, the authorities were to apply for confiscation in every case, whether property had been found in Germany or not. Complaining about the small number of denaturalization proposals received from some State Police offices, Heydrich demanded that in future

---

[86] LAB, A Rep. 092/50479, pp. 117–24, Denaturalization Proposal of Gestapo Nuremberg dated June 30, 1937.

[87] See PAAA, Inl. II A/B, R 99671, no. 6420, Gestapo Düsseldorf Denaturalization Proposal against A. L. on May 25, 1937.

denaturalization proceedings be initiated in all cases in which the prescribed grounds clearly existed.[88]

Subsequently, the number of cases related primarily to alleged economic "crimes" rose considerably. In May 1939, the Gestapo in Stuttgart proposed the denaturalization of "F.," a Jewish businessman, not for any political activity but because of "foreign currency and economic interests." F. was the joint owner of a Stuttgart-area paper-manufacturing plant that had a subsidiary company in London. The company was Aryanized in March 1939, but the Jewish owners had already emigrated and blocked all payments to Germany from the London-based branch. The Gestapo feared that, due to the loss of existing contracts, the company's valuable export business would fall to the former subsidiary in Britain. The report concluded that the conditions for denaturalization and the seizure of property in Germany outlined in Himmler's guidelines were fulfilled.[89]

Processing of Cases Involving Property

In view of the increasing importance of property considerations for denaturalization cases from 1937 onward, it is worth examining the process of property confiscation more closely. After the Gestapo began denaturalization proceedings, the Finanzamt Moabit-West commissioned the relevant Tax Offices to rapidly prepare a precise listing of the financial circumstances of those named, including any outstanding debts or other relevant details, so that the Gestapo could secure their property without delay. It also confidentially requested that the Currency Office not approve any more financial transactions involving the subjects of denaturalization proceedings.[90]

A detailed memorandum from December 1938 describes the diverse work of the Finanzamt Moabit-West with regard to denaturalization. In cases of property confiscation, it had to notify all debtors and creditors, name trustees, and correct the title deeds to real estate. It then had to sell the property. All cases were registered in a card index organized by type of property, with incoming payments of rent or interest recorded to ensure their continued collection. The Finanzamt Moabit-West found it especially difficult to administer the more than fifty medium-sized companies (employing between 50 and 250 workers). Although appointed trustees

---

[88] BAL, R 58/62, Gestapo Central Office to all State Police Offices on January 11, 1938.

[89] PAAA, Inl. II A/B, R 99805 Denaturalization Proposal of Gestapo Stuttgart against D.M.F. on May 2, 1939.

[90] LAB, A Rep. 092/54564, FA Moabit-West circular to Tax Offices (S 1110-) undated (1933) probably distributed as O 1300 – I 1/33 on September 8, 1933; see also LAB, A Rep. 092/50477, Instruction No. 1304 to FA Moabit-West on June 20, 1938.

carried out much of the everyday work, it still had to make a number of important decisions. It had either to dismiss employees or renew their contracts, examine creditors' claims, sign contracts, and pursue legal cases. The Finanzamt Moabit-West had to hold discussions with interested parties, such as businessmen, lawyers, banks, trustees, and liquidators. In all these matters, deadlines had to be observed.[91]

Despite some inevitable rivalries within the administration, property seizure relied on a very effective combination of the executive authority of the Gestapo and the technical expertise of the Tax Offices. In December 1938, Himmler proposed that the relevant Tax Offices be made responsible for the administration of secured property prior to denaturalization, as the police did not have sufficient skilled personnel to deal with complex property cases.[92] The Finanzamt Moabit-West, however, reacted skeptically on practical grounds, as more of its own staff would be required to deal with an increased workload. In addition, the Finanzamt argued that only the Security Police had sufficiently wide-ranging powers and the operational flexibility to secure property in advance of denaturalization, for example, using the extraordinary powers granted under the Reichstag Fire Decree of February 28, 1933.[93]

After the introduction of the new guidelines in spring 1937, the number of denaturalization cases rose sharply, from only 155 in 1936 to 1,028 in 1937, 4,242 in 1938, and some 10,000 each in 1939 and 1940. Correspondingly, the number of new cases involving property confiscation received by the Finanzamt Moabit-West rose steadily from 93 in 1936 to 566 in 1938 and then to 1,300 in 1939. Thus, the intensified confiscation of Jewish property using the denaturalization law began in 1937–1938 with the new guidelines, prior to the devastating effects of Kristallnacht that in turn stimulated intensified emigration by Jews.[94]

Official statistics on the income to the Reich from denaturalization reveal that up to the end of 1938 only just over RM 6 million had been booked officially as received – a very small amount in comparison with the large

---

[91] LAB, A Rep. 092/54564, FA Moabit-West to OFP Berlin on December 15, 1938.
[92] LAB, A Rep. 092/54564, RFSS B. NR. S-PP (II-B), no. 4575/37 on December 28, 1938.
[93] Ibid., FA Moabit-West to OFP Berlin O.1300 – 2/39 February 3, 1939, and OFP Berlin, memo of March 8, 1939.
[94] For figures on denaturalization by year, see M. Hepp (ed.), *Die Ausbürgerung*, vol. 1, p. LVII; figures for cases processed by FA Moabit-West, see LAB, A Rep. 092/54564 Report by FA Moabit-West December 15, 1938, and also M. Friedenberger, K.-D. Gössel, and E. Schönknecht (eds.), *Die Reichsfinanzverwaltung im Nationalsozialismus*, p. 29; for Jewish emigration figures see for example S. Mehl, *Das Reichsfinanzministerium*, p. 45.

sums raised by the Reich flight tax. These official figures, however, do not include the income from securities or from real estate handed over to the Real Estate Administration Office (*Liegenschaftsverwaltung*).[95] In addition, the process of selling off property was quite slow so that it might take more than two years to book as income much of the money received . Thus, these official figures are considerably lower than the actual amounts received, owing to internal bureaucratic delays and exclusions.

The annual income from denaturalizations (calculated with the above-noted significant exclusions) did jump sharply to more than RM 12 million in 1939 and probably exceeded RM 20 million in 1940.[96] This large increase reflected the considerable intensification of property-motivated denaturalizations after the start of the war in 1939,[97] when the seizure of material resources for the Reich in advance of the possible naturalization of Jews in other states (which would shield their assets from confiscation) acted as an increased incentive for the "mass denaturalization" of propertied Jewish emigrants.[98] Indeed, it is probable that a significant portion of the income generally viewed as resulting from the Eleventh Decree after November 1941 actually came from the mass denaturalization of propertied Jewish emigrants in the period from 1939 to 1941.

Dissolution of the Masonic Lodges

Completed in the summer of 1935, the dissolution of the German Masonic lodges and the subsequent confiscation of their property by the state provide an interesting comparison to the confiscation of Jewish property. In spite of the very different circumstances and the more benign treatment of former Masons,[99] several common features are illuminating.

In November 1934, the Political Police in Bavaria issued instructions for the treatment of recently confiscated property from certain Masonic

---

[95] M. Friedenberger, K-D. Gössel, and E. Schönknecht (eds.), *Die Reichsfinanzverwaltung*, p. 29.

[96] Ibid.

[97] See Chapter 5 for more details.

[98] See M. Dean, "The Development and Implementation of Nazi Denaturalization and Confiscation Policy," pp. 226–28.

[99] Renate Endler and Elisabeth Schwarze (eds.), *Die Freimaurerbestände im Geheimen Staatsarchiv Preussischer Kulturbesitz: Bd. 1, Grosslogen und Protektor Freimaurerische Stiftungen und Vereinigungen* (Frankfurt am Main: Peter Lang, 1994), pp. 44–45; this book notes that 1,265 former masons were recognized in 1947 by the "KZ-Stelle" in Hamburg as victims of fascism, although it is not clear that they were persecuted for their membership of Masonic lodges.

lodges. Buildings were to be locked and sealed, and their temporary use by Nazi Party organizations was recommended – to avoid the payment of taxes! Claims by third parties against the property of the lodges could be made, but were to be checked carefully, to hinder any attempts by former lodge members to recover property. Any payments to widows and other dependents from confiscated lodge funds required the permission of the Bavarian Political Police.[100]

The leading Masonic lodges buckled under Nazi pressure and were dissolved "voluntarily" in the course of 1935, partly because their patriotic principles led them to avoid a direct conflict with the state.[101] Consequently, they also concluded with the Interior Ministry certain vague agreements about the subsequent disposition of Masonic property. The lodges' records, archives, and libraries, as well as ritual items, were to be handed over to the Gestapo. Furniture and real estate were to be sold by a liquidator overseen by the Gestapo and the proceeds used for charitable purposes. In practice, once a lodge was dissolved, the Gestapo would lock and seal the building. The *Sicherheitsdienst* (the SD, Security Service of the SS) would then take for itself relevant documentary materials and ritual objects for evaluation in the SD Central Office (*SD-Haputamt*) in Berlin. The documents were used to generate a card index of former lodge members and for research on "freemasonry," whereas some duplicates of books were subsequently transferred to public libraries.[102]

The forced dissolution of remaining lodges (with the temporary exception of B'nai B'rith, a Jewish organization with chapters that bore some similarities to Masonic lodges) that was decreed by Interior Minister Wilhelm Frick on August 17, 1935, included provisions for the confiscation of lodge property on the grounds that it served purposes "hostile to the people and the state." Thus, their property was handled slightly differently from that of the lodges that had dissolved themselves "voluntarily."[103]

To help clarify matters, in April 1936 the Central Office of the Gestapo issued additional instructions on the handling of confiscated Masonic objects. Most gold and silver items were to be melted down. Less valuable items might be given to the *Nationalsozialistische Volkswohlfahrt* (National

---

[100] NARA, RG-242, T-580, reel 112 Bavarian Political Police circular, November 8, 1934.

[101] Ralf Melzer, *Konflikt und Anpassung: Freimaurerei in der Weimar Republik und im "Dritten Reich"* (Vienna: Bramüller, 1999), pp. 148–49.

[102] Helmut Neuberger, *Winkelmass und Hakenkreuz: Die Freimaurer und das Dritte Reich* (Munich: Herbig, 2001), pp. 264–71. Just as they created a "Jewish Museum" in Prague, the SD also established a "Museum of Freemasonry" in Berlin while using the archival material of the lodges to carefully observe their former members; R. Melzer, *Konflikt und Anpassung*, pp. 150–53.

[103] R. Melzer, *Konflikt und Anpassung*, pp. 149–50.

Socialist People's Welfare, NSV) and other charitable organizations, provided that the Masonic symbols were removed.[104] Despite pressure for the rapid sale and disposal of lodge property, the process of liquidation dragged on in some cases into 1941. The Gestapo closely supervised the management and sale of real estate, and some of the choice properties were sold to Party and state offices for well under market value. For example, the SD took over some lodge buildings to house part of the confiscated archival and library collections. According to a 1940 Himmler decree, the remaining financial proceeds were to be used for charitable purposes. The actual beneficiaries included the *Nationalsozialistische Kriegsopferversorgung* (National Socialist War Victims Fund), several old people's homes previously linked to freemasonry, and a pension fund for former employees of the lodges.[105]

Several underlying principles developed by the Nazi authorities for the handling of confiscated Masonic property were also applied toward some seized Jewish property. For example, the Gestapo played an active role in sealing and securing both Masonic and Jewish property; seized documentary records and some of the spoils were exploited in both cases to further persecution of the group; and choice items were diverted (especially real estate) for Party and state use, as well as for selected "charitable ends." The Gestapo maintained close control over the entire operation against the Masonic lodges, as large amounts of private or business property were not involved.

After the subsequent dissolution of the B'nai B'rith organizations on April 10, 1937, for "activities hostile to the state," the Gestapo applied very similar practices to the confiscation of their property. In particular, the membership records seized by the SD were carefully evaluated for denaturalization purposes. The Gestapo, for example, prepared a denaturalization proposal in June 1939 against the Jewish emigrant, "M. G.," citing his membership in the "Swabian Lodge" of B'nai B'rith as the main reason for the case brought against him. An examination of the denaturalization proposals kept by the German Foreign Office reveals that many former members of B'nai B'rith were so targeted after April 1937. Where the tax authorities uncovered property, denaturalization also included its confiscation.[106]

---

[104] NARA, RG-242, T-175, roll 414, fr. 2940026-27, Gestapoamt to Stapostellen, April 6, 1936.

[105] H. Neuberger, *Winkelmass und Hakenkreuz*, pp. 271–72; Ralf Melzer, *Konflikt und Anpassung*, pp. 149–53.

[106] PAAA, Inl. II A/B, R 99836, Gestapo Augsburg denaturalization proposal against M. G. on June 7, 1939; LAB, A Rep. 092/50478, Gestapo Kassel to Gestapo Central Office – denaturalization of the Jewish Dr. H. K., March 22, 1938; for other cases involving so-called Jewish lodges, see, for example, PAAA, Inl. II A/B, R 99711, no. 6597, Gestapo

Progress of the Aryanization and Liquidation of Jewish Businesses up to 1938

Avraham Barkai argues forcefully that the sale and liquidation of the bulk of Jewish businesses had to a large extent already taken place before the introduction of the extensive battery of legal measures for the completion of Aryanization in the summer and fall of 1938.[107] His arguments are in part confirmed by subsequent, more detailed regional studies, even if the trend is not so clear for larger cities, such as Hamburg. For example, in a comparison of the dynamics of the Aryanization process for three medium-sized German towns, Alex Brüns-Wüstefeld reveals a clear pattern shared by all three. There was a steady decline in the number of Jewish businesses, such that some 50 percent or less remained at the beginning of 1938: in Heidelberg (53 percent), Göttingen (44 percent), and Marburg (31 percent). Another important finding was that even before 1938 considerably more Jewish businesses had been liquidated than were transferred into "Aryan" ownership.[108]

The evidence for the port city of Hamburg is somewhat different, as here, according to Bajohr's figures, only a small proportion of those Jewish firms that were Aryanized (fewer than 10 percent) changed hands before 1938.[109] There are a number of reasons for the slower pace of Aryanization in Hamburg, but the importance of foreign currency earned by Jewish import-export businesses was clearly a key factor. In addition, larger cities such as Hamburg and Berlin also saw an influx of Jews from the countryside during the 1930s, replacing some of the losses due to emigration. This meant that it was somewhat easier for Jews to sustain businesses there, based primarily on trade within the Jewish community. The anonymity of the big city may also have made it easier for non-Jews to continue visiting Jewish shops without suffering reprisals.

From 1936 onward, the Party increasingly sought to intervene directly in the Aryanization process, claiming the right to review Aryanization contracts. This intervention occurred, for instance, in the Gau of southern Westphalia, where the Gau economics adviser issued guidelines in August 1937 for conducting "the takeover of Jewish companies by members of the German community." This foreshadowed the system introduced in

Frankfurt denaturalization proposal against K. F. on April 21, 1938; and R 99925, Gestapo München report on May 13, 1941.

[107] Avraham Barkai, *Vom Boykott zur "Entjudung": Der wirtschaftliche Existenzkampf der Juden im Dritten Reich 1933–1943* (Frankfurt am Main: Fischer, 1987), pp. 80 and 122–26.

[108] Alex Brüns-Wüstefeld, *Lohnende Geschäfte: Die "Entjudung der Wirtschaft am Beispiel Göttingens* (Hannover: Fackelträger, 1997), pp. 122–25.

[109] F. Bajohr, '*Aryanisation*,' p. 314.

April 1938 for regulating the Aryanization of remaining Jewish businesses, which granted the Party, in the person of the Gau economics adviser, precisely this right to review and, if necessary, intervene in all Aryanizations.[110]

The degree of direct coercion in the Aryanizations and liquidations of the mid-1930s varied considerably from case to case. For example, in Hanau, the Jewish owner of a fashion business was arrested and convicted on trumped-up charges of *Rassenschande* in June 1935, after which the windows of his shop were also smashed and defaced. The owner's wife then attempted to run the business, but was forced to sell in 1936 at a low price that was knocked down again after the contract was signed, when she was threatened with incarceration in a concentration camp. After her husband was released, they both migrated to Uruguay in August 1938.[111]

In many cases, it was the effectiveness of the boycotts that forced Jewish businesses into liquidation or to be sold. In the fall of 1937, the Gau economics adviser in southern Westphalia reported that no members of the Party and its organizations, no officials, and, in the countryside, few farmers were still buying in Jewish shops.[112] Despite some degree of exaggeration, this boycott no doubt had an effect.[113] Naturally, a business that had lost most of its customers soon ran into debt and even became difficult to sell, accounting in part for the large number of liquidations. In addition, the Four-Year Plan applied further direct pressure, as at the end of 1937 Hermann Göring introduced the discriminatory tightening of raw materials supplies.[114] In some cases, the passports of Jews were confiscated and held ransom until all their business debts had been paid.[115]

Erosion of Jewish Wealth

Reliable figures are not available for the overall amount of Jewish wealth at the time of the Nazi seizure of power. Neither are reliable figures available

---

[110] See Gerhard Kratzsch, *Der Gauwirtschaftsapparat der NSDAP: Menschenführung – "Arisierung" – Wehrwirtschaft im Gau Westfalen-Süd* (Münster: Aschendorffsche, 1989), pp. 146–53 and 178–85.

[111] M. I. Pfeifer, "Entrechtung und Verfolgung," pp. 52–53.

[112] G. Kratzsch, *Der Gauwirtschaftsapparat*, p. 165.

[113] Examples from Rheinland – Pfalz in 1936 and 1938 demonstrate that the Party there organized economic reprisals against those who traded with Jews; see J. Simmert and H-W. Herrmann (eds.), *Die nationalsozialistische Judenverfolgung in Rheinland – Pfalz*, pp. 87–88, 101.

[114] H. James, *The Deutsche Bank*, p. 51.

[115] Barbara Händler-Lachmann and Thomas Werther, *Vergessene Geschäfte – verlorene Geschichte: Jüdisches Wirtschaftsleben in Marburg und seine Vernichtung im Nationalsozialismus* (Marburg: Hitzeroth, 1992), pp. 92–93.

for the subsequent decline of that wealth due to emigration, Aryanization, and confiscation. The estimate for Jewish wealth in Germany in 1933 lies somewhere in a range between RM 8 and 12 billion, given that the total amount registered in the Jewish property census taken in the summer of 1938 for both Germany and Austria was just under RM 8 billion.[116] In a speech quoted in the *Frankfurter Zeitung* just after the Kristallnacht pogrom in November 1938, Walter Funk, the Reich Minister of Economics, estimated that more than RM 2 billion of Jewish property had already been transferred into German possession since April of that year.[117] However, since many businesses were sold at less than their real value or simply forced into liquidation, the loss of value to the Jewish owners was considerably greater than this amount. Much of this wealth was simply wiped out by the effects of boycotts, forced sales, and confiscations.

These rough figures indicate that probably in excess of one-third of German Jewish wealth was eroded in the period from 1933 to 1938. This erosion was partly due to the emigration of nearly one-third of the German Jewish population, but it also reflected the enforced sale of property, especially businesses, at reduced prices. As Ronald Zweig argues, Jewish prosperity was "based on intangibles, such as education, expectations, motivation, professional standing, and experience," as much as it was on the ownership of capital.[118] The effects of Nazi economic discrimination devastated these key foundations and provoked the emigration of experienced businessmen, craftsmen, and employees, together with their productive capabilities. Increasingly, those who remained behind were the elderly, the sick, and those with family dependents to support.

---

[116] See Helen B. Junz, "Report on the Pre-War Wealth Position of the Jewish Population in Nazi-Occupied Countries, Germany and Austria" in Independent Committee of Eminent Persons (eds.), *Report on Dormant Accounts of Victims of Nazi Persecution in Swiss Banks* (December 1999), Appendix S, pp. A-165–66.

[117] USHMM, RG-6.005.02, OCCWC Nuremberg, Germany. Preliminary Briefs of Economics Division, vol. 1, fr. 01377, 'The Aryanization of Jewish Property in Germany' quoting Nbg. Doc. 3545-PS. Cited also by Raul Hilberg, *The Destruction of the European Jews*, 3 vols, 3rd Edition (New Haven: Yale University Press, 2003), vol. I, p. 135.

[118] Ronald W. Zweig, "Der ungarische Goldzug oder Der Mythos vom jüdischen Reichtum," in Constantin Goschler and Philipp Ther (eds.), *Raub und Restitution: "Arisierung" und Rückerstattung des jüdischen Eigentums in Europa* (Frankfurt am Main: Fischer Taschenbuch, 2003): 169–83. An expanded version of this anthology also appears in English: Martin Dean, Constantin Goschler, and Philipp Ther (eds.), *Robbery and Restitution: The Conflict over Jewish Property in Europe* (New York: Berghahn Books in association with the United States Holocaust Memorial Museum, 2007), pp. 211–22.

State Manipulation of Trade and Capital Markets

One of the main aims of Nazi economic policy was to reduce the costs of its own massive borrowing for rearmament. Therefore, the gradual reduction of interest rates, especially on government bonds, was accompanied by measures designed to make alternative investments less attractive.[119] For example, the untranslatable *"Anleihestockgesetz"* (Bond Intermission Law) of December 1934 fixed limits on the dividends that joint stock companies could pay, thereby considerably reducing the attractiveness of owning shares. As a result, new issues of shares remained at a low level throughout the 1930s.[120] Foreigners had their investments fixed into blocked accounts by foreign exchange control restrictions, and they were permitted to buy only government bonds and not German shares with these funds.[121] Share prices did rise as the economy recovered, but the government was most concerned to divert available funds to low-interest government bonds, calculated to finance rearmament as cheaply as possible, while trying not to undermine business confidence at the same time. As Harold James comments,

> With the exception of the racially motivated attack on Jewish possessions, the fundamental principle of private ownership was left untouched. The laws defining what ownership involved, people's "property rights," however, were utterly transformed. Germany remained a private economy, but without the guidance of those signals usually associated with the operation of a market: freely determined (not administered) prices, interest rates, or exchange quotations. It was an economy without a market mechanism that was supposed to behave as its new masters wished.[122]

In a book entitled *The Vampire Economy*, published in 1939, Guenter Reimann painted a revealing picture of the operation of the Berlin Stock Exchange under the Nazis:

[119] On the continual decline of interest rates, see Otto Nathan, "Nazi War Finance and Banking," National Bureau of Economic Research, *Our Economy in War* (Occasional Paper 20: April 1944), p. 93, Appendix, Table 3, Interest Rates in Germany, 1932, 1938–42.

[120] Harold James, "Die Deutsche Bank 1933–45," in Lothar Gall, Gerald D. Feldman, Harold James, Carl–Ludwig Holtfrerich, and Hans E. Büschgen, *Die Deutsche Bank 1870–1995* (Munich: C.H. Beck, 1995), pp. 325–26.

[121] Guenter Reimann, *The Vampire Economy: Doing Business under Fascism* (New York: Vanguard, 1939), p. 177.

[122] H. James, *The Deutsche Bank and the Nazi Economic War against the Jews*, pp. 32–33.

The Berlin Stock Exchange still exists – as a building, as an institution with large offices, with brokers and bankers, with a huge organization for daily announcement of stock and bond quotations. But it is only a pale imitation of what a stock exchange is supposed to be. For the stock exchange cannot function if and when the state regulates the flow of capital and destroys the confidence of investors in the sanctity of their property rights.

The glorious days when millions of marks daily poured into the Stock Exchange. . . . have long since departed. . . . [T]he "Aryan" members of the Berlin Stock Exchange have lost much more than they gained by the removal of the "non-Aryans". . . . because the stock exchange no longer functions as such. It has become an empty husk.[123]

These comments confirm the extent to which the Nazis, primarily through the policies of rearmament and autarky, rapidly transformed and distorted the German economy, from one based on free capital and markets to a heavily state-directed economy that still operated through private firms. This is not the place to detail the strategies by which German business adapted to this new world. Nevertheless, the policy of Aryanization and economic discrimination against the Jews was another major field in which business leaders all too willingly adapted to the new ground rules laid down by the government in order to pursue advantage.

In particular, the increasing financial pressure created by rearmament moved Göring to eye greedily the remaining "reserves" of Jewish wealth as a further resource with which to stoke Germany's economic preparations for war. By 1938, he was seeking ways to mobilize that wealth directly for the government, specifically by converting much of it into treasury bonds bearing little interest. This conversion would enable him to tap into Jewish assets directly without officially confiscating them until a later date.

At the same time, as Frank Bajohr notes, the Nazis' massive intervention in the economy and the opportunities for enrichment thereby created brought with them necessarily a culture of graft, mutual back-scratching, and endemic corruption. From opportunistic businessmen who sought to drive out their Jewish competitors, to Party officials who enriched themselves and their cronies by forcing Aryanization, there was clearly a "profit motive" to much antisemitic activity, which also reflected a more general pattern of institutionalized corruption that was built into the structures of Nazi rule.[124] As Gerald Feldman comments, it is "important to understand

---

[123] G. Reimann, *The Vampire Economy*, pp. 175–77.
[124] Frank Bajohr, *Parvenüs und Profiteure: Korruption in der NS-Zeit* (Frankfurt am Main: S. Fischer, 2001), pp. 189–95.

that for Nazi officials and businesses, the organized state-sponsored thievery was viewed more or less as 'business as usual.'"[125]

Increasing Economic Pressure

In summary, the 1930s witnessed considerable continuity in the development of Nazi property-confiscation methods. These methods were applied first in a radical and improvised fashion against the Nazis' political opponents as a key element in the consolidation of power. At the same time, the Nazis exploited the extraordinary powers of the Enabling Act to pass specific laws legitimizing their confiscations, which in turn opened up opportunities for additional confiscations in the future. The example of the denaturalization of Jewish emigrants, applied with increased intensity after the circulation of new guidelines by the Gestapa in the spring of 1937 and vastly increased after the outbreak of war, demonstrates this clearly. However, other laws directed against the property of "Communists" and "enemies of the people and the state" were also used widely thereafter for the confiscation of Jewish property.

Among the Jewish victims, there were both prescient individuals who suspected the terrible threat behind the Nazi rhetoric and prepared to leave the country and a few who protested vigorously against their treatment. As Marion Kaplan describes it, many Jews "clung to mixed signals from the government as well as from non-Jewish friends and strangers – a lull in antisemitic boycotts here, a friendly greeting there."[126] Except for a few minor legal victories and an honest price occasionally paid for businesses or other assets sold, the majority of economic actors, far from protesting the unfairness of Nazi discriminatory measures, instead adapted to the mood of the times and took advantage of the opportunities for private gain at the Jews' expense, only worsening their plight.

Essential to the dynamic of Nazi policies was the gradual and opportunistic increase of economic pressure on the Jews. The authors of those policies, however, were careful not to scare off key economic interests until those interests' independence and power had been tamed. Thus, Aryanization proceeded in a piecemeal fashion and was closely intertwined with pressure on the Jews to emigrate. Nonetheless, the chicanery of both the

---

[125] Gerald D. Feldman, "Confiscation of Jewish Assets and the Holocaust," in *Confiscation of Jewish Property in Europe, 1933–1945: New Sources and Perspectives* (Washington, DC: United States Holocaust Memorial Museum, 2003), p. 6.
[126] M. Kaplan, *Between Dignity and Despair*, p. 5.

Party and the authorities – seen for example in the interaction between local boycotts and the discriminatory application, against Jews, of existing laws and regulations – steadily increased the economic pressure to shut down businesses and leave. Yet, before 1938, radical plans to tax the Jews specifically as a group or moves to more wholesale expropriation were postponed, mainly due to fears of their effects on international markets and business confidence. It was the dynamic unleashed by the *Anschluss* with Austria and subsequently Kristallnacht that rapidly accelerated plans for the wholesale expropriation of the Jews.

In the meantime, Nazi efforts focused mainly on forcing Jewish emigration and stripping their wealth as part of the process. The dilemma facing Jews caught between the need to emigrate and the inability to take their property with them is the subject of the next chapter.

2

MOUNTING OBSTACLES TO JEWISH EMIGRATION, 1933–1939

The aim of Nazi "Jewish policy" during the initial years of the Third Reich was to pressure the Jews to emigrate. The intention, however, was that the Jews should leave most of their wealth behind for the benefit of "the German people." The Third Reich therefore applied considerable taxes and fees as part of the emigration process, making it a major source of revenue

Figure 2.1. A German customs official checks the emigration of a Jewish family in Bielefeld, 1936. *Source:* Stadtarchiv und Landesgeschichtliche Bibliothek Bielefeld. USHMM, WS # 45073.

for the state. In particular, the Reich Flight Tax (*Reichsfluchtsteuer*) exacted 25 percent of the wealth of propertied emigrants; in more than 90 percent of cases, this tax was applied against Jews.[1] As the Nazis intensified the network of regulations and currency restrictions during the 1930s, the process of emigration became a bureaucratic and financial obstacle course that by no means had a certain outcome. Nevertheless, other Nazi policies tried to reconcile the inherent contradiction between the aims of confiscation and emigration by channeling Jewish wealth toward the payment of emigration costs.

For example, the Ha'avara Agreement, signed in 1933, made available limited amounts of foreign currency to meet the large cash sums required for legal entry into Palestine while also boosting German exports. From the end of 1936, the Currency Offices (*Devisenstellen*) played a key role in forcing emigration. They blocked a considerable part of the wealth of individual Jews merely on suspicion of their emigration plans, releasing it only for the payment of taxes or other costs linked directly to emigration.[2] After the Evian Conference in the summer of 1938, the Nazi leadership opened negotiations with the Intergovernmental Committee on Refugees, under the chairmanship of George Rublee, with the aim of "mobilizing" Jewish wealth in support of emigration. Furthermore, the Nazis introduced a special emigration tax in 1938 with the intention of extracting money from propertied Jewish emigrants to help finance the emigration of some of the impoverished majority who remained.

Many emigration plans of Jewish families and individuals fell through in the late 1930s, often due to the lack of sufficient financial means. This chapter examines on the basis of individual case files the many costs imposed on Jewish emigration by the Nazi state and looks at how Jews responded. In particular, several cases of the emigration of Jewish businessmen are investigated to illustrate the many practical obstacles to the transfer of Jewish capital. The experiences of individual emigrants are also described to show

[1] Martin Friedenberger, "Die Rolle der Finanzverwaltung bei der Vertreibung, Verfolgung und Vernichtung der deutschen Juden," in Martin Friedenberger, Klaus Dieter Gössel, and Eberhard Schönknecht (eds.), *Die Reichsfinanzverwaltung im Nationalsozialismus: Darstellung und Dokumente* (Bremen: Edition Temmen, 2002): 10–94, here p. 12.

[2] See especially the paper of Claus Stolberg, "The Role of the Central Fiscal Authority in the Plundering and Expulsion of the German Jews 1933–1941," first presented at the German Studies Association Conference in San Diego, 2002. I am grateful to Professor Stolberg for showing me this paper before publication. It demonstrates clearly how the implementation of "security orders" (*Sicherungsanordnungen*) by the Currency Offices helped reconcile the contradiction between forced emigration and confiscation.

how the daily bureaucratic persecution of the "regulated individual"[3] took its toll on the lives of even those who were fortunate enough to leave Germany before October 1941 when Heinrich Himmler banned further Jewish emigration. In particular, the extensive records of the Currency Offices reveal not only their key role in the policy of forced emigration but document also the rapid impoverishment of the Jews at this time.

Approaching the issue of Jewish emigration through the lens of individual case studies spotlights the options and costs facing Jews seeking to emigrate; it also illuminates the operations of the Nazi bureaucracy. Even those Jews who emigrated successfully did so only at a considerable loss in terms of property confiscated, abandoned, taxed, or stolen and of families torn apart, in very many cases never to be reunited.

Discriminatory Measures against Jewish Emigrants

In Nazi Germany there was almost nothing that Jews could do right. After taking power, the Nazi-dominated government made it clear that it wanted to be rid of the Jews. However, the flood of regulations and especially financial restrictions and penalties made it quite difficult for Jews to leave and establish a new existence abroad. Indeed, over time the conditions for Jews emigrating became more difficult rather than easier, as Germany's principle was that the Jews should leave the country but that their money (and property) should remain. It is necessary to outline the main discriminatory measures applied against Jewish emigrants before examining their practical impact on those seeking to leave.

The Flight Tax (*Reichsfluchtsteuer*)

The Reich flight tax was introduced in 1931 as a measure aimed at preventing capital flight during the economic crisis. At that time, it was not intended as a specifically anti-Jewish measure. However, its harsh provisions – entailing the confiscation of 25 percent of all domestic wealth – meant that it soon became a severe obstacle to the transfer of Jewish-owned capital out of Germany after the large-scale emigration of Jews began in 1933.[4]

---

[3] The phrase is used in recognition of the groundbreaking analysis in H. G. Adler, *Der verwaltete Mensch: Studien zur Deportation der Juden aus Deutschland* (Tübingen: J. C. B. Mohr, 1974).

[4] See Dorothee Mussgnug, *Die Reichsfluchtsteuer* (Berlin: Duncker & Humblot, 1993).

In particular, an amendment in May 1934 reduced the tax threshold for assets to RM 50,000 and for income to RM 10,000, greatly increasing the number of Jewish emigrants affected. At the same time, the tax authorities were granted powers to demand a security payment equivalent to the expected flight tax from those planning to emigrate.[5] In practice, the tax usually amounted to more than 25 percent of current capital, as the last tax assessment was used for the calculation, and most Jews had in the meantime expended part of their wealth on their emigration. Although non-Jews were often able to gain exemptions if they could prove their emigration was in the economic interests of the Reich, such exemptions were very rarely granted to Jews.[6] The official justification for the tax was that emigrants owed something to the state for the nonpayment of future taxes.[7]

Among the measures taken to enforce the flight tax was the publication of tax citations (*Steuersteckbriefe*) in the official gazettes. Emigrants named for nonpayment were threatened with arrest if encountered on German soil.[8] Whereas only 14 names were published in 1932, this number had risen to 179 in 1936. More than 150 names were published in 1937 and in 1938, but the number fell in wartime as emigration became more difficult.[9]

The rising number of tax citations reflected also the considerable amount of income received by the Reich from the flight tax. Rising steadily from RM 1,000,000 in 1932–33 to RM 45,337,000 in 1935–36 and RM 81,354,000 in 1937–38, it reached a peak of RM 342,621,000 in the budget year that ended March 1939. In total, more than RM 925 million was

[5] Bettina Hindemith and Susanne Meinl (eds.), *Legalisierter Raub: Der Fiskus und die Ausplünderung der Juden in Hessen 1933–1945* (Frankfurt am Main: Sparkassen-Kulturstiftungen Hessen-Thüringen, 2002), pp. 13–14.

[6] Susanne Heim, "Vertreibung, Raub und Umverteilung: Die jüdischen Flüchtlinge aus Deutschland und die Vermehrung des 'Volksvermögens,'" in *Beiträge zur Nationalsozialistischen Gesundheits- und Sozialpolitik* 15: 107–38, here pp. 110–11. From December 1937 on, the Reich Finance Minister expressly opposed granting exemptions for Jews; see Susanne Meinl, "The Expropriation of Jewish Emigrants from Hessen during the 1930s," in *Confiscation of Jewish Property in Europe, 1933–1945: New Sources and Perspectives* (Washington, DC: U.S. Holocaust Memorial Museum, 2003): 93–104, here p. 95. For examples of appeals for reduction of the flight tax, dating from 1933, see BLHAP, Pr. Br. Rep. 36A (OFP Berlin-Brandenburg)/165 Reichsfluchtsteuer 1931–33.

[7] Gerald Feldman, "Confiscation of Jewish Assets and the Holocaust," in *Confiscation of Jewish Property in Europe, 1933–1945*, p. 4; D. Mussgnug, *Die Reichsfluchtsteuer*, p. 37.

[8] M. Friedenberger, "Die Rolle der Finanzverwaltung," p. 12.

[9] See Kerstin and Frank Wolf (eds.), *Reichsfluchtsteuer und Steuersteckbriefe 1932–42*, p. 10. The names of those who failed to pay outstanding taxes were also published in the relevant official gazettes (*Reichsanzeiger* and *Reichssteuerblatt*). See also the Web site on this topic at http://home.arcor.de/kerstinwolf, which was still being updated as of January 5, 2003.

raised by March 1943. This made a considerable contribution to Germany's finances, as in 1940 total annual revenue was only some RM 24 billion.[10]

Observation Network

From 1933 onward, along with the implementation of the flight tax came the introduction of extensive measures of observation and persecution relating to Jewish emigration. For example, the post office was expected to report to the relevant Tax Offices any changes of address to abroad made by Jews; moving companies were to notify them of all Jewish removal contracts; and from 1936 on, notaries were obliged to inform them of any real estate sales involving Jews.[11] Some measures resulted from local initiatives within the bureaucracy. The Tax Office in Mannheim set up a regional central office in October 1935 to register emigration plans in advance. Jews were specifically targeted, and 600 Jews with assets in excess of RM 20,000 were placed on a watch list. Tax officials in Mannheim also recommended that banks and insurance companies notify the relevant authorities of any liquidated accounts or repurchased policies, as these were seen as clear indications of the intention to emigrate. In January 1936 the president of the regional Tax Office (*Landesfinanzamt*) in Berlin pointed to the centralization of flight tax processing in Mannheim as an example that should be adopted in his region. It was mainly a lack of sufficient personnel that prevented the full application of the "Mannheim model" throughout the Reich.[12]

Nevertheless, the Nazi authorities developed an increasingly close coordination among the various arms of the bureaucracy. In Berlin, a Central Information Office was created at the Tax Office to coordinate all information with regard to nonpayment of taxes, capital flight, and property transfer. This activity was directed primarily against Jewish emigrants. In October 1935, the Gestapo urged that the local Tax Offices and Customs Investigation Offices (*Zollfahndungsstellen*) give immediate notice to the Central Information Office regarding any cases of Jews, especially Jewish businessmen, who were planning to leave the country.[13] By the end of 1936, the Gestapo had further refined the system of mutual notification with the Tax, Customs, and Currency Offices, as well as the local authorities, with regard

[10] Stefan Mehl, *Das Reichsfinanzministerium und die Verfolgung der deutschen Juden 1933–1943* (Berlin, 1990), p. 44; S. Heim, "Raub und Umverteilung," p. 111.

[11] M. Friedenberger, "Die Rolle der Finanzverwaltung," p. 13.

[12] BAL, R 2/5973, pp. 58–96.

[13] BAL, R 58/276, pp. 27–28 Polit. Polizeikommandeur der Länder B. Nr. II 1 E -2746/35, September 11, 1935 and 38662/35 II 1 E -2746/35, October 10, 1935.

to individuals' suspected intentions to emigrate. There were even a series of preprinted forms designed to standardize the procedure. In June 1936, the Central Office of the Gestapo described cooperation with the financial administration in this sphere as "effective," successfully preventing the secret departure with their capital of persons liable to the flight tax.[14] For example, in one case, the local Currency Office received information about a Jewish man who planned to give each of his three children RM 15,000 prior to their emigration. This scheme would have brought his own assets below the RM 50,000 limit for the flight tax. Because the Currency Office learned of this scheme in time, it was able to secure RM 23,245 of his wealth in accordance with paragraph 7 of the flight tax law.[15]

Role of Currency Offices in Forcing Emigration

Blocking of Accounts ("Security Orders")

As Frank Bajohr shows with regard to the development of Aryanization in Hamburg, the radicalization of currency and customs control measures in the period 1936–37 was such that Currency and Customs Offices began to play a decisive role in forcing the liquidation of Jewish businesses.[16] On December 1, 1936, a new currency law extended the powers of the Currency Offices to the issuance of "security orders" (*Sicherungsanordnungen*) blocking property in Germany and enabling them to appoint trustees for those assets on the mere suspicion of capital flight. By 1938, the Nazi authorities viewed all Jews as potential smugglers of capital.[17] The Currency Offices thus became instrumental in imposing state control over a large portion of Jewish wealth through the issuance of security orders.

The new powers issued to the customs and currency authorities to block accounts began to interfere considerably with Jewish lives.[18] The case of a Jewish doctor and his wife demonstrates some of the practical consequences

---

[14] M. Friedenberger, "Die Rolle der Finanzverwaltung," pp. 44–46.

[15] BAL, R 2/5978, Regional Tax Office Berlin, report on cooperation with the Gestapo, February 27, 1936.

[16] F. Bajohr, *"Arisierung" in Hamburg*, p. 190.

[17] Ibid., p. 193.

[18] Gerd Blumberg, "Etappen der Verfolgung und Ausraubung und ihre bürokratische Apparatur," in Alfons Kenkmann and Bernd-A. Rusinek (eds.), *Verfolgung und Verwaltung: Die wirtschaftliche Ausplünderung der Juden und die westfälischen Finanzbehörden* (Münster: Oberfinanzdirektion Münster, 1999): 15–40, here p. 25; see also Gerd Blumberg, "Die Zollverwaltung," in Wolfgang Leesch, et al. (eds.), *Geschichte der Finanzverfassung- und verwaltung in Westfalen seit 1815* (Münster: OFD, 1998), pp. 326–27.

of the registration of "suspected emigration plans."[19] The family members returned from their holiday abroad in August 1937 to find that tax officials had confiscated their furniture during their absence. They succeeded in removing the confiscation order and recovering their furniture only after setting up a considerable "security deposit" for the flight tax in government bonds. Thus, it can be seen that the application of the flight tax gave German officials considerable powers to impound Jewish property even prior to the escalation of anti-Jewish measures in 1938.[20] In Düsseldorf, the Central Union (*Central Verein*) of German Jews received many complaints about such "security deposits" being demanded by the Tax Offices in the first months of 1937.[21]

Beyond merely freezing the assets of potential emigrants, with the intention of preventing these assets from being smuggled out of the country, there was an additional twist to the way the currency laws were applied, especially by the Currency Offices. As Claus Stolberg argues convincingly on the basis of a regional case study of the financial administration of Hanover, the activities of the Currency Offices actually forced Jews to emigrate by leaving them little alternative in how they could spend their money:

> The suspicion of intent to emigrate expressed in the provision (Para. 37a of the Currency Law) was thereby effectively turned into coercion to emigrate, because only those applications for the release of assets that were not aimed at remaining in the country were granted. However, it would be unrealistic to maintain that in 1938 there was anyone among the Seligmanns who still saw a future for himself in Germany. Nevertheless, regardless of this, the coercive measures taken by the fiscal authorities left no alternative to this fundamental decision. From now on the Currency Offices dictated how things proceeded, right down to the ramifications of daily life. The reach of their jurisdiction, which derived from paragraph 37a of the Currency Law, made the Currency Office the most effective instrument in expelling and plundering the German Jews.[22]

Stolberg's research focuses especially on the period from 1937 onward. He notes that five of seven male members of the extended Seligmann family from Ronnenberg were sent to Buchenwald in the wake of Kristallnacht,

---

[19] The names of many individuals have been rendered anonymous in accordance with the terms of use stipulated by many German public archives operating under German data protection laws.

[20] OFDB, Reichsfluchtsteuer file of FA Charlottenburg Ost, Reg. Bez. 138, 361-end, File of Dr. M.S. and Frau C.S.

[21] USHMM, RG-11.001M (copies from RGVA, Moscow), reel 133, 721-1-2884, CV Landesverband Rheinland/Westfalen to CV Berlin, March 15, 1937.

[22] See C. Stolberg, "The Role of the Central Fiscal Authority."

also hastening their emigration, but in all but one case the blocking of assets by the Currency Office had started prior to this action. Certainly, their departure from the country was expedited by the circumstance that "all expenses directly connected with 'emigration' – the passage fare, money on board, visa fees, &c. – were permitted without exception and were approved by the Currency Office without any fuss. The various compulsory fees – the tax on leaving the Reich, wealth tax, &c. – were deducted straight away."[23]

In this way the Currency Offices in Germany acted much as a decentralized version of the infamous Central Office established in Vienna in 1938,[24] stripping Jews of their assets and coercing them into emigration by leaving them little practical alternative after much of their property had been blocked.

Currency Transfer Restrictions

From 1934 onward, the amount of cash emigrants could take out on their person was strictly limited to only RM 10 in foreign currency.[25] Therefore, if they wished to transfer money legally, emigrants had to rely on the official procedures for money transfers, which acted as a considerable tax on emigration. These transfers could be conducted only via the Deutsche Golddiskontbank (DeGo) from blocked emigrant accounts. This levy was only 20 percent in 1934, but the authorities increased it successively to 65 percent and then 68 percent in 1935, reaching 81 percent in October 1936 and 90 percent in June 1938. From September 1939 the rate was increased to an excruciating 96 percent – leaving only 4 percent of the actual value at the disposal of an emigrant in foreign currency overseas.[26] According to an internal Finance Ministry memorandum from 1935, Jews attempting to transfer remaining funds by legal means suffered a loss of almost 80 percent.[27]

A further complication was the system of currency transfer approvals administered by the Currency Offices, which from 1935 onward was linked directly to a declaration from the relevant tax authorities that no outstanding taxes remained to be paid.[28] This key document was also required as a

---

[23] Ibid.

[24] For further details on the operation of the Zentralstelle in Austria and also on the impact of the mass arrest of Jews in the wake of Kristallnacht, see Chapter 3.

[25] M. Friedenberger, "Die Rolle der Finanzverwaltung," p. 14.

[26] F. Bajohr, *"Arisierung" in Hamburg*, pp. 153–54.

[27] BAL, R 2/5977, RFM undated Memo 330/35.

[28] This document was called a *Steuerliche Unbedenklichkeitsbescheinigung*. See G. Blumberg, "Die Zollverwaltung," p. 324.

prerequisite for emigration. Obtaining this document became increasingly difficult after additional special taxes and levies were introduced toward the end of the 1930s. Sometimes, the Tax Offices might also uncover back taxes owed from previous years, which might delay emigration and add further costs.

The high costs of the transfer procedure for Jewish emigrants can be seen from the example of Fritz G., who migrated to London in 1938. On April 26, he had a balance of RM 10,500 in various German banks. This amount was transferred under the slightly more favorable conditions offered by the *Allgemeine Treuhandstelle für die jüdische Auswanderung GmbH* (General Trusteeship for Jewish Emigration Ltd [Altreu]) in Berlin on May 15, 1938, at a rate of 35 percent minus additional costs for the transfer, so that RM 3,500 was wired to Barclays in London. He there received only £281, which, as he subsequently reported, "on account of my stay here, where I still do not have any possibility of earning money, has been reduced further by about GB £45."[29]

Thus, for those still in Germany, the very poor rate of exchange acted as a considerable obstacle to emigration. As Arthur Stern of Münster expressed it to local tax officials in October 1938, "I currently have the intention to emigrate, which I have been unable to realize owing to the unfavorable conditions for transferring funds and the bans on immigration."[30]

The "Punitive Tax"

In the wake of Kristallnacht in November 1938, Göring introduced the "Punitive Tax," which was applied to all Jewish property worth more than RM 5,000. Initially set at 20 percent, in the fall of 1939 it was raised to 25 percent of registered Jewish property. By 1940 this measure had raised more than RM 1.1 billion in revenue for the state.[31] The impact of this very harsh "property tax" is examined more closely in the next chapter. However, more than any other measure, this tax dealt a severe blow to the financial position of all Jews with property and greatly complicated their emigration plans, as now not just 25 percent but 50 percent of registered wealth became blocked to cover their tax obligations.

---

[29] OFDB, JuVa, file of Fritz G., 907/5068.

[30] Gisela Möllenhoff and Rita Schlautmann-Overmeyer, eds., *Jüdische Familien in Münster, Teil 2,2: Abhandlungen und Dokumente 1935–45* (Münster: Westfälisches Dampfboot, 2001), p. 599.

[31] S. Mehl, *Das Reichsfinanzministerium*, p. 78.

Taxes Applied to Removal Goods on Emigration

During the course of the 1930s, a series of ever more restrictive regulations were applied to the items Jews were permitted to take with them on emigrating. This created increased anxiety among prospective emigrants, who remained unclear about the specific details of those restrictions. For instance, an elderly man from Mannheim requested help from the newspaper of the Central Union of German Jews (*Centralverein der Juden in Deutschland*) in assessing his liability to special taxes on emigration. He was planning to join his son, who had already migrated to France, and he was expecting to receive RM 7,000 from his life insurance policy soon. His emigration goods included furniture, clothing, some old tin plates, silver bowls, family heirlooms, and a stamp collection of some 30 years (valued at RM 2,000–3,000). He wanted to know if he could take his property with him, if he would have to pay a tax, or if he could dispose of his goods freely only inside Germany.[32]

Marion Kaplan illustrates vividly the impact these regulations had on Jewish emigrants:

> To emigrate with one's belongings, one had to receive a permit from the Finance Department. This permit was obtainable only after preparing lists of all the items one wished to take. Lisa Brauer spent an entire week writing "endless lists, in five copies each, . . . every item entered, every list neatly typed, and in the end I could only speak and breathe and think in shoes, towels, scissors, soap, and scarves." Another woman recalled how "a science of emigration advisement came into being [and these advisors] prepared the lists. For example, one was not allowed to say 'one bag of sewing supplies,' but had to detail every thimble, every skein of wool, every snap." Also one could not just take anything: "only those things were allowed which had been purchased before 1933." Other items could be taken only in limited amounts, and only "if the complete price was paid to the Gold-Discount-Bank once again."[33]

Some idea of the additional expenses accruing from this "export tax" can be gleaned from the case of Jakob Goldmann of Frankfurt, who had to pay an additional RM 15,650 to export his "removal" goods. In addition, he was not allowed to take out an electric hotplate, a sewing machine, or a

---

[32] USHMM, RG-11.001M.31 (RGVA), reel 133, 721-1-2884 A.M. to CV Zeitung, August 8, 1937.

[33] Marion A. Kaplan, *Between Dignity and Despair: Jewish Life in Nazi Germany* (New York: Oxford University Press, 1998), p. 133.

radio on his original list. For his vacuum cleaner he had to pay a "tax" of RM 135 and for a fur coat RM 250.[34]

Copies of the carefully prepared lists of removal goods can be found in various files of the Currency Offices or the financial administration.[35] In many cases, the items never left German soil, as the moving containers became trapped at the ports on the outbreak of war and the contents were subsequently sold off to cover the storage costs, with the balance being confiscated by the Reich. The DeGo issued receipts for the sums paid by individual Jews to receive permission to transport the items, most of which totaled a few hundred Reichsmark.[36] These emigration lists provide a very detailed impression not only of the items carefully packed up for shipment but also of the exhausting and painstaking preparations for emigration, as people packed up their most prized possessions, hoping to see them again on arrival in their new country.

Strategies for the Export of Capital

Under these increasingly harsh circumstances, the temptation for Jews to attempt "illegal" transfers of foreign currency rose commensurately. On an individual level, Jews attempted using a number of methods for the export of capital, which became familiar to the German customs and currency authorities. For example, the purchase of expensive photographic equipment just prior to emigration was known by the Gestapo to be a preferred smuggling device that also offered a prospective livelihood on arrival at the emigrant's chosen country of refuge. Other valuable items that

---

[34] B. Hindemith and S. Meinl (eds.), *Legalisierter Raub*, p. 27.

[35] For a fairly typical example of the lengthy lists of removal goods that had to be prepared, see ZAM, Devisenstelle, file of R. U., *Umzugsgutverzeichnis* dated October 25, 1939. The list includes more than 100 individual items R. U. wanted to take out of Germany with him by boat, mostly clothing and practical household objects purchased before 1933. I am grateful to Alfons Kenkmann and Gerd Blumberg for providing me access to these files.

[36] See BAL, R 182 Receipts of the Deutsche Golddiskontbank (DeGo) for payments made for relocation goods (*Umzugsgut*) by Jewish emigrants. These loose files generally include the name and last German address of the Jewish emigrants, as well as the payment sum and the transferring bank. Some payments were made by relatives living overseas. In certain cases, the passports of Jews were retained by the authorities until the requested sum had been paid; see R 182/49, OFP-Hessen, Darmstadt, October 17, 1938 regarding Kurt Dietrich David.

could be smuggled out for sale abroad included rare postage stamps or diamonds.[37]

Another very effective method, if a suitable partner could be found,
was the direct exchange of property, such as real estate, with a non-Jewish
partner who was returning home to Germany from abroad.[38] A similar
exchange could be made with cash if, for example, an emigrating Jew left
his remaining funds to an impoverished Jewish family in Germany whose
relatives then made foreign currency available to him overseas.[39]

Available legal records reveal the case of one female emigrant who
attempted to pay off the debts of foreign companies in Germany using
her own money, in order to collect the equivalent in foreign currency from
the companies overseas. Clearly, this operation did not remain undetected,
although proceedings against her were not opened until after she was safely
abroad.[40]

Especially suspect for the currency officials were those Jewish businesses
that had regular contacts abroad. For example, a memorandum prepared
within the Economics Ministry for a meeting with the heads of the Currency Offices on November 22, 1938, noted that general permissions issued
previously to Jewish transport companies for making payments abroad were
difficult to police. Therefore, the author of the memorandum recommended
the withdrawal of such general permissions or the taking of other measures
to plug this loophole.[41]

As Frank Bajohr argues, given the intolerable conditions for Jews in
Germany during the 1930s, the surprising thing is how few resorted to the
"illegal" methods the Nazis repeatedly denounced as "typically Jewish."[42]

---

[37] PAAA, Inl. 11 A/B, R 99887, Gestapo Aachen Denaturalization Proposal in the case of
G.H.H., July 22, 1940; see also S. Meinl, "The Expropriation of Jewish Emigrants from
Hessen during the 1930s," p. 97.

[38] G. Blumberg, "Die Zollverwaltung," p. 323.

[39] R. Hilberg, *Die Vernichtung*, p. 150; for the case of an attempt, uncovered by the Currency
Office, to transfer money from a Jewish account in Germany to a German-American
partner, see PAAA, R 99921, Denaturalization Proposal of Gestapo Karlsruhe against F.
I. B., May 16, 1941.

[40] Landesarchiv Magdeburg, Landeshauptarchiv (LMLHA), Rep. G 11 Devisenstelle, Nr.
4309, pp. 64–66. The case was uncovered when some of the German creditors recognized
the illegal nature of these payments, probably fearing punishment after the money was
detected in their accounts.

[41] BAL, R 7/3153.

[42] Frank Bajohr, "'Arisierung' als gesellschaftlicher Prozess," in Irmtrud Wojak and Peter
Hayes (eds.), *"Arisierung" im Nationalsozialismus: Volksgemeinschaft, Raub und Gedächtnis*
(Frankfurt am Main: Campus, 2000), p. 21.

It would be wrong to give the impression that smuggling occurred on the large scale the Nazis feared, based on their own ideology and propaganda. One young Jewish emigrant to the United States recalls a heated discussion between his parents in the mid-1930s. His mother objected strongly to an "illegal" transaction by his father intended to rescue some money from the depredations of the flight tax. She insisted on reversing the transaction, not so much out of a fear of being caught, but rather because of her own firm belief in obedience to the law. She was determined to remain honest and not to behave the way that the Nazis characterized the Jews in their propaganda. Trying to save money for a new beginning by smuggling meant for her becoming a "Jewish swindler," which she was not prepared to do.[43]

The Ha'avara and Other Transfer Agreements

The Ha'avara Transfer Agreement that operated from 1933 until the outbreak of war offered the best opportunity and conditions for the legal export of Jewish capital.[44] More than 50,000 German Jews took advantage of this opportunity, some 36 percent as so-called capitalists entering the Mandate of Palestine with £1,000 "entry money" (*Vorzeigegeld*) in their possession.[45] Goods worth a total of RM 139.5 million had been transferred under the agreement by 1939.[46] This large migrant group still faced many bureaucratic hurdles, as well as the difficult political, economic, and even climatic conditions in Palestine. For example, one man was eager to have his application approved in time for the rainy season, as he planned to open a business specializing in the chemical waterproofing of clothing (using German products).[47]

The Ha'avara agreement was an unusual special case of permitting capital export in return for the purchase of German goods.[48] Essentially, the transfer functioned by having prospective emigrants pay money into an account in

---

[43] S. Meinl, "The Expropriation of Jewish Emigrants from Hessen during the 1930s," p. 101.

[44] This is demonstrated most explicitly in a numerical table prepared by Werner Feilchenfeld; see Werner Feilchenfeld, Dolf Michaelis, and Ludwig Pinner, *Haavara-Transfer nach Palästina und Einwanderung Deutscher Juden 1933–1939* (Tübingen: J.C.B. Mohr, 1972), p. 69.

[45] Ibid., p. 77.

[46] Herbert A. Strauss (ed.), *Jewish Immigrants of the Nazi Period in the USA*, vol. 4, p. 253.

[47] Brandenburgisches Landeshauptarchiv, Potsdam (BLHAP), Rep 36A (Devisenstelle), A 529.

[48] For a brief summary regarding the agreement, see Juliane Wetzel, "Auswanderung aus Deutschland," in Wolfgang Benz (ed.), *Die Juden in Deutschland 1933–1945: Leben unter nationalsozialistischer Herrschaft* (Munich: C.H. Beck, 1988), pp. 464–68.

Germany, which was then used to buy German goods for export to Palestine. The company buying the goods then repaid the emigrant in Palestine. Germany benefited by increasing its exports, whereas Jews obtained a better rate of exchange through this method than was otherwise possible. However, there were fierce critics of the agreement on both sides, with the Germans limiting its application as it was clearly costing them valuable foreign currency.[49] By the end of 1938, the exchange rate used for British pounds was less than one-third of the real value, so that it was only marginally more beneficial than the other transfer options available.[50]

In 1937, the Altreu was founded. This organization also offered a slightly better rate of exchange (losses between 27 percent and 50 percent depending on the amount) for Jews transferring less than RM 30,000, while in return some money was also paid to the *Reichsvertretung der Juden* (Jewish national organization) to assist with the emigration of indigent Jews.[51]

Use of Overseas Branches

One somewhat successful method that Jewish businessmen employed to export capital was the establishment of a foreign branch or a depot that might subsequently be used to transfer or smuggle out funds at the time of emigration. Jewish publishers and booksellers were confronted immediately after the Nazi seizure of power with the banning of their products and the threatened closure of their businesses. Thus, they were among the first group to take active measures in response. For example, a publishing company in Halle/Saale owned by Martin F. established a branch office in Prague at the end of 1933. According to a German investigation, it then forwarded books and journals with an actual value in excess of RM 100,000 to this address with a fraudulent customs description, claiming that they were only free samples or propaganda material. In this way the hard-pressed bookseller was able to rescue some of his capital by shipping it abroad.[52]

A branch office or production facility overseas also opened up a number of possibilities for transferring capital or protecting it from confiscation.

---

[49] For examples of the arguments within the German bureaucracy on the continuation of the Agreement, see Herbert A. Strauss (ed.), *Jewish Immigrants of the Nazi Period in the USA*, vol. 4, *Jewish Emigration from Germany 1933–1942*, pp. 261–72.

[50] S. Heim, "Vertreibung, Raub und Umverteilung," p. 113.

[51] Ibid., p. 114.

[52] According to the available records, the outcome of the currency case against the bookseller was a fine of RM 10,000; see LMLHA, Rep. G 11 Devisenstelle, Nr. 794, pp. 12–15; for a similar case, see PAAA, Inl. II A/B, R 99664, Fiche 6388, denaturalization proposal against B. K., February 18, 1937.

Overseas plants, stocks, existing contracts, debts owed by international clients, and even good will were all assets that could be realized abroad, if necessary. There they were generally protected from the most sweeping German measures of confiscation and extortion and retained their real market value. Successful tactics used by emigrant businessmen included the diversion of payment for outstanding debts and even the transfer of contracts and patents to the overseas branch. To cite only one example, a wine exporter migrated to England and from there collected almost RM 10,000 of money owed to him from his previous export activities.[53]

To counteract "illegal" transfers, the German authorities conducted spot checks and frequently examined the accounts of those companies trading overseas. From an examination of the results of these investigations in Hamburg, Bajohr concludes that most Jewish companies in fact complied with the repressive German currency regulations.[54] The ingrained habit of obedience to legal authority made it difficult for many Jews to adjust to the reality of a state-organized threat to their very existence.

The following case studies of capital export by Jewish businesses reveal much about both the nature of the process and why some strategies proved more successful than others.[55]

Large-Scale Transfers of Capital

The case of the Julius Petschek Group, run by the brothers Walter and Paul Petschek, is a good example of how an international basis for a Jewish company could reduce the scale of losses caused by Nazi expropriation measures. Having already moved their corporate office from Berlin to Prague,

---

[53] PAAA, Inl. II A/B, R 99877, denaturalization proposal of Gestapo Frankfurt am Main against L. S., May 8, 1940. As Hilberg demonstrates, Aryanized Jewish businesses with foreign branch offices had the possibility of making good their claims against the new owners by blocking remaining assets held in those branches; see Raul Hilberg, *Die Vernichtung*, p. 149. See also Reichsbankstelle Wuppertal-Barmen to Präsidenten des Landesfinanzamtes (Devisenstelle) Münster, October 20, 1936, warning that overseas credit balances of a recently Aryanized company (Hugo Wolf, Schwelm) had not been transferred on the sale of that company; photocopy from OFD Münster files; I am grateful to Alfons Kenkmann for making this material available to me at the Villa ten Hompel Geschichtsort in Münster.

[54] F. Bajohr, *"Arisierung" in Hamburg*, p. 158.

[55] An extended version of this analysis of the problem of exporting capital abroad can be found in Martin Dean, "Multinational Jewish Businesses and the Transfer of Capital Abroad in the Face of 'Aryanization', 1933–39," in Chris Kobrak and Per Hansen (eds.), *European Business, Dictatorship and Political Risk: 1920–1945* (New York: Berghahn, 2004), pp. 103–21.

at the end of 1937 the Petscheks initiated talks with the American- and British-owned United Continental Corporation (UCC) to create a holding company to "cloak" their continuing influence in the company.

When Aryanization negotiations began in 1938 with a consortium led by the Friedrich Flick group, this holding company gave the appearance at least to the German parties that they were dealing with an American partner. The Petscheks, represented by the UCC, demanded to be paid in foreign currency as they intended to terminate all their business activity in Germany. It was primarily these international connections that gave them some measure of protection from Aryanization measures at that time.

In May 1938, a deal was signed whereby the RM 24 million nominal value of the company was bought by a consortium, including the Friedrich Flick concern, for US $4.75 million, paid in foreign currency made available by the Economics Ministry. This deal was made in spite of an earlier commitment by Göring that the Petscheks would not receive any foreign currency. Flick's good connections to the Economics Ministry, however, helped reverse this decision. Even though the sale price was only half of the Petscheks' original demand, it was still much better than subsequent Aryanizations, in which the proceeds were paid in Reichsmarks into blocked accounts that were then successively depleted by emigration taxes, levies, and outright confiscation.

The existence of a private consortium of Aryanizers who were keen to gain control of the company and who responded positively to the Petscheks' offer (in part fearing competition from the state) facilitated this outcome. Above all, the appearance of foreign ownership, created by the British and American holding companies, provided extra leverage that enabled some precious foreign currency to be extracted from the usually tight-fisted Economics Ministry.[56]

Harold James's work on the involvement of the Deutsche Bank in several large-scale Aryanizations confirms that the experience of the Petscheks was not an isolated incident. For example, the Hirschland Aryanization case also included a detailed agreement with the Reich that enabled some of the proceeds to be exported. James observes that, due to its strong international contacts, the Deutsche Bank was often involved in Aryanization deals that included the transfer of funds abroad.[57]

[56] L. M. Stallbaumer, "Big Business and the Persecution of the Jews: The Flick Concern and the 'Aryanization' of Jewish Property Before the War," *Holocaust and Genocide Studies*, vol. 13, no. 1 (Spring, 1999): 1–27; see also R. Hilberg, *The Destruction*, pp. 131–36. The family of Ignaz Petschek was much less successful in its attempt to hang on to its property.

[57] Harold James, *The Deutsche Bank and the Nazi Economic War against the Jews* (Cambridge: Cambridge University Press, 2001), pp. 77–82, 112.

Battling the Bureaucracy: A Failed Attempt to Establish a Manufacturing Business in Italy

As Susanne Heim observes, the process of emigration in the 1930s required an enormous effort to complete all the paperwork and overcome the numerous bureaucratic hurdles. Unfortunately, the emigrants were entirely at the mercy of government officials, who could wreck the entire effort by the arbitrary withholding of a single stamp.[58] The example of a failed attempt to migrate to Italy in connection with the favorable terms for exporting capital to that country illustrates how the efforts undertaken by prospective emigrants might ultimately prove fruitless.

In November 1935, the businessman W. F. made an application to the Currency Office for the export of RM 25,000 (in lira) for the purpose of emigration to Italy, requesting additional permission to export machinery with a total value of RM 40,000 to establish a screw manufacturing plant in Milan. The application was signed by Dr. G., a non-Jewish Lord Mayor (*Oberbürgermeister*) and currency adviser who even traveled to Milan on behalf of the applicant and helped prepare the paperwork. The original plan envisaged the emigration of the family of the applicant's wife, whose living costs would be financed from the expected profits of the new business. W. F. hoped to take advantage of the prevailing favorable transfer arrangements with Italy.[59]

According to the supporting statement of Dr. G., there was strong demand for a screw factory in Milan as the Siemens plant there had reported difficulties in obtaining screws. (In Italy, most screws were purchased from Switzerland.) Dr. G. argued that the establishment of the new business would help the export of German machine products to Italy, setting an example that could well lead to more export business in the future. The emigrant, however, would need to export some production equipment and cash reserves to establish the new company in Milan.

Negotiations were conducted with the German company of Hahn & Kolb for the required machines, which would guarantee production of 15,000 screws per day by each of five machines to be exported. The necessary legal steps toward the establishment of a company in Italy were initiated with the assistance of a local Italian lawyer. The emigrant, W. F., was described in the application as being well suited by personality and experience for the direction of such an enterprise. He supposedly had some relevant technical knowledge (he was an experienced motorist!), work

---

[58] S. Heim, "Vertreibung, Raub und Umverteilung," p. 107.
[59] See F. Bajohr, *"Arisierung" in Hamburg*, p. 155.

experience in marketing (for the coal industry), and a good knowledge of languages. In addition, he had in Milan a number of friends who would be able to help him through the difficult initial transition period.

The application prepared by Dr. G. estimated that RM 40,000 would be required to pay for the machinery. These machines would produce an income of RM 36 per day to set against raw material costs of RM 22 per day, enabling a profit of RM 14 per day per machine. The estimated costs in terms of depreciation, rent, personnel costs, and other fixed running costs would leave a net income of RM 4 per machine per day or RM 6,000 per year.

This income was deemed sufficient to enable W. F. to live reasonably well, in spite of his large family, in view of the lower cost of living in Italy. An additional cash transfer of some RM 25,000 was proposed to cover his initial costs until the business started to make a profit. The application was accompanied by a supporting certificate issued by the Information Section of the Emigration Advice Office.[60] An additional supporting letter from the German Chamber of Commerce for Italy advised that the planned factory would provide the applicant with the possibility of maintaining himself there and would not be contrary to German economic interests.

One problem with the application, however, was that the start-up capital consisted almost exclusively of W. F.'s share in an inheritance (real estate) that was currently leased out and therefore not immediately realizable. Essentially, the applicant was planning to take out a new loan of RM 100,000 backed by his share of the property to finance his emigration plans.

The application was assessed by the Currency Office, which in December 1935 requested the expert advice of the regional Chamber of Industry and Commerce (*Industrie und Handelskammer*), asking whether the planned investment would be in the interests of the German economy.[61] In its reply, the Chamber of Industry and Commerce expressed concern that the Swiss producers of most Italian screws were already using German parts and therefore the Chamber would like to see existing contracts ensuring that the Milan company would also order these from Germany.

On the basis of this reply, the Currency Office wrote to W. F. at the end of January 1936 that it would have to deny the application. Dr. G.

---

[60] Auskunftsabteilung der Vereinigung für Deutsche Siedlung und Wanderung – Auswanderungsberatungsstelle.

[61] BAL, R 2/5977, Circular on Foreign Currency Regulations 1/36, January 2, 1936, noted that in cases of companies being established overseas (Betriebsauswanderung), the opinion of the Chamber of Industry and Commerce was always to be requested to determine if the project was in the interests of the German economy (i.e., whether it would increase German production and exports and return a profit for Germany).

then approached the Chamber of Industry and Commerce, requesting the opportunity to discuss the matter with them personally. In March 1936, however, the Chamber of Industry and Commerce returned the file to the Currency Office, considering the case closed.

In April 1936, Dr. G. wrote again to the Currency Office, now applying for the transfer of only RM 45,000 in cash on behalf of his client, requesting the most favorable application of conversion deductions. He explained that "the long duration of the emigration preparations had already seriously damaged the interests of the applicant." Hopes of transferring the full amount from W. F.'s share of his inheritance had now been dashed, as the property had since been sold, producing only a fraction of the originally expected amount.

Nevertheless W. F. persevered, now planning to open a smaller screw factory in Milan, if the transfer of the RM 45,000 was to be approved. This meant that he could no longer include his relatives in the emigration project, as the resulting income would also be much lower. In a last appeal, Dr. G. argued that this plan would definitely benefit the German economy, as W. F. still intended to purchase the screw-manufacturing machines in Germany. But in May 1936, the Currency Office once again denied the application, stating that currently the transfer of funds abroad from the named account for emigration purposes was not possible.[62]

The exact reasons for the denial of this investment plan are not entirely clear from the files. Yet, the key role played by the regional Chamber of Industry and Commerce cannot be doubted. Arguments of economic nationalism were advanced as the main reasons for denying the application, but it is possible that this may have been a cover for antisemitic motivations, despite the avowed Nazi intention of furthering Jewish emigration.

In this case, the absence of an existing overseas branch almost certainly made it harder to achieve the export of capital. Insufficient funding and a lack of practical experience constituted additional obstacles. However, the main hurdles were the difficulties in obtaining permission for the transfer of funds and the still disadvantageous rate of exchange. The poor return on the sale of Jewish real estate, due partly to the need to sell in a hurry, in turn prevented the emigration of needy family members.[63] This case

---

[62] BLHAP, Rep. 36A (Devisenstelle), file of W. F., A1073. This file does not explicitly refer to the Jewishness of the applicant, but his sister, who is mentioned in the file, was subjected to the punitive tax applied only against Jews.

[63] For examples of the effects on the value of Jewish real estate after 1933, see Britta Bopf, "Economic Discrimination and Confiscation: The Case of Jewish Real Estate," in *Confiscation of Jewish Property in Europe, 1933–1945*, pp. 105–26.

demonstrates several of the main hindrances to overseas investment as a form of capital transfer in the very hostile economic and political climate for Jews in Nazi Germany.

Deceptive Transfers: A Factory in Nuremberg with an Overseas Depot

Another case from the denaturalization files shows how Jews easily became criminalized due to the pervasive reach of the currency regulations. The Jewish businessman J. F. was the co-owner of a metal products factory in Nuremberg. In a confidential report, the Nuremberg Chamber of Industry and Commerce denounced J. F. as a "dirty competitor" who dumped his wares at very low prices, causing considerable damage to other metal products companies in the region.

The Gestapo's 1935 proposal for J. F.'s denaturalization also noted that "when German soil became too hot for him after the national uprising, on account of his unspeakable business practices," J. F. sent the sum of £700 abroad without the approval of the Currency Office. According to the Gestapo, he also instructed foreign firms to make part of their payments into foreign accounts. To cover up these payments, he also falsified receipts for smaller amounts to deceive the Currency Office. Finally, he allegedly established in London a depot of goods worth £2,800, which he had used to support himself after his flight to London.

A criminal case was opened, but the authorities soon closed it due to the defendant's absence. His remaining property in Germany, however, was confiscated. The Gestapo proposed canceling his citizenship because of his alleged "severe infractions of Germany's currency laws."[64] This example demonstrates how the establishment of a depot in London helped considerably in salvaging some capital from the clutches of the Currency Office. The highly irritated tone of the Gestapo reports would have perhaps offered the refugee a wry smile of satisfaction in preserving a small part of his property from a system designed to take everything while driving him from his home.

Emigration Attempts That Failed

Unfortunately, many attempts at emigration and capital transfer failed. The bicycle parts import/export business of Labowsky & Co. in Hamburg was one of the few Jewish businesses that remained highly profitable after the

---

[64] LAB, A Rep. 092/50479, Interior Ministry Report, September 9, 1935.

Nazis' takeover of power. In 1937, the company still brought in almost £15,000 in foreign currency for the Reichsbank. The company's downfall began, however, with the opening of a currency investigation against the co-owners for the unauthorized transfer of just RM 80 at the end of 1937.

Shortly afterward, the owners began preparing their emigration to Amsterdam. Following an inspection of the company's books, the Currency Office imposed a security order against the company on January 20, 1938, blocking its accounts and requiring approval for all further commercial transactions. Applied against an import/export company, this measure effectively rendered further business activity impossible. In response, the owners left for Amsterdam, collected outstanding foreign debts there, and opened a new company called Novex Trading. As they wrote to their attorney in Hamburg, "You know the circumstances that caused us to leave Hamburg, and you can imagine that it is with very heavy hearts that we give up a company that . . . represents our life's work."

The Currency Office denied attempts to obtain reasonable compensation for the company. As Frank Bajohr notes, the Jewish owners in fact demonstrated a surprising readiness to cooperate with the Currency Office, not only paying a fine of RM 4,100 but also paying back some of the foreign currency they had collected (£660) in Amsterdam. They transferred ownership of the company to its former attorney in Hamburg at no cost, and he was even permitted to retain cash balances in excess of RM 70,000. The new Dutch company, however, did not benefit from its cooperation and was put on a "black list" prepared by the Reich Export Office (*Reichsstelle für den Aussenhandel*) in 1939 with the aid of the Currency Office.

After the Nazi occupation of the Netherlands in 1940, even the owners' emigration proved unable to save them from the Nazi net. The former owner of the company, Walter Labowsky, was deported to the Theresienstadt ghetto in 1943 and did not survive the war. The fate of his business partner, Sally de Leeuw, is not known.

In this case, the extensive powers of the Currency Office achieved the company's Aryanization by forcing the owners abroad. Despite the ability of the Jewish owners to start a new business in Amsterdam using some capital they had salvaged, the unfortunate choice of destination still left them exposed to Nazi deportations.[65]

For many Jews, the goal of emigration was to prove illusory. Max Leffmann, for instance, was the co-owner of a small family drapery business in Münster from October 1934 until its Aryanization in November 1938. After

---

[65] F. Bajohr, *"Arisierung" in Hamburg*, pp. 200–201.

the Kristallnacht pogrom, he made preparations together with his sister to migrate to Trinidad and open a similar drapery business there, even taking Spanish lessons. But this plan fell through after he had already paid his special tax to the DeGo for permission to transport his removal goods. Their attempts in 1939 to migrate to the United States were also unsuccessful, as the U.S. quota system contributed to further fatal delays.[66]

Many Jews attempting to emigrate encountered frustrations similar to those that Gerson Rosen experienced. In a letter dated May 1939, the Jewish Help Society (registered as an Emigration Advice Office) reported that his emigration could not be completed by June 5, because nearly all berths to almost the only remaining destination of Shanghai were sold out until the autumn. Therefore, it was necessary to extend the deadline for his departure by five months until November 1939. In the meantime the start of the war made the chances of successful emigration even slimmer, so that Rosen was unfortunately still in Germany when the large-scale deportations to the east began in 1941.[67]

Removal Goods, Customs Control, and Smuggling

The Customs Investigations Offices and the customs officials at the borders were responsible for enforcing the currency restrictions and the regulations on removal goods (see Figure 2.1). According to the research of Gerd Blumberg, relatively few Jews were arrested in the act of trying to smuggle currency or valuables across the "green border" to Holland. As the customs forces were increased (the personnel strength on the Dutch-Westphalian border was more than doubled from 317 to 661 officers between 1935 and 1939), a number of Jews were detained trying to cross "illegally." However, because the Gestapo viewed it as in Germany's interests to be rid of the Jews, most were released and deported unless they were found to be carrying illegal currency or valuables.

In some cases, Jews managed to smuggle part of their wealth out of the country. The grain dealer Walter Stein sold his shares in a cement company for cash shortly before Kristallnacht and fled to the Netherlands with his mother and the proceeds. The German authorities charged the non-Jewish

---

[66] Gisela Möllenhoff and Rita Schlautmann-Overmeyer, *Jüdische Familien in Münster 1918 bis 1945, Teil 1: Biographisches Lexikon* (Münster: Westfälisches Dampfboot, 1995), p. 254.

[67] USHMM, RG-11.001M.31, reel 77, 505-2-57, correspondence concerning Gerson Rosen, 1939–41.

purchaser of the shares with aiding in the breach of the currency regulations, but the court subsequently acquitted him. After Stein sold his vehicle in Krefeld on September 26, 1938, investigators could find no further trace of him in Germany.[68]

Designed to combat currency smuggling, circulars issued by the Berlin Central Information Office reported a number of "typical" ruses allegedly used by Jews. These included hiding currency under a plaster cast, concealing money belts under ladies clothing, posting letters just before departing, and taking out curtain rings made of solid gold.[69] In some instances, however, non-Jews also assisted emigrants in circumventing the regulations, as they were less likely to be checked, although in many cases they received payment or some other reward for this help. Marion Kaplan describes one incident of deception:

A few women bribed officials without consulting their husbands. They knew full well that their plans would have been vetoed, but they hoped to save some valuables for their immediate needs abroad. Else Gerstel, the wife of a judge, hid silverware with "Aryan" friends until the night before she packed. She then paid off the packers to hide the silver while "seven Gestapo men were watching."[70] She also smuggled other valuables in a secret compartment of her desk, built especially for this purpose: "I had risked of course the concentration camp and my life, probably all our lives. Alfred had no idea of what I had done. The night before we arrived in Cuba I whispered the whole story in his ear."[71]

Difficulties Faced by Jews in Emigrating

Constantly Escalating Expenses

A particular problem facing all emigrants, including those who were relatively well off, was the incalculable and constantly escalating costs of emigration. Most soon found themselves tapping into their last financial reserves, such as real estate and life insurance policies, to scrape together the necessary cash. One academic who managed to get a post in the United States by 1938 still faced considerable costs in transporting his family and their belongings.

[68] G. Blumberg, "Etappen der Verfolgung," pp. 20–28.
[69] BAL, R 2/5977, Präs. Landesfinanzamt (LFA) Berlin Zentrale Nachrichtenstelle, Rundschreiben Nr. 6, November 12, 1935.
[70] These were probably customs inspectors rather than Gestapo men.
[71] M. Kaplan, *Between Dignity and Despair*, p. 135.

To cash in his life insurance policy he had to write to the Currency Office for permission:

> I have been living in Princeton since September 1937, where I received a guest professorship. . . . Since I have been offered a position here, I intend to bring my wife and child as well as the rest of our belongings over in the autumn. However, I do not have the means to pay for this. Therefore, I need to cash in my life insurance policy in order to pay for the transportation expenses.[72]

Enormous Paperwork

Particularly wearing for prospective Jewish emigrants was the enormous mass of paperwork required before they could leave the country. They had to contact and make payment to a number of offices and agencies to obtain passports, visas, and certificates demonstrating that they had never broken the law and had paid all their taxes. This activity also involved additional expenses in processing fees and hidden charges. For example, in 1937 new regulations stipulated that emigrants could leave the country only by traveling with a few specific (mostly German) shipping companies. By limiting the number of berths available, this measure drove up prices.[73] In addition, many charges for visas had to be paid in foreign currency, which also had to be obtained at the current unfavorable rates.[74]

Marion Kaplan conveys the plight facing all German Jews by citing the words of Bella Fromm: "'So far I have gathered a collection of twenty-three of the necessary documents. I have made a study of the employees and furniture in fifteen official bureaus . . . during the hours I have waited.' Bewildered, she reported that she did not yet have all the papers she needed – and this was a few months before the November Pogrom."[75] An additional problem was that some documents, including visas and tickets, remained valid only for a limited time, so it was always a scramble to gather all the necessary stamps and documents in time.

Of course, the bureaucracy was not always sympathetic to the plight of emigrants, even though the official policy was to encourage emigration. In August 1938, for instance, the Tax Office in Wilmersdorf noted that

---

[72] ZAM, Devisenakte, file of Prof. O. P., letter of emigrant to Finanzpräsidenten on June 7, 1938. I am grateful to Alfons Kenkmann and Gerd Blumberg for providing me with access to these files.

[73] S. Heim, "Vertreibung, Raub und Umverteilung," p. 125.

[74] S. Meinl, "The Expropriation of Jewish Emigrants from Hessen during the 1930s," p. 96.

[75] M. Kaplan, *Between Dignity and Despair*, p. 130.

emigrating Jews generally needed a number of copies of their "taxes paid" certificates, but that the Tax Office usually issued only one copy to applicants to save time and effort, recommending that the applicant make several copies of the original. Unfortunately, the Tax Office reported that some police authorities were not recognizing the copies.[76] This experience reflected in part the frequently arbitrary manner in which regulations were applied. As Hermann Simon concluded in a retrospective report in 1942, "Due to the fact that the application of these legal provisions was left in the hands of government officials acting in accordance with their discretion, Hitler's officials could easily use this discretion in a discriminatory manner against Jewish emigrants from Germany."[77]

Corruption and Bribery

Corruption on the part of the Nazi authorities took a number of different forms. One of the most notorious cases was the Berlin Police President, Wolf-Heinrich Graf von Helldorf, who was a *bon vivant* who could always use more cash. He extorted money from wealthy Jews (particularly those owning property worth more than RM 300,000) by confiscating their passports. The Jews were able to obtain permission to emigrate only in return for a compulsory contribution known as the "Helldorff-charity gift," which often exceeded several hundred thousand Reichsmark. That the money never reached the Jewish charitable organizations for which it was nominally intended became clear in one case when Helldorff requested a second donation, the victim complained, and the Jewish community denied ever having received the first payment. It is assumed that Helldorff kept most of the money for himself.[78] At a lower level, even the employees of shipping offices might ask for RM 100 extra simply for putting a family on the waiting list for a precious place on a ship.[79] Most notorious were several South and Central American embassies,[80] which asked for hefty bribes, even for visas that were forged or issued without proper authority,

---

[76] Finanzamt Wilmersdorf-Nord report on cooperation with the police authorities, August 11, 1938, in M. Friedenberger, K.-D. Gössel, and E. Schönknecht (eds.), *Die Reichsfinanzverwaltung im Nationalsozialismus*, pp. 47–48.

[77] Report of Hermann E. Simon to the "American Federation of Jews from Central Europe," November 10, 1942, published in Herbert A. Strauss (ed.), *Jewish Immigrants of the Nazi Period in the USA*, vol. 4, *Jewish Emigration from Germany 1933–1942*, pp. 249–52.

[78] Frank Bajohr, *Parvenüs und Profiteure: Korruption in der NS-Zeit* (Frankfurt am Main: S. Fischer, 2001), pp. 123–24.

[79] M. Kaplan, *Between Dignity and Despair*, p. 131.

[80] NARA, RG-242, T-120, roll 4653, K338522–24, Reichsstelle für das Auswanderungswesen an AA, October 5, 1939.

but which just might help Jews to leave the country. One emigration adviser in Berlin reported that in the months from November 1938 to August 1939 he paid RM 8,000 in bribes for passports, tax payment certificates, currency approvals, residency permits, and the release of inmates from prison.[81] The Emigration Advice Office in Berlin reported in December 1938 that "obtaining visas has become a business, which by the way is very lucrative. Many agents make a profit from it."[82]

Emigration Figures and Destinations

Of approximately 525,000 Jews living in Germany in 1933, about 295,000 had emigrated by 1939.[83] The largest annual figure was 80,000 who left in 1939 in the immediate wake of Kristallnacht and the intensification of persecution.[84] From Hessen, to take one case, about half of the estimated 70,000 Jews of the region had emigrated by 1941. Most Hessian Jews migrated to Britain, the United States, Palestine, and the Netherlands; however, many Jews from rural backgrounds went to countries such as Brazil, Argentina, and Chile that were more willing to take permanent migrants. A number of Jews even went to Shanghai.[85] A precise breakdown of emigration destinations is available for the Jews of Mainz for the period from 1933 to summer 1938: of 649 known emigrants, 207 went to the United States, 140 to Palestine, 53 to the Netherlands, 49 to France, 35 to South America, 32 to Switzerland, 30 to Britain, 28 to South Africa, and 75 elsewhere.[86]

German regulations depriving Jewish emigrants of most of their wealth acted as a considerable hindrance to their emigration, as no state was

---

[81] Susanne Heim, "Vertreibung, Raub und Umverteilung," p. 126.

[82] Bericht über die Tätigkeit der gemeinnützigen öffentlichen Auswandererberatungsstelle Berlin, Oktober bis Dezember 1938, cited in Gabriele Anderl, Dirk Rupnow, and Alexandra-Eileen Wenck, (eds.), *Die Zentralstelle für jüdische Auswanderung als Beraubungsinstitution* (Vienna: Historikerkommission, 2002), p. 35.

[83] Walter Rummel and Jochen Rath, (eds.), *"Dem Reich verfallen" – "den Berechtigten zurückzuerstatten": Enteignung und Rückerstattung jüdischen vermögens im Gebiet des heutigen Rheinland-Pfalz, 1938–1953* (Koblenz: Verlag der Landesarchivverwaltung Rheinland-Pfalz, 2001), p. 40.

[84] For a breakdown by year, see S. Mehl, *Das Reichsfinanzministerium*, p. 45; Mehl's overall total is slightly lower than that found in Rummel and Rath (see note above).

[85] S. Meinl, "The Expropriation of Jewish Emigrants from Hessen," p. 94.

[86] Johannes Simmert and Hans-Walter Herrmann (eds.), *Die nationalsozialistische Judenverfolgung in Rheinland-Pfalz 1933 bis 1945: Das Schicksal der Juden im Saarland 1920 bis 1945* (Koblenz: Landesarchivverwaltung Rheinland-Pfalz, 1974), pp. 112–13, Report of the Police President in Mainz concerning the Jews in Mainz in the years 1936 and 1937, dated August 15, 1938.

prepared to accept large numbers of penniless refugees.[87] Even countries that accepted Jewish refugees from Germany passed measures to limit their access to the local labor market and to encourage them then to emigrate somewhere else.[88] For many German Jews, the United States was the destination of first choice. According to the emigration guidelines for the United States distributed by a Jewish organization, however, persons without independent capital or any friends or relations willing to support them in America had almost no chance of receiving a prized immigration visa.[89] In particular, the quota system also caused unbearable delays, so that many sought first to flee Germany, preferring to wait for their number to come up from a safer vantage point.

Mounting Obstacles to Emigration

Starting with the implementation of the flight tax, the various special taxes, compulsory payments, and economic restrictions created a closely meshed network of measures designed to deprive Jews of most of their wealth on emigration. From 1934 on, it was possible to "secure" (that is, block) Jewish property to ensure payment of the flight tax; by 1937, even the "suspected intention" to emigrate, indicated by the application for a passport or the liquidation of a bank account, could trigger the blocking of remaining accounts.[90] These discriminatory measures, combined with the high costs of emigration itself, made it increasingly difficult for even wealthy Jews to leave. In addition, the legal transfer of money was subjected to such a punitive rate of exchange that it meant the effective confiscation of nearly all of it.

Historians hitherto have stressed the contradiction between the Nazi aims of forced emigration and fleecing potential Jewish emigrants of their wealth to raise revenue.[91] This contradiction was apparent to some Nazi authorities. For example, a memorandum from the files of the Reich Finance Ministry in 1935 noted that from the "racial standpoint" the emigration of as many Jews as possible offered the most favorable solution of the "Jewish Problem." The strict currency transfer laws, however, constrained this policy. The memorandum noted that the near-complete prohibition of currency

[87] S. Heim, "Vertreibung, Raub und Umverteilung," p. 109.

[88] Ibid., pp. 117–18.

[89] USHMM, RG-11.001M.31 (RGVA), reel 99, 721-1-93 (Centralverein der Juden in Deutschland), undated informational leaflet of the Hilfsverein der Juden in Deutschland.

[90] See M. Dean, "Cooperation and Rivalry," pp. 13–14.

[91] W. Rummel and J. Rath, "Dem Reich verfallen," pp. 39–40.

transfers also severely limited the readiness of other countries to take Jews and made it harder for them to settle down permanently abroad.[92]

The continued operation of the Ha'avara Transfer Agreement, in spite of much opposition within the bureaucracy, and the proactive application of security orders by the Currency Offices from 1937 onward reflected attempts to reconcile these contradictions. In particular, the increasing use of security orders to block property served to increase the pressure to emigrate, as large expenditures could be made only toward this end. Together with the loss of professions and businesses, these security orders added financial to the physical and psychological pressure to emigrate.

Cases of Jewish businessmen attempting to export themselves and their businesses abroad reveal both the opportunities and difficulties involved. The establishment of foreign production facilities or a distribution office could provide the basis for continued business activity after emigration; foreign stocks, cash reserves, or business contracts outside the immediate grasp of the Reich provided foreign capital that could be drawn upon after emigration. The exasperated tone of some Gestapo reports complaining about the "illegal" export of capital shows that a few Jewish businessmen did succeed in frustrating the Nazi aim of mobilizing Jewish wealth in support of Germany's feverish military preparations.

Despite the attempt to criminalize the Jews by discriminatory laws and inflammatory propaganda, the internal correspondence of the financial bureaucracy includes some honest assessments. A February 1936 report by the regional Tax Office in Dresden stated that only a few Jews had left the country without paying their taxes, whereas many were emigrating legally.[93] Because discriminatory taxation and strict currency restrictions had rendered legal capital transfers extraordinarily difficult, even in "successful" cases, Jewish emigrants usually left behind well over 50 percent of their original capital. Factories and other fixed assets in Germany usually had to be abandoned completely, as by mid-1938 the proceeds from a sale could be paid only into blocked accounts.[94]

The planned manufacturing project in Italy mentioned earlier pointed to some of the practical obstacles hindering capital export. Here the regional Chambers of Industry and Commerce as well as the Currency Offices played a key role. The inevitable delays arising from bureaucratic procedures also

---

[92] BAL, R 2/5977, undated memo 330/35 from the files of the Finance Ministry.

[93] BAL, R 2/5978, Präs. Landesfinanzamt (LFA) Dresden report, February 28, 1936.

[94] See, for example, G. Möllendorf and R. Schlautmann-Overmeyer, *Jüdische Familien in Münster 1918 bis 1945, Teil 1: Biographisches Lexikon* (Münster: Westphälisches Dampfboot, 1995), p. 288.

caused the value of remaining Jewish capital to decline. Many plans for emigration had to be abandoned due to lack of sufficient time or means to complete the necessary preparations. After November 1938, the greatly increased tax burden and other intensified forms of persecution (arrest, denaturalization) made the export of capital virtually impossible. The only aim then was to try to escape before it became impossible.

Conclusion: The Role of Property in Emigration

Despite the enormous losses, it still remained easier for those with property to fight their way through the hurdles. For a few, especially those middle-aged or older, the sacrifices required, the difficulties entailed in starting new lives, and the reluctance to leave familiar surroundings and precious belongings inclined them to stay put or delay departure, waiting at least until their children had established themselves abroad. A report by the regional Tax Office in Darmstadt noted in 1936 that "the vast majority of those Jews who possessed greater amounts of property have by and large already emigrated. Remaining behind are mostly those Jews whose property is tied down in real estate or businesses that cannot easily be liquidated." Through their possession of real estate or large companies, these Jews were so closely linked to Germany that for them the thought of emigration remained quite distant. Other groups forced to remain behind were mostly the "indigent" or less well off.[95] A similar report from Dresden noted that there were not many wealthy Jews left in the city. However, the regional Tax Office had noted an increased level of emigration after the introduction of the Nuremberg Laws. Since September 1935, a total of sixty-eight Jews from Dresden had emigrated legally, transferring some RM 600,000 abroad.[96]

The events of 1938, however, which are examined in the next chapter, dramatically increased the pressure to emigrate, so that nearly all Jews sought to leave. Unfortunately after the outbreak of war in 1939, international emigration became much more difficult, permitting only a few thousand more to escape by 1941. Nevertheless the considerable losses involved in emigration, including during the early 1930s, demonstrate quite clearly that even the "lucky ones" who were able to get out in time – when viewed in terms of their traumatic experience navigating their way through a capricious and hostile bureaucracy and the loss of their homes, livelihoods, and often family as well – should be seen in certain respects as "survivors"

---

[95] BAL, R 2/5978, Präs. LFA Darmstadt report, February 29, 1936.
[96] Ibid., Präs. LFA Dresden report, February 28, 1936.

of the Holocaust. No amount of restitution or compensation, which in any case would be quite modest, could make up for the wrenching effects of uprooting oneself and having to make a fresh start, usually with only a fraction of the capital that had been built up over years, decades, or even generations. Consequently, those few items that were packed up and sent abroad often became a most invaluable link with a world that was lost.

3

THE ANSCHLUSS AND KRISTALLNACHT: ACCELERATING
ARYANIZATION AND CONFISCATION IN AUSTRIA
AND GERMANY, 1938–1939

Two key events in 1938, the Anschluss with Austria in March and the Kristallnacht pogrom in November, radically accelerated the Nazi expropriation of Jewish property. After Austria's annexation, local Nazis commandeered Jewish businesses and plundered apartments. In response, the Nazi authorities in Vienna retroactively authorized and attempted to regulate the ongoing "wild Aryanizations." Göring's plans for more extensive state confiscation also began to mature at this time. The registration of Jewish property during the summer, prompted by developments in Austria, was a major step in this direction. However, the violence and destruction of property during the November pogrom prompted Göring to introduce a comprehensive package of forced Aryanization measures, including a special punitive tax, which supplanted his earlier, more cautious approach.

What were Nazi intentions toward Jewish property? Before 1938 the Nazis had introduced a series of partial attacks on Jewish property rights. Yet, in spite of the strongly aggressive tone of their antisemitic propaganda, the Nazi leadership had not yet embarked on a systematic program of expropriation. Instead, initiatives often came from the local level: Party officials deployed coercion and boycott actions to force many Jewish businesses into liquidation or sale at well below market prices. Progressive exclusion from the civil service and many professions had severely undermined the economic position of most Jews, but the Reich government initially shied away from a frontal attack on property rights, partly to avoid unsettling key domestic business interests and foreign governments.

Nevertheless, the intention of the Nazi leadership to carry forward confiscation measures against Jewish property became quite explicit during the first months of 1938.[1] For example, on March 1 the Economics Ministry issued new guidelines for the exclusion of Jews from all public contracts, except in cases where it was unavoidable.[2] By April, economic advisers close to Hermann Göring had drawn up detailed plans for the conversion of Jewish wealth into government bonds, in order to deny Jews any further influence within the German economy. This scheme would also make Jewish wealth immediately available to the state for financing rearmament, leaving the Jews with only a type of pension to prevent them from becoming a burden on the state. Ultimately, the plan was only partially implemented; however, an examination of its details reveals much about Nazi intentions and some of the expropriation methods that were applied more thoroughly in the occupied territories during the war.

It was the dynamic of radical antisemitism unleashed in Austria after the Anschluss in March 1938, however, that served both as a catalyst and a model for resolving economic Aryanization within the Reich. As several commentators observe, in Austria developments with regard to both Aryanization and the forced emigration of the Jewish population quickly ran ahead of those in Germany.[3] Many key innovations evolved from efforts by the Party and the state to regain control over events taking place on the ground. The results were sometimes improvised responses to local developments, rather than the implementation of carefully laid plans drawn up in Berlin.

Initial "Wild Aryanizations" in Austria

The lasting images of the Austrian Anschluss in 1938 are those of the warm reception given by many Austrians to the arriving Nazi German forces

---

[1] A. J. van der Leeuw, "Der Griff des Reiches nach dem Judenvermögen," in A. H. Paape (ed.), *Studies over Nederland in oorlogstijd* ('s-Gravenhage: Martinus Nijhoff, 1972), pp. 211–36, here, p. 212; see also NARA, RG-238, T-1139, Nbg. Doc., NG-1793, German Foreign Ministry report dated January 25, 1938 on economic aspects of the Jewish question, which dates the start of measures for the removal of Jews from the economy to an internal directive of January 4, 1938, which specifically defined a "Jewish business" for the first time.

[2] BAL, R 7/4740, Economics Ministry (secret) instruction to all higher Reich authorities and all regional governments, March 1, 1938 (Betr.: Ausschluss von Juden von der Vergebung öffentlicher Aufträge); see also Wolf-Arno Kropat, *"Reichskristallnacht": Der Judenpogrom vom 7. bis 10. November 1938 – Urheber, Täter, Hintergründe* (Wiesbaden: Kommission für die Geschichte der Juden in Hessen, 1997), p. 28.

[3] Wolfgang Seibel (ed.), *Holocaust und "Polykratie" in Westeuropa 1940–1944: National Berichte* (December, 2001) (Introduction), p. ix; Helmut Genschel, *Die Verdrängung der Juden aus der Wirtschaft im Dritten Reich* (Göttingen: Musterschmidt Verlag, 1966), p. 166.

and the widespread scenes of public humiliation inflicted on Austria's Jews. Columns of Jews were forced to clean the streets, synagogues were vandalized and their Torah scrolls burned, and young SA men forced their way into Jewish apartments and seized money, jewelry, and savings books.[4] During the "revolutionary" atmosphere of the first days, Austrian Nazi "Old Fighters" or persons only loosely linked to the Party simply commandeered Jewish businesses, driving out the owner or considerably limiting his commercial influence. At the same time these "wild commissars" exploited their positions ruthlessly and bled the businesses dry for their own benefit. As Gerhard Botz maintains, many Austrian Nazis demanded "compensation" for all the disadvantages they alleged they had suffered before 1938: There was a deeply rooted local antisemitism that led Austrians to expect personal material benefits from forcing Jews out of their businesses and apartments. According to a retrospective report by the Austrian Minister for Economy and Labor, Hans Fischböck, at least 25,000 Jewish businesses fell prey to wild commissars during this initial phase.[5]

The newly established Gestapo offices were also very active in the redistribution of wealth, organizing large-scale arrests of political opponents and Jews – arrests that frequently were accompanied by confiscations and extortion.[6] The properties of the Jewish community in Vienna were searched and any cash or valuables confiscated. Many Jewish businesses were openly plundered, and probably as many as 7,000 were forced to close down as a result of these initial depredations.[7] The widespread extent of the confiscations, not only of Jewish property, is evident from a list prepared by Himmler in

[4] *Deutschland-Berichte der Sozialdemokratischen Partei Deutschlands (Sopade) 1934–1940, 5. Jahrgang, 1938*, 7 vols. (Frankfurt am Main: P. Nettelbeck, 1980) (hereafter *Sopade Berichte*), p. 738; Peter Longerich, *Politik der Vernichtung: Eine Gesamtdarstellung der nationalsozialistischen Judenverfolgung* (Munich: Piper, 1998), p. 162.

[5] See Hans Safrian and Hans Witek, *Und keiner war dabei: Dokumente des alltäglichen Antisemitismus in Wien 1938* (Vienna: Picus, 1988), pp. 95–102; Gerhard Botz, *Nationalsozialismus in Wien: Machtübernahme und Herrschaftssicherung 1938/39* (Buchloe: Obermayer, 1988), pp. 328–31; H. Genschel, *Die Verdrängung*, pp. 161–62; Gertrud Fuchs, "Die Vermögensverkehrsstelle als Arisierungsbehörde Jüdischer Betriebe" (Diplomarbeit eingereicht an der Wirtschaftsuniversität Wien, Oktober 5, 1989), pp. 55–56; Hans Witek, "'Arisierungen' in Wien: Aspekte nationalsozialistischer Enteignungspolitik 1938–1940," in Emmerich Talos et al. (eds.), *NS-Herrschaft in Österreich: Ein Handbuch* (Vienna: öbv & hpt, 2001): 795–816, here pp. 796–97, 801–802.

[6] See BAL, R 104 F/7, Dr. C. Koenig to Vizepräsident Barth, August 6, 1938; Hans Safrian, "Expediting Expropriation and Expulsion: The Impact of the 'Vienna Model' on Anti-Jewish Policies in Nazi Germany, 1938," *Holocaust and Genocide Studies*, Vol. 14, No. 3 (Winter 2000), p. 397; W-A. Kropat, "*Reichskristallnacht*," p. 31.

[7] *Sopade Berichte, 1938*, vol. V, pp. 735–37; Herbert Rosenkranz, *Verfolgung und Selbstbehauptung: Die Juden in Österreich 1938–1945* (Vienna: Herold, 1978), p. 69.

the summer of 1938 of 162 cases. Valuations are given for only forty-nine of these confiscations, but their total estimated worth alone exceeded RM 93 million. Included are several businesses and real estate properties confiscated from Jews, as well as property seized from non-Jewish political opponents of the Nazis.[8]

The Anschluss with Austria actually increased the Jewish population of the Reich by some 200,000.[9] Göring complained in March 1938 that Vienna was not a German city because so many Jews lived there. He declared that in the sphere of culture as well as economics, the presence of the Jew could no longer be tolerated. One of the tasks he set for the new government in Austria was "to take any steps necessary for the redirection of Jewish commerce, i.e., for the Aryanization of business and economic life, and to execute this process . . . legally but inexorably."[10] As officials of the Finance Ministry noted, "The impulse for a more complete . . . implementation of Aryanization was the incorporation of Austria, where the Jewish Question was comparatively much more significant within the overall economy."[11]

The main problems involved with the rapid, largely spontaneous seizures of Jewish businesses in Austria were the high degree of corruption and inefficiency with which they were carried out and the lack of any legal basis for them. As Hans Witek describes, the business practices of the wild commissars ranged from corruption and misuse of company funds to massive self-enrichment.[12] However, the newly appointed Reichskommissar for the Reunification of Austria with the Reich, Josef Bürckel, felt compelled to recognize the commissar system as a necessary evil. He argued that the existing situation could not be reversed, as doing so might lead to severe disturbances that would undermine the rule of law and damage the image of the Reich in Central Europe. Instead, he provided the commissars with a legal framework and attempted to limit their worst excesses by establishing institutions of state oversight.[13]

---

[8] *International Military Trials: Nazi Conspiracy and Aggression* [Red Series] (Buffalo, NY: William S. Hein, 1996), vol. VI, pp. 153–55, 3446-PS.

[9] P. Longerich, *Politik der Vernichtung*, p. 162.

[10] *International Military Trials: Nazi Conspiracy and Aggression*, vol. VI, p. 160, 3460-PS.

[11] "Anstoss für eine umfassendere und innerhalb des Vierjahresplans durchzuführende möglichst totale Arisierung sei die Eingliederung Österreichs gewesen, in dessen Wirtschaft die Judenfrage eine verhältnismässig grosse Bedeutung habe," NARA, RG-238, T-1139, NG-4029, memo. of RFM. Betr.: Arisierung der gewerbl. Wirtschaft, June 4, 1938.

[12] H. Witek, "'Arisierungen' in Wien," p. 803.

[13] H. Rosenkranz, *Verfolgung und Selbstbehauptung*, p. 60; G. Botz, *Nationalsozialismus in Wien*, pp. 330–33 citing Bürckel's report to Göring of April 29, 1938.

A struggle for control over the process of Aryanization also took place among various factions within the Nazi administration in Austria. Although Göring initially commissioned Reichsstatthalter Arthur Seyss-Inquart in March to carry out Aryanization, the real power in Austria lay with Bürckel, who organized the plebiscite after German troops marched in and who was nominated as Reichskommissar by Hitler on April 23rd. Bürckel announced shortly after his appointment that he would personally direct Aryanization in Austria on a strictly legal basis. He viewed the Jewish Question mainly as a practical economic and administrative task and intended to implement Aryanization in a way that would bring in revenue for the state. He faced challenges both from Staatsrat Wilhelm Keppler within Göring's Four-Year Plan administration and from local Party leaders, but he made most of the decisions implementing the radical Aryanization of the Austrian economy in close consultation with Hans Fischböck.[14]

The first measures to restrain the wild commissars were issued at the end of March 1938. Property confiscated by the Party was to be handed over to the security authorities, and "commissary administrators" (the commissars) were obliged to register with the newly appointed State Commissioner for the Private Economy, Walter Rafelsberger. New regulations in April gave the authorities the power to set wage levels for the commissars. Even the registration of Jewish property, ordered on April 26, served partly as a measure to make the commissars more accountable for formerly Jewish capital now under their control.[15]

Registration of Jewish Property

As Hans Safrian demonstrates, the registration of Jewish property was conceived initially as a measure for Austria alone. However, it was quickly taken up by Göring and applied to the Old Reich as well in April 1938. The registration decree now became an integral part of Göring's rapidly developing plans to remove the Jews completely from active participation in the economy.[16] Data from the property census subsequently facilitated the systematic stripping of Jewish wealth through successive levies, taxes, and confiscations, as well as the liquidation of remaining personal assets in the wake of the deportations.

---

[14] H. Rosenkranz, *Verfolgung und Selbstbehauptung*, pp. 61–64; G. Fuchs, "Die Vermögensverkehrsstelle," pp. 35–37.

[15] G. Fuchs, "Die Vermögensverkehrsstelle," pp. 59–61.

[16] H. Safrian, "Expediting Expropriation," p. 396; see also, for example, "Registrierung des jüdischen Vermögens," *Berliner Börsen Zeitung*, April 27, 1938.

The two key elements of the decree of April 26, 1938, were that Jews had to register and value their property and that the sale of Jewish businesses would be subject to government approval. Ominously, the Commissioner for the Four-Year Plan was now authorized "to take necessary measures to ensure the deployment of [Jewish] property in accordance with the needs of the German economy."[17] As van der Leeuw comments, most Jews in Germany understood that soon they would no longer be able to dispose freely of their own property.[18] An internal Foreign Office memorandum, prepared in response to complaints received from various foreign countries, stated that "the deployment of the property . . . in accordance with the needs of the German economy formulated in . . . the decree represents a confiscation."[19] This conclusion was unavoidable despite strenuous efforts by the drafters to use language that would appear innocuous.[20] Already in July 1938, the Economics Ministry issued instructions for the property census to be used to complete the compulsory sale to the state of foreign securities remaining in Jewish hands.[21]

Plan to Convert Jewish Property into State Bonds

As Interior Minister Frick reported to Göring in June, "Through the decree on the registration of Jewish property . . . and the instructions issued . . . on the same day, the solution of the Jewish Question in the economic sphere has been initiated. In a meeting on April 29 at the Prussian State Ministry, plans were made for the final removal of the Jews from German economic life by transforming their property into forms that denied them any further economic influence."[22]

At this key ministerial meeting, an overall plan for removing Jewish influence from the economy was outlined and agreed on. Its kernel was the conversion of Jewish property into state bonds:

> The Jewish Question is now to be resolved organically in that all Jewish property will be offered to the Reich, which will compensate the Jews with

---

[17] *RGBl.* (1938) I, pp. 414–15, "VO. über die Anmeldung des Vermögens von Juden," April 26, 1938, published in *Schriftenreihe des Bundesamtes zur Regelung offener Vermögensfragen, Heft 6: Behandlung der vermögensrechtlichen Ansprüche der NS-Verfolgten* (Berlin, 1994), pp. 143–44.

[18] A. J. van der Leeuw, "Der Griff," p. 213.

[19] NARA, RG-238, T-1139, NG-3802.

[20] A. J. van der Leeuw, "Der Griff," p. 213.

[21] BAL, R 7/4740, Economics Ministry circular, July 25, 1938 (Betr.: Erfassung ausländischen Wertpapiere auf Grund der Anmeldung des Vermögens von Juden).

[22] NARA, RG-238, T-1139, NG-3937, Interior Minister Frick to Göring, June 14, 1938.

new state bonds at a low rate of interest and will implement the corresponding transfer of property into German hands. On account of the obligation to sell, Jewish property will automatically fall in value and can be bought at lower prices. The involvement of the state will specifically prevent especially skillful and cunning German businessmen from profiting from the liquidation of Jewish property, ensuring that the state is the beneficiary of the action.[23]

Göring's plan to convert Jewish property into government bonds offered the advantage that the money could be used directly to relieve the critical financial position of the Reich. By 1938, it seemed that the only way to continue to finance rearmament was to print more money. To complete the confiscation that was clearly in Göring's mind when he proposed this scheme, it would be necessary only to transfer the money from one state account to another by canceling the bonds.[24] Other elements of the plan included preparations for the marking of Jewish businesses, the removal of any remaining tax exemptions from the Jews, and the intention to proceed with the Aryanization of Jewish real estate.[25]

On June 14, 1938, the Interior Ministry distributed a draft of the measures designed to achieve Aryanization in accordance with the plan outlined in April. Essentially, the Jews were to exchange their business assets for a pension in the form of government bonds paying 4.5 percent annually (2.5 percent interest, 2 percent repayment). Thus, these bonds would be worth only about 50 percent of their nominal value (as most interest rates were then roughly twice this level, at about 5 percent).[26]

The plan, however, met with detailed practical criticism from the Finance Ministry and the Reichsbank, and it disappeared into departmental filing cabinets following deadlocked discussions over the summer.[27] The conversion of Jewish property into state bonds was, however, pursued along with other policies: The Economics Ministry issued a decree at the end of

---

[23] Ibid.

[24] A. J. van der Leeuw, "Der Griff," p. 214.

[25] BAL, R 104 F/10, Extract copy of minutes of meeting held on April 29, 1938, sent to Reichskommissar Bürckel on May 2, 1938, by the Deputy to the Führer of the NSDAP (NI-1062).

[26] NARA, RG-238, T-1139, NG-3937, Reich and Prussian Interior Minister (Frick) to Göring, June 14, 1938; A. J. van der Leeuw, "Der Griff," p. 215.

[27] A. J. van der Leeuw, "Der Griff," p. 215; for Schacht's criticism, see PAAA, Inl. IIg, 169, S. D 520 322–29, cited by A. Barkai, *Vom Boykott zur "Entjudung": Der wirtschaftliche Existenzkampf der Juden im Dritten Reich 1933–1943* (Frankfurt am Main: Fischer, 1987), p. 218, fn. 27; at the Air Ministry meeting on November 12, 1938, Göring complained that the nice plans drawn up during the April meeting had been pursued only very tardily ("nur sehr schleppend verfolgt worden sind"): see IMT, *The Trial of the Major War Criminals* (Blue Series) (Nuremberg, 1947–1949), vol. XXVIII, p. 499.

August 1941 compelling Jews to convert remaining securities at an unfavorable fixed price.[28] However, in practice this belated measure was soon overtaken by the terms of the Eleventh Decree to the Reich Citizenship Law in November 1941, which initiated outright confiscation through the denaturalization of Jews in connection with their deportation.[29]

During the summer of 1938, further steps toward full confiscation were delayed as individual Reich ministries raised practical objections. For example, in June 1938, Interior Minister Frick opposed the confiscation of business assets without compensation because of the possible consequences for German assets overseas. At the same time, however, he stressed that, insofar as Jews in Germany were able to live off the capital sums arising from the sale of their businesses and other property, their accounts would require strict control by the state.[30]

Application of the Currency Laws

Much of the remaining Jewish wealth had already been secured through the application of the Currency Laws. In June 1938, the Ministry of Economics even issued temporary instructions to halt all currency transfers by Jews, as these might sabotage the measures for securing the "application" of Jewish property. The Ministry of Economics instructed the approval authorities to notify the relevant Currency and Tax Offices of all Aryanizations, so that security orders (blocking the property) could be issued promptly. All remaining loopholes were gradually closed, making it almost impossible for Jews to transfer property overseas. In particular, the proceeds Jewish sellers received from Aryanization also became subject to blocking measures. The expanding network of regulations was designed to ensure that the greater part of Jewish wealth would ultimately fall into the hands of the Reich.[31]

All these Nazi plans for confiscation derived from their ideological view of the Jews: For the Nazis, it was necessary to take back that which the Jews, through their activities as "financial and trading parasites," had acquired illicitly from the unsuspecting and hard-working German people.[32] In the

---

[28] A. J. van der Leeuw, "Der Griff," p. 226; J. Walk (ed.), *Das Sonderrecht für die Juden im NS-Staat*, 2nd edition (Heidelberg: C.F. Müller, 1996), IV 224. For more details, see Chapter 6.

[29] See Chapters 4 and 6.

[30] NARA, RG-238, T-1139, NG-3937, Reich and Prussian Interior Minister Frick to Göring, June 14, 1938.

[31] A. J. van der Leeuw, "Der Griff," pp. 216–17.

[32] Ibid.; for an example of this ideological standpoint, see BAL, NS 6/230, pp. 14–19, Stellvertreter des Führers, Anordnung Nr. 89/38, August 2, 1938: "Auf diese Weise wird

summer of 1938, the Party drew up provisional plans for a law making the Jews compensate the Reich for the material damages they allegedly had inflicted.[33] This principle was also applied on an individual basis, as many Nazi Party members sought "compensation" for supposed personal losses suffered due to Jewish "exploitation" during the economic crisis.

The *Vermögensverkehrsstelle* (VVS)

The Property Transaction Office (VVS) was established in Vienna on May 18, 1938. Its director was Walter Rafelsberger, and it was initially under the auspices of the Ministry for Trade and Transport, which by the end of May had been integrated into Fischböck's Ministry for Economy and Labor.[34] Preparations for the establishment of the VVS had already begun in April, around the time of the announcement of Jewish property registration. Its main tasks included the registration of all Jewish property, the approval of sales or rental contracts involving Jewish businesses (i.e., overseeing their Aryanization or liquidation), and the administration of proceeds derived from sales of Jewish businesses.[35]

For Austrian Nazis, another important reason for the establishment of the VVS was to act as a brake on the extensive German investment in Austria, caused by the weakness of the Austrian economy. On April 14, 1938, the Law for the Protection of the Austrian Economy was introduced, and the VVS was also intended to limit excessive inward investment from the Old Reich.[36] As Harold James notes, all businesses in Austria were adversely affected by the inappropriate exchange rate adopted by the Austro-German monetary union. Thus, there was pent-up demand for new capital from Germany to help make Austrian businesses competitive within the enlarged Reich market.[37] Austrian officials were concerned that the sale of Jewish property be exploited to restructure the economy to the benefit of Austrians.

---

das Judentum einen Teil der Schäden wieder gutmachen, die es dem deutschen Volk zugefügt hat." (In this way the Jews will repair a part of the damage that they have inflicted on the German people).

[33] BAL, R 104 F/11, Draft Law on Compensation for Damage Resulting from the Jews, July 18, 1938.

[34] Fischböck was also Austrian Finance Minister at the same time.

[35] G. Fuchs, "Die Vermögensverkehrsstelle," pp. 29–33.

[36] Ibid., pp. 31–32; Helmut Genschel, *Die Verdrängung*, p. 161.

[37] Harold James, *The Deutsche Bank and the Nazi Economic War against the Jews* (Cambridge: Cambridge University Press, 2001), p. 138

In practice, however, considerable inward investment still took place due to Austria's urgent need for capital.[38]

The VVS became Bürckel's central mechanism for implementing closer Party and state control over Aryanization.[39] This centralized institution was intended to match requests for Aryanization with available properties. In particular, the strong competition for Jewish assets in Austria provoked Reichskommissar Bürckel to wrest the initiative back from the "wild commissars" and direct energies toward specific objectives. A purge of the commissars in July opened the way for the "rationalization" of the Austrian economy, by liquidating many small Jewish businesses deemed to be inefficient and unsustainable.[40]

On July 2, 1938, Seyss-Inquart issued an order for all commissary administrators to be dismissed if the VVS had not confirmed them in their posts by the end of the month. Rafelsberger explained that this measure was designed "to facilitate the complete elimination of the wild commissars and to secure the orderly administration and transfer of Jewish property." In the *Völkischer Beobachter*, there was even a report in July that twelve commissars had been arrested and sent to Dachau following an investigation initiated by Bürckel. A new oversight office henceforth exercised closer supervision over the remaining commissary administrators. As a result of these measures, most of the thousands of wild commissars were dismissed – considerably dampening the mood within the Party in Austria.[41]

The files of the VVS have been largely preserved intact, revealing a great deal about Jewish wealth, its confiscation, and its redistribution. Not only are the original property declarations from the summer of 1938 included but also are subsequent reductions, including the payment of special taxes and the Aryanization of businesses and real estate.[42] There is also extensive documentation on the purchasers of Jewish property, who had to prove both that they were not Jewish and that they were qualified in terms of available capital, business experience, and Party loyalty. The files contain contracts

---

[38] G. Fuchs, "Die Vermögensverkehrsstelle," pp. 151–53.

[39] H. Witek, "'Arisierungen' in Wien," p. 800.

[40] BAL, R 104 F/3, Bürckel to Göring, July 19, 1938.

[41] G. Fuchs, "Die Vermögensverkehrsstelle," pp. 63–64; H. Rosenkranz, *Verfolgung und Selbstbehauptung*, pp. 67–68.

[42] As Hans Safrian argues, it would be a mistake to take the results of the property census as a complete measurement of Jewish wealth in Austria, as much had already been plundered and liquidated in the first four months following the Anschluss; see H. Safrian, "Expediting Expropriation," n. 51, pp. 410–11; see also H. Rosenkranz, *Verfolgung und Selbstbehauptung*, p. 69.

of Aryanization and details of the government levy usually imposed on the purchase price.[43]

Within the VVS, there was a growing conflict between the aims of Rafelsberger and of Bürckel, who oversaw its operations. Rafelsberger sought to use Jewish enterprises as a means of rewarding "deserving Party members," which Bürckel viewed as a dangerous waste of state resources. Therefore, Bürckel appointed trusted men to key positions within the VVS, limiting Rafelsberger's authority, until eventually in the summer of 1939 Bürckel was able to exploit Rafelsberger's open differences with the Reich Economics Ministry to have him replaced.[44]

The progress of Aryanization in Austria during the course of 1938 and 1939 can be charted fairly effectively from the records of the VVS. The number of businesses controlled by the newly recognized commissary administrators jumped quickly from 1,624 in July to 5,210 in September, falling to only 868 in December 1938 after Kristallnacht, as many were liquidated or sold.[45] At that time, the VVS had 296 employees, and some 80 percent of all business Aryanizations had been completed. By the end of 1939, this figure had reached 96 percent. The running costs of the VVS were paid from income raised by its own activities.[46]

The VVS introduced a series of new mechanisms that were subsequently adopted widely throughout Europe to expedite Aryanization. For instance, after a time the VVS began to appoint salaried trustees, whose wages it paid, to replace the unreliable system of more independent commissary administrators. In addition, it became customary in all large-scale Aryanizations to have the sale price set more or less independently on the basis of the calculations of a business accountant (*Wirtschaftsprüfer*). These detailed analyses also provided the data necessary to calculate the amount of the profiteering penalty to be paid to the state, in recognition of the artificially low sale prices.[47]

The final sale price and contracts for Aryanizations also had to be approved by the VVS. Essentially, Jewish owners received only the basic value of the remaining material assets of the company; no payment at all

---

[43] See Hubert Steiner and Christian Kucsera (eds.), *Recht als Unrecht: Quellen zur wirtschaftlichen Entrechtung der Wiener Juden durch die NS-Vermögensverkehrsstelle. Teil I: Privatvermögen, Personenverzeichnis* (Vienna: Österreichisches Staatsarchiv, 1991), which lists all the names of Jews who had files (that is, registered property) with the VVS, including their dates of birth.

[44] G. Fuchs, "Die Vermögensverkehrsstelle," pp. 40–52.

[45] H. Rosenkranz, *Verfolgung und Selbstbehauptung*, p. 127.

[46] G. Fuchs, "Die Vermögensverkehrsstelle," pp. 48–54.

[47] Ibid., pp. 82–85, 107–108.

was made for "good will"; that is, expected future profits, loyal customers, or brand names. In addition, a number of other costs were deducted from the price, including all charges associated with the Aryanization itself. Often the German Labor Front (DAF) could insist on improvements to factory facilities, which would also be deducted from the sale price. In any case, the proceeds had to be paid into blocked accounts from which the Jewish owner could withdraw only a small amount per month. The bulk was generally deducted to pay for the punitive tax, possibly the flight tax, or other "contributions," which considerably diminished the initial sum.[48]

Who were the main beneficiaries from the accelerated process of Aryanization in Austria? In the first place, some two-thirds of the approved applications to take over Jewish firms came from Party members. As this group made up only one-third of the more than 33,000 applicants, they were considerably more likely to benefit than nonmembers, which may explain in part the flood of applications to join the Nazi Party in Austria at this time. Deserved Party stalwarts also received several additional perks, especially during the first few months before the system became more bureaucratized. There were opportunities for them to receive special credits at low interest rates, and they might be permitted to pay back much of the "start capital" in monthly installments from the expected profits. Up to May 1939, the complete value of the Aryanizations approved by the VVS had reached RM 81 million. This, of course, was only a fraction – certainly less than 50 percent – of the real value of the companies sold. A portion of the profits also went to the state, both through the "profiteering payment" and other charges; for instance, those for running the VVS itself.[49]

After August 1938, the larger Aryanizations in Austria (businesses worth more than RM 100,000) were conducted separately via the Kontrollbank, with only limited participation by the VVS. This was done partly to prevent the excessive enrichment of individual Party members at the expense of the state and to ensure that purchasers of key industries had sufficient capital and business experience. The Kontrollbank was a consortium of the Creditanstalt and the Länderbank (Austria's main banks) and also Nicolai & Co., but it was closely supervised by Party and state institutions. It initially took direct control over the businesses to be Aryanized, paying only the material value and administering them until a suitable buyer was found.[50] As it made a considerable profit on each sale, the proceeds were then used

---

[48] Ibid., pp. 89–98; see also BAL, R 8135 (Dt. Rev. u. Treuhand AG, Wien)/272, 334, and 215.

[49] G. Fuchs, "Die Vermögensverkehrsstelle," pp. 97–100, 143–44.

[50] H. Rosenkranz, *Verfolgung und Selbstbehauptung*, p. 130.

to make further purchases. Up until July 1941, the Kontrollbank made more than RM 7.25 million in net profits from its purchase and sale of large Jewish businesses, but nearly half of this had already been paid to the Reich, indicating that it could not keep these profits for itself. Nevertheless, the Kontrollbank received nearly RM 400,000 in commissions, which it was allowed to keep.[51] In the case of the larger Aryanizations, generally experienced and wealthy investors and large firms, including some from Germany, bought up most of the objects. The more thorough background checks and greater capital sums needed made it much harder for ordinary Party members to make realistic bids. In this way the Aryanization process actually accelerated the concentration of capital in Austria and did not necessarily match the anticapitalistic rhetoric that was particularly strong within the Austrian Nazi Party.

At the start of the Aryanization process, there was a clear expectation inside the Austrian Party that the proceeds from Jewish property would be used directly to compensate long-standing Party members, many of whom had suffered imprisonment, exile, or loss of employment for their political convictions during the 1930s. As Bürckel put it in an undated memorandum on the Jewish Question in Austria,

> Many Party members expected that for reasons of "compensation" (*Wiedergutmachung*), Jewish property should be sold to them considerably under its real value.... Many Party comrades came along, who are excellent people but have no knowledge of business affairs, and who would inevitably fail in a very short time. Therefore, I established the principle that Aryanization and compensation should have nothing to do with each other.... This idea of mine met with stiff resistance, especially from the head of the Vermögensverkehrsstelle [Rafelsberger].[52]

Bürckel succeeded in reducing the opportunistic exploitation of Jewish wealth by Party members, but as we have seen, they remained a very strongly favored group. The Party initially used the profits from Aryanization in other ways to assist its members. By December 1938, about RM 70,000 had been used for various "compensation" projects. However, after Kristallnacht, Göring insisted that the state and not private individuals should be the main beneficiary of Jewish property.[53]

In fact, the bulk of Jewish businesses in Austria were liquidated rather than Aryanized. According to VVS statistics published in December 1939, only 4,755 Jewish businesses had been Aryanized, and the remaining 21,143

---

[51] G. Fuchs, "Die Vermögensverkehrsstelle," pp. 122–34.

[52] Cited in G. Fuchs, "Die Vermögensverkehrsstelle," pp. 137–38.

[53] Meeting held at the Air Ministry on November 12, 1938, 1816-PS, see IMT, Blue Series, vol. XXVIII, pp. 502–503; ibid., pp. 138–40.

dealt with so far were liquidated.[54] Many of those liquidated were small businesses that simply collapsed after the flight or exclusion of the proprietor. The initial plundering at the time of the Anschluss, together with further vandalism, thefts, and confiscations during Kristallnacht – especially violent in Austria – contributed considerably to the rapid demise of many Jewish businesses. The non-Jewish business class benefited handily from these developments without necessarily Aryanizing Jewish businesses directly. The liquidations removed much of the intense competition in Austria's shrunken interwar domestic market. At the same time, remaining stocks from liquidated businesses were mostly divided up among the relevant trade groups, which sold them to their own members well below the usual wholesale price.

The sale of Jewish real estate, also coordinated mainly by the VVS, took much longer than the process of business Aryanization. In total, there were more than 10,000 real estate objects in Austria, most in Vienna. By August 1939, only some 3,500 sales contracts had been approved, and another 4,000 applications were still being processed.[55] Real estate was not given priority by the Nazi leadership and was not subjected to compulsory measures until the law of December 3, 1938 – although the effects of flight, discriminatory taxes, and Gestapo pressure forced many Jews to sell before this date. According to a sample survey of more than 1,000 Jewish real properties conducted by the official Austrian Historians' Commission (*Historikerkommission*), just under 50 percent were transferred through a sales contract (up to 1940 signed mainly by the Jewish owner), whereas nearly 30 percent were confiscated (either after the Eleventh Decree in November 1941 or as property of "enemies of the people and the state"). Many houses had to be sold to pay outstanding taxes, and it is estimated that at least one-third of the sales price went directly to the state for this reason.[56]

Case Studies of Implementation of Aryanization in Austria

The records of the *Deutsche Revisions- und Treuhandanstalt* provide some interesting insights into the Aryanization process, as they include economic assessments of Aryanized companies conducted several months after Aryanization. In the case of a clothing and furniture combined production and sales outlet (Haber brothers), sold via the Kontrollbank with approval

---

[54] "21,000 jüdische Betriebe stillgelegt," *Warschauer Zeitung*, December 2, 1939. I am grateful to my colleague Joseph White for bringing this document to my attention.

[55] G. Fuchs, "Die Vermögensverkehrsstelle," p. 139.

[56] Historikerkommission (ed.), *Vermögensentzug während der NS-Zeit sowie Rückstellungen und Entschädigungen seit 1945 in Österreich: Schlussbericht* (Vienna: Historikerkommission, 2003), pp. 92–95.

by the VVS in April 1939, accountants judged that the sale price of RM 575,000 was under half of the estimated market value (*Verkehrswert*) of RM 1.3 million. They noted that, as in many Aryanization cases, the value of existing stocks had been considerably underestimated by the assessor. Two main reasons were identified for why the Kontrollbank accepted what was essentially a very low offer. First, none of the other interested parties was prepared to offer more, and second, the Tax Office was keen to complete the sale in order to reclaim some of the RM 834,000 in taxes owed by the previous Jewish owners.

Another interesting, though typical, feature in this case was the meager capital resources of the successful Austrian bidders. These bidders made an initial payment of RM 350,000 based on a bank credit of RM 100,000 and a state-guaranteed loan of a further RM 250,000, and the remainder of the purchase price was to be paid back in installments from the expected profits of the company. At the end of 1939, when the assessment was made, it appeared that the company was making a good profit, benefiting from the upswing in the Austrian economy, so that the owners could pay themselves a salary of RM 18,000 each per year. However, many of the customers were still buying on credit, and the business itself had considerable debts to pay back over the coming years. In addition, the start of the war would affect the outlook for the company, as further investment was planned to bring the production and sales sites together on the Mariahilfestrasse (one of Vienna's main shopping streets) and additional investments would be required to convert to military production.[57]

In the case of another company, sold in April 1938 before implementation of the new legislation on Aryanization, a subsequent examination of the books revealed that the price of RM 6,700 had been little more than a token payment. In this case the Jewish owner had already left Austria before the Anschluss and was therefore unable to export the proceeds in any case. Here the VVS retrospectively increased the price to RM 24,700 by adding an Aryanization payment of RM 18,000; fortunately for the new owners this could be made in installments from the expected profits. Yet, this higher price still bore little relation to the real value, believed to exceed RM 100,000.[58]

In fact, not all Aryanizations were necessarily guaranteed to bring a profit. In some cases existing equipment was so run down, or the loss of business due to boycotts and destruction so severe, that it might be difficult to

---

[57] BAL, R 8135 (Wien)/54 Brüder Haber, Kaufhaus für Bekleidung und Wohnkultur, Wien. Dt. Rev. u. Treuhand AG, Sonderprüfung, October 9, 1939.

[58] BAL, R 8135 (Wien)/226 Rudolf Korff, Damenhutfabrikation und Einzelhandel, Sonderprüfung, September 8, 1939.

restore the company to profitability without some considerable investment, especially given the growing competition from German firms.

Political events and geography had a considerable impact on the profitability of Aryanized businesses. For example, the conflicting experiences of two small cafés demonstrate both the risks and benefits involved. One, in a working-class district, actually made good profits right away as political tensions over Czechoslovakia in September 1938 brought in many customers to listen to the news on the radio. The new owner soon paid off the purchase price of RM 9,000 into a blocked Jewish account, as well as part of the levy charged by the VVS. Another café, taken over by an employee, failed to make a profit initially because 90 percent of the former clients were Jewish and he had been obliged to ban Jews from the premises. This created immediate financial problems, as the district remained predominantly Jewish, at least during the first year after the Anschluss.[59]

Value and Structure of Jewish Property in Austria

Because of the property census taken in the spring of 1938, detailed information survives about the structure of remaining Jewish wealth in Austria as of summer 1938. In the census, an effort was also made to register the capitalized value of pensions and salaries (calculated by the use of actuarial tables). These capitalized values, however, are somewhat misleading, as many Jewish employees were in the process of losing their jobs. One assumes that the share of business capital had declined considerably since March 1938, although the value of other types of assets had also diminished in the months before the census.

The gross value of Austrian Jewish assets calculated by the Nazis on the basis of 47,768 property declarations was RM 2,295,085,000, which decreased to RM 2,041,828,000 after deducting registered liabilities.[60] The sums may be categorized according to types of property as follows:

Real estate and land	34.9%
Business capital	19.9%
Other tangible values	3.4%
Financial assets	41.8%

[59] BAL, R 8135 (Wien)/299 Kaffee Rebekka Schreiber, Favoritenstr. 59 & Kaffee Morzin, Wien I, Salzgries 2.

[60] Helen B. Junz, "Report on the Pre-War Wealth Position of the Jewish Population in Nazi-Occupied Countries, Germany and Austria," prepared for the Independent Committee of Eminent Persons and included as Appendix S in *Report on Dormant Accounts of Victims of Nazi Persecution in Swiss Banks* (December 1999), p. A-143.

In a more detailed analysis of a sample of Austrian property census returns, Helen Junz discovered that, within the financial assets class, fixed interest securities predominated over equities, but that foreign issues were also strongly represented. Many of these foreign securities were physically held abroad. Overall, she estimates that probably more than 20 percent of all financial assets were invested in foreign securities.[61]

As the historian Herbert Rosenkranz points out, the census figures represent a considerable underestimate of the value of Jewish property in March. For example, they do not include the market values of some 7,000 businesses that had been closed soon after March 13, 1938. In addition, more than 16,000 Jews had emigrated by the initial registration deadline of June 30, 1938. Some emigrants still registered their remaining property from abroad, but the value doubtlessly was diminished due to emigration costs and various Nazi depredations. In addition, some personal property, such as silverware, was not declared, as people did not intend it to be sold. However, the values for some businesses may have been overstated, at least in comparison with the VVS valuations for their sale.[62]

The Central Office for Jewish Emigration

The radicalization of anti-Jewish policy in Austria was also linked to concerted efforts directed by the SD toward the emigration and even forced expulsion of Austrian Jews – a task viewed by Adolf Eichmann as much more difficult than the Aryanization of their property.[63] On August 20, 1938, the Central Office for Jewish Emigration (*Zentralstelle für jüdische Auswanderung*) was founded in Vienna on the authority of Reichskommissar Bürckel. It was created partly in response to the bureaucratic difficulties Austrian Jews faced in obtaining all the necessary paperwork for emigration. Nominally, the new office was subordinated to SS-Standartenführer Dr. Walter Stahlecker of the Security Police, but in practice it was held closely under the control of Eichmann and the SD.[64] The Central Office aimed both to expedite the departure of Austria's Jews and to extract much

---

[61] Ibid., p. A-147.

[62] H. Rosenkranz, *Verfolgung und Selbstbehauptung*, pp. 68–69.

[63] Eichmann Trial, Document T-130, Eichmann to Hagen, Vienna, May 8, 1938.

[64] BAL, R 58/486, pp. 8–11, Zentralstelle für jüdische Auswanderung an das Sicherheitshauptamt II 112, z. Hd. v. SS-OStF Hagen September 14, 1938; and pp. 13–14, Bürckel letter on the establishment of the Central Office and its tasks, August 20, 1938.

of their remaining wealth in the process.[65] However, its establishment also represented considerable continuity in the development of the SD's policy toward the Jews.

In a lengthy December 1937 report, uncovered in the former Stasi Archives in East Berlin, Herbert Hagen, the head of Referat II 112 (which dealt with the Jews) within the SD main office, closely foreshadowed the policy later adopted in Austria: "The central offices of the Jewish organizations should be so directed in terms of personnel and organization, that for the Jews the only possible way out remains emigration." The same report also argued in detail that the SD and Gestapo should implement a radical solution to Jewish policy: exploiting the funds of overseas aid organizations to help pay for Jewish emigration.[66]

Such were the methods employed by Eichmann almost as soon as the Nazis took control in Austria. On March 16, 1938, the Gestapo broke into offices of the Jewish community (*Israelitisches Kulturgemeinschaft*, or IKG) and discovered evidence of a large donation to the Vaterländischen Front in support of the aborted plebiscite against the Anschluss. In response, Eichmann imposed a large fine of RM 500,000 (equivalent to the donation) on the IKG. At the same time, he set about turning the officials of the IKG into his instruments for the achievement of the SD's specific goal of forcing Jewish emigration. On May 8, 1938, Eichmann claimed that he had received the agreement of both the IKG and the Zionists to the emigration of some 20,000 indigent (*mittellose*) Jews by May 1, 1939.[67] It was the large number of impoverished Jews in Austria lacking sufficient money to pay for emigration who were seen as the major hindrance to the SD's aim of driving all Jews out.

The main organizational principles applied by the Central Office were also foreshadowed by earlier schemes. For example, the idea of streamlining the complex paperwork necessary for emigration was proposed first by the IKG itself. A further aim of the Central Office was to overcome the widespread corruption within the bureaucracy, which enabled a few wealthy Jews to jump the long queues for visas and other paperwork with the

---

[65] A. J. van der Leeuw, "Der Griff," p. 223; Hans Safrian, *Eichmann und seine Gehilfen* (Frankfurt am Main: Fischer, 1995), pp. 41–46.

[66] Bericht von II 112, gez. Oscf. Hagen, December 11, 1937, BA-Hoppegarten, ZB I, 1330. Quotation and arguments, see Gabriele Anderl, Dirk Rupnow, and Alexandra-Eileen Wenck (eds.), *Die Zentralstelle für jüdische Auswanderung als Beraubungsinstitution* (Vienna: Historikerkommission, 2002), pp. 56–60.

[67] Gabriele Anderl et al. (eds.), *Die Zentralstelle*, pp. 56–60; see also, Eichmann Trial Document, T-130, Eichmann to Hagen, May 8, 1939.

assistance of bribes, often coordinated by lawyers.[68] Similarly, the idea of an "emigration fund" exploiting the assets of the wealthier Jews to help pay the emigration costs of those less well off was developed during the expulsion of the Jews from Burgenland after April 1938[69] and also as part of the "Gildemeister Aktion."[70] The Central Office later adapted this concept in the form of the so-called *Passumlage* or progressive emigration tax that it administered.

Reinhard Heydrich outlined the principles behind the *Passumlage* at the infamous Wannsee Conference in January 1942:

> The financing of emigration was provided by the Jews, that is the Jewish political organizations themselves. In order to prevent the proletarianized Jews from being left behind, the principle was applied that the propertied Jews were to finance the emigration of those without property; they had to pay a corresponding fee or emigration tax, based on a sliding scale according to their property, which was used to cover the financial obligations incurred in the course of the emigration of the indigent Jews.[71]

According to German records, the income from this tax was to be applied to advance Jewish emigration ("*die Förderung der jüdischen Auswanderung*"). Recent research has revealed that in the period 1938–41, more than RM 8 million was collected via the *Passumlage* and related fees. Unfortunately the exact expenditure of these funds is not clear from the available files.[72]

Exploiting Foreign Aid Organizations

In the summer of 1938, several competing plans sought to exploit the potential support of foreign Jews, especially that provided by overseas aid organizations, to assist in financing the emigration of the less well off. In June 1938, the SD was keen to use a gift of $100,000 offered by Jewish aid organizations abroad to further the emigration of up to 700 indigent Jews from Austria. At the same time, the emigration of propertied Jews was even temporarily hindered to boost the emigration of those with insufficient

---

[68] Gabriele Anderl et al. (eds.), *Die Zentralstelle,* p. 74.

[69] Historikerkommission (ed.), *Schlussbericht,* p. 86; BAL, R 58/486, pp. 60–61, Gestapo Wien an Inspekteur der Sipo. Wien, April 28, 1939.

[70] H. Rosenkranz, *Verfolgung und Selbstbehauptung,* p. 85.

[71] PAAA, Inl. IIg/117, pp. 165–82, Protocol of the Wannsee Conference held on January 20, 1942.

[72] Gabriele Anderl et al. (eds.), *Die Zentralstelle,* pp. 138–40, 222; H. Rosenkranz, *Verfolgung und Selbstbehauptung,* p. 124.

means.[73] The SD in Vienna also achieved veto powers over emigration applications sent to the Currency Office for approval, thereby tightening its control over all Jewish emigration.[74]

A particular problem was the reluctance of foreign aid organizations to put any funds directly at the disposal of the Reich, as they did not want to reward its brutal policies. At the same time, the SD was obliged to comply with Göring's exhortations that none of the Reich's precious foreign currency should be expended for Jewish emigration.[75] Therefore, Eichmann's close control over the IKG was essential to resolve these contradictions. The aid agencies agreed to continue supplying foreign currency to the IKG, which would then be paid to emigrants once abroad. These contributions, however, were made with the proviso that a large part of the Reichsmark sums collected from the emigrants in Vienna was to be used directly for welfare programs of the IKG. For example, the "Joint" (American Jewish Joint Distribution Committee) gave considerable financial aid to Austrian Jews throughout 1938, as it feared that without this support the poorer Austrian Jews might starve or be sent to concentration camps as "asocial elements."[76]

This complex relationship also required some flexibility from the SD if they were not to lose a key source of revenue for Jewish emigration. For example, the SD succeeded in excluding the IKG from the removal of tax exemptions that was applied to Jewish communal organizations in the Old Reich in March 1938, arguing that "charitable gifts" (*Spenden*) to the IKG were helping finance emigration. Even Himmler agreed that removing the IKG's charitable status might only cause many Jews to become a burden on the state, and he won a further deferral in April 1939.[77] The SD even made efforts to prevent the withdrawal of state welfare support from the Jewish community, for similar self-interested financial reasons.[78]

From March 1938 to the end of October 1941, the IKG received $4.2 million from aid organizations abroad. This sum was spent mainly on "landing money" for emigrants and paying for their transportation, for which

---

[73] Eichmann Trial, Document T/37(300), report on the journey of Reichsbankrat Dr. Wolf and Assessor Siegert to Vienna, June 20, 1938; Gabriele Anderl et al. (eds.), *Die Zentralstelle,* pp. 100–104.

[74] Eichmann Trial, Document T/135, letter from Eichmann on his meeting with Dr. Wolf, June 16, 1938.

[75] Gabriele Anderl et al. (eds.), *Die Zentralstelle,* pp. 18, 180.

[76] H. Rosenkranz, *Verfolgung und Selbstbehauptung,* p. 81.

[77] Gabriele Anderl et al. (eds.), *Die Zentralstelle,* pp. 82–83 and 162–64.

[78] Ibid., pp. 142–43.

the IKG received in return RM 21.2 million for its own internal costs. This income (directly or indirectly) from emigrants made up more than 50 percent of all the income received by the IKG and was vital for the continuation of its welfare operations at a time of rapidly increasing poverty among those Jews who remained.[79]

Operations of the Central Office

The streamlining of bureaucratic procedures also ensured that all taxes and debts were paid before emigration.[80] In this sense, the SD acted as the central coordinating office for the systematic plundering of the Jews on emigration, in accordance with the tax and currency laws introduced previously in the Old Reich. However, the various offices concerned (e.g., Tax Offices, Currency Offices, Visa Offices, and others) still retained much of their autonomy. In some respects, the Central Office acted as little more than a passport office, as these other agencies still conducted their own inquiries before approving any application.[81] As Herbert Rosenkranz put it, the Jews who queued up at the Rothschild Palace still had to go to one window after another, paying various taxes and fees and obtaining necessary certificates before their emigration finally was approved.[82]

A close degree of cooperation prevailed between the Central Office and the VVS; credits were sometimes granted in lieu of unsold real estate, for example, to expedite the SD's goal of emigration. Even Reichskommissar Bürckel praised the relatively good cooperation between the two institutions. In addition, the Central Office requested information from the VVS about all large-scale Aryanizations, especially when emigration was involved.[83]

In practice, the Central Office did not give detailed advice to emigrants or actively secure emigration possibilities for them. These tasks still were performed by officials of the IKG.[84] As documents uncovered in Vienna since 2000 show, all Jews interested in emigration were registered by the

---

[79] Ibid., p. 191. In addition to foreign currency from Jewish organizations, some $1.5 million was raised by the relatives of emigrants.

[80] See the preprinted forms of the *Zentralstelle* in USHMM, RG-11.001M.01, reel 8 (RGVA, former "Osobyi archive," 500-1-625).

[81] Gabriele Anderl et al. (eds.), *Die Zentralstelle*, p. 225.

[82] H. Rosenkranz, *Verfolgung und Selbstbehauptung*, p. 124.

[83] Gabriele Anderl et al. (eds.), *Die Zentralstelle*, p. 133.

[84] Ibid., p. 110.

IKG on index cards, and clearly these records were intended to help steer emigration in accordance with the policies of the SD.[85]

The procedural streamlining achieved by the Central Office brought with it the submission of the Jews to the SD's arbitrary power. SD men routinely humiliated Jews in the course of their daily business while they plundered their property. There was also a high degree of personal enrichment and corruption, as some SD officials exploited their position to extort bribes or simply steal property. Eichmann's colleagues could measure their social advancement in tangible form as they moved into Aryanized apartments, appointed with Jews' furnishings.[86]

Concentration of Austria's Jews and Confiscation of Communal Property

Shortly after the Anschluss, in April or May 1938, Himmler ordered that all Austrian Jews be concentrated in Vienna. Initially the SD aimed to have this task completed by the end of October 1938. In total some 10,000 people were affected by the order.[87] For instance, in May 1938, there were 120 Jews living in Gänserndorf in Lower Austria; in November 1938, they were deported to Vienna and the property of the community confiscated. By January 1939, no Jews remained in the town.[88] In May 1939, the SD reported that the concentration of Austria's Jews in Vienna was more or less complete (about 800 still resided in the provinces).[89] This rapid concentration resulted in the dissolution of all Jewish communal organizations in Austria, apart from the IKG, and the liquidation of their property.

In March 1938, a Liquidation Office (*Stillhaltekommission*) was established in Austria, which was soon under the control of Reichskommissar

---

[85] For a brief overview of the recent archival finds in Vienna, see Anatol Steck, "The Archives of the Jewish Community of Vienna: A Cooperative Microfilming Project to Preserve Holocaust-Relevant Records," *Stammbaum: The Journal of German-Jewish Genealogical Research*, no. 24 (Winter 2004): 4–9.

[86] H. Safrian, *Eichmann und seine Gehilfen*, p. 56

[87] BAL, R 58/486, p. 169, SD-Hauptamt II 112 4, note of November 2, 1938 (Betr.: Konzentrierung der Juden in der Ostmark auf Wien); Wolf Gruner, *Zwangsarbeit und Verfolgung: Österreichische Juden im NS-Staat 1938–45* (Innsbruck: Studien, 2000), p. 41.

[88] Shmuel Spector and Geoffrey Wigoder (eds.), *The Encyclopedia of Jewish Life Before and During the Holocaust* (Jerusalem: Yad Vashem, 2001), p. 412.

[89] BAL, R 58/486, pp. 52–56, Report of II 112 (SD Hauptamt) on May 16, 1939 (Betr.: Jüdische Auswanderung aus der Ostmark).

Bürckel. It was responsible for registering and disposing of the property of organizations liquidated by the Nazis in the wake of the Anschluss. These organizations included sports clubs and Masonic lodges, as well as political and religious organizations. In practice, the Liquidation Office closely served the interests of the Nazi Party; many governmental and Party organizations profited directly from the liquidation process, acquiring prime real estate and other property under very favorable conditions.[90]

The property of the IKG and other Jewish communities and organizations was administered initially by the Liquidation Office, and in May 1939, part of it was placed in a "Trust Fund for Jewish Welfare." In December, Bürckel named Eichmann the special agent for the property of the Jewish communities and the Trust Fund, including some real estate outside Vienna. The Liquidation Office sold a number of properties in 1939, and Eichmann appointed Anton Brunner to oversee the rapid sale of most of the remaining real estate outside Vienna, in many cases to the local authorities. In any case, the properties outside Vienna were worth much less than those in Vienna (many of which exceeded RM 100,000 in value). The total value of real estate was more than RM 5 million, even according to the low Nazi estimates; because of those low estimates, some properties were simply given away.[91] From the available evidence, it appears that at least some of the income raised by the liquidation of Jewish communal property was made available to the IKG for the support of emigration and urgent welfare needs.[92]

Rapid Impoverishment of Jews

Even before the Anschluss, Austria's Jewish community was less well off per capita than their co-religionists in Germany. According to one calculation, by April 1938 one-third of Austrian Jews were receiving regular welfare payments.[93] Soon, the effects of Aryanization, loss of employment,

---

[90] Gabriele Anderl et al. (eds.), *Die Zentralstelle*, p. 162.

[91] Eichmann Trial, document T/147, unsigned letter from IKG to Löwenherz, Vienna, June 26, 1939; BAL, R 8135 (80 re. 3)/69, Bericht der Deutschen Revisions und Treuhand AG, Zweigniederlassung Wien, September 25, 1940.

[92] Gabriele Anderl et al. (eds.), *Die Zentralstelle*, pp. 149–51; see also Eichmann Trial, Document T/37(303), memo by Löwenherz on his meeting with Eichmann on August 14, 1939.

[93] Michael Wildt (ed.), *Die Judenpolitik des SD 1935 bis 1938: Eine Dokumentation* (Munich: Oldenbourg, 1995), p. 200, doc. no. 32, situation report of the SD II 112 for 1938; Gabriele Anderl et al. (eds.), *Die Zentralstelle*, p. 85.

confiscations, and plunder produced a severe economic crisis among the Jewish population. By the end of 1938, the IKG had a monthly deficit of more than one million RM, and it urgently needed foreign aid to plug this gap. The SD gave responsibility to the IKG not only to organize emigration but also to maintain Jewish welfare organizations.[94] Now, the main restriction on emigration consisted of the high financial and bureaucratic hurdles to be overcome to obtain the necessary visas. These costs meant that most remaining potential emigrants became reliant on IKG support to cross those hurdles.

An indication of the rapid impoverishment inflicted on even quite wealthy Austrian Jewish families can be seen from an IKG official's notes regarding the planned emigration of a twenty-nine-year-old medical doctor, Fritz Offenberger, who was released from Buchenwald in January 1939 after seven months in "protective custody." The IKG official, who spoke only with Dr. Offenberger's mother, concluded, "Previously, very orderly conditions; educated middle class (*gutbürgerlich*); now misery (*jetzt Elend*). Well-behaved pious Jews (*brave fromme Juden*). Very warmly support possible aid."[95]

After the German invasion of Poland, which provoked a general European war, most escape routes were closed. From July to October 1939, the number of people receiving financial support from the IKG rose from just over 20,000 to about 33,000, and the amount paid to each was reduced as overall spending fell in line with reduced IKG income. By the end of 1939, about 117,000 Jews had emigrated from Austria, with the result that 70 percent of those remaining were more than forty-five years old.[96]

Therefore, the IKG had to balance the aim of supporting emigration with the need to pay for the rapidly growing burden of welfare support. In this sense, their dealings with the SD were a necessary evil, as they combined support for emigration with the raising of cash for immediate welfare needs, shifting much of the burden onto the remaining wealthy Jews, who had much better chances of getting out. In assessing these difficult moral choices facing the Jewish leadership, one must bear in mind the key

---

[94] W. Gruner, *Zwangsarbeit und Verfolgung*, p. 71.

[95] Central Archives for the History of the Jewish People, Jerusalem, Archives of the Israelitische Kultusgemeinde Wien, reel Alpha 01, Fritz Offenberger, interview notes, January 9, 1939 (copies held also at the USHMM in RG-68). Dr. Offenberger still needed RM 250 to cover his outstanding emigration costs, but was able to leave for the United States via Britain shortly after these notes were written. I am most grateful to Ilana Offenberger for this information she uncovered during her PhD research on Jewish families in Vienna during the Holocaust period.

[96] Gabriele Anderl et al. (eds.), *Die Zentralstelle*, pp. 210–11.

context of the need to maintain hospitals and support life for those who remained.[97]

Austrian Models and Lessons

What was the significance of the Austrian experience for the development of property confiscation measures in the Old Reich and subsequently in the occupied territories during the war? An important point is that pressure from below did make a difference. The rapid seizure of many Jewish businesses by the "wild commissars," the thousands of applications for Aryanized property, and the direct plundering of Jewish property during Kristallnacht and on other occasions all served to accelerate the pace of antisemitic measures in Austria and throughout the Reich. As Hans Safrian concludes, one of the reasons for the systematic radicalization of antisemitic policy, in addition to ideological considerations, was the concrete material interest – the greed – of those directly involved.[98]

In many key respects, the "Austrian model" was not so much a carefully planned development as an interactive steering by key Nazi dual Party/state institutions of organic developments that accompanied the annexation of Austria. As noted, Bürckel felt compelled to legitimize the wild commissars in order to tame them and direct the energy thereby unleashed into channels more favorable to the state. Both the VVS and the Central Office served primarily to coordinate and expedite the ongoing processes of expropriation and emigration in accordance with Party and state goals. These processes were created and evolved in accordance with the needs of a fluid situation on the ground.

The so-called Vienna model has not been strictly defined in the historiography.[99] However, it is important to recognize that it comprised two distinct and ultimately competing versions of how to organize the expropriation of Jewish property. From the start, the Austrian model represented a division of labor between the SD, which was working primarily toward Jewish emigration, and the state administration, under Bürckel, responsible

[97] Ibid., pp. 86, 181–82, 190–91.
[98] H. Safrian, *Eichmann und seine Gehilfen*, p. 24; ibid., p. 223.
[99] See Dirk Rupnow, "'Zur Förderung und beschleunigten Regelung der Auswanderung...' Die Wiener Zentralstelle für jüdische Auswanderung als Modell," unpublished paper presented at the conference "'Arisierung' und Restitution: Die Rückerstattung jüdischen Eigentums in Deutschland und Österreich nach 1945 und 1989," held at Freiburg in Breisgau in October 2000. I am grateful to the author for making this paper available to me.

for "cleansing" the Austrian economy of Jewish influence.[100] Nevertheless, there was always a certain conflict of interest between the systematic plundering of business and financial assets by "legal means," developed by Bürckel and Fischböck, exploiting the considerable appetite for Jewish property in Austria, and the combination of emigration and expropriation pursued by the SD.

The efforts of the VVS and the Central Office achieved significant results in advancing the Nazis' objectives. In August 1939, Rafelsberger of the VVS reported to Himmler the successful liquidation of 21,000 Jewish businesses and the Aryanization of 5,000 others. He concluded that "through the activity of the VVS the given task of removing Jews from the Austrian economy had been practically solved within less than eighteen months. In particular, Jewish shops and companies in Vienna had completely disappeared."[101] In a similar vein, an internal report by Herbert Hagen of the SD in June 1939 claimed credit for achieving the emigration of some 110,000 Jews from Austria since August 1938. Hagen's claim is perhaps overstated, as some emigration had been illegal (in spite of the SD's efforts), but he aimed also to further consolidate the SD's central role within Nazi anti-Jewish policy.[102]

Helmut Genschel has characterized Aryanization in Austria as a giant plunder campaign, initially in favor of the Old Fighters and then increasingly to the benefit of the Party and finally the state.[103] This evolution reflected the ability of Bürckel and Fischböck to gain control over and redirect this process. Fischböck and his officials developed in Austria a number of key mechanisms that were subsequently deployed for the systematic confiscation of Jewish property in Germany and elsewhere. Significantly, both the registration of Jewish property and the universal blocking of Jewish accounts receiving the proceeds of Aryanization were implemented first in Austria. Indeed, much of the carefully coordinated system of expropriation laws and institutions employed in the occupied Netherlands from 1940 onward was based directly on Fischböck's earlier experiences and plans. These measures included increased safeguards against corruption, such as valuations by external business accountants, and the payment of Jewish owners in the form of a pension, which easily could be confiscated after their deportation.[104] However, in transferring the expropriation methods

[100] Eichmann Trial, document T-130, Eichmann to Hagen, Vienna, May 8, 1938.
[101] BAL, NS 19/836, Staatskommissar in der Privatwirtschaft an RFSS (Himmler), August 14, 1939. Quoted also by H. Safrian and H. Witek (eds.), *Und keiner war dabei*, pp. 97–98.
[102] H. Safrian, *Eichmann und seine Gehilfen*, pp. 46–49.
[103] H. Genschel, *Die Verdrängung*, pp. 165–66.
[104] For further details, see Chapter 7.

to the occupied countries, where lines of jurisdiction still were unresolved, the potential for conflicts over control of the expropriation mechanisms (and therefore also over the proceeds) remained high.

Eichmann's skill in building up the Central Office lay less in the originality of its methods than in his ruthlessness in making the SD the decisive force in the implementation of anti-Jewish policy in Austria, thereby establishing principles and gaining experience that could be applied in both the Old Reich and the occupied territories.[105] As noted, the Central Office was not primarily concerned with expropriation, but rather the mobilization of both domestic and foreign Jewish funds in support of its program of forced emigration. Control over Jewish communal finances was an important aspect of this program. Already by fall 1938, the SD was holding up the model of its experiences in Vienna as the basis for the establishment of similar organizations in the rest of the Reich. The Reich Central Office for Jewish Emigration, however, did not achieve similar results, as by the time of its establishment in January 1939 the prospects for further large-scale emigration had considerably diminished.[106] Yet, such as it was, the operation of the Reichsvereinigung from 1939 was based in part on the experiences made with the Austrian Jewish communities.

The activity of the Central Office for Jewish Emigration in Prague demonstrates the flexibility of the mechanisms established in Vienna: the Prague Central Office became the main instrument for the expropriation of Jews in the Protectorate of Bohemia and Moravia during the process of concentration and successive deportation via Theresienstadt. In the Netherlands, however, attempts by Heydrich and the SD to expand the Central Office there into a similar role coordinating deportation and expropriation policy had to give way to Fischböck's more sophisticated methods of "legal confiscation."

The pattern of events in Austria, however, was not the only case in which confiscation methods evolved from a combination of direct violence on the ground and subsequent legislation seeking to redirect this destructive energy.

---

[105] Gabriele Anderl et al. (eds.), *Die Zentralstelle*, p. 113; BAL, R 58/486, pp. 6–7, report of Hagen to I 112 on his official journey to Vienna on August 31 to September 1, 1938 (received September 12, 1938).

[106] *Trials of War Criminals before the Nuernberg Military Tribunals under Control Council Law No. 10, Nuernberg, October 1946–April 1949* [Green Series] (Washington, DC: U.S. Government Printing Office, 1949–1953; Reprinted in Buffalo, NY: William S. Hein, 1997), vol. XIII, pp. 129–30, NG-2586-A, Göring directive to Reich Minister for the Interior, January 24, 1939, on the appointment of Heydrich as Chief of the Reich Central Office for Jewish Emigration. On preparations for the establishment of Central Offices for Jewish emigrants in Berlin, Frankfurt, Hamburg, and Breslau and coordination with the Berlin Tax Offices in February 1939, see BAL, R 2/5973, pp. 222–26.

Kristallnacht, in November 1938, reflects a similar pattern of "popular violence" instigated from above but also running out of control, which led ultimately to a more systematic and comprehensive form of legal expropriation designed to limit and channel the negative impact of these "excesses."

Kristallnacht

The original April 1938 plan to convert Jewish wealth into government bonds was not implemented as envisaged, mainly due to the unforeseen acceleration of Jewish policy in November 1938. On October 14, Göring again expressed his firm determination that "the Jewish Question must now be grasped with every possible means, as they must be removed from the economy." On that occasion, Göring stressed that Aryanization was a matter for the state and not the Party. The wild actions in Austria, where according to the report of Minister Fischböck, the Party combined Aryanization with compensation for Old Fighters, had to stop.[107] Göring's statements in the period from April 1938 to December 1938 make clear his intention to confiscate all Jewish property in the classic Nazi fashion of "*so oder so*," by one means or another. It was only a matter of timing and opportunity as to which mechanism of several available options would prove most effective and beneficial. However, although much of the groundwork for the Aryanization of the economy was laid during the first nine months of 1938, it took a catalytic event to jolt the Nazi bureaucracy into action.[108]

During the summer of 1938, renewed antisemitic actions occurred in Germany along with the registration of Jewish property and the application of approval procedures for Aryanization contracts. In mid-June, many Jews were arrested as part of the action against "asocial elements," and in Berlin especially, encouraged by Goebbels, Nazi-inspired rioters broke shop windows and in some cases plundered the contents. On the night of June 18–19, three synagogues were demolished. Yet, on June 22, partly in response to foreign protests, the action was called off; as the SD and other forces within the administration preferred to achieve their aims by more controlled and orderly means. Additional attacks on shops outside Berlin followed in July, but it was not until October (after the Munich Agreement) that widespread attacks on Jewish shops started again.[109]

The SS's weekly journal, *Das Schwarze Korps*, made an appeal on November 3 for separate Jewish residential areas to be created so the Jews' activities

---

[107] 1301-PS, IMT, Blue Series, vol. XXVII, pp. 160–64.
[108] A. J. van der Leeuw, "Der Griff," pp. 215–16.
[109] P. Longerich, *Politik der Vernichtung*, pp. 175–90.

could be better "controlled." The same article justified further Aryanization and confiscation measures on the grounds that Jewish wealth in Germany rightly belonged to the German people and should be used to pay for the weapons necessary to protect Germany, especially as the Jews were encouraging other countries to make war against her.[110] It was in this charged atmosphere of anti-Jewish propaganda, directed in part against Jewish property ownership, that the events of Kristallnacht took place.

On November 7, 1938, a seventeen-year-old Jewish youth, Herschel Grynszpan, shot the Third Secretary at the German Consulate in Paris, Ernst vom Rath. Grynszpan was the son of Polish Jews living in Germany, and he wanted to protest the previous weeks' mass deportation of Jews with Polish citizenship to Poland; his parents were among those deported. Secretary vom Rath died of his wounds on November 9, 1938.[111]

Goebbels and Hitler responded by launching the Kristallnacht pogrom that same day. This exhibition of open violence removed the last legal and political restraints on the treatment of the Jewish population. On the night of November 9–10 alone, more than one hundred Jews were killed, hundreds of synagogues were set on fire and destroyed or severely damaged, and some 7,500 businesses and many private homes were also damaged or plundered. German police and auxiliary Nazi forces arrested about 30,000 Jewish men and sent them to Dachau, Buchenwald, and other detention sites.[112]

On the following day when Göring spoke to the Führer, Hitler gave him instructions to start immediately the "removal of the Jews from the economy."[113] Now Göring directed all his energies toward a swift and radical achievement of this goal.[114]

Meeting at the Air Ministry on November 12, 1938

At an infamous meeting on November 12, 1938, attended by a number of key Nazi officials, Göring insisted emphatically that he would now introduce the necessary measures for the Aryanization of the economy blow by blow. He repeated many of the ideas that had been discussed in April; in

---

[110] *Das Schwarze Korps*, November 3, 1938, p. 2.

[111] G. Fuchs, "Die Vermögensverkehrsstelle," pp. 69–71.

[112] Frank Bajohr, *"Aryanisation" in Hamburg: The Economic Exclusion of the Jews and the Confiscation of their Property in Nazi Germany* (New York: Berghahn, 2002), p. 224; Ian Kershaw, *Hitler 1936–45: Nemesis* (New York: W.W. Norton, 2002), p. 148.

[113] IMT, Blue Series, vol. XIII, p. 116, testimony of Funk, May 6, 1946; cited in I. Kershaw, *Nemesis*, p. 143, n. 87.

[114] A. J. van der Leeuw, "Der Griff," p. 217.

particular, that the Jews were to be excluded from the economy and would be compensated with state bonds as a type of pension.[115] But this time, the discussions were followed by a series of concrete measures implementing Göring's aims by means somewhat different from those previously discussed. On that same day, Göring decreed the exclusion of Jews from further activity as shopkeepers and craftsmen. With only a few exceptions, all such businesses were to be liquidated. For all remaining Jewish businesses, compulsory Aryanization was decreed in accordance with detailed measures published later, on December 3.[116]

Only portions survive of the stenographic record of the revealing discussions at the Air Ministry. Nevertheless, those minutes deserve close examination, as this was a rare occasion when the Nazis openly debated the pros and cons of various economic persecution measures. In his presentation, Göring advocated direct state intervention to speed up Aryanization and also sought to gain maximum benefit for the Reich's strained finances. For example, he wanted to secure part of the profits of Aryanization for the state by imposing a surcharge (*Aufschlag*) on Aryanization transactions; at the same time, he wanted to restrain the excessive corruption of regional Party leaders. Only those Nazi Party members who had been deprived of their own business on political grounds before 1933 would be entitled to special treatment; otherwise strict economic principles would be applied to Aryanization. Göring's plans also envisaged the liquidation of many Jewish businesses to rationalize the structure of industry, whereas some Aryanized factories would be converted to meet the needs of war production.[117]

The most dramatic initiative taken by Göring was the imposition of a "contribution" (the "punitive tax") of RM 1 billion on the Jews, intended as a reprisal to discourage any repetition of the murder of the Nazi official in Paris.[118] The Reich Finance Ministry had considered schemes for a special tax on the Jews in 1936–37, in response to the murder of the Swiss Nazi leader, Wilhelm Gustloff, in Davos in 1936. However, before Kristallnacht Göring had rejected these proposals, partly from concern about their impact abroad.[119] The initial response of Finance Minister Lutz Graf Schwerin von Krosigk at the Air Ministry meeting was fear that Jews would be tempted

---

[115] Meeting held at the Air Ministry on November 12, 1938, 1816-PS, in IMT, Blue Series, vol. XXVIII, pp. 500–501.

[116] A. J. van der Leeuw, "Der Griff," pp. 217–19.

[117] Meeting held at the Air Ministry, November 12, 1938, 1816-PS, in IMT, Blue Series, vol. XXVIII, pp. 501–505.

[118] Ibid., pp. 537–38.

[119] Stefan Mehl, *Das Reichsfinanzministerium und die Verfolgung der deutschen Juden 1933–1943* (Berlin, 1990), pp. 58–59; ibid., p. 511; the German press also referred specifically to the

to sell off their stocks and shares, causing a run on the markets. Göring, however, remained confident that Jews would "wait and see," as they didn't know how much "each would have to pay."[120]

A significant part of the Air Ministry discussions was devoted to the issue of insurance. Gerald Feldman examines this question in close detail and argues persuasively that Eduard Hilgard, the head of the corporatist Reich Group for Insurance (*Reichsgruppe Versicherung*), was largely wrong-footed by Göring with Heydrich's help. Göring took advantage of Hilgard's incautious statement that the insurance companies would meet their legal obligations by slapping an extra levy on the insurance companies for the benefit of the state. Göring announced that "the compensation owed to the Jews . . . has to be paid [by the insurance companies instead] to the Finance Minister. (Hilgard: Aha!)." Only lengthy negotiations over the ensuing months enabled the insurance companies to reduce very considerably the scale of this unusual Kristallnacht tax on their industry (to just more than RM 1 million). To achieve this reduction, the industry's representatives, including Hilgard, had no compunction in adopting the same antisemitic rhetoric as Göring and Heydrich. The Jews were still obliged to repair all the damages themselves, the only small concession being that some were able to count part of these expenses against their payment of the punitive tax.[121]

In the view of Herbert Rosenkranz, it was Hans Fischböck's mastery of figures and careful plans for the confiscation of Jewish property that enabled Göring to overcome the scruples of more conservative ministers, such as Economics Minister Walther Funk and Finance Minister von Krosigk. During the November 12th meeting, Fischböck whetted Göring's appetite for booty, encouraging him to initiate a series of extensive and lucrative confiscation measures.[122] The record of these discussions demonstrates how the experience of more radical Aryanization in Austria served to embolden Göring.

For example, Fischböck allayed Göring's concerns about the impact of closing all Jewish shops at once by referring to the systematic plans for the rapid liquidation of the majority of Jewish businesses in Austria. Göring's fears that the proceeds from Aryanization might go astray if Jews were able to buy jewels and flee the country were also assuaged when Fischböck assured

---

Gustloff incident as additional justification for the punitive tax. See for example *Berliner Börsen Zeitung*, November 13, 1938, "1 Milliarde Mark Busse für Pariser Mord."

[120] PS-1816, IMT, Blue Series, vol. XXVIII, pp. 537–40.
[121] See G. Feldman, *Die Allianz*, pp. 233–84.
[122] H. Rosenkranz, *Verfolgung und Selbstbehauptung*, p. 165.

him that in Austria all such proceeds were put into blocked accounts or paid only in installments over a long period.[123]

At the Air Ministry meeting, Fischböck also proposed plans for exchanging both Jewish real estate and securities for Reich bonds paying only 3 percent interest – a profitable arrangement for the Reich. Göring reiterated that the Jews had to surrender all securities, as otherwise they would retain considerable influence within the economy. However, von Krosigk noted that this was a completely novel idea, that now the Jews, "who previously were to be left as the holders of pensions, would now be subjected to forced confiscation."[124]

Economics Minister Funk warned that "if details of this debate were to become public, it will cause a run on the financial markets." However, these concerns only prompted Göring to insist on more stringent measures to punish non-Jews for buying Jewish capital assets, thus freezing Jewish transactions more effectively. Fischböck stressed the need to introduce measures quickly to prevent Jewish wealth from escaping, remarking that perhaps it was a good thing that "we are putting ourselves under pressure in this way."[125]

After this discussion, Göring and Fischböck gave instructions for the initiation of measures designed to freeze and convert all types of Jewish assets into low-interest Reich bonds. However, the first stage of actual confiscation now came in the form of the punitive tax (*Sühneleistung*), which Göring had decreed at the meeting.

The Punitive Tax

For Jews who still had some private property remaining, the punitive tax was the most important consequence of Kristallnacht. This outrageous measure actually punished the Jews for the atrocities committed against them. Within fifteen months, it raised more than RM 1.1 billion for the Reich's hard-pressed finances.

The punitive tax affected all Jews with property in excess of RM 5,000 and who held German citizenship, including those living abroad. The tax level was initially set at 20 percent of the net property value as registered by Jews in response to the April 26 decree. It was to be paid in four installments up to August 15, 1939. On October 19, 1939, the rate of the punitive tax

---

[123] PS-1816, IMT, Blue Series, vol. XXVIII, pp. 524–27; see also Hans Safrian, "Expediting Expropriation and Expulsion," pp. 400–402.

[124] PS-1816, IMT, Blue Series, vol. XXVIII, pp. 528–29.

[125] Ibid., pp. 531–40.

payments was raised from 20 percent to 25 percent, as new calculations showed that the first four payments would not reach the arbitrary total of RM 1 billion. Thus, an additional installment was simply added, equal to the previous four, "to ease collection."[126]

The punitive tax mobilized the German Tax Offices and the powers of a modern tax system to implement the persecution of the Jews. The German tax journal, *Die Deutsche Steuer-Zeitung*, commented that "the Tax Offices are . . . being sent into the front line in the struggle against the Jews."[127] The legal consequences of nonpayment of the tax included the accretion of late fees and the Currency Offices' refusal to grant approvals for transactions. As an ultimate sanction, the Tax Offices also had recourse to forced confiscation measures. Thus, the new sanctions paralleled those already being used to enforce payment of the flight tax.

Many Jews encountered great difficulties in paying the tax, as much of their wealth was tied up in fixed investments that were difficult to sell without a great loss. Gerdy Stoppleman recalled, for instance, that "to pay the . . . tax, I sold our furniture, valuable paintings, and carpets . . . dirt cheap. Many a home of true Aryans, SA and SS, became exceedingly well furnished."[128] Some Jews tried to negotiate a reduction in their payments, claiming that the value of the property had fallen sharply since registration or they had already been forced to sell off assets as part of their preparations for emigration.

The punitive tax also applied to the property that remained in Germany of Jews who had emigrated. Many Jews living abroad thought it was better to register this property, in an effort to save at least part of it, as it was impossible to transfer more than a small fraction abroad by legal means. However, the effect of these registrations from abroad was only to make it easier for the German authorities to confiscate this wealth, using the mechanism of denaturalization as well as the punitive tax.[129]

Control over Jewish Securities and Government Intervention in the Stock Market

This large-scale confiscation of Jewish property required close control by the Finance and Economics Ministries to regulate any possible effects on a jittery market. In his 1939 book, Guenter Reimann commented that

[126] S. Mehl, *Das Reichsfinanzministerium*, pp. 72–75.

[127] Ibid., p. 73.

[128] M. Kaplan, *Between Dignity and Despair*, p. 71.

[129] A number of punitive tax files registered from abroad with the *Finanzamt Moabit-West* can be found in the Archives of the Oberfinanzdirektion Berlin.

"the expropriation of Jewish capital would have led to large-scale sales of stocks and bonds with resultant price disturbances if the government had not stepped in."[130]

Soon after the announcement of the punitive tax, Jews began to submit applications to sell off their securities to meet this expected burden. At the end of November, the Economic Group for Private Banking (*Wirtschaftsgruppe Privates Bankgewerbe*) had to stress to its members that Jews would only be permitted to liquidate their assets if they made a declaration that they possessed no other liquid assets with which to pay specific obligations.[131] Shortly afterward, paragraph 11 of a new Decree on the Application of Jewish Property, issued on December 3, 1938,[132] stipulated that all Jews except those with foreign citizenship were obliged to place all their securities in a bank "depot" (safe deposit) and to confirm with the bank their status as Jews. All subsequent transactions with regard to the investments in these Jewish depots required explicit permission from the Reich Economics Ministry.[133] These measures effectively made it impossible for Jews to sell their securities other than to pay taxes or to meet other specific circumstances, such as covering emigration expenses.[134]

Later that month, additional regulations were passed permitting Jews to pay part of the punitive tax, first in stocks and shares and then in government bonds if they lacked sufficient cash reserves. A circular of the Economic Group for Private Banking argued that "in view of the large sums concerned, the release of stocks and shares for sale can only be permitted in limited amounts due to the current state of the stock market."[135] This instruction, of course, implied much greater government intervention in the stock market. Of the punitive tax payments made up to September 1939, securities comprised RM 293 million of the first RM 804 million received (about 36 percent).[136]

---

[130] Guenter Reimann, *The Vampire Economy: Doing Business under Fascism* (New York: Vanguard, 1939), p. 177.

[131] USHMM, RG-14, Accession 2000.10, Historical Archives of the Deutsche Bank (HADB), P276, p. 158, Deutsche Bank, Mitteilungsblatt der Zentrale, M, 273/38 vom 24.11.38.

[132] *VO über den Einsatz des jüdischen Vermögens* in *RGBl.* (1938) I, p. 1709.

[133] *Berliner Börsen Zeitung*, December 12, 1938, USHMM, RG-14, Acc.2000.10, Historical Archives of the Deutsche Bank (HADB), P10563.

[134] On the use of securities to pay for emigration expenses see for example GSPK, I Rep. 109/6253 (*Haushalte Seehandlung 1925–42*), internal memo, Generaldirektion der Preuss. Staatsbank, January 24, 1939.

[135] *Wirtschaftsgruppe Privates Bankgewerbe*, circular no. 170, December 10, 1938, USHMM, RG-14, Acc.2000.10 (HADB), P10563.

[136] S. Mehl, *Das Reichsfinanzministerium*, p. 75.

During the ensuing years, the confiscation and resale of Jewish securities were closely integrated into the Third Reich's overall monetary policy. The Prussian State Bank released Jewish shares gradually onto the market, specifically to slow down the sharply rising price of shares. This deliberate policy of intervention was freely reported in the financial press. The *Berliner Börsen-Zeitung*, for example, reported in February 1939 how the government itself had become a major market player:

> The liquidation of Jewish share investment property is now conducted differently than before.... Alongside the stock exchange a large reservoir of investments has arisen. The shareholder Reich has been accepting stocks and shares instead of cash in payment. This form of conversion confirms that the state does not intend to become a long-term shareholder in specific companies, but will sell off the shares as soon as a convenient possibility offers itself.... In any case it offers the chance for the state to directly influence the stock market.[137]

Aryanization

The Aryanization of Jewish businesses before 1938 was conducted primarily on a private basis in response to boycotts, economic discrimination, and pressure to emigrate.[138] According to a speech by the Minister of Economics Funk on November 17, 1938, RM 2 billion of registered Jewish property had already been brought into German possession.[139] After Kristallnacht, however, Göring sought to assert greater state control over the process of Aryanization. On December 10, 1938, he published a decree stressing the need for a strict legal basis for the transfer of Jewish property into German hands. Any benefits from the elimination of the Jews from the economy were to go to the state. If individuals or offices obtained an unjustified advantage from Aryanization, they could be forced to make a compensation payment.[140] This decree was directed primarily against the excessive corruption of certain regional Party bosses in connection with Aryanization procedures, especially in Franconia.[141]

In the assessment of Frank Bajohr, however, the impact of such centralizing measures should not be overestimated. In contrast to the interpretation of Helmut Genschel, who saw the role of the Party now weakened in

---

[137] *Berliner Börsen-Zeitung*, February 9, 1939, USHMM, RG-14, Acc.2000.10 (HADB), P10563.

[138] See especially A. Barkai, *Vom Boykott*, pp. 80–88.

[139] 3545-PS, IMT, Red Series, vol. VI, pp. 239–40.

[140] 1208-PS, IMT, Blue Series, vol. XXVII, pp. 69–71.

[141] A. J. van der Leeuw, "Der Griff," p. 221; PS-1757, Blue Series, vol. XXVIII, pp. 55–234.

favor of a more bureaucratic process run by the state, Bajohr argues that Göring's attempts to assert state control still remained mostly rhetoric. He sees claims, such as Göring's on December 10, 1938, that Aryanization was now a function of the state, rather as "helpless attempts to ensure that developments that had run out of control did not go completely off track."[142] In practice, the opportunities for enrichment opened up in the wake of Kristallnacht – for example, in buying up the businesses of Jews deported to concentration camps or purchasing liquidated stock at favorable prices – were exploited mainly by Party members. The regional Party Gau Economic Advisors (Gauwirtschaftsberater) continued to play a dominant role in overseeing Aryanizations, and the role of the central Reich authorities was still confined primarily to the collection of taxes, foreign exchange levies, and confiscations on an individual basis. The state drew up the new regulations, but institutions at the local level and under strong Party influence were still primarily responsible for implementing them. The proceeds raised by the state through taxes on the profits made in Aryanizations (Entjudungsgewinnsteuer) remained modest compared to the overall value of property Aryanized.[143]

Whatever the division of spoils, the practical effects of Kristallnacht combined with the new legislation to accelerate the pace of Aryanization. Already on November 10, 1938, the Schutzpolizei in Munich ordered that all Jewish shops be closed and that they should be clearly marked as Jewish businesses. This reflected orders issued by the Gestapo at this time for all Jewish shops to remain closed.[144] In many cases, negotiations were soon opened to complete their liquidation or transfer into Aryan hands. Many Jews had already taken the final deadline for the registration of Jewish property on August 31, 1938, as a last warning and rapidly concluded unfavorable contracts, fearing outright confiscation by the Party or the state thereafter. The banks also sharply tightened up their credit practices toward Jewish businesses during 1938: the Commerzbank officially began distinguishing clearly between Jewish and non-Jewish customers in June 1938, in November the bank made all new credits to Jews dependent on the approval of the Currency Offices, and from December 9, 1938, the Commerzbank stopped issuing new loans to Jews.[145] These key shifts in policy undoubtedly quickened the pace of liquidations, foreclosures,

---

[142] F. Bajohr, "*Aryanisation*," p. 234.

[143] Ibid., pp. 230–37.

[144] See BAL, R 58/276, p. 164, Müller an alle Stapo(leit)stellen, December 7, 1938.

[145] Ludolf Herbst and Thomas Wiehe (eds.), *Die Commerzbank und die Juden 1933–1945* (Munich: C. H. Beck, 2004), pp. 90–91.

and rapid sales. In accordance with the December 3, 1938 Decree on the Utilization of Jewish Property, businesses could be subjected to forced sales. Sometimes, several potential buyers competed over the most sought-after objects, but the Jewish owners received very little after various arbitrary deductions were made. The money was paid into a blocked account so that almost nothing could be transferred abroad on emigration.

Only in the case of the Aryanization of real estate did Göring order a temporary delay on December 28, 1938, as he did not want Jews to rent from Aryan owners of property. Therefore, the Nazis accepted some continued Jewish ownership of residential property during the process of concentrating the Jews into specific buildings (*Judenhäuser*).[146] Indeed, in April 1939, a new law on rental contracts involving Jews was introduced, giving the authorities the power to force Jewish apartment owners to take in other Jews as sub-tenants.[147] In this manner Jews were to be concentrated mainly in the few remaining buildings they owned, even if it also tended to slow down the Aryanization of real estate, as some Jewish properties were required to house those Jews unable to emigrate.

Vandalism and Confiscation of Property during and after Kristallnacht

The events of Kristallnacht were marked by the massive destruction of property. As one letter subsequently passed on to the American Jewish Joint Distribution Committee in New York described it, "Wherever the work of destruction during the night was not thorough enough, as in Berlin, it was repeated the afternoon of November 10th. Merchandise was thrown out on the street or completely ruined on the premises. In a large Jewish department store, for example, nothing at all was left of the porcelain, glass, and bric-a-brac. The offices of this store were also entirely demolished."[148] Widespread plunder accompanied the sheer vandalism, often carried out by the local Party members who organized and incited the pogrom.

---

[146] F. Bajohr, "*Aryanisation,*" p. 243. See BAL, NS 6/330, Anordnung 1/39, Göring, (secret) Führer Decisions Regarding the Jewish Question, December 28, 1938.

[147] Johannes Simmert and Hans-Walter Herrmann (eds.), *Die nationalsozialistische Judenverfolgung in Rheinland-Pfalz 1933 bis 1945: Das Schicksal der Juden im Saarland 1920 bis 1945* (Koblenz: Landesarchivverwaltung Rheinland-Pfalz, 1974), pp. 184–86, Gesetz über die Mietverhältnisse mit Juden vom April 30, 1939 (*RGBl.,* I, 864).

[148] Henry Friedlander and Sybil Milton (eds.), *Archives of the Holocaust: An International Collection of Selected Documents,* 22 vols. (New York: Garland, 1991), vol. 10, doc. 18, p. 173.

One German Jew, who had converted to Christianity and later fled to Britain, described the scene of destruction in his home wrought by Nazi thugs as follows:

> The inside of our little house looked bad. Floors and carpets were strewn with broken glass, covering the floors like snow. Scattered around were the rocks that had been thrown, overturned chairs, pictures that had fallen down, and other things, for instance an iron rake and a watering can that these criminals had found on the patio and thrown through the windows as well as a broken iron patio chair.... The only unbroken windowpanes were the ones in Barbara's room, where Jean-Pierre had been sleeping that night.[149]

In the wake of Kristallnacht, Göring argued that future demonstrations should be careful not to destroy property so wantonly, especially those goods that would otherwise have to be imported.[150] This vandalism was certainly difficult to reconcile with the Four-Year Plan's jealous hoarding of foreign exchange. In Gräfenhausen in Hesse, SA troops arrived from the larger nearby town of Darmstadt on Kristallnacht and vandalized Jewish property. In Hörde, Westphalia, the synagogue was set on fire, and Jewish homes and stores were damaged. Jews were subsequently forced to sell off their businesses at a fraction of their value.[151] The Criminal Police in Munich reported that forty-two shops were either destroyed or damaged; six fires were set, including one in the synagogue; and a goldsmith's and a shoe shop were looted. The French consul in Munich noted that about sixty Jewish businesses (that is most of those remaining) were affected.[152]

Despite Gestapo instructions that attempted to prevent theft and looting, a very large amount of Jewish property was looted or confiscated during Kristallnacht. Reichskommissar Bürckel in his report to Göring even described it as the "night of the long fingers."[153] As one local Party leader (Ortsgruppenleiter) subsequently described his understanding of events,

---

[149] USHMM, RG-02.061.*01, "Homeless in Exile: Days of Persecution in Fall and Winter, 1938–1939," typewritten testimony of Harry Richard Loewenberg, p. L5. I am grateful to Michael Berkowitz of the University of London for drawing this source to my attention during his fellowship at the USHMM.

[150] 1816-PS, IMT, Blue Series, vol. XXVIII, p. 500. The destruction of glass was especially damaging economically, as most of it had to be imported from Belgium; see G. Feldman, *Die Allianz*, p. 245.

[151] S. Spector and G. Wigoder (eds.), *Encyclopedia of Jewish Life*, pp. 450 and 519.

[152] Andreas Heusler and Tobias Weger (eds.), *Kristallnacht: Gewalt gegen die Münchner Juden im November 1938* (Munich: Buchendorfer, 1998), pp. 51, 152.

[153] 2237-PS in *International Military Trials: Nazi Conspiracy and Aggression*, Red Series, vol. IV, pp. 918–19; see also Jacob Presser, *The Destruction of the Dutch Jews* (New York: E.P. Dutton, 1969), p. 357.

"During the 'Jewish action' I was under the impression that all Jewish property was to be confiscated and subsequently handed over to the National Socialist People's Welfare (NSV) or to long-standing Party members and SA-men."[154] Instructions issued by Heydrich in the early hours of November 10 stressed that no threat to German life or property should be presented and that Jewish businesses and apartments should be destroyed, but not plundered. In addition, citizens of foreign countries, even if they were Jewish, were not to be interfered with.[155] Despite these specific orders against looting, many participants understood the "action" as an opportunity to help themselves or simply could not resist the clear temptation. For example, in the synagogue "Friedberger Anlage" in Frankfurt the safe was broken into on the day after the fire and the silver ritual items stolen.[156]

As one participant in another looting incident brazenly claimed, his own actions stemmed from a desire to save valuable items from needless destruction:

> I saw that various people broke into the apartment of the Jew E. on the second floor in order to demolish his furnishings. Out of curiosity I also entered the apartment of the Jew and assisted in the destruction of a bookshelf and various other items. Suddenly I saw how a youth smashed a large and valuable camera on the arm of a chair and that he wanted to do the same with a second camera. To prevent this, I took the camera from the youth, and claimed it for myself, then I thought it would be better to take it with me, to make practical use of it, rather than deliberately destroying it, which wouldn't help anybody.[157]

The Gestapo, Order Police, and local authorities took much Jewish property into "safe-keeping," but a substantial part of that property was never returned to the original owners.[158] The Gestapo seized the art collections of more than fifty Jews in Munich and kept it initially in local museums. In March 1942 (after issuance of the Eleventh Decree), the local tax administration wrote to the Finance Ministry stating its intention to sell off the

---

[154] J. Simmert and H.-W. Herrmann (eds.), *Die nationalsozialistische Judenverfolgung in Rheinland-Pfalz*, p. 189.

[155] Ibid., pp. 129–31, Heydrich instruction to Gestapo Darmstadt, sent from Munich at 1.20 am, November 10, 1938.

[156] Kommission zur Erforschung der Geschichte der Frankfurter Juden (ed.), *Dokumente zur Geschichte der Frankfurter Juden 1933–1945* (Frankfurt am Main: Waldemar Kramer, 1963), p. 45.

[157] J. Simmert and H.-W. Herrmann (eds.), *Die nationalsozialistische Judenverfolgung in Rheinland-Pfalz*, p. 142, interrogation of a 17-year-old apprentice concerning theft during the "Jewish Action," November 18, 1938.

[158] See for instance BAL, R 58/276, p. 164, Müller to all Stapo(leit)stellen, December 7, 1938.

paintings as Reich property. Among the confiscated works, the most valuable included Italian masters of the fourteenth and fifteenth centuries, a Canaletto, and several paintings by Spitzweg.[159] In Frankfurt, the city purchased some artworks directly from the Jewish owners at bargain prices in the immediate aftermath of Kristallnacht, whereas other items, including ritual silver, were confiscated from the "Museum of Jewish Historical Objects" and subsequently sold on the authority of the Gestapo.[160]

According to Gestapo orders, money and valuables secured at the time of Kristallnacht were to be returned to their Jewish owners, once any outstanding taxes had been paid and any related "costs" had been deducted.[161] However, this did not apply to money or items valued over RM 1,000, unless the owner was in the process of emigrating.[162] Some Jews did receive a small part of their confiscated property back. For example, Richard Frank of Pirmasens was arrested on November 10, 1938. During a concurrent search, RM 760 and many valuable pieces of jewelry were confiscated from his house. By January 1939, he had received RM 200 back in cash.[163] This was another example of how Nazi anti-Jewish measures were supposed to be "self-financing": in one case, local Party members had spent part of the secured funds "to cover the costs" of blowing up the synagogue, guarding the Jews, and cleaning up damaged apartments.[164]

Some non-Jews also suffered material damage during the pogrom and naturally applied for compensation.[165] Even nine months after the pogrom, some Jews were still being forced to pay for the damages suffered by non-Jews. Caecilie Rotschild, a Jewish homeowner in Alzey who in July 1939 was in the process of selling her house, still had to pay for the damage incurred in November 1938 or face having the costs deducted from the

---

[159] See BAL, R 2/51098, pp. 104–105 and 119–20, OFP Munich to RFM, March 2 and March 9, 1942.

[160] See Monica Kingreen, "Wie sich Museen Kunst aus jüdischem Besitz aneigneten," *Frankfurter Rundschau*, May 9, 2000. This article is a revised version of an academic presentation given by the author.

[161] J. Simmert and H.-W. Herrmann (eds.), *Die nationalsozialistische Judenverfolgung in Rheinland-Pfalz*, p. 180, order of the Gestapo office in Koblenz to the Landräte, February 23, 1939.

[162] D-183, IMT, Red Series, vol. VI, pp. 1075–76, Gestapo Darmstadt to SS-Abt. Kassel, December 7, 1938.

[163] J. Simmert and H.-W. Herrmann (eds.), *Die nationalsozialistische Judenverfolgung in Rheinland-Pfalz*, pp. 164–65.

[164] Ibid., pp. 173–75, interrogation of Ortsgruppenleiter R. on use of funds placed in his safekeeping after the Jewish action, Neustadt a. d. Weinstrasse, February 23, 1939.

[165] Ibid., pp. 167–68.

selling price, in accordance with the laws passed in November 1938 obliging Jews to repair all damages arising from the pogrom.[166]

Kristallnacht was especially brutal in Vienna. Here forty-two houses of prayer were destroyed and some 7,800 Jews arrested, including more than 1,000 whose preparations for emigration had already been processed by the Central Office. The destruction of property was especially severe. According to Herbert Rosenkranz, 4,083 businesses were closed, and in Vienna's First District alone, some 1,950 Jews were forcibly evicted from their apartments.[167]

The damage in the Austrian provinces was also quite considerable. In Krems, windows were smashed on the orders of the SS, and around Wiener Neustadt, furniture, jewelry, and savings books were confiscated from hundreds of Jewish homes, including those of some foreign Jews. In Salzburg, seven Jewish businesses that had not yet been Aryanized were destroyed and the Jewish owners forced to deliver the remaining wares directly to the National Socialist Welfare organization (NSV), from which much property was subsequently pilfered.[168] Even in the view of the SD, the effect of such destruction was mainly negative, as (for example) the departure of one group of 600 Jews destined for Palestine had to be postponed.[169]

According to internal SD reports, in Vienna the local Party leaders (*Ortsgruppenleiter*) organized the confiscations together with the SA, Party officials, and also the SS. They cleared out the contents of Jewish houses and shops, but despite strict orders, many items went astray. According to Odilo Globocnik's estimate, the Party in Austria confiscated valuables worth about RM 25 million. It took five days and nights for Party officials to make an inventory of all the secured property. Two thousand Party members received new apartments.[170]

Nearly all of the synagogues in the Reich were destroyed or vandalized, and specific orders were given to secure property found inside them. Of seven synagogues in Saxony before Kristallnacht, all but one in Leipzig were burned down, and the one not burned suffered serious damage.[171] There was also considerable destruction of property inside the synagogues and other buildings of Jewish religious communities.[172] Moreover, the Jewish

---

[166] Ibid., pp. 194–95.
[167] H. Rosenkranz, *Verfolgung und Selbstbehauptung*, p. 159.
[168] Ibid., p. 160.
[169] Ibid., p. 161.
[170] Ibid., pp. 162–63; G. Fuchs, "Die Vermögensverkehrsstelle," pp. 72–73.
[171] USHMM, RG-14.011M (Sächsisches Hauptstaatsarchiv Dresden), reel 13, 11136/4, report of Saxon Interior Ministry, December 14, 1938.
[172] See for example photographs in A. Heusler and T. Weger (eds.), "*Kristallnacht*," pp. 82–83.

communities were assigned financial responsibility for removing the rubble. In many towns, such as Frankfurt am Main the city then bought the land on which the synagogues had stood at a favorable price, with the intention of developing it for public use.[173] In Schenklengsfeld, even the rubble from the synagogue was sold – some of the material was used to build a barracks for the Reich Labor Service (Reichsarbeitsdienst).[174] Only delays caused by the war left a number of synagogue sites undeveloped as of 1945.

Jews Arrested and Compelled to Emigrate

In connection with Kristallnacht, the Gestapo ordered, just before midnight on November 9, the arrest of 20,000 to 30,000 Jews, especially those owning significant property.[175] Accordingly on November 10 and during the ensuing days, between 25,000 to 30,000 Jewish men were arrested; most of them were sent to the concentration camps in Dachau, Buchenwald, and Sachsenhausen. A number of them died over the ensuing weeks from the brutal treatment they received. On November 14, 1938, Heydrich issued instructions to State Police offices that Jews could be released temporarily from protective custody if their presence was urgently required during Aryanization of their business or shop, or they could be released permanently if they already had all the necessary paperwork to emigrate immediately.[176] Many of the arrested Jews had been released by the turn of the year 1938/39. However, this release was only on condition that they could demonstrate their intention to emigrate within a certain period. Frequently, they had to sign financial documents under duress. Some even had to sign over their entire property.[177]

In Gleiwitz in Upper Silesia, for example, which had a Jewish population of 1,443, hundreds of Jews were locked in a building during the Kristallnacht

---

[173] See Jürgen Steen and Wolf von Wolzogen (eds.), *"Die Synagogen brennen . . . !" Die Zerstörung Frankfurts als jüdische Lebenswelt* (Frankfurt am Main: Historisches Museum Frankfurt am Main, 1988), p. 163. In Höchst, on the site of one synagogue an air raid shelter was constructed.

[174] Karl Honikel (ed.), *Geschichte der Jüdischen Gemeinde Schenklengsfeld* (Schenklengsfeld: Christlich-Jüdischer Arbeitskreis Schenklengsfeld, 1988), p. 237.

[175] BAL, R 58/276, p. 124, Fernschreiben an alle Stapoleitstellen, Berlin, November 9, 1938, 11:55 PM.

[176] Ibid., p. 142, Chef der Sicherheitspolizei Heydrich an alle Staatspolizei(leit)stellen, November 14, 1938.

[177] W. Seibel (ed.), *Holocaust und "Polykratie" in Westeuropa: National Berichte*, p. XIII; A. Heusler and T. Weger (eds.), *"Kristallnacht,"* pp. 130–34; Kurt R. Grossmann, *Emigration: Die Geschichte der Hitler-Flüchtlinge 1933–1945* (Frankfurt am Main: Europäische Verlagsanstalt, 1969), p. 115; for an example of this practice, see PAAA, Inl. II A/B, R 99921, denaturalization proposal of Gestapo Neustadt a.d. Weinstrasse against G. I. H., May 19, 1941. Trustees and liquidators were often appointed to Jewish businesses while their

rioting. On the following day, 235 men were sent to Buchenwald, where at least six perished.[178] In response to these arrests, wives and families scrambled to sell property and make all the complex arrangements for departure within the tight deadlines set.[179] As Marion Kaplan has recorded, one wife "accompanying her husband home after his imprisonment...explained that she had just sold their house and bought tickets to Shanghai for the family."[180]

This policy, combined with the obvious shock of the pogrom, caused a further upsurge in emigration, just as the final laws regulating the compulsory Aryanization of Jewish businesses were published in December 1938.[181]

Confiscation of Jewelry and Precious Metals in February 1939

As was apparent during the Air Ministry discussions on November 12, 1938, the Nazi leadership was very concerned about the possibility of capital flight, especially through the smuggling of valuable items by Jewish emigrants. Indeed, a few Jewish emigrants did succeed in smuggling items out, sometimes with the assistance of non-Jews.[182] To forestall this activity, as well as to secure precious metals for the benefit of the state, the Reich government ordered the compulsory surrender by Jews of almost all precious metals and jewelry in February 1939.[183]

Shortly after the publication of the decree, Hanna Bernheim packed a suitcase and headed for a Nazi "purchasing post" to give up her valuables:

> There were many people who had three, five suitcases, full of marvellous things: old [bridal] jewelry, Sabbath candles and goblets...beautiful old and modern plates.... The young officials were in high spirits.... These treasures, often collected by generations, were thrown together.... They were small-minded enough to take jewelry not at all precious as to the...value, but precious to us as souvenirs of beloved persons.[184]

owners were under arrest; see Frank Bajohr, *Parvenüs und Profiteure: Korruption in der NS-Zeit* (Frankfurt am Main: S. Fischer, 2001), p. 117.

[178] S. Spector and G. Wigoder (eds.), *The Encyclopedia of Jewish Life*, p. 433.

[179] See n. 176 above; see also BAL, R 58/276 for Nazi guidelines on these policies.

[180] Kaplan, *Between Dignity and Despair*, p. 128.

[181] J. Walk (ed.), *Das Sonderrecht*, III 46.

[182] See, for example, BAL, R2/5906, Report of the Reichsstelle für Außenhandel, February 25, 1939.

[183] See, for example, Wolf Gruner, "The German Council of Municipalities (*Deutscher Gemeindetag*) and the Coordination of Anti-Jewish Local Politics in the Nazi State," in *Holocaust and Genocide Studies* vol. 13, no. 2 (Fall 1999): 181–87.

[184] Kaplan, *Between Dignity and Despair*, p. 132.

One family that lived in the Charlottenburg district of Berlin surrendered an entire silver dinner service for eighteen persons, including coffee spoons, fish cutlery, desert spoons, three silver baskets, and a soup ladel.[185] The amounts received in return, paid belatedly (if at all) into blocked accounts, were usually only a fraction of the real value of the items. According to Frank Bajohr, the sums paid were usually less than 20 percent and often less than 10 percent of the real worth.[186]

The onerous regulations were strictly enforced. For example, Olga Meyer in Konstanz surrendered her precious metals on April 18, 1939, but when, on May 9, customs officials searched her house (probably in connection with emigration preparations), her husband was found to have withheld certain items. In consequence, the Currency Office confiscated the illegal items on May 22; in a decision issued on June 1, 1939, the district court confirmed that they should be forfeited to the Reich and also blocked the Meyers' bank account.[187] Those Jews caught with any gold, silver, or jewels when trying to emigrate could be punished for the failure to surrender them, as happened to Minna Adler, Betty Siebenschein, and Friedrich Loebl, arrested on their way to Switzerland in 1939.[188] Thus, by 1939, not even the silver cutlery in the cupboard was safe from the legalized depredations of the Nazi state.

The Economic Final Solution

The central idea underlying another Nazi strategy related to Jewish emigration and Jewish property – a notion entertained by Hitler during the fall of 1938 and early 1939 – was that of establishing a central fund or bank that would contain all Jewish wealth, estimated from the July registration returns

---

[185] OFDB, Restitutionsakte 7–2397/57, Case of F. E. In this postwar restitution case, a former employee of thirty-one years was able to give details of the cutlery, and the family received DM 1,929 in compensation.

[186] F. Bajohr, "Aryanisation," p. 247. On the role of Degussa in resmelting much of the metal surrendered during the "Pawnshop Action," see Peter Hayes, *From Cooperation to Complicity: Degussa in the Third Reich* (Cambridge: Cambridge University Press, 2004), pp. 159–70. Hayes also gives an estimate of only 10–15 percent of the real value of the items being received by Jewish owners.

[187] Rolf Böhme and Heiko Haumann (eds.), *Das Schicksal der Freiburger Juden am Beispiel des Kaufmanns Max Mayer und die Ereignisse des 9./10. November 1938* (Freiburg im Breisgau: Schillinger, 1989), p. 50.

[188] *Widerstand und Verfolgung in Wien 1934–1945*, 3 vols. (Vienna: Oesterreichischer Bundesverlag für Unterricht, Wissenschaft und Kunst Jugend und Volk Verlagsges. MbH, 1975), vol. 3, p. 238.

to be about RM 7.1 billion.[189] These financial resources would then be used to finance emigration for the mass of the Jews, as well as the "welfare costs" for those unable to leave. Above all, in the view of the Nazi bureaucrats who drew up these plans, Jewish emigration should not be allowed to drain away any of Germany's currency reserves at all, but rather it should enhance them by also mobilizing international support for the Jews in the form of foreign currency to be placed at the disposal of the German government. In one form of this plan advocated by Hjalmar Schacht (president of the Reichsbank until January 1939), Germany was supposed to benefit from concomitant increased exports, in a similar manner to the Ha'avara Transfer scheme for emigrants to Palestine.[190]

The initial starting point for the so-called Schacht Plan was the evident failure of the Evian Conference in the summer of 1938, which Germany had in any case boycotted because the German Foreign Office viewed the Jewish Question as an internal matter not to be discussed with foreign governments. In the wake of the Evian Conference, an Intergovernmental Committee on Refugees (IGC) was founded under the direction of the American lawyer George Rublee and given the task of finding an international solution to the growing refugee crisis in concert with German authorities, it was hoped.[191]

Two days after the November 12th meeting at the Air Ministry, Dr. Hans Fischböck, on Göring's instructions, proposed that the main German ministries now take up Rublee's offer of talks. Fischböck had already activated his own contacts with the Bank of England. He envisaged "a plan linking Jewish emigration with the promotion of exports, which would make it possible for the Jews to transfer their government bonds to foreign countries."[192]

Fischböck's initial contacts, in spite of the hostility of Ribbentrop's Foreign Office, led in turn to the Schacht-Rublee negotiations conducted with Hitler's approval in December 1938 and January 1939. At about this

---

[189] This figure comes from the net result of the 1938 Jewish property census, see A. Barkai, *Vom Boykott zur "Entjudung,"* p. 125.

[190] A. J. Van der Leeuw, "Der Griff," pp. 224–25; on the Ha'avara Transfer Agreement, see especially Werner Feilchenfeld, Dolf Michaelis, and Ludwig Pinner, *Haavara-Transfer nach Palästina und Einwanderung Deutscher Juden 1933–1939* (Tübingen: J. C. B. Mohr, 1972).

[191] Magnus Brechtken, "Zwischen Rassenideologie und Machtpragmatismus – 'zerstreuende' Auswanderung, Palästinafrage, und die Entwicklung des 'Endlösungs'-Begriffs (1933–1940)," unpublished conference paper given in Gainesville, Florida, pp. 19–20.

[192] *Documents on German Foreign Policy*, Series D (Washington DC: U.S. Government Printing Office, 1953), vol. V, pp. 905–906, no. 650, Memo. by the Director of the Political Department (Woermann) on November 14, 1938. See also Magnus Brechtken, *"Madagaskar für die Juden": Antisemitische Idee und politische Praxis 1885–1945* (Munich: Oldenbourg, 1997), pp. 202–203.

time, additional practical measures were taken to secure and mobilize Jewish wealth and to organize mass emigration through the establishment of a single Reich Union (*Reichsvereinigung*) for all Jews and the creation of a Reich Central Office for Jewish Emigration in imitation of that in Vienna.[193]

The details of the Schacht plan emerged following a meeting in London in December. A trustee fund for the Jews was to be established using 25 percent of the Jewish wealth that was recently registered. The remainder was to be placed at the disposal of the Reich to pay the living costs of the mainly elderly Jews who would be unable to emigrate. A careful examination of the negotiations reveals that the proposed deal was linked to increased German exports in the form of equipment for the emigrants. This mechanism would assist in the conversion of money from the internal trustee fund into hard currency for the use of Jews overseas. Meanwhile, the governments represented at Evian would be asked to establish an external fund that would "lend" the emigrating Jews RM 10,000 each.[194]

Despite both sides' initial interest in the Schacht plan, it proved impossible to establish the preconditions for the acceptance of large groups of Jewish emigrants by other countries. British and American bankers also disagreed on how to raise funds for the external trustee account. In 1939, Rublee's successor, Sir Herbert Emerson, suggested that individual emigration would remain more important than any large-scale emigration projects.[195] The inflexible nature of German demands and the unrealistic nature of such plans amid heightened international tension gave this project almost no practical prospect of realization.

On the German side, the scheme was torpedoed by a combination of factors. Ribbentrop and other Foreign Office officials opposed it, as they saw their own turf being invaded by amateurs. Then, Schacht resigned as president of the Reichsbank in January, primarily over Göring and Hitler's intention to continue printing money so they could forge ahead with rearmament against the advice of the Reichsbank board.[196] Göring continued to pursue similar semi-official initiatives, mostly using his subordinate Helmut Wohlthat, with the aim of keeping some diplomatic options open to outflank his rival Ribbentrop. The outbreak of the war finally rendered the

---

[193] *Trials of War Criminals*, Green Series, vol. XIII, pp. 129–30, NG-2586-A, Göring to RMdI, January 24, 1939; A. J. van der Leeuw, "Der Griff," p. 224; R. Hilberg, *Die Vernichtung*, pp. 193–95.

[194] A. J. Van der Leeuw, "Der Griff," pp. 224–25; for a summary of the British interpretation of the talks, see USHMM, RG-11.001M.01 (RGVA), 500-1-638, Rublee to Wohlthat, February 1, 1938.

[195] A. J. Van der Leeuw, "Der Griff," p. 225.

[196] 3724-PS, IMT, Blue Series, vol. XXXII, p. 536, Testimony of Schacht, July 11, 1945.

plan more or less obsolete by further reducing the possibilities for Jewish emigration.

Instrumentalization of Jewish Wealth

Nevertheless, the serious consideration given to the "Schacht Plan" and other similar schemes is quite revealing of the thinking at that time within the Nazi leadership and the German bureaucracy. Göring, who played such a key role in decisions concerning the Jewish Question at this stage, was also preoccupied with financing rearmament and clearly looked to Jewish wealth as a valuable windfall that could help him bridge the gap until Hitler's aggressive foreign policy started to reap serious material dividends. As recorded in the notes of his speech on November 18, "the critical financial position will be relieved for now by the RM 1 billion fine imposed on the Jews and the expected income for the Reich from the Aryanization of Jewish businesses."[197]

At the same time, the main policy goal remained the emigration of the Jews, as reflected in the official invitation to a meeting organized by the Interior Ministry. The conference on the Jewish Question involving regional officials was scheduled for December 16, 1938. The invitation also announced the planned establishment of the Reich Central Office for Jewish Emigration and noted that "under certain circumstances the rich Jews would be an important bargaining chip [Pfand] in the Führer's hand."[198] In late November 1938, the Ministry of Economics expressed increasing concern about the emigration of those Jews without financial means: "the latest developments have also led to the impoverishment of the previously propertied Jews."[199] In January 1939 (in connection with the Schacht-Rublee negotiations), officials of the Reichsbank even calculated the expected burden on the Reich if some 300,000 Jews aged 45 and over were to remain in Germany, as they were unable to emigrate. They estimated that, after ten or eleven years, their remaining property (assumed to be worth about RM 3 billion after deducting the punitive tax and losses during the Aryanization process) would be used up, creating a burden of

---

[197] 3575-PS, ibid., p. 415, Göring address to the Reich Defense Council, November 18, 1938.

[198] BAL, R 18/5519, Notiz für die Teilnehmer an den Veranstaltungen des Reichsministers des Innern am 16. Dezember 1938 in Berlin, December 15, 1938, p. 285, cited by Magnus Brechtken, "Zwischen Rassenideologie und Machtpragmatismus," pp. 17–18.

[199] BAL, R 7/3153, Übersicht über die mit dem Judenproblem zusammenhängenden Fragen für die Besprechung mit den Leitern der Devisenstellen am Dienstag, dem 22. November 1938.

some RM 2.5 billion over the following thirty years until the last of them had died.[200] Of course, one should not read too much into such documents, but they reflect a clear tendency among German bureaucrats to treat Jewish property and the fate of the Jews as intertwined aspects of a specific financial problem for the Reich — a tendency that had very serious consequences for the lives and ultimate fate of individual Jews.

[200] BAL, R 2501/6641, pp. 44–47, Vertrauliche Reichsbanksache, Über die finanzielle Seite der Entfernung der Juden aus Deutschland, January 18, 1939.

4

BLOCKING JEWISH BANK ACCOUNTS AND PREPARATIONS FOR MASS CONFISCATION, 1939–1941

One aspect of Nazi persecution of the Jews that has been largely neglected is the blocking of accounts by the Currency Offices (*Devisenstellen*). In the summer of 1939, this measure was extended to almost all Jews, shortly after its widespread application in the occupied Czech lands. Jews could not spend more than a fixed amount each month without obtaining permission from the Currency Offices. Combined with the impact of the punitive tax, their exclusion from the economy, the introduction of forced labor, and the withdrawal of social benefits, the blocking of accounts contributed to rapid pauperization among Jews. At the same time, the Nazis forced the Jewish communal organization, the *Reichsvereinigung* (RV), to maintain some welfare support, paid for by the liquidation of remaining communal property and the imposition of compulsory contributions on the Jews. The pauperization and isolation of the Jews now that private employment was almost impossible also prompted demands for their deportation to "the East," so that Jewish apartments could be made available for "needy" Aryans.

By the spring of 1940, the interest of the *Reichssicherheitshauptamt* (Reich Security Main Office, RSHA) in securing resources for the war caused it to initiate the denaturalization of all Jewish emigrants who owned significant property in Germany. The resulting generation of thousands of denaturalization orders for individual Jews required a huge bureaucratic effort that took some considerable time to implement. Thus, from the fall of 1940, the Nazi bureaucracy started to look for ways to streamline the denaturalization procedure. The resulting Eleventh Decree to the Reich Citizenship Law, published in November 1941, also provided a highly convenient mechanism for conducting the automatic confiscation of property from Jews deported to the East.

Beginning in August 1939, tax officials began the lengthy process of issuing security orders (*Sicherungsanordnungen*) to almost every Jew in Germany with a domestic bank account, limiting withdrawals to a fixed amount, usually not more than RM 300 per month.[1] This measure marks roughly the point at which the majority of Jews lost control over their private property. Deprived of their own financial means, it became very difficult for Jews to defend themselves against Nazi measures of forced expulsion, deportation, and murder. The last vestiges of independence and economic freedom were removed by these administrative measures initiated just before the German attack on Poland.

Blocking of Jewish Accounts

Early Instances in the 1930s

An early precedent for the blocking of Jewish bank accounts was set in March 1933. In Rhineland-Pfalz, controlled by Gauleiter Fritz Bürckel, the blocking of bank accounts was applied briefly as a means to ensure that Jews paid all outstanding debts before they were forced to leave the region. This measure was applied only to Jews who had moved into Rhineland-Pfalz after 1914, and the blocking of accounts was reversed on the orders of the Bavarian Interior Minister after a few days. Nevertheless at least fifty-seven Jewish accounts were blocked at this time in the district of Landau.[2]

As the 1930s progressed, increasing numbers of Jewish bank accounts were blocked, mainly as a result of the implementation of foreign currency regulations.[3] Even before the stricter currency regulations of December 1936, Jewish emigrants were obliged to deposit their remaining bank balances into special blocked accounts for emigrants (*Auswanderersperrkonten*), which they could dispose of only with permission of the Currency

---

[1] Gerd Blumberg, "Etappen der Verfolgung und Ausraubung und ihre bürokratische Apparatur," in Alfons Kenkmann and Bernd-A. Rusinek (eds.), *Verfolgung und Verwaltung: Die wirtschaftliche Ausplünderung der Juden und die westfälischen Finanzbehörden* (Münster: Oberfinanzdirektion Münster, 1999): 15–40, here p. 32. That this was more than just a regional phenomenon can be seen from an examination of the Devisenstelle records available for Thüringen; see, for example, BAL, R 139 II/113.

[2] Johannes Simmert and Hans-Walter Herrmann (eds.), "Die nationalsozialistische Judenverfolgung in Rhineland-Pfalz 1933 bis 1945," in *Dokumentation zur Geschichte der jüdischen Bevölkerung in Rhineland-Pfalz und im Saarland von 1800 bis 1945* (Koblenz: Landesarchivverwaltung Rheinland-Pfalz in Verbindung mit dem Landesarchiv Saarbrücken, 1974), vol. 6, p. 10.

[3] See Chapter 2.

Offices.[4] As the pace of Aryanization increased during the summer of 1938,[5] new security orders directed more Jewish assets into blocked accounts that were newly created to receive the proceeds. For example, in August 1938, the *Zollfahndungsstelle* (Customs Investigation Office, ZfS) in Dortmund issued a "provisional security order" against the Jewish manufacturer C. S. on learning that he intended to sell his share of a cotton waste recycling plant and then emigrate.[6]

The events surrounding the Kristallnacht pogrom produced both a rapid increase in Jewish emigration and many new regulations, compelling Jews to place an increasingly large proportion of their wealth under the control of the Nazi financial administration. There were even some regional initiatives to block all Jewish bank accounts. On November 11, the Gestapo in Hanover, on instructions from Higher Police Leader, SS Obergruppenführer Friedrich Jeckeln, ordered the blocking of all Jewish accounts and safe-deposit boxes at bank and credit organizations. The order stipulated that the maximum sum Jews could withdraw was RM 50 per week.[7] The *Oberfinanzpräsident* (senior finance president, OFP) in Munich issued a similar instruction on November 12, 1938. There, up to RM 100 could be withdrawn per week for living expenses, but all other transactions would require permission.[8] However, on that same day, Reich Interior Minister Wilhelm Frick ordered that all measures lacking a sound legal basis be stopped immediately, mentioning specifically the blocking of accounts. These initiatives were apparently abandoned as a result,[9] although they foreshadowed the more general blocking of Jewish accounts legally applied by the Currency Offices about nine months later.

---

[4] For examples of emigrant blocked accounts from 1935 and 1936, see *Brandenburgisches Landeshauptarchiv* Potsdam (BLHAP), Rep. 36A (*Devisenstelle*) A1415 and A23.

[5] The deadline for registering Jewish assets in the summer of 1938 produced a flurry of sales contracts concluded by people trying to beat this deadline.

[6] Devisenakte of C. S., Zollfahndungsstelle report, Dortmund, August 15, 1938, held at the archive of the Zollamt (Customs Office) in Münster (ZAM). I am grateful to Alfons Kenkmann, the former director of the Villa ten Hompel Geschichtsort in Münster, and also Gerd Blumberg of the customs administration in Münster for granting me access to the Currency Office files of the city.

[7] Eichmann Trial Documents, T/112, Instruction by Gestapo Hanover, November 11, 1938.

[8] A. J. van der Leeuw, "Der Griff des Reiches nach dem Judenvermögen," in A. H. Paape (ed.), *Studies over Nederland in oorlogstijd* ('s-Gravenhage: Martinus Nijhoff, 1972), p. 222 – first published in *Rechtsprechung zum Wiedergutmachungsrecht* (1970): 383–92; this document is referred to also by Andreas Heusler and Tobias Weger (eds.), *"Kristallnacht": Gewalt gegen die Münchner Juden im November 1938* (Munich: Buchendorfer, 1998), p. 172.

[9] BAL, R 58/276, p. 140, SSD Berlin Nr. 82, November 12, 1938.

The transition to compulsory Aryanization in the fall of 1938 brought with it increasing restrictions on many forms of Jewish property. At the infamous meeting at the Air Ministry on November 12, 1938, Hans Fischböck explained that, in Austria, insofar as cash was paid to Jews for Aryanized property at all, it was done on the condition that it would be paid into a blocked account. Göring heartily approved of this, interjecting, "We can do that too."[10] According to the decree on the "use of Jewish property" ("*Verordnung über den Einsatz des jüdischen Vermögens*") issued on December 3, 1938, the approval necessary for the sale of Jewish businesses would be conditional on the Jewish seller receiving the proceeds only in state bonds.

The same decree also ordered the compulsory deposit of Jewish securities with banks (*Depotzwang*) and included strict regulations on when they could be sold.[11] Henceforth, only up to RM 1,000 in securities could be sold per month without specific permission and only in cases of urgent need, for instance to pay expenses due to sickness or death, and then only in the absence of cash reserves. Securities could be used to an unlimited extent to pay taxes and other contributions, including emigration expenses, but again only when other ready means, including jewelry, had been exhausted.[12] The implementation of these regulations was effectively delegated to the banks via the *Wirtschaftsgruppe Privates Bankgewerbe* (Economic Group for Private Banks), the corporatist banking organization, under tight Nazi control.[13]

Finally, the compulsory surrender of gold, silver, and other valuable items by Jews that was ordered in February 1939 also produced more blocked accounts.[14] Although partial compensation was supposed to be paid, any

[10] See Hans Safrian, "Beschleunigung der Beraubung und Vertreibung: Zur Bedeutung des 'Wiener Modells' für die antijüdische Politik des 'Dritten Reiches' im Jahr 1938," in Constantin Goschler and Jürgen Lillteicher (eds.), *"Arisierung" und Restitution: Die Rückerstattung jüdischen Eigentums in Deutschland und Österreich nach 1945 und 1989* (Göttingen: Wallstein, 2002): 61–89, here p. 82; International Military Tribunal (IMT) (ed.), *Trial of the Major War Criminals* [Blue Series] (Nuremberg, 1947), vol. XXVIII, p. 527.

[11] *Reichsgesetzblatt* (RGBl.), I (1938), p. 1709, VO. über den Einsatz des jüd. Vermögens, December 3, 1938.

[12] On the use of securities to pay for emigration expenses, see for example, GSPK, I Rep. 109/6253 (Haushalte Seehandlung 1925–1942), internal memo., Generaldirektion der Preuss. Staatsbank, January 24, 1939.

[13] Michael Gruber and Michael Tüchler, *Rechtliche Regelungen im Zusammenhang mit der Entziehung, Bereinigung und Rückstellung von Wertpapieren* (Vienna: Historikerkommission, 2002), pp. 48–49. Regrettably this study is of only limited value as it is confined to a normative description of the relevant Nazi laws concerning securities with no discussion of how they were actually implemented.

[14] *RGBl.* I (1939), p. 282, Dritte Anordnung auf Grund der VO. über die Anmeldung des Vermögens von Juden, Feb. 21, 1939. For the details of this action, see Wolf Gruner, "The German Council of Municipalities (Deutscher Gemeindetag) and the Coordination of

sum exceeding RM 2,000 was to be paid into a blocked account, and cash payments were not to exceed RM 500.[15]

As regional studies indicate, the efforts of the financial and customs authorities to hinder the transfer of capital abroad intensified after November 1938 as more Jews sought to emigrate. The ZfS in Dortmund reported in April 1939 that through various measures it had been possible "to secure Jewish property – especially the liquid part of it – adequately and in time." Up to March 1939, customs investigators had issued 418 provisional security orders and processed 3,162 reports of suspected plans to emigrate. It was the task of the Currency Offices to check and approve the security orders.[16]

As a result of the increasing numbers of security orders arising from forced Aryanization and increased emigration, not to mention the heightened activism of the Nazi authorities, the number of applications for permission to release funds began to pile up at the Currency Offices. In many cases, the applications were approved, but some were rejected without explanation. By this time, the authorities treated all propertied German Jews as potential currency smugglers, and sooner or later they were likely to become entangled in the network of observation and pre-emptive measures. However, the universal imposition of blocked accounts for Jews did not occur first in Germany, but rather in the recently occupied Protectorate of Bohemia and Moravia.

Mass Blocking of Jewish Accounts in the Protectorate

After German occupation in March 1939, the new Nazi authorities in Bohemia and Moravia took advantage of special measures taken to "stabilize the currency" to introduce the blocking of all Jewish bank accounts. A circular sent to financial institutions in the Protectorate by Finance Minister Dr. Kriz on March 25, 1939, froze all safes and safe-deposit boxes so that they could be opened only in the presence of government officials. Banks and other credit institutions were prohibited from making payments to Jews, except for those funds necessary for the continued running of a business. The decree also restricted Jewish withdrawals from "non-Aryan blocked accounts" to 1,500 Kronen per week for living expenses. At the same time, lists of Jewish bank accounts were prepared for official use.[17] The authorities

---

Anti-Jewish Local Politics in the Nazi State," in *Holocaust and Genocide Studies*, 13, no. 2 (Fall 1999): 171–99.

[15] BAL, R 139II/110, instruction of the Devisenfahndungsamt, March 8, 1939.

[16] Gerd Blumberg, "Etappen," p. 31.

[17] USHMM, RG-48.005M (Czech State Archive in Prague), reel 1, Finance Ministry to all financial institutions, Prague, March 25, 1939. The decree 6766/39 VI "über

at this stage registered only the contents of Jewish safe-deposit boxes,[18] but in 1940, valuable items (such as gold and silver) were subjected to compulsory purchase at fixed prices well below market values. These new measures were directed against the bank accounts of all Jews.

A child survivor from Mährisch Ostrau has described the impact of these measures:

> For my mother and me, it was a difficult time as we had to solve all our problems on our own without a father [who had been sent to Sosnowiec]. And there were many problems. Slowly our money began to run out, as our bank account, like the accounts of all Jews, was blocked. We made an effort to sell various items, but we did not have much left. They wanted to throw us out of our apartment, and it was only thanks to the efforts of good people that they didn't do it. Even then, as an eight-year-old, I frequently asked myself why we were different from everybody else. I was still too young to understand.[19]

On June 21, 1939, the Reichsprotektor of Bohemia and Moravia, Konstantin von Neurath, issued a further decree making the sale of many types of Jewish property contingent on state permission. Then in early 1940, the rules on blocking Jewish bank accounts were reformulated: "All payments to Jews, Jewish businesses, and Jewish associations can be made into a blocked account only at a currency bank or another . . . authorized financial institution."[20] The same implementation decree confirmed that "a Jew can withdraw from only blocked accounts at one or several financial institutions (for example, giro account, savings book, or safe deposit) for himself and his dependents not more than 1,500 Kronen per week."[21]

Shortly after this in 1940, a further decree established the "Emigration Fund of Bohemia and Moravia." In the name of the Jewish community, but under the strict control of the Security Police, this fund was to become the collecting point for a major part of the money secured in blocked accounts

einige Massnahmen zum Schutze der Währung" was published on March 25, 1939, with supplemental decrees issued on May 6 and June 26, 1939.

[18] Ibid., Finance Ministry, Investigation Dept., circular of April 1939.

[19] Moshe Har El, *"Ich habe nicht gewusst, dass wir noch eine schlimmere Zeit vor uns hatten": Von Mährisch-Ostrau in die Berge der Tatra und nach Israel*, eds. Jolanda Rothfuss and Olaf Schulze (Konstanz: Labhard, 2001), p. 21.

[20] Walther Ütermöhle and Herbert Schmerling, *Die Rechtsstellung der Juden im Protektorat Böhmen und Mähren: Eine systematische Darstellung der gesamten Judengesetzgebung* (Prague: Böhmisch-Mährische Verlags-Druckerei-Gesellschaft, 1940), pp. 8–11, 28–30; on these financial measures, see also Wolf Gruner, "Das Protektorat Böhmen und Mähren und die antijüdische Politik 1939–1941," in *Theresienstädter Studien und Dokumente* (2005): 27–62.

[21] W. Ütermöhle and M. Schmerling, *Die Rechtsstellung*, pp. 8–11, 28–30.

during the course of the deportations of Czech Jews to Theresienstadt and on to their probable death in the East.[22]

The example of the universal blocking of Jewish accounts in Bohemia and Moravia was followed throughout the Reich shortly afterward. In Germany, however, this measure was justified primarily as a logical extension of existing foreign currency control legislation.

General Application of Security Orders from August 1939

It is not clear precisely what link there was between the blocking of accounts in the Protectorate and its more widespread implementation in the Reich. However, developments in the Protectorate were well known to Göring's Four-Year Plan Office, which was busy expanding its influence there.[23] The directive initiating the intensified blocking of accounts in the rest of the Reich was Currency Office Circular 108/39, issued by the Economics Ministry on August 16, 1939. It expanded the previous security orders issued under the Foreign Currency Law and was intended to be applied to all Jews with significant property or income.

Internal documentation justified the measure mainly in terms of simplifying existing procedures, thereby reducing the bureaucratic effort involved. As had occurred previously with safe-deposit boxes, this meant shifting part of the burden of handling routine requests to the banks so that the Currency Offices dealt only with exceptional requests. The new regulation stipulated that "persons concerned [i.e., Jews] are forced to make payments for all expenses not related to daily needs from one single account at a Currency Bank and all payments received cannot be made in cash, but have to be paid into this secured account with limited access."[24]

To meet current living expenses, the Currency Office set a monthly maximum sum for withdrawals, which was usually not to exceed RM 300. Withdrawals were to be calculated according to "actual needs." Otherwise, only taxes, existing debts, and other levies (such as compulsory contributions

---

[22] Ibid., p. 58; in December 1941, the Reichsprotektor made the Zentralstelle für jüdische Auswanderung responsible for the remaining property of the deported Jews. It was instructed to make use of the Emigration Fund in winding up the assets; see Henry Friedlander and Sybil Milton (eds.), *Archives of the Holocaust*, vol. 22, *Zentrale Stelle der Landesjustizverwaltungen, Ludwigsburg* (New York: Garland, 1993), pp. 89–94.

[23] Jan Björn Potthast, *Das jüdische Zentralmuseum der SS in Prag: Gegnerforschung und Völkermord im Nationalsozialismus* (Frankfurt am Main: Campus, 2002), pp. 59–60.

[24] BAL, R 139 II/110 (reel 80011), RWM Allgem. Erlass Nr. 108/39 Berlin, August 16, 1939. Attention is drawn to this circular by A. J. Van der Leeuw; see LAB, B. Rep. 039–01/320, A. J. Van der Leeuw, Gutachten, December 11, 1969, p. 22.

to the Jewish community) could be paid without express permission. Day-to-day control over the accounts was left to the banks, which had to check the receipts.

As the preamble to the new directive explained, the aim was to prevent capital flight by the systematic securing of Jewish property. At the same time, this effort would also make possible the emigration of remaining Jews who possessed no property. The idea behind the measure was to force Jews to place all their money into bank accounts, so that it could be expended only for certain specifically stated purposes.

The directive instructed Currency Offices to obtain the addresses of the Jews from the Tax Offices, which had received the registration forms for Jewish property in 1938, or from the police authorities, which had registered all Jews in July 1938. Only currency officials entrusted with issuing security orders were to be assigned to this task. The Economics Ministry recommended close cooperation with the banks, so that all applications for special access to accounts would be brought to the Currency Office by a particular bank on a specific day of the week.[25]

In Münster, two officials of the Currency Office sent out the standardized security orders daily beginning in October 1939. By March 1940, they had issued 4,162 orders to the Jews living in Westphalia.[26] For example, the security order for Arthur Spanier of Herford was issued on October 27, 1939, informing him that he could no longer freely dispose of his own property.[27] A brief examination of security orders imposed on accounts held with the Deutsche Bank in Mannheim reveals that large numbers were issued in 1940, setting a monthly allowance for each of its Jewish customers.[28] The examination of security orders issued by the Currency Office in Rudolstadt, Thuringia, indicates that very many were issued in September and October 1939, the more wealthy cases (in which often a higher limit was set) being dealt with first.[29]

The initial correspondence with Jews requested a detailed inventory of their regular monthly expenditures so that the monthly allowance could be set at the appropriate level. Thus, some Jews with high monthly expenses for rent, mortgages, dependents, or other items initially received allowances

---

[25] Ibid.

[26] Gerd Blumberg, "Etappen," p. 32.

[27] Herbert Wolf, "Zur Kontrolle und Enteignung jüdischen Vermögens in der NS-Zeit: Das Schicksal des Rohtabakhändlers Arthur Spanier," in *Bankhistorisches Archiv* (1990): H. 1, 55–62, here p. 56.

[28] See, for example, HADB (Historisches Archiv der Deutschen Bank), Mannheim collection, F 28/53.

[29] See BAL, R 139 II/112–115.

in excess of RM 300. Of course, this detailed accounting exercise also represented a considerable invasion of privacy.

Confirmation of the timing of this measure can also be found in the diary of Victor Klemperer. On September 20, 1939, Klemperer wrote, "Our situation grows daily more catastrophic. Order yesterday: restricted access to bank account, surrender of all ready cash." Two days later, he wrote, "When I went to the Deutsche Bank yesterday to open my restricted account and wanted to deposit RM 300, they were astonished (What for? You can freely dispose of 400!). I should first of all go to the Currency Office today in person, in case there is some error." Finally on September 25th, he noted, "I *had to* open the restricted account. Running around, expenses, obstructions."[30]

A not untypical response to the receipt of a security order in the fall of 1939 was that of Bertha Blüth on September 28th. She replied that a monthly limit would not be needed in her case, as her money was in two savings banks and she would require very little over the course of the year. She explained that she lived with her daughter rent-free, and because her daughter wanted to emigrate, she needed the money later for an old people's home.[31] A number of the recipients replied sharply to the Currency Offices, protesting that they had next to no money anyway. In such cases, the Currency Office asked them to demonstrate their lack of means in a signed declaration. This declaration in turn might lead to the withdrawal of a security order.[32]

At this time when emigration was still possible and was clearly the aim of most Jews of working age, the main thrust of these regulations remained primarily to prevent the possibility of Jews' smuggling currency or valuable items. Even some private individuals shared this concern. For example, on November 9, 1939, employees of Carl Zeiss, Jena, the famous maker of optical instruments, wrote to the Currency Office in Thuringia to warn of a ruse used by Jews to transfer property overseas. Apparently, Jews intending to emigrate went to the American consulate and burned their U.S. securities before the eyes of U.S. officials, who documented it. With this evidence, the Jews could subsequently obtain duplicate certificates overseas. The staff at Carl Zeiss felt it was their loyal duty to warn the Currency Office of this practice.[33] In November 1939, the Economics Ministry wrote to the

---

[30] Victor Klemperer, *Ich will Zeugnis ablegen bis zum letzten: Tagebücher 1933–1941* (Berlin: Aufbau, 1996), pp. 490–500; translation based mainly on V. Klemperer, *I Will Bear Witness: A Diary of the Nazi Years*, transl. Martin Chalmers (New York: Random House, 1998), pp. 312–13.

[31] BAL, R 139 II/113, Bertha Blüth an OFP Thüringen, Devisenstelle, Eisenach, September 28, 1939.

[32] See, for example, R 139 II/119, case of Clothilde Goldmann.

[33] BAL, R 139 II/110, p. 254, Carl Zeiss, Abt. Wirtschaftspolitik an OFP Thüringen, November 9, 1939.

Senior Finance President in Breslau opposing the granting of permission for large sums to be paid from blocked accounts for emigration purposes. The Ministry wished to prevent any possible smuggling of money or the payment of bribes to foreign embassy staff.[34]

During this period, both the Jews inside the Reich and most who had successfully emigrated experienced a rapid deterioration of their financial position. In October 1939, officials of the Tax Office (*Finanzamt*, FA) in Münster attempted to secure the fifth installment of the punitive tax from all Jews who had emigrated or were about to emigrate. During this process, the Tax Office established that many Jews now no longer had sufficient funds to pay the additional installment, as most of their money had been consumed by the high costs of preparing for emigration. It noted that the collection of this tax would in many cases either endanger Jews' emigration or cause them to become a burden on the welfare authorities. In particular, it recommended that debts incurred to Aryans be paid first before the tax was collected to ensure that Aryans would not end up actually paying for the tax.[35]

The file of M. I. P., a Jewish emigrant to Chile, is typical. Having already been subjected to a security order in 1938 because of his preparations to emigrate, he was forced to cash in his life insurance policies in 1938, and he requested permission to cash in some of his shares in April 1939 to cover his rising expenses. Then in November 1939, a further security order reduced his monthly allowance to only RM 400, despite rent payments of RM 126 per month for himself and three children and living expenses estimated at an additional RM 500, including the cost of Spanish lessons necessary for his emigration plans. Of RM 45,000 to his name in 1937, less than RM 6,000 remained by November 1939, as almost RM 20,000 was now frozen in security for the flight tax and the punitive tax, just as he faced ever-spiraling costs for his visa and tickets. He was fortunate to leave the country in December 1939, having been deprived of most of his assets in just two years.[36] Others were not able to escape, and many consumed all their remaining financial reserves even before the deportations, only to die in poverty. Erich Frey noted in his diary that "from a financial point of view, Aunt Clara died at the right time. Of the RM 1,600 left by her children at the time of their emigration only about RM 70 remained after payment of funeral costs, gravestone inscription, and other incidentals. The

---

[34] Ibid., RWM an OFP Breslau, November 18, 1939.

[35] FA Münster Stadt an OFP Westfalen, Betr.: Judenvermögensabgabe V. Rate – Erfahrungen und Zweifelsfragen, Münster, October 26, 1939. Copy received from the collections of the Villa ten Hompel, Münster.

[36] ZAM, Devisenakte of M. I. P.

remaining money will be used for grave maintenance."[37] Within the Reich, although most Jews retained formal access to their blocked accounts up to their deportation, the small amounts remaining in them were rapidly used up.

Despite the considerably greater obstacles after September 1939, approximately 25,000 Jews were able to emigrate from Germany from the beginning of the war up to the prohibition of further emigration in October 1941.[38] Some were permitted to transfer money abroad from their blocked accounts in Germany to countries that had not joined the anti-Axis coalition, provided all outstanding taxes and fees had been paid. However, the effective rate of exchange was so poor that it amounted to the confiscation of almost all of their money. In September 1939, this "surcharge" was increased again to reach 96 percent, so that only 4 percent remained for the emigrants. In fact, the end result was generally even worse, due to commission charges and other expenses, such as for telegrams or legal representation in connection with the transfer. One successful transfer of RM 20,000 in March 1941 resulted in the ultimate receipt of only some $320 in New York, not counting cable costs totaling an additional RM 235.[39] In addition, the property of Jews who succeeded in obtaining citizenship in an enemy nation such as Great Britain before being denaturalized was frozen in accordance with the Enemy Property regulations. In these cases, however, the German authorities initially decided not to confiscate such property for fear of reprisals against German property abroad.[40]

Administration by Private Banks

A key aspect of the blocking of accounts was the extent to which they were administered directly by private banks. In August 1940, the Economics Ministry issued guidelines confirming that the guiding principle of the new policy in August 1939 had been to shift much of the work onto the banks. The circular detailed payments that did not require permission from the Currency Offices: all taxes; contributions to the Jewish community

[37] USHMM, RG-10.041 #03, diary of Erich Frey, pp. 19–20.

[38] Avraham Barkai, *Vom Boykott zur "Entjudung": Der wirtschaftliche Existenzkampf der Juden im Dritten Reich 1933–1943* (Frankfurt am Main: Fischer, 1987), p. 168. These figures do not include the Austrian Jews who emigrated.

[39] USHMM, RG-14.003M (Reichsvereinigung der Juden), 146; see also H. Wolf, "*Zur Kontrolle und Enteignung*," p. 58. The official exchange rate was fixed at RM 2.5 to $1.

[40] See Stephan H. Lindner, *Das Reichskommissariat für die Behandlung feindlichen Vermögens im Zweiten Weltkrieg: Eine Studie zur Verwaltungs-, Rechts- und Wirtschaftsgeschichte des nationalsozialistischen Deutschlands* (Stuttgart: Franz Steinert, 1991).

or the RV; gifts to social or religious institutions; legal fees, especially in connection with emigration; medical expenses; costs of asset management; purchases of securities when bought through a bank; purchases of items needed for emigration; travel costs for emigration; debts incurred prior to the security order; and fees to the *Deutsche Golddiskontbank* (DeGo) in connection with the transfer of money or goods abroad.[41] The banks were to screen applications for special permissions. Jews were urged to pay small obligations first from the monthly allowance before appealing to the Currency Office. The banks were to require proper documentation in support of claims for the release of larger amounts. Only in doubtful cases should they refer applicants to the Currency Offices, to ensure "that the reduction of work intended by the introduction of general blocked accounts in the summer of 1939 would actually be achieved."[42] The monthly fees for maintaining a blocked account were, needless to say, considerably higher than those for regular accounts, as Jewish customers soon noticed when they examined their statements.[43]

Because of the small amount of his financial assets, Erich Frey in Berlin was not subjected to a security order until June 1941. Then, he had to indicate his "current expenditures to the foreign exchange [currency] office and . . . received permission to withdraw monthly a set amount. All my income, including wages, had to be deposited in a bank trust account to which I had only limited access. This caused more work for me, since I had to give up my postal checking account. There were also extra costs because bank fees are higher than those of the postal checking system."[44]

In September 1941, the Economic Group for Private Banks again reminded its members that Jews were permitted to make certain special payments from their accounts (for medical expenses and the like), and in particular for taxes owed, but that in every case the bills had to be presented in order to prevent overpayment.[45] That same month, the Economics Ministry instructed banks not to issue any further checkbooks to Jews and to recall those in circulation to prevent Jews from writing "illegal" checks in excess of their monthly limit.[46] Given the close involvement of the banks in

[41] BAL, R139 II/110, p. 144, circular of RWM in currency matters, August 9, 1940.
[42] Ibid.
[43] For example, the Deutsche Bank in Mannheim charged one customer the fee of RM 25 for implementing the security order (*Sicherungsanordnung*) imposed by the Gestapo!
[44] USHMM, RG-10.041 #03, diary of Erich Frey, p. 26.
[45] BAL, R 139 II/110, p. 133, Wirtschaftsgruppe Privates Bankgewerbe (WiGrPrB) circular, September 25, 1941.
[46] Ibid., p. 212, RWM an WiGrPB, September 24, 1941.

freezing their accounts, it is not surprising that many long-standing Jewish clients felt very bitter at their treatment.[47]

Main Effects of Blocked Accounts

As Marion Kaplan demonstrates, the blocking of Jewish bank accounts was an additional humiliation for the Jews, emphasizing their powerlessness in the face of Nazi dictates: "For access to their money, Jews had to apply to the government and bring proof of why they needed it. Thus, Jews had to write for special permission to take their own savings out of these blocked accounts. They had to submit formal requests for funds to buy a new winter coat, pay doctor's bills, or pay off old debts."[48]

Historians have not previously focused on the role of blocked accounts in the Nazi confiscation process. As noted above, their creeping introduction in Germany, mainly as a result of the new Currency Law of December 1936, has meant that their more widespread introduction from August 1939 has often been overlooked. This was partly a result of the lack of access to individual Currency Office files, which have only recently been opened up to historians.

However the significance of the phenomenon lies in the rapid pauperization of the German Jews, resulting primarily from the vast tax burden imposed on them by the flight tax and the punitive tax (JuVa), compounded by the effects of compulsory Aryanization and the high costs of emigration. By the end of 1939, when the universal blocking of Jewish accounts was introduced, it served primarily as a means for the German government to supervise rapidly diminishing Jewish savings and force Jews to divert these resources – mostly in vain – toward the vanishing goal of emigration.[49] At the same time, the government also preserved some money in the bank accounts of the more wealthy Jews, which was then collected directly by the German state in connection with the mass deportations from October 1941.

[47] See, for example, HADB, Filiale Mannheim, F 28/24.
[48] Marion A. Kaplan, *Between Dignity and Despair: Jewish Life in Nazi Germany* (New York: Oxford University Press, 1998), p. 146.
[49] I am indebted to Prof. Claus Stolberg for showing me his paper presented at the German Studies Association conference in San Diego in fall 2002, "'Wie mir bekannt geworden ist, beabsichtigen Sie auszuwandern . . .': Die Rolle der Oberfinanzdirektion Hannover bei der Vertreibung der Juden." This paper helped reconcile the contradiction between Nazi policies of forced emigration and those of confiscation by demonstrating that all expenses in relation to emigration were actively supported by the Currency Offices, which otherwise severely restricted Jewish expenditures through the blocking of accounts.

The Initial Deportations and the Treatment of Jewish Property, 1938–1941

Between 1938 and 1941, the Nazi authorities conducted a series of deportations of specific groups of Jews or of Jews from particular regions, raising the question of how to deal with the property they left behind. A brief analysis helps reveal the development of thinking on this issue within the German bureaucracy and provides background to the drafting of the Eleventh Decree to the Reich Citizenship Law and the regulation of Jewish property matters in the wake of the full-scale deportation of Jews from Germany beginning in the fall of 1941.

The Deportation of Polish Jews, October 1938

On October 26, 1938, Heydrich issued instructions for a large number of Jews who were Polish citizens to be given notice that they had to leave the Reich by October 29.[50] This was in direct response to a Polish measure of early October denying re-entry into Poland for Polish citizens abroad if they did not have a requisite approval issued by the Polish Embassy. This Polish measure was designed specifically to deny a right of return to Polish Jews resident abroad, especially those in Germany, who were suffering from intensified persecution at this time. In accordance with Heydrich's directive, the German police arrested more than 15,000 Polish Jews in late October and rapidly deported them to Poland to beat the deadline set by the Poles. From the Leipzig district in Saxony, for instance, 1,598 Jews were deported on October 28.[51]

This was the first large-scale deportation of Jews to a destination outside the Reich, and the special legal status of these Jews created a number of difficulties in regard to their property. In Saxony, the police sealed the deportees' apartments to prevent looting. Questions soon arose concerning the costs incurred by the police and others due to the deportations. The sudden arrests left a number of companies without their owners, so that no one could be found with the authority to continue paying wages or other

---

[50] See USHMM RG–14.01M (Selected Records from the Sächsischen Hauptstaatsarchiv Dresden), reel 2, file Ministerium des Innern Nr. 11180, Heydrich Schnellbrief to regional governments, October 26, 1938. I am grateful to Wolf Gruner for bringing this collection to my attention.

[51] USHMM RG–14.01M (Sächs. HStA Dresden), reel 2, Min. des Innern Nr. 11180, p. 25, Pol. Präs. Leipzig to Sächs. Min. des Innern, Dresden, October 29, 1938; on this deportation, see also Karol Jonca, "The Expulsion of Polish Jews from the Third Reich in 1938," in *Polin* 8 (1994): 255–81.

urgent debts. The local government in Leipzig was compelled to appoint trustees to administer the firms (as had been done with "Marxist property" before) in order to limit damage to the local economy.[52]

The empty apartments posed another problem. As in most cases access to them was now denied, the landlords were unable either to rent them out or to get the back rent from the deportees. Within the German bureaucracy, some officials were concerned that the financial interests of the state might lose out in a general "run" on the remaining property by creditors, applied through forced sales using court orders.[53] However, because an agreement concerning the property was being negotiated with the Polish government, which even permitted Jews to return briefly to sort out their financial affairs, Heydrich preferred to let the courts deal with claims for compensation. In an agreement signed in January 1939, he even handed over responsibility for the property to Polish consular officials, although some refused to accept this burden. Therefore, although these events foreshadowed many of the issues and problems that developed during subsequent deportations, diplomatic considerations did not permit the direct seizure of property by the state other than to pay for taxes or other legally recognized debts.[54]

The Start of the War and Deportation Plans

After Hitler's attack on Poland on September 1, 1939 and the onset of a general European war, Nazi policy toward the Jews changed in certain key directions. As historian Wolf Gruner demonstrates, it soon became clear that the policy of forced expulsion to other countries was no longer feasible, as most borders were now closed and in any case the *Reichsfinanzministerium* (Reich Finance Ministry, RFM) was no longer prepared to make available any foreign currency for Jewish emigration. As early as September 19, 1939, the Ministerial Council for Defense of the Reich discussed "the future population of the Polish 'protectorate' and the accommodation [*Unterbringung*] of the Jews living in Germany." Thus, plans got underway for the expulsion of Jews into the newly occupied territories.[55]

---

[52] USHMM RG–14.01M (Sächs. HStA Dresden), reel 2, file Min. des Innern Nr. 11180, p. 24, Kreishauptmann Leipzig to Sächs. Min. des Innern, Dresden, October 29, 1938; and pp. 41–42, Saxon Interior Minister to RFSS, November 1, 1938.

[53] Ibid., Saxon Interior Minister to RFSS, December 6, 1939.

[54] Ibid., see especially p. 162, Heydrich to Saxon Interior Minister, January 4, 1939; ibid., pp. 181–84, RFSS Schnellbrief, January 26, 1939, re.: expulsion of Polish Jews.

[55] Wolf Gruner, "Von der Kollektivausweisung zur Deportation der Juden aus Deutschland (1938–1945) – Neue Perspektiven und Dokumente," in *Beiträge zur Geschichte des Nationalsozialismus* 20, *Die Deportation der Juden aus Deutschland: Pläne – Praxis – Reaktionen 1938–1945* (Göttingen: Wallstein, 2004): 30.

In early October, Eichmann received instructions from Gestapo chief Heinrich Müller to begin expelling Jews from the areas of Kattowitz, Mährisch-Ostrau, and Vienna across the River Vistula for the purpose of gaining experience for subsequent larger "evacuations." At the same time, Eichmann also began to draw up regional lists of Jews in the "Old Reich," the "Protectorate" (Bohemia and Moravia), and the "Ostmark" (Austria), while also planning for the extraction of remaining property from the Jews being expelled. As Gruner points out, in contrast to previous deportations, the expropriation of those Jews being deported was now envisaged from the outset.[56]

When Eichmann started the deportations in mid-October, the police issued instructions for any cash to be confiscated from the deportees and converted into Polish złoty at an unfavorable rate and for 1 percent of all their remaining property to be collected as a "contribution." These instructions closely resembled those issued in fall 1941 for the mass deportation of Germany's Jews: already part of their property was being robbed during the process of deportation, whereas the remainder was left behind in blocked accounts. In total, Eichmann organized the deportation of well over 5,000 Jews into the Nisko area in October 1939 before the action was broken off due to "technical difficulties."[57]

Deportation of the Jews from Stettin and Pomerania, February 1940

On the night of February 12/13, 1940, the Gestapo office in Stettin, assisted by the local Nazi Party, organized the deportation to the Lublin district of some 1,200 Jews from Stettin, Greifenhagen, Greifswald, and other towns in Pomerania, comprising about one-third of the Pomeranian Jews.[58] According to international press reports, the confiscation of property during these deportations was even more comprehensive and brusque. Members of the SS or the SA visited the affected families and told them that they would be deported to an unknown destination within a few hours. They were permitted to take only one suitcase per person and had to leave all their furniture behind. Any cash or valuables, with the exception of wedding rings, had to be surrendered, and they were forced to sign declarations effectively renouncing ownership of their bank accounts or real estate.[59] The remaining

---

[56] Ibid., pp. 31–32.

[57] Ibid., pp. 33–35.

[58] Ibid., p. 37; Shmuel Spector and Geoffrey Wigoder (eds.), *The Encyclopedia of Jewish Life before and during the Holocaust* (Jerusalem: Yad Vashem, 2001), pp. 451–52.

[59] NARA, T-120 (German Foreign Office), reel 4651, fr. K336600–2, extract from *Politiken*, Copenhagen, February 17, 1940; see also the Gestapo instructions for the operation, cited by W. Gruner, "Von der Kollektivausweisung zur Deportation," p. 37.

property was then placed under the trusteeship of the regional authorities (*Regierungspräsidenten*). Over the following weeks, their household items were sold and the income received paid into blocked accounts. Much property was stolen, and some items, including children's books, were passed on to the Nazi welfare organization (*Nationalsozialistische Volkswohlfahrt*, NSV).[60]

The fate of these deportees was particularly harsh. They suffered severely on the trains for three days without food or water, and from the city of Lublin many were forced to continue on by foot or sled to smaller towns under extreme winter conditions. Within a month, some 230, including a number of children, were reported to have died. During a subsequent transport from Schneidemühl on March 12, the deportees were apparently not permitted to take any luggage or even any money with them.[61]

Correspondence from the files of the Stettin Gestapo demonstrates how this deportation also affected Jews who had emigrated earlier. Alice Busch migrated to Palestine in July 1937, leaving her husband Max behind in Stettin. In early 1941, the Gestapo initiated investigations toward the denaturalization of Alice Busch, primarily because of her possible inheritance of real estate worth RM 48,000 from her husband Max (who had been deported to the General Government in February 1940); this sum of money would make it worth their while to proceed with denaturalization in accordance with guidelines issued in September 1940. However, in May 1941 the Gestapo in Stettin had still received no information of Max's death. In November 1941, the OFP seized the property, before the lengthy denaturalization procedures could be completed, as both marriage partners had been automatically denaturalized and expropriated under the Eleventh Decree.[62]

Deportations from Baden and the Palatinate, October 1940

The next large-scale deportation from the Reich took place on October 22/23, 1940, on orders from Hitler and Himmler with the involvement of the regional authorities in Baden and the Palatinate (Saarpfalz). This deportation was probably a practical consequence of the Madagascar Plan

---

[60] W. Gruner, "Von der Kollektivausweisung zur Deportation," pp. 37–38.

[61] NARA, T-120 (German Foreign Office), reel 4651, fr. K336608–9, Polish-Jewish Welfare Committee, Cracow March 14, 1940 – appeal to Göring; David Silberklang, "The Holocaust in the Lublin District" (Unpublished English version of his PhD Dissertation submitted to Hebrew University in Jerusalem in February 2003), pp. 69–70.

[62] USHMM, RG-11.001M.04 (RGVA, Gestapo Stettin), reel 73, 503-1-356, file on Alice Busch.

that was prepared in the summer of 1940 after the fall of France. A larger deportation involving the Jews of Hessen was planned, but then abandoned, partly because of the resistance of Vichy, France. The deportation affected 6,504 Jews, nearly all of whom were then held in the camp at Gurs in southern France, from where more than 2,000 were subsequently deported to Auschwitz or Lublin-Majdanek.[63] The deportees were obliged to hand over the keys to their apartments and could only take up to 50 kilograms of luggage and up to RM 100 with them.[64] As one deportee, Berty Friesländer-Bloch, recalled, the deportation took place on the Jewish holiday of Sukkot. Two Gestapo men ordered the family to get ready within 30 minutes and informed them they could take with them only the most urgent necessities; that is, one woolen blanket and RM 100 each. "We also had to sign a piece of paper that said that we had voluntarily surrendered the rights to our property," she recalled.[65]

On November 9, 1940, Himmler's office issued guidelines regarding certain aspects of this recent deportation, including detailed instructions on the administration and sale of the property left behind. Whereas furniture was to be sold quickly by the local authorities to enable apartments to be rented out again, real estate was not to be sold for the time being, and most stocks and shares were to be converted (into state bonds) and placed in blocked safe-deposits. Himmler ordered that 10 percent of the cash sums collected be paid into a special account to cover the costs of the deportation. At the same time, individual accounts were to be opened to collect most of the proceeds for each Jew, and in certain special circumstances, payments could still be made from these accounts, for example, to dependents who were receiving support before the deportations. Prior to their deportation, Jews were also required to sign an authorization empowering the RV to have access to their accounts.[66] Thus, the trusteeship ordered at this time

---

[63] For example, twelve Jews from Grötzingen in Baden were deported to Gurs on October 22, 1940. See S. Spector and G. Wigoder (eds.), *Encyclopedia of Jewish Life*, p. 459.

[64] W. Gruner, "Von der Kollektivausweisung zur Deportation," pp. 41–42; see also Paul Sauer, *Die Schicksale der jüdischen Bürger Baden-Württembergs während der nationalsozialistischen Verfolgungszeit 1933–1945: Statistische Ergebnisse der Erhebungen der Dokumentationsstelle bei der Archivdirektion Stuttgart und zusammenfassende Darstellung* (Stuttgart: W. Kohlhammer, 1969).

[65] Erhard R. Wiehn (ed.), *Oktoberdeportation 1940: die sogenannte "Abschiebung" der badischen und saarpfälzischen Juden in das französische Internierungslager Gurs und andere Vorstationen von Auschwitz: 50 Jahre danach zum Gedenken* (Konstanz: Hartung-Gore, 1990), pp. 155–56.

[66] BAL, R 2/12222, RFSS S – IV A 5 b – 802/40, Richtlinien für die Erfassung, Verwaltung und Verwertung der zurückgelassenen Vermögenswerte, November 9, 1940; see also R 58/276, pp. 267–71, RFSS Ergänzende Richtlinien, March 25, 1941.

actually stopped short of outright confiscation, although the measures clearly tended toward this goal. The Security Police conducted the confiscation of property accompanying the deportations in 1940 in close conjunction with the regional governments. At a meeting held on December 4, 1941, between the representatives of the Gestapo and the RFM, responsibility for this property was transferred from the Plenipotentiary of the Reichsführer SS (Himmler) to the relevant OFPs.[67]

The Confiscation of Property from Polish Jews in the Reich

The property of Polish Jews inside the Reich became subject to general confiscation under the Decree for the Confiscation of the Property of Polish Citizens, issued on September 17, 1940. This policy was administered by a separate bureaucracy, the *Haupttreuhandstelle Ost* (Main Trustee Office East, HTO), reporting directly to Göring's Office of the Four-Year Plan. The HTO was active mainly in the territories incorporated into the Reich from Poland in the fall of 1939, but in December 1940, it officially established a Special Section for the Old Reich (*Sonderabteilung Altreich*) in Berlin to deal with the property of the former Polish state and individual Polish citizens (including Jews) inside the Reich's pre-1939 borders. According to the head of the HTO's Legal Section, Bruno Pfennig, the main aim of the Special Section for the Old Reich was to "complete the removal of the eastern Jews (*Ostentjudung*) from the economy."[68]

This measure was another forerunner of the wholesale confiscations of Jewish property enacted under the Eleventh Decree and had quite considerable scope. In the mid-1930s, more than 11 percent of Jews in Germany held Polish citizenship.[69] Despite the forced deportation of more than 15,000 Polish Jews from the Reich in late October 1938, many thousands remained. In addition, the incorporation into the Reich of extensive Polish territory in late 1939 made the September 1940 decree the basis for massive property

---

[67] NARA, RG-242, T-1139, reel 53, NG-5373 RFM O 5210 – 1724 VI, December 8, 1941, Niederschrift über eine Besprechung am 4. Dezember 1941.

[68] On the organizational structure of the HTO, see Jeanne Dingell, "Property Seizures from Poles and Jews: The Activities of the Haupttreuhandstelle Ost," in *Confiscation of Jewish Property in Europe, 1933–1945: New Sources and Perspectives* (Washington, DC: United States Holocaust Memorial Museum, 2003): 33–41; on the Sonderabteilung Altreich, see Bernhard Rosenkötter, *Treuhandpolitik: Die "Haupttreuhandstelle Ost" und der Raub polnischer Vermögen 1939–1945* (Essen: Klartext, 2003), pp. 146–49.

[69] Helen B. Junz, *Where Did All the Money Go?: The Pre-Nazi Era Wealth of European Jewry* (Bern: Staempfli, 2002), p. 72.

confiscations from Jews and Poles there. These confiscations were carried out by the HTO acting together with the Security Police.

Some 6,000 case files of the HTO (Sonderabteilung Altreich) have survived in the archives in Berlin.[70] They cover the administration and sale of various types of assets, including businesses, life insurance policies, bank accounts, securities, real estate, silverware, and other household items. Mixed together are two categories of files: those of Poles, many of whom attempted over several years to regain their confiscated property by claiming that they were actually of German blood, and those of Jews who suffered the confiscation of everything except a few items for personal use and had almost no means of recourse.[71]

Much of the property belonging to Polish Jews, especially businesses, had previously been brought under the control of trustees during the course of Aryanization. Beginning in the fall of 1940, these trustees had to report to the HTO, which was responsible not only for the administration but also the sale of the property. A number of files concerned real estate in Vienna owned in whole or in part by Polish Jews. In one case, the property was sold in the fall of 1941 before the publication of the Eleventh Decree.[72] Many files also contain application letters from prospective buyers. One applicant claimed that his father had built the house in 1914, but lost it in the inflation period, as he wrote "due to Jewish interest rates."[73] In some cases, properties were difficult to sell as they were owned by multiple parties, and in others, lengthy bureaucratic battles were fought among the HTO, the Tax Offices, and also the *Reichskommissar für die Behandlung feindlichen Vermögens* (Reich Commissar for the Treatment of Enemy Property, RKBfV) over which institution was responsible for them.

Among the files is one of a German Jewish woman who had married a Polish citizen and thereby forfeited her German citizenship. She wrote a series of heart-rending letters, maintaining vehemently her German origins and protesting the confiscation of all her clothing and household property, which had been packed up in preparation for a failed emigration attempt in August 1939. Noting the value and the date of purchase of each item,

---

[70] OFDB, Div. Ordner I (RFM Handakte Scheerans), "Über diskriminierende Massnahmen des Dritten Reiches gegen jüdische Staatsbürger und die heraus resultierenden Aufgaben des Archivs des ehem. Reichsfinanzministeriums," p. 4.

[71] For an example of the attempt to confiscate even small amounts of personal property of little or no monetary value, see OFDB, HTO 18927.

[72] OFDB, HTO 17153.

[73] Ibid., HTO 17166.

the list of possessions prepared for the customs includes everything from an umbrella and a thermos flask to her jewelry and lingerie. In one particularly moving letter she pleads,

> Unfortunately I fell into the hands of a confidence trickster (*Hochstapler*) and after only three months of marriage I immediately applied for a divorce, which I received.... If you want to take away from me my very last possessions, my dowry chest (of linen) and all my clothes, I would be left completely naked with nothing to wear and thereby would be much poorer than a beggar, as now neither my parents nor I have any means left in order to buy other things.[74]

Sadly, another letter from a transport company addressed to the HTO reported "that our request... to the residential registration office (Einwohnermeldeamt) in Berlin has revealed that Frau E. S. was deported to Minsk on November 14, 1941."

Because revenues from Poles and from Jews were mixed together, it is not possible to give a figure for the amount of Jewish property confiscated by the HTO. Nevertheless, one source reported that this authority had confiscated and administered more than RM 100 million by January 1945.[75]

Jewish Forced Labor

The initial impulses for the imposition of forced labor on the German Jews emerged in the fall of 1938 through a combination of their progressive removal from the workforce, their impoverishment, and the practical limitations on their emigration. For Hermann Göring, the Nazi leader primarily responsible for Jewish policy at this time, it was clear that, rather than become a burden on the state, Jews should be put to work. In a speech in early December 1938, he argued that "those Jews who have no position, and are healthy and able to work, and who have no property (such that they might live from the interest on it), will be assembled in certain worker columns.... they don't need to be concentration camps.... here they will

---

[74] See ibid., HTO 19596.
[75] *Legalisierter Raub: Der Fiskus und die Ausplünderung der Juden in Hessen 1933–1945* (Ausstellungskatalog) (Frankfurt am Main: Fritz Bauer Institut, 2003), p. 15. I am grateful to Susanne Meinl for sharing with me some of the results of her research on the HTO collection at the OFDB.

receive food. . . . a little bit of pocket money. . . . And [we will] keep them in certain [work] camps."[76]

On December 20, 1938, the president of the Reich Institute for Work Placement and Unemployment Insurance, Friedrich Syrup, ordered that the Labor Exchanges (*Arbeitsämter*) should find work for all unemployed Jews or for those Jews receiving welfare assistance.[77] It still took several months for these instructions to be implemented at a local level by the Labor Exchanges, but by May 1939, it is estimated that more than 13,500 Jews were subjected to forced labor, nearly 6,000 of them on road or similar construction projects. Many Jews were engaged by the municipal authorities in various forms of manual labor, such as cleaning the streets, clearing rubbish, or loading trains. In the summer of 1939, the forcible recruitment of Jews was intensified to meet the growing labor shortage.[78]

The start of the war again focused attention on those Jews remaining in the Reich, as their prospects of emigration had been greatly diminished. In mid-September 1939 at a meeting on Jewish emigration in the office of Göring's deputy, Staatsrat Helmut Wohlthat, it was noted that some 50,000 men and 60,000 to 70,000 women could be mobilized, although about 60 percent of the Jews would not be eligible for "work deployment" as they were younger than age sixteen or older than fifty-five. It was noted, however, that at this time the Führer had not yet taken a decision on the matter.[79]

The impact of these measures on individual Jews was quite profound. In May 1940, Max Leffmann, a Jewish man from Münster who was subjected to forced labor at a brick factory, complained to the Tax Office that he could barely live on the monthly "allowance" from his bank account of RM 125 as he had to maintain his work clothes and had additional expenses for travel and food. It was also impossible for him to get to the bank due to his long work hours on Monday to Friday (6:30 AM to 6:30 PM) and until 3:30 PM on Saturday. He therefore asked to receive his weekly pay of RM 25–30 directly in cash.[80] In many cases, pay was very low, sometimes

[76] Besprechung Görings "über die Judenfrage" mit den Gauleitern, Oberpräsidenten und Reichsstatthaltern am 6.12.1938 im RLM, cited in Wolf Gruner, *Der geschlossene Arbeitseinsatz deutscher Juden: Zur Zwangsarbeit als Element der Verfolgung 1938–1943* (Berlin: Metropol, 1997), pp. 60–61.

[77] W. Gruner, *Der geschlossene Arbeitseinsatz*, pp. 66–67.

[78] Ibid., pp. 92 and 103.

[79] BAL, R 2/14195, RFM, Referat V/3, note on a meeting re: Jewish emigration, Berlin, September 16, 1939.

[80] ZAM, Devisenakte of M. L.; see also, Gisela Möllenhoff and Rita Schlautmann-Overmeyer (eds.), *Jüdische Familien in Münster, Teil 2,2: Abhandlungen und Dokumente 1935–45* (Münster: Westfälisches Dampfboot, 2001), p. 809.

only RM 0.10 per hour with no insurance; the families of forced laborers, sometimes now separated from their menfolk, often had to rely on Jewish welfare support.[81]

During 1940, Jewish men were increasingly deployed in industry; some women were also recruited. By early 1941, about 24,500 men and 16,500 women were so mobilized in the "Old Reich."[82] For many, hard physical labor was unpleasant and dangerous, sapping their last reserves of strength. Thus, both Jewish monetary and physical capital were being drained for the German war effort. The property declarations signed by Jews just prior to deportation often provide details of their forced labor at this time, in terms of outstanding pay owed to them by specific firms, while also recording the rapid decline of their financial position since the previous property census in 1938. The same files also often reveal recent changes of address resulting mainly from administrative decisions, which also contributed to their pauperization.[83]

The Eviction of Jews and Their Concentration in "Jewish Houses"

Another measure that seriously affected the material situation of German Jews and drained their financial reserves was their eviction from parts of many cities and their concentration in "Jewish houses" (*Judenhäuser*). In November 1938, the SS propaganda journal *Das Schwarze Korps* called for the isolation of the Jews in separate houses or residential quarters. In December 1938, Göring indicated that the Nazi aim was to concentrate Jews only in houses under Jewish ownership. Then in April 1939, the legal basis for this policy was defined with the Law on Rental Contracts with Jews.[84] The main aim of this law was that Jews should not be tenants of Aryans and Aryans should not be tenants of Jews. It made forcible evictions of Jews possible, if not yet compulsory. In many towns, the implementation of this

---

[81] Wolf Gruner, *Der geschlossene Arbeitseinsatz*, pp. 119 and 129.

[82] Ibid., p. 176.

[83] See individual files examined from the collection LAB, Rep. A 092. These files have since been transferred to BLHAP.

[84] *RGBl.*, I (1939), pp. 864–65, "Gesetz über Mietverhältnisse mit Juden" vom 30.4.39, cited in Angela Schwarz, "Von den Wohnstiften zu den 'Judenhäusern,'" in Angelika Ebbinghaus and Karsten Linne (eds.), *Kein abgeschlossenes Kapitel: Hamburg im "Dritten Reich"* (Hamburg: Europäische Verlagsanstalt, 1997): 237; Gisela Möllenhoff and Rita Schlautmann-Overmeyer, *Jüdische Familien in Münster, Teil 2,2*, p. 804.

policy was linked to other considerations, such as local town planning, or, later, even the impact of Allied bombing.

In Hamburg, beginning in May 1939, Jews received a wave of eviction notices. In desperation, they turned to the Jewish community organization, which assumed the task of assigning them an apartment or frequently only a single room in a house with other Jews. Thus the authorities exploited the Jewish community organization to help implement the policy. For its part, the local Jewish communal officials hoped thereby to ameliorate the worst consequences of the evictions.[85] The experience was no less distressing for that. In July 1939, Meta Seelig in Münster wrote, "We try not to think about anything, for how many memories does this house hold that are reawakened when we have to leave it." In Münster, the concentration of all Jews in *Judenhäuser* was not completed before the deportations, but some people had to move more than once as Jewish landlords emigrated or had their property auctioned off. The available space was progressively reduced, and several families had to share small apartments.[86]

The research of Susanne Willems shows that in Berlin the *Generalbauinspektor für die Reichshauptstadt* (Office for the Reconstruction of the Capital, GBI) under the authority of Albert Speer played a key role in organizing the mass evictions and subsequently also the deportations of Berlin's Jews, as it used the reallocation of apartments occupied by Jews for its own city planning schemes.[87] Already in the first half of 1939, the GBI began incorporating the idea of Jew-free zones, seeking to clear more desirable areas, such as the streets around the Kurfürstendamm, and making space for non-Jews displaced by its own massive construction projects.[88] In September 1940, the Law on Rental Contracts with Jews was amended to permit the eviction of Jews even from houses owned by other Jews in the three most important cities of the Reich: Berlin, Vienna, and Munich.[89]

The implementation of this policy on a massive scale was underway by the spring and summer of 1941 as hundreds of Berlin Jews received eviction notices. Among the beneficiaries were Security Police officials declared in

---

[85] A. Schwarz, "Von den Wohnstiften," pp. 237–39.

[86] G. Möllenhoff and R. Schlautmann-Overmeyer, *Jüdische Familien, Teil 2,2*, pp. 804–807; on the "Judenhäuser," see also Marlis Buchholz, *Die hannoverschen Judenhäuser: Zur Situation der Juden in der Zeit der Ghettoisierung und Verfolgung 1941 bis 1945* (Hildesheim: A. Lax, 1987); see also M. Kaplan, *Between Dignity and Despair*, p. 171.

[87] Susanne Willems, *Der entsiedelte Jude: Albert Speers Wohnungsmarktpolitik für den Berliner Hauptstadtbau* (Berlin: Hentrich, 2000), pp. 14–16.

[88] Ibid., pp. 135–36.

[89] Ibid., pp. 165–66.

need of housing.[90] The war administration report of the Pankow District of Berlin for March 1941 noted that evicted Jews were "accommodated with other Jewish families, who had to make room for them as subtenants, or in houses specially selected for accommodating Jews." Those houses were chosen mainly on account of "the poor conditions of the buildings."[91]

The traumatic nature of these resettlements even within Berlin is revealed by comments in the diary of Erich Frey. He received notification to leave his apartment in December 1941 and was assigned a single room in an apartment already occupied by Jews in Karlshorst. He wrote, "I again made telephone calls to moving companies. Mom packs, is desperate and close to a nervous breakdown." It was difficult to arrange a moving company as most did not want to do business with Jews. In addition, various disputes with the other tenants of the new house had to be settled before Frey and his wife could move in: "As so-called intruders, we were received with mixed feelings by the other parties involved." The room was cold and cramped. For the first time in twenty-five years Frey and his wife had to sleep separately, one in a small bed and the other on the couch. Not only did he have to donate much of his furniture to the Jewish community, as it could not be moved, but he also was forced to pay RM 540 to the GBI for the cost of renovating the old apartment.[92]

The *Reichsvereinigung* and Jewish Welfare Efforts

In February 1939, the newly established compulsory central organization of the Jews, the Reich Union (*Reichsvereinigung*, RV) imposed an emigration tax on all Jews in the process of emigrating. According to regulations issued in 1940, this tax consisted of 1 percent of their total property for those having property valued between RM 10,000 and RM 20,000, with progressively higher rates for those who had more property.[93] Beginning in the

[90] Ibid., pp. 183–84, 227, and 379. The GBI was careful to avoid being specifically mentioned in the eviction notices. In Berlin, the Jewish community also established an advice center that helped victims find space in existing Jewish houses and apartments.

[91] Kriegsverwaltungsbericht Pankow for the period 1.9.39–31.3.41, cited by Wolf Gruner, "Die Reichshauptstadt und die Verfolgung der Berliner Juden 1933–1945," in Reinhard Rürup (ed.), *Jüdische Geschichte in Berlin* (Berlin: Hentrich, 1995): 229–66, here p. 243.

[92] USHMM, RG-10.041 #03, diary of Erich Frey, pp. 26–31. In the case of those deported, the GBI deducted the renovation costs from any remaining property of the deportees administered by the Tax Office; see S. Willems, *Der entsiedelte Jude*, p. 381.

[93] Gudrun Maierhof, "Selbsthilfe nach dem Novemberpogrom: Die jüdische Gemeinde in Frankfurt am Main 1938 bis 1942," in Monica Kingreen (ed.), *"Nach der Kristallnacht":*

summer of 1939, the remaining separate Jewish organizations and communities were successively dissolved and their property transferred to the RV in accordance with the Tenth Decree to the Reich Citizenship Law, issued on July 4, 1939.[94] For example, in the local property register, the title to the property of the "Israelitische Synagogengemeinde (Adass Jisroel) in Berlin" at Sigismundhof 11 was transferred to the RV on November 25, 1940.[95]

With the start of the war, the financial position of Jewish welfare organizations had deteriorated considerably as they were suddenly cut off from most overseas support.[96] At the same time, their services were needed more than ever, as Jews were by now largely excluded from public welfare. In the first half of 1940, the RV had total expenditures of RM 22.5 million, of which about RM 9.5 million went to welfare measures. The RV's budgeted expenditures at this time were financed primarily from "assets" (RM 11.7 million) and the emigration tax (RM 10.6 million). During the second half of the year, the projected expenditure on welfare was RM 10.4 million.[97] However, subjected to strict budgetary controls by the Security Police, the RV was compelled to reduce its expenditure on welfare, despite the flow of money raised from the sale of remaining communal property. Its leadership had no access to the RV's funds without express permission from the RSHA.[98] At the local level, Gestapo officials oversaw the activities of the Jewish welfare organizations within the RV, aiming to cut down expenditures and increasing the recruitment of Jews for forced labor.[99]

In December 1940, a further special tax, first introduced for Polish citizens, the inappropriately named Social Equalization Tax (*Sozialausgleichsteuer*), was extended to Jews as well. This tax deducted 15 percent of earned income directly at the source.[100] By this time the RV could raise money only from among its own members to cover increased welfare needs; therefore, the impact of such a tax was to make it even harder to scrape together funds.

Jüdisches Leben und antijüdische Politik in Frankfurt am Main 1938–1945 (Frankfurt am Main: Campus, 1999), p. 164.

[94] Ibid., p. 161.

[95] Mario Offenburg (ed.), *Adass Jisroel Die Jüdische Gemeinde in Berlin (1869–1942): Vernichtet und Vergessen* (Berlin: Museumspädagogischer Dienst, 1986), p. 258.

[96] Gerhard Botz, *Wohnungspolitik und Judendeportation in Wien 1938 bis 1945* (Vienna: Geyer, 1975), p. 72.

[97] Wolf Gruner, "Poverty and Persecution: The Reichsvereinigung, the Jewish Population, and Anti-Jewish Policy in the Nazi State, 1939–1945," *Yad Vashem Studies* XXVII (1999): 23–60, here p. 45.

[98] S. Willems, *Der entsiedelte Jude*, pp. 400–401.

[99] G. Maierhof, "Selbsthilfe," p. 171.

[100] W. Gruner, "Poverty and Persecution," p. 47.

The Intensification of Denaturalization against Jewish Emigrants[101]

After the German invasion of Poland, the RSHA issued new guidelines on the denaturalization of Jewish emigrants. A circular sent to Gestapo offices on May 8, 1940, stressed the necessity of concentrating available resources on those cases that were "important for the war." Such cases included not only emigrants who were engaged in "anti-German" activities but also emigrants who possessed significant assets that would be lost to the Reich if they were to become citizens of another state before denaturalization.[102]

Then, in a circular to the Gestapo offices dated September 24, 1940, Heydrich again stressed that the previous strict preconditions for denaturalization had allowed many Jewish emigrants with considerable wealth in Germany to evade denaturalization. Even the broader interpretations of this law had left many untouched. As a result, a great deal of property had escaped confiscation, especially when Jews had obtained the citizenship of other countries in time.

The rapid processing of "war-important" cases urged in May 1940 was limited initially to Jews who still possessed identifiable property in Germany. In all cases in which property in excess of RM 5,000 was uncovered, the Gestapo was to secure it immediately to deny Jewish emigrants further access to it.[103] In response, the Münster Gestapo office requested in August 1940 the property registration files of all local Jews who had since emigrated, with a view to determining if sufficient property remained for initiating denaturalization[104]; this practice probably was widespread throughout the Reich.

The tax affairs of Jewish emigrants were dealt with by the Finanzamt (FA) Moabit-West in Berlin as the designated central office for the tax affairs of all German emigrants after their departure. According to a November 1941 report by this office, the punitive tax files of emigrant Jews who owned

---

[101] The second half of this chapter is based in part on my article, "The Development and Implementation of Nazi Denaturalization and Confiscation Policy up to the Eleventh Decree to the Reich Citizenship Law," *Holocaust and Genocide Studies,* vol. 16, no. 2 (Fall 2002): 217–42.

[102] BAL, R 58/62, RSHA to State Police offices on May 8, 1940; Himmler stressed this point again in the decree he issued a few days later: LAB, A Rep. 092, Acc. 3924, Nr. 769 (Handakte Möser) RFSS decree, May 17, 1940.

[103] Ibid.

[104] Gestapo Münster to OFP Münster, II B 3 – 180.01 Nr. 97/40, August 1, 1940. I am grateful to Alfons Kenkmann at the Villa ten Hompel Geschichtsort for making this document available to me.

property in Germany worth more than RM 5,000 were routinely forwarded to the RSHA for assistance in determining which ones to denaturalize.[105] This made sense, as only Jews who possessed more than RM 5,000 in Germany were subject to the punitive tax. A detailed examination of the remaining punitive tax files held by the *Oberfinanzdirektion* (Regional Financial Office, OFD) in Berlin confirms the close cooperation between the FA Moabit-West and the Gestapo. On the original cover page of some of the files can be seen clearly in red pencil the comment "returned from the SS." In a few files, one can also find a brief letter from the head of the Security Police and the SD: "to the FA Moabit West (to Juva) [in red]. Enclosed I return your file. No domestic property values could be established."[106]

The case of A. B., a Jewish man who was recommended for denaturalization by the Berlin Gestapo on May 26, 1941, is typical of those wartime cases that were directed mainly against property. A. B. was accused of nonpayment of his punitive tax and other tax obligations. His undeveloped piece of land in Berlin-Zehlendorf had already been secured on these grounds.[107] He was denaturalized on August 27, 1941, and in November a German official opened private negotiations with the FA Moabit-West regarding possible purchase of the land. By June 1942, however, this formerly Jewish property had been reserved for the construction of Reich-owned housing.[108] As a result of a 1942 block on the sale of Jewish real estate to private individuals, some of the property seized from the Jews was still in state possession at the end of the war.[109] Other forms of property took many months or years to be registered, collected, and sold. For example, in the case of L. L., who

[105] LAB, A Rep. 092, Acc. 3924, Nr. 769 (Handakte Möser), OFP Berlin-Brandenburg Vermögensverwaltung, FA Moabit-West, Vermerk über eine Besprechung mit der Gestapo, November 1, 1941. I am grateful to Klaus Dettmer of the LAB for making this file available to me.

[106] OFDB, JuVa 907/5071. My research indicates that only those files that recorded that no property had been found appear to have been returned by the RSHA.

[107] PAAA, Inl. 11 A/B, R 99921, Gestapo Berlin denaturalization proposal (den. p.) against A. B., May 26, 1941.

[108] BAL, R 2/26599, ORR Lorenz an RFM, November 26, 1942, and note of Referat Maedel, June 18, 1942.

[109] On the limitation of sales, see for example Wolfgang Dressen (ed.), *Betrifft: "Aktion 3". Deutsche verwerten jüdische Nachbarn. Dokumente zur Arisierung* (Berlin: Aufbau Verlag, 1998), pp. 189–92. This did little to stem the flood of applications to buy Jewish property. After the war, more than 1,800 Jewish properties remained under state administration: see OFDB, Div. Ordner I (RFM Handakte Scheerans), "Die Massnahmen gegen die jüdische Bevölkerung und ihre Einrichtungen seit 1933" (Ausarbeitung des Archivs des ehem. RFM, Februar 1949), p. 168. According to the available records, in the case of A. B., the entry in the deed book (Grundbuch) was not corrected in favor of the Reich until October 1944, see OFDB, Restitutionsakten, 1–97/49 A. B.

immigrated to the Netherlands in 1933 and was recommended for denaturalization in 1937, the relevant banks did not deliver some of his shares to
the Reichsbank until December 1944.[110]

The denaturalization of emigrant Jews sometimes affected their relatives
inside the Reich, as can be seen from the experiences of Dr. Walter Ostwald,
who arrived in England in September 1938 on a visitor's passport. His
apartment furnishings reached him, having been plundered and severely
damaged, shortly after the outbreak of the war. He struggled to make a
living in London, first washing dishes and later as an accountant in a legal
office. On October 16, 1941, his German citizenship was revoked and all of
his property in Germany confiscated. As a result, regular payments from his
German bank account to his mother and penniless sister in Germany were
cut off.[111]

The Sale of Jewish Property Trapped in the Ports

On August 1, 1940, Himmler issued new instructions concerning the treatment of property held in storage for Jewish emigrants being considered for
denaturalization.[112] This property had become a problem for the transport
companies, because it could no longer be exported after the outbreak of war
and increasingly Jews abroad were unable or unwilling to pay the high storage fees demanded. Another consideration was the fear that Allied bombing
might destroy the property.[113] In Hamburg, the RSHA began the confiscation of this stored property in January 1941, and public auctions began
there shortly afterward. At a meeting in March, Hamburg's social welfare

---

[110] L.'s furniture from Amsterdam was cleared out of his residence in May 1943 during the
course of the "Möbelaktion" following his deportation to Theresienstadt, where he died
in February 1944. PAAA, Inl. 11 A/B, R 99671, Nr. 6420, Gestapo Central Office to
Interior Ministry, April 23, 1937; and OFDB, Restitutionsakten, 8–456/57, 8–455/57
and 221540/IRSO.

[111] Gisela Möllenhoff and Rita Schlautmann-Overmeyer, *Jüdische Familien in Münster 1918 bis
1945, Teil 1: Biographisches Lexikon* (Münster: Westfälisches Dampfboot, 1995), pp. 325–26.

[112] BAL, R 58/276, RSHA to Stapo(leit)stellen, March 5, 1941. See also A. J. Van der
Leeuw, "Zur Vorgeschichte der Enteignung jüdischen Vermögens durch die Elfte VO-
RbürgerG," in *Rechtsprechung zum Wiedergutmachungsrecht*, vol. 1 (January 1962): 1–4.

[113] Frank Bajohr, *"Aryanisation" in Hamburg: The Economic Exclusion of the Jews and the
Confiscation of their Property in Nazi Germany* (New York: Berghahn, 2002), p. 278; Kurt
Schilde, *Bürokratie des Todes: Lebensgeschichten jüdischer Opfer des NS-Regimes im Spiegel
von Finanzamtsakten* (Berlin: Metropol, 2002), p. 47; and NARA, RG-59, Lot File
52D408, Records of the Intergovernmental Committee on Refugees, 1942–1947, Misc.
Sub's Files Box 4, Archer Woodford, American Consul, Hamburg to American Embassy
Berlin, March 3, 1941; I am grateful to Richard Breitman for bringing this document to
my attention.

administration discussed the ongoing auctions of this property, which was valued at more than RM 20 million. It noted that the auctioneers had instructions not to exceed certain fixed price levels. The city was also in the process of buying up a reserve stock of items that would be needed for the local population in the event of catastrophic air raids. For this purpose, a contract was signed with the city's moving companies concerning the transport and storage of these items.[114]

In early 1941, the Gestapo in Hamburg wrote to the Gestapo in Stettin concerning a Jewish man from Stettin whose property was stored in the port of Hamburg, asking them to check whether there were grounds for denaturalization. When they replied in the negative, the Hamburg Gestapo then exploited an apparent currency offense in connection with the property instead (the nondeclaration of specific items) as a pretext to proceed with its confiscation and sale just the same.[115] The significance of these public auctions was that the practice of selling off Jewish personal property to alleviate the needs of the German population and raise revenue began even before the mass deportations and the introduction of the Eleventh Decree, providing a clear precedent for the treatment of household items and clothing left behind by the deportees.

Drafting of the Eleventh Decree

In September 1940, the RSHA began talks with the relevant ministries with the aim of denaturalizing all emigrant Jews, charging that all of them were hostile toward the Third Reich. Preparations were made so that all of the denaturalization cases could be carried out quickly once the new legislation was in place.[116] In December 1940, as planning began for what was to become the Eleventh Decree to the Reich Citizenship Law, the Interior Ministry noted that depriving Jews of their citizenship might hinder their emigration, as countries were less likely to accept stateless immigrants. The Ministry was prepared to accept this disadvantage, however, because after the war Germany would find a "solution to the Jewish Question" that would not depend on the voluntary participation of other countries.[117]

In many respects, the model for the new decree was provided by the denaturalization procedures applied to Jewish emigrants. During discussions

---

[114] Konrad Kwiet, "Nach dem Pogrom: Stufen der Ausgrenzung," in Wolfgang Benz (ed.), *Die Juden in Deutschland 1933–1945: Leben unter nationalsozialistischer Herrschaft* (Munich: C. H. Beck, 1993): 545–69, here p. 561.

[115] USHMM, RG–11.001M.04 (RGVA), reel 73, Gestapo Stettin, 503-1-364.

[116] BAL, R 58/62, RSHA to State Police offices, September 24, 1940.

[117] BAL, R 43 II/136a, pp. 43–44, Interior Ministry express letter, December 9, 1940.

in the spring of 1941, an early draft was entitled "Draft Decree on the Property of Jews Abroad Who Are to Lose Their German Citizenship."[118] Reich Chancellory correspondence concerning this measure makes it clear that by December 1940 the Nazis intended that all Jews be removed from German territory in the near future, even if their ultimate destination remained unknown.[119]

Ministerial representatives met to draft the decree in January and March 1941.[120] The drafters envisaged the confiscation of all property belonging to German Jews abroad. The draft specifically referred to the July 14, 1933, Law for the Revocation of Citizenship as the model for this more extensive measure and proposed that all those leaving the Reich would forfeit their property the instant they crossed the Reich's borders.[121] This proposal became the basis for the property aspects of the subsequent Eleventh Decree.

During these meetings, the plans for the future use (*Zweckbestimmung*) of seized Jewish property were revised by removing references to "the support of Jewish emigration" (*Förderung der Judenauswanderung*). The sums raised were now to serve only the "solution of all Jewish questions" (*Lösung aller Judenfragen*) or, as it was finally worded, "the furtherance of all purposes in connection with the solution of the Jewish Question." According to notes of the March meeting, even this statement of purpose was not binding for the RSHA or the RFM. These semantic discussions represent the last lingering shadows of earlier plans to finance the emigration of Germany's poorer Jews through a levy or confiscation of property from those Jews who were better off.[122]

---

[118] BAL, R 2/5980, pp. 46–51, Interior Ministry express letter, March 13, 1941, with appendices.

[119] BAL, R 43 II/136a, pp. 43–44, Reich Chancellory to Interior Ministry, December 17, 1940. "Im übrigen fragt es sich, ob im Hinblick darauf, dass in nicht ferner Zeit die Juden aus Deutschland verschwunden sein werden, es sich noch lohnt, ihnen eine besondere Rechtsstellung einzuräumen."

[120] For a detailed analysis of the genesis of the Eleventh Decree, see Cornelia Essner, "Das System der 'Nürnberger Gesetze' (1933–1945) oder der verwaltete Rassismus" (Ph.D dissertation Berlin, 1999), pp. 363–403. I am grateful to Prof. Hans Mommsen for bringing this thesis to my attention.

[121] Ibid., pp. 369–70. See also, NARA, RG-238, T-1139, reel 4, NG-300, notes of the conference on January 15, 1941, concerning citizenship conditions in the Reich.

[122] NARA, RG-238, T-1139, reel 4, NG-300, notes of the conference on January 15, 1941, and attached draft; BAL, R 43 II/136a, pp. 83–86, Interior Ministry invitation to the meeting on March 15, 1941, to discuss a draft for the Eleventh Decree, with enclosed drafts, dated March 13, 1941; BAL, R 2/5980, p. 52, note of a meeting at the RFM on March 15, 1941. For the eventual wording of the Eleventh Decree, see *RGBl.*, I (1941), pp. 722–24, November 26, 1941. On the so-called *Treuhandfonds* proposal (representing

During the March meeting, the RSHA withdrew its original request for control over all Jewish real estate that would fall to the Reich. In return for this concession, the RFM withdrew its demand to publish all the names of those affected by the general ordinance. The two agencies also agreed that the OFP Berlin would be designated as the reporting office in order to simplify the many resulting administrative instructions that would have to be issued.[123]

A follow-up letter issued by the Interior Ministry on March 19, 1941, made it clear that, because the General Government was not Reich territory, German Jews living there (or deported there) would also lose their property. The Ministry also noted that the new decree would simplify the work of the Foreign Office overseas with regard to the issuance of passports and the liquidation of property belonging to emigrant Jews; previously, the confiscation of the latter's property had been possible only on an individual basis, and in each case the embassy had to establish in written form the damaging conduct of individual Jews toward the Reich.[124] The new decree would simplify the procedures considerably for a number of separate ministries involved in the hitherto lengthy denaturalization process.[125]

However, the RFM warned that speeding up the process would greatly increase the workload of the financial administration. The FA Moabit-West was already heavily burdened with property confiscations involving thousands of complex cases. Before, such work had come in over a period of time; this decree would add tens of thousands of new cases overnight. The FA Moabit-West argued that it would be unable to cope with this burden. Thus, it was agreed to designate the Senior Finance President Berlin as the responsible office. The RFM concluded that it could accept the burden only if every effort was made to simplify the work, for example, by such measures as delegating responsibility to the Security Police and SD for establishing whether a case for property confiscation existed.[126]

---

25 percent of Jewish property intended to support emigration) see BAL, R 2501/6641, Reichsbank confidential note on the financial aspects of the removal of the Jews from Germany dated January 18, 1939. On the financial aspects of the proposed Madagascar Plan in the summer of 1940, see especially Nuremberg Document NG-5764, NARA, RG-238, T-1139.

[123] BAL, R 43 II/136a, pp. 83–86, Interior Ministry invitation to the meeting on March 15, 1941 to discuss a draft for the Eleventh Decree, with enclosed drafts, dated March 13, 1941; R 2/5980, p. 52, note of a meeting at the RFM on March 15, 1941.

[124] See Chapter 1.

[125] BAL, R 2/5980, Interior Ministry circular concerning the Eleventh Decree, March 19, 1941.

[126] BAL, R 2/5980, undated reply (draft) to Interior Ministry from March 1941.

Propaganda and ideological considerations also lay behind the planning for this decree. In the invitation to the March meeting, the Interior Ministry noted that the Foreign Office wanted to publish the decree in conjunction with the date on which U.S. Lend-Lease legislation in support of Britain would take effect. This was reiterated in a March 19, 1941, letter that set a deadline of March 26 for comments.[127] Thus, a measure directed partly at Jewish emigrants' property in Germany was also viewed by the German Foreign Office as a reprisal against the United States for financial aid to Britain.

In June 1941 the head of the Reich Chancellory, Hans Heinrich Lammers, wrote confidentially to Martin Bormann, the head of the Party Chancellory, concerning the drafting of the Eleventh Decree. Lammers wrote that the Führer thought that after the war there would be no Jews left living in Germany.[128] The expropriation of German Jews living outside the Reich, therefore, also provided a mechanism for Germany's comprehensive expropriation of Jewish property. Those who were not affected by confiscation upon the publication of the decree would become subject to it subsequently upon deportation. This was reaffirmed in a July 7, 1941, Interior Ministry circular confirming Hitler's decision to confine the measure to Jews outside the Reich's frontiers so as to avoid complications and exceptions in drafting the law.[129] In anticipation, the RSHA had already announced in June 1941 a stop to further denaturalization proposals against German Jews living abroad.[130]

Because of its central role in the confiscation of Jewish property up to 1941, the FA Moabit-West was also consulted in planning for the implementation of the Eleventh Decree.[131] The enormous increase in work, however, made some decentralization desirable. A memorandum prepared by the FA Moabit-West on November 7, 1941, argued for a central coordinating role for the FA Moabit-West (subsequently incorporated directly within the OFP Berlin-Brandenburg) and the retention of certain tasks while delegating other tasks to the regional OFPs: "The FA Moabit-West has control

---

[127] BAL, R 43 II/136a, pp. 83–86, Interior Ministry invitation to the meeting on March 15, 1941 to discuss a draft for the Eleventh Decree, with enclosed drafts, dated March 13, 1941; ibid.

[128] BAL, R 43 II/136a, pp. 123–25.

[129] BAL, R 2/5980, Interior Ministry invitation to a meeting on July 14, 1941, regarding the Eleventh Decree, July 7, 1941; A. J. Van der Leeuw, "Zur Vorgeschichte," pp. 1–4, also underlines this key point.

[130] BAL, R 58/276, RSHA an alle Stapo(leit)stellen, June 13, 1941.

[131] Stefan Mehl, *Das Reichsfinanzministerium und die Verfolgung der deutschen Juden 1933–1943* (Berlin, 1990), p. 33.

over certain institutions and experience that deserves to be exploited further. . . . In addition a certain practical knowledge in dealing with the cases has been developed at the FA Moabit-West, which ought not to be left untapped."[132]

In a subsequent report dated November 19, 1941, the FA Moabit-West again stressed its eight years as a central repository of experience. The agency recommended registration of all propertied persons who were being denaturalized; as before, information about them was to be centralized on index cards at Moabit-West, making it possible to answer the numerous requests by the ministries, state police offices, banks, and other agencies. Yet because at least 20,000 more cases were expected in the event of the general collection of all property from emigrant Jews (including some 5,000 with full or partial ownership of real estate), the FA Moabit-West simply had to decentralize the work. The complex processing of real estate cases would be delegated to the regional OFPs to ease the burden on Moabit-West.[133]

Large-scale systematic deportations of Jews from the Reich began in October 1941.[134] The experience that had been gathered from large-scale denaturalizations, as well as during the deportations from Baden and the Palatinate in October 1940, provided the main reference points for regional financial administrations in processing the property of the deported Jews. Finance officials from Frankfurt am Main (OFP Kassel) held preparatory discussions with representatives of the RFM in the offices of the FA Moabit-West on October 9, 1941.[135] In practice, the Tax Office in Frankfurt decided to rely more heavily on external staff such as legal assessors and administrators during the deportations, due to the lack of available personnel. The main difference to the emigration cases, in addition to the sudden increase in workload created by the deportation of more than 1,000 Jews from Hessen in one fell swoop, was the urgent need to clear the vacated apartments of

---

[132] LAB, A Rep. 092, Acc. 3924, Nr. 769 (Handakte Möser), FA Moabit-West O 5210 1/310, November 7, 1941.

[133] OFDB, Div. Ordner IV (RFM Handakte Scheerans), FA Moabit-West O 5300/O 5400 to OFP Berlin, November 19, 1941; this memo is quoted extensively by S. Mehl, *Das Reichsfinanzministerium*, pp. 100–101.

[134] Wolf Gruner, "Die Reichshauptstadt und die Verfolgung der Berliner Juden," p. 248; Monica Kingreen, "Gewaltsam verschleppt aus Frankfurt: Die Deportationen der Juden in den Jahren 1941–45," in Monica Kingreen (ed.), *"Nach der Kristallnacht": Jüdisches Leben und antijüdische Politik in Frankfurt am Main 1938–1945* (Frankfurt am Main: Campus, 1999): 357–402, here p. 358.

[135] OFDB, Div. Ordner IV (RFM Handakte Scheerans), pp. 276–77, OFP Kassel, Re.: Collection of Jewish Property, November 5, 1941. I am grateful to Monica Kingreen for bringing this correspondence to my attention.

mostly low-value household goods in order to reduce the compensation the government would have to pay to the apartment owners for loss of rent.[136]

On November 4, 1941, the RFM issued a *Schnellbrief* (express letter) to the regional OFPs, delegating to them responsibility for the administration and disposal of the property of deported Jews and issuing procedural guidelines. At this time (i.e., just prior to the Eleventh Decree), the laws for the confiscation of the property of "enemies of the people and of the state" and of "communists" were applied, and confiscation notices were handed out to the deportees individually. In each case, a file was to be opened and an index card created to provide an overview. Examples of the preprinted forms used by the FA Moabit-West were included with the circular.[137]

Himmler's October order banning the further emigration of Jews from Germany was distributed in November 1941 to the regional Gestapo, police, and state registration offices (*Standesämter*). Only in very special cases where a positive Reich interest was established could the RSHA permit exceptions.[138] The close temporal conjunction of the ban on further emigration with the beginning of the deportations in October underlines the links that existed among emigration, deportation, and property seizure and that were realized in the Eleventh Decree to the Reich Citizenship Law on November 25, 1941.[139]

The new decree ordered the mass confiscation of property from emigrants and deportees via denaturalization from the moment they crossed the Reich's borders.[140] This replaced the principle of examining each case individually under the former denaturalization procedure.[141] In practice,

---

[136] Ibid., see also pp. 278–81, reports of FA Frankfurt am Main – Aussenbezirk dated October 23 and 31, 1941.

[137] BAL, R 2 Anh./7, RFM express letter O 5205 740 VI g, November 4, 1941; this circular is published in *Schriftenreihe des Bundesamtes zur Regelung offener Vermögensfragen*, vol. 6, pp. 230–34.

[138] NARA, RG-242, T-175, reel 280, fr. 2774161, Gestapo Aachen to the Landräte, November 4, 1941, regarding the emigration of Jews. The Himmler order dated October 23, 1941, and issued by the RSHA, has been published in *Widerstand und Verfolgung in Wien 1934–1945*, vol. 3 (Vienna: Oesterreichischer Bundesverlag für Unterricht, Wissenschaft und Kunst Jugend und Volk Verlagsges. MbH, 1975), doc. no. 147, p. 277.

[139] *RGBl.*, I (1941), pp. 722–24 (November 26, 1941), Elfte VO. zum Reichsbürgergesetz. Vom 25. November 1941.

[140] According to a confidential circular of the Interior Ministry dated December 3, 1941, the General Government and the Reich Commissariats Ostland and Ukraine were deemed to be outside the Reich for these purposes. See H. G. Adler, *Der verwaltete Mensch: Studien zur Deportation der Juden aus Deutschland* (Tübingen: J. C. B. Mohr, 1974), pp. 503–504 (NG-5336 and NG-2650).

[141] See Diemut Majer, *"Fremdvölkische" im Dritten Reich* (Boppard am Rhein: Harald Boldt Verlag, 1993), p. 212.

however, the Gestapo continued to issue confiscation orders against many of the deported Jews on the basis of the 1933 laws, as several of the main destinations, including Auschwitz, Theresienstadt, and Łódź, lay within the Reich's frontiers.[142]

Effects of Blocked Accounts and the Eleventh Decree

After the November pogrom and the start of the war, the Jews in Germany were stripped of their last remaining rights and economically degraded to bare subsistence, an underclass with no hope of respite. In the words of Konrad Kwiet, they were "impoverished and deprived of their rights, decimated and elderly, separated from their families and cut off from the outside world, obliged to perform forced labor and crammed together in 'Jewish houses,' undernourished and exhausted, limited in their freedom of movement [and after September 1941] brand-marked by a star the size of a side-plate."[143]

A further array of discriminatory measures followed the German attack on Poland. In September 1939, on the holiday of Yom Kippur, Jews were obliged to surrender their radios, and in December they were excluded from clothing rations. In July 1940, they were also denied access to telephones.[144] There were also restrictions on when Jews could shop. In Berlin in the summer of 1940, in many shops Jews were officially forbidden to shop until late in the afternoon, by which time many items had been sold out. They received reduced food rations and for certain items, such as cocoa or rice, none at all.[145]

The history of Germany's Jews from 1938 to 1942 has been little studied, partly due to the lack of sources, but mainly because these painful experiences were overshadowed by the deportations and murder that followed. In

[142] A. J. Van der Leeuw, "Zur Vorgeschichte," p. 4, notes that Jews deported to Łodz and Theresienstadt received individual confiscation orders (*Einziehungsverfügungen*) after November 25, 1941, as these towns were inside the expanded Reich. There are also some examples of Jews, deported to Auschwitz, who were issued Einziehungsverfügungen prior to their deportation; see for example LAB, Rep. 092, Nr. 8498, file of F. E., born September 28, 1884, deported to Auschwitz on March 1, 1943. H. G. Adler, *Der verwaltete Mensch*, p. 577, cites an example of a transport to Auschwitz from Würzburg in June 1943 for which no Einziehungsverfügungen were prepared. I am grateful to Joachim Neander for his assistance with this question.

[143] K. Kwiet, "Nach dem Pogrom," p. 545; cited also by S. Willems, *Der entsiedelte Jude*, p. 7.

[144] USHMM, RG-10.041 #03, diary of Erich Frey, pp. 42–43.

[145] W. Gruner, "Die Reichshauptstadt," p. 244; M. Kaplan, *From Dignity to Despair*, p. 151.

recent years, many local studies have examined this period in more detail, and the recent opening of the financial archives adds a vast store of information on the rapid deterioration of the Jews' material circumstances, which took place largely before the deportations.[146]

This chapter has focused particularly on two key aspects of the Nazi exploitation of Jewish wealth during this period that have largely escaped the attention of historians. First, the application of blocking measures (security orders) to the majority of Jewish bank accounts from August 1939 has often been mentioned by historians, but not previously analyzed systematically. The availability of extensive records on how these accounts were monitored on a daily basis reveals the key role played by the private banks that took over much of the day-to-day administration from the Tax Offices. This measure was applied by the financial administration with little interference by the Gestapo before the advent of the deportations.

Another aspect overlooked by historians is the impact of the mass denaturalization of Jewish emigrants carried out during the war but prior to the Eleventh Decree as a means to raise revenue. As noted, the number of new denaturalization cases involving property dealt with by the FA Moabit-West rose only slowly, from thirty-three in 1933 to ninety-three in 1936. It then accelerated to 203 cases in 1937, 566 in 1938, and 1,300 in 1939. By September 1940, a further 1,268 had been added. The income for the Reich from denaturalization was in excess of RM 12 million during 1939 and reached a total of RM 23,794,371 by September 1940. However, these figures do not include revenue from the sale of securities and the net value of most of the real estate; the overall total must have been considerably greater. And it must be borne in mind that, as of September 1940, of the 3,562 property cases received, only 847 had been settled.[147]

The snowballing scale of income from property confiscation can be illustrated by figures for the period from April 1 to December 31, 1940, during which time RM 37,620,125 was booked to the Reich from Jewish emigrants alone, again not including income from securities or unsold real estate.[148] By comparison with the income obtained from the punitive tax (RM 1.12 billion) and the flight tax (RM 900 million), the income gained from denaturalization up to September 1940 appears small. However, it is likely that a considerable proportion (almost certainly in excess of RM 100

---

[146] See especially the remarkable volumes for Münster edited by G. Möllenhoff and R. Schlautmann-Overmeyer.

[147] LAB, A Rep. 092/54589, FA M-W, O 1300 – Ordn. No. 8/40, Berichterstatter Regierungsrat Boetcher, September 13, 1940.

[148] LAB, A Rep. 092, Acc. 3924, No. 769, OFP Berlin to RFM, February 3, 1942.

million) of the RM 778 million estimated to have been collected as a result of the Eleventh Decree actually derived from the thousands of emigration cases initiated before November 25, 1941, against emigrants still possessing more than RM 5,000 in Germany.[149]

The head of the FA Moabit-West complained in September 1940 about the growing demands on his office:

> In 1937 the number of denaturalizations involving the seizure of property grew considerably and had a particularly burdensome effect, as many of the cases left over from previous years had not been completed. Nevertheless in 1937 the work had to be done without any additional staff. The year 1938 brought a renewed increase in denaturalizations involving property confiscation. This rise continued sharply into the years 1939 and 1940. As a result the requirement for additional personnel became urgent, but so far has still not been met adequately. The level of staff given for September 1940 is insufficient for the smooth conduct of the work and, in view of the continuing rise in the number of denaturalizations, is too low.[150]

As the number of cases increased, the size of the staff at the FA Moabit-West was gradually expanded. A small office of two or three workers in the period from 1933 to 1936 had mushroomed by September 1940 into a full-time staff of five senior civil servants (*Beamten*) with twenty-two additional staff and eighteen typists, and the leadership of the office argued strenuously for further increases in spite of the war.[151]

A high degree of institutional continuity therefore facilitated the transition from the denaturalization and property seizure of individual Jewish emigrants to the confiscation of the remaining property of all Jews. The FA Moabit-West, which had acted as a central office for denaturalization cases, was converted into the Property Processing Office of the OFP Berlin-Brandenburg after publication of the Eleventh Decree, and it retained part of its central coordinating role for the utilization of remaining Jewish property in the Reich.[152] For example, it continued to administer the central card

---

[149] Raul Hilberg, *Die Vernichtung der europäischen Juden* (Frankfurt am Main: Fischer, 1982) vol. 3, p. 1074; OFDB, Div. Ordner I (RFM Handakte Scheerans), Die Massnahmen gegen die jüdische Bevölkerung und ihre Einrichtungen seit 1933, memorandum dated February 2, 1949.

[150] LAB, A Rep. 092/54589, FA M-W, O 1300 – Ordn. No. 8/40, Berichterstatter RR Boetcher, September 13, 1940.

[151] Ibid.

[152] LAB, A Rep. 092, Acc. 3924, No. 769 (Handakte Möser), OFP Berlin O 1741 – 2/41 – P II/O, December 23, 1941.

index for all of Germany, although the regional OFPs dealt with most matters concerning real estate and businesses, as well as the household property of Jews deported from their own districts.[153]

In many respects, the law for the revocation of citizenship introduced in 1933 served as an important model for the development of the complete expropriation of remaining Jewish wealth on the basis of the Eleventh Decree in 1941. Both the methods and the institutional infrastructure for the implementation of the Eleventh Decree – in the form of the FA Moabit-West – were already in existence as a result of earlier experience with denaturalization. A steady and logical intensification of the measures can be seen from the first laws for property confiscation introduced in 1933 through to their refinement with regard to the Jews in the form of the Eleventh Decree.

Following the outbreak of the war, the new guidelines issued by Himmler and Heydrich in the summer of 1940 expanded the target group for denaturalization to all emigrant Jews with significant property in Germany. This expansion was motivated specifically by a concern to accelerate the seizure of these resources for the wartime needs of the Reich. This measure in turn opened the door to the general confiscation of all Jewish property when the Eleventh Decree extended existing denaturalization procedures not only to all Jewish emigrants but also to those Jews deported from the Reich. The technical details of this measure were driven more by the practical need of the bureaucracy to simplify procedures than by legal considerations of defining the "citizenship status" of Germany's Jews.

The measures directed against Jewish emigrants and their property developed in conjunction with plans to deport from Germany all remaining Jews. Indeed, the correspondence concerning the drafting of the Eleventh Decree from December 1940 onward spells out the intentions of the Nazi leadership, signaled first during the Polish campaign, to remove all Jews from Germany.[154]

Ultimately, the bureaucracy itself developed a strong interest in the simplification of the vast task of processing individual denaturalizations. The

---

[153] H.G. Adler, *Der verwaltete Mensch*, pp. 531–32; see also S. Mehl, *Das Reichsfinanzministerium*, pp. 98–100. For an example of the regional responsibility for the property of deported Jews, see H. Wolf, "Zur Kontrolle," p. 61. The remnant of the central card index was available for consultation on microfiche at the Landesarchiv in Berlin (LAB) in 1999.

[154] On the development of "resettlement plans" for Jews from the Reich in connection with the occupation of Poland in September 1939, see for example Götz Aly, *"Endlösung": Völkerverschiebung und der Mord an den europäischen Juden* (Frankfurt am Main: S. Fischer, 1995), pp. 29–35, 59–62; Peter Longerich, *Politik der Vernichtung: Eine Gesamtdarstellung der nationalsozialistischen Judenverfolgung* (Munich: Piper, 1998), pp. 251–57.

Eleventh Decree permitted the respective ministries to streamline considerably the enormous bureaucratic effort involved. Thus, the rational calculations of bureaucrats seeking to increase revenue and simplify procedures played a role in perfecting the mechanisms of persecution. Despite this rationalization, remaining complexities prevented the Nazi bureaucracy from completing the process of confiscation before the end of the war in 1945. A vast paper trail of correspondence among many offices remained behind, which has been augmented since by the equally mammoth documentation of postwar restitution cases.

Analysis of the day-to-day implementation of denaturalization policy reveals a high degree of cooperation between the financial and police administrations. A sampling of the files also illustrates many sides of the lives of the Jewish victims. The considerable documentation collected for the purposes of bringing to an end people's citizenship and controlling and then stealing their property also brings to light the very difficult choices that faced all of those caught up in the Nazi web of persecution and destruction.

Part II: Jewish Property and the European Holocaust, 1939–1945

5
DESTRUCTION AND PLUNDER IN THE OCCUPIED EAST:
POLAND, THE SOVIET UNION, AND SERBIA

The German invasion of Poland started with the widespread seizure of property linked both to Aryanization and the needs of the German war economy. Jews were hit particularly hard by this initial looting and suffered also from the blocking of accounts, trade restrictions, and demands for contributions. The effects of resettlement and ghettoization further undermined Jewish private assets, so that little remained to the bulk of the Jewish population once the deportations to the death camps began in 1942. The

Figure 5.1. Jewish men tasked with clearing out Jewish homes after a deportation Aktion in Kraków, c. 1942. *Source:* USHMM, courtesy of Archiwum Panstwowe w Krakowie, 1024. USHMM, WS # 07120.

Trustee Office (*Treuhandstelle*) managed seized Jewish businesses and real estate for the benefit of the civil administration, defending itself against the claims of institutional rivals. Finally the processing of personal property at Auschwitz and the "Operation Reinhard" death camps reveals both the immense bureaucratic effort devoted to handling Jewish property and the inevitable corruption and waste that accompanied its direct exploitation at the extermination sites.

In the occupied Soviet territories, the German authorities displayed a similar combination of rapacious exploitation, bureaucratic formalism, and jurisdictional conflict. Confronted with the immediate question of how to handle Jewish property, military and police units who secured it at killing sites initially treated much of it like other "war booty." The creation of ghettos by the civil administration to isolate those Jews not murdered in the initial wave of mass shootings also accelerated the rapid deterioration of their material situation, as much property was seized and the little that remained was rapidly used up for the Jews' own subsistence. The management of Jewish property once it was secured by the civil administration, as demonstrated in the case of Latvia, reveals a considerable bureaucratic effort scarcely justified by the financial results. In these eastern regions, the acquisition of Jewish property acted more as an incentive for the participation of impoverished local collaborators in the Holocaust than it did for the SS, which murdered the Jews for ideological reasons.

In the case of Serbia, a similar pattern of direct exploitation by the German Army in the Balkans can be discerned. Here, the interests of local ethnic Germans and the desire to prop up the puppet Serbian state competed with the needs of Germany's war finances. The Reich's financial experts attempted to reconcile these differences by allowing the Serb state to retain seized Jewish property while they extracted the available profits from its sale, with interest, by forcing Serb financial institutions to borrow against the value of unsold Jewish real estate to meet urgent German demands for "war compensation." However, in view of the high costs of administering Jewish property in Serbia, the benefits derived from this improvised solution were limited.

The recent study by Itamar Levin on the impact of German policies in the Warsaw ghetto hammers home the point that the theft of property combined with physical isolation resulted in death on a massive scale through disease and starvation, even before the mass shootings started in the occupied Soviet territories in the summer of 1941.[1] Quoting extensively from

---

[1] Itamar Levin, *Walls Around: The Plunder of Warsaw Jewry during World War II and Its Aftermath* (Westport, CT: Praeger, 2004), pp. 5–7.

the main primary narrative sources for the ghetto, Levin demonstrates the numerous ways in which the progressive German expropriation of Warsaw's Jews (as well as the Jews' relations with their Polish neighbors) directly contributed to the gathering genocide. Precisely in such a situation of desperate need, the possession or loss of property could make a difference between life and death. Needless to say – although Warsaw was in many respects an extreme case – a similar dynamic played out over Jewish property throughout Europe, especially in the smaller ghettos in occupied Polish and Soviet territory.

Levin's work on the Warsaw ghetto reflects a wider historiographical focus on the issue of property in recent years. The development, during the 1990s, of regional studies of the Holocaust[2] has now also been followed by more focused regional studies devoted to the issue of Jewish property.[3] In the late 1990s, the international diplomatic interest in stolen Jewish property even prompted government publications on this subject in Belarus and Ukraine.[4] Scholars have begun to examine the issue of Jewish property

---

[2] See especially the works of Christian Gerlach, *Kalkulierte Morde: Die deutsche Wirtschafts- und Vernichtungspolitik in Weissrussland 1941 bis 1944* (Hamburg: HIS, 1999); and Dieter Pohl, *Nationalsozialistische Judenverfolgung in Ostgalizien 1941–1944* (Munich: Oldenbourg, 1996). Other more recent regional studies include: Wendy Lower, *Nazi Empire-Building and the Holocaust in Ukraine* (Chapel Hill: University of North Carolina Press in association with the United States Holocaust Memorial Museum, 2005), which focuses on the Zhytomyr region.

[3] See for example articles by Yitzhak Arad, "Plunder of Jewish Property in the Nazi-Occupied Areas of the Soviet Union," *Yad Vashem Studies* XXI (2000): 109–48; and Dieter Pohl, "Der Raub an den Juden im besetzten Osteuropa 1939–1942," in Constantin Goschler and Philipp Ther (eds.), *Raub und Restitution: "Arisierung" und Rückerstattung des jüdischen Eigentums in Europa* (Frankfurt am Main: Fischer Taschenbuch, 2003), pp. 58–72. Pohl argues that generally in Eastern Europe the robbery of Jewish property was motivated more by ideological than economic motives and that these confiscations were of only limited significance to the German war economy, see p. 66; see also Martin Dean, "Die Enteignung 'jüdischen Eigentums' im Reichskommissariat Ostland 1941– 1944," in Irmtrud Wojak and Peter Hayes (eds.), *"Arisierung" im Nationalsozialismus: Volksgemeinschaft, Raub und Gedächtnis* (Frankfurt am Main: Campus, 2000), pp. 201–18.

[4] Vladimir Adamushko, Galina Knat'ko, and Natalia Redkozubova (eds.), *"Nazi Gold" from Belarus: Documents and Materials* (Minsk: National Archive of the Republic of Belarus, 1998); see also the review by Leonid Smilovitsky, "Nazi Confiscation of Jewish Property in Belorussia," *Jews in Eastern Europe* 3 (37) (Winter 1998): 75–79; Hennadii Boriak, Maryna Dubyk, and Natalia Makovska (eds.) *"Natsystske zoloto" z Ukraïny: u poshukakh arkhivnykh svidchen*, 2 vols. (Kiev: Ukraïnskyi natsionalnyi fond "Vzaiemorozuminnia i prymyrennia", 1998). The focus on "Nazi gold" conveyed by these titles misrepresents the comprehensive nature of Nazi expropriation of Jewish property, as well as much other state and private property in the Occupied Eastern Territories.

at a national and even a local level, looking more closely at the role of the local non-Jewish population.[5]

What happened to the property, and which organizations processed it and profited directly from its theft? Is it possible to assess the degree of corruption involved? What was the role of the local population, and to what extent did Jewish property act as a motive for participation in the killings? Finally, what does the perspective of the victims add to our understanding of the expropriation process? What measures did Jews take to preserve some small part of their property in the hope that it might help them survive? These are some of the questions that are addressed in this chapter. A careful examination of these issues can tell us much about the implementation of the Holocaust and about the role Jewish property played within the dynamic social processes involved.

With the assistance of much previously inaccessible documentation from the archives of Eastern Europe, it is now possible to examine in much greater local detail the role that Jewish property played. Although only a fraction of the material has been preserved, information regarding seized Jewish property includes in some cases the victims' names and detailed lists of the property taken; its contemporaneous value and the income derived from property sales are often recorded. Sadly, these property records are some of the few remaining testimonies to the many Jewish communities that were completely wiped out in Eastern Europe. For example, on August 15, 1941, the local German commandant in the town of Korzec (Korets) in Volhynia made a list of the property taken from 77 named Jews who were most probably among 250 people shot on that day, among them Taube Dussai, who surrendered "two rings."[6]

Such rare contemporaneous documentation can help us establish both who was murdered and what they once owned. It provides a vital key to the names of many thousands of individuals whose lives were so cruelly cut short. However, these documents can only be understood fully when contextualized with the aid of parallel sources, such as survivor testimony, administrative correspondence, and the evidence from postwar investigations.

---

[5] See, for example, Katrin Reichelt, "Der Anteil von Letten an der Enteignung der Juden Ihres Landes," in *Beiträge zur Geschichte des Nationalsozialismus*, vol. 19, *Kooperation und Verbrechen: Formen der "Kollaboration" im östlichen Europa 1939–1945* (Göttingen: Wallstein, 2003), pp. 224–42.

[6] BAL, R 2104/23, pp. 972–89. Geographical names used here are according to the political conventions of 1938;, thus, the Polish spellings are given for many towns in present-day Belarus and Ukraine.

Throughout the occupied East, a considerable share of Jewish property was collected from the victims at the killing sites. This reflected the more direct temporal and geographic link between the robbery and murder of the Jews in this region. Here, the nature of the local economy, reflected in less developed banking and taxation systems, forced the Germans to rely more on extortion and direct force than on legal and bureaucratic instruments. Indeed, right from the start, the invasion of Poland was accompanied by economic plunder on an unprecedented scale.

Poland: Effects of the German Onslaught

The devastating effects of the German military campaign and of the initial weeks of military administration on the Polish economy are easily under-estimated because of the short duration of the fighting. The records of the Berlin Restitution Archive,[7] however, provide ample evidence of the massive destruction and looting in Poland during the first few months of German occupation. During that time, officials under Göring's direction sought to strip Poland of everything that could be of use to the war effort. Jewish businesses and shops were hit especially hard, as many Jewish pro-prietors fled before the advancing Wehrmacht, and Jewish businesses were dominant in many industries, such as leather, fur, and textiles, that were of particular interest to German looting agencies.

Almost immediately, the military administration issued decrees restrict-ing Jewish economic activities. On September 12, 1939, it prohibited the movement or sale of Jewish property.[8] A further military decree on Septem-ber 18 blocked Jewish-owned bank accounts. Henceforth, they could not receive any payment in excess of 550 złoty in cash – anything more had to be paid into a blocked account. In addition, the amount that Jewish fami-lies could withdraw from banks was limited to 250 złoty per week, with a maximum amount of only 2,000 złoty in cash permitted outside the bank per family. In November, the withdrawal limit was reduced to 500 złoty per month. These stringent regulations made the conduct of trade virtually

---

[7] The "Archiv für Wiedergutmachung," created to assist with the settlement of restitution cases by the Berlin courts in the 1960s, is now located in the Landesarchiv Berlin (LAB), B Rep. 039-01.

[8] LAB, B Rep. 039-01/244 (Polen-Allgemein 1), VO betr.: Das Verbot der Verlagerung und Übertragung jüdischen beweglichen und unbeweglichen Vermögens in den von den deutschen Truppen besetzten Gebieten, September 12, 1939.

impossible for Jews and led to searches for concealed cash. Many businesses were soon forced into liquidation.[9]

The blocking of bank accounts probably affected a smaller percentage of Jews in Poland than in the Reich, because many small Jewish traders there did not customarily use banks. In addition, some Jews had withdrawn their savings as a precautionary measure when war broke out. German measures taken to manage the Polish currency, such as converting it to Reichsmark on a limited scale inside the Reich, and stamping it in the General Government to forestall the import of old notes from the Soviet or German-incorporated territories, also wiped out much of Jewish savings in cash. In addition, the *Devisenschutzkommandos* (Currency Protection Squads, DSKs) were active in occupied Poland, securing gold and foreign currency held by Jews in bank safes and paying it into the *Reichskreditkassen* (Reich Credit Banks, RKKs) for transfer to the Reichsbank.[10]

At the start of the war, many Jews fled their homes and took refuge in towns and cities farther east, especially in Warsaw, where probably some 100,000 Jewish refugees gathered. The Germans bombed Warsaw heavily before its capture, concentrating particularly on Jewish residential areas. Estimates suggest that more than 20,000 Jewish apartments were destroyed or burned and that more than 5,000 Jews were killed directly in the bombardment of Warsaw alone.[11] For those who survived, the physical and economic disruptions were considerable, as the German occupying forces robbed many Jewish businesses in the chaotic conditions that ensued.

The flood of new restrictions made life very hard for Jewish refugees, who were separated from their customary infrastructure. The enforcement of a curfew at night and prohibitions on traveling by train made it hard for them to return home or conduct business. Then in December, as the civil administration was being established, new decrees forbade Jews from relocating without permission, introduced forced labor, and restricted Jews' ability to sell tools or machines. The German administration banned Jews from certain professions such as the law and denied them public pensions and welfare support. Under these conditions, many Jews relied on the support of

---

[9] LAB, B Rep. 039-01/244 (Polen-Allgemein 1), "Die Zerstörung der jüdischen wirtschaftlichen Positionen in Polen," undated German report, probably from July 1940.

[10] See Werner Präg and Hans Jacobmeyer (eds.), *Das Diensttagebuch des deutschen Generalgouverneurs in Polen 1939–1945* (Stuttgart: Deutsche Verlags-Anstalt, 1975), p. 183.

[11] Władysław Bartoszewski, *Warsaw Death Ring, 1939–1944* (Warsaw: Interpress Publishers, 1968), p. 18, notes that the German bombing and shelling of Warsaw resulted in some 60,000 civilian casualties and the destruction of 12 percent of the city's buildings. For slightly different figures, see also Shmuel Spector and Geoffrey Wigoder (eds.), *The Encyclopedia of Jewish Life before and during the Holocaust* (Jerusalem: Yad Vashem, 2001).

their own welfare organizations and what little help they still received from abroad. The new "Jewish Councils" appointed by the Germans organized recruitment for forced labor together with the Labor Offices (*Arbeitsämter*) of the local administration, mainly to prevent the Germans from simply abducting Jews from the streets.[12]

Initial Confiscations

The initial wave of confiscations in Poland demonstrated both the overlapping competencies of various German agencies and the exploitation of confiscation decrees to cover abuses both private and official. For instance, during the first few weeks, the SS and other Nazi authorities confiscated large stocks of fur coats and unfinished pelts from Jewish furriers and fur traders in cities such as Warsaw and Cracow.[13] The more valuable furs were destined for Leipzig, the center of the German fur industry, to be exported; many were exported to Sweden, where they were used to pay for vitally needed iron ore. Less valuable items were sold on the German market. However, one SS-Standartenführer came under investigation for sending furs from Warsaw to Munich to be sold by a relative. After this scandal the SS had to hand over to the Four-Year Plan administration of the remaining furs it had collected at the depot in Warsaw.[14]

One Jewish woman recalled after the war that in the fall of 1939 her husband, who owned a fur shop in Warsaw, received orders in the name of the German commandant that Jews had to surrender all valuables, including gold, silver, furs, and electrical equipment. This order was published on the streets, and Jews who did not comply were threatened with the death penalty. In consequence, her husband gave up her personal jewelry together with a list of the contents of the shop to the SS command post at the office of the Jewish Council. Soon afterward, six SS men came with a lorry to

---

[12] LAB, B Rep. 039-01/244 (Polen-Allgemein 1), "Die Zerstörung der jüdischen wirtschaftlichen Positionen in Polen." The same article estimates there were 500,000 Jewish refugees in the General Government.

[13] LAB, B Rep. 039-01/274 (Polen-Fabrikeinrichtungen 5), Verbindungsoffizier OKW Wi Rü. Amt zur HTO report of June 10, 1940. On the confiscations, see also the statement of Fritz Schultz on May 28, 1964 and those of other witnesses to be found in file LAB, B Rep. 039-01/251 (Polen-Pelze).

[14] LAB, B Rep. 039-01/251 (Polen-Pelze), statement of Hans Schultz on October, 2, 1964; Beschluss LG Berlin October 30, 1964; statement of Dr. von Wendorff on March 3, 1967; statement of Carlos Kropp on August 27, 1964; (148 WGK) 81 WGA 6707.59(42.64), Beschluss Landgericht (LG) Berlin April 1, 1965, summary of statement of former official Hildebrandt.

transport away more than seventy fur coats and thousands of untreated skins. The SS men did not issue any receipts.[15]

According to decrees issued on November 16, 1939, and on January 24, 1940, the requisition of Jewish property was permitted only when it was needed specifically for public purposes. In practice, however, confiscations were frequently conducted arbitrarily and without receipts. German officials would enter Jewish houses and remove furniture and other items even from quite poor Jews. Such requisitions were intended primarily to equip German offices, but much was diverted into private channels.

One large-scale source of confiscations was the property left behind in the houses of Jews and Poles who had fled before the advancing German forces or been arrested by the German security forces. For example, a Polish railway worker observed in Cracow at the end of 1939 how the Germans organized the loading of furniture, paintings, carpets, furs, and crystal onto a train destined for the Reich. He was able to establish that these items had been removed from the apartment of a wealthy Jew who had fled.[16]

An Austrian civilian, L. W., was assigned to Cracow by the Four-Year Plan to assist with the valuation of fur stocks confiscated there. He recalled that his "duties were very burdensome, as he appeared there merely as an instrument of the Nazi authorities." L. W. claimed that he tried to be generous in his valuations and even hid the odd fur when inspecting shops so that the Jewish owners (often present) would not lose everything. The assessed prices were subsequently to be paid into blocked accounts and the inspected goods transported to Berlin. From one firm, "Ament," German officials removed more than RM 13,000 worth of goods. L. W. observed that "in Cracow a great many things were taken from the Jews." He discovered that large amounts of jewelry and silver had been collected and stored in a gym hall in large chests. He was surprised that few security measures were taken and believed that items were stolen from this hoard.[17]

Another German official who served in Radom stated that the confiscations from Jewish tanners and furriers continued up until the summer of 1940 and that large amounts of leather were dispatched from there to the Reich.[18] The trustee of a Jewish tannery in Radom recalled that, after the confiscations in the fall of 1939, only a small amount was paid into the blocked account of the company, which in any case was of no assistance to

[15] LAB, B Rep. 039-01/251 (Polen-Pelze), (148 WGK) 41 WGA 6659 verbunden mit 6661/59 (112/63) Beschluss, February 18, 1965.

[16] LAB, B Rep. 039-01/252 (Polen-Hausrat), statement of Roman Jasiewicz on September 26, 1959; D. Pohl, "Der Raub," p. 63.

[17] LAB, B Rep. 039-01/251 (Polen-Pelze), statement of L. W. on April 13, 1965.

[18] Ibid., statement of H. K. on January 17, 1967.

the former Jewish owner, who was permitted no access to these funds at all.[19] In Łódź – which was in the incorporated territories – the owners of Jewish textile businesses were requested through public announcements to hand over their wares to the Łódź Public Trading Company (*Litzmannstädter Warenhandelsgesellschaft*) in exchange for receipts. No compensation was paid, but the Jewish owners were promised that payments would follow later. Because the Polish textile industry was largely in Jewish hands, soon only a few companies remained in business due to the shortage of raw materials.[20]

A rough idea of the scale of these early confiscations can be gained from the correspondence between the Economic Armaments Office of the Wehrmacht High Command and the *Haupttreuhandstelle Ost* (Main Trustee Office East, HTO) in June 1940. Since November 15, 1939 (when the civil administration was established), more than 20,000 railroad cars of materials had been transported to the Reich, and the HTO sought compensation on behalf of the businesses now under their control. For example, it was reported that leather and furs worth RM 2.75 million had been sent to the Reich, as well as RM 3.2 million of cotton from Łódź. The total value of all such raw materials exceeded RM 73 million. In the face of these claims, the Wehrmacht agreed to pay some modest compensation to the HTO. These delayed negotiations explain the slow repayment of sums to businesses, most of which had been liquidated, placed under trusteeship, or sold in the meantime.[21] As a former official of the Trustee Office in Warsaw noted, "Doubtless, there were also many 'wild confiscations,'" in addition to those where some record was kept.[22]

The initial phase of the occupation was characterized by the systematic seizure of raw materials for the German war effort, which in part degenerated into private exploitation and unrestricted plundering beyond even the broad scope authorized by official decrees. However, as in the Reich before, precisely such excesses forced the authorities to require a more careful accounting of Jewish property, including the investigation and punishment of egregious offenders. By January 1940, Hans Frank, who was in charge of the General Government, had changed the direction of economic

---

[19] LAB, B Rep. 039-01/272 (Polen-Fabrikeinrichtungen 5), statement of M. D. on April 24, 1967.

[20] LAB, B Rep. 039-01/271 (Polen-Fabrikeinrichtungen 5), statement of K. K. on December 22, 1966.

[21] LAB, B Rep. 039-01/274 (Polen-Fabrikeinrichtungen 5), Report of Verbindungsoffizier OKW Wi Rü. Amt zur HTO, June 10, 1940.

[22] LAB, B Rep. 039-01/271 (Polen-Fabrikeinrichtungen 5), statement of Dr. B. on April 28, 1964.

policy from the initial asset stripping toward a more sustainable exploitation of local resources. To implement this strategy, reliable bureaucratic structures were created to manage and exploit formerly Jewish businesses and real estate in the interests of the Reich.

The Treuhandstelle (and Haupttreuhandstelle Ost)

According to Max Winkler, the man appointed by Hermann Göring to establish the HTO, which operated in those Polish territories directly incorporated into the Reich, its main objectives included the "elimination of any unauthorized confiscation or enrichment of individuals," as well as the uniform administration of confiscated properties. The HTO provided credits where necessary, oversaw trustees, and either liquidated or sold many of the businesses it took over.[23] The administrative split between the HTO, which was under the direct control of Göring's Four-Year Plan, and the *Treuhandstellen* (Trustee Offices) in the General Government, which occurred shortly after the establishment of the civil administration there, reflected the competing claims to Polish and Jewish property. Once Hans Frank began to administer the General Government with an eye to maintaining its economic viability, he did not want a separate organization operating within his administration answerable directly to Göring's Four-Year Plan, intent mainly on stripping assets.[24] Therefore, the Treuhandstelle became one of the the the main mechanisms by which Jewish property was exploited in the East.

A report on the first year of the Treuhandstelle's work in Cracow noted that, in November 1939, it had initially taken over many of the trustees appointed by the military. Among its main tasks were the registration and administration of factories and businesses abandoned by their owners (including many belonging to Jews) and the enforcement of the prohibition on the transfer or sale of Jewish businesses. In October 1940, the Trustee Office in the Cracow district administered 297 industrial enterprises; 849 trade and craft businesses; 2 banks; 2,640 houses and apartments; 534 hotels,

---

[23] *Trials of War Criminals before the Nuernberg Military Tribunals under Control Council Law No. 10, Nuernberg, October 1946-April 1949* (hereafter Green Series) (Washington, DC: USGPO, 1952), vol. 13, pp. 742–45, Extracts from an Affidavit of Max Winkler, May 7, 1948.

[24] Jeanne Dingell, "Property Seizures from Poles and Jews: The Activities of the Haupttreuhandstelle Ost," in *Confiscation of Jewish Property in Europe, 1933–1945: New Sources and Perspectives, Symposium Proceedings* (Washington, DC: United States Holocaust Memorial Museum, 2003), p. 34; Dieter Pohl, *Von der "Judenpolitik" zum Judenmord: Der Distrikt Lublin des Generalgouvernements 1939–1944* (Frankfurt am Main: Peter Lang, 1993), p. 74.

bars, and restaurants; and 37 pharmacies.[25] Yet, the Trustee Office took over more than abandoned businesses. From the start, it had instructions to take over or liquidate all Jewish businesses of economic significance. Therefore, in 1940 a more systematic policy of Aryanization focused on strategic industries and locations. Shortages of reliable trustees and qualified entrepreneurs held back full-scale "Aryanization" in some locations, as it was not desired that Poles themselves should establish a middle class by taking over Jewish businesses. At the same time, plans were made to hold back the sale of some businesses to give men returning from the front a chance to benefit at the end of the war.[26] However, in Warsaw it is estimated that 75 percent of Jewish businesses and enterprises had been liquidated by the middle of 1940.[27] By this time, the denial of access to raw materials had already starved out many. Ghettoization finished off the last remnant in 1941.[28]

The transfer of businesses and real estate into the hands of the state or other new owners necessarily required an elaborate legal framework and administration. Inside the Reich, Polish and Jewish property could be confiscated in accordance with the decrees for the Confiscation of Former Polish State Property (January 15, 1940) and for the Confiscation of Property of Citizens of the Former Polish State (September 17, 1940).[29] No single decree regulated the exclusion of the Jews from the economy in the General Government, but sufficient legal authority had been provided at the start of the occupation when regional authorities (Trustee Offices) were given the power to appoint trustees and conduct confiscations.

The management and the sale of former Jewish real estate provided an important source of income for the German administration. However, the civil administration had to compete with the *Reichskommissar für die Festigung deutschen Volkstums* (Reich Commissar for the Strengthening of the German Racial Community, RKFDV), headed by Himmler, and other Party organs for control of this resource. As in Germany, deed books had to be changed and businesses legally registered. By 1943, in the absence of a strict legal basis for the confiscation of real estate belonging to the murdered Jews, the civil authorities applied the "confiscation order" of January 1940, originally

[25] LAB, B Rep. 039-01/244 (Polen-Allgemein 1).

[26] LAB, B Rep. 039-01/244 (Polen-Allgemein 1), Lagebericht Kreishauptmannschaft Tarnow für Sept. 1940. In the Danzig region, a special trustee company (*Auffangsgesellschaft für Kriegsteilnehmerbetriebe des Handels in Danzig-Westpreussen GmbH*) was created to manage companies until they could be sold to former soldiers later.

[27] Isaiah Trunk, *Judenrat: The Jewish Councils in Eastern Europe under Nazi Occupation* (Lincoln: University of Nebraska Press, 1996), p. 64.

[28] D. Pohl, Von der "Judenpolitik," p. 75.

[29] J. Dingell, "Property Seizures," pp. 36–37.

intended for "abandoned properties," so that Jewish real estate could be sold promptly without incurring further costs.[30]

The staff of the Trustee Offices included many private individuals, such as bankers and lawyers from inside the Reich.[31] Trustees paid themselves generous salaries and sometimes charged high expenses to the companies they ran. Although the Trustee Office was designed to regulate the temporary administration of confiscated property, it became synonymous with inefficiency and graft. Even the attempt to bureaucratize the confiscation process suffered from the "wild East" mentality, and the veneer of legality served here mainly as an additional tool for rampant exploitation.

In Rzeszów, the local German administration boasted in October 1940 of the continued successful progress of Aryanization. The author of the report was pleased to confirm that even a town so thoroughly "infested" with Jews as Rzeszów could be Aryanized without bringing industry to a halt. Nearly all the main streets would soon be cleared of Jewish shops, and the few remaining all had Aryan personnel so that their "Jewish character" was not apparent. The removal of Jewish shops from the main streets had resulted in their concentration in streets of their own. The creation of a ghetto had not proved possible. Instead, Aryan and Jewish streets for living and shopping had been demarcated. The Aryanization of the countryside had also been started. In two country towns "Aryan" ironmongers were established after the Jewish shops had been liquidated.[32]

What was the outcome of this enormous program of trustee administration in occupied Poland, comparable in scale with the privatization of state industries in East Germany after 1989? In his recent analysis of the activities of the HTO in the Incorporated Territories, Bernhard Rosenkötter stresses the difficulty in obtaining reliable figures by which to assess them. Although the Four-Year Plan estimated the value of property under HTO supervision at RM 6 or 7 billion in 1942, the final figures published by the HTO in March 1945 came to only RM 2.17 billion, to which should be added another RM 900 million in real estate. Much property had been sold by then at less than market price to further the economic integration of ethnic Germans. The value of administered property, including that of businesses, had frequently declined due to lack of investment or

---

[30] See Bogdan Musial, *Deutsche Zivilverwaltung und Judenverfolgung im Generalgouvernement: Eine Fallstudie zum Distrikt Lublin 1939–1944* (Wiesbaden: Harrassowitz, 1999), pp. 312–18.

[31] LAB, B Rep. 039-01/271 (Polen-Fabrikeinrichtungen 5), statement of Bruno Stahlke on March 3, 1965.

[32] LAB, B Rep. 039-01/244 (Polen-Allgemein 1), report from Dist. Krakau, Reichshof (Rzeszow), October 30, 1940.

adverse wartime conditions. Rosenkötter stresses in particular that the net income going directly to the benefit of the Reich, only RM 1-1.5 billion, was piteously small in comparison with what was extracted from occupied France (RM 10 billion up to the end of 1941) in "occupation costs." It was clearly well below the expectations of Göring's Four-Year Plan Office and of the Reich Finance Ministry.[33]

The bulk of administered property consisted of industrial plant facilities, factory equipment, and real estate, much of which, it should be stressed, had previously been in Polish rather than Jewish hands. However, from the reports of the regional offices, between 5 percent and 17 percent of the property they handled came from furniture and other personal items confiscated from the houses and apartments of people who had fled, were arrested, or had actually or euphemistically been resettled. This proportion was especially high in Eastern Upper Silesia. Banks, insurance companies, and savings institutions made up about 14 percent of the total property administered.[34] However, the income from Polish securities was very limited, and the Reichsbank proposed closing down this section within the HTO in August 1944, as it had realized only about RM 1 million and the income from dividends was not even covering the cost of its collection.[35] Much HTO property still remained unsold at the end of the war, partly because of the loss of staff as the war progressed.[36] This picture of limited utilization of the extensive resources administered applies also to the Trustee Offices in the General Government. It is perhaps surprising that the bureaucratic management of these considerable assets contributed comparatively little to the financing of the war.

Cultural Looting

In this more general study, it is not possible to give detailed attention to the looting of cultural items that was also an integral part of German occupation policies in Poland. As elsewhere, several special agencies competed

---

[33] Bernhard Rosenkötter, *Treuhandpolitik: Die "Haupttreuhandstelle Ost" und der Raub polnischer Vermögen 1939–1945* (Essen: Klartext, 2003), pp. 278–79; Reich Finance Minister Schwerin von Krosigk also complained about the high costs of administration and the small net income to the Reich from the Occupied Eastern Territories in a letter dated September 4, 1942, NG-4900.

[34] B. Rosenkötter, *Treuhandpolitik*, pp. 281–85.

[35] LAB, B Rep. 039-01/252 (Polen-Hausrat), p. 98, Reichsbank Direktorium, August 24, 1944.

[36] As of March 1944, massive quantities of gold, silver, and jewelry were also being held by the HTO until transfer to the Reichsbank for processing and sale; see NI-13819, NARA, RG-238, T-301.

over the spoils from the start. For example, Kommando Paulsen, acting under the authority of the RSHA, was active in Warsaw and seized what it viewed as objects of "German" cultural value. Beginning in October 1939, Governor Hans Frank authorized Dr. Kajetan Mühlmann and his staff to secure artifacts to augment German cultural property.[37] There was also much wanton destruction of Jewish cultural treasures. For example, most of the 400,000-volume library of the Talmudic seminary in Lublin, was burned on the market square in early 1940.[38] Among several organizations that collected Jewish literature from Poland for their own research purposes were the *Rasse- und Siedlungshauptamt* (Race and Settlement Main Office), the *Hohe Schule* (Party Research Institute) in Frankfurt, and the Nazi Party's *Hauptarchiv* (Main Archive). The *Einsatzstab Reichsleiter Rosenberg* (Rosenberg Operational Staff, ERR) that was active in most other occupied territories had no collecting operations in the General Government, as it was not established until after most of the treasure there had already been plundered.

Ghettoization

Jewish property was widely seized and exploited in western and central Poland during ghettoization. Even prior to the formation of ghettos, the German authorities subjected Jewish communities to forced contributions, coerced by threats or the taking of hostages, in order to raise cash or collect furniture for the newly arrived German officials. Jewish councils often organized the payment of these contributions in the form of a tax within the community.[39] Nevertheless, these methods remained local and quite primitive compared with the results achieved through the centralized tax system in Germany or even by tapping blocked accounts in France or Bulgaria.[40] Certainly, the flight of capital from Polish banks at the start of

---

[37] See Andrzej Mezy'nski, *Kommando Paulsen: Organisierter Kunstraub in Polen 1942–45* (Cologne: Dittrich-Verlag, 2000), pp. 7–10. See also IMT, Blue Series, vol. XXVIII, pp. 293–98 (1773-PS) and vol. XXI, pp. 512–13 (3042-PS).

[38] LAB, Archiv für Wiedergutmachung, Gutachten des Instituts für Zeitgeschichte, March 13, 1963.

[39] D. Pohl, *Von der "Judenpolitik,"* p. 79.

[40] In Bulgaria, part of the contents of blocked accounts was transferred to a "Jewish communal fund" that was also to be used to finance Jewish "resettlement" by the Commissariat for Jewish Affairs; see LAB, B Rep. 039-01/318, German translation of Ministerial Decision no. 4,567 (anti-Jewish legislation establishing the Commissariat) issued by the Interior Ministry and published in the *Bulgarian Official Journal* 192 (August 29, 1942). I am grateful to Götz Aly for bringing this document to my attention. The Bulgarian practice was based on a similar French model; see Jean-Marc Dreyfus, "French Banks and

the war and the subsequent currency reforms made financial mechanisms of exploitation less effective here.

The forced resettlement of Jews and Poles from the Incorporated Territories beginning in the fall of 1939 and the formation of ghettos resulted in considerable material losses. Jews could take only a limited amount of property and had to leave in haste. In Łódź (Litzmannstadt), the confiscation of Jewish property was closely linked to the establishment of the ghetto. On April 3, 1940, the mayor of Litzmannstadt decreed that because, "in accordance with Reich laws Jewish property was considered confiscated," all Jewish property was to be registered on lists and secured, with the exception of just a few items required for immediate daily use.[41] The police organized many arbitrary confiscations. However, a considerable portion of Jewish property was collected by the ghetto administration to help pay for its own operations. The introduction of a special ghetto currency also drained off most remaining exchangeable values from within the ghetto.[42] When the other Jewish communities around Łódź were liquidated during the course of 1942, their remaining property was collected and sold with the income paid to the Łódź ghetto administration.[43] This again reflected the Nazi practice of making anti-Jewish measures self-financing.

Although there were many reasons why ghettoes were established, one of their effects was to drain remaining property out of the Jewish population, as Jews were forced to sell their last possessions in the search for food. This employment of starvation to complete spoliation had little to do with legal norms. It was a further act of terror inflicted on the Jews before consigning them to their deaths. Any remaining valuables were taken away in repeated searches during the deportations. By systematically stripping Jewish property both before and inside the ghettos, and by physically isolating the Jews, the German authorities drove whole communities toward destruction by rendering them unable to sustain themselves from their own resources and by their own efforts.

Aryanization 1940–1944," in Oliver Rathkolb (ed.), *Revisiting the National Socialist Legacy: Coming to Terms with Forced Labor, Expropriation, Compensation, and Restitution* (Innsbruck: Studien Verlag, 2002): 145–53, here, p. 151.

[41] *Dokumenty i materiały do dziejów okupacji niemieckiej w Polsce*, vol. 3 (*Ghetto Lodzkie*) (Łódź, 1946), pp. 74–75, Der Oberbürgermeister Litzmannstadt an den Ältesten der Juden, Herrn Rumkowski, April 30, 1940.

[42] Ingo Loose, "Die Enteignung der Juden im besetzten Polen, 1939–45," in Katharina Stengel (ed.), *Vor der Vernichtung: Die staatliche Enteignung der Juden im Nationalsozialismus* (Frankfurt am Main: Campus, 2007), pp. 283–307. I am grateful to the author for making his paper available to me before its publication.

[43] *Dokumenty i materiały*, vol. 3, pp. 209–12.

Inside the ghettos, a harsh black market based around the barter of remaining mobile assets came to dominate what economic life still existed. In the Warsaw ghetto, the inflated prices for food soon drained people's reserves until only the "wealthiest" could afford to buy on the black market.[44] In the smaller ghettos, the economic restrictions were sometimes easier to circumvent. In Glowno, for example, close to the border with the Reich, through bribery Jews continued to have access to the city outside the ghetto and were able to continue working, smuggling food, and trading on the black market. Thus, there was no massive starvation in Glowno from the establishment of the ghetto in April 1940 up to the deportation of the majority of the population to the Warsaw ghetto in February 1941.[45]

As the well-known conflict between "productionists" and "attritionists" (the former wished to exploit the Jews, the latter to starve them out) among the German ghetto administrators described by Christopher Browning illustrates,[46] the physical impact of the establishment of ghettos on the Jewish population was clear to the German authorities. In January 1941, the Germans confiscated all Jewish property in Warsaw located outside the ghetto walls, and many people lost in one blow most of their life savings. The affected properties included 1,700 grocery shops and 2,500 other businesses.[47] Inevitably, the shortages of food and material goods within the ghettos put added strain on the Jewish councils and their administrative organs as they attempted to distribute fairly what was left. Inequalities in distribution, corruption, and any harsh treatment of other Jews caused many to recall with considerable bitterness the activities of some Jewish councils.[48]

Even for those who managed to escape from the ghettos and live on the "Aryan" side, life and death often depended on their ability to salvage something of their former property. For example, Celina Greenspan and her husband managed to sell most of the valuables they had stored with friendly Poles, garnering several thousand złoty. They used this money to buy "Aryan" papers that helped at least Celina to survive.[49] However, the

---

[44] I. Levin, *Walls Around*, pp. 18–19.

[45] See S. Spector and G. Wigoder (eds.), *The Encyclopedia of Jewish Life*, p. 435.

[46] See Christopher Browning, *The Path to Genocide: Essays on Launching the Final Solution* (Cambridge: Cambridge University Press, 1992), pp. 28–56.

[47] I. Levin, *Walls Around*, p. 69

[48] I. Trunk, *Judenrat*, Appendix I, pp. 577–85; as Spector notes, in the testimonies and memorial books "extreme expressions – both positive and negative" are to be found, largely uncensored; see S. Spector, *The Holocaust of Volhynian Jews*, pp. 165–66.

[49] USHMM, RG–02.208M, Pamietniki Żydów (Memoirs of Jews, 1939–1945, Jewish Historical Institute, sygn. 302), reel 6, #53 Celina Grünszpan testimony. Her husband was unfortunately killed in the Warsaw Uprising in August 1944.

blackmailers (*szmalcowniks*) – probably several thousand individuals around Warsaw – made survival an expensive business for Jews living on the "Aryan" side and made the ability to preserve part of one's prior wealth both more crucial and more difficult.[50]

"Aktion Reinhard": Exploitation and Corruption

The most notorious example of the theft of gold and other property from Holocaust victims in the East was that recovered directly from the death camps. In particular, the seventy-six deliveries of foreign exchange, precious metals, coins, and jewelry to the Reichsbank by SS officer Bruno Melmer from mid-1942 have been the subject of much intensive research.[51] The Final Report of the Independent Commission of Experts (ICE) appointed by the Swiss government concluded that, although the Reichsbank had sold 120 kilograms of "Melmer" gold to Switzerland, this sale represented only a small proportion of the total of gold recovered – at least 2,580 kilograms – most of which was sold via Germany's two largest commercial banks, Deutsche Bank and Dresdner Bank.[52] As Peter Hayes notes, the last thirty-three Melmer deliveries were not even processed for sale, but were recovered in bags at the end of the war by U.S. forces from a salt mine in Thuringia, reflecting the Reich's ability to retain considerable reserves of precious metals through the very end of the war.[53]

The stripping of property from Jewish victims during the round-ups and the systematic collection and sorting of the items they had left behind were an integral part of the so-called Aktion Reinhard mass murder campaign. Bertrand Perz and Thomas Sandkühler argue that the processing of all Jewish property in the General Government, together with that collected in

---

[50] Gunnar S. Paulsson, *Secret City: The Hidden Jews of Warsaw 1940–1945* (New Haven, CT: Yale University Press, 2002), pp. 148–52.

[51] NARA, RG 260, OMGUS (Office of Military Government, U.S. Zone (Germany)), records of the Finance Advisor, Specific Functional Policy Programs, Records re. FED 1947–49, Box 167, 2/167/5, Non-Monetary Gold: statement of SS Capt. Melmer on 15 July 1947; see also, for example *U.S. and Allied Efforts to Recover and Restore Gold and Other Assets Stolen or Hidden by Germany during World War II: Preliminary Study*, coordinated by Stuart E. Eizenstat (Washington DC: Department of State, May 1997), especially Chapter 9, "Disposal by the U.S. of captured gold looted by Germany from individual victims of Nazi persecution and from European central banks"; Independent Commission of Experts, *Switzerland and Gold Transactions in the Second World War* (Bern: EDMZ, 1998), pp. 35–36 and 48–49.

[52] Independent Commission of Experts: Switzerland – Second World War, *Switzerland, National Socialism and the Second World War: Final Report* (Zürich: Pendo, 2002), p. 249.

[53] Peter Hayes, *From Cooperation to Complicity: Degussa in the Third Reich* (Cambridge: Cambridge University Press, 2004), pp. 181–82.

Auschwitz, was viewed by some SS officials as comprising a single coordinated operation.[54] In any case, SS and Police Leader Odilo Globocnik prepared a detailed report listing about RM 180 million worth of textiles, cash, precious metals, foreign currency, jewels, and other valuables collected during Aktion Reinhard; the report also explained that much other property, such as furniture, food, shoes, and so on, was utilized for the benefit of ethnic Germans or to cover the cost of operations and so did not appear in the accounts.[55] At the local level, groups of Jewish prisoners were forced to gather remaining items from the emptied ghettos and sort them in warehouses; the more valuable items were forwarded to Lublin, whereas less desirable articles were auctioned locally and the proceeds paid into special accounts (see Figure 5.1).[56]

In spite of Himmler's repeated warnings to the SS to avoid any hint of personal corruption, the temptations in the concentration camps and death camps, which themselves existed in effect outside the law, were too great to be resisted. The investigations conducted by Dr. Morgen of the RSHA did not succeed in causing the dismissal of any of Himmler's chosen camp commanders, mainly because the Nazi leaders did not want to compromise the secrecy surrounding the camps. Nevertheless, the files reveal widespread venality among SS guards and officials.[57]

What is known about the SS death camps in German-occupied Poland derives in part from the reports of a few surviving Jewish prisoners who had been ordered to sort the property of those murdered and to perform other functions necessary to the running of the camp. For example, after her deportation from Westerbork to Sobibor on April 9, 1943, Selma Engel (née Wijnberg) was assigned to sort clothes and to search them for any valuables. She escaped during the uprising later in 1943. Her future husband, Chaim, who helped her flee, managed to take with him an eyeglasses case filled with diamonds and gold. This proved vital to their survival, as they were able to use the valuables to bribe farmers to hide them for a while. However, by the time of the liberation the pair had absolutely no money left and did not possess any proper clothes, due to the heavy toll of surviving in

---

[54] Bertrand Perz and Thomas Sandkühler, "Auschwitz und die 'Aktion Reinhard' 1942–1945: Judenmord und Raubpraxis aus neuer Sicht," *Zeitgeschichte*, 26. Jg., Heft 5 (Sept./Okt. 1999): 283–316.

[55] NO-059 and NO-62, *Trials of War Criminals*, Green Series, vol. V, pp. 725–31.

[56] Jacek A. Młynarczyk, "Organisation und Durchführung der 'Aktion Reinhard' im Distrikt Radom," in Bogdan Musial (ed.), *"Aktion Reinhardt": Der Völkermord an den Juden im Generalgouvernement 1941–1944* (Osnabrück: Fibre, 2004): 165–95, here, p. 187.

[57] Rainer Weinert, "Die Sauberkeit der Verwaltung im Kriege": Der Rechnungshof des Deutschen Reiches 1938–1946 (Opladen: Westdeutscher Verlag, 1993), pp. 140–41.

the Polish countryside.[58] Even after the Red Army had driven out the German occupying forces, some marauding Poles, many of them motivated primarily by greed, continued to attack some of the few surviving Jews. Jews attempting to reclaim their property, especially houses, were often greeted with open hostility, antisemitic insults, and even violence.[59]

Systematic Plunder in the Occupied Soviet Territories

In the occupied Soviet Union, the rapid progression to mass shooting of the Jewish population during the first months of the German invasion created a situation different from the more gradual deportation of the Jews in Western Europe and even central Poland. Certainly, the value of Jewish-owned property per family in this region was lower than in much of the rest of Europe.[60] Because few of the Jews in these particular occupied territories owned real estate or businesses, the German authorities were not so concerned with exploiting the existing financial infrastructure or with allaying fears about the effect on business confidence. Therefore, they made almost no effort to conceal the goal of confiscation from the Jewish victims; here the Germans murdered, extorted from, and plundered the Jews from the start.

In any case, Soviet expropriation policies had considerably diminished Jewish property-holding prior to the German invasion. In eastern Poland and the Baltic States, the Soviet authorities had nationalized most private property, especially businesses and real estate. Craftsmen were compelled to work within state-run cooperatives (*artels*) for fixed wages. In Lithuania, the number of private shops was reduced from some 25,000 to about 4,500; all large stores were nationalized. German estimates indicate that only 5 percent of retail trade remained in private hands.[61] In Riga, only about 350 Jewish real estate properties (approximately one-third) escaped

---

[58] USHMM, RG-50.030-0067, Oral History with Selma Wijnberg Engel, July 16, 1990. See also Jules Schelvis, *Vernichtungslager Sobibor* (Münster: Unrast, 2003), p. 276.

[59] See Jan T. Gross, *Fear (Anti-Semitism in Poland after Auschwitz)* (New York: Random House, 2006).

[60] For a rough estimate of per capita wealth that places "Western USSR" very firmly at the bottom of the list, see Sidney Zabludoff, *"And It All But Disappeared": The Nazi Seizure of Jewish Assets* (Policy Forum No. 13) (Jerusalem: Institute of the World Jewish Congress, 1998), p. 30.

[61] USHMM, RG-53.002M, National Archive of the Republic of Belarus (NARB), reel 22, 370-6-20, pp. 178–80, Bericht über Stand und Leistungen der Gesamtwirtschaft des Generalbezirks Litauen 1 September 1941 bis 1 September 1943.

Soviet nationalization.[62] In the Baltic States, Soviet authorities dissolved or incorporated private Jewish banks and credit institutions into the State Bank.[63]

The killing process in this region developed rapidly following the German invasion. The majority of Jews in the Baltic States had been murdered by December 1941. In western Belorussia and western Ukraine, widespread killing "Aktions" in the summer and fall of 1941 were followed by the clearance of most of the ghettos and the murder of their inhabitants in 1942 and the first half of 1943. For the victims, expropriation came in a series of brutal steps linked closely to their physical oppression and murder. Restrictions on trade, the imposition of forced labor, the formation of ghettos, and the raising of forced contributions all followed in rapid succession. The local population also exploited the Jews' ever-present threat of death by demanding high prices for illegal food, extracting bribes, and stealing from empty houses after the massacres.

The extensive surviving archival trail records the considerable efforts undertaken by the Germans to collect, register, and administer Jewish property, primarily for the benefit of the local German administration. Detailed inventories indicate that silver items and money, as well as furniture, clothing, jewelry, and housing, made up the bulk of Jewish property. Gold and foreign currency formed a small, but most valuable part of the loot, as the Germans could use it to buy vital raw materials abroad via the neutral countries. Only the most valuable items were sent to Berlin for sorting and sale. Most household and personal items were used directly by the German administration, sold locally to raise revenue, or distributed among the local populace, with priority given to ethnic Germans. Rents were even collected on some household items and real estate. Jewish forced labor was viewed as a financial asset and booked accordingly in German accounts.

Although all Jewish property was officially declared confiscated by the German civil administration, in practice several separate organizations were involved in its collection, administration, and distribution. Among these were the police, the Wehrmacht, the ERR, and even local collaborationist organizations, such as the Belorussian Self-Help Organization. Corruption was rife at all levels, and the overall income was not large compared to the costs of war.

---

[62] NARA, T-459, reel 21, Wohnungs- u. Immobilienamt Riga-Stadt, May 4, 1942.

[63] BAL, R 29/110, RKK (Reichskreditkasse) Libau report of August 1941; USHMM, RG-53.002M NARB, reel 22, 370-6-20, pp. 178–80, Bericht über Stand und Leistungen der Gesamtwirtschaft des Generalbezirks Litauen, September 1, 1941 to September 1, 1943.

Initial Military Occupation and Deliveries to the War Booty Office

The arrival of the Germans in the summer of 1941 was accompanied by the looting of stores (most of them now state-owned) by local inhabitants. In some places there were also pogroms that almost always involved the plunder or devastation of Jewish property.[64] Among the earliest measures taken by the Germans was the imposition of "contributions" on Jewish communities. In the Belorussian town of Nieśwież (Nesvizh) in mid-October 1941, for example, the local German commandant demanded a ransom of a half-million rubles (RM 50,000) and 2.5 kilograms of gold in exchange for the release of 200 Jewish hostages.[65] In Minsk, forced tax payments by the Jewish population provided a vital initial source of income for the German administration.[66]

From the start, Nazi seizures of Jewish property in the occupied Soviet Union were closely linked to the extermination program. Evidence from the records of the *Reichshauptkasse Beutestelle* (Reich Treasury War Booty Office) demonstrates that the Einsatzgruppen and other mobile killing units sent collections of valuables to Berlin in the wake of the first anti-Jewish Aktions in the summer of 1941. Valuables were routinely collected from victims just prior to mass shootings and initially were treated in a fashion similar to other so-called war booty.[67] Finance Ministry officials in Berlin transcribed detailed reports from the collecting units, some of which left no illusions as to the means by which these valuables had been acquired.[68]

One report consists of a list of mainly silver tableware and jewelry confiscated from Jewish apartments by SS-Hauptscharführer Kaiser of Einsatzkommando 3 on July 22, 1941, following the large-scale arrests and shootings of adult male Jews in Daugavpils, Latvia.[69] Units of Einsatzgruppe A made a particularly weighty delivery via the head of the Security

---

[64] S. Spector, *The Holocaust of Volhynian Jews*, pp. 64–67.

[65] M. Dean, *Collaboration*, p. 44; for further examples, see Y. Arad, "Plunder of Jewish Property," p. 123.

[66] B. Chiari, *Alltag hinter der Front*, pp. 261–62.

[67] See Martin Dean, "Jewish Property Seized in the Occupied Soviet Union in 1941 and 1942: The Records of the *Reichshauptkasse Beutestelle*," *Holocaust and Genocide Studies*, vol. 14 no. 1 (Spring 2000): 83–101. On the actual distinction between "war booty" and Jewish property, see OFDB, Archiv Div. Ordner I (Ausarbeitungen des Archivs des ehem. RFM – Handakte Scheerans), p. 310, Referent Eckhardt, Y 5205/1 – 243 V, October 29, 1942.

[68] M. Dean, "Jewish Property," p. 95.

[69] BAL, R 58/214, Ereignismeldung UdSSR, no. 24, July 16, 1941; Hans-Heinrich Wilhelm, *Die Einsatzgruppe A der Sicherheitspolizei und des SD 1941/42* (Frankfurt am Main: Peter Lang, 1996), pp. 105–106.

Police and SD in Berlin on January 16, 1942. It consisted of 32,446 items packed into 150 chests, cases, and sacks, which reportedly originated from Jewish apartments searched by Einsatzkommando 3 in Daugavpils and also from safe-deposit boxes of Jews seized at the Lithuanian State Bank in Kaunas.[70] The shipment included more than 60 kilograms of gold in various forms. Only one victim is named, Sora Krupit of Panevezys, who owned $45 worth of U.S. Treasury bonds. Among the items carefully recorded in the ledgers for this shipment were U.S. $1,822 in cash, 2,850 teaspoons, 527 silver serviette rings, 1,141 small coffee spoons, more than 5,000 mens' watches, 15.5 kilograms of gold wedding rings, 6.5 kilograms of gold earrings, 61 diamonds, 9.3 kilograms of gold chains, and 0.57 kilograms of dental gold. Household objects, foreign currency, bonds, and jewelry were also included among the loot.[71] A number of the items proved to be of little value. On examining crates newly arrived from the East in April 1942, SS-Brigadeführer Frank of the newly created SS *Wirtschafts- und Verwaltungshauptamt* (SS Main Economic Administration Office, SS WVHA) reported that much of the jewelry was fake or damaged and that many watches were completely worthless.[72] Damaged watches collected in Riga, Latvia, were sent to the ghetto for repair.[73]

During the course of 1942, the Reich Treasury's War Booty Office received considerable amounts of silver from the East, reflecting the fact that many Jewish ritual and household objects are made of silver rather than gold. Shipments containing hundreds of kilos of silver collected by the Wehrmacht were sent from Volhynia and Galicia. From Ortskommandantur II/935, one delivery consisting of more than 2,500 kilos, mostly of silver items collected by the end of August 1941, included 64 kilograms of ritual items from the synagogue in Ostrog.[74] Gold items made up only a small portion of this delivery, partly due to official restrictions on the possession of gold in the Soviet Union (gold wedding rings were among the few such valuables permitted). Surprisingly, much of this loot was stored in Germany and was not rapidly sold off or converted into foreign currency to aid

[70] BAL, R 2104/20, pp. 468–516. Two further chests with metal, silver, and crystal items confiscated from Kaunas were forwarded by the RSHA on April 14, 1942. See also R. Hilberg, *Die Vernichtung der europäischen Juden*, vol. 2, pp. 380–81, citing the value of 3,769,180 rubles for the items taken from Lithuanian banks by EK 3 and noting the protests of Reichskommissar Lohse to HSSPF Prützmann (25 September 1941) against these confiscations in violation of the prerogatives of the civil administration.

[71] BAL, R 2104/20, pp. 468–516.

[72] BAL, R 2104/21, p. 81.

[73] BAL, R 92/10312.

[74] M. Dean, "Jewish property," p. 89; BAL, R 2104/21, pp. 256–57.

the war effort. As late as spring 1944, the Finance Ministry issued urgent instructions to expedite the processing of remaining "war booty" and SS property, such as watches, rather than leaving it lying in the vaults.[75]

German military and police units sometimes collected property directly in conjunction with the mass shootings of Jews, as, for example, in Mir in western Belorussia. On January 27, 1942, a delivery arrived at the War Booty Office in Berlin with 1,822 złoty, seven dollars, and fifty-five old coins "found on the Jews shot on 9 November 1941."[76] The documentation confirms the active role that soldiers of the 8th Company, Infantry Regiment 727, played in Mir, together with the local Belorussian police, as reported also by eyewitnesses and the contemporary report of Hauptkommissar (regional commissar) Friedrich Fenz in Baranowicze.[77] The degree of Wehrmacht participation in such Aktions varied widely, and in many cases they played only a supporting role to the Einsatzgruppen, for example, securing property from former Jewish houses after an Aktion.[78]

In some areas under military administration the wave of murderous killing scarcely abated during the winter of 1941–42. In early 1942, Einsatzgruppe B, assisted by local collaborators and other German personnel, liquidated the remaining ghettos and Jewish settlements in eastern Belorussia and in nearby occupied Russian territory. One example is the town of Chashniki, in the Vitebsk district. After collecting the Jews in a former church building

---

[75] NARA, RG-238, T-301, reel 112, docs. NI-13818-20; see also Nuremberg documents 3942-PS and NO-4096; extract copy of Monthly Report May 1945, published as Anlage 1 in Bundesarchiv, *The Whereabouts of the Records of the Deutsche Reichsbank: A Research Report* (Bundesarchiv R 4 - 2850/18, August 1998); and LAB, A Rep. 092/54622, Verwertung von Beutegut. According to one postwar estimate, approximately RM 280 million in war booty had been resold (*verwertet*) by April 1945, although clearly Jewish property comprised only a small fragment of this total; see NARA, RG-238, T-1139, NG-5342, RFM Restverwaltung, January 5, 1946.

[76] BAL, R 2104/14, p. 181. The cover letter from the paymaster of Second Battalion, Infantry Regiment 727 notes, "The money originates from the shooting of Jews in Mir, which was carried out on November 9, 1941." See BAL, R 2104/14, p. 185. A full English translation of this document is published also in M. Dean, "Jewish Property," p. 88.

[77] Statements by witnesses in the committal proceedings at Dorking in England in the spring of 1996 against the former police chief in Mir, Semion Serafinowicz, indicate clearly the active role of the local police during the November 9 massacre. NARA, RG-238, PS-3667, Report of Hauptkommissar Fenz in Baranowicze on February 10, 1942. See also Martin Dean, "Microcosm: Collaboration and Resistance during the Holocaust in the Mir Rayon of Belarus, 1941–1944," in D. Gaunt, P.A. Levine, and L. Palosuo (eds.), *Collaboration and Resistance during the Holocaust: Belarus, Estonia, Latvia, Lithuania* (Bern: Peter Lang, 2004), pp. 223–60.

[78] M. Dean, "Jewish Property," pp. 85 and 90.

that had been turned into a cultural center under the Soviets, the Secret Field Police and local collaborators shot the remaining 1,000 or so Jews of Chashniki on February 15:

> After the Aktion, the belongings of the murdered Jews were collected, sorted, and, under the auspices of the SD, handed over to the "Bürgermeister" to be sold to the Belorussian population. The receipts were paid into the town's account. Some days later, a group of youngsters, prodded by the rumors of "Jewish gold" left behind by the victims in the underground part of the "church," sallied forth to the crypt, but did not find anything.[79]

The district commissar in Borisov reported in August 1942 that the "Jewish Aktions" took place there prior to the establishment of the civil administration. He maintained that probably the SD and the Wehrmacht had collected most of the portable wealth. Furniture and other usable items had been given to the Wehrmacht and other German offices. Local mayors utilized the remainder for their budgets. Twenty-five gold rubles were forwarded to the *Reichskreditkasse* (Reich Credit Bank, RKK) in Minsk at the beginning of December 1941. Other measures with regard to Jewish property were not deemed necessary.[80] Reports by officials of the Wehrmacht Economic Inspectorate confirm that the town administration had collected a contribution of 300,000 rubles (RM 30,000) from the Jews. The money and other valuables collected during the mass shooting of 7,000 Jews by the SD and the local police in October 1941 were also forwarded to the RKK.[81] Clothes and items of lesser value worth RM 157,000 were sold or distributed free to the poor on the orders of the local mayor, Stanislav Stankevich.[82] Subsequently a few pieces of jewelry, probably of Jewish provenance, were found in the possession of the chief of the local police, D. Ehoff.[83]

---

[79] BA-MA, RH 26-201/17, p. 4; and interviews conducted by Daniel Romanovsky. I am grateful to Daniel Romanovsky for bringing this incident to my attention in connection with work on a forthcoming encyclopedia volume on "Ghettos under German Occupation," in preparation by the Center for Advanced Holocaust Studies at the USHMM.

[80] V. Adamushko, et al. (eds.), *"Nazi Gold" from Belarus*, p. 92, Gebietskommissar Borissow to Generalkommissar Weissruthenien, August 8, 1942; see also C. Gerlach, *Kalkulierte Morde*, p. 681.

[81] LAB, B Rep. 039-01 Archiv für Wiedergutmachung (AfW), vol. 55, pp. 923–25, report of Dr. Wenz, October 22, 1941. Presumably the Reichskasse refers to the Reich Credit Bank (RKK) in Minsk.

[82] USHMM, RG-53.002M NARB, 845-1-206, pp. 318–23, Extract from the interrogation of Ehoff on February 28, 1947; C. Gerlach, *Kalkulierte Morde*, pp. 681–83.

[83] BAL, R 2104/26, pp. 605, 610, and 618.

Jurisdictional Conflicts and Corruption

A particular problem was the array of German agencies handling Jewish property. Naturally, they came into conflict with each other over jurisdiction. Initially, the Wehrmacht was responsible in conjunction with the newly established local administration.[84] However, the establishment of a civil administration in the western districts of the occupied Soviet Union in the summer and fall of 1941 created the infrastructure for the more orderly registration, administration, and sale of Jewish property. Reich Commissar Hinrich Lohse in Ostland proclaimed in October that he would take over all Jewish property, and he ordered its registration, including that already in the possession of non-Jews.[85] The processing of Jewish property kept part of the civil administration busy throughout the entire occupation.[86] Valuables were to be sent to Berlin for processing, with the proceeds booked to the budgets of the Reich Commissars in Ostland and Ukraine.[87] Less valuable items were to be used on the spot.

Subsequent directives divided responsibility among various sections of the civil administration. In December 1941, responsibility for many types of property went to the Treuhand.[88] Finally, in summer 1942, the administration of movable property was reassigned to the Financial Department, with only commercial property remaining under the Treuhand's responsibility.[89] Cultural property, including Jewish books, was dealt with mainly by the ERR.[90] Given the flood of instructions and the rival competencies, it is

---

[84] BAL, R 2104/14, pp. 421–25; NARA, T-459, reel 21, fr. 66, District Commissar Daugavpils report, May 26, 1942; BAL, R 92/10318, report of District Commissar Jelgava, June 9, 1943.

[85] V. Adamushko, et al. (eds.), *"Nazi Gold" from Belarus*, pp. 28–29, Verkündungsblatt des Reichskommissars für das Ostland, October 24, 1941; NARA, RG-242, T-459, reel 21, Anordnung über die Anmeldung jüdischen Vermögens, October 11, 1941.

[86] See Martin Dean, "Seizure, Registration, Rental and Sale: The Strange Case of the German Administration of Moveable Property in Latvia (1941–1944)," in *Latvia in World War II: Materials of an International Conference, 14–15 June 1999, Riga* (Riga: Latvijas vestures institute apgads, 2000): 372–78, here p. 373.

[87] V. Adamushko, et al. (eds.), *"Nazi Gold" from Belarus*, pp. 110–13, Reichsminister für die besetzten Ostgebieten an RKO u. RKU, September 7, 1942; see also NARA, T-459, reel 3, fr. 731, Städt. Pfandleihanstalt Berlin an RKO, August 4, 1942.

[88] R. Hilberg, *Die Vernichtung*, vol. 2, p. 382; NARA, T-459, reel 24, fr. 975, District Commissar Riga, February 21, 1942.

[89] USHMM, RG-18.002M, reel 5 (70-5-19), p. 93.

[90] On the activities of the ERR and cultural looting in the occupied Soviet Union, see, for example, B. Chiari, *Alltag hinter der Front*, pp. 80–95; Wolfgang Eichwede and Ulrike Hartung (eds.) *"Betr.: Sicherstellung" – NS-Kunstraub in der Sowjetunion* (Bremen: Temmen, 1998); Patricia Kennedy Grimsted, "Twice Plundered or 'Twice Saved'? Identifying

not surprising that not all property flowed correctly and promptly through the designated channels.[91] In the areas under military administration, the Wehrmacht remained primarily responsible through the *Wirtschaftsstab Ost* (Economic Staff East) and the *Ortskommandanturen* (local commandants) together with the Einsatzgruppen.

Despite the official transfer of responsibility for Jewish property to the civil administration in the summer and fall of 1941, the executive forces of the police continued to play an important role in its collection. As the agents primarily responsible for the murder of the Jews, they were on the spot and also had the available manpower for the collection of valuables at the killing sites. Some property remained in their safekeeping from earlier Aktions, and not all was swiftly handed over to the civil administration. Friction between civil and police agencies over the administration of Jewish property persisted for much of the occupation.

One of the first conflicts emerged in the district of Siauliai, Lithuania. Reich Commissar Ostland Lohse wrote to the Higher SS and Police Leader (HSSPF) Hans-Adolf Prützmann on September 25, 1941, requesting that the police hand over confiscated Jewish property to the relevant District Commissars.[92] Mounting criticism of the police by the civil administration culminated in a letter from Reich Minister for the Occupied Eastern Territories Alfred Rosenberg to the head of the Reich Chancellery, Hans Heinrich Lammers, on October 14, 1941. Rosenberg complained vigorously that police leaders in the East were not adhering to the Führer decree of July 17, 1941, regarding jurisdiction, but referred instead to "secret orders unavailable to the civil administration." In particular he charged that the SS had removed large amounts of silver and gold;[93] and indeed, the "war booty" records indicate that large collections of valuables were arriving in Berlin from Einsatzgruppe A in early 1942.[94]

Russia's 'Trophy' Archives and the Loot of the Reichssicherheithauptamt," *Holocaust and Genocide Studies*, vol. 15 no. 2 (Fall 2001): 191–244; and Patricia Kennedy Grimsted, "The Postwar Fate of Einsatzstab Reichsleiter Rosenberg Archival and Library Plunder, and the Dispersal of ERR Records," *Holocaust and Genocide Studies*, vol. 20 no. 2 (Fall 2006): 278–308.

[91] For an example of confusion over the correct channels, see NARA, RG-242, T-459, reel 21, fr. 75, instructions of General Commissar to District Commissar Riga-Land, June 4, 1942.

[92] USHMM, Acc.1996.A.0169, reel 5, (YVA) M41/307 (NARB, 391-1-39), RKO to HSSPF, September 25, 1941; see also R. Hilberg, *Die Vernichtung*, vol. 2, pp. 380–81.

[93] NARA, RG-238, T-1139, reel 21, NG-1683, Reich Minister for the Occupied Eastern Territories (RmfdbO) Rosenberg an Chef der Reichskanzlei Lammers, October 14, 1941. The Führer decree on "Police and Security in the newly occupied eastern territories" can be found in BAL, R 43 II/686a.

[94] See M. Dean, "Jewish Property," p. 85.

The example of the mass shooting of Jews in Riga demonstrates that, despite the proclaimed jurisdiction of the District Commissar over Jewish property matters, the executive authority of the police could still override it. Officials subordinate to the District Commissar complained bitterly of their inability to restrain the actions of the SS.[95] The police had carried out the murder of the Jews without prior consultation, wrecking plans for an orderly collection of Jewish property and rendering any effective accounting by the district commissar impossible.[96] The response of the District Commissar on this occasion – which was to renounce all responsibility – demonstrated that defense of his competence was less important to him than covering his back against possible criticism.

The responsibility of the civil administration for confiscated Jewish property was, however, confirmed by a Himmler order to the HSSPFs (I/1630/41) headed, "Concerning: the Treatment of Items Confiscated during House Searches and the Evacuation of Jews," and distributed at the beginning of 1942. The order stipulated that gold and silver items were to be collected and administered by the relevant Security Police offices, but that they were then to be sent to the finance departments of the civil administration. The only exception was for certain monetary sums required for the purposes of the SS and police.[97]

These instructions to transfer secured items to the civil administration were partially implemented during the following months. The office of HSSPF Ostland (now Friedrich Jeckeln) handed over a large cache of valuables from the Riga ghetto to the Reich Commissar's Section III (Trustee Office). The loot included more than RM 12,000 worth of foreign currency and silver items with a value in excess of RM 1,000, as well as watches, coins, and jewelry. Citing the Himmler Decree I/1630/41, the HSSPF requested a receipt for the items, which was issued by the Trustee Office on February 20, 1942.[98]

Another Himmler instruction, issued on August 12, 1942, ordered that all precious metals should be delivered to the SS-WVHA either directly in

---

[95] NARA, RG-242, T-459, reel 21, fr. 158–59, Riga, December 8, 1941.

[96] Ibid., fr. 145–46, Gebietskommissar an HSSPF, December 13, 1941; fr. 147, Gebietskommissar an HSSPF, December 11, 1941; fr. 149–50, Vermerk Riga, December 11, 1941; fr. 163, an den Reichskommissar, December 4, 1941.

[97] USHMM, RG-18.002M, reel 5, (Latvian State Historical Archives, 70-5-24), especially RSHA order to BdS Riga and others on November 26, 1942, and RFSS to HSSPFs I/1630/41 (copy undated).

[98] NARA, RG-242, T-459, reel 2, fr. 1113–14, Generalkommissar Abt. III/Treuhand an HSSPF Ostland, February 20, 1942 and HSSPF Ostland an RKO Abt. Treuhand, Feb. 11, 1942.

Berlin or via Globocnik's receiving office in Lublin.[99] It is therefore possible that some valuables from the occupied Soviet territories may have arrived in conjunction with the Melmer deliveries from "Aktion Reinhard" in the General Government.

An examination of the context in which this order was issued reveals that it was probably precipitated by several requests for access to gold and other proceeds from the Jewish Aktions for current use by SS institutions.[100] Himmler's strategy was to avoid carefully any accusation that the SS was exploiting Jewish valuables for its own purposes and without permission. Instead, he sought to centralize all deliveries of valuables from the East into the hands of the SS-WVHA to maximize their impact. Oswald Pohl would then report to the Finance Ministry that a certain sum from the "Jewish evacuations" had been delivered to the Reichsbank without a single penny being held back by the SS or the RKFDV. "In this manner," he wrote, "it will be easier to obtain the corresponding funds correctly from the Finance Ministry."[101] With regard to the use of gold supplies to repair the teeth of members of the SS and the police, very similar language was used: "The RFSS expects that after the SS and police has delivered larger quantities of old gold and other precious metals, the Economics Ministry will treat this sort of request from us more generously."[102]

This modest strategy of Himmler's resulted in the Melmer deliveries to the Reichsbank, the first of which arrived on August 26, 1942.[103] Himmler's intention was to convince the Reich leadership of the irreproachable

[99] This August 12 order is cited in USHMM, RG-18.002M, reel 5, (Latvian State Historical Archives 70-5-24), pp. 37 and reverse, RSHA to BdS Riga et al., November 26, 1942 (Abschrift).

[100] Regarding the request for the use of Jewish gold for dental purposes from the SS-dentist Grawitz, see NARA, RG-238, NO-3165, NO-3166, and NO-3192; regarding the request for Jewish funds for the equipment of schools, see NARA, T-175, reel 54, fr. 2568620-23; regarding the use of Jewish silver for the manufacture of cutlery and other things, see NO-3192. The significance of the request for dental gold in stimulating this order was identified by the Independent Commission of Experts: Switzerland – Second World War, *Switzerland and Gold Transactions in the Second World War: Interim Report* (Bern: May 1998), pp. 34–35.

[101] NARA, T-175, reel 54, fr. 2568620, RFSS Pers. Stab an Chef des Stabsamtes SS Gruppenführer Greifelt, August 14, 1942.

[102] NARA, RG-238, NO-3192, RFSS Pers. Stab an Oswald Pohl, August 12, 1942.

[103] *U.S. and Allied Efforts to Recover and Restore Gold and Other Assets Stolen or Hidden by Germany During World War II: Preliminary Study,* coordinated by Stuart E. Eizenstat (Washington, DC: Department of State, May 1997), see chapter 9, "Disposal by the U.S. of Captured Gold Looted by Germany from Individual Victims of Nazi Persecution and from European Central Banks."

efficiency of the SS and thereby to strengthen its position in budget negotiations by the impressive scale of these shipments.

Wrangling still continued, however, over sums backlogged with the
police. For example, the failure of Gendarmerie officials to deposit valuables with the civil administration after the clearance of the ghetto in
Ilja, Belorussia, produced another flurry of correspondence. In July 1943,
Reich Commissar Lohse reiterated his competence by referring to a further instruction of the SS-WVHA issued in June.[104] The Security Police
meanwhile transferred RM 1.8 million from confiscated Jewish property to
the General Commissar in Riga in April 1943.[105] In December 1943, the
financial department of the General Commissar in Weissruthenien reported
having received more than RM 300,000 from the *Befehlshaber der Sicherheitspolizei* (Senior Commander of the Security Police, BdS) Ostland. The
gold and silver items were forwarded to the Berlin Municipal Pawnshop
for sale.[106]

How is one to interpret these gradual and apparently reluctant transfers
by the police? Clearly, the very existence of competing jurisdictions and
the reliance of the civil administration on the police for the implementation of certain aspects of policy contributed to these frictions. Further
light is shed on the dispute by a request from the BdS Ostland to use RM
25,000 from confiscated monies for the purchase of "Schnaps" for the "Son-
derkommandos" involved in partisan warfare. As Untersturmführer Wittke
explained, "The BdS requires money for things that could not be put into
the budget, but at the same time are urgently needed" for official purposes
(such as intelligence operations).[107] A similar practice was commonplace in
the neighboring Białystok region, where money taken from individual Jews
shot after the ghetto liquidations was put into a special fund to reward local
policemen who had distinguished themselves in partisan warfare.[108] The
request for the diversion of funds in Ostland was also linked to ongoing
negotiations about the division of personnel and material costs between
the Reich government in Germany and the occupation administration in
the East.[109] Thus, the temporary withholding of large sums realized from

---

[104] USHMM, RG-18.002M, Latvian State Historical Archives (LSHA), reel 5, 70-5-24.

[105] Ibid., p. 21, BdS to RKO, May 1, 1943.

[106] Ibid., p. 48, Generalkommissar Weissruthenien Abt. II Finanzen an Reichskommissar,
December 6, 1943.

[107] Ibid., p. 11, BdS Ostland an Reichskommissar, March 5, 1943.

[108] USHMM, RG-53.004M State Archives of the Grodno Oblast', reel 1, 1-1-54, p. 39.

[109] USHMM, RG-18.002M LSHA, reel 5, 70-5-24, p. 23, RKO Abt. Finanzen, Vermerk,
June 8, 1943, p. 10, RKO Abt. Finanzen, Vermerk, February 19, 1943; and p. 11, BdS
Ostland an Reichskommissar, March 5, 1943.

confiscated Jewish property may also have been connected to battles over the division of resources within the hard-pressed budget for the Occupied Eastern Territories.

The Impact of Ghettoization: The Case of Głębokie

A detailed chronology of the numerous forms of exploitation experienced by one Jewish community can be found in the Głębokie memorial book.[110] This account reveals the recurring depredations by the Germans and the local population that preceded the physical destruction of the Jews. The bookkeeping of the German civil administration in the town provides corroboration of the events recounted more graphically by Jewish survivors.

The town of Głębokie had a Jewish population of about 5,000 at the onset of the German occupation, which comprised more than half of its population.[111] On the arrival of the German Army at the beginning of July 1941, local non-Jews plundered Jewish homes. The military administration soon introduced food rationing for the Jews and demanded the surrender of any "surplus." The local indigenous police then killed the family of Ascher Hoffmann, alleging that he had concealed flour. The Germans also strictly prohibited Jews from consuming "luxury items," such as butter or eggs. To forestall the arbitrary seizure of Jews from the streets, the Jewish Council assumed responsibility for assigning people to forced labor according to the Germans' instructions.[112]

The German civil administration established its operations in Głębokie.in the fall of 1941. On arrival, German civil officials requisitioned Jewish furniture to equip their offices. They also complained that Wehrmacht units passing through had taken large amounts of movable property. At the end of September, the administration demanded a large sum of money,

---

[110] *Memorial Book of Glebokie*, a translation into English of *Khurbn Glubok (Głębokie)* by M. and Z. Rajak, which was originally published in 1956 in Yiddish in Buenos Aires by the Former Residents' Association in Argentina, 1994. "The major portion of this book is devoted to recounting the destruction of Gluboke, which the two brothers, Michael and Tzvi, who were Gluboke teachers, wrote." The book also includes some information about the neighboring communities of Sharkoystzene (Szarkowszczyna), Dunilovitch (Dunilowicze), Postav (Postawy), and the surrounding area collected from survivors by the Landsleit Fahrein (Association) in Argentina.

[111] In 1921, 2,844 Jews lived in the town of Głębokie (63 percent of the total population); see *Encyclopaedia Judaica* (Jerusalem: Keter, 1972). The population of the ghetto rose to a figure of 6,000 to 8,000 Jews, including refugees and Jews resettled from neighboring towns and villages. The Soviet Extraordinary Commission Report of March 23, 1945 gives 8,000 ghetto inhabitants; see USHMM, RG-53.002M NARB, reel 6, 845-1-206.

[112] *Memorial Book of Glebokie*, pp. 23–40.

threatening to shoot all the Jews if the ransom were not met. On October 2–3, the Jews had to hand over their valuables, in particular gold and silver. Nevertheless the amount turned over disappointed German expectations, amounting to less per head than the amount Jews were officially permitted to retain.[113] The *Memorial Book of Głębokie* records how people stood in line to give up small family heirlooms; some hid property with non-Jewish neighbors they deemed reliable. A few of the latter denounced their Jewish neighbors, causing their deaths in order to retain what they had received.[114]

The German authorities established a ghetto in Głębokie on October 22, 1941, cramming the Jewish population into overcrowded conditions within the area of just a few streets. This forced relocation provided another opportunity for neighbors to loot Jewish property. Young girls helped themselves to items the Jews were unable to take with them in their enforced haste. Local police guards obtained bribes for permitting Jews to smuggle wood into the ghetto for fuel. Non-Jews also sold food "illegally" at inflated prices, sometimes cheating the Jews in the process. After the establishment of the ghetto, acting District Commissar Petersen demanded further Jewish "contributions," which raised the sum of RM 200,000.[115] On November 14, an inspection by officials of the civil administration from Minsk noted that Jewish property had been inventoried and registered on lists. But it also commented that "since Jews provide the craftsmen and other workers that are absolutely necessary, a liquidation Aktion should not be conducted."[116]

In the spring of 1942, the land area of the ghetto in Głębokie was reduced in size. Jewish property was again stolen from the vacated rooms, and German officials and policemen took the best houses for their own use. In return for a fee, local policemen offered to warn Jews of forthcoming Aktions. When members of the SD (Security Police) appeared in Głębokie in May 1942 at the start of the summer wave of massacres of Jews in the region, the Głębokie Jews began to prepare for the worst and construct hiding places. They scraped together remaining valuables in the hope that a

---

[113] Ibid., pp. 39–43; V. Adamushko, et al. (eds.), *"Nazi Gold" from Belarus*, pp. 66–67, Acting District Commissar Petersen to General Commissar Weissruthenien, June 22, 1942 (facsimile); this important document summarizes the measures taken with regard to Jewish property and some of the problems encountered.

[114] *Memorial Book of Glebokie*, pp. 42–51; on the giving of property into "safe-keeping," see also V. Adamushko, et al. (eds.), *"Nazi Gold" from Belarus*, pp. 83–84, District Commissar to General Commissar Weissruthenien, July 10, 1942.

[115] *Memorial Book of Glebokie*, pp. 46–51; V. Adamushko, et al. (eds.), *"Nazi Gold" from Belarus*, pp. 66–67, Acting District Commissar Petersen to General Commissar Weissruthenien, June 22, 1942 (facsimile).

[116] USHMM, RG-53.002M NARB, reel 11, 370-1-55, inspection report on visit to Głębokie on November 14, 1941.

bribe would encourage the SD to leave. The SD officials murdered twenty Jews on this visit before departing.[117]

In June, the German authorities established a separate ghetto for those unable to work. "The Germans decided to use the second ghetto for a financial Aktion," as one survivor recalled; "people could pay money to avoid being sent to it."[118] Then on June 19, 1942 the Germans liquidated the "second ghetto." During this Aktion more than 2,200 Jews were murdered. The German authorities could not prevent large-scale theft from the empty ghetto. The sale of confiscated items also proved problematic as "the population was so desperate to get its hands on the old Jewish stuff" that it was impossible to guarantee an orderly public sale.[119] Food supplies found in the ghetto were passed on to the German agricultural administration to be sold to the population.[120]

German civil administration reports from the summer of 1942 provide a detailed picture of the wealth officially looted from the Jewish community. Petersen calculated that, up to August 31, a total of RM 358,000 had been collected and transferred to the RKK in Minsk. The main components of this income were the Jewish contributions (mentioned above); profits received from the sale of clothing, livestock, and real estate; and income from Jewish labor farmed out on a contract basis, mainly to the Wehrmacht. Not included were 5,875 gold rubles (in coins), almost 10 kilograms of gold objects, more than 112 kilograms of silver coins, and 36 kilograms of Polish nickel coins that were sent separately to the RKK in Riga. Still in local storage in the autumn of 1942 were 351 kilograms of various silver items and a number of bond certificates, which were kept in the safe.[121]

---

[117] *Memorial Book of Glebokie*, pp. 60–64; on the wave of killing in the Głębokie District (Gebiet), see V. Adamushko, et al. (eds.), *"Nazi Gold" from Belarus*, p. 75, Acting District Commissar Petersen to General Commissar Weissruthenien, July 1, 1942 (facsimile).

[118] Ilya Ehrenburg and Vasily Grossman (eds.), *The Black Book: The Ruthless Murder of Jews by German-Fascist Invaders throughout the Temporarily-Occupied Regions of the Soviet Union and in the Death Camps of Poland During the War of 1941–1945* [Translated by John Glad and James S. Levine] (New York: Holocaust Library, 1981), p. 191.

[119] "Die Bevölkerung ist auf den alten jüdischen Kram so versessen, dass auch ein Verkauf örtlichen Charakters unter Aufbietung aller zur Verfügung stehenden deutschen Kräfte niemals in geordneten Bahnen zu halten wäre." Quoted by B. Chiari, *Alltag hinter der Front*, p. 259.

[120] *Memorial Book of Glebokie*, pp. 71–100; V. Adamushko, et al. (eds.), *"Nazi Gold" from Belarus*, pp. 75 and 83–4, Acting District Commissar Petersen to General Commissar Weissruthenien, July 1 and July 10, 1942; B. Chiari, *Alltag hinter der Front*, p. 259.

[121] V. Adamushko, et al. (eds.), *"Nazi Gold" from Belarus*, p. 107, District Commissar Głębokie to General Commissar Weissruthenien, September 4, 1942; and pp. 66–67, Acting District Commissar Petersen to General Commissar Weissruthenien, June 22, 1942;

After the liquidation of the second ghetto, the remaining property was collected in local storage sites. A large laundry was established to clean clothing suitable for sale. During the process, some Jewish forced laborers recognized items belonging to loved ones. Manye Freydkin recognized the shirt of her recently murdered husband Shimon.[122] The *Memorial Book* records in detail the scale of these operations:

> There were also workshops where things were pressed, repaired, and restored. After they were repaired the things were displayed in the stores. The merchandise was first recovered from Jewish homes, and afterwards brought from the surrounding towns. From these towns were brought whole wagons loaded with crates of utensils and dishes, packed in the pages of holy books. The wagons with these things were covered with torn, bloody clothing, often with torn, bloody *taleisim* (prayer shawls).

German officials in Głębokie took some of the most valuable stored items and also much of the production of Jewish craftsmen in the ghetto, sending large quantities home for friends and relatives or simply lining their own pockets.[123] Dozens of train cars left Głębokie loaded with cloth, leather, wool, footwear, knitted items, and foodstuffs packed by a special office of the District Commissar. The Jewish population became impoverished, but German pockets continued to swell.[124]

In the summer of 1943, the Germans liquidated the ghetto in Głębokie as they became increasingly concerned about the partisan danger. The burning of the ghetto and the massacre of its residents resulted in the death of more than 3,000 Jews.[125] The main author of the *Memorial Book*, the schoolteacher M. Rajak, was among the few who managed to escape into the forests. He recalls an encounter with local peasants one week after the destruction of his community, where for more than ten years he had educated hundreds of students:

> I came to a village and entered a house, which was bright, happy and holiday-like. The house was filled with parents and children. Everything was normal, as if nothing had occurred. Before my eyes there again opened a bottomless pit, into which we had rolled. I entered a few more houses. Almost

an extract of this document is also published in Wolfgang Benz, Konrad Kwiet, and Jürgen Matthäus (eds.), *Einsatz im "Reichskommissariat Ostland"*, doc. 110, pp. 145–46 (this edited version unfortunately omits the reference to the amount of silver collected; see also B. Chiari, *Alltag*, p. 260).

[122] *Memorial Book of Glebokie*, p. 94.
[123] Ibid., pp. 94–100.
[124] I. Ehrenburg and V. Grossman (eds.), *The Black Book*, p. 193.
[125] *Memorial Book of Glebokie*, p. 127.

everywhere the same! I encountered furniture from the city: nice beds, chests, mirrors, tables, stools and grandfather clocks. In one house I saw two nice buffets – they did not harmonize with the poor peasant houses, something looked strange? But I wasn't surprised. It was well known that a large portion of Jewish furniture during the murders had gone to the villages.[126]

The Strange Case of the Administration of Jewish Property in Latvia

The treatment of Jewish property in Latvia reveals an unusual combination of strict legal formalism, corruption, inefficiency, and bureaucracy. Here, the detailed registration of Jewish property produced extensive documentary records.[127] Repeatedly, the German authorities in Latvia attempted to register Jewish property, not while it was in the possession of the Jews themselves, nearly all of whom had been murdered by the end of 1941, but while it was in the possession of the local Latvians and German officials who had "inherited" the property.

The first registration campaign occurred at the end of 1941 following a series of registration decrees and instructions issued in September and October.[128] In many places, local officials registered Jewish and other "ownerless" property that had been collected and often redistributed in the wake of the Soviet deportations, arrests of suspected communists, and the mass shootings of Jewish communities. Jewish-owned farm animals were sometimes passed on to local peasants, dental equipment or musical instruments made available to hospitals and schools, and apartments and furnishings taken over by officials of the German Army, police, or civil administration, initially at no cost.[129] The disorganized nature of some of these early confiscations conducted under the military administration did, however, create a number of problems for the civil administration that followed it.

Once the civil administration had firmly established itself, it requested detailed reports on Jewish property from the District Commissars in

---

[126] Ibid., p. 160.

[127] See especially NARA, RG-242, T-459, reel 21, fr. 1-86; for examples of registration files, see BAL, R92/10258-89. The Latvian case is examined also in M. Dean, "Seizure, Registration, Rental and Sale."

[128] V. Adamushko, et al. (eds.), *"Nazi Gold" from Belarus*, pp. 28–29, Verkündigungsblatt des Reichskommissars für das Ostland, October 24, 1941; NARA, RG-242, T-459, reel 21, p. 60, Aufruf, Dünaburg, September 26, 1941, and Anordnung über die Anmeldung jüdischen Vermögens, Riga, October 11, 1941. The decree of Reichskommissar Lettland is dated October 13, 1941.

[129] BAL, R 92/10221.

May 1942.[130] The report from Daugavpils noted that movable property had been registered on preprinted forms and collected on behalf of the District Commissar. Foreign currency was exchanged at the Reich Credit Bank and credited to the District Commissar's account. Stocks and bonds remained in safekeeping locally. Watches had been distributed to the Wehrmacht, police, and railway employees. Real estate was being administered by the local authorities and rented out. "Derelict" houses were sold for demolition. Furniture and personal items were issued to the Wehrmacht or members of the local population for use "on a temporary basis." Low-value and damaged items as well as clothing had been sold. The money raised from Jewish property had reached RM 241,468 by the end of March 1942, of which RM 36,468 had been spent under the District Commissar's budget. The remainder was transferred to the account of the civil administration in Riga. Still to be processed were large amounts of silver (cutlery, goblets, and so on) then in local storage.[131]

Subsequently, responsibility for Jewish property was handed over to specific departments within the civil administration, and new registration and accounting exercises were conducted. In the fall of 1942, a renewed registration effort aimed at retrieving some of the Jewish property previously distributed and either renting or selling it, following an evaluation process.[132] This plan was implemented in a desultory fashion into 1944, although its administration costs drained away a large proportion of the expected revenue.

The income anticipated from the administration of confiscated real estate was considerable. In May 1942, the Property Company (*Grundstücksgesellschaft*), entrusted with administering real estate, reported that it controlled 8,200 buildings, including 85,500 apartments, worth an estimated RM 400 million. The annual rent for these properties was estimated at RM 24.7 million. However, the estimated net profit was only some RM 750,000, and considerable costs for repairs were expected.[133] A report by the administration in Daugavpils in 1944 complained that expenses for the management of Jewish property, including the salaries of those administering it, were consuming more than 50 percent of the income.[134]

---

[130] NARA, RG-242, T-459, reel 21, fr. 30-32, instruction from Reich Commissar, May 2, 1942; and instruction from General Commissar, May 15, 1942.

[131] NARA, RG-242, T-459, reel 21, fr. 58-59, report of District Commissar Dünaburg to General Commissar, May 6, 1942.

[132] LAB, AfW, Bd. 49, pp. 283–86, (ZSL, Vers. Heft III) RmfdbO an RKO u. Ukraine, September 7, 1942; see also BAL, R 92/835.

[133] BAL, R 2301/6000, Grundstücksgesellschaft Lettland, report of May 31, 1942.

[134] BAL, R 92/10306, Abt. II Fin.H.1356, report of May 8, 1944.

Throughout Latvia, individual Jewish bank accounts and any outstanding debts owed to them were to be registered. Some 3,000 individuals had registered Jewish property in Daugavpils, but the Germans still suspected widespread evasion by the locals.[135] An investigative department, run by the SD and employing local officials, was established to search for concealed Jewish property. This effort opened the door to denunciations and investigations of those suspected of concealing new-found wealth. Even some Jews in hiding or living on the "Aryan" side were uncovered by these investigations.[136]

My interpretation of the entire bizarre spectacle is that the civil administration was trying to repair the damage caused by the wild looting that had inevitably occurred in conjunction with the bloody early massacres of Jews. However, neither registrations nor denunciations did much to reestablish the rule of law. Rather, a further layer of corruption, arbitrariness, and inefficiency settled on top of the initial wave of crime, as German and local officials continued to skim off the best items and the real profits for themselves. Sometimes, this skimming took place at the expense of the local population who had bought items in "good faith" or had been denounced by jealous neighbors.

Nevertheless, the effort to give the whole procedure a veneer of legality is significant. A leading principle remained that the state and the German "national community" (*Volksgemeinschaft*), and not individuals, should profit from Jewish property. After the detailed registration of former Jewish property in Latvia, police offices and individuals were subsequently charged rent or required to purchase specific items already in their possession.[137] Thus, bureaucracy gradually tamed the "wild" nature of the initial expropriation process. Those who paid the generally cheap prices received legal title to the possessions, and the circulation of Jewish property supplied sorely needed consumer goods – in the short term. The thousands of registration forms, many still preserved as originals in German archives, serve as a paradoxical link to the victims of the Holocaust through the counting of their material possessions; they are "strange legal forms" that served ultimately to document the massive scale of official crimes.

Beneficiaries

A detailed accounting of the income derived from Jewish property in the East remains highly problematic. The successive participation of the

[135] K. Reichelt, "Der Anteil von Letten," p. 236.
[136] BAL, R 92/10296.
[137] See, for example, BAL, R 92/10304 and 10306.

Einsatzgruppen, the military administration, the civil administration, German police, and local officials in the process means that no centralized accounting of all property was maintained. The presence of Jewish property from Einsatzgruppen and Wehrmacht units among German war booty is just one example of sums going astray. Other amounts were claimed by the Wehrmacht Economic Inspectorate or used for urgent administrative expenses at the local level.

Christian Gerlach rightly warns against overestimating the importance of Jewish property as a source of income for the German civil administration. Using various sources, including a speech given by the head of the Finance Department in Reich Commissariat Ostland, State Secretary Dr. Friedrich Vialon, Gerlach estimates that Jewish property collected by the civil administration provided only some RM 10 million (between 1 and 3 percent) of the Commissariat's total budget.[138] Widespread corruption and the distribution of less valuable items to the local population further reduced the net sums left for the Commissariat.[139] The high costs of administration, the large numbers of items on loan or unprocessed by the end of the war, and income applied to the budgets of local mayors also diminished what was left for the Reich Commissariat. In comparison with the large sums extracted from the German Jews (RM 3 to 4 billion), the amounts registered within Reich Commissariat Ostland remain surprisingly small.[140]

Who benefited most from the looting? The lion's share of the revenue was destined for the shaky finances of the civil administration in the East. Income from valuables sent to Berlin was supposed to be booked to the account of the Reich Commissar, but delays meant that not all of it had been received before the evacuation of the region in 1944. Of course, given the comparatively small sums raised and the intention of the civil administration to profit from Jewish labor, the seizure of Jewish property cannot be viewed as the decisive motive for the German killings. Nevertheless, the seizure of all Jewish property was demanded by the internal logic of the same ideology that led to the physical destruction of the Jews.

Assessing the extent of corruption during the process of expropriation is an almost impossible task. These indeterminate sums have to be added to the looted amount that was recorded in official figures. They also reveal much about the motives of those involved. The sources for Głębokie and many

---

[138] C. Gerlach, *Kalkulierte Morde*, pp. 681–83; this estimate is probably slightly low, but not unreasonable in light of the local figures reported from Głębokie and Daugavpils in the summer of 1942.

[139] Ibid., pp. 678–83.

[140] The sum of about RM 3-4 billion directly netted by the Reich from Germany's Jews seems reasonable, as almost RM 3 billion was brought in by the combined effects of the punitive tax, the "flight tax," and the Eleventh Decree alone.

other places indicate the active role of both Germans and the indigenous local police in acquiring items for their own use. For example, Gendarmerie officials in the town of Kosów Poleski near Słonim were court-martialed for stealing Jewish property (among other offenses).[141] Jewish property also played a key role in helping finance patronage and embezzlement among officials in the Belorussian Self-Help Organization, established officially to provide charitable aid to needy Belorussians.[142] The destruction of the Jews and the associated struggle over their material legacy have been identified by historians such as Bernhard Chiari as instrumental in the wider breakdown of social cohesion under German occupation.[143]

There is evidence that funds derived from Jewish property were kept in illegal accounts to finance Security Police operations outside regular budgetary controls. Throughout the Occupied Eastern Territories, both the civil administration and the police were involved in any number of corruption scandals involving Jewish property.[144] Control over Jewish property provided access to the means of institutional and personal enrichment, an opportunity widely exploited throughout the East.

Collaboration

Shalom Cholawsky and Shmuel Spector, studying events from the perspective of Jewish survivors, see the fate of Jewish property as a barometer of local relations between Jews and non-Jews.[145] For parts of the local population, the acquiring of Jewish property was an important incentive for participating in the anti-Jewish measures. Precisely because of the desperate shortage of material goods in these areas, the prospect of personal enrichment served effectively to implicate and integrate local collaborators within the process of destruction. For the few Jewish survivors subjected to repeated attacks on their lives and possessions, the base motives of their former neighbors left some of the most indelible wounds, a painful human story that lies behind the numerous property lists preserved in the archives.

---

[141] NARA, RG-242, A 3343 (BDC collection), SSO File for Karl Zenner (11.6.1899).

[142] B. Chiari, *Alltag*, pp. 114–22 and 259. Dieter Pohl and Christian Gerlach emphasize the widespread corruption within German offices in the East, especially among the police and civil administrations, which organized the property seizures. D. Pohl, *Nationalsozialistische Judenverfolgung*, pp. 302–304; C. Gerlach, *Kalkulierte Morde*, pp. 678–79.

[143] B. Chiari, *Alltag*, p. 269.

[144] See for example M. Dean, *Collaboration*, pp. 96–97 and 109; C. Gerlach, *Kalkulierte Morde*, pp. 679–81.

[145] Shalom Cholawsky, *The Jews of Bielorussia during World War II* (Amsterdam: Harwood, 1998), pp. 275–77; Shmuel Spector, *The Holocaust of Volhynian Jews, 1941–44* (Jerusalem: Achva Press, 1990), pp. 239–41.

One case from Soviet investigative records concerning the town of Horodziej (Gorodeya), near Nieśwież in Belorussia, illustrates the looting behavior of the local police. Shortly after the mass execution of Jews there on July 16, 1942, the head of the town's Belorussian police, Matskalo, gave orders that the head of the Judenrat, Zygmuntovich, be escorted back into the ghetto by two local policemen to reveal hidden loot.[146] After Zygmuntovich recovered twenty-five rubles in gold coins from the wooden beams of a house, Matskalo seized the money. When the Jew said that there were no more valuables, the police chief shot him in the back. Other local policemen took Zygmuntovich's boots and other Jewish clothing to buy illegally brewed alcohol from local peasants.[147]

In Włodzimierzec, in the Wołyń region of Poland, when the Jews were assembled on the market square just prior to their murder in August 1942, a Ukrainian policeman called out, "Whoever has hidden gold, silver, or other valuables can come with us and remove them from their hiding places. Those who do this will be allowed to remain alive." According to one survivor, most Jews did not believe that thereby their lives would be spared.[148] Just before the liquidation of the Łokacze ghetto, some Jews tried to bribe local policemen to let them escape. One militiaman replied, "Get along with your valuables. I will take them ... anyway, after your death." A few Jews met policemen they knew who said they would have liked to have let them through, but that they were afraid of their colleagues and especially of the German policeman in charge, who had forbidden any Jews to leave on pain of death. Subsequently a group of eight escapees got out after bribing two policemen with a watch and a jacket. However, the Wachtmeister soon appeared and shots pursued the escapees.[149]

Jewish property was often used to reward local police and others who helped track down Jews in hiding. In Riga, a number of Latvian Schutzmänner (local police) applied for items of furniture from the ghetto, citing participation in anti-Jewish "Aktions" in support of their claims.[150] Local policemen moved into the houses of Jews after the mass shootings, for

---

[146] On the date of the Horodziej Aktion, see M. Dean, *Collaboration*, p. 87.

[147] Minsk Oblast' KGB Archive, archive file no. 902, Criminal Case no. 35930, Case against A.N.S. (1950–51), pp. 23–25, 45–56, 71–72, 126–27, 208–30, and 331–37.

[148] Mordechai Weissman, "My Escape from the Ditches of Slaughter," in A. Meyerowitz (ed.), *Sefer Vladimerets, galed lezekher iranu* (The Vladimirets Book, Testimony to the Memory of Our City) (Tel Aviv: Former Residents of Vladimirets in Israel, 1963).

[149] Michael Diment, *The Lone Survivor: A Diary of the Lukacze Ghetto and Svyniukhy, Ukraine* (New York: Holocaust Library, 1991), pp. 124–40.

[150] NARA, RG-242, T-459, reel 2, fr. 815-1002; and reel 3, fr. 546-48. I am grateful to my friend and colleague Robert G. Waite for bringing these documents to my attention.

instance in Nowa Mysz, near Baranowicze.[151] Stanisław Szepel, a blacksmith from Domaczów, denounced a Jew who had survived a mass execution and came to his house asking for bread. In return for bringing the Jew to the police (with the aid of another local inhabitant), Szepel was rewarded. His position as a considerable beneficiary from the massacre of his neighbors is underlined by the fact that he took over both a house and a blacksmith's forge from former Jewish property.[152]

Despite the clear intent for all Jewish property to be confiscated for the benefit of the German administration, material rewards clearly acted as an incentive for collaboration at the regional level. Administrators recognized this motive and tolerated or encouraged it as they saw fit, often taking their own cut. The process of genocide, once unleashed, released dynamic currents that could not necessarily be foreseen or fully controlled from the center.

Property and Jewish Survival

Documents of the local commandant (OK II/335) in Polotsk illustrate measures that Jews undertook to conceal property. Reports of the German field gendarmerie and Belorussian police (OD) in August 1941 noted that Jews in the ghetto were bartering clothing with local peasants; searches revealed large amounts of food and also valuables, some of which had been buried.[153] Looting by local inhabitants after ghetto liquidations had grave consequences for the surviving Jews. For example, in Siemiatycze (Białystok region), a group of Jews hiding in a bunker after the ghetto had been cleared were counting on their hidden supplies of food and valuables to help them survive. When one of them went to check, however, this is what he found:

> My brother reported that there was no food to be found in our house, which had been stripped to its bare walls. He had snuck around to the side of the house to the small storage cellar where we kept perishable foods cool in the summer. Not only was there no food there but scavengers had found the valuables we had hidden behind some wooden boards at the onset of the war. Our Polish neighbors were so proficient that they even dismantled an outdoor oven that we had built to disguise the location of the cellar. . . . Only our Polish neighbors could have known about such things. They were quite expert at detecting every possible place where Jews might

---

[151] M. Dean, *Collaboration*, p. 97.

[152] KGB Archive for the Brest Oblast', file no. 42, Trial of Stanislav Dmitrevich Shepel (1944). Shepel was sentenced to twenty years of forced labor on November 14, 1944.

[153] BAL, R 2104/15, pp. 18–19. On the concealment of property in Polotsk, see also BAL, R 2104/23, p. 1514. The items confiscated were forwarded to Berlin.

have hidden anything of value. . . . We did not know where to turn, what to do to get some scraps of food that might keep us alive.[154]

Jacob Biber, a Jewish survivor from Maciejów (Wołyń, Poland), recalled that at the end of the German occupation a local villager (Taras) informed him of the following:

> The farmers said that they missed the Jews, that when the Jews were alive they had provided the farmers with everything . . . the Ukrainians in the city on the other hand still sympathized with the Germans . . . [They] were still searching for Jews, since they had robbed most of them of their property and they wanted no surviving witnesses when the Soviets returned. Taras added, "The Ukrainians in the city don't care about independence any more, as long as they can keep the property they took from the Jews."[155]

Even after the war, Jews in the Soviet Union encountered great difficulty recovering their property due to the loss of documents and to government obstruction.[156]

Serbia

The availability of detailed German reports makes Serbia an informative case study for assessing both German aims and the actual outcome of their plunder campaign in the East. During 1941, the confiscation of Jewish property took place at an accelerated pace in Serbia. Laws (similar to those issued in France) defining who was a Jew, ordering the registration of property, asserting state control, and authorizing the appointment of trustees were applied in quick succession within four months. The murder of Serbia's Jews also proceeded rapidly, carried out by the Security Police and the Wehrmacht, so that by April 1942 only their property remained.[157] Initially

---

[154] Miriam and Saul Kuperhand, *Shadows of Treblinka* (Urbana, IL: University of Illinois Press, 1998), pp. 35–36.

[155] Jacob Biber, *Survivors: A Personal Story of the Holocaust* (San Bernadino, CA: Borgo Press, 1986), p. 142.

[156] Leonid Smilovitsky, *Katastrofa evreev v Belorussii 1941–1944 gg.* (Tel-Aviv: Biblioteka Matveia Chernogo, 2000), p. 23.

[157] Götz Aly, *Hitlers Volksstaat: Raub, Rassenkrieg und nationaler Sozialismus* (Frankfurt am Main: S. Fischer, 2005), pp. 213–16, also available in English as *Hitler's Beneficiaries* (New York: Metropolitan Books, 2007). Aly cites Serbia as a key example of how the Third Reich used Jewish property to support the German war effort by utilizing it immediately to prop up the budget and economies of occupied and allied states so that more could be extracted in occupation costs and war contributions. However, although this appears to be confirmed by some of the sources for Serbia, detailed study shows that it was in fact an

the proceeds, after outstanding taxes and debts had been paid, were placed into blocked accounts at the disposal of the General Commissioner for the Economy in Serbia (*Generalbevollmächtigte für die Wirtschaft in Serbien*).

During 1942, 33.5 million dinars were diverted from the special accounts derived from seized Jewish property to defray the costs of maintaining the concentration camps where the Jews had been held before their murder. This use of the funds was considered legitimate even by the Reich Audit Office (*Reichsrechnungshof*), presumably in accordance with the principle that measures for the "solution of the Jewish problem" should be self-financing.[158]

An early mistake was the failure to register Jewish property until after the Jews had been removed from their residences, leaving much research to be done in the property registers to identify the houses that had belonged to them. Because a lot of movable property had escaped collection due to "dubious transactions," those individuals who had acquired that property were obliged to register it in March 1942. Within the Office of the General Commissioner for the Economy in Serbia, a special section for Jewish property was established, based on the experiences of the HTO with regard to the administration of property by official trustees.[159] Initially, however, it was not clear exactly how the proceeds from Jewish property would be used, and this uncertainty served to delay its efficient exploitation.

Between March and June 1942, key discussions were held regarding the ultimate disposition of the proceeds from Jewish property in Serbia. As Götz Aly notes, these discussions are quite revealing of the principles behind German policy in the occupied territories.[160] After November 25, 1941, any property belonging to German Jews in Serbia had fallen to the Reich

---

unusual case. In Serbia, the revenue from Jewish property (and borrowing against it) was used to settle the war compensation claims of German and ethnic German individuals as well as the Reich against the Serb state, with probably only a limited direct benefit for the Reich's war finances.

[158] NARA, RG-238, T-75, reel 65, fr. 187–94, Rechnungshof an Generalbevollmächtigte für die Wirtschaft in Serbien (GBS), Betr.: Verwaltung des Judenvermögens, June 23, 1942; reel 65, fr. 197–205, Referat 17 an Rechnungshof, September 8, 1942; fr. 206–208, Referat 17 an RM Göring VjP/Dr. Gramsch, Betr.: Ausgaben zu Lasten des Judenvermögens, September 18, 1942.

[159] BAL, R2/30663, Collection of Jewish Property in Serbia, RFM note dated August 28, 1942; see also Karl-Heinz Schlarp, *Wirtschaft und Besatzung in Serbien, 1941–1944: Ein Beitrag zur Nationalsozialistischen Wirtschaftspolitik in Südosteuropa* (Wiesbaden: Franz Steiner, 1986), pp. 294–302; Walter Manoschek, *"Serbien ist judenfrei": Militärische Besatzungspolitik und Judenvernichtung in Serbien 1941/42* (Munich: R. Oldenbourg, 1995), pp. 35–40.

[160] Götz Aly, *Hitlers Volksstaat*, pp. 213–16.

under the Eleventh Decree. The property of Jews of enemy nationality in Serbia was to be administered as enemy property, whereas that of Jews from neutral states was to be left untouched. In June 1942, Göring's Office of the Four-Year Plan, in concert with the other German offices involved, decided that property belonging to Yugoslav and "stateless" Jews was to be confiscated in favor of Serbia.[161] The official reasoning was that, in all occupied territories, the liquidation of Jewish property was to be carried out by the local authorities according to German guidelines, in favor of the occupied territories and never the Reich, for these political and financial considerations:

> The solution of the Jewish Question should be a matter for the occupied territories themselves.

> All income from the occupied territories should on principle be available for the local administration, while the Reich, without resort to special sources of income of an occupied territory or infringement of its financial sovereignty, requests occupation expenses in one sum.

There were other political reasons for the Reich not to become too directly involved in disputes over the use of Serbian Jewish property, as Hungary still had outstanding claims to the northern part of Serb territory.

The implementation of property seizure in Serbia was, however, placed firmly in the hands of the German administration. One German concern was to ensure that detailed records were kept; the German authorities also worried that the local Serbian administration might not favor non-Serb minorities, excluding even the local ethnic German population from the spoils. Therefore, the German authorities in effect administered Jewish property and the proceeds on behalf of the Serbian state. They were also concerned that at the end of the war Serbia would be unable to pay the considerable "war damages" claims they demanded, including those owed to German and ethnic German individuals. Therefore, soon after the decision to transfer Jewish property nominally to Serbia, they started to make payments for war compensation from the proceeds of Jewish property managed by the Serbian State Mortgage Bank (*Staatliche Hypothekenbank*), thereby exploiting their direct control over Serbian finances. Indeed, these payments soon ran ahead of the actual money received from the liquidation of Jewish property, and the State Mortgage Bank had to borrow money

---

[161] NARA, RG-238, T-75, reel 65, fr. 197, Referat 17, Betr.: Verwaltung des Judenvermögens, September 8, 1942; NARA, RG-238, T-75, reel 53, Treuhandverwaltung und Judenvermögen, Verwaltungsbericht, signed Gurski, in Eggerding on March 23, 1945 (henceforth Verwaltungsbericht), pp. 13–14.

against the value of unsold Jewish real estate transferred to its name to make these large payments.[162]

By August 1942, the fate of Jewish movable wealth – that is, clothing, household furniture, and other personal effects – had largely been resolved. The SD and the Wehrmacht had confiscated most household items from the Jews, using some to equip the residences and offices of the German military administration in Serbia. The SD had sold off part of the rest. The German financial authorities decided that the Wehrmacht could keep its furniture, but that the SD should pay the sums it had collected into the Serbian budget (i.e., the War Damages Compensation Fund). Other remaining furniture could be offered to the Reich Ministry for the Occupied Territories to equip its offices in the East (as had been proposed in Western Europe).[163]

The most valuable part of Jewish property in Serbia consisted of real estate, which in Belgrade alone supposedly was worth 2.5 billion dinars according to fixed 1941 prices.[164] However, the wartime administration of this newly gained asset did not produce large sums for the German war effort. A detailed June 1943 report by the Trustee Organization for Jewish Real Estate in Belgrade revealed that the administration of more than 1,000 Jewish residential properties had only broken even since it started its work in July 1941. Income of 62 million dinars, mainly from rent, was largely eaten up by operating costs, taxes, repairs, and other expenses amounting to almost 54 million dinars, and the Trustee Organization deducted another 8 million for its own expenses. The only real profit received was a net income of 126 million dinars (RM 6.3 million) from the sale of 138 properties, which was paid into a special account for "Aryanization proceeds" at the Bankverein A. G. Belgrade. Of the properties sold, twenty-three had gone to Reich Germans, forty-four to ethnic Germans, and sixty-four to Serbian buyers; in terms of price, the Reich Germans had paid 31 percent, the ethnic Germans 29 percent, and the Serbs 33.6 percent of total sales income.

---

[162] BAL, R2/30663, Collection of Jewish Property in Serbia, RFM note dated August 28, 1942; see also K.-H. Schlarp, *Wirtschaft und Besatzung*, pp. 296–301; NARA, RG-242, T-75, reel 65, fr. 1065, Staatl. Hypothekenbank an Dr. Josef Kamm, Kriegsverwaltungsrat, Betr.: Financierung der Entschädigung Deutscher für Kriegsschäden, December 1, 1942; reel 53, Verwaltungsbericht, March 23, 1945, p. 17.

[163] NARA, RG-242, T-75, reel 65, fr. 187, Reichsrechnungshof an GBS, June 23, 1942.

[164] NARA, RG-242, T-75, reel 53, Verwaltungsbericht, March 23, 1945, estimated real estate outside Belgrade at another 1 billion dinars; RG-242, T-75, reel 56, fr. 728-37, Kommissarische Verwaltung des jüd. Haus u. Grundbesitzes, Belgrad, Schlussbericht, June 22, 1943, however, claims that the 1,041 former Jewish properties it administered in Belgrade had an estimated value of only 1.5 billion dinars. Some other properties were not under its control.

Most of the report consists of a list of excuses for the failure to make a profit from the rental properties. Among the most important reasons were the damages caused by German bombing of the city that had to be repaired, the fact that 200 apartments remained empty for six months because the SD sealed them after the Jews were removed, the imposition of rent reductions and rent controls in the city, contracts giving the Wehrmacht very low rents, nonpayment of rent by some tenants, the cost of pulling down heavily damaged buildings, and so on.[165] This case is quite informative, revealing a pattern not untypical for the rest of occupied Europe: much of the anticipated income from former Jewish real estate and other property was largely swallowed up by administrative costs under generally unfavorable wartime conditions. The only real income to be gained was by selling off capital at prices held at artificially low levels by the Germans' own price restrictions. By January 1943, even this revenue source began to dry up, as prospective buyers began to fear that in the event of an Allied victory they would have to return former Jewish real estate without compensation.[166]

The Aryanization of Jewish businesses in Serbia also met with only limited success in the face of difficult economic conditions. The German authorities were keen to sell businesses quickly, as they soon noticed that administration by trustees generally led only to a rapid decline in a business's capital assets and sale price. According to one source, more than 900 businesses were sold or liquidated, producing an income of more than 320 million dinars[167] or roughly one-third of the total amount realized from Jewish property in Serbia before the German retreat. However, many businesses that were Aryanized had to close down shortly afterward, mainly due to the lack of raw materials. German control of the process enabled them to sell off certain key strategic businesses to German buyers and also favor local ethnic Germans, especially in the Banat. However, for German firms, the fixed low prices of the businesses were less attractive, as they had to exchange their Reichsmarks at unfavorable rates. Some businesses were bought by former trustees, as there was a dearth of other qualified buyers.[168]

Some of the valuables and securities secured by the SD in Serbia were delivered to Berlin; however, German authorities decided against paying an equivalent sum to the Serbian government because the amount was not

---

[165] RG-242, T-75, reel 56, fr. 728-37, Kommissarische Verwaltung des jüd. Haus u. Grundbesitzes, Belgrad, Schlussbericht, June 22, 1943; see also K-H. Schlarp, *Wirtschaft und Besatzung*, pp. 296–98.

[166] BAL, R2/30663, RFM Berlin, January 18, 1943; NARA, RG-242, T-75, reel 53, Verwaltungsbericht, March 23, 1945, p. 15.

[167] NARA, RG-242, T-75, reel 53, Verwaltungsbericht, March 23, 1945, pp. 87–88.

[168] K.-H. Schlarp, *Wirtschaft und Besatzung*, pp. 296–302.

large and the nationality of the former Jewish owners could no longer be determined.[169] In April 1943, jewelry and other valuables seized from the Jews in Serbia were transferred to the War Booty Office for reasons of security.[170] After the Finance Ministry learned that not all the confiscated items had necessarily belonged to Jews, but some might also have belonged to non-Jews from throughout the former Yugoslavia, they requested a detailed inventory, including details about the former owners and the place of confiscation.[171] It can be assumed that only a small part of this loot was actually sold before 1944, so that its contribution to the German war effort was limited.

Surviving documentation on Jewish jewelry that remained in Serbia at the disposal of the General Commissioner for the Economy indicates a value of more than 1 million dinars; some was sold on the black market abroad, raising more than $10,000 in hard currency (in U.S. dollars and Swiss francs). This money was to be used in turn to buy scarce commodities such as livestock from Romania that were desperately needed for the Serbian economy. However, these transactions brought no hard currency into Serbia before December 1943, so any real economic impact for the occupation authorities was also belated.

Götz Aly's recent analysis in *Hitlers Volksstaat* (published in English as *Hitler's Beneficiaries*) represents a major contribution, as he examines the plunder of Jewish property firmly within the context of German war finances. He links the exploitation of Jewish property to the broader problem of how the Reich plundered both occupied states and collaborating allies through a combination of mechanisms: requisitions, the payment of soldiers in local currency, war contributions, controlled inflation, and the use of Jewish property as a means to soak up local demand and stabilize weak currencies by recycling it for the benefit of local budgets. Aly cites Serbia as a particularly transparent example of his thesis: in this puppet state, the German authorities stated openly their intentions to recycle Jewish property through the country's financial system in order to extract more effectively its resources for themselves.[172] As one German report concludes, among the reasons for crediting Jewish property to the Serbian state, rather than seizing it for the Reich, was to provide "financial aid for the Serbian state

---

[169] BAL, R2/30663, RFM, Referent Breynan, July 10, 1942.

[170] Ibid., RFSS an RFM, April 9, 1943.

[171] Ibid., RFM note, May 28, 1943.

[172] Götz Aly, *Hitlers Volksstaat*, pp. 213–16. Aly's figure for occupation costs of 500,000 dinars per month seems too low, in the light of his calculation that 3-4 billion dinars from Jewish property would cover these costs for about six months.

budget, already heavily burdened by German occupation costs."[173] Still, the figures for the exploitation of Jewish property in Serbia call into question some of Aly's assumptions, especially when the intentions of German actors are compared with the much more limited results achieved.

In any event, very little Jewish property was sold to Serbs, and virtually all the income from the property that was sold went to pay Germany's war compensation claims, including those of private individuals. A close reading of the documents indicates, however, that even these limited efforts to mobilize resources from Jewish property were hardly an overwhelming success. A report by the State Mortgage Company in December 1942 claims that originally compensation payments were to be made only from the cash paid to the Mortgage Company from the sale of Jewish property. However, by that month, more than 500 million dinars had already been paid for German damage claims, whereas only seventy-eight properties had been auctioned, valued at just 193 million dinars, of which only a small amount had actually been received. Indeed, the State Mortgage Company was driven close to bankruptcy and had to borrow money secretly by mortgaging its unsold Jewish real estate to continue functioning![174] Far from proceeding smoothly, this method of using Jewish property to favor German interests was a rickety structure at best. After an initial payout of some 500 million dinars for war compensation claims in the second half of 1942, only another 250 million dinars were paid out during the rest of the occupation. This was the only large net gain for the Reich from Jewish property in Serbia. Although the gross cash income from Jewish property was probably in excess of 900 million dinars, the high administration costs, especially for managing unsold real estate (the bulk of Jewish property), meant that the cash income received was probably 200 million dinars less than the total of 756 million paid out in war damages. Serb borrowing made up the difference.

Although aggressive German intervention to obtain compensation payments forced the Serb state to borrow against Jewish property almost immediately, it seems that this resource was rapidly exhausted, especially as further sales of real estate had become difficult by early 1943. In any case, it is not clear to what extent these war compensation payments were actually used for the German war effort. Rather, it seems that the German administration of Jewish property on behalf of the Serb state produced only limited wartime returns in relation to the manpower and resources invested in its extraction. In the Banat, there was even a proposal to release several hundred ethnic

---

[173] NARA, RG-242, T-75, reel 53, Verwaltungsbericht, March 23, 1945, p. 15.
[174] NARA, RG-242, T-75, reel 65, fr. 10657, Staatl. Hypothekenbank an Dr. Josef Kamm, Kriegsverwaltungsrat, December 1, 1942.

Germans from service in the Waffen SS "Prinz Eugen" Division so they could return home to act as urgently needed trustees for Jewish property.[175] The lasting impressions left by the exploitation of Jewish property in Serbia are of high administration costs and the great difficulties encountered in turning Jewish property into cash in a situation of fixed prices and the growing uncertainties of war.

Conclusions: The Role of Jewish Property in "Cleansing" the East

The Nazi authorities went to considerable lengths in the East not only to seize all Jewish property but also to give these confiscations at least a veneer of legality. Their grand aims of cleansing the region of entire population groups, redistributing some of the confiscated wealth, and thereby defraying the costs of occupation and war all necessitated a complex legal framework and bureaucracy to manage the plunder in the interests of the Reich. Despite the very high levels of corruption and personal enrichment, a lawless free-for-all could not be permitted, and counter-measures were occasionally taken within the German administration.[176]

In the Reich Commissariats Ostland and Ukraine, the civil administration won most jurisdictional battles over Jewish property. The Security and Order Police, however, fought a prolonged rearguard action, based mainly on their direct executive powers. This civil administration viewed the actions of the police as undermining its authority. The dual chain of command that the police defended so fiercely also caused much friction and duplication, as well as the oft-described competitive eagerness to achieve specific aims.

With regard to the widespread collaboration of parts of the local populace in measures against the Jews, the distribution of some Jewish property provided a useful incentive that strongly reinforced local antisemitism and other political and personal motives. The Germans were quite aware that retention of Jewish property would give local people a material stake in the occupation regime.

---

[175] K.-H. Schlarp, *Wirtschaft und Besatzung*, p. 299.

[176] On the role of law in the seizure of Jewish property in the occupied East, see Martin Dean, "The Role of Law in the Seizure of Property in Nazi-Occupied Eastern Europe," in Johannes Bähr and Ralf Banken (eds.), *Das Europa des "Dritten Reichs": Recht Wirtschaft, Besatzung* (Frankfurt am Main: Klostermann, 2005), pp. 81–104. I am grateful to the editors for inviting me to contribute to this volume, which led to several new insights by forcing me to examine events from a legal perspective.

For the Jews, deprivation of property reduced considerably their chances for survival. That many firearms obtained by Jewish resistance groups were purchased and also that even the most selfless of "righteous gentiles" still needed money to buy extra food illustrate the obvious link between property confiscation and the terrifying effectiveness of genocide in these regions. The seizure of Jewish property was not just a byproduct of Nazi genocidal policies, but an integral part of the murder process, reinforcing and accelerating the intended destruction.

6

SETTLING ACCOUNTS IN THE WAKE OF THE DEPORTATIONS

In mid-October 1941, the Nazi leadership began the mass deportation of German Jews from the Reich. Taking into account its experience with previous deportations, the German bureaucracy made detailed preparations for handling the deported Jews' remaining property. The regional financial administrations organized the dissolution of bank accounts, the confiscation of securities and real estate, and the payment and collection of outstanding debts. Apartments sealed by the Gestapo had to be cleared of furniture and other possessions as soon as possible to minimize landlords' rental claims against the Reich before the dwellings could be leased again. The financial administration arranged for the sale of this movable property, giving some priority to needy groups within the population.

Before their deportation, each Jewish family had to prepare a final property inventory to assist the bureaucratic process of liquidating their estates. These final testaments present a snapshot of the meager resources remaining to German Jews on the eve of their destruction. From those with some means remaining, the Security Police collected a further payment to cover the costs of deportation.

The dissolution of Jewish accounts was a prolonged process that in many cases had not been completed by the end of the war. In pursuing this aim, the financial administration conducted a detailed correspondence with banks, utilities, and insurance and transport companies, as well as many other private and public entities. Thus, despite efforts to maintain secrecy, many members of German society must have been aware of and complicit in the sudden removal of their former clients and neighbors.

The Beginning of Mass Deportations from the Reich

After the deportation of the Jews from Baden and the Palatinate in October 1940, the next large-scale deportation dispatched about 5,000 Jews into the Lublin and Radom Distrikts from Vienna between February 15 and March 12, 1941.[1] The affected Jews were required to prepare a list of all their property, including debts owed to them; the proceeds from the sale of that property were to be used to pay for transport costs and in general for the "Final Solution of the Jewish Problem."[2] In mid-March, the Reich Security Main Office (RSHA) even informed the leaders of the compulsory Jewish communal organization, the *Reichsvereinigung der Juden* (RV), that "for the complete emigration of all Jews capable of 'establishing settlements' (*siedlungsfähig*), considerable sums of money would be required" from the RV.[3]

Almost as soon as the deportations from Vienna raised expectations that deportations from other German cities would soon follow, a general cessation of deportations was imposed in March due to the transportation demands associated with preparations for the invasion of the Soviet Union. It was not until September, probably reflecting Hitler's confidence in victory, that he decided to start the mass deportation of Germany's Jews, previously scheduled for after the war.[4] It is unlikely that seizing Jewish property served as the main motive, but for some leading Nazis, such as Gauleiter Kaufmann in Hamburg, demands for the removal of the Jews were linked to the expectation of using former Jewish property to assist Germans affected by British bombing.[5]

---

[1] Götz Aly, *"Endlösung": Völkerverschiebung und der Mord an den europäischen Juden* (Frankfurt am Main: S. Fischer, 1995), pp. 220–21 (available in English as *"Final Solution": Nazi Population Policy and the Murder of the European Jews* (London: Arnold, 1991); Wolf Gruner, "Von der Kollektivausweisung zur Deportation der Juden aus Deutschland (1938–1945) – Neue Perspektiven und Dokumente," in *Beiträge zur Geschichte des Nationalsozialismus 20, Die Deportation der Juden aus Deutschland: Pläne – Praxis – Reaktionen 1938–1945* (Göttingen: Wallstein, 2004): 21–62, here p. 43.

[2] Hans Safrian, *Eichmann und seine Gehilfen* (Frankfurt am Main: Fischer, 1995), p. 97.

[3] W. Gruner, "Von der Kollektivausweisung," p. 45.

[4] On Hitler's buoyant mood in early October, see Richard Overy, *Russia's War: Blood upon the Snow* (New York: TV Books, 1997), pp. 127–28; Christopher Browning, *Initiating the Final Solution: The Fateful Months of September-October 1941* (Washington, DC: United States Holocaust Memorial Museum, 2003), p. 3; C. Browning and J. Matthäus, *Die Entfesselung der 'Endlösung': nationalsozialistische Judenpolitik 1939–1942* (Berlin: Propyläen, 2003), pp. 471–72; and ibid., pp. 46–51. Gruner argues persuasively that the decision in September to start deportations to Łodz was the outcome of a longer process that had begun in August, see ibid.

[5] Peter Witte, "Two Decisions Concerning the 'Final Solution of the Jewish Question': Deportations to Łódź and Mass Murder in Chelmno," *Holocaust and Genocide Studies*, vol. 9, no. 3 (Winter 1995): 318–45, p. 325.

In early November 1941, shortly after the start of the deportations but before publication of the Eleventh Decree, the Finance Ministry issued detailed instructions on how to process the property of deported Jews. The Gestapo was initially to secure the property and seal the empty apartments, leaving the keys with the janitor. The regional financial administration entrusted with administering and selling the property was to obtain from the Security Police the property declarations prepared by the Jews just before their departure. Emphasis was laid on clearing the empty apartments quickly to avoid the state having to pay the apartment owners for lost rent. Once items that could be used by the financial administration itself had been set aside, the remaining movable property was to be sold locally to individuals or in bulk to the Nazi Welfare Organization (NSV) or bomb-damaged cities. Valuable cultural items were also to be secured and offered first to the regional chambers of culture.[6]

A clear illustration of the close cooperation of the regional financial administration with the Gestapo and other local authorities appears in the minutes of a November 19, 1941, meeting in Münster, held to prepare for the first deportations from the city, scheduled on December 13, 1941. Chaired by the deputy Gauleiter Peter Stangier, Senior State Counselor Heinrich Heising from the office of the regional Senior Finance President (OFP), Dr. Busse of the Gestapo, the mayor, and other local officials also participated in the meeting. Heising spoke about some of the difficulties encountered during the recent deportations from Düsseldorf: for example, the Reich was unable to pay for repairing all the apartments, as in some cases insufficient property remained to cover these expenses. Auctioning items proved difficult as fixed prices were in effect, but bids often exceeded those limits. Many Jews had simply given property away, ignoring the official confiscation announced on October 15. A separate account had to be maintained for each individual Jew, to receive the proceeds from the sale of his or her property, so that outstanding debts could be paid off. Scarcely 20 percent of the property declarations had been properly filled out, as the victims had no interest in this exercise, so two finance officials had to make an inventory of the property in the apartments and seal them as soon as they were vacated.

The meeting's participants recommended that most apartments and much of the property, apart from that allocated for the administration, be used to assist bomb-damage victims. It recommended that a special committee be created to examine the expected flood of requests to buy real estate. Dr. Busse of the Gestapo promised to prepare a list of the Jews designated

[6] BAL, R 2 Anh./7, RMF Schnellbrief, Nov. 4, 1941.

for deportation to make it clear which apartments would be vacated, so that the remaining approximately 115 Jews still exempted (those in mixed marriages, on work deployment, or too old or too sick to be deported) could be concentrated in "Jewish houses." The deportation was to be organized as follows: the Jews would be taken to the Gertrudenhof and searched there. They would not be permitted to take any jewelry or cash, but would receive RM 50 in Reich Credit Bank notes (German occupation money)[7] on arrival. They could take only 50 kilograms of luggage, consisting of blankets, clothing, and household items. There would be two transports, one to Riga and one to Minsk.[8]

The Introduction of the Eleventh Decree

In anticipation of the Eleventh Decree in November 1941, the RSHA distributed a circular noting that, in unclear cases, the head of the Security Police and the SD would determine whether the property of specific Jews had "fallen" into the possession of the Reich. The same circular noted that the bulk of property belonging to Jewish emigrants had already been secured in accordance with Security Police circular no. 1433 of September 24, 1940.[9]

The Eleventh Decree was issued on November 25, 1941, and published the following day in the *Reichsgesetzblatt* (Reich Law Gazette). In addition

---

[7] On the extensive use of this form of payment in the occupied and Allied countries to the benefit of the Reich's finances, see Götz Aly, *Hitlers Volksstaat: Raub, Rassenkrieg und nationaler Sozialismus* (Frankfurt am Main: S. Fischer, 2005), pp. 107–13.

[8] Notes of a confidential meeting, Der Oberbürgermeister, Münster, November 20, 1941. I am grateful to the staff of Villa ten Hompel for making a copy of this document available to me. Original source: Stadtarchiv Münster, Stadtregistratur Fach 26, 18 d, pp. 122–24, cited also by Gerd Blumberg, "Etappen der Verfolgung und Ausraubung und ihre bürokratische Apparatur," in Alfons Kenkmann and Bernd-A. Rusinek (eds.), *Verfolgung und Verwaltung: Die wirtschaftliche Ausplünderung der Juden und die westfälischen Finanzbehörden* (Münster: Oberfinanzdirektion Münster, 1999): 15–40, p. 36. In fact, only one transport left Münster for Riga on December 13, 1941, with 400 Jews from the district (*Bezirk*) of Münster, Westfalen. The second transport to Minsk was redirected to Riga before its departure on January 27, 1942, and only twelve Jews from Münster were included, according to the records of the resident registration office (*Einwohnermeldeamt*); see Gisela Möllenhoff and Rita Schlautmann-Overmeyer (eds.), *Jüdische Familien in Münster, Teil 2,2: Abhandlungen und Dokumente 1935–45* (Münster: Westfälisches Dampfboot, 2001), pp. 846–47.

[9] BAL, R 2/9172b, pp. 1–7, RSHA Runderlass undatiert (November 1941), betr.: 11. VO. The same circular confirmed that the General Government would be deemed as "abroad" for the purposes of the new law. On the concerted efforts of the RSHA to confiscate the property of Jewish emigrants after September 1940 using the Denaturalization Law of July 1933, see Chapter 4.

to depriving Jews of German citizenship the moment they left the Reich's boundaries, thereby confiscating their property, the decree proclaimed that the Reich was responsible for their debts only up to the sale value of the remaining property of each individual Jew. In the case of non-Jewish dependents, some "hardship" payments might be made.[10] On December 3, 1941, a secret supplemental instruction of the Reich Interior Ministry specified that the loss of citizenship applied also to those Jews in the German-occupied territories: the General Government, or the Reich Commissariats Ostland and Ukraine.[11] The intention of this supplemental instruction was to simplify the procedure for expropriating Jews deported to the East, as well as previous emigrants who had not obtained another citizenship.

The impact of the new measure was not lost on remaining staff at the U.S. Embassy in Berlin. A telegram addressed to the U.S. Secretary of State briefly summarized the practical implications of the Eleventh Decree. In particular, the U.S. officials noted not only the complete expropriation of Jewish emigrants but also its connection to the deportation of Jews to the East: "the many thousands of Jews now being deported into . . . [the Occupied Eastern Territories] each week will soon be de jure as well as de facto deprived of their citizenship and their worldly goods."[12]

The Eleventh Decree also had a negative impact on German Jews who had migrated to Palestine. Until November 1941, these people had been largely protected against expropriation as they had been regarded as foreign Jews (as if they had acquired "Palestinian citizenship"), and their property was administered by the Commissioner for Enemy Property. In early December 1941, however, the Finance Ministry instructed the Commissioner for Enemy Property to transfer all such cases to the OFP Berlin unless there was clear evidence that individuals had actually acquired "Palestinian citizenship" before the publication of the Eleventh Decree.[13] German Jews who had obtained the citizenship of an enemy country before November 25, 1941, still enjoyed some protection of their property under the Enemy Property regulations.[14]

[10] Matthias Lichter, *Das Staatsangehörigkeitsrecht im Grossdeutschen Reich* (Berlin: Heymanns, 1943), pp. 147–50.

[11] BAL, R 2/9172b, p. 11, RMdI confidential circular, December 3, 1941.

[12] NARA, RG-59, Decimal File, 1940–1944, 862.4016/2213.

[13] BAL, R 2/9172b, pp. 20–21, RFM note of a conference on December 4, 1941; see also, however, BAL, R 87/114, pp. 51–53, Vermerk, Reichskommissar für die Behandlung des feindlichen Vermögens, December 9, 1941, which noted that the FA Moabit-West was currently overwhelmed (überlastet).

[14] BAL, R 139 II/111, correspondence of OFP Rudolstadt with Städtische Sparkasse, January 1942.

Deportation Lists and Individual Files

The considerable efforts made by the bureaucracy of the Third Reich to track down and confiscate Jewish property left very detailed records. For example, the Security Police prepared the deportation lists, still available for most deportations from the Reich, as official certificates of property confiscation. As instructions issued by the Finance Ministry on December 9, 1941, explained, these lists constituted "official notification that the preconditions exist for the property to fall to the Reich."[15]

In fact, the deportation lists generally do not detail specific property, but state only whether the persons concerned owned property and whether it fell to the Reich under the Eleventh Decree or had been confiscated under other laws. Individual property declarations were appended to the lists and were subsequently transferred to individual files created for those possessing property. Because of the the technical legal nature of the process, it appears that the Gestapo stuck rigidly to the terms of the law. Those Jews of German citizenship or who were stateless had their property automatically confiscated on crossing the borders of the Reich according to the Eleventh Decree; however, because many transports were destined for locations still inside the Reich, including Terezin (Theresienstadt), Łódź (Litzmannstadt), and Oświęcim (Auschwitz), in these cases their property had to be confiscated on the basis of the 1933 laws for the confiscation of the property of "communists" and of "enemies of the people and the state." Therefore, in many files may be found a receipt (*Zustellungsurkunde*) certifying that deportees had been notified of the seizure of property under the 1933 laws prior to departure. In the case of suicides or deaths of Jews just before their deportation, the Gestapo had to seize property by means of an individual confiscation certificate (*Einziehungsverfügung*) as the Reich border had not been crossed.[16] Despite the Gestapo's efforts to remain within the law, the financial administration was not very impressed with its work, complaining in February 1942 that the transport lists of the Security Police were inadequate, as they were not organized alphabetically.[17]

---

[15] BAL, R 2 Anh./7, RMF Schnellbrief, December 9, 1941.

[16] Henry Friedlander and Sybil Milton (eds.), *Archives of the Holocaust, Volume 22: Zentrale Stelle der Landesjustizverwaltungen, Ludwigsburg* (New York: Garland, 1993), pp. 21–22.

[17] LAB, A Rep. 092, Acc. 3924, No. 769, Generalia – Judenvermögensverwertung, Handakte Moser, OFP Berlin Brandenburg Vermoegensverwaltung, OFP Berlin Verv.-Auss. O 5205 – Allgemein – P II Verv., February 9, 1942. Theresienstadt was in the Protectorate of Bohemia and Moravia, but was deemed to be "Reich" territory for the purposes of the Eleventh Decree. On this point, see also Chapter 4.

Despite Hitler's expressed desire to reduce the bureaucratic efforts necessary for property confiscation,[18] individual files were opened for each Jewish victim, as debts still had to be paid off up to the level of the value of the remaining property collected. Each file began with the victim's property declaration, which was filled out just before deportation; the ensuing correspondence in the files is mainly concerned with the collection of outstanding sums from bank accounts, the sale of property, the return of security deposits, and the like, together with eventual payments to legitimate creditors.[19] These files offer snapshots of victims' lives at the time of the deportations, not only listing furniture and other remaining property but also documenting matters such as forced labor and unpaid bills.[20] However, most of the documents – usually typewritten on preprinted forms – are concerned with the administration and liquidation of the property left behind. The sheer number of different form letters, the wide array of organizations involved, and the frequent references to "evacuation" or "deportation" leave no doubt that the disappearance of Berlin's Jews was an everyday reality and no secret at all.

The property declarations usually were filled out at the collecting points just prior to deportation. Siegmund Weltlinger, who worked for the Jewish community in Berlin at the collecting point (the synagogue building) in the Levetzowstrasse, described the experience: "I sat there with a staff of co-workers throughout the night, preparing the property registration forms and checking the lists. I will never forget the nights that I had to spend there. Heartbreaking scenes were played out. There were always suicides or attempted suicides. Some women jumped from upstairs onto the marble floor; a more terrible desecration of a place of worship could not be imagined."[21] In any case, by the time of their deportation, most Jews had very little property left. For example, Max Neuberger, born in 1880 in Frankfurt am Main, worked as an employee of the RV with monthly net wages of RM 190 just before his deportation to Auschwitz on May 17, 1943, on the thirty-eighth transport. His monthly rent was RM 131.

---

[18] Cornelia Essner, Die "Nürnberger Gesetze" oder die Verwaltung des Rassenwahns 1933–1945 (Paderborn: Schöningh, 2002), p. 302.

[19] See, for example, LAB, A Rep. 092/1152 and 092/3235; for further examples, see Inka Bertz, "Ein Karteiblatt für jeden abgeschobenen Juden erleichtert die Übersicht," in Dorothea Kolland (ed.), Zehn Brüder waren wir gewesen . . . : Spuren jüdischen Lebens in Berlin-Neukölln (Berlin: Edition Hentrich, 1988): 372–86. A detailed analysis of one individual file can be found in Kurt Schilde, Bürokratie des Todes: Lebensgeschichten jüdischer Opfer des NS-Regimes im Spiegel von Finanzamtsakten (Berlin: Metropol, 2002), pp. 77–187.

[20] See LAB, A Rep. 092, file of N. W., born 1913 Berlin.

[21] Cited in K. Schilde, Bürokratie des Todes, p. 70.

According to his property declaration, his entire wealth consisted of RM 35 he had left in his apartment and RM 1.88 still in his wallet.[22]

Regardless of the size of the sums, officials wrote in turn to banks and life insurance companies to dissolve remaining accounts "legally," with the capitalized values being transferred directly to the Reich. The recovery of outstanding obligations and loans demanded enormous bureaucratic efforts. Regional financial offices also had to deal with the outstanding debts of many victims; for example, some of these debts were reclaimed by gas and electricity companies from remaining bank balances using printed forms signed with the Nazi greeting, "Heil Hitler." Individuals wrote hopeful letters of application for the opportunity to purchase Jewish real estate, stressing their loyalty to and sacrifices for the regime. The Dresdner Bank requested permission to sell off Jewish securities directly to favored customers.[23] In all this correspondence, the participants acted strictly in accordance with Nazi legal regulations. The courts had to amend the ownership records in deed books from the name of the former Jewish owner to the "German Reich (Reich Financial Administration)," leaving an indelible imprint in surviving property registers.[24]

The only objections to this expropriation were phrased in terms of legal propriety or possible political implications abroad. The legal department of the Deutsche Bank, for example, expressed concern at the procedures adopted by the OFP Berlin-Brandenburg, arguing that the possibility could not be ruled out that some Jews abroad had in the meantime obtained the citizenship of another country before the Eleventh Decree had come into force, which would render the declared confiscation illegal and open the bank to possible legal action overseas.[25] The main effect of such objections was to slow down the process of confiscation. As the OFP in Westphalia noted at the end of March, in those cases where confirmation from the head of the Security Police and SD had been specifically requested, not one had been completed over the preceding two and a half months.[26] Subsequently, the Finance Ministry instructed the OFP Berlin-Brandenburg

---

[22] Mario Offenburg (ed.), *Adass Jisroel: Die Jüdische Gemeinde in Berlin (1869–1942): Vernichtet und Vergessen* (Berlin: Museumspädagogischer Dienst, 1986), pp. 244–45.

[23] Wolfgang Dreßen (ed.), *Betrifft: "Aktion 3". Deutsche verwerten jüdische Nachbarn. Dokumente zur Arisierung* (Berlin: Aufbau Verlag, 1998), pp. 42 and 227.

[24] Monika Schmidt, "'*Arisierungspolitik*' des Bezirksamtes," in Karl-Heinz Metzger et al. (eds.), *Kommunalverwaltung unterm Hakenkreuz: Berlin-Wilmersdorf 1933–1945* (Berlin: Hentrich, 1992): 169–228, here p. 224.

[25] BAL, R 2/9172b, pp. 26–35, Deutsche Bank an OFP Berlin-Brandenburg, March 10, 1942.

[26] Ibid., p. 55, OFP Westfalen in Münster an RFM, March 31, 1942.

not to issue further confiscation orders other than for deported Jews, unless a determination from the head of the Security Police and SD had already been issued. The consequent delays meant that, with respect to the property of Jewish emigrants, the Eleventh Decree largely failed to achieve its goal.[27]

In the case of one Jewish emigrant, E. L., a Security Police determination was not issued until November 23, 1944. Then on January 18, 1945, the Property Processing Office of the OFP Berlin-Brandenburg requested that the Gestapo in Hamburg transfer RM 10,266 to the account entitled "property fallen to the Reich," comprising the proceeds from the much earlier sale of E. L.'s removal goods that the Gestapo had been handling.[28] With regard to the processing of securities in particular, the income expected from the Eleventh Decree did not flow as quickly as the finance officials had anticipated.

Using Jews' Securities to Manipulate the Financial Markets

Securities formed a considerable part of assets owned by Jews in the Reich in the late 1930s. According to the property census for Austria, more than 10 percent of Jewish property lay in securities; for the Old Reich, the proportion was higher.[29] Some 35 percent of revenue from the "punitive tax" came in the form of securities, as payment in this form was strongly encouraged.[30] Almost 25 percent of the revenue from the implementation of the Eleventh Decree was reportedly in the form of securities (although part of this actually derived from the thousands of denaturalizations ordered before November 1941).[31]

An examination of surviving files among the 20,000 at the Oberfinanzdirektion in Berlin (the so-called Patzer files) demonstrates that most Jews owning securities had relatively small portfolios, worth a few thousand Reichsmark or less. Just a few files reveal large-scale investments of more than RM 20,000 or even in excess of RM 100,000. Most of the larger amounts belonged to individuals who had succeeded in emigrating before

---

[27] Ludolf Herbst and Thomas Wiehe (eds.), *Die Commerzbank und die Juden 1933–1945* (Munich: C. H. Beck, 2004), pp. 166–67.

[28] LAB, A Rep. 092/23119, file of E. L., Vermögensverwertungsstelle (Vv) an Gestapo Hamburg, January 18, 1945.

[29] H. G. Adler, *Der verwaltete Mensch: Studien zur Deportation der Juden aus Deutschland* (Tübingen: J. C. B. Mohr, 1974), p. 534.

[30] Of the punitive tax payments received up to September 1939, securities made up some RM 293 million of the first RM 804 million paid by individual Jews, about 35 percent; see Stefan Mehl, *Das Reichsfinanzministerium und die Verfolgung der deutschen Juden 1933–1943* (Berlin, 1990), p. 75.

[31] See Chapter 4.

implementation of the Eleventh Decree and were registered earlier in the expropriation process. It is difficult to generalize about the types of shares held by Jewish investors, but they do not appear to have differed much from those held by other private investors. Familiar names of prominent German companies, such as I. G. Farben, Löwenbräu, Siemens & Halske, and Degussa, appear in Jewish-owned portfolios.

A concern expressed during the Air Ministry conference in November 1938 was that a sudden massive sale of Jewish-owned shares might lead to a sharp fall in the stock market, damaging the economy and embarrassing the government.[32] Therefore, when the imposition of the punitive tax caused Jews to surrender large numbers of securities to the Reich, including many shares in payment, the government appointed the Prussian State Bank (*Seehandlung*) as the sole agent for receiving shares. The intention was for the Prussian State Bank to sell these shares gradually, giving the Economics Ministry the side benefit of a convenient instrument for manipulating the level of the stock market in its own interest.[33] In the months after November 1938, the section of the Prussian State Bank dealing with shares surrendered in payment of the punitive tax had its hands full, despite doubling its initially assigned manpower by February 1939.[34]

In the first months of the war, share prices rose appreciably, boosted by German military success and the prospect of a victorious peace. As one of the main financial newspapers, the *Frankfurter Zeitung*, put it in December 1940, "The reservoir of Jewish shares had for a long time helped to limit the rise in share prices."[35] The same article noted that large companies had amassed considerable holdings of shares, but were reluctant to sell because of the high taxes they would have to pay. The proposal at that time for all shares to be registered was also seen as a step toward stricter government controls, intended to dissuade companies from continuing to buy shares with surplus cash.[36]

---

[32] PS-1816, IMT, Nuremberg, *Trial of the Major War Criminals* (hereafter, Blue Series) (Nuremberg, 1948), vol. XXVIII, pp. 537–40.

[33] BAL, R 2/9172b, pp. 16 and reverse, RFM note on the treatment of securities fallen to the Reich according to the 11. VO., Dec. 9, 1941: "The [Prussian State Bank] Seehandlung put the shares on the market in accordance with the instructions of the Economics Ministry, in order to facilitate the damping down of prices on the stock market, which the Economics Ministry desired."

[34] GSPK, I Rep. 109 Preussischer Staatsbank (Seehandlung)/6253, Haushalte Seehandlung 1925–42, report of Preussischer Staatsbank, Berlin, February 17, 1939.

[35] GSPK, I Rep. 109/1121, Lage an den Geld u. Effektenmärkten, 1938–1942, "Konzentration des Aktienbesitzes," extract from *Frankfurter Zeitung*, December 3, 1940.

[36] Ibid.

In spring 1941, expectations of a new tax on dividends helped depress the stock market briefly; however, prices recovered even before the law was finally announced.[37] A government plan for the registration of shares bought since the start of the war again emerged in November 1941, which no doubt raised the specter of a further wartime tax on profits as a means to restrain stock market gains.[38] Thus, the government used not only the gradual release of Jewish shares but also active threats to the profitability of shareholding to try to tilt the market in favor of government bonds. Eventually, in the spring of 1942, a cap was put on the selling price of certain shares, starting with those of I. G. Farben, to prevent further rapid rises.[39] Nevertheless, as Götz Aly observes, the demand for shares remained insatiable even after Germany's military fortunes started to decline, as companies saw stocks as a much better long-term investment than government bonds, despite the restriction on dividends and the manipulation of share prices. Finally, in early 1943, the government froze all share prices, effectively putting an end to further public trading.[40]

Compulsory Exchange of Jewish Shares for Government Bonds

Part of Göring's strategy, proposed in 1938 to remove Jewish influence from the economy and to mobilize Jewish wealth for the German war effort, was the compulsory exchange of Jewish shares for government bonds. His plan was not entirely new, as foreign securities, including those held by non-Jews, had already been subjected to compulsory surrender (with compensation) earlier in the 1930s as a means to generate foreign exchange.[41] However, it was not until August 28, 1941, that the Economics Ministry prohibited the free sale of shares owned by Jews and ordered that they be surrendered to the Prussian State Bank in exchange for government bonds paying 3.5 percent interest.[42] This order continued the policy of containing stock market rises to keep interest rates low and help the government sell its own bonds. The timing of this measure almost certainly reflected the observed need for more reserves of (Jewish) shares to throw onto the market in light of continued stock market rises, rather than any direct connection with the planned

---

[37] Ibid., *Frankfurter Zeitung*, April 20, 1941.

[38] Ibid., *Frankfurter Zeitung*, November 2, 1941.

[39] See GSPK, I Rep. 109/1121.

[40] G. Aly, *Hitlers Volksstaat*, p. 85.

[41] See, for example, Ralf Banken, "Die nationalsozialistischen Goldreserven und Devisenpolitik 1933–1939," *Jahrbuch für Wirtschaftsgeschichte* 1 (2003): 49–78.

[42] J. Walk (ed.), *Das Sonderrecht für die Juden im NS-Staat*, Second edition (Heidelberg: C. F. Müller, 1996), IV-224.

Eleventh Decree. By this time, further denaturalization proposals had already been stopped in anticipation of the forthcoming law.[43] Interestingly, a similar exchange of Jewish-owned shares for government bonds was initiated in the Netherlands just a few of months later, in November 1941.[44]

Implementation of the share exchange in the Reich resulted in considerable financial losses to Jews still holding shares, as share values were calculated as of March 31, 1941, in spite of the sharp stock market rise since that time. Officials of the RV calculated in September 1941 that it would suffer a loss of several hundred thousand Reichsmark due to this measure and protested (in vain) to the Economics Ministry.[45] An example of how this measure was implemented can be found in the flight tax records of the Tax Office Charlottenburg-Ost. A Jewish man (initials A. I. M.) held I. G. Farben shares with a nominal value of RM 11,000 in a bank depot, as a security for his anticipated flight tax payment. After the Economics Ministry instruction in August, the bank requested permission from the Tax Office in September to convert the shares into government bonds bearing 3.5 percent interest.[46] However, it was not until late December 1941 that the bank reported having sent the share certificates to the Prussian State Bank, and it was not expecting to receive the government bonds for another two or three months.[47] In fact, the bureaucratic effort involved in these conversions proved to be quite an embarrassment to the Prussian State Bank, for by the time it began making the conversions in October 1941, the RSHA had already initiated mass deportations of Jews from Germany, causing most of the shares concerned to come directly into the Reich's possession anyway as a result of the Eleventh Decree.

Effects of the Eleventh Decree on the Compulsory Conversion of Shares

In a letter from the Economics Ministry to Bayrhoffer at the Finance Ministry (RFM), dated February 3, 1942, Dr. Kohler drew attention to the difficulties arising for the Prussian State Bank from the implementation of the

---

[43] BAL, R 58/276, RSHA an alle Stapo(leit)stellen, June 13, 1941.

[44] Gerard Aalders, *Geraubt! Die Enteignung jüdischen Besitzes im Zweiten Weltkrieg* (Cologne: Dittrich, 2000), p. 273; see also Chapter 7.

[45] See USHMM, RG-14.003M (Reichsvereinigung der Juden), no. 125, pp. 111–20.

[46] OFDB, Sammlung FA Charlottenburg-Ost, Reichsfluchtsteuer file of A. I. M., letter from Bank Haslinger Söhne to FA Hansa, September 26, 1941.

[47] Ibid., letter from Bank Haslinger Söhne to FA Hansa, December 29, 1941; see also, for example, LAB, A Rep. 092, Nr. 7082, file of H. I. D., September 11, 1941, shares delivered to Pr. Staatsbank, converted to 3.5 percent Reichsschatzanweisungen and received back in depot of Deutsche Bank on February 5, 1942.

Eleventh Decree. Apparently, it was very difficult for the bank to obtain the confiscated Jewish shares quickly, and as a result, its interventions on the stock market to regulate share prices had broken down. For more than a week, all market activities by the Prussian State Bank had to be stopped.[48]

A subsequent letter from Hermann Schilling of the Prussian State Bank to Walther Bayrhoffer of the RFM on April 28, 1942, clarifies the nature of these "difficulties." The Prussian State Bank, in close cooperation with the Economics Ministry, was using formerly Jewish-owned shares reported to them to influence the stock market. The Prussian State Bank assumed large-scale obligations to deliver specific shares by a fixed date. In other words, it conducted a form of futures trading using anticipated supplies of Jewish shares.

After the proclamation of the Eleventh Decree in November 1941, a large part of the Jewish shares expected by the Prussian State Bank from the conversion operation failed to arrive promptly at the bank. As other correspondence demonstrates, there was some confusion among the banks and the regional financial administrations whether to send share certificates to the Reich Treasury or to the Prussian State Bank.[49] In addition, the process of converting shares to government bonds itself took several months on average to implement, and the implementation of the Eleventh Decree was also subject to delays, especially for Jews living abroad whose citizenship status was not clear.[50] Therefore, the Prussian State Bank got into serious difficulties. The shortfall of shares caused by these effects of the Eleventh Decree amounted to about 3,000 transactions. Reserves of reported shares foreseen for later interventions had to be drawn on immediately, and some deliveries were met only several months after the due date. Overall, the Prussian State Bank managed to avoid large-scale damage, but they did have to make some emergency purchases on the free market (at higher prices) to meet the shortfall. In general, however, the price differential paid remained within reason. Again, Schilling of the Prussian State Bank requested prompt delivery by the relevant financial offices (the OFPs) of the previously requested shares. He commented, "If we had known that a large part of the reserves registered here would not come to us, then we would not have intervened on the same scale."[51]

---

[48] OFDB, Div. Ordner I (Ausarbeitungen des Archivs des ehem. RFM – Handakte Scheerans), p. 238, RWM an RMF, February 3, 1942.

[49] BAL, R 2/9172b, pp. 82–83, OFP Hamburg to RFM, January 6, 1942 and reply of RFM to OFP Hamburg, April 15, 1942.

[50] See, for example, the correspondence with the Deutsche Bank cited above.

[51] OFDB, Div. Ordner I (Ausarbeitungen des Archivs des ehem. RFM – Handakte Scheerans), p. 239, Preuss. Staatsbank an RWM, April 28, 1942. The official accounts of the

This surprising story reveals the extent to which the Reich government was drawn into market manipulation through the use of Jewish shares temporarily in its possession. There were, however, some limits to government intervention. When I. G. Farben offered a large-scale reinvestment opportunity in 1942 on favorable terms for existing shareholders, it was deemed inappropriate for the government to participate and invest public money in a speculative manner to take advantage of Jewish shares temporarily in their possession.[52]

Slow Processing of Shares

It is difficult to estimate the balance among shares, interest-bearing certificates, and government bonds held by Jews. It should be noted that only some 6,000 companies were traded on German stock exchanges in the 1930s and this number was declining, partly due to the effects of increasing government regulation and intervention. Only under specific conditions were companies allowed to raise share capital through new issues, as the government was keen to direct available liquid savings into government bonds. Most attractive were the fixed-interest private bonds of 5 percent or higher, which when available usually were sold directly by the banks to their favored customers.

After discussions held in early December 1941 at the RFM, it was decided that the OFP in Berlin was to be informed directly about the sale of all Jewish shares by the Prussian State Bank.[53] In the archives of the Oberfinanzdirektion Berlin have been preserved lists of the shares sold by the Prussian State Bank recording the amounts booked to the Reich Treasury. These lists provide a rough overview of the progress made in processing and selling shares between 1942 and 1944. In June 1999, access was granted to examine these so-called *Verwertungslisten*, which consist of two "*Leitz Ordner*" files, numbered 49 and 50. The first contains the sales receipts for the period from March 1, 1942 to June 30, 1943; the second file covers the period from July 10, 1943 to January 26, 1945. Between March and December 1942, just over RM 12 million from this source was booked to the Reich Main Treasury in budget section (*Haushaltsplan*) XVII, chapter 7,

Prussian State Bank are hard to decipher, but in February 1942 a discrepancy between expected (*Soll*) and actual (*Haben*) levels of Jewish shares of some RM 5 million appears in the ledgers, although the real meaning of this is not clear from the document. See GSPK, I Rep. 109/6068 (monthly results, February 1942). By the end of December 1942, the overall total on Konto 31 (Übernahme aus Judenbesitz) had reached some RM 70 million, up from about 30 million in February 1942.

[52] OFDB, Div. Ordner I (Ausarbeitungen des Archivs des ehem. RFM – Handakte Scheerans), pp. 308–309, RFM note, September 9, 1942.
[53] BAL, R 2/9172b RFM, Niederschrift über eine Besprechung am 6. Dezember 1941.

heading, 1 or 2. Throughout the whole of 1943, a similar sum was paid in, and for the whole of 1944 an additional sum in excess of 7 million RM – making a total of more than RM 31 million.[54]

These rough tallies estimated from the ledgers correspond fairly well with a report of the Reichsbank directorate in August 1944 on the progress in processing various kinds of securities. The report noted that, on the basis of the Eleventh Decree, 52,000 security certificates (*Effektenposten*) had been received, of which roughly 33,000 had so far been sold or otherwise credited to the Reich, leaving about 19,000 to be processed. The Reich debt administration had so far received about RM 70 million in government bonds, whereas from the shares, bonds, foreign securities, and other industrial obligations so far about RM 50 million had been received. According to the rough calculations of the Reich Treasury, approximately 25,000 more security certificates from Jewish sources were still expected.[55]

These figures confirm the relatively slow progress made in reselling Jewish-owned shares obtained as a result of the Eleventh Decree. Subsequent estimates suggest that, in total, approximately RM 186 million in securities were raised by the Eleventh Decree up to the end of 1944,[56] although in fact part of this income almost certainly derived from the intensified denaturalizations pursued from the summer of 1940 and directed at emigrant property in Germany. In any case, the bulk of the revenue obtained from Jewish-owned securities did not stem from 1942–44, as the punitive tax and the flight tax operations combined netted considerably more in securities during 1938–41. Significantly, only about half of the share certificates expected from the Eleventh Decree had actually been processed by summer 1944. Progress slowed toward the end of the war, as staffing levels were further reduced and processing offices were dislocated by Allied bombing.[57]

An analysis of individual files from the so-called Patzer Section, which dealt with securities in the Reich Finance Ministry, largely confirms the impression gained from these general reports. However, it is clear that some shares were bought directly by the deposit-holding banks, cutting out the

---

[54] OFDB, Leitz Ordner 49, Preuss. Staatsbank (Seehandlung) Verwertungslisten vom 1.3.42 bis 30.6.43 and Leitz Ordner 50, Preuss. Staatsbank (Seehandlung) Verwertungslisten vom 10.7.43 bis zum 26.1.45.

[55] LAB, B Rep. 039-01/252 (Polen-Hausrat), p. 98, Reichsbank Direktorium, August 24, 1944; M. Offenberg (ed.), *Adass Jisroel: Die Jüdische Gemeinde in Berlin*, p. 260, gives the figure of 33,000 completed and 12,000 unfinished files from the Patzer Section being preserved by the RFM at the end of the war.

[56] H. G. Adler, *Der verwaltete Mensch*, p. 545.

[57] LAB, B Rep. 039-01/376, pp. 149–59, Gutachten Berliner Zentralbank, December 16, 1953.

middleman (the Prussian State Bank) and remitting the proceeds directly to the Reich Treasury. In addition, among the files are some denaturalization cases that had been initiated before the Eleventh Decree, whereas other files concern individuals deported to destinations, such as Auschwitz, Łódź, or Theresienstadt, where the Eleventh Decree did not apply as they were inside the Reich. Thus the above-cited estimate of RM 186 million from the Eleventh Decree alone needs to be considered with some caution.

Administrative Organization of Property Processing

On December 1, 1941, at the instigation of the Gestapo, the RV issued a circular forbidding Jews from selling or giving away their remaining movable property prior to deportation. The instruction tried to counteract this widespread practice that diverted many valuable items away from the clutches of the financial administration.[58] The officials of the RV were compelled to participate in the deportations in a number of ways, including being involved in the distribution of deportation notifications or assisting the deportees with the preparation of required paperwork and with their other immediate needs at the collecting points.[59]

After the proclamation of the Eleventh Decree, the Security Police reduced to RM 150 per month the maximum that could be withdrawn from blocked Jewish accounts. In response, the Economics Ministry instructed the Currency Offices to adjust previous security orders, especially those issued before the summer of 1939, as these often still had higher monthly limits. Clearly, the aim was to secure the bulk of remaining Jewish assets for confiscation under the Eleventh Decree. For example, applications to make gifts were henceforth to be refused if there was any suspicion that the aim was to avoid subsequent confiscation.[60] During the first weeks of February 1942, numerous new security orders were issued by Currency Offices, such as that in Rudolstadt, reducing the monthly limit to RM 150. In one case, a Jewish doctor who had been living from the money in her business account died upon being informed of her reduced limit.[61] Even

---

[58] BAL, R 58/276, RV Rundschreiben, December 1, 1941.
[59] K. Schilde, *Bürokratie des Todes*, p. 68; Beate Meyer, "Handlungsspielräume regionaler jüdischer Repräsentanten (1941–1945) – Die Reichsvereinigung der Juden in Deutschland und die Deportationen," in *Beiträge zur Geschichte des Nationalsozialismus 20, Die Deportation der Juden aus Deutschland: Pläne – Praxis – Reaktionen 1938–1945* (Göttingen: Wallstein, 2004): 63–83, here p. 66.
[60] BAL, R 139 II/110, p. 130, RWM an OFP Devisenstellen, January 19, 1942.
[61] BAL, R 139 II/114, file of Dr. med. Leonie Cohen.

after February 1942, there remained some flexibility in the application of the rules by the Currency Offices. One family's appeal of the reduction of the limit to RM 150 resulted in a slightly higher limit temporarily, as the money was required to pay for domestic help. However, the limit was enforced once the domestic assistant left the family.[62]

The enormous increase in work following the Eleventh Decree required a special division of labor within the financial administration. A circular dated February 27, 1942, confirmed the delegation (initiated in November 1941) to the regional OFPs of responsibility for processing the property of the deported Jews. However, the OFP Berlin-Brandenburg still maintained a central card index for the whole of Germany, requiring notification from the regional OFPs of business conducted at the local level.[63] Within the financial bureaucracy, strict distinctions were made between the denaturalization cases (reference: O 5210) and the deportation cases (reference: O 5205), as the regulations differed in key points and the income was also booked separately within the Reich's accounts.[64]

The section of the Finanzamt Moabit-West that processed emigrant property (denaturalizations) was renamed the *Vermögensverwertungsstelle* (Property Processing Office) and became integrated within the OFP Berlin in December 1941.[65] This office retained responsibility for all cases concerning emigrant Jews and the processing of property from all Jews deported from Berlin. Because of the enormous increase in work arising from the Eleventh Decree, the Property Processing Office was also rapidly expanded, accelerating the continuous growth experienced by the Finanzamt Moabit-West since 1937. Internal correspondence reflects constant concerns about staff shortages and the ever-mounting burden of work. At a staff meeting in March 1942, the leadership even stressed the need to reply to incoming mail promptly, so as not to give the impression that the office had been brought

---

[62] BAL, R 139 II/115, file of Renate Eckmann.

[63] George Weiss (ed.), *Einige Dokumente zur Rechtsstellung der Juden und zur Entziehung ihres Vermögens 1933–1945: Schriftenreihe zum Berliner Rückerstattungsrecht VII* (Germany: G. Weiss, 1950), pp. 59–61, RFM o 5210 – 1839 VI, February 27, 1942.

[64] LAB, A Rep. 092, Acc. 3924, Nr. 769 (Handakte Moser), OFP B-B Vv – Aussenstelle o 5210 – Allg – P II Verv, Vfg., April 4, 1942.

[65] S. Mehl, *Das Reichsfinanzministerium*, p. 102; LAB, A Rep. 092, Acc. 3924, Nr. 769, OFP Berlin Vv-Aussenstelle o 5210 – Allgemein.: notes of the office meeting of December 6, 1941. Martin Friedenberger, "Das Berliner Finanzamt Moabit-West und die Enteignung der Emigranten des Dritten Reichs 1933–1942," *Zeitschrift für Geschichtswissenschaft* 49:8 (2001): 677–94, stresses the loss of competence by the Finanzamt Moabit-West as a result of this reorganization, but the key point was that its staff remained the core of the newly created office.

to a standstill since November 1941.[66] By October 1942, at the height of its operations, its staff had expanded to more than four hundred people.[67]

Deportation Waves and Destinations

The deportations of Jews from the Reich took place in a series of waves with different destinations. Between mid-October 1941 and March 1942, 60,000 Jews were deported from Germany, Austria, and the Protectorate. The destinations of these transports included Łódź (Litzmannstadt), Warsaw, Riga, Kaunas (Kovno), and Minsk. Among the largest deportations in this period were those from Berlin, Hamburg, Cologne, Frankfurt am Main, Munich, and Nuremberg. Then from mid-March until mid-June 1942 another 55,000 Jews were deported into the ghettos and camps (especially Izbica, Piaski, and Zamość) of the Lublin district of the General Government.[68] Beginning in June 1942, some deportations were directed to Theresienstadt, where mostly elderly Jews, but also some other privileged groups, were sent with the intention of creating the propaganda impression that those who were deported were receiving decent treatment.[69] However, more than 80,000 Jews from Theresienstadt were deported on to Auschwitz and other extermination or labor camps where most died, and nearly 34,000 people died from the poor living conditions in Theresienstadt itself.[70] By 1943, the main destination for Jews from the Reich was Auschwitz; between the end of January and the middle of March 1943, more than 10,000 Jews were sent there from Berlin, as a result of an effort to comb out those still working in factories.[71] After this time, smaller transports, mostly of groups previously exempted, continued to depart from the Reich right up to the end of March 1945.

---

[66] LAB, A Rep. 092, Generalia, note of internal meeting on March 14, 1942.

[67] LAB, A Rep. 092/54619.

[68] *Beiträge zur Geschichte des Nationalsozialismus 20, Die Deportation der Juden aus Deutschland*, p. 12 (Editorial); *Gedenkbuch: Opfer der Verfolgung der Juden unter der nationalsozialistischen Gewaltherrschaft in Deutschland, 1933–1945* (Frankfurt am Main: J. Weisbecker, 1986), vol. II, p. 1743.

[69] See the film *Der Führer schenkt den Juden eine Stadt* (Waltham, MA: National Center for Jewish Film, 1991).

[70] See Vojtech Blodig, *Terezín in the "Final Solution of the Jewish Question" 1941–1945: Guide to the Permanent Exhibition of the Ghetto Museum in Terezin* (Prague: Oswald, 2003); *Gedenkbuch: Opfer der Verfolgung*, vol. 2, pp. 1772–73; Freie Universität Berlin, Zentralinstitut für sozialwissenschaftliche Forschung (ed.), *Gedenkbuch Berlins: Der jüdischen Opfer des Nationalsozialismus* (Berlin: Druckhaus Hentrich, 1995), pp. 1421–22.

[71] *Gedenkbuch Berlins*, p. 1420.

Monica Kingreen has analyzed the main deportation waves from Hessen, examining also correspondence received from a few individuals after their arrival in some of the camps. Among the deportations from Frankfurt were large transports to Riga, Minsk, and Kaunas in October and November 1941; in the spring of 1942, deportees from Hessen were sent to the Piaski ghetto near Lublin, where most died of hunger or were sent to be gassed at Sobibor. In May and June, others were deported from the collecting points in Frankfurt and Kassel to Lublin (that is, the Majdanek camp) or to Izbica fifty miles to the south. From some transports, there were no survivors at all. In August and September 1942, there were several large transports to Theresienstadt, mostly of elderly Jews. From there, one elderly Jewish woman wrote to her son in Sweden: "I am sorry that I always swore at you for putting your feet on the good sofa – it was all for nothing – but really. I am no longer attached to that stuff – only my good bed [I miss]. . . . "[72]

From the small town of Nordhausen in Thuringia, most Jews were deported in successive waves during 1942: twenty on May 10 into the General Government, fifty-four on September 19 to Theresienstadt, and six on March 2, 1943 "to the East." There were also deportations of single individuals, the last in March 1945, when so-called privileged Jews were deported. Most had little money remaining, but the financial administration collected some RM 8,000 from Harri Hermann and his wife Rosa (deported on September 19, 1942, to Theresienstadt) after the Gestapo issued an official confiscation certificate.[73]

The progressive humiliation and robbery of German Jews on the way to their deaths continued after the confiscation of the property left behind in their apartments. In Nuremberg, Jews were beaten and robbed while awaiting deportation in a camp on the Reich Party rallying grounds.[74] In 1961, Heinz Lohmüller recalled some of his experiences on the first transport from Dortmund to Riga on January 15, 1942. Before departure the Jews had to surrender their money and jewelry. They were also kept in isolation for five days before and were searched repeatedly for concealed property. In Dortmund, they had been permitted to retain only one bag on boarding the train, and their other luggage was put onto a separate car that was detached in Königsberg. On arrival at the Shiritova station near Riga,

---

[72] Monica Kingreen, "'Wir werden darüber hinweg kommen': Letzte Lebenszeichen deportierter hessischer Juden. Eine dokumentarische Annäherung," in *Beiträge zur Geschichte des Nationalsozialismus 20, Die Deportation der Juden aus Deutschland*: 86–111, quotation on p. 107.

[73] D. Reschwamm, "Die Vertreibung und Vernichtung der Juden im Spiegel der Akten des Finanzamtes Nordhausen," *Geschichte, Erziehung, Politik* 7 (1996): 404–13, pp. 411–12.

[74] See B. Meyer, "Handlungsspielräume," pp. 76–77.

the Jews were required to leave their remaining luggage on the platform and were escorted into the ghetto. The bags left at the station in Riga were eventually returned, but only after they had been searched. Those who braved the beatings of the SS to reclaim their bags generally discovered that less than half of the original contents remained. The Jewish deportees were subjected to further body searches in Riga. Their best clothes were taken, leaving them practically in rags. The few valuables they retained could be exchanged for food or other badly needed goods (at inflated prices) only when they were escorted out of the ghetto for forced labor.[75]

Clearing Property from Emptied Apartments

The task of clearing the emptied Jewish apartments was a rather eerie one. The predominant image left behind by the vast correspondence about outstanding gas bills, the winding up of bank accounts, the recall and sale of remaining securities, and the administration of real estate is one of emptiness – the whole infrastructure of a person's life in terms of housing and possessions being tidied up and put away. The impression made on an intruder who glimpsed this emptiness is conjured up in a description by one of the men who helped clear out the "evacuated" apartments:

> On our arrival the lock on the apartment door had only been patched up, but the door was sealed. This apartment, or rather how the Nazis had treated it, is still in my mind. On the kitchen table there were two half-empty cups and next to them two half-eaten rolls. There were still ration cards on the table and a notice for Jews concerning things they were forbidden to do.... In the rooms everything had been turned upside down. The drawers of the furniture had been partially emptied on the floor. Someone had clearly been searching for valuables and stolen them.[76]

This petty pilfering in the immediate wake of the deportations reflected also more systematic corruption among Gestapo and other officials involved in organizing the deportations. In Berlin, the head of the Gestapo, SS Obersturmbannführer Otto Bovensiepen, was transferred in disgrace in November 1942, as several of his subordinates were under investigation for personal enrichment; they were accused of taking property from Jews at the collecting point in the Levetzowstrasse and from empty Jewish apartments.[77] The investigation revealed that (at least initially) the Gestapo officials had

---

[75] LAB, B Rep. 039-01/248 (Polen- Edelmetalle 2), statement of Heinz Lohmüller, January 28, 1961.

[76] Cited in K. Schilde, *Bürokratie des Todes*, pp. 74–75.

[77] Ibid., pp. 64–65.

kept no proper accounts, leading to "gross irregularities" in handling funds and property.[78]

An example of how the apartments were cleared emerges from the file of P. A., preserved among the thousands of records of the OFP Berlin-Brandenburg. After P. A.'s deportation in September, the contents of his apartment were examined by a court assessor on October 14, 1942, and valued at RM 811.00. Among the items listed in the property declaration just for the dining room were a dining table, five chairs, an armchair, a glass cabinet, a cupboard, a lamp, a carpet, and a tea trolley. The estimator's fee for his work was RM 14. The contents were sold en bloc to the trader A. S., who paid the assessed amount minus 30 percent, or RM 567.70, after clearing the apartment on February 11, 1943. The net profit to the Reich from this clearance, however, was limited, as an additional RM 480 in rent had to be deducted for the period before the apartment was emptied, offset slightly by the RM 4.47 collected from the electrical utility company (Bewag), from the deportee's security deposit. The main revenue claimed by the Reich from P. A. consisted of just over RM 10,000 still in a blocked bank account and more than RM 6,600 in securities in a blocked bank "deposit," although it is likely that these funds had already been signed over to the RV at the time of P. A.'s deportation to Theresienstadt.[79]

In Berlin, the financial administration expressed dissatisfaction with the distribution of remaining property from the apartments, which was initially organized by the Economic Group of Traders (a corporate consortium). Therefore, at the beginning of December 1942, the OFP Berlin-Brandenburg argued that the RFM should sign a new contract with the city authorities. The Economic Group of Traders had kept its promise to clear the emptied apartments promptly, but there were complaints that the war wounded and certain government agencies had been unable to obtain sufficient goods and also that prices had been charged above the official fixed levels. The Berlin city administration now offered to clear the apartments quickly itself, which had the advantage for the OFP of enabling it to deal with one centralized agency, rather than with a loose collection of businessmen. In particular, this arrangement would spare the financial administration from having to deal with numerous requests for confiscated

[78] Frank Bajohr, *Parvenüs und Profiteure: Korruption in der NS-Zeit* (Frankfurt am Main: S. Fischer, 2001), p. 122.

[79] LAB, A Rep. 092/1152, file of P. A. (born 1862). The file notes only in late 1944 that the account was no longer in the name of P. A.; for similar examples, see also Alfred Konieczny, *Tormersdorf, Grüssau, Riebnig: Obozy przej'sciowe dla Zydów Dolnego 'Slaska z lat 1941–1943* (Wroclaw: Wydawn. Uniwersytetu Wroclawskiego, 1997), pp. 169–217; and K. Schilde, *Bürokratie des Todes*, pp. 77–187.

property by prominent individuals, a process that had become a consider-able burden on the workload of officials and that hardly could be justified during the war.[80]

The Reich Finance Ministry accepted the city's proposal, and by June 1943 a new contract was ready to be signed. The city would pay the OFP the assessed market price minus 30 percent. The contract specified that various classes of items were excluded from general sale, as they were reserved for specific departments within the government; for example, gramophone records were to go to the Propaganda Ministry, books and newspapers to the RSHA, sewing machines to the Łódź ghetto administration, and Jewish cultural items to the Einsatzstab Reichsleiter Rosenberg (ERR). In the final contract, the city administration also agreed that, in its sale of confiscated items, victims of Allied bombing, the war wounded, decorated soldiers, families with many children, and other individuals worthy of special consideration would be taken care of first.[81]

Deportations of Sinti and Roma

There were considerable similarities between the handling of Jewish prop-erty and that belonging to Sinti and Roma following the deportations. Ulrich Opfermann's case study of the small town of Berleburg in northern Germany demonstrates that virtually the same process of expropriation was applied to this victim group.[82] For example, the Tax Office in Siegen con-fiscated land belonging to deported Sinti and Roma in Berleburg and then leased it out to private individuals at a yearly rate.[83] In Berlin, the municipal gas company wrote to the Property Processing Office of the OFP, inform-ing them that the "female gypsy" (*Zigeunerin*) Johanna Herzenberger had been deported to Auschwitz and claiming the sum of RM 17.06 that she owed to the gas company, as her remaining property had been confiscated by the OFP.[84] Property was confiscated in accordance with the 1933 laws for the confiscation of communist property and that of "enemies of the

---

[80] LAB, A Rep. 092/54623, OFP Berlin-Brandenburg an RFM, December 1, 1942.

[81] Ibid., RFM an OFP, January 4, 1943, draft contract of January 14, 1943 and contract sent by OFP to city mayor on June 19, 1943, for signature.

[82] See Ulrich Friedrich Opfermann, "Zigeunerverfolgung, Enteignung, Umverteilung: Das Beispiel der Wittgensteiner Kreisstadt Berleburg," in Alfons Kenkmann and Bernd-A. Rusinek (eds.), *Verfolgung und Verwaltung*, pp. 67–86.

[83] Finanzamt Siegen, file concerning "Sinti und Roma." I am grateful to Alfons Kenkmann and the staff of the Villa ten Hompel Memorial Site for access to this file.

[84] USHMM, RG-07.008M*1, Oberfinanzdirektion: Property seized from the apartments of Roma and Sinti – 1943.

people and the state"; the names were published in the *Reichsanzeiger* to make the confiscations "legal."[85] Individual files were opened for each person deported, and the "costs of the evacuation" were even deducted from remaining accounts before the sums were transferred to the OFP.[86]

Treatment of Real Estate, Life Insurance, Pensions, Valuables, and Cultural Property

After the publication of the Eleventh Decree, the regional OFPs took over the administration of real estate belonging to deported Jews, reserving part of it for government offices or housing for civil servants. On April 22, 1942, the Finance Ministry ordered that the sale of formerly Jewish real estate be discontinued, so that soldiers returning from the front might have the opportunity to purchase it later. Only certain categories of people, such as war wounded and veterans of the "National Uprising," were exempted from this prohibition, as well as those who had already been in negotiation with the financial administration for some time.[87] In May 1942, the Economics Ministry also stressed that formerly Jewish real estate should be sold at roughly market prices, as it was important that no money should be lost to the Reich.[88] The flow of applications to buy properties continued, and some sales of real estate were conducted through the end of 1942, as the exempted categories were quite broad. However, in a number of cases awaiting official approval, the sales were stopped, as the Economics Ministry had instructed the Price Control Offices not to approve sales contracts if it was likely that the Jewish owner was going to be deported in the near future.[89] Then in February 1943, the RFM put a complete stop to all further sales, again to protect the interests of soldiers absent at the front who otherwise would be denied an opportunity to benefit from them.[90] At the end of the war, the OFP Berlin-Brandenburg was reportedly in possession of some 2,000 Jewish

[85] Ibid.

[86] USHMM, RG-07.008M*3, Oberfinandirektion – property of Roma and Sinti, Bürgermeister Bernau an OFP, Vv, March 5, 1943.

[87] Walter Rummel and Jochen Rath (eds.), *"Dem Reich verfallen" – "den Berechtigten zurückzuerstatten": Enteignung und Rückerstattung jüdischen Vermögens im Gebiet des heutigen Rheinland-Pfalz, 1938–1953* (Koblenz: Verlag der Landesarchivverwaltung Rheinland-Pfalz, 2001), pp. 329–31; H. G. Adler, *Der verwaltete Mensch*, pp. 638–39; LAB, A Rep. 092, Generalia – 357, Pressenotiz RFM, May 1, 1942.

[88] BAL, R 139 II/110, p. 204.

[89] Karl-Heinz Metzger, et al. (eds.), *Kommunalverwaltung unterm Hakenkreuz: Berlin-Wilmersdorf 1933–1945* (Berlin: Hentrich, 1992), pp. 224–25.

[90] H. G. Adler, *Der verwaltete Mensch*, p. 641.

real estate properties,[91] although the effects of Allied bombing, rent control, and lack of repairs meant that many properties had declined in value.

The management of confiscated Jewish property also opened up many opportunities for corruption by property administrators. For example, the authorities were looking for a certain Meyer, who had disappeared after being accused of having exploited his position as a trustee of former Jewish properties to buy up the mortgages, foreclose on them, and then purchase the real estate cheaply.[92]

After the publication of the Eleventh Decree, the OFPs tried to track down all life insurance policies and pensions belonging to deported Jews and emigrants, claiming the capitalized value on behalf of the state. A considerable portion of Jewish property was in the form of annuities or pensions: according to the 1938 property census, some 20 percent of all Jewish assets in Austria were in this form. The Nazi authorities had already started to undermine Jewish state pension rights during the 1930s; in December 1938, for example, Jews were excluded from further annual increases.[93] According to the Eleventh Decree, all state pensions were canceled on deportation, whereas the financial administration claimed 75 percent of the capitalized values of private pension insurance contracts.[94] Many private companies refused, or at least tried to delay, their payment of these capitalized sums to the Reich.[95] In practice, some state pensions had already been canceled prior to deportation: the elderly Jew P. A., deported to Theresienstadt in September 1942 wrote in his property declaration form that his pension from the city of Berlin had not been paid since February 1942.[96]

As Gerald Feldman's research shows, a large proportion of Jewish life insurance policies had already been cashed in or converted to noncontributory polices before November 1941 to pay the punitive and flight taxes, as well as other emigration or living costs. In general, insurance companies complied with government instructions to transfer capitalized sums to the Reich in accordance with legal confiscation orders. In the first years after

[91] OFDB, Div. Ordner I (Ausarbeitungen des Archivs des ehem. RFM – Handakte Scheerans), p. 171.

[92] LAB, A Rep. 092/50244.

[93] J. Walk (ed.), *Das Sonderrecht*, III-66.

[94] BAL, R 2/9172b, p. 127, Reichsaufsichtamt für Privatversicherung an die beaufsichtigten Unternehmen, July 29, 1942.

[95] Raul Hilberg, *Die Vernichtung der europäischen Juden* (Frankfurt am Main: Fischer, 1961, 1982), p. 496; see also Dieter Ziegler, *Die Dresdner Bank und die deutschen Juden* (Munich: R. Oldenbourg, 2006), pp. 98–105.

[96] LAB, A Rep. 092/1152, file of P. A. (born 1862), pp. 1–8, Vermögenserklärung, September 3, 1942.

the end of the war, some very limited compensation was paid in a number of cases, at least for German Jews, as the documentary trail was clear and the West German government assumed responsibility.[97]

After the Kristallnacht pogrom, several mechanisms were established for dealing with Jewish valuables and cultural items that were subject to compulsory surrender or seizure or otherwise were taken by the state in payment of taxes or as a result of confiscation orders. The compulsory surrender of precious metals and jewelry to the municipal pawnshops in early 1939 has been described in connection with the events of Kristallnacht.[98] Special regulations dealt with the handling of artworks, books, and archives.

In June 1939, for example, the Finance Ministry issued instructions for confiscated Jewish and Hebrew literature to be sent to the Prussian State Library, which became the central clearinghouse for deciding whether specific books should be preserved. These instructions covered items confiscated by customs officials at the borders, those seized by the financial administration, and books secured by the police. However, before being transferred to the Prussian State Library, books first had to be evaluated both on security grounds and also with regard to their possible usefulness for research.[99] In August 1940, another RFM circular instructed that, henceforth, Jewish and Hebrew literature should be sent first to the RSHA, which would then pass on to the Prussian State Library those items not required for its own purposes.[100]

Once the deportations got underway in Berlin, the books of evacuated Jews were examined first by an employee of a large bookstore, who estimated their prices and then forwarded most on to various book dealers for sale, with the net proceeds accruing to the Reich. At the same time, he also checked both for restricted items on behalf of the Gestapo and those required for research, which would be offered to the ERR.[101] The ERR did not pay for the items it took, as it did not intend to resell them.[102] A subsequent

[97] Gerald Feldman, *Die Allianz und die deutsche Versicherungswirtschaft 1933–1945* (Munich: C. H. Beck, 2001), pp. 617–26.

[98] See Chapter 3.

[99] USHMM, RG-11.001M.01, reel 5, 500-1-399, RFM Instruction, June 12, 1939, and preceding correspondence, as copies in files of SD. On the robbery and subsequent treatment of Jewish books in several European countries, see Regine Dehnel (ed.), "Jüdischer Buchbesitz als Raubgut," *Zeitschrift für Bibliothekswesen und Bibliographie, Sonderheft* 88 (2005).

[100] LAB, A Rep. 092, Generalia, RFM circular, August 2, 1940; see also BAL, R 139II/110.

[101] LAB, A Rep. 092, Generalia, OFP B–B Vv, circular of June 12, 1942, Betr.: Verwertung der dem Reich mit dem Judenvermögen verfallenen Bücher.

[102] LAB, A Rep. 092, Generalia, RFM, March 21, 1942 (printed instruction) O 5400 – 94 VI.

instruction reaffirmed that books confiscated by the Reich could be sold only after the Gestapo had examined them, retaining any forbidden items or those it still needed.[103] Similar detailed instructions issued by the financial administration dealt with various other types of property, ranging from stamp collections to bicycles.

Beneficiaries

Hundreds of officials, even at the height of the war, were employed to handle the administration and sale of Jewish property. A great many government contractors and private individuals, including property assessors, auction houses, trustees, estate agents, notaries, and transport companies, were also involved. At the bottom of the food chain, thousands of individuals benefited from the sale of cheap household items or the availability of apartments, even if the Nazi administration always tried to preserve a hierarchy based on the Party's racial and social priorities.

Among the main beneficiaries from the resale of Jewish property at generally low fixed prices were members of the financial administration itself. A not inconsiderable part of former Jewish real estate was set aside to provide housing for finance officials, whereas furniture and other items were evaluated first as to whether they could be used for official purposes. The offices of the financial administration and the Gestapo generally obtained the best pieces from confiscated Jewish property.[104] No regulations explicitly excluded finance officials from purchasing items directly for themselves. The senior finance president in Dresden, Dr. Meyer, called up the Reich Finance Ministry in Berlin himself to request permission to buy a small carpet left over from the auctions. The official reply granted his request, noting that, although it was important that finance officials not be seen to enrich themselves in any way from property entrusted to them on behalf of the *Volksgemeinschaft* (German people's community), such purchases would be permitted so as not to disadvantage officials, as long as the full assessed prices were paid.[105] The personal attitudes of officials in the financial administration are difficult to decipher from the very dry official correspondence: The

---

[103] LAB, A Rep. 092, Generalia, Gestapo Berlin Stapo IV B 7 – B 4593/42, July 15, 1942.

[104] Monika Schmidt, "'Arisierungspolitik' des Bezirksamtes," in Karl-Heinz Metzger et al. (eds.), *Kommunalverwaltung unterm Hakenkreuz*: 169–228, here p. 223; Christiane Kuller, "'Erster Grundsatz: Horten für die Reichsfinanzverwaltung': Die Verwertung des Eigentums der deportierten Nürnberger Juden," in *Beiträge zur Geschichte des Nationalsozialismus 20, Die Deportation der Juden aus Deutschland*, pp. 160–79.

[105] BAL, R 2/9172b, p. 90 and reverse, note of a telephone conversation with OFP, Dr. Meyer, Dresden, April 29, 1942.

specific wording was closely regulated, and a great deal of correspondence was conducted using preprinted forms.[106] Yet, in postwar restitution cases, many former finance officials appeared as witnesses and property assessors, revealing quite openly their conviction that the confiscations had been completely legitimate as legal transactions sanctioned by the state. Most remained indifferent to the enormous injustice inflicted on the Jews.

Public Auctions and the Operations of the Vugesta

The widespread auctions of household items reveal the extent to which the general population shared this indifference to the fate of their Jewish neighbors. Frank Bajohr, who found that there were roughly ten separate buyers for the property of each Jew, estimates that at least 100,000 people profited in this way in the Hamburg region alone.[107] Some auctions were actually held in the former apartments of the Jews, although the financial administration soon discouraged this practice as it made the circumstances behind the transaction too transparent. For the town of Bad Driburg in the Höxter district (*Kreis*) near Münster, receipts from auctions of Jewish property have been preserved in the financial archives. In one instance, the Höxter Tax Office auctioned the household items of the Jewish deportee S. B. on May 1, 1942, in the town gymnasium. Among items sold was a leather sofa for RM 115, a wardrobe for RM 69, six plates for RM 2.30, a lemon squeezer for RM 0.65, three tea towels for RM 1.15, and a large tablecloth for RM 3.45. The inventory includes the last names of the various purchasers and also their hometowns.[108] Ironically, detailed auction lists from the archives such as these were able to stir up public debate and controversy more than fifty years after the war.[109]

---

[106] This thorny question of reconstructing the motives and mindset of the finance officials concerned is dealt with in greater detail by several contributors in Katharina Stengel (ed.), *Vor der Vernichtung: Die Staatliche Enteignung der Juden im Nationalsozialismus* (Wissenschaftliche Reihe des Fritz Bauer Instituts, Bd. 15) (Frankfurt am Main: Campus, 2007).

[107] Frank Bajohr, *"Aryanisation" in Hamburg: The Economic Exclusion of the Jews and the Confiscation of Their Property in Nazi Germany* (New York: Berghahn, 2002), p. 279.

[108] F. A. Höxter, Versteigerungsverzeichnisse der jüd. Haushaltungen – Bad Driburg, 1942. I am grateful to the staff of the Villa ten Hompel in Münster for access to this file.

[109] See W. Dreßen (ed.), *Betrifft: "Aktion 3."* The exhibition accompanying this publication drew criticism, as Dreßen decided to publish the names of beneficiaries in contravention of his agreement to black out the names when receiving access from the archives. Some commentators defended his action on the grounds that data protection should not also protect perpetrators or beneficiaries. See for example the newspaper article in the *"taz"* (*die tageszeitung*) on January 23, 2000.

In Austria, a special constellation of private economic interests, working closely with the Gestapo, developed in the fall of 1940 to deal with more than 5,000 crates of Jewish removal goods stranded in the depots of transport companies. As most emigrants were no longer able to pay the mounting storage costs and, by summer 1940, many were being proposed for denaturalization to seize their property, the Gestapo approached a consortium of transport firms to establish a private company, the so-called *Vugesta* (Processing Office for Jewish Removal Goods of the Gestapo). The main idea behind this company was that, rather than having each case treated separately, which might lead to considerable losses for the transport firms, it would treat all the seized property as a single mass.[110]

By the end of 1942, the sale of removal goods in Vienna was largely completed. Therefore, the Gestapo also approached the Vugesta to assist with the sale of items left behind in the thousands of apartments of Jews deported from Vienna. The movable items were collected with the assistance of employees of the Gestapo-controlled Jewish community organization.[111] As the Vugesta was paid on commission, it was eager both to maximize its turnover and profit, auctioning the most valuable pieces through the renowned Viennese auction house, the Dorotheum. However, its activities also reflected the social policy of the Nazi leadership, as victims of bomb damage, the war wounded, and other specific groups received preference in the sale of Jewish property. According to one report, more than 14,000 soldiers on the front, war wounded, war widows, and prioritized individuals received furniture from party member Witke, a senior official of the Vugesta (who also ran his own "antique shop"). In total, the Vugesta sold items for more than RM 15 million, of which some RM 11 million derived from auctions at the Dorotheum. However, in this case, the proceeds did not go directly into the coffers of the Gestapo, as some RM 7 million was transferred to the OFPs in Vienna and in Berlin.[112]

Rivalry between the Security Police and the Financial Administration

The start of mass deportations from the Reich also exacerbated the existing rivalry between the Security Police and the financial administration for control over remaining Jewish property. The executive authority of the Security

---

[110] Robert Holzbauer, "Einziehung volks- und staatsfeindlichen Vermögens im Lande Österreich: Die 'VUGESTA' – die Verwertungsstelle für jüdisches Umzugsgut der Gestapo," *Spurensuche*, 1–2 (2000): 38–50.

[111] H. Safrian, *Eichmann*, p. 176.

[112] R. Holzbauer, "Einziehung," pp. 38–50.

Police in organizing the deportations and its control over the RV enabled it to coerce Jews into signing over part or all of their property, thereby diverting considerable sums from the accounts of Jews being deported. First, the Security Police issued instructions for Jews to pay at least 25 percent of their remaining property into the "Special Account W" and to pay outstanding contributions owed to the RV. These sums ostensibly covered various costs of the deportations and were not supposed to appear in the property declarations.[113] Once regional preparations for the deportation of German Jews had begun, the Gestapo contacted the Currency Offices directly to ensure approval of transfers from blocked Jewish accounts to the Special Account W. In March 1942, for example, the Gestapo in Weimar wrote to the Currency Office in Rudolstadt informing it of plans to "evacuate" a number of local Jews.[114]

Another devious method by which the Security Police gained control of the assets of many elderly German Jews deported to Theresienstadt was getting them to sign so-called *Heimeinkaufverträge* or "[Old-Age] Home Purchase Contracts." As Susanne Willems shows, these contracts originated in the spring of 1941 when the RV developed special "acceptance contracts" for Jews entering homes for the elderly inside the Old Reich. The aim was for the better situated Jews, especially those with no dependents in Germany, to contribute more than the actual cost of their care so as to help pay for those who had insufficient funds. The high "entrance fees" (at least RM 11,000) were assessed from remaining assets declared on a detailed property form, and applicants had only one week to decide whether to accept these harsh conditions.[115]

When the deportations of elderly Jews to Theresienstadt began in summer 1942, the RV, under Gestapo pressure, urged deportees to sign new "Home Purchase Contracts," specifically for Theresienstadt and supposedly to cover their living costs there. Under these contracts, Jews transferred large sums – in some cases all their remaining money – to another special account (*Sonderkonto H*), for transfer to Theresienstadt.[116] The RV also converted some previous "Home Purchase Contracts" to this new format, transferring funds already collected in local accounts to the new Special Account H.

---

[113] H. G. Adler, *Der verwaltete Mensch*, pp. 562–69; Avraham Barkai, *Vom Boykott zur "Entjudung": Der wirtschaftliche Existenzkampf der Juden im Dritten Reich 1933–1943* (Frankfurt am Main: Fischer, 1987), p. 196.

[114] BAL, R 139 II/111, Gestapo Weimar an Devisenstelle Rudolstadt, March 18, 1942.

[115] Susanne Willems, *Der entsiedelte Jude: Albert Speers Wohnungsmarktpolitik für den Berliner Hauptstadtbau* (Berlin: Hentrich, 2000), pp. 403–406.

[116] For examples of the *Heimeinkaufverträge*, see USHMM RG-14.003M (RV), files #501–84.

Nine thousand "Home Purchase Contracts" for Theresienstadt were issued with a value of about RM 125 million between June 1942 and July 1943. Of this sum, about RM 110 million had been collected on Special Account H by mid-1943 when the RFM took over control of the RV's property.[117]

There was some local resistance by the financial administration to these large-scale transfers. For example, in September 1942, the regional financial administration in Thuringia was reluctant to permit a payment to the RV in one case, as apparently the RV had applied for the transfer of funds three weeks after the evacuation, by which time the property had already fallen to the Reich under the Eleventh Decree. After detailed investigation, however, it was established that the Gestapo had in fact obtained a signed declaration of transfer before the deportation, so that the financial administration withdrew its objections.[118] Such disputes over the booking of the proceeds of confiscation should nevertheless not obscure the close cooperation that prevailed between the financial and police authorities in organizing the system of financial exploitation.

In practice, most of the demarcation disputes arising from the dual nature of the confiscation systems operated by the Security Police and the financial administration were resolved by mutual consultation. Dr. Walter Mädel of the RFM commented on the essential difference in approach of the two institutions in a December 1942 memorandum. He complained about Himmler's management of the funds collected through the RV by the SS: "The RFSS expresses on the one hand the opinion that all Jewish property must go to the Reich. On the other hand he has the intention of disposing of funds extracted from this property mass freely, without reference to budgetary controls. This shows once again the effort where possible to finance operations outside the regular control of funds through the budgetary process, with only net returns appearing in the official accounts."[119]

In the absence of detailed accounts, it is difficult to assess the impact of the Security Police's diversions of Jewish property on the Reich budget. As noted, in any case, the Reich Finance Ministry took over administration of the property of the RV according to a decree issued on August 3, 1943 (O 5210 − 350 VI),[120] and its criticism seems to have stopped short of

---

[117] S. Willems, *Der entsiedelte Jude*, pp. 407–11; on the *Heimeinkaufverträgen*, see also H. G. Adler, *Der verwaltete Mensch*, pp. 569–71.

[118] BAL, R 139 II/111, pp. 8–10.

[119] BAL, R 2/12222, pp. 226–29, Referat Mädel, "Finanzierung der Massnahmen zur Lösung der Judenfrage," December 14, 1942; see also H. G. Adler, *Der verwaltete Mensch*, p. 571.

[120] Oberfinanzdirektion: Div. Ordner I (RFM Handakte Scheerans), "Die Massnahmen gegen die jüdische Bevölkerung und ihre Einrichtungen seit 1933" (Ausarbeitung des

accusing the Security Police of using the funds from Jewish property for "illegitimate" purposes.[121]

The management of this dispute is in itself revealing. Far from provoking an open conflict with the Security Police, most Finance Ministry criticism remained within the RFM itself. Patzer of the General Office wrote to Mädel on December 24, 1942, listing several examples of diversions of funds in the RV's favor by the Security Police and requesting that clarity be established.[122] The outcome was a compromise that recognized de facto the diversions in favor of the Gestapo (using the RV), provided they occurred within the framework of the existing laws.

A Finance Ministry memorandum of March 17, 1943, signed by Schlüter, noted resignedly that the head of the Security Police had been informed previously of the possibility of financing the deportation of the Jews through the regular budget and had ignored this advice. "Therefore," Schlüter wrote, "it appears pointless to oppose the system of self-financing that the head of the Security Police has chosen. It is to be assumed that the head of the Security Police will simply find other ways of reaching his goal of financing it where possible outside the budget."[123]

In effect, the transfers in favor of the RV were recognized, provided that they took place prior to the deportee's crossing of the Reich's border. According to the Eleventh Decree, Jewish property fell to the Reich and was legally transferred at precisely this instant. The main concern of the Finance Ministry was that "Aryan" creditors might be disadvantaged by diversions of Jewish property.[124] This system of apparent "honor" among murderous thieves should be seen against the background of the more acrimonious tone accompanying similar disputes in the East.[125]

Archivs des ehem. RFM Febr. 1949), pp. 165–68; see also M. Offenburg (ed.), *Adass Jisroel*, p. 269.

[121] On the avowed intent of the RSHA, Bormann, and Heydrich to use the funds of the RV to finance the deportations, see Wolf Gruner, "Die Grundstücke der 'Reichsfeinde': Zur 'Arisierung' von Immobilien durch Städte und Gemeinden 1938–1945," in Irmtrud Wojak and Peter Hayes (eds.), *"Arisierung" im Nationalsozialismus: Volksgemeinschaft, Raub und Gedächtnis. Jahrbuch 2000 zur Geschichte und Wirkung des Holocaust* (Frankfurt am Main: Campus, 2000): 125–56, here p. 142.

[122] NARA, RG-238, T-1139, reel 47, NG-4584, Generalbüro an Abt. VI (Ref. Dr. Maedel), December 24, 1942.

[123] NARA, RG-238, T-1139, reel 47, NG-4583, RMF O 5205 – 495/42 VI g, Betr.: Beschaffung der Mittel für die Abschiebung der Juden, March 17, 1943.

[124] Ibid.

[125] See Chapter 5.

Seizure of Jewish Property by the SS in the Protectorate of Bohemia and Moravia

In the Protectorate of Bohemia and Moravia, the Security Police applied a more comprehensive model to deal with remaining Jewish property in the wake of the initial concentration of Czech Jews in Theresienstadt (Terezin), before most were deported to Auschwitz and other camps. In the Protectorate, all remaining Jewish property was to be credited to the Central Office for Jewish Emigration in Prague (*Zentralstelle für jüdische Auswanderung*, renamed *Zentralamt* in August 1942), ostensibly to cover the "costs of emigration and evacuation."[126] Among the costs paid from these funds was compensation to non-Jews who were resettled to make space for the establishment of the Jewish "ghetto."[127] For the clearing of property from the emptied apartments in Prague and its immediate vicinity, a *Treuhandstelle* (Trustee Office) staffed by Jews retained for this task was established under the Central Office (most of these Jews were deported to Auschwitz in 1943–44). Part of the collected property was sold directly to Germans and ethnic Germans locally, and part was delivered to bomb-damaged cities in Germany.[128]

According to one witness who worked in the Treuhandstelle, the transport section had twenty trucks that made eighty to one hundred trips every day to collect furniture from apartments.[129] In total, more than 9,200 Jewish apartments were cleared in the Protectorate.[130] Enormous loads of furniture were stored in more than fifty provisional warehouses – synagogues, sports halls, and some of the vacated apartments themselves. Among items stored were more than 20,000 carpets, 1.3 million household and kitchen items, 55,000 paintings, and more than 770,000 books (some of the books were bought directly by a German bookshop, Andre, in Prague).[131] The

---

[126] H. Friedlander and S. Milton (eds.), *Archives of the Holocaust, Volume 22: Zentrale Stelle*, doc. 43, pp. 89–94, Reichsprotektor an alle Oberlandräte, December 15, 1941; LAB, B Rep. 039-01/306, pp. 394–95, URO letter dated April 24, 1964; Jan Björn Potthast, "Antijüdische Massnahmen im Protektorat Böhmen und Mähren und das 'Jüdische Zentralmuseum' in Prag," in I. Wojak and P. Hayes (eds.), *"Arisierung" im Nationalsozialismus*: 157–201, p. 158.

[127] LAB, B Rep. 039-01/306, *Verordnungsblatt des Reichsprotektors*, February 16, 1942.

[128] H. G. Adler, *Der verwaltete Mensch*, p. 597.

[129] LAB, B Rep. 039-01/305, statement of Ernst Recht, head of Treuhandstelle in 1944, May 18, 1961.

[130] R. Hilberg, *Die Vernichtung*, p. 500.

[131] J. B. Potthast, "Antijüdische Massnahmen," p. 158; LAB, B Rep. 039-01/305, statement of Ernst Recht, May 18, 1961.

Treuhandstelle even prepared propaganda on its activities, boasting of its achievements in "returning Jewish property to the possession of the German people (*Volksgut*)."[132]

An interesting aspect of the treatment of Jewish property in the Protectorate was the establishment of the Jewish Museum in Prague as a repository for ritual objects from synagogues and archival material belonging to Czech Jewish communities. In total, more than 100,000 items were eventually registered there. The original initiative for this project came from the leaders of the Jewish community themselves, but surprisingly it also gained the support of Hans Günther, the SS officer in charge of the Central Office. Soon, the thinking of the Germans became clear: The objects in the museum would be the only surviving relics of one thousand years of Jewish culture in the Czech lands, and the Nazis intended the museum to remain as a propaganda warning about the threat posed by the Jews. The Jewish officials working there, however, tried to subvert this intention while helping preserve these precious objects. Nearly all the Jewish employees were deported to Theresienstadt between 1943 and 1945, but the vast collection remained as a unique cultural legacy.[133]

In the Protectorate, where in 1941 Reinhard Heydrich was the Reichsprotektor, the Security Police was able to retain control over almost all seized Jewish property, diverting the proceeds to its own accounts administered by the Central Office. This was the model envisioned by the Security Police for all of Europe, but in most other places – including the Occupied Eastern Territories – the civil or military administrations retained official jurisdiction over most property from Jewish sources. Even in the Protectorate, however, a separate organization, known as the *Vermögensamt* (Property Office), subordinate to the civil administration, also played a role in the confiscations. As the Finance Ministry noted, the main aim of the Security Police in controlling the proceeds from Jewish property was to cover its costs incurred while implementing the Final Solution.

Interpretations of the Liquidation of Jewish Assets after the Deportations

This detailed review of the historical evolution of property confiscation in the Reich helps put Hans Adler's critical analysis of the relationship between

---

[132] LAB, B Rep. 039-01/314. I am grateful to Götz Aly for bringing this file to my attention. See also J. B. Potthast, "Antijüdische Massnahmen," p. 197.
[133] J. B. Potthast, "Antijüdische Massnahmen," pp. 163–79; see also idem., *Das jüdische Zentralmuseum der SS in Prag: Gegnerforschung und Völkermord im Nationalsozialismus* (Frankfurt am Main: Campus, 2002).

the Finance Ministry and the Security Police in its proper perspective. In his study, Adler acknowledges the importance of the close cooperation between these two institutions, if the deportation process were to run on smooth bureaucratic rails. He concludes,

> In connection with the Eleventh Decree to the Reich Citizenship Law a remarkable perfection of the co-operation between the RSHA and the Finance Ministry developed, initially with regard to these central offices, but then also for the Gestapo as well as the OFPs and Finance Offices as the executing agencies. The Finance Ministry intervened in this game so resolutely and unscrupulously, that solely on account of this, its participation in the deportations becomes one of considerable shared responsibility for the "Final Solution."[134]

From the confiscation process within the Reich evolved a complex system of mutual consultation between officials, a system that also incorporated private institutions such as banks and insurance companies within the network. The confiscation of property following the deportation of German Jews relied very heavily on a derivative system of mutual notification. The deportation lists prepared by the Gestapo[135] were intended now to replace the lists of persons proposed for denaturalization and subsequently published in the *Reichsanzeiger*.[136] The system developed for the phase of emigration was thereby adapted for the confiscation of the property of the deportees. Its goal was to achieve the most complete exploitation of Jewish property by enforcing "legal confiscation" under the Eleventh Decree, itself an extension of previous denaturalization and confiscation policies. In practice, this networking strategy actually slowed down implementation, due to the sheer weight of the bureaucracy involved. However, the system also proved to be less prone to the confusion and corruption that characterized the looting of Jewish property in the East.

The very scale of the measures taken to seize and distribute Jewish property demonstrates both widespread knowledge of the deportations and the crucial "legal" aspect of the Final Solution. The administration and sale of Jewish property employed hundreds of officials, even at the height of the war. Many thousands of other officials and private individuals were drawn into the process. High administration costs, however, often consumed much of the income generated, as many organizations and individuals took their

---

[134] H. G. Adler, *Der verwaltete Mensch*, p. 506.

[135] See USHMM, RG-30, Acc.1996.A.0342, for examples of deportation lists from Berlin. I am grateful to Peter Lande for bringing this key collection to my attention.

[136] For examples of the lists of those proposed for denaturalization, see LAB A Rep. 092; all of the lists published can be found in Michael Hepp (ed.), *Die Ausbürgerung*, 3 vols.

cut, often concealed as expenses and salaries. Among the lesser beneficiaries were tens of thousands of private individuals who bought household items cheaply or moved into vacated apartments. Nevertheless, the Nazi administration also preserved a strict hierarchy among beneficiaries, ranked according to the Party's racial and social priorities. At the same time, systemic corruption ensured that Nazi potentates, as well as low-ranking police and finance personnel, secured the best items for themselves.

In conclusion, the comments of Inka Bertz regarding the exhaustive processing of Jewish property in the Reich seem close to the mark. The German financial administration undertook an enormous bureaucratic effort, but in perhaps the majority of cases little if any profit resulted for the Reich and many files had not yet been closed at the end of the war. Therefore, it appears that correct bureaucratic implementation of the confiscation process was perhaps the most important aspect of this whole procedure: it was required to legitimize the robbery.[137] In this way, the "elimination of Jewish influence from the economy" was still being remorselessly completed as a state-sanctioned legal process even after the lives of most of the victims had been extinguished.

---

[137] I. Bertz, "Ein Karteiblatt für jeden abgeschobenen Juden," p. 385.

7

"PLUNDER BY DECREE": THE CONFISCATION OF JEWISH PROPERTY IN GERMAN-OCCUPIED WESTERN EUROPE

Figure 7.1. A moving van of the Puls Company, which collaborated with the Germans in emptying the apartments of deported Jews in the Netherlands, 1942–1943. *Source:* Nederlands Instituut voor Oorlogsdocumentatie, 5J Jodenverfolging, Neg # 04658. USHMM, WS # 45175.

In the countries of Western Europe occupied by the Nazis in 1940, the economic persecution of the Jews took the form primarily of legal decrees and administrative measures.[1] The Nazi policy of removing the Jews from the economy ("*Entjudung der Wirtschaft*") required a clear legal framework to be effective. Potential buyers and middlemen were reluctant to invest in Jewish property without obtaining secure legal title to businesses or real estate. This problem became critical in occupied countries as most exile regimes, including those of the Netherlands, Belgium, France, and Norway, proclaimed laws outlawing cooperation in German confiscation measures.[2]

Probably the most efficient example of the spoliation of Jewish property throughout Europe was in the Netherlands, where the German civil administration applied a number of lessons learned from experiences inside the Reich. The clear aim was to secure Jewish property, especially in the form of businesses, bank accounts, and securities, prior to the removal of the Jewish population, which began in 1942. By first centralizing all Jewish assets at a single bank, the German authorities greatly simplified the subsequent intended confiscation, which could be achieved by then concentrating all the money in one collective account.[3] Nevertheless, even here they encountered a number of problems and complications, so that they were unable to complete all cases before the end of the occupation.

In Western Europe, a considerable number of Jews had been able to flee by the time of the German invasion, and their property, along with that of Germany's political opponents, was among the first to be seized by German security forces. This seizure often took place in conjunction with more general measures directed at freezing enemy property, and these initial seizures did not always result in immediate confiscation, as enemy property was generally placed under temporary German administration for fear of Allied reprisals against German property overseas. During the first few months of occupation, the German authorities also directed their attention toward the property of associations, ranging from trade unions and political parties to churches and Jewish communal institutions. The Germans liquidated this property quickly, paying the proceeds into collective accounts.

Beginning in the fall of 1940, the occupation authorities introduced a series of decrees and procedures for the Aryanization of Jewish businesses,

---

[1] Wolfgang Seibel (ed.), *"Holocaust und 'Polykratie'" in Westeuropa, 1940–1944: Nationale Berichte* (December, 2001) (Einleitung), p. iv.

[2] See Gerard Aalders, *Geraubt! Die Enteignung jüdischen Besitzes im Zweiten Weltkrieg* (Cologne: Dittrich, 2000), p. 398; *The Reisel/Bruland Report on the Confiscation of Jewish Property in Norway* (Part of Official Norwegian Report 1997: 22) (Oslo, 1997), p. 24.

[3] See, for example, Joseph Billig, *Le Commissariat General aux Questions Juives, 1941–1944*, 3 vols. (Paris: Editions du Centre, 1955–1957), vol. 1, p. 46.

although implementation varied from country to country depending on the type of German occupation (civilian or military) and the extent of local participation in the process.[4] This chapter pays greater attention to Aryanization, as it was integral to the overall process of confiscation in the West, creating institutions and structures that also played a role in the confiscation of other forms of property. In all countries, the Germans sought to secure most Jewish private property prior to the deportations by using methods similar to those developed in Germany: the registration of property and the use of blocked accounts, special taxes, currency restrictions, and restrictions on the sale or transfer of Jewish property.

Throughout occupied Western Europe, considerable tension developed among the various institutions of confiscation, especially, as elsewhere, between the Security Police and the administration, whether civil or military. However, in Western Europe, the role of the Security Police was largely confined to securing the property of emigrant Jews and those deported. Although some funds were diverted to pay expenses incurred during the deportations, including the construction of transit camps, such as Westerbork, and the railway transport costs, the bulk of Jewish wealth was retained within German occupation budgets, much of it in blocked or collective accounts that remained traceable at the end of the war. Cultural looting, which took place on a large scale in the West, reflected both the rivalry between different German occupational institutions and the corrupt inclinations of the Nazi leadership itself. In particular, the *Einsatzstab Reichsleiter Rosenberg* (Rosenberg Operational Staff, ERR) operated throughout Western Europe, not only seizing archives and libraries but also providing part of the infrastructure for the massive removal of furniture to the Reich. Once again, the methods and infrastructure initially developed to deal with the property of Jews who fled were quickly adapted to exploit the remaining property of those deported as well.

Luxembourg: Confiscation before Deportation

As a microcosm of occupied Western territories, the Grand Duchy of Luxembourg provides an example of the rapid and largely unproblematic application of methods developed in the Reich to the liquidation of Jewish

---

[4] See, for example, Jean-Marc Dreyfus, "Die Enteignung der Juden in Westeuropa," in Constantin Goschler and Philipp Ther (eds.), *Raub und Restitution: "Arisierung" und Rückerstattung des jüdischen Eigentums in Europa* (Frankfurt am Main: Fischer Taschenbuch, 2003), pp. 41–57.

property. After an initial phase of registration and legislative preparation, the civil administration implemented the Aryanization of Jewish businesses and the liquidation of other private property, first of those who had fled and then of the deportees, with comparative efficiency, drawing on experienced personnel from within the Reich.

Up until May 10, 1940, about 3,500 Jews lived in Luxembourg. The majority fled to neighboring Belgium and France during the invasion, so that in July 1941 only 796 were known to be in the country. Although formally under the control of the military commander for Belgium and northern France, Luxembourg soon received a civil administration ruled by the neighboring Gauleiter of Koblenz-Trier, Gustav Simon, who was answerable directly to Hitler. It should therefore come as little surprise that Simon, as *Chef der Zivilverwaltung* (Head of the Civil Administration, CdZ) published during the first year of his rule a series of decrees that in a simplified form rapidly caught up with, and even overtook developments with regard to Jewish property in the Reich.[5]

When the draft of the first anti-Jewish decree was considered at the beginning of September 1940, Simon expressed reservations about introducing so many German laws all at once, fearing presumably that this might alienate the local population. The Führer responded that he had already approved the drafts prepared by Hans Globke of the Interior Ministry: the rapid assimilation of Luxembourg in terms of anti-Jewish (and other) legislation reflected Hitler's stated intention that Luxembourg should soon be "brought back" to the German people.[6]

Since more than three-quarters of Luxembourg's Jews had already fled, the Aryanization of businesses was relatively straightforward. In accordance with the Decree on the Administration and Application of Jewish Property issued on September 5, 1940, all Jewish property had to be registered, and the civil administration could also appoint trustees for and compel the sale of Jewish businesses. The aim was to liquidate or to transfer rapidly into Aryan hands the 335 businesses registered as Jewish.

A detailed report on the progress of Aryanization in Luxembourg was published in the German newspaper *Die Judenfrage* at the end of May 1941. Responsibility for Aryanization was placed in the hands of Gauinspektor Jospeh Ackermann, who had very successfully implemented it

---

[5] Raul Hilberg, *Die Vernichtung der europäischen Juden*, 3 vols. (Frankfurt am Main: Fischer, 1961, 1982), vol. II, p. 630; LAB, B Rep. 039-01/327 Luxembourg 26, Report of Institut für Zeitgeschichte, January 9, 1962.

[6] NARA, RG-238, T-1139, NG-2297; LAB, B Rep. 039-01/327 Luxembourg 26, Report of Institut für Zeitgeschichte, January 9, 1962.

in the Moselle district previously. To reduce competition that harmed efficiency and profitability, Ackermann liquidated most Jewish businesses: Only seventy-five businesses were Aryanized, and the civil administration employed mainly Luxembourgers of German descent as trustees. Three hundred and eighty buildings and 155 plots of land were registered as being in Jewish hands. Most of the agricultural land was rented out and the remainder made available for purchase by local ethnic German farmers. The civil administration took over most of the Jewish houses for its own use or gave them to affiliated organizations, such as the German National Railway (*Deutsche Reichsbahn*), the Post Office, or the Hitler Youth. A small amount of real estate was sold to local Germans.[7]

Having initiated Aryanization in the fall of 1940, the government's next step was to deal with the private property of those who had fled, including bank accounts, securities, the contents of safe-deposit boxes, and furniture and household goods, as well as artworks, jewelry, and other valuables. On February 7, 1941, Simon decreed that the property of persons who had fled at the time of the German occupation on May 10, 1940, and had not returned by February 1, 1941, as well as the property of Jews who had emigrated, would be placed under German administration and could be confiscated. This measure was directed not only against Jewish property but also against the property of other emigrants viewed as "enemies of the Reich." Financial records of the CdZ administration indicate that the sale of confiscated property began shortly afterward in the spring of 1941.

On April 18, 1941, an implementation order supplementing the above decree extended its scope to the property of all Jews in Luxembourg, including inheritances. The order stated that "the head of the civil administration can also order that the property of those Jews who are still resident in Luxembourg be placed under German administration."[8] This is a clear example of how measures taken initially to deal with the property of emigrant Jews could then be extended to the remaining Jewish population.

In practice, the CdZ waited in most cases until after the start of the deportations in October 1941, when more than five hundred Jews were "sent to the East," before liquidating the remaining Jewish private property.[9] Nonetheless, as in Germany, the CdZ imposed a succession of new regulations on the Jewish community before this time, including the wearing

---

[7] LAB, B Rep. 039-01/327 Luxembourg 26, *Die Judenfrage*, May 31, 1941.

[8] LAB, B Rep. 039-01/327 Luxembourg 26.

[9] R. Hilberg, *Die Vernichtung*, vol. II, p. 631, indicates that Gauleiter Simon deported 512 Jews to the Łódź ghetto in October 1941 and another 310 Jews to Theresienstadt (Terezin) between 1942 and 1944.

of the Jewish star (earlier than in Germany), forced labor for some, and numerous economic restrictions.

As recalled by local Jews, the occupation started with the confiscation of property from Jewish apartments, mainly to equip German offices, followed by the compulsory surrender of radios and typewriters. The CdZ also enforced the blocking of Jewish bank accounts, permitting only between RM 150 and RM 250 to be withdrawn per month, depending on family size. All means of transport were confiscated, and the CdZ decreed (as in Germany) that Jews had to surrender silver cutlery and other precious metals. As a particular insult, the German authorities forced the Jewish community to demolish the synagogue at its own expense. Subsequent collections included items such as cameras, furs, and linen, and ultimately even shoes – Jews were allowed to retain only one pair.[10] Thus, in Luxembourg, the German occupation was experienced by Jews as a period of progressive impoverishment, in which their private property officially no longer belonged to them.

The confiscation of Jewish property in the wake of the deportations also followed a pattern reminiscent of events in Germany. The keys to apartments had to be surrendered to the Jewish Council (*Ältestenrat*), which had also been involved in the registration of the Jews. On government instruction, banks transferred the contents of Jewish accounts to a collective account at the Luxembourg branch of the Bank der Deutschen Arbeit, from where it was subsequently sent to the Reich. Much Jewish private property had been in the form of securities. Fleeing Jews had taken a considerable amount of these to neighboring countries for safekeeping, but the rapid German advance and the efficient work of the *Devisenschutzkommandos* (Currency Protection Squads, DSKs) enabled most to be recovered. As in Germany, not all securities were resold by June 1944, when the Dresdner Bank turned down the opportunity to purchase the remaining shares.[11]

According to the account books of the CdZ, most of the confiscated furniture of emigrant Jews was sold for the benefit of needy local families – after local German offices had taken their pick of the best items. Records of the sums raised from individual estates still exist.[12] In the wake of the deportations, much of the furniture collected was probably sent to the Reich to

---

[10] LAB, B Rep. 039-01/330 Luxembourg 26, "Verfolgung und Deportation der Juden in Luxembourg" (translated) article from the *Revue Luxembourg*, May 31, 1969, based in part on the testimony of Alfred Oppenheimer; see also Eichmann Trial, session 68.

[11] LAB, B Rep. 039-01/327-30 Luxembourg 26; see especially numerous statements by Willi Brauckmann, who acted as a "professional witness" in numerous German restitution cases in the 1960s, having had "first-hand experience" in organizing the confiscations.

[12] LAB, B Rep. 039-01/327-8 Luxembourg 26, Information from the Bundesminister der Finanzen, dated December 3, 1962; for an example of surviving records, see those for the family of H. W.'s estate.

be made available to bombed-out families. According to the postwar statements of Willi Brauckmann, one of the main organizers of the confiscation program, precious metals were bought by a dealer from Germany, linen was given to the Nazi welfare organization (*Nationalsozialistische Volkswohlfahrt*, NSV), furs were sent to a collecting point in the Moselle district, and valuable paintings were put in the local art gallery.[13] These examples are by no means comprehensive, but indicate the wide variety of intermediaries and beneficiaries of Jewish property.

In practice, the processing of confiscated property did not go quite as smoothly as the simple wording of the decrees implies. For example, at the start of the occupation, some former Jewish houses were simply occupied by employees of the Security Police. The CdZ became aware of this when one house owner began to demand rent. However, when an inventory was made, it became clear that some of the furniture was missing. Apparently, the Security Police had taken it to Germany to equip its offices there. Ultimately, the CdZ permitted the Security Police to retain these items.[14]

This example reflects the ubiquitous conflicts between competing German agencies. In Luxembourg, the prime agency responsible for the confiscations was Section IV of the CdZ, which had roughly one hundred employees. Not all of them worked with confiscations, but Section IVa, which dealt with confiscated items, was itself divided into five departments according to different forms of property. By late 1941, when the deportation of the Jews began, responsibility for processing the items left behind had been transferred to the *Deutsche Umsiedlungs und Treuhand-Gesellschaft* (German Resettlement and Trustee Company, DUT), reflecting the concern that household goods be made available at a reasonable price to needy Germans.

In Luxembourg, the CdZ also exploited the redistribution of Jewish property to foster German economic penetration, favoring local Germans both as trustees and purchasers of businesses and land. The local population was offered the opportunity to buy only less valuable household goods. Nonetheless, local companies were also actively involved in the liquidation of Jewish property. Not only were the banks required to transfer Jewish accounts and to open safe-deposit boxes, but landlords were required to register former Jewish tenants and transport companies had to report items left behind by emigrants. One local furniture store was able to purchase former Jewish property for resale to its customers.

Despite the survival of confiscation records of certain types of property, restitution by the postwar Luxembourg authorities remained limited.

---

[13] LAB, B Rep. 039-01/327-8 Luxembourg 26, statement of Willi Brauckmann, October 6, 1964.

[14] Ibid., statement of Willi Brauckmann, July 28, 1964.

According to one source, only thirty-six of those Jews who were deported ever returned. Although much of the information regarding bank accounts was available, the sums in them could not be restored initially as the money had been transferred to Germany, where the Allies had confiscated it along with the property of the Bank der Deutschen Arbeit, an organization deemed to be closely affiliated to the Nazi Party.

In conclusion, the confiscation of Jewish property by the German civil administration in Luxembourg was conducted both efficiently and comprehensively. Nevertheless, some indications of corruption appear in the restitution files, as a number of companies and individuals, mostly Germans, benefited from the process both legally and illicitly. In particular, the example of Luxembourg demonstrates well the important role of large-scale Jewish emigration at the time of the invasion in opening the door for the subsequent, more comprehensive confiscation of Jewish property. In Luxembourg, the German administration simply amended the initial confiscation laws directed against those who had fled to extend official control to encompass all Jewish property several months before the deportations began.

The Netherlands

The spoliation of Jewish property in the Netherlands also proceeded in accordance with streamlined practices developed previously inside the Reich. Reichskommissar Dr. Arthur Seyss-Inquart and his *Generalkommissar für Finanzen und Wirtschaft* (Minister for Financial and Economic Affairs, GkFW) Hans Fischböck – both of them from Austria – were careful to apply lessons learned previously to ensure firm state control over the process.[15] The Dutch historian, Gerard Aalders, characterizes the Nazi looting of the Jews in the Netherlands as an orderly confiscation decreed by the state – "robbery by decree."[16] The main complications resulted from the need to conceal the ultimate aim of the German measures, including through the

---

[15] See Götz Aly and Susanne Heim, *Vordenker der Vernichtung: Auschwitz und die deutschen Pläne für eine europäischer Neuordnung* (Hamburg: Hofmann und Campe, 1991), pp. 44–45; and A. J. van der Leeuw, "Reichskommissariat und Judenvermögen in den Niederlanden," in A. H. Paape (ed.), *Studies over Nederland in oorlogstijd* ('s-Gravenhage: Martinus Nijhoff, 1972), pp. 237–49, here pp. 237–38. Seyss-Inquart and Fischböck drew upon experiences from Austria, Germany, and the Protectorate of Bohemia and Moravia in drawing up their plans.

[16] Gerard Aalders, "Die Arisierung der niederländischen Wirtschaft: Raub per Verordnung," in Alfons Kenkmann and Bernd-A. Rusinek (eds.), *Verfolgung und Verwaltung:*

use of camouflaged institutions, to enable the goal of complete confiscation to be achieved. Despite considerable cooperation by some Dutch financial institutions, there were no indigenous plans for any form of spoliation, and so the entire policy had to be imported and directed by the Germans.

As part of the concealment strategy, the German civil administration sought to bring all forms of Jewish property under its control in a series of carefully prepared stages. A report prepared by the Security Police in the Netherlands at the end of 1942 explained that the first step had been to restrict the ability of Jews to freely dispose of their own property, followed by compulsory registration measures and finally the obligation to surrender property. The aim of these measures was to prevent Jewish property escaping in an uncontrolled fashion, so that it could be prepared for important tasks of the Reich, especially covering the costs incurred by the removal of the Jews.[17]

It was not the Security Police that was primarily responsible for this "softly, softly" approach that proved remarkably successful, but rather the German civil administration. The attempts of the Security Police to gain control over Jewish property through the creation of its own institutions remained largely unsuccessful, with the exception of schemes to blackmail wealthy Jewish individuals in return for permission to emigrate or deferment of their deportation. Nevertheless, competition for control over the process of looting is a revealing aspect of spoliation in the Netherlands and confounds the myth of an all-powerful Security Police within the German administrative structure.

The major innovation in the Netherlands was the rapid concentration of nearly all Jewish movable wealth at the Bank of Lippmann, Rosenthal & Co., Sarphistraat (LiRo) under the provisions of two decrees issued in August 1941 and May 1942. In practice, this was a refined version of the measures taken in the Reich to register Jewish property and control it in blocked accounts overseen by the Currency Offices. Nominally, the property remained in the possession of Dutch Jews in blocked accounts at LiRo, at least until the beginning of 1943 when it was transferred into a single collective account. By this time, the deportation of Jews from the Netherlands was already in full swing. The concentration of all Jewish property in one financial institution considerably simplified both the collection of property and its ultimate confiscation.

Die wirtschaftliche Ausplünderung der Juden und die westfälischen Finanzbehörden (Münster: Oberfinanzdirektion Münster, 1999), pp. 122–37.

[17] Eichmann Trial, document T-536, Gestapo Report on the development of the Jewish Question in Holland, December 31, 1942.

Seizure of Property of Persons Who Fled and of "Enemies"

After its establishment on May 29, 1940, initially the new civil administration under Reichskommissar Seyss-Inquart was concerned to avoid civil disturbances and therefore did not move immediately against Jewish property. As in Luxembourg, the first measures were directed instead against "enemy property," which of course affected the property of Jews and others who had fled the country during the invasion.[18] Under a decree of June 14, 1940,[19] "enemy property" had to be registered with the *Deutsche Revisions- und Treuhand AG* (DRT), a German accountancy firm. The DRT, acting together with Fischböck's Ministry for Financial and Economic Affairs (GkFW), directed the appointment of administrators and their subsequent supervision. In total, the "Enemy Property" section of the GkFW managed capital with a value of about 1.2 billion florins (or RM 900,000).[20]

As in the Reich, the Germans administered non-Jewish enemy property in the Netherlands in trust until the end of the war, but it was not confiscated for fear of possible reprisals against their own investments that had been frozen abroad.[21] The property of several hundred Dutch Jews who had fled was initially also placed in trust in accordance with the "Enemy Property" regulations. Subsequently, however, it was unlawfully sold in 1942 and 1943, together with other Jewish property, and the proceeds paid into an account of the DRT at the LiRo bank.[22]

The "Enemy Property" regulations did, however, serve as a potential model for the treatment of Jewish property, perhaps allaying the fears of some Jews when the civil administration ordered Jewish property registration in the summer of 1941. Significantly, Fischböck subsequently charged the "Enemy Property" section of the GkFW with the supervision of the administration of Jewish property by the LiRo Bank, revealing the close connections between these two policies.[23]

---

[18] G. Aalders, "Niederlande: Wirtschaftliche Verfolgung," in W. Seibel (ed.), *Holocaust und "Polykratie" in Westeuropa, 1940–1944: Nationale Berichte* (December, 2001), p. 129.

[19] VO 26/1940 über die Behandlung des feindlichen Vermögens.

[20] The exchange rate was 1 florin = RM 0.75.

[21] See Stephan H. Lindner, *Das Reichskommissariat für die Behandlung feindlichen Vermögens im Zweiten Weltkrieg: Eine Studie zur Verwaltungs-, Rechts- und Wirtschaftsgeschichte des nationalsozialistischen Deutschlands* (Stuttgart: Franz Steinert, 1991).

[22] G. Aalders, "Niederlande: Wirtschaftliche Verfolgung," pp. 136–37. This was the property of several hundred Dutch Jews who fled to Britain in May 1940, but not all of them were wealthy and the total amount was only a small proportion of all "enemy property" seized. For these reasons, the Germans may have been less concerned about the prospect of reprisals concerning this property, although as Aalders points out, it was a clear violation of international law.

[23] BAL, R 177/203, Dr. Schröder, GKFW an Herrn von Karger, LiRo, March 4, 1942.

Communal Organizations

Reichskommissar Seyss-Inquart ordered the registration and reformation of non-commercial organizations and foundations in two decrees issued on September 20, 1940,[24] and February 28, 1941.[25] With regard to non-Jewish organizations, such as the trade unions, the Nazi aim was mainly to gain control over them and their finances. The second decree resulted in the liquidation of Jewish organizations, with the funds being paid into accounts at the *Vermögensverwaltungs- und Rentenanstalt* (Property Administration and Pension Institute, VVRA)[26] under the direction of the Commissioner for Non-Commercial Organizations and Foundations, Hans Werner Müller-Lehning. The liquidation of about one thousand Jewish organizations is estimated to have brought in 10 million fl. Other organizations affected by these measures included the Masonic lodges, whose archives were looted by the ERR after their liquidation.[27]

Aryanization of Jewish Businesses

With regard to Aryanization, Reichskommissar Seyss-Inquart and Generalkommissar Fischböck were eager to avoid the excesses that had occurred in Austria during the initial "wild Aryanizations" in March 1938. Therefore, they were careful to establish several new institutions to maintain close state control over the process. Their aim was to ensure that a realistic price was paid in the Netherlands and that applicants had suitable business experience and adequate capital.[28]

The first stage in the process of Aryanization was the registration of Jewish businesses, according to the terms of Decree 189/1940[29] of October 22, 1940. The decree included a definition of who was a Jew and made the sale of Jewish businesses subject to official permission. All "Jewish businesses" (those with one Jewish partner or director, or in which Jews owned more than 25 percent of the capital) had to register their assets and liabilities with the *Wirtschaftsprüfstelle* (Office of Economic Investigation, WPS) by November 30, 1940. By the end of November, 19,000 businesses had complied, and ultimately about 21,000 "Jewish" firms were registered. A Security Police report from this period notes that Dutch Jews were reluctant to sell their companies voluntarily, partly because of the difficulties

---

[24] VO 145/1940.

[25] VO 41/1941.

[26] Vermögensverwaltungs- und Rentenanstalt, established on May 31, 1941.

[27] G. Aalders, *Geraubt!*, pp. 192–95.

[28] G. Aalders, "Niederlande: Wirtschaftliche Verfolgung," p. 130.

[29] VO 189/1940 über die Anmeldung von Unternehmen.

involved in emigrating and also their inability to convert the Dutch guilders they would receive into hard currency that would be of use abroad. There was also a fear on the German side that the best objects might fall into the wrong hands, and so the Nazis began to prepare at the local level for a compulsory Aryanization program similar to that implemented in Germany during 1938.[30]

At the end of 1940, Seyss-Inquart obtained the Führer's approval in principle to proceed with compulsory Aryanization. Following the disturbances that culminated in the Amsterdam dockworkers strike in February 1941, fear of public opinion no longer remained a reason for delay.[31] Therefore, in March a further "Aryanization decree"[32] was introduced to provide the legal basis for the forced sale and liquidation of Jewish enterprises and their placement under the control of trustees. The WPS, which had been built up around the economic staff that had served in the German General Consulate in Amsterdam, then proceeded to appoint trustees and supervise their work. The Jewish enterprises bore the costs of administration.[33] A few Jewish businesses had already been placed in trusteeship under the "Enemy Property" laws, which had prepared the way for their Aryanization prior to the March 1941 decree.

As elsewhere, implementation of Aryanization still took considerable time, as difficult decisions had to be made in thousands of cases about the appointment of trustees, whether to Aryanize or liquidate, and how to find suitable buyers. According to a report by Reichskommissar Seyss-Inquart to the head of the Party Chancellery, Martin Bormann, dated January 27, 1942, of the approximately one thousand businesses dealt with to that date, some four hundred had been taken over by Dutch businessmen (valued at 60.5 million fl.) and 340 by Germans (valued at 103 million fl.); the remaining 260 were reserved for veterans of the ongoing war (Kriegsteilnehmer). The German authorities exploited their control over Aryanization to support German businesses and entrepreneurs trying to gain a foothold in the Netherlands while allowing some Dutch entrepreneurs to pick up many of the smaller businesses. In particular, the Dresdner Bank established its own subsidiary in the Netherlands, the Handelstrust West, which

---

[30] USHMM, RG-41, Acc.1997.A.1007, Netherlands Institute for War Documentation (NIOD), reel 301, Meldungen aus den Niederlanden (BdS reports), November 29, 1940.

[31] NARA, RG-242, T-120, reel 3271, E554244-45, Aufzeichnung betr. Arisierung in Holland, March 1, 1941.

[32] VO 48/1941, über die Behandlung anmeldepflichtiger Unternehmen, March 12, 1941.

[33] G. Aalders, "Niederlande: Wirtschaftliche Verfolgung," pp. 139–40.

became very active in support of German Aryanization bids.[34] Other individuals in Germany made applications for Aryanization opportunities in the Netherlands via the Regional Economic Advisers (*Gauwirtschaftsberater*) of the Party.[35]

Ultimately, about two thousand firms were Aryanized and about ten thousand liquidated, although the WPS had still not decided on the fate of one thousand cases by the end of the occupation. Roughly 8,000 of the 21,000 firms originally identified as Jewish-owned or under Jewish influence managed to escape this definition by reducing the level of Jewish ownership and paying a fine (1 percent of capital).[36] The Dutch historian Jos Scheren questions both the efficiency and the carefully planned nature of Aryanization in the Netherlands, citing both its slow progress and also the fairly chaotic, sometimes contradictory policies pursued with regard to Jewish market vendors and peddlers in Amsterdam.[37] However, the German authorities were most concerned with the large and profitable companies suitable for Aryanization and took less interest in the small businesses that hardly brought any net profit, even from their liquidation. Indeed, the significance of Austrian and German prototypes is readily apparent when one examines the new institutions created for implementing Aryanization, especially with regard to the management of the proceeds.

Most revealing is the way Aryanization led directly to confiscation in the Netherlands, thereby applying certain plans that had been considered, but not implemented, in the Reich. The proceeds from Aryanization sales were paid into accounts at the VVRA, which in turn was supposedly to make one hundred quarterly payments over twenty-five years into blocked accounts opened for the former Jewish owners at LiRo (with no interest paid).[38] This was a modified form of Austrian plans to finance Aryanization through long-term repayments and to manage the process through a central "Control Bank"; actually, these plans were employed only for the large-scale Aryanizations there. As the name "Property Administration and Pension Institute" indicated, this was also the realization of Göring's plan "to Aryanize the . . . economy; that is, to throw out the Jews and enter them into

[34] R. Hilberg, *Die Vernichtung*, vol. II, pp. 599–601.

[35] Jacob Presser, *The Destruction of the Dutch Jews* (New York: E. P. Dutton, 1969), pp. 367–68.

[36] G. Aalders, *Geraubt!*, p. 202; R. Hilberg, *Die Vernichtung*, vol. II, pp. 602–603.

[37] See Jos Scheren, "Aryanization, Market Vendors, and Peddlers in Amsterdam," in *Holocaust and Genocide Studies*, vol. 14, no. 3 (Winter 2000): 415–29.

[38] G. Aalders, *Geraubt!*, pp. 200–201; see also Jean-Marc Dreyfus, "L'aryanisation économique aux Pays-Bas (et sa comparison avec le cas français), 1940–1945" (unpublished paper presented at the United States Holocaust Memorial Museum in summer 2001), p. 8.

the debt register, pensioning them off."[39] The last part of this plan was also realized, as the money paid to the Property Administration and Pension Institute was mostly converted into both Reich and Dutch government bonds, placing this large financial resource directly at the government's disposal.[40]

After the beginning of large-scale deportations from the Netherlands in July 1942, the VVRA ceased further payments into individual Jewish accounts at LiRo, and on instructions from Fischböck the existing accounts were consolidated into a single collective account in 1943.[41] Thus, ultimately the proceeds from Aryanization flowed conveniently to the state. It is very hard to assess the precise amount raised from Aryanization in the Netherlands, as most prices paid were still well below market value.[42] In general, Aryanization was conducted more quickly and with greater central direction in the Netherlands than in Germany or other parts of Western Europe; its implementation was linked closely in time to plans for the deportation of Dutch Jews from the summer of 1941 onward. Thus, the Nazi civil administration was able to direct Aryanization centrally in a very comprehensive manner, making it an instrumental part of the confiscation process.[43]

"Austrian Models" – The May 1941 Decision and Its Aftermath

In one respect, Scheren's critique of the monolithic view of Nazi confiscation policies in the Netherlands is justified. The outcome was by no means predetermined, but rather it emerged from the competing schemes and political maneuvering of different organizations within the Nazi administration. Reichskommissar Seyss-Inquart sought to distribute responsibility for Jewish policy among different departments so that he could remain in overall control. In particular, he firmly resisted the strong pressure exerted

---

[39] A. J. van der Leeuw, "Der Griff des Reiches nach dem Judenvermögen," in A. H. Paape (ed.), *Studies over Nederland in oorlogstijd*, pp. 211–36, here p. 214, quoting Nüremberg Document PS-1816, transcript of the conference on November 12, 1938, IMT, *The Trial of the Major War Criminals* (Blue Series) (Nuremberg, 1948), vol. XXVIII, pp. 499–540.

[40] A. J. van der Leeuw, "Reichskommissariat und Judenvermögen in den Niederlanden," in A. H. Paape (ed.), *Studies over Nederland in oorlogstijd*, pp. 237–49, here p. 242.

[41] Ibid., pp. 244–47; see also, for example, BAL, R 177/214, GkFW an DSK Niederlande, February 26, 1943.

[42] Gerard Aalders, *Nazi Looting: The Plunder of Dutch Jewry during the Second World War* (Oxford: Berg, 2004), p. 281, gives an estimate of 150 to 200 million fl.

[43] For this comparative insight, I am indebted to J-M. Dreyfus, "L'aryanisation économique," pp. 23–26.

by the Security Police and SD to take control over all aspects of Jewish policy, including the economic side, which developed in the wake of the February 1941 strike.[44]

In practice, two "Austrian models" competed for the privilege of collecting and administering Jewish wealth in Holland. While Dr. Fischböck was preparing for the comprehensive confiscation of Jewish wealth, based on the pseudo-legal confiscation by decree developed in Austria and the "Old Reich," the Security Police (on instructions from Heydrich) was also developing its own variant of comprehensive expropriation.[45] In a letter sent to Seyss-Inquart in April 1941, the local head of the Security Police, Hanns Rauter, outlined a plan to establish a Central Office for Jewish Emigration in the Netherlands that would serve as a "model" for the solution of the Jewish Question throughout Europe. The plan envisaged the creation of a Central Fund to procure the necessary financial support for emigration and the "total solution of the Jewish Question." A key figure in the development of this plan was Dr. Erich Rajakowitsch, who had gained experience with similar operations in Vienna and Prague.[46]

To decide which plan to implement, Reichskommissar Seyss-Inquart convened a meeting of ministerial chiefs on May 19, 1941. The historian Joseph Michman convincingly summarizes the decisive results of this meeting:

> There was no disagreement among those present that the final goal was the removal of all Jews from Holland. With regard to the economic side of the Jewish question Seyss-Inquart adopted the idea that the confiscated Jewish property would be used for financing the "Final Solution," but for the time being he rejected the proposal to set up an emigration fund. Dr. Fischböck put forward a "plan in stages for achieving the general objective": the economy was to be rid of Jews; income from the sale of Jewish businesses or their liquidation was to be deposited with a company set up specially for this purpose, with responsibilities toward dispossessed Jews (its liability was extremely reduced and in most cases was not honored); Jewish land was also to be confiscated and ownership transferred to another special company; Jews were to deposit their money and securities in one bank which would handle only this type of transactions. The novelty, which distinguished Fischböck's plan

[44] In February 1941, there was some civil unrest in Amsterdam and a strike in support of the Jews following the intensification of repressive measures against them.

[45] G. Aalders, "Die Arisierung der niederländischen Wirtschaft," pp. 122–37; for the origins of some of these policies, see especially A. J. van der Leeuw, "Der Griff," pp. 211–23.

[46] Joseph Michman, "Planning for the Final Solution against the Background of Developments in Holland in 1941," *Yad Vashem Studies*, vol. XVII (1986): 145–80, here pp. 148–53.

from the established practices in Austria and the Reich, was centralization achieved by the founding of special companies controlled by the German authorities. This system had the advantage of ensuring the seizure of all Jewish property on the one hand, and eliminating the corruption, which had plagued the Aryanization campaign in Austria and Germany, on the other. In his plan Fischböck realized the proposals he had advanced in a meeting with Göring following Kristallnacht; at that time those proposals had been enthusiastically endorsed by Göring. The Fund for Jewish Emigration, conceived by Rajakowitsch, could not accommodate this comprehensive and professionally conceived plan, and Fischböck was charged with its implementation. By stripping the SS of control over economic matters, the independence of the Central Office was considerably reduced, especially since Fischböck did not place at its disposal the proceeds from Jewish property. The SS complained that Seyss-Inquart's principle of financing the Final Solution was thereby violated, but to no effect. As a result, the Central Office, which was planned to be a large organization, remained a very limited enterprise until the beginning of the deportations.[47]

As Joseph Michman demonstrates, responsibility for Jewish matters in the occupied Netherlands was divided between the civil administration and the Security Police, reflecting their underlying rivalries. Although Reichskommissar Seyss-Inquart appointed the Commissioner in Amsterdam, Dr. H. Böhmcker, as *Judenkommissar*, the Security Police Commissioner Dr. W. Harster was appointed to the post of deputy for Jewish affairs by Heydrich.[48]

One interpretation might depict this rivalry as one Austrian model being set up in competition against another. The centralized model applied by Adolf Eichmann and his SD colleagues in Austria and Prague, linking emigration with confiscation and finally also to the deportations, was trumped here by Seyss-Inquart with the help of Fischböck's technical expertise. Despite being sidelined, the Security Police continued to play an important role, especially after the deportations started in the summer of 1942. Seyss-Inquart's skill lay in trying to coordinate and limit the underlying rivalries by playing his subordinates off against each other.[49]

---

[47] J. Michman, "Planning for the Final Solution," pp. 163–65; see also G. Aalders, "Niederlande: Wirtschaftliche Verfolgung," p. 141.

[48] J. Michman, "Planning for the Final Solution," pp. 162–63.

[49] The internal resolution, or rather the institutionalization, of rivalries can be seen in the instructions on the "Jewish Question" issued by Seyss-Inquart on November 25, 1941. In the introduction, he stressed that the Commissioner for Amsterdam, Böhmcker, and the head of the Security Police there were instructed to work in mutual consultation and to resolve important issues by mutual agreement; see BAL, R 177/203, Reichskommissar Seyss-Inquart, Zur Behandlung der Judenfrage, November 25, 1941.

The Registration of Jewish Property – The First LiRo Decree

After the May meeting, the comprehensive confiscation of private property from the Dutch Jews was implemented in a "pseudo-legal" and concealed manner. The first stage was the concentration of Jewish liquid property at LiRo, in accordance with the so-called First LiRo Decree issued on August 8, 1941.[50] The new centralized LiRo Bank, created in summer 1941, involved a deliberate deception: in an attempt to allay Jewish fears, the new bank used the same name as a well-established Jewish bank that had already been Aryanized.[51]

All Dutch financial institutions were obliged to transfer Jewish bank accounts and share certificates to LiRo. When they complained that they would lose about 5 percent of their current business as a result, they received assurances that they would receive commissions in connection with the conversion of Jewish wealth into fixed interest securities.[52] Top-secret guidelines on the treatment of the Jewish bank accounts and securities holdings (depots) established at LiRo made clear that these were intended to be blocked accounts, from which only a fixed amount could be withdrawn each month by the Jewish owners to meet their ordinary living expenses. The regulations permitted only a few exceptions to these limits, for extraordinary payments such as taxes or doctor's bills, in response to written applications to the Inspection Department at LiRo.[53]

Jacob Presser notes that a significant aspect of the First LiRo Decree was that, of eleven articles, five dealt with penalties for any infringements. Certainly, the complex requirements of the decree were an onerous burden for the Jews and the banks, which had to cope with a morass of new regulations.[54] A Jewish man who was arrested in Amsterdam for the illegal possession of share certificates in November 1941 protested that he thought it was the responsibility of the bank to transfer the shares automatically and that therefore he had not known anything about it himself.[55] Officials at LiRo complained repeatedly about "passive resistance" to the measure by Dutch banks that had failed to transfer their Jewish accounts. In particular, they feared that wealthier individuals were escaping the net. For example,

---

[50] VO 148/1941, über die Behandlung des jüdischen Vermögens.

[51] For details of this process, see G. Aalders, *Geraubt!*, pp. 221–326.

[52] USHMM, RG-41, Acc.1997.A.1007 (NIOD), reel 391, Nbg. Doc. NID-13754, LiRo internal memo, August 19, 1941.

[53] BAL, R 177/203, undated guidelines on LiRo accounts created under VO 148/1941.

[54] J. Presser, *The Destruction of the Dutch Jews*, pp. 72–73.

[55] USHMM, RG-14.001M (Gestapo Düsseldorf), reel 5, statement of J. S., November 19, 1941.

a number of prominent Jewish former stockbrokers had not registered any property with LiRo by November.[56] Despite the careful registration in August 1941 of 140,522 "full-blooded" Jews in the Netherlands by the German authorities, it remained a difficult task for the Dutch banks and insurance companies to identify their Jewish customers.[57]

Not all Jews remained passive witnesses as the new restrictions threatened to engulf their savings. Information on transfers of assets at the time of the German invasion is difficult to obtain, but there was only a short window of opportunity to make them, as by June 1940 the German authorities had authorized the DSKs to prevent currency transfers. However, from 1941 on, there is evidence of various special contracts prepared by Jews in an effort to get around the German restrictions. For example, a Jewish man, A. A., made a contract with the firm Pierson & Co. to pay them 450,000 fl. on the condition that it would be returned three months after the conclusion of a peace treaty between Britain and Germany. However, the Germans did not hesitate to declare such contracts invalid, as their clear intention was to subvert the terms of the anti-Jewish laws.[58]

The Conversion of Shares into Government Bonds

A considerable portion of Jewish assets in the Netherlands was invested in shares and government securities. According to the internal accounts of LiRo, by 1945 it had received about 300 million fl. in securities – nearly three-quarters of all incoming Jewish property. By comparison, cash and bank deposits came to only 55 million fl.[59] Therefore, the treatment of Jewish share capital is of considerable significance for understanding the confiscation process.

On November 17, 1941, Reichskommissar Seyss-Inquart instructed the LiRo Bank to begin converting Jewish assets into German and Dutch government bonds, as soon as the process of concentration had "been largely

---

[56] BAL, R 177/203, LiRo Inspectie an GkFW, November 24 and November 26, 1941; see also similar correspondence on March 18, 1942.

[57] See G. Aalders, "Niederlande: Wirtschaftliche Verfolgung," p. 133: of these, 22,252 were foreign nationals (14,652 from the Reich). The Dutch banks did not have records telling them which customers were Jewish and which were not.

[58] BAL, R 177/203, GkFW an LiRo, June 23, 1942; even as early as February 1941, the Germans reported Jews requesting special contracts from insurance companies designed to protect them against anticipated confiscation measures; see USHMM, RG-41, Acc.1997.A.1007 (NIOD), reel 301, Meldungen aus den Niederlanden (BdS reports), February 4, 1941.

[59] G. Aalders, Geraubt!, p. 388: the total income received by LiRo was just over 425 million fl.

completed."[60] This conversion was postponed initially, due to concerns at LiRo that compliance with the First Decree had been slow and incomplete. However, in the first months of 1942, LiRo started the conversion process with a massive sale of Jewish shares. The timing could hardly have been worse though, as it coincided with a fall in the stock market caused by Japanese advances in the Far East. The financial press was well informed about the action, as LiRo did little to conceal the origins of these sudden large sales.[61]

The conversion of Jewish property into government bonds in this way was a revival of Göring's 1938 plans – to convert Jewish assets into low-interest government bonds and help finance rapidly mounting state debt. At the same time, it represented an important further step toward confiscation, as the nominal owners of the shares were (of course) not consulted. The Jews of Amsterdam were quite shocked when it was revealed in March 1942 that many of their shares had already been converted into government bonds. The Jewish Council protested that there was no legal basis for these sales and expressed the fear that they would inevitably accelerate the impoverishment of the Dutch Jews.[62]

The large-scale sale of Jewish shares in the Netherlands was facilitated by the cooperation of many Dutch stockbrokers. With regard to the sale of most shares, it is difficult to reconstruct precisely who was involved. However, throughout the war, trade continued in so-called American certificates issued by Dutch financial institutions based on U.S. shares. Their value rose steadily, as the Dutch currency fell against the dollar with the increasing expectation of an Allied victory. From the available records, Gerard Aalders concludes that 136 of the 375 members of the Amsterdam stock exchange dealt in formerly Jewish-owned shares of this type and that most must have been aware of the fact that they were stolen.[63]

The massive sale of Jewish shares in the Netherlands was exploited by the Nazis to repatriate some foreign shares to boost their foreign currency reserves.[64] In addition, German companies took an interest in purchasing shares of some Dutch companies in order to penetrate the local market.

---

[60] USHMM, RG-41, Acc.1997.A.0117 (NIOD), reel 131 (Collection 97, Alfred Flesche, 1940–1945) RK to LiRo, November 17, 1941; see also G. Aalders, *Geraubt!*, p. 273.

[61] G. Aalders, *Geraubt!*, pp. 273–78.

[62] See BAL, R 177/203, Joodsche Raad an Beauftragten des Reichskommissars für die Stadt Amsterdam, Böhmcker, April 1, 1942.

[63] G. Aalders, *Geraubt!*, pp. 278–82; see also Jaap Barendregt, *Securities at Risk: The Restitution of Jewish Securities Stolen in the Netherlands during World War II* (Amsterdam: Aksant, 2004), pp. 25–34.

[64] For further details, see Chapter 9.

For example, the German insurance company Allianz purchased 300,000 fl. in shares of the Dutch insurance company, Ass. Mij. de Nederlanden van 1945, from Jewish or "Enemy Property" sources in April 1942.[65] The main purchasers of Jewish-owned shares were in fact Dutch stockbrokers, though some may have been acting as intermediaries for German buyers.

The Second LiRo Decree

In May 1942, the Second LiRo Decree secured the funds already registered and demanded the surrender to LiRo of almost all remaining Jewish valuables. In addition, it reduced the limit for monthly withdrawals by Dutch Jews to 250 fl.[66] This decree completed the official transfer of Jewish private wealth to the LiRo Bank initiated in August 1941, although it did not openly specify actual confiscation. Hitler preferred to defer acknowledgment of the confiscation policy until the Jews had been physically removed, partly out of concern for public opinion.[67]

The drafting of the Second LiRo Decree provides insight into the decision-making process with regard to confiscation issues. As was the First LiRo Decree, it was prepared mainly by the officials of Fischböck's Ministry for Economics and Finance (GkFW) in close cooperation with the section of the Ministry for Justice and Administration responsible for drafting new legislation. Even though drafts were sent to the other relevant ministries and some adjustments were made as a result, the final word remained with the Reichskommissar.[68] Thus, both knowledge and responsibility were spread widely throughout the German occupation administration, and the confiscation decree was carefully coordinated with the other anti-Jewish measures.

Despite the careful preparations and adoption of existing German models, the implementation of the Second LiRo Decree was not without its problems. In particular, the Inspection Department of LiRo, under the guidance of the GkFW, had to oversee the Jewish accounts and consider

---

[65] Gerald Feldman, *Die Allianz und die deutsche Versicherungswirtschaft 1933–1945* (Munich: C. H. Beck, 2001), p. 463; see also R. Hilberg, *Die Vernichtung*, vol. II, p. 601.

[66] A copy of the "Second LiRo Decree" can be found in BAL, R 177/214, VO 58/42, May 21, 1942; see also R 177/203, GkFW Abt. Feindvermögen an Ministerialrat von Böckh, enclosing report for Reichskommissar Seyss-Inquart, June 3, 1942.

[67] BAL, R 177/213, Lammers an Seyss-Inquart, February 12, 1942: "Der Führer hat auf eine Anfrage des OKHs zur Vermeidung unerwünschter politischer Rückwirkungen … entschieden: 1. Die Beschlagnahme jüdischer Wohnungseinrichtungen soll möglichst wenig Aufsehen erregen. 2. Eine Beschlagnahme kommt nur in Frage, soweit die jüdischen Besitzer der Einrichtungen nicht mehr anwesend und die Wohnungen unbewohnt sind."

[68] See the extensive correspondence on the drafting of the decree in BAL, R 177/213.

the numerous applications for withdrawals over the limit of 250 florins per month. A report by the Inspection Department from mid-September 1942 noted that, even with one hundred employees, it was very hard pressed, constantly working overtime, especially as the Jews were using every possible means to evade the regulations. While complaining that his department had become the "most hated people," its head, Otto Witscher, was concerned to retain a "free hand" with regard to special requests and not lose his power to the GkFW. In support of his claim to retain considerable independence, Witscher boasted that he had always favored the reduction of the limit to 250 fl., as it was not acceptable that "Jews should have more money than an 'Aryan worker' supporting his family by hard work."[69]

The cessation of further payments to Jews from LiRo ordered in November 1942 and the ensuing liquidation of individual accounts marked the final steps in the confiscation process. As one subsequent German report put it, with the transfer to a collective account, "the individual property of the respective payees [individual Jewish account owners] is submerged and the delivered values are to be viewed as confiscated by the Reichskommissar."[70] Beginning in January 1943, account holders no longer received statements from LiRo, and the remaining Jews in need of support had to make applications to the Jewish Council, which paid them from funds made available by LiRo.[71] This reflected another element of prewar German schemes: using the Jewish communal organization to ensure that Jews did not become a burden on the state.[72] The conversion from individual blocked accounts to one single combined account also destroyed the record of the money's original provenance, considerably complicating the process of postwar restitution to surviving Jews and the heirs of those murdered in the Nazi concentration and death camps.

Diamonds, Precious Metals, Jewelry, and Other Cultural Property

The value of precious metals, diamonds, jewelry, and cultural property (just over 5.1 million fl. according to internal records) surrendered to the LiRo Bank was relatively small compared with the financial assets collected.[73] However, LiRo had to compete with other agencies, including the ERR,

---

[69] BAL, R 177/214, Arbeitsbericht der "Inspectie," September 15, 1942.

[70] LAB, B. Rep. 039-01/320, A. J. van der Leeuw, Gutachten, December 11, 1969, p. 22. I am grateful to Götz Aly for bringing this source to my attention.

[71] G. Aalders, Geraubt!, pp. 245–47; Joods Historisch Museum Amsterdam (ed.), Documents of the Persecution of the Dutch Jewry (Amsterdam: Polak and Van Genneo, 1979), p. 44.

[72] See, for example, A. J. van der Leeuw, "Der Griff," p. 221.

[73] G. Aalders, Nazi Looting, pp. 187–88.

for many items,[74] and some jewelry and precious metals were extracted by the confiscation and blackmailing efforts of the Security Police. LiRo processed its share of these items fairly quickly, completing the resale of most by the end of 1943. Valuations were performed by a variety of auction houses and brokers who received commissions of 1 or 1.5 percent. Many artworks and other cultural items were sold at less than their value or were simply surrendered to other German agencies, such as the Dienststelle Mühlmann, which acquired artworks in the Netherlands under the authority of Seyss-Inquart.[75]

The total value of the silver processed by LiRo was almost twice that of the gold, but the prices paid were well below the international market value, as LiRo also paid for the smelting costs of silver bullion and gold was sold at official prices kept artificially low. In agreement with the *Reichsstelle für Edelmetall* (Reich Office for Precious Metals), the most valuable silver was to be sent to Berlin and the remainder smelted locally or sent to Degussa.[76] Jewelry was sold mainly to German firms or government agencies. The main purchaser was General Commissar Schmidt, who put a stop to the sale of diamonds in January 1943 and then purchased more than 1 million fl. in jewelry and precious stones from LiRo between March and May 1943. The distorted priorities of the Nazi regime are reflected in the fact that these diamonds were intended primarily as ornaments to be worked into the casings of Germany's highest military decorations.[77]

The Amsterdam diamond industry itself was treated initially with some caution due to the fragile nature of the trade, which relied heavily on the skills and business connections of the many Jewish craftsmen and brokers who owned some 80 percent of it. In this industry, Aryanization was largely deferred until 1944, as maintaining the supply of diamonds – especially industrial – was vital to the German war effort. Dutch diamond workers and their families were protected at first from the deportations, although by June 1943 most had been rounded up and carried off to the transit camp at Westerbork, from where some were subsequently deported to the East.[78]

---

[74] See, for example, BAL, R 177/203, ERR an LiRo, May 14, 1942.

[75] G. Aalders, *Nazi Looting*, pp. 187–89 and 213–16.

[76] Ibid., pp. 186–89; BAL, R 177/203; see also Peter Hayes, *From Cooperation to Complicity: Degussa in the Third Reich* (New York: Cambridge University Press, 2004), p. 187, noting the receipt of 225 kilograms of fine silver by Degussa from LiRo.

[77] G. Aalders, *Nazi Looting*, pp. 187–91; see also A. J. van der Leeuw, "Die Käufe des Generalkommissars z.b.V. Fritz Schmidt," in A. H. Paape (ed.), *Studies over Nederland in oorlogstijd* ('s-Gravenhage: Martinus Nijhoff, 1972), pp. 278–82.

[78] G. Aalders, *Nazi Looting*, pp. 120–22; J. Presser, *The Destruction*, pp. 371–74.

As the German authorities were particularly concerned to recover any hidden stocks of diamonds and to prevent them being smuggled out of the country, the offer of protection from deportation was also used to extract remaining diamonds via blackmail, although in many cases German officials subsequently reneged on their promises of protection. After their arrests in May and June of 1943, some diamond company owners were released, as the Four-Year Plan had commissioned the company of Bozenhardt brothers to buy up remaining diamond stocks for sale on the world market in exchange for foreign currency. The official fixed price was actually paid during this action to facilitate resale on the world markets with acceptable paperwork.[79]

By the end of 1944, only part of the extorted diamonds had been sold, as their sale in neutral countries was encountering growing difficulties. Nevertheless, diamond workers had better chances of survival than most Dutch Jews, not only because they were arrested later but also thanks to Himmler's plans (never realized) to continue exploiting their special skills at the Bergen-Belsen concentration camp.[80]

Blackmail Schemes: Stamps for Emigration and Deferral of Deportation

In the Netherlands, the early "voluntary" Aryanizations (up to the spring of 1941) included certain contracts that featured permission to emigrate as an encouragement to sell businesses. This method is documented in about thirty cases, although the complicated nature of the arrangements meant that some Jews did not actually leave the Netherlands for a neutral country until as late as spring 1943. In some instances, the surrender of additional foreign currency from overseas was included in the deal.[81]

A version of this model was then adapted increasingly by 1942 with the aim of extorting overseas investments, foreign currency, or concealed valuables, especially diamonds. The DSKs and the Currency Institute, which were subordinate to Fischböck's GkFW, played an increasingly important role, together with LiRo and the Security Police, in authorizing emigration

---

[79] G. Aalders, *Nazi Looting*, pp. 120–22; A. J. van der Leeuw, "Die Aktion Bozenhardt und Co.," in A. H. Paape (ed.), *Studies over Nederland in oorlogstijd*, pp. 257–77.

[80] A. J. van der Leeuw, "Die Aktion Bozenhardt," p. 270; J. Presser, *The Destruction*, pp. 373–74.

[81] R. Hilberg, *Die Vernichtung*, vol. II, p. 604; for specific cases, see Bettina Zeugin and Thomas Sandkühler (eds.), *Die Schweiz und die deutschen Lösegelderpressungen in den besetzten Niederlanden: Vermögensentziehung, Freikauf, Austausch 1940–1945: Beiheft zum Bericht Die Schweiz und die Flüchtlinge zur Zeit des Nationalsozialismus* (Bern: Unabhängige Expertenkommission Schweiz, Zweiter Weltkrieg, 1999), pp. 38–39.

permits. With the onset of the deportations in summer 1942, the Security Police also practiced similar extortion methods as the price for issuing so-called deportation deferrals (*Sperrstempel*), usually valid for less than three months. Such negotiations helped determine the fate of more than one thousand Jews in the Netherlands, and the money thereby extorted was in the realm of 40–100 million fl. Because of the large sums involved and the need to tap foreign currency reserves overseas, a number of shady middlemen, such as Walter Büchi, played a key role in these negotiations, some of them extracting commissions of 10 percent or more. More than 154 Jewish men and women managed to survive through such payments, but the German authorities still deported to death camps or concentration camps the majority of those involved in such deals.[82]

Life Insurance and Pensions

Life insurance policies had to be registered with LiRo both by the Jewish owners and the companies themselves following the Second LiRo Decree; LiRo then proceeded to recall the capitalized values of the registered policies in accordance with the deadline of April 1, 1943, set for the completion of all of LiRo's work.[83] However, officials at LiRo confronted a number of practical difficulties and were not satisfied with the level of cooperation by Dutch insurance companies. For example, in July 1942, the Inspection Department of LiRo complained about new policies being issued after the First LiRo Decree in which the payee was a Dutch company, but the beneficiary was a Jew. In December 1942, it reported that a major life insurance company was refusing to make further pension payments for deported Jews unless it received a declaration from the commandant of Westerbork Camp that the beneficiary was still alive.[84] In response to such tactics, a more explicit decree covering the termination of insurance policies and pensions was issued in June 1943 (VO 54/1943), intended to overcome such legal obstruction. LiRo's own research revealed that not all Jewish policies were being declared by the companies, and ultimately it seems that barely 80 percent of Jewish polices were ultimately surrendered. In total, some 22,368 policies were surrendered, with a combined value of about 25 million fl.[85]

---

[82] G. Aalders, *Geraubt!*, pp. 371–82; Bettina Zeugin and Thomas Sandkühler (eds.), *Die Schweiz und die deutschen Lösegelderpressungen*, pp. 115–17.

[83] G. Aalders, *Nazi Looting*, pp. 180–83. The deadline can be found in an undated LiRo memo from 1942; see BAL, R 177/214.

[84] BAL, R 177/209, Liro an GkFW, July 1 and December 12, 1942.

[85] G. Aalders, *Nazi Looting*, pp. 180–83; in both the German and English editions of Aalders' book there is some confusion about the date of "54/1943," which should be June 11,

Real Estate

Jewish real estate in the Netherlands was dealt with under a separate decree of August 11, 1941, which called for its registration with a new institution, the *Niederländische Grundstücksverwaltung* (Dutch Real Estate Administration, NGV) that was founded five days later.[86] Subsequently, the NGV was responsible for the administration and sale of registered Jewish real estate and mortgages, with the assistance of trustees. As with industrial property, the proceeds were initially to be paid into blocked accounts for the former owners at LiRo via the VVRA, in installments over twenty-five years. In total, 20,000 properties and 5,600 mortgages were registered, with an estimated value of 150 million and 22 million florins, respectively.[87]

In practice, the prices paid were frequently well below the market value. This was partly a result of the reluctance to buy former Jewish property, especially in the countryside, reinforced by the wariness of Dutch mortgage institutions to lend money for this purpose. Germany's declining military fortunes after the battle of Stalingrad in February 1943 certainly made investment in former Jewish property an increasingly risky proposition. As Aalders points out, however, it is not clear whether the reluctance of Dutch institutions and individuals to participate in sales of Jewish-owned real estate was motivated primarily by political or economic calculations.[88]

Clearing Jewish Apartments after the Deportations

The processing of Jewish household effects actually began in the Netherlands before the deportations, as the ERR confiscated and exploited the property of Jews who had managed to flee during the Nazi invasion. The process of concentrating Jews before the deportations, which began in early 1942, also involved the registration of their household property by the *Hausraterfassungsstelle,* a special section affiliated with the Central Office for Jewish Emigration; it had both Jewish and Dutch staff. The ERR then cleared the

---

1943. According to the conclusions of the various official Dutch investigations, insurance policies were the only sorts of Jewish assets not reported to LiRo on a large scale; see the Web site of the Dutch Ministry of Finance: http://www.minfin.nl/ttw/english.htm, as of February 8, 2001.

[86] According to VO 154/1941 (über den jüdischen Grundbesitz), Jewish real estate had to be registered with the NGV by September 15, 1941.

[87] G. Aalders, *Geraubt!*, pp. 210–11. The "Algemeen Nederlandsch Beheer van Onroerende," or General Dutch Management of Real Estate, also became involved in the management and sale of Jewish properties after a while. Like the NGV, it was staffed mainly by Dutch Nazis and claimed a commission of 5 percent for "management fees."

[88] Ibid., pp. 212–20.

houses.[89] This division of labor was maintained after the mass deportations began in July 1942. Ultimately, the Germans deported more than 75 percent of the Jewish population in the Netherlands (107,000 out of 140,000).[90]

By the end of June 1944, the contents of more than 29,000 dwellings had been cleared, with most of the property being sent to Germany in the course of the so-called Furniture Action (*Möbel-Aktion*) for the benefit of German victims of Allied bombing. Furniture remaining in the Netherlands was either given to the Wehrmacht for its own use, or the low-quality pieces were sold to Dutch wholesalers. The sort of benefits obtained by some Dutch collaborators can be seen from the May 1943 example of the Dutch SS-Standartenführer Feldmeijer, who requested an apartment equipped with items "suitable for entertaining prominent guests." His request was duly met with articles removed from a former Jewish residence.[91]

As in Germany, a major problem was posed by the claims for outstanding rent from the owners of apartments, especially if they could not rent out apartments while the belongings of former Jewish occupants were still there.[92] According to the regulations drawn up by the GkFW, LiRo had to pay rent only for the period from the deportation to the clearing of the flat. The cost of any renovations to the apartment could be claimed only if this condition had been specifically written into the original lease. Outstanding debts from the period prior to deportation could not be recouped from the sale of property left behind.[93]

As Presser observes, the process of clearing Jewish apartments took place in full view (see Figure 7.1): "Everyone in the vicinity, even those who had not seen the victims dragged away under cover of darkness, could not but observe the furniture vans being loaded up in broad daylight."[94]

Beneficiaries and Corruption

A large bureaucracy requiring numerous forms in multiple copies was necessary to organize the plundering of the Dutch Jews. According to Presser,

---

[89] Bob Moore, *Victims and Survivors: The Nazi Persecution of the Jews in the Netherlands 1940–1945* (London: Arnold, 1997), p. 88; J. Presser, *The Destruction*, pp. 360–61.

[90] Wolfgang Seibel, "Perpetrator Networks and the Holocaust: Resuming the 'Functionalism' versus 'Intentionalism' Debate," paper prepared for delivery at the 2000 Annual Meeting of the American Political Science Association, p. 19. Only about 5,200 Jews returned to the Netherlands after the war from the concentration and death camps; see G. Aalders, *Nazi Looting*, p. 228.

[91] J. Presser, *The Destruction*, pp. 361–62.

[92] See BAL, R 177/203, J. A. Duyndon an GkFW, August 20, 1942.

[93] BAL, R 177/203, LiRo an GkFW, November 21, 1942.

[94] J. Presser, *The Destruction*, p. 359.

"some of the laborers in this vineyard were not beyond collecting a few windfalls. But . . . most did their work meticulously and honestly." Today, the extensive records they created mean that, despite the loss of some important documents, the process of confiscation can still be reconstructed. The documents do reveal several notable cases of corruption within LiRo itself, mainly because there was no effective way to control the activities of the staff and most of the "clients" had been deported.[95]

The various opportunities for enrichment certainly facilitated the progressive removal of the Jews, despite the lack of widespread support for German anti-Jewish policies among the Dutch population as a whole. According to one German report, the Dutch police were especially interested in stealing coffee, tea, tobacco, and cash while arresting Jews. They frequently forbade Jews to take any luggage with them on the grounds that the Germans would take it anyway.[96]

The role of the "bounty hunters" in the Netherlands, who collected rewards for exposing Jews in hiding, has recently become a topic of more intensive research. Despite denials during their postwar trials, it appears that financial rewards were the prime motives for the Dutch civilian staff of the "Recherchegruppe Henneicke" under the control of the Central Office for Jewish Emigration, who helped arrest for deportation as many as eight or nine thousand Jews.[97] Funds to reward these people were advanced from confiscated Jewish property.[98] The DSKs also set up a similar system of local informants to track down concealed Jewish property. In March 1942, the DSK proposed offering rewards to attract informants, to be paid as a percentage of the amount recovered on a sliding scale.[99] It is still not clear how widespread participation in these activities was.

As elsewhere, there were also local initiatives to mop up Jewish property overlooked by the house-clearing squads. A fifty-one-year-old housewife wrote in her diary on July 3, 1943, "I and Truus went over some Jewish homes, but there was little to get – all the essentials had gone, including underclothes and linen. The next-door neighbors had got there first; all I could find was a few trifles and Truus got a pedal car and some other toys.

---

[95] G. Aalders, *Nazi Looting*, pp. 139–41.

[96] NARA, RG-238, T-1139, Nbg. Doc. NG-2631, Reichskommissar an AA, Betr.: Abschiebung der Niederländischen Juden, March 26, 1943.

[97] See Ad van Liempt, *Kopgeld: Nederlandse premiejagers op zoek naar joden 1943* (Amsterdam: Balans, 2002); for an example of an arrest report by W. C. H. Henneicke himself, see USHMM, RG-41, Acc.1997.A.0117 (NIOD), reel 392, Bericht Betr.: die Jüdin Mina Rubins und das Judenkind Rozette v/d Stam. A note on the file indicates they were gassed shortly afterward on September 3, 1943.

[98] J. Presser, *The Destruction*, p. 366.

[99] BAL, R 177/203, DSK memo, March 30, 1942.

But the whole business is highly dangerous, for if they catch you they send you to the Vught concentration camp."[100] Support for Jews in hiding was often rendered in return for financial rewards.[101] Therefore, the effectiveness of the asset-stripping campaign, begun comprehensively before the start of the deportations, also reduced the chances of Jews surviving to the liberation. To salvage something of their property, some Jews turned to Dutch friends and neighbors, the so-called *Bewahrier*, to "look after" their property until their return. However, even for those few Jews who did return, it was not always easy to reclaim their possessions.

Assessment of Confiscations in the Netherlands

The most striking aspects of the confiscation process in the Netherlands were (1) the careful preparation of the action in coordination with planning for the deportations and (2) its rapid and comprehensive implementation. In the key months from August 1941 to May 1942, the legislative framework of confiscation in the Netherlands was assembled, accompanying the key transition in German policy from forced emigration to deportation and physical destruction.[102] By the fall of 1941, detailed planning for the removal (*Aussiedlung*) of the Jews from the Netherlands was already underway, with Hitler's explicit approval.[103] The actual implementation still took time to prepare, but in the meantime the two LiRo Decrees effectively concentrated and secured almost all Jewish assets at the LiRo Bank. As one internal LiRo report maintained, "it was important to secure Jewish property as far as possible before the deportations, as otherwise considerable amounts would inevitably go astray."[104] Thus, there was even a parallel between the concentration of Dutch Jews for deportation and the concentration of their assets. As the Inspection Department at LiRo also managed the blocked accounts, this represented a considerable simplification in comparison with

---

[100] J. Presser, *The Destruction*, p. 363.

[101] See, for example, Eichmann Trial doc. T/536, Gestapo report on "The Development of the Jewish Problem in the Netherlands," December 31, 1942.

[102] W. Seibel (ed.), *Holocaust und 'Polykratie' in Westeuropa, 1940–1944: Nationale Berichte*, pp. xxxvi and xlix. Seyss-Inquart was careful to insist on a unified approach toward Jewish policy at a meeting on October 8, 1941.

[103] J. Michman, "Planning for the Final Solution," pp. 167–69; B. Moore, *Victims and Survivors*, pp. 76–79; the reference to "Aussiedlung" can be found in USHMM, RG-41 (Acc.1997.A.0117), reel 302 (NIOD Collections 77–85), File 53A, BdS den Haag, circular re. "Sonderreferat J," August 28, 1941.

[104] BAL, R 177/214, Arbeitsbericht der "Inspectie," September 15, 1942, p. 3; the report also noted that hidden property was much harder to track down after the Jewish owners had gone.

the way blocked accounts were administered by the banks and tax offices in the Reich.[105]

What happened to confiscated Jewish property in the Netherlands? In practice, only a small part was actually used for financing the Final Solution. Of the total income from Jewish property, almost certainly in excess of one billion fl.,[106] only about 25 million fl. were made available to the Gestapo for the establishment of two Jewish camps and other administrative costs in the Netherlands. The bulk of the money remained in the accounts of LiRo and the VVRA. According to Seyss-Inquart, in talks with Reich Finance Minister Graf Lutz Schwerin von Krosigk, it had been agreed that the major part would be retained for purposes inside the Netherlands.[107] However, the rapid processing of Jewish property provided an almost immediate boost to Germany's shaky war finances, as much of it was quickly converted into Dutch and German government bonds, starting even before the deportations. The haul also brought in some vital foreign currency, though only part of the diamonds and foreign securities collected were actually sold in the neutral countries due to increasing difficulties encountered in these markets by 1944.[108]

Most striking is the effectiveness of the confiscation policy, securing according to the rough calculations of Helen Junz as much as 94 percent of Jewish property on Dutch soil.[109] Even some overseas assets were repatriated through the blackmail schemes and extensive registration of property. Significantly, a very large part of the proceeds went directly into the hands of the state, correcting the free-for-all of "wild Aryanizations" in Austria and the destruction of property during Kristallnacht. The German authorities also exploited the policy of Aryanization to pursue other German aims, including German penetration of the Dutch economy and its "rationalization" through the liquidation of many smaller and inefficient firms. The

---

[105] Ibid.

[106] G. Aalders, *Nazi Looting*, p. 224; see also, Helen B. Junz, *Where Did All the Money Go?: The Pre-Nazi Era Wealth of European Jewry* (Bern: Staempfli, 2002), p. 65; Second World War Assets Contact Group (ed.), *Second World War: Theft and Restoration of Rights. Final Report of the Second World War Assets Contact Group* (Amsterdam, 2000), pp. 84–87, gives a rough breakdown of known amounts: LiRo – fl. 370 million; businesses – fl. c. 300 million; real estate and mortgages – fl. 196 million; household effects – fl. c. 118 million; valuables and cash surrendered to the Security Police and others for blackmail – fl. c. 43 million; noncommercial organizations – fl. 7 million.

[107] Report by Seyss-Inquart in 1944, see Eichmann Trial doc. T-571, letter from Seyss-Inquart to Martin Bormann, February 28, 1944; see also G. Aalders, *Geraubt!*, pp. 388–89.

[108] On the sale of Dutch securities in Switzerland, see Chapter 9.

[109] H. B. Junz, *Where Did All the Money Go?*, p. 65.

looting was also used to reward some Dutch collaborators, although the role of the Dutch as beneficiaries remained limited, as the appetite for Jewish property was restrained and much of the furniture was shipped to Germany.

What was the role of Dutch institutions and Dutch society in this massive and highly effective plunder campaign against Jewish property? It is important to stress that very few initiatives came from the Dutch population or the Dutch administration. Although many Dutch citizens were prepared to take a risk and invest in former Jewish property, the reservations they expressed here were much greater than in Austria or Germany. The warnings against purchasing Jewish property – warnings issued by the Dutch government in exile – were widely known and to some extent heeded, especially as faith in an Allied victory always remained alive and grew steadily from 1943.[110]

The legalistic approach taken by the German authorities to the confiscation of Jewish property in the Netherlands was successful, as Dutch civil servants and private institutions were generally law-abiding and obeyed German instructions. It would be wrong, of course, to deny that the Germans encountered some problems; for example, banks permitted Jews access to their safe-deposit boxes. There were also the inevitable corruption and friction between the German authorities involved, even if they remained at lower levels than in most other countries. In many respects, the system of bureaucratic "confiscation by decree" in the Netherlands proved very successful for the Germans, even by comparison with other Western European countries. The clear priorities of the Nazi-run civil administration planning for the eventual incorporation of the Netherlands into the Reich also played a role.[111]

In assessing the implementation of confiscation in the Netherlands, Joseph Michman concludes that "Fischböck's methods of plundering the Jews were more sophisticated and effective than the emigration fund of the SS, and in the final analysis the Reich was the main beneficiary of his victory, which raked in more money and assets."[112] This important finding confirms the need to examine the role of the financial bureaucracy, as well as of the Security Police, in the implementation of the Final Solution. In the Netherlands, the comprehensive confiscation of Jewish property was carefully coordinated with the development of the Final Solution, transferring

---

[110] G. Aalders, *Geraubt!*, pp. 398–99. On June 7, 1940, the Dutch government in exile banned any transactions with the German occupation regime. On January 5, 1943, the "Inter-Allied Declaration against Acts of Dispossession Committed in Territories under Enemy Occupation and Control" specifically warned against offering any assistance to German looting policies.

[111] J.-M. Dreyfus, "Die Enteignung der Juden in Westeuropa," pp. 53–54.

[112] J. Michman, "Planning for the Final Solution," p. 174.

the bulk of Jewish wealth directly into the hands of the state by methods first conceived in Austria and the Reich.

Norway

In Norway, there was some antisemitic activism during the 1930s, including the demand in one newspaper, *Exstrablad*, for a boycott of Jewish businesses.[113] However, under German occupation, most Jews retained access to their personal property and bank accounts prior to their arrest and deportation.[114] Probably due to the small size of the country's Jewish population (2,173 souls in 1941–42), detailed legislation for the confiscation of Jewish property was not introduced before the start of the deportations.

In April 1941, the Germans confiscated the synagogue in Trondheim and completely vandalized it. They subsequently used the main sanctuary as a barracks and removed all Hebrew inscriptions. In October 1941, a circular was sent to all county governors instructing them to register Jewish property. Confiscation of Jewish stores started in the fall of 1941 in the city of Trondheim. On October 21, 1941, the German Security Police confiscated three stores belonging to the Abrahamsen family. A Norwegian agent of the Gestapo, Reidar Johan Duner Landgraff, placed these stores under "Aryan" managers who reopened them at the beginning of November. The Jewish owners fled to Sweden. Other stores were seized in Trondheim, Ålesund, and Kristiansand, but no Aryanization legislation along the model of that imposed in Belgium, France, and the Netherlands was passed in 1940–41. The Administration Office that oversaw the confiscated businesses answered directly to the German Security Police, which also received any profits beyond the costs of administration.[115]

---

[113] Daniel J. Elazar, et al. (eds.), *The Jewish Communities of Scandinavia – Sweden, Denmark, Norway, and Finland* (Lanham, MD: University Press of America, 1984), p. 118.

[114] For example, shortly after the start of the German occupation in April 1940, Margrit Rosenberg Stenge, a minor, was able to withdraw her family's savings from a bank in Oslo using a power of attorney in the name of her neighbor, Mrs. Prager. Her family had already gone into hiding and desperately needed the money to pay for their upkeep, see *Margrit Rosenberg Stenge, Margrit's Story: Narrow Escape to and from Norway* (Montreal, Quebec: Concordia University Chair in Canadian Jewish Studies; Montreal Institute for Genocide and Human Rights Studies, 2004), pp. 29–30.

[115] *The Reisel/Bruland Report on the Confiscation of Jewish Property in Norway* (Part of Official Norwegian Report 1997: 22) (Oslo, June 1997), pp. 9–12; Samuel Abrahamsen, *Norway's Response to the Holocaust* (New York: Holocaust Library, 1991), pp. 87–90.

The legal process of confiscation in Norway was improvised, legitimizing retrospectively executive measures already taken in connection with the deportation of the Jews.[116] At the beginning of October 1942, the commander of the German Security Police in Trondheim, Gerhard Flesch, ordered the arrest of the Jews in his area, which was accompanied by the confiscation of all property. Then on October 25, 1942, coded telegrams were sent to the various regional police offices in the rest of Norway ordering them to arrest local Jews. According to the telegrams, at the time of their apprehension, the Jewish prisoners were also to sign a statement agreeing to the confiscation of their property. The telegrams instructed the police to search for securities, jewelry, and cash; to block bank accounts; and to empty safe-deposit boxes.[117]

Only on October 26, 1942, did the Norwegian authorities introduce a Decree on the Confiscation of Property Belonging to the Jews. This comprehensive measure stated simply that assets of any kind, belonging to Jews with Norwegian citizenship or who were stateless, would be confiscated for the benefit of the state. The second paragraph assigned responsibility for implementation to the Ministry of Internal Affairs of the Quisling government and mandated that the names of the persons affected were to be published in the official newspaper of the Norwegian Nazi Party, *Fritt Folk*. The following paragraphs guaranteed the rights of third parties who were owed money, threatened severe punishment for those concealing Jewish property, and stipulated that the decree came into force immediately. According to an instruction of November 12, 1942, from Minister President Vidkun Quisling to Reichskommissar Terboven, an exception was to be made for confiscated gold, silver, and jewelry, which were to be handed over to the German Security Police as a contribution to the war effort. Wristwatches were also to be handed over to the German Army "for military use." The property of any German Jews in Norway was to be retained by the German authorities, in accordance with a separate agreement.[118]

In November 1942, the Norwegian government established a Liquidation Board under the Minister of Finance to manage the confiscation, administration, and liquidation of Jewish assets. As in Germany, separate files were

---

[116] This game of catch-up is in some respects reminiscent of the way the first Nazi confiscation decrees were introduced in the summer of 1933; see Chapter 1.

[117] R. Hilberg, *Die Vernichtung*, vol. II, p. 583; Oskar Mendelsohn, *The Persecution of the Norwegian Jews in World War II* (Oslo: Norges Hjemmefrontmuseum, 1991), p. 15; *The Reisel/Bruland Report*, p. 10.

[118] S. Abrahamsen, *Norway's Response*, p. 90; *The Reisel/Bruland Report*, pp. 10–13 and 113. The Reisel/Bruland Report assumes that the gold and silver assets were used by the German authorities to help pay for the transport of Jews to Auschwitz.

kept for each Jewish household, managed by an official receiver to facilitate the settlement of outstanding debts and the liquidation of assets, but the proceeds were all paid into a Communal Fund. Some types of property, such as office furniture and equipment, motor vehicles, paintings, and furs, were forwarded directly by the Liquidation Board for use in Norwegian government and Norwegian Nazi Party offices and therefore did not contribute to the Communal Fund. Only part of the confiscated real estate was sold, with the remainder being managed by the Liquidation Board. Life insurance policies were cashed in, bank accounts dissolved, and some securities sold; proceeds from the securities either went to the Communal Fund or were deposited with the Christiana Bank to collect the accruing interest. Some furniture and movable property were sold at auction or through special distribution centers, which favored specific groups within the population and marketed the items at knockdown prices. One beneficiary of low-value items was the Norwegian Nazi Party's welfare organization. Most of the unsold merchandise from liquidated stores was sold to other Norwegian businesses, usually in large batches and below market value.[119]

Shortly after the confiscation decree, on December 18, 1942, the Norwegian government-in-exile in London issued a provisional Decree Concerning the Invalidity of Legal Transactions Connected with the Occupation. This guaranteed the restitution of homes, stores, apartments, personal belongings, and communal property, dampening the appetite for Jewish property.[120] Nevertheless, many Norwegian individuals benefited from the confiscations, especially those directly involved in the process; they paid themselves high salaries and in some cases engaged in embezzlement. Businessmen bought up stock or whole companies cheaply, whereas Party members and others acquired furniture and apartments. In a small number of cases, in contrast, non-Jewish friends purchased items on behalf of Jews, securing the items for them until their return.

In total, the Germans deported more than 740 Jews from Norway (mainly in shipments on November 26, 1942, and on February 24, 1943), and most of the others (about 1,300) fled to Sweden. Of the deportees, only twenty-four returned.[121] According to an official report of 1952, the total received in the Communal Fund was 11,361,507 Norwegian crowns, derived from 1,053 separate estates. However, the same report indicated that (high) administration costs had already been deducted from this total, consisting of salaries

[119] *The Reisel/Bruland Report*, pp. 13–21.
[120] S. Abrahamsen, *Norway's Response*, p. 150.
[121] R. Hilberg, *Die Vernichtung*, vol. II, p. 585; S. Abrahamsen, *Norway's Response*, p. 148; *The Reisel/Bruland Report*, p. vi.

paid to administrators, and that other costs incurred during the liquidations and sales were probably equivalent to about one-third of the initial income received. In addition, a number of estates confiscated before November 1942 or belonging to German Jews were not included in the Fund.[122] The main beneficiary was the Norwegian state, which ironically had the advantage that at least some of the money and most of the records were still available after the war to assist the process of restitution. However, here again the Norwegian government claimed a share in administration fees, and death duties were sometimes applied to one estate several times, following the precise chain of inheritance in extended families in which only one member had survived.[123]

Denmark

In Denmark, there was no state policy of confiscation, as Danish politicians made protection of the Jewish minority a part of their modus vivendi with the Germans,[124] up to the German effort to deport the Jews in October 1943. As one German Jew who had already escaped to Sweden from Denmark reported prior to the flight and rescue of the Danish Jews,

> There is not the slightest [anti-] Jewish legislation. . . . the Danish Government, in spite of the German occupation, possesses extensive autonomy. . . . in spite of repeated demands on the part of the Germans, they have refused successfully, to introduce any [anti-] Jewish laws. The Jewish question, for the Danish Government, has become a direct question of the existence or the non-existence of an independent Denmark, and it has. . . . refused to be daunted by threats of [loss of independence].[125]

---

[122] *The Reisel/Bruland Report*, pp. 22–23.

[123] *The Reisel/ Bruland Report*, pp. 55–61; given the small Jewish population in Norway and the wealth of the country, it was easier here than in many other places to resolve the issue of material compensation during the 1990s. In the summer of 1998, the Norwegian government offered some $60 million to Norwegian Jews and international Jewish organizations as compensation for property seized during World War II: *New York Times*, June 27, 1998.

[124] See for example Dr. Werner Best's comments on the Danish attitude to the Jewish Question in January 1943, published in *Akten zur Deutschen Auswärtigen Politik, Serie E: 1941–45* (Göttingen: Vandenhoeck & Ruprecht, 1975), vol. V, pp. 77–78.

[125] Cited by Myrna Goodman, "Resistance and Rescue: German-Occupied Denmark, 1940–1943 – Ideology, Politics, and Culture" (PhD Diss., University of California, Davis, 2002), pp. 137–38.

After the Danish rescue operation, in which hundreds of Jews escaped with Danish help by boat to Sweden, the Jewish community arranged from Stockholm to pay many of the fishermen for their services. The Danish Ministry of Social Welfare then actively intervened to secure the property of both deported Jews and those who had fled, taking care of the affairs of 1,970 Jewish families until their return. Inventories of valuables and furniture were made; cash, savings books, and other property were placed into a municipal safe in Copenhagen for safekeeping.[126] As Leni Yahil notes, a large number of Jews found their apartments ready for them on their return, as Gentile relatives and friends had ensured that everything was in order. A few, however, returned to find their furniture gone and their apartments rented out to other people. In particular, some of those who had formally transferred their businesses to acquaintances found that the new "owners" were not prepared to admit the fictitious nature of the arrangement, but adhered to the letter of the law.[127] Yet, despite these minor blemishes, the Danish example still stands out in stark contrast to the other occupied countries of Europe: no legal confiscation was implemented, and most property was taken into safekeeping by the Danish authorities, to be returned soon after the end of the German occupation.

Belgium

The Belgian government fled to London as German forces occupied the country, but in an emergency law published on May 10, 1940, it authorized the Secretaries-General (heads of departments) who remained in place to carry on the administration under German occupation.[128] Both sides had learned from the brutal and rather bitter occupation during World War I and sought to achieve for the duration a modus vivendi that would reduce the impact of war on the Belgian population.[129] Therefore, the Secretaries-General largely cooperated with the German military administration, but in October 1940 they refused to enact proposed anti-Jewish legislation as part

[126] Leni Yahil, *The Rescue of Danish Jewry: Test of a Democracy* (Philadelphia: Jewish Publication Society of America, 1983), pp. 286–88; on the financing and other aspects of the rescue operation, see also R. Hilberg, *Die Vernichtung*, vol. II, pp. 594–96.

[127] L. Yahil, *The Rescue*, pp. 372–73.

[128] W. Seibel (ed.), *Holocaust und 'Polykratie' in Westeuropa, 1940–1944: Nationale Berichte*, p. xxix.

[129] For this insight, I am grateful to David Watts, who presented a very informative unpublished paper entitled "German Forced-Labor Policy in Belgium, 1916–1917 and 1942–1944" at a Research Workshop on "Forced and Slave Labor" hosted by the United States Holocaust Memorial Museum in summer 2003.

of the Belgian domestic code, compelling the Germans to issue their own decrees as an occupying power. Despite this official refusal to participate, there was widespread "passive collaboration" by the local Belgian administration in implementing the German decreed anti-Jewish measures.[130]

Another important context for the confiscation policies applied by the German military administration in Belgium was the nature of the Jewish population. Only a small proportion (between 5 and 10 percent) of the approximately 90,000 Jews living in Belgium in 1940 had Belgian citizenship.[131] In Antwerp, in particular, Flemish right-wing political parties had agitated against the growing influx of Jewish immigrants in the late 1930s. As in Germany, there was also an economic aspect to antisemitism, as elements of the middle class sought to use it as a weapon against their supposed Jewish economic competitors. The extreme right-wing parties, namely the *Vlaamsch Volksblok* (Flemish Popular Block) and the Rexists, did not make a breakthrough in the elections held in Antwerp in 1938, but in May 1939 the Antwerp Bar Association voted to exclude Jewish lawyers from practicing in the city.[132] This measure reflected Antwerp's position as a stronghold of Flemish nationalism; it witnessed considerable radical antisemitic agitation in the period before the war.

Seizure of Property of Those Who Fled and "Enemy Aliens"

It has been estimated that some 10,000 German Jewish refugees fled to Belgium between 1933 and 1938.[133] After the German attack on May 10,

---

[130] David Fraser, "National Constitutions, Liberal State, Fascist State and the Holocaust in Belgium and Bulgaria," in *German Law Journal*, no. 2 (1 February 2005); see also Maxime Steinberg, "The Judenpolitik in Belgium within the West European Context: Comparative Observations," in Dan Michman (ed.), *Belgium and the Holocaust: Jews, Belgians, Germans* (Jerusalem: Yad Vashem, 1998), pp. 199–224, here pp. 210–11; and Maxime Steinberg, *L'etoile et le fusil: La Question Juive 1940–42*, 3 vols. (Brussels: Vie ouvrière, 1983), vol. 1, pp. 108–13.

[131] Julianne Wetzel, "Frankreich und Belgien," in Wolfgang Benz (ed.), *Dimension des Völkermords: Die Zahl der jüdischen Opfer des Nationalsozialismus* (Munich: Oldenbourg, 1991), p. 109. Precise figures for the Jewish population of Belgium are not available due to the large and fluctuating number of Jewish refugees there at this time.

[132] Lieven Saerens, "Antwerp's Attitude toward the Jews from 1918 to 1940 and its Implications for the Period of Occupation," in Dan Michman (ed.), *Belgium and the Holocaust: Jews, Belgians, Germans* (Jerusalem: Yad Vashem, 1998), pp. 159–94, here pp. 180–88.

[133] *Les biens des victimes des persecutions anti-juives en Belgique: Spoliation – Rétablissement des droits. Resultats de la Commission d'etude. Rapport Final de la Commission d'etude sur le sort des biens des members de la Communaute juive de Belgique spolies ou delaisses pendant la guerre 1940–45* (Brussels: Services du Premier Ministre, 2001), p. 146.

1940, the Belgian authorities interned about five or six thousand people as suspicious persons. These internees were mostly German nationals, and as the German forces advanced, the Belgian authorities sent many to the south of France to prevent them falling into German hands. The Belgian prison service impounded their property. Many were German Jewish refugees, and more than 3,500 remained in France after the armistice, from where most were subsequently deported to the East via the notorious camp in Drancy.[134]

As in Luxembourg, hundreds, perhaps several thousand, Jews fled the country at the time of the invasion, and Group XII within the Economic Section (*Wirtschaftsabteilung*) of the German Military Administration impounded their property under "enemy property" decrees issued shortly after the start of the occupation. The German occupation forces also took over the apartments of many such refugees for their own use as offices and residences.[135] Hitler authorized the ERR to collect books and archives throughout Western Europe, intended for the planned Nazi ideological institute, the *Hohe Schule*, and its research into the Jewish Question. According to one estimate, during the occupation, the ERR looted more than 100,000 publications from 150 major libraries in Belgium and sent them initially to Berlin; of these libraries, approximately one hundred were Jewish.[136] The ERR also looted the private homes of Jews who had fled, collecting in July 1941, for example, eighty-two books from the former apartment of Roger Lévy at Avenue des Nations 74 in Brussels; at the time it was occupied by a German Army paymaster named Müller who had informed the ERR of the presence of books left behind.[137]

Registration of Property and Aryanization of Jewish Businesses

After the occupation of Belgium in 1940, Jewish property was registered according to German decrees issued in October 1940 and at the end of May 1941. The assets of about 23,000 persons were recorded on official registration forms. According to the declarations, their cash totaled RM 3 million, securities RM 100 million, real estate RM 100 million, and business

---

[134] *Les biens des victimes*, pp. 146–47; M. Steinberg, *L'etoile et le fusil*, vol. I, pp. 86–88.

[135] Maxime Steinberg, "Belgien: Polizeiliche und wirtschaftliche Verfolgung," in Wolfgang Seibel (ed.), *"Holocaust und 'Polykratie'" in Westeuropa, 1940–1944*, pp. 194–373, here pp. 222–23.

[136] *Les biens des victimes*, p. 141.

[137] USHMM, RG-31.002M (Central State Archives Kiev), reel 7, 3676-1-168, p. 28. These ERR documents ended up in Kiev after the war, having been looted from the Germans by the Soviets in Central Europe.

property about RM 80 million (for a total of RM 283 million).[138] However, the research of the Belgian Historical Commission indicates that, except for businesses and real estate, which were difficult for people to conceal, most other assets were underrepresented in the declarations.[139]

The German military authorities organized the systematic Aryanization of Jewish companies in Belgium using the *Brüsseler Treuhandgesellschaft* (Brussels Trustee Company, BTG), a public company under Belgian law. By July 1941, the German authorities had decreed that all Jewish businesses had to be marked distinctively as "Jewish enterprises."[140] Some 7,700 Jewish companies were registered and subsequently either Aryanized or (in more than 6,000 cases) liquidated.[141] In mid-June 1942, of 129 provisional administrators (*kommissarische Verwalter*) active in Belgium under the auspices of the BTG, only 9 were of Belgian nationality.[142]

The Final Report of the Belgian Historical Commission describes in detail one liquidation case, giving valuable insight into what it entailed. The BTG charged an administrator, Hauck, with the liquidation of Similex, a leather business, in March 1942. Hauck closed down the firm and prepared an inventory of its assets. By October 2, 1942, the liquidation was more or less completed. The employees' wages were paid up to March 1943 and other debts settled. Hauck notified the military commandant in Brussels of the 2,000 kilograms of coal remaining in the firm's cellars. On November 8, the remaining industrial equipment was removed, and on November 9, the firm's name was removed from the commercial register. The remaining proceeds from the liquidation (6,600 Belgian francs) went into the BTG account.[143]

---

[138] For details of the property registration results, see M. Steinberg, "Belgien: Polizeiliche und wirtschaftliche Verfolgung," pp. 240–41.

[139] Rudi van Doorslaer, "Raub und Rückerstattung jüdischen Eigentums in Belgien," in Constantin Goschler and Philipp Ther (eds.), *Raub und Restitution: "Arisierung" und Rückerstattung des jüdischen Eigentums in Europa* (Frankfurt am Main: Fischer Taschenbuch, 2003), pp. 134–53, here p. 135. The concluding report of Group XII of the German military administration gives a lower figure of RM 225 million. The reasons are discussed below.

[140] Viviane Teitelbaum-Hirsch, *Comptes d'une mort annoncée* (Brussels: Edition Labor, 1997), p. 32 and document appendix, pp. 201–206, Ordonnance complétant l'ordonnance relative aux juifs, May 31, 1941. Hotels, restaurants, and cafés had already been marked in accordance with a previous decree.

[141] V. Teitelbaum-Hirsch, *Comptes d'une mort annoncée*, p. 35; for a full breakdown of the Aryanization of 7,729 Jewish businesses by sector from German sources, see R. Hilberg, *Die Vernichtung*, vol. II, p. 635; *Les biens des victimes*, pp. 82–94.

[142] W. Seibel (ed.), *Holocaust und 'Polykratie' in Westeuropa, 1940–1944: Nationale Berichte*, p. lviii.

[143] *Les biens des victimes*, pp. 86–87.

The income from Aryanization was initially paid into blocked, named accounts at Belgian banks. Only after October 1942 did the German authorities order the transfer of these funds to a central account at the *Société Française de Banque et de Dépôts* (French Society for Banking and Secure Deposits, SFBD).[144] At the end of the occupation, the final report of Group XII, in charge of Aryanization within the German Military Administration, put the net income to the Reich from the "administration" of Jewish industrial property in Belgium at RM 12 million, of which a large part was remitted to Germany via clearing. The BTG benefited from various taxes and fees charged to the administered companies to cover its own expenses, including a 5 percent fee on the proceeds of liquidations. Because of the legal methods applied, however, it was not possible for the German authorities to gain access to much of the overall proceeds, which remained in blocked accounts in Belgium or tied up in businesses not yet sold.[145] In this respect, German policy did eliminate Jewish "influence" from the Belgian economy, but except for the German penetration of certain sectors of industry, no large gain accrued to the German war effort from Aryanization in Belgium.[146]

Diamond Industry

The experience of the Belgian diamond industry, based in Antwerp, reflects a pattern similar to developments in Amsterdam, where Jews were also prominent in the industry.[147] At the time of the invasion, some diamond merchants managed to escape to the United States, Britain, and Portugal, whereas others put part of their stocks into safekeeping in France. The German authorities initially treated the merchants with some caution in the hope of recovering at least some of these hidden diamonds. First, diamond traders were required to register their stocks in the summer of 1940. Beginning in November 1940, the Germans asserted progressively tighter controls: The authorities confiscated diamonds belonging to "enemies" (including

---

[144] W. Seibel (ed.), *Holocaust und 'Polykratie' in Westeuropa, 1940–1944: Nationale Berichte*, p. lvii.

[145] The value of the 637 firms still controlled by the BTG (unsold) at the end of the occupation was estimated to be RM 100 million, but this sum had never become available for the German authorities to spend. See R. van Doorslaer, "Raub und Rückerstattung," pp. 136–37.

[146] *Les biens des victimes*, pp. 89–94.

[147] Some 350 of 400 diamond traders in Antwerp were Jewish; see V. Teitelbaum-Hirsch, *Comptes d'une mort annoncée*, p. 82; the same figure can be found in Etienne Verhoeyen, *La Belgique Occupée: de l'an 40 à la libération* (Brussels: De Boeck Université, 1940), p. 255.

Jews), and safe-deposit boxes were emptied by the DSKs, which then also conducted raids at the diamond exchanges. These actions forced some of the remaining merchants to flee, so that by the end of 1941, the Germans had successfully purged all but a handful of Jewish dealers from the industry. Promises of protection from deportation offered to those who surrendered their diamond stocks to the head of the Diamond Control Office, William Frensel, generally proved to be worthless.[148] On the basis of the fragmentary evidence available, the Belgian Historical Commission concluded that diamonds worth more than 72 million Belgian francs were forcibly sold or confiscated by the German authorities during the occupation.[149]

Real Estate

The seizure and resale of Jewish real estate in Belgium encountered a number of local difficulties that diminished the ability of the German occupation authorities to mobilize these assets during the war. One was the refusal of Belgian notaries to register sales of Jewish real estate. The Germans got around this obstacle in December 1943 by issuing a decree enabling German notaries to carry out this function, but this did little to whet the appetite of the Belgian population for stolen real estate. The fragmentary records indicate that less than 10 percent of Jewish real estate could be sold during the occupation.[150] In addition, the fixed prices on which most sales were based (beginning in June 1940) were 50 percent below the market level, limiting German income from those sales that did take place. Much of the gross income received from sales had to be paid to those institutions that had issued mortgages.[151]

In Antwerp, four Belgian trustees administered Jewish real property, receiving a commission from the BTG for their work. The main agency involved in the administration of Jewish real estate outside of Antwerp was the *Verwaltung des Jüdischen Grundbesitzes in Belgien* (Administration of

---

[148] Eric Laureys, "The Plundering of Antwerp's Jewish Diamond Dealers," in *Confiscation of Jewish Property in Europe, 1933–1945: New Sources and Perspectives* (Washington, DC: United States Holocaust Memorial Museum, February 2003), pp. 57–74.

[149] *Les biens des victimes*, pp. 117–18.

[150] R. van Doorslaer, "Raub und Rückerstattung," pp. 137–38. The level of sales was slightly higher in Antwerp than elsewhere, perhaps because of the greater degree of Belgian involvement in the administration and sale of property; see *Les biens des victimes*, pp. 58–67; see also Götz Aly, *Hitlers Volksstaat: Raub, Rassenkrieg und nationaler Sozialismus* (Frankfurt am Main: S. Fischer, 2005), p. 231.

[151] BAL, R 2/32063, Besprechung am Dezember 11–12, 1942 im RFM; R. van Doorslaer, "Raub und Rückerstattung," pp. 137–38.

Jewish Real Estate in Belgium, VJGB), which had about 10 million Belgian francs in more than five hundred accounts at the end of the occupation, although about sixty had negative balances. As with industrial property, the net proceeds of both the sales and administration of real estate – estimated at about 20 million Belgian francs – were paid into a variety of different accounts, most of which remained blocked in Belgium in the names of the Jewish owners until the end of the occupation.[152]

Blocked Bank Accounts and Shares

It is difficult to obtain a precise picture of how the blocking of Jewish bank accounts in Belgium was implemented. The German Military Administration decreed at the end of May 1941 that Jews had to transfer their money into "Jewish" accounts at currency banks and that securities could no longer be disposed of without permission. The income from the Aryanization of Jewish businesses was paid into blocked named accounts at Belgian banks. However, it was not until September 1942 that Jewish liquid wealth was subjected to direct control by the local military commandants, effectively blocking all individual accounts. German regulations set a monthly limit of 1,875 Belgian francs on the amount Jewish families could withdraw from bank accounts.[153] After October 24, 1942, the Belgian banks were instructed to centralize all funds from Jewish accounts at the SFBD. This order was intended to bring those funds under direct German control as the SFBD was administered under the "Enemy Property" regulations, and it probably anticipated the outright confiscation of all funds after the deportations. However, recent research based on the records of the Belgian banks indicates that in practice exceptions were often permitted and that the concentration of bank accounts beginning in the fall of 1942 was only partially implemented. One reason for the delayed centralization of Jewish accounts was the banks' concern that any Belgian creditors should be paid off before Jewish accounts were transferred.[154]

It appears that the military administration did give the blocking of Jewish bank accounts in Belgium a high priority, although it was also linked to the deportations and planned confiscations. It is probable, however, that,

---

[152] *Les biens des victimes*, pp. 58–74.

[153] For a published version of the ordinance dated May 31, 1941, see V. Teitelbaum-Hirsch, *Comptes d'une mort annoncée*, pp. 201–206; W. Seibel (ed.), *Holocaust und 'Polykratie' in Westeuropa, 1940–1944: Nationale Berichte*, p. lviii, and in the same volume M. Steinberg, "Belgien: Polizeiliche und wirtschaftliche Verfolgung," pp. 237–38.

[154] *Les biens des victimes*, pp. 47–55; M. Steinberg, "Belgien," pp. 238–39.

because a very large proportion of Jews were not Belgian nationals, a significant share of Jewish property had already been secured earlier under the "Enemy Property" regulations issued in 1940 (especially from those who had fled) or by the special legislation regarding German Jews.[155] Nevertheless, once the deportations got underway, the blocking of bank accounts had a serious economic impact on the victims: in November 1942, the German Foreign Office reported that the financial position of the remaining Jews in Belgium had so deteriorated that they were compelled to cash in their last remaining assets.[156]

Confiscation of Property from German Jews

German reports mention the difficulties they encountered in establishing the nationality of all Jews whose property had been seized.[157] Many German Jews found refuge in Belgium prior to 1940, and according to a decree issued on April 22, 1942, all of their property was to be credited to the Reich under the Eleventh Decree.[158] Most German Jews in Belgium fled again or were deported by the Belgians to France at the time of the German invasion, and the German authorities were keen to seize their remaining assets. From the registration reports on the blocked accounts at Belgian banks, the Germans established that about RM 140,000 belonged to German Jews. This money was then confiscated in connection with the planned deportation of all Jews in Belgium.[159] Furniture belonging to German Jews in Belgium was destined for the relief of bomb-damage victims in Germany, but the payment for these items – which in the case of other Jews was owed to the BTG – was to be settled directly with the Reich Finance Ministry instead, to avoid the transfer of Reichsmarks to Belgium. The German military adminstration in Belgium exchanged information with the senior finance presidents (OFPs) in Germany in an effort to identify assets belonging to German Jews who had fled to Belgium. These were to be identified on the basis of lists prepared of Jews who had left behind "tax debts."[160]

---

[155] *Les biens des victimes*, pp. 147–51; M. Steinberg, "Belgien," pp. 206 and 222–23.
[156] *Akten zur Deutschen Auswärtigen Politik, Serie E: 1941–45*, vol. IV, p. 418. At that time, more than 16,000 Jews had already been deported.
[157] NARA, RG-238, T-1139, reel 53, NG-5369.
[158] *Les biens des victimes*, p. 147.
[159] BAL, R2/32063, RFM Vermerk, November 6, 1942.
[160] Ibid., RFM Vermerk, October 29, 1942; OFP Köln an RFM, January 6, 1943; Militärbefehlshaber in Belgien und Nordfrankreich an RFM (Mädel), March 31, 1943.

Liquidating Remaining Assets in the Wake of the Deportations

From a population of between 65,000 and 90,000 Jews still in Belgium, the Germans deported about 25,000 between July 1942 and the end of 1944. As in the Netherlands, massive amounts of furniture belonging to the Jews in Belgium were transported to the Reich beginning in early 1942. The German authorities planned initially to use it to furnish the offices of the *Reichsministerium für die besetzten Ostgebiete* (Reich Ministry for the Occupied Eastern Territories, RMfdbO), but in practice much was used to replace the material losses inflicted by Allied bombing. First, the Germans looted the furniture of Jews who had fled and left behind items stored in the port of Antwerp, beginning in March 1942. Then the RMfdbO delegated the clearing of apartments in the Netherlands, Belgium, and France to the ERR, also under the direct control of Reichsleiter Alfred Rosenberg. In an effort not to attract attention, confiscations were to take place only from empty apartments where the owner was no longer present.[161] According to a report prepared by the RMfdbO, between September 1942 and August 1943, 3,868 dwellings in Belgium were completely cleared, and from them 54,059 cubic meters of furniture were transported to the Reich.[162] Among the private firms involved was the renowned German transport company, Kühne & Nagel, which in October 1943 chartered a ship to take Belgian furniture from Antwerp to a number of cities in the Rhineland.[163] Several Belgian transport companies assisted the Germans in clearing the apartments and shipping the contents. As in Germany, many landlords tried to recoup lost rent by seizing the contents of Jewish apartments. The Germans countered by sealing apartments, but it appears that landlords were later reimbursed, at least up to the value of furniture seized from the apartments concerned.[164] Income from the sale of furniture from the West was booked to Einzelplan XVII of the German budget, which, as Götz Aly points out, became the repository for much of Germany's ill-gotten gains, of which Jewish property formed probably only a small part within a very large "extraordinary budget" that helped Germany finance the enormous costs of the war.[165]

[161] NARA, RG-242, T-120 (Auswärtiges Amt), reel 1205, fr. 478668-70, Luther Fernschreiben, Berlin, May 19, 1942.

[162] *Les biens des victimes*, pp. 130–31.

[163] Wolfgang Dreßen (ed.), *Betrifft: "Aktion 3." Deutsche verwerten jüdische Nachbarn. Dokumente zur Arisierung* (Berlin: Aufbau Verlag, 1998), p. 48.

[164] *Les biens des victimes*, pp. 126–27.

[165] BAL, R 2/32063, RFM memo, October 29, 1942; G. Aly, *Hitlers Volksstaat*, pp. 174–75.

Assessment of Confiscation in Belgium and the Basis for Restitution

As Jean-Marc Dreyfus concludes, the Belgian case falls somewhere in the middle between the very comprehensive securing of Jewish assets in the Netherlands and the far less complete and more bureaucratic pursuit of Aryanization and confiscation in occupied and Vichy France.[166] The confiscation in Belgium would not have been possible without the passive collaboration of the Belgian authorities, but the denial of that cooperation in certain cases, such as the refusal to notarize real estate contracts, limited considerably the profits gained by the Reich. Most important, the application of Belgian law to the BTG's accounts and most other blocked Jewish accounts meant that a large proportion of the proceeds from the liquidation and freezing of assets remained within Belgium in identifiable accounts at the end of the occupation, their planned centralization at the SFBD having been only partially implemented. This at least facilitated the restoration of some financial assets to survivors and heirs. However, considerable sums remained unclaimed at the banks, and other "heirless" property fell to the Belgian state rather than Jewish successor organizations. The fact that most Jews did not hold citizenship excluded them from receiving other forms of war-related compensation from the Belgian government.[167] On a personal level, the relations of Jews with their non-Jewish neighbors also reflect a mixed picture: although a few locals helped Jews go underground,[168] in some cases Jews returning after the war to reclaim property left with neighbors for safekeeping met with hostile denials.[169]

Occupied and Vichy France

In France, the complex relationship between the German and Vichy authorities resulted in a plethora of legislation concerning Jewish property, with significant differences in timing and implementation between the Occupied (Northern) and Unoccupied (Southern) Zones. For the purpose of comparison with other Western European countries, the focus in this section is primarily on the zone of German military occupation in northern France. In general, the measures applied here resembled those in Belgium and the Netherlands, but the degree of participation by the French administration

---

[166] J.-M. Dreyfus, "Die Enteignung der Juden in Westeuropa," p. 53.
[167] R. van Doorslaer, "Raub und Rückerstattung," pp. 141–51.
[168] R. Hilberg, *Die Vernichtung*, vol. II, pp. 639–40.
[169] V. Teitelbaum-Hirsch, *Comptes d'une mort annoncée*, p. 59.

in Aryanization and confiscation measures was greater. The French administration deliberately sought to limit the extent to which the Germans could gain control over key elements of the French economy; in so doing, however, it became an active participant in the implementation of much of the Nazi anti-Jewish program.

At the time of the invasion in May 1940, more than 70,000 Jews fled Paris and other towns in northern France to what was to become the Unoccupied Zone. In October 1940, the Germans deported more than 22,000 Jews from Alsace and Lorraine across the demarcation line into the Unoccupied Zone. As elsewhere, these initial displacements opened the door to the seizure of property left behind and the establishment of institutions to carry it out.[170]

Vichy Law for the Revocation of Citizenship

The first measure directed at the confiscation of Jewish assets in France was a purely French initiative, albeit based on mechanisms developed earlier in Nazi Germany. On July 22, 1940, the new Vichy authorities introduced a law for the revocation of citizenship from French citizens living abroad. As in Germany, concrete cases of revocation of citizenship were accompanied by the confiscation of domestic assets. The law was aimed primarily at political opponents and at Jews who had fled the country – in particular, a number of wealthy Jewish families, such as the Rothschilds, who had fled as the Germans advanced in May and June of 1940, leaving much of their property behind.[171]

Art, Archives, and Libraries

The looting of artwork and cultural property in France began with the German occupation. On June 30, 1940, after Hitler traveled to Paris, he entrusted the German ambassador, Otto Abetz, with securing artworks in public ownership and also listing and seizing cultural treasures owned by Jews.[172] This measure was "justified" in part by some Jews' practice of turning their collections over to museums for safekeeping before fleeing. Together with the *Geheime Feldpolizei* (Secret Field Police), in June and

---

[170] R. Hilberg, *Die Vernichtung*, vol. II, pp. 647–48.

[171] W. Seibel (ed.), *Holocaust und 'Polykratie' in Westeuropa, 1940–1944: Nationale Berichte*, p. xl; Michael Curtis, *Verdict on Vichy: Power and Prejudice in the Vichy France Regime* (New York: Arcade, 2002), pp. 105–106.

[172] Lynn Nicholas, *The Rape of Europa: The Fate of Europe's Treasures in the Third Reich and the Second World War* (London: Macmillan, 1994), pp. 119–20. Hitler was in Paris on June 28, 1940: see Hector Feliciano, *The Lost Museum: The Nazi Conspiracy to Steal the World's Greatest Works of Art* (New York: Basic Books, 1997), p. 16.

July 1940, Abetz's subordinates secured the collections of numerous Jews, especially those who had fled, including the stocks of a number of Jewish art dealers.[173]

By September 1940, however, authority for most art looting in the West had been transferred to the ERR. It appears that with Göring's support Rosenberg had been able to trump Ribbentrop's initial efforts to monopolize art plunder through Abetz. The looting agencies moved swiftly; it is estimated that three-quarters of the plunder secured by the ERR had been collected by mid-1941. A special depot was set up in the historic Jeu de Paume building in central Paris, from which the best works were selected for the collections of Hitler and Göring. After these two potentates, the Hohe Schule and German museums were also given privileged access; remaining works were passed on to local French art dealers for auction, with the proceeds going to the widows and children of deceased French soldiers.[174]

The case of art in France exemplifies Jonathan Petropoulos's arguments that rivalry between German agencies generally spurred them on to more rapacious looting practices, whereas the creation of broad networks (including, for example, a number of dealers in France) facilitated the broad scope and large scale of the operation.[175]

The Aryanization of Jewish Businesses and the Commissariat Général aux Questions Juifs (CGQJ)

At the start of the occupation on May 20, 1940, the German military administration assumed the power to appoint "provisional trustees" to head any business that had been deprived of its owners or directors. This power enabled them to take control over enterprises belonging to Jews and other persons who had fled before the German advance. After the Vichy government was established during the summer of 1940 – asserting its sovereignty also over the occupied territories – the new Minister of Industrial Production, Jean Bichelonne, wanted to limit German control over French enterprises. A new Vichy law on September 10, 1940, gave the French

[173] Anja Heuss, *Kunst- und Kulturgutraub: Eine vergleichende Studie zur Besatzungspolitik der Nationalsozialisten in Frankreich und der Sowjetunion* (Heidelberg: Winter, 2000), p. 298. Many of the items secured were subsequently handed over to the ERR.

[174] Jonathan Petropoulos, *Art as Politics in the Third Reich* (Chapel Hill: University of North Carolina Press, 1996), pp. 127–39.

[175] Jonathan Petropoulos, "The Polycratic Nature of Art Looting: The Dynamic Balance of the Third Reich," in Wolfgang Seibel and Gerald Feldman (eds.), *Networks of Nazi Persecution: Division-of-Labor in the Holocaust* (New York: Berghahn, 2005), pp. 103–17, here pp. 112–14.

administration the right to appoint provisional administrators.[176] In October, the German military authorities issued a decree requiring the registration of "Jewish" companies (those with at least one-third Jewish ownership or with a Jewish administrator) and authorizing the appointment of provisional administrators, but conceding to the French government the right to nominate the administrators. This was the first step toward a comprehensive Aryanization program modeled on experiences gained in the Reich. It came just prior to similar decrees in the Netherlands and Belgium.[177] In December, Bichelonne also created a new layer of administration, the *Service du Contrôle des Adminstrateurs Provisoires* (Service for the Control of Provisional Administrators, SCAP), to oversee their work. In northern France many Jews were able to discern the pattern of events and sold their businesses in the autumn of 1940, taking what assets they could with them into the Unoccupied Zone.[178]

The creation of the General Commissariat for Jewish Questions (CGQJ) by the Vichy government in March 1941, partly as a result of German pressure, created another rival authority that by July 1941 had been given control over SCAP and the activities of the provisional administrators. Throughout its existence, the CGQJ was primarily concerned with Aryanization; of the 1,044 CGQJ agents throughout France in 1944, more than two-thirds were concerned with Aryanization and other economic measures.[179] As a new institution, the CGQJ encountered frequent jurisdictional conflicts with other arms of the French bureaucracy, and its place in the bureaucracy was changed twice: from the office of the prime minister to the Ministry of Interior in the summer of 1941 and then back again in May 1942. Under the direction of Xavier Vallat, there could be little doubt about its determination to enforce rigorously antisemitic legislation, even in the Unoccupied Zone, but it always lacked adequately qualified staff, and Vallat himself possessed only weak administrative skills.[180] Among the tasks of the CGQJ was also the drafting of new anti-Jewish legislation. According to the preliminary

[176] Marc-Olivier Baruch, "Perpetrator Networks and the Holocaust: The Spoliation of Jewish Property in France, 1940–44," in W. Seibel and G. Feldman (eds.), *Networks of Nazi Persecution*, pp. 189–212, here pp. 193–94.

[177] J.-M. Dreyfus, "Franco-German Rivalry and 'Aryanization' as the Creation of a New Policy in France, 1940–44," in *Confiscation of Jewish Property in Europe, 1933–1945: New Sources and Perspectives*, Symposium Proceedings (Washington, DC: United States Holocaust Memorial Museum, 2003), pp. 75–92, here pp. 76–77.

[178] Republique Française, *Summary of the Work by the Study Mission on the spoliation of the Jews in France* (Paris, 2000), p. 21.

[179] Michael R. Marrus and Robert O. Paxton, *Vichy France and the Jews* (New York: Basic Books, 1981), pp. 129–30 and 294.

[180] Ibid., pp. 128–30 and 153.

plans of the German SD, the CGQJ was "to administer the concentration of the Jews and their property prior to deportation."[181]

The Germans had prompted these French initiatives, thereby involving the French administration and population in the exclusion of Jews from the economy while also sparing German personnel. However, the *Militärbefehlshaber in Frankreich* (German Military Commander in France, MBF) recognized that the French authorities might lack the necessary energy and conviction to implement them. As one German report concluded, "The task of the German military administration will be to watch over carefully and control the activity of the French authorities."[182]

French officials, however, had their own concerns about the dangers of corruption during Aryanization. Therefore, the Ministry of Economy and Finance was authorized to appoint its own auditors, charged with overseeing the accounts kept by provisional administrators.[183] On February 2, 1941, a new French decree confirmed the right of provisional administrators to liquidate Jewish businesses, signaling French acceptance of Aryanization, if not without compensation. (At this time, proceeds from Aryanization were still paid to Jewish owners without restrictions.) On April 26, 1941, however, a new German decree denied Jews free disposal of these proceeds, signifying in effect confiscation, as in Germany after the decree of December 3, 1938.[184]

The French law – Regarding Businesses, Property and Assets Belonging to Jews, issued on July 22, 1941 – required that all Jewish property be registered and placed under the control of the CGQJ. Money from assets sold was to be paid into blocked accounts at the state-owned bank, *la Caisse des Dépôts et Consignations* (CDC), and could be disposed of only with the permission of the CGQJ. Provisional administrators were now to be appointed for all Jewish businesses and other property, except for state bonds or real estate that constituted a principal residence.[185]

German legislation in April 1941 followed by similar Vichy decrees excluded Jews from a long list of professions in commerce and the public sector, including banking, shipping, insurance, real estate, armament

---

[181] J. Billig, *Le Commissariat Général aux Questions Juives*, vol. I, p. 46.

[182] Der Militärbefehlshaber in Frankreich, Verwaltungsstab, Wirtschaftsabteilung, Az.: Wi I 426/40, November 1, 1940, CDJC, CL-1, quoted in W. Seibel (ed.), *Holocaust und 'Polykratie' in Westeuropa, 1940–1944: Nationale Berichte*, p. lxi.

[183] W. Seibel (ed.), *Holocaust und 'Polykratie' in Westeuropa, 1940–1944: Nationale Berichte*, p. xxxiii.

[184] Wolfgang Seibel, "A Market for Mass Crime? Inter-institutional Competition and the Initiation of the Holocaust in France, 1940–42," *International Journal of Organization Theory and Behavior*, vol. 5, nos. 3 and 4 (2002): 219–257, here p. 227.

[185] M. O. Baruch, "Perpetrator Networks," p. 196.

sales, antiques, wholesale trading in grains and livestock, periodical publishing, and other media-related employment. War veterans could be granted exemptions, although comparatively few Jews benefited from this measure.[186]

In the implementation of Aryanization, the French authorities and also newly formed local economic organizations (Organizing Committees) displayed concern about the impact on the local economy, thereby permitting specific exemptions or even the release of key workers from arrest.[187] In general, the roughly 8,000 provisional administrators, almost all of whom were French citizens, were held in low esteem, and despite attempts to maintain bureaucratic oversight, certain abuses were commonplace. The director of the SCAP, Even Bralley, drew attention to provisional administrators who were timorous, clumsy, negligent, or "unscrupulous," the last type often acting in collusion either with Jews or with buyers. Some profited considerably from their activities, managing as many as fifteen or twenty properties, and several ended up in jail. Prices paid were usually well below market value; those for real estate, for example, were lower by about 30 percent. However, this discount reflected also the slowness and uncertainties involved in such sales, as well as the decline in enthusiasm for Jewish property by early 1943, especially as resale in less than three years was forbidden. Under Vallat's successor as head of the CGQJ, Darquier de Pellepoix, nepotism and cronyism became even more marked among the provisional administrators.[188] The staff of the CGQJ itself suffered from low morale, as it was looked down upon by the rest of the administration as only a temporary branch.[189]

One of the avowed aims of French Aryanization policy was to "restructure" the economy by eliminating small inefficient companies in "overcrowded" industries. This rationalization appealed to French companies seeking to benefit from the elimination of Jewish competitors. In practice, this "rationalization" did not go far, in part because of rival competencies within the bureaucracy and the poor organizational ability of the CGQJ.[190] The implementation of Aryanization also varied considerably from one

[186] Donna F. Ryan, *The Holocaust and the Jews of Marseille: The Enforcement of Anti-Semitic Policies in Vichy France* (Urbana: University of Illinois Press, 1996), pp. 65–67.

[187] M. R. Marrus and R. O. Paxton, *Vichy France and the Jews*, pp. 134–35, 160.

[188] Ibid., pp. 157 and 295; D. F. Ryan, *The Holocaust and the Jews of Marseille*, pp. 71–74; J.-M. Dreyfus, "Die Enteignung der Juden in Westeuropa," p. 48.

[189] Alexandre Doulut, "La spoliation des biens juifs dans le Lot-et-Garonne," in *Revue d'histoire de la Shoah*, no. 186, *Spoliations en Europe* (Janvier-Juin 2007): 291–328, here pp. 292–93.

[190] M. R. Marrus and R. O. Paxton, *Vichy France and the Jews*, p. 158; J. -M. Dreyfus, "Die Enteignung der Juden in Westeuropa," p. 53.

region to another, depending on the attitude of the local administration, even if its validity was largely accepted by the bureaucracy and the courts.[191] In French North Africa, beyond the immediate reach of German military power before 1943, the Vichy authorities applied their own Aryanization measures quite stringently in Algeria and also evicted the Jews from specific professions in Tunisia. The economic measures taken against Morocco's Jews were much less systematic.[192]

Blocking of Bank Accounts

Following the April introduction of blocked Jewish bank accounts for receiving the proceeds of Aryanization, a further German decree blocked private Jewish accounts on May 28, 1941, again only in the German Occupied Zone. The response of the French banks is interesting. As rumors of the decree's contents spread in advance of its publication, the German authorities instructed French banks to block the accounts a few days in advance to prevent Jews from pre-empting the measure by withdrawing large sums and transferring them to the Unoccupied Zone. The French banks complied, but actual implementation remained problematic, as Jews had not yet been issued special identity cards and the banks had difficulties in identifying their Jewish customers.[193]

As elsewhere, Jews were subjected to a monthly allowance set by the authorities, which could lead to considerable hardship. Suzanne W. applied to the CGQJ in October 1941 requesting an increase in her monthly allowance from 1,000 to 2,000 French francs, citing her serious health condition (diabetes), which required constant attention and prevented her from working. In her case, the request was granted, on the condition of documentary proof of real expenses, but the invasion of privacy and inconvenience were considerable.[194]

On July 22, 1941, the Vichy authorities "codified" much of the German legislation as a central measure for all of France. Nevertheless the blocking of private accounts was not implemented in the Unoccupied Zone, even

[191] D. F. Ryan, *The Holocaust and the Jews of Marseille*, pp. 77–78.

[192] Michael Abitbol, *The Jews of North Africa during the Second World War* (Detroit: Wayne State University Press, 1989), pp. 71–74; see also R. Hilberg, *Die Vernichtung*, vol. II, pp. 659–60.

[193] Jean-Marc Dreyfus, "French Banks and Aryanization 1940–1944," in Oliver Rathkolb (ed.), *Revisiting the National Socialist Legacy: Coming to Terms with Forced Labor, Expropriation, Compensation, and Restitution* (Innsbruck: Studien Verlag, 2002), pp. 145–53, here, pp. 148–49.

[194] Claire Andrieu, et al. (eds.), *Mission d'étude sur la spoliation des Juifs de france, vol. 1 La spoliation financière* (Paris, Documentation française 2000), pp. 38–39.

after German troops entered it in November 1942.[195] Historians have not fully explained this major difference in policy between the two zones, but it clearly demonstrates the ability of the Vichy authorities to limit the effects of measures initiated by the German occupants when they chose to do so. However, the proceeds from the Aryanization of Jewish businesses, real estate, securities, and other property sold or liquidated in all of France were paid into blocked accounts at the CDC. From these sums, 10 percent was deducted, although most of this was made available for the relief of needy Jews by the central Jewish communal organization, the *Union générale des Israélites de France* (General Union of French Jews, UGIF).[196]

Nevertheless, the retention of individual accounts and extensive record keeping by the French authorities facilitated the restitution of financial assets after the Occupation, assisted also by the continued presence of the majority of French Jews. According to the Final Report of the Study Mission on the Spoliation of the Jews in France (Matteoli Commission), in the Occupied Zone, where anti-Jewish measures were more comprehensive, probably more than 70 percent of blocked assets (in value) were reactivated. Thus, despite the French exploitation of blocked accounts for actual confiscation measures, careful accounting enabled a considerable portion of assets to be returned to those still around and able to make claims. The rate of restitution for the property of those who were deported, in many cases leaving no clear heirs, was, however, less satisfactory. There never was any systematic attempt made to verify that assets had actually been returned to their owners or legitimate heirs.[197]

The "Punitive Tax" Imposed on French Jews (l'amende)

Ostensibly in response to the attacks on German military personnel in the fall of 1941, and especially as a result of pressure from the RSHA to take more drastic action, the MBF decreed on December 17 a "contribution" of 1 billion French francs (equivalent to RM 50 million) to be paid by the Jews of the Occupied Zone to the Reich Credit Bank (RKK) in four installments up to March 31, 1942.[198] The punitive tax imposed on Germany's Jews after Kristallnacht provided the model for this measure.[199]

---

[195] Ibid., p. 51; J.-M. Dreyfus, "French Banks", p. 149.

[196] W. Seibel (ed.), *Holocaust und 'Polykratie' in Westeuropa, 1940–1944: Nationale Berichte*, p. lxiii; J.-M. Dreyfus, "French Banks," p. 151.

[197] Republique Francaise, *Summary of the Work by the Study Mission*, pp. 24–25.

[198] W. Seibel (ed.), *Holocaust und 'Polykratie' in Westeuropa, 1940–1944: Nationale Berichte*, p. lxiv.

[199] See C. Andrieu et al. (eds.), *Mission d'étude sur la spoliation des Juifs de France, vol. 1 La spoliation financière*, 3–6, L'amende imposée en zone occupée en decembre 1941.

To raise the money, the French Economics and Finance Ministry and the Professional Association of Banks arranged a loan to the UGIF,[200] mainly to prevent the Germans from intervening directly in the banking sector. The idea was in part to use the funds already deposited at the CDC to pay the fine, though these were insufficient to cover the full amount. A new law issued on January 16, 1942, officially authorized the loan. In March 1942, the UGIF was authorized to draw on the funds deposited in blocked accounts at the CDC to pay off the loan. An important result of the forced contribution was to normalize state confiscation of Jewish property in France, resting as it did on close cooperation between the government and the banks, just as German plans for the deportation of French Jews were being prepared.[201]

The consequence of the various persecution measures was considerable economic hardship among Jews throughout France. The UGIF provided aid to an increasing number of Jews until the deportations started in 1942, but it lacked sufficient funds. By 1943, the authorities permitted Jews to make contributions to the UGIF from blocked accounts, and an individual tax of 120 French francs in the Occupied Zone (360 French francs in the Unoccupied Zone) was imposed; it was to be paid, however, in the Occupied Zone from permitted subsistence allowances, rather than frozen deposit balances.[202]

Valuables Confiscated from Deportees at the Drancy Camp

In total, the German authorities deported 76,000 Jews from France. The costs of the deportations, or at least those for the segment that went through French territory, were charged to the Military Commander in France to be paid in French francs out of occupation costs.[203] Beginning in 1942, the internment camp at Drancy, near Paris, became the main transit point for French Jews being deported to Auschwitz. Up to August 17, 1944, 80,000 people passed though Drancy, of whom 67,000 were deported to the death camps. Until June 1943, the French authorities administered the camp. Those internees who arrived before July 1942 and who surrendered their money had accounts opened at the City of Paris Municipal Savings Bank

[200] The UGIF was established by Vichy on November 29, 1941, as a result of pressure by the MBF as a compulsory union of all Jews. It was also subordinated to the CGQJ; see W. Seibel (ed.), *Holocaust und 'Polykratie' in Westeuropa, 1940–1944: Nationale Berichte*, p. lx.

[201] W. Seibel (ed.), *Holocaust und 'Polykratie' in Westeuropa, 1940–1944: Nationale Berichte*, pp. lxiv–lxv; W. Seibel, "A Market for Mass Crime?" pp. 230–31.

[202] Michael Curtis, *Verdict on Vichy*, p. 144; D. F. Ryan, *The Holocaust and the Jews of Marseille*, pp. 76–77.

[203] R. Hilberg, *Die Vernichtung*, vol. II, p. 683.

and, after February 1942, at the CDC. Just over 1 million French francs were deposited on behalf of Drancy internees into 7,410 separate accounts in the CDC's books, of which 10 percent was paid as a levy to the CGQJ.

Beginning in June 1943, Alois Brunner, one of Eichmann's chief deportation specialists, took charge of the camp, and presumably thereafter the German authorities confiscated most of the property from the inmates directly "for the benefit of the Reich." The deportees were subjected to repeated searches and plunder carried out by French Gendarmes, German camp staff, and the Jewish Affairs Police. Thefts and black market dealing were also rampant within the camp. Similar confiscations, searches, and thefts took place in the camps at Pithiviers and Beaune-la-Rolande.[204]

Furniture Action

As in the Netherlands and Belgium, a "Furniture Action" was implemented in northern France, beginning with the apartments and property of those who fled and followed from the summer of 1942 on by those of the deportees. In northern France, the ERR secured and successively looted nearly 38,000 Jewish apartments.[205] The research of Jean-Marc Dreyfus and Sarah Gensburger describes three special camps in Paris – named Austerlitz, Lévitan, and Bassano. More than 700 Jews were kept in these camps as "slave laborers" to assist the ERR in processing much of the furniture from its looting activities. Many Paris moving companies were ordered by the German authorities to empty the apartments promptly. Oberstführer Kurt von Behr and the officials of the Dienststelle Westen (the main office of the ERR in the West) who ran these camps skimmed off some of the best items for themselves and even ran a small *haute couture* shop, mainly to pamper the wives and mistresses of German officers.[206]

The recollections of the inmates, many of whom were spared from deportation as they were half-Jews or were married to non-Jews, shed some light on the character of the deportations. One lady, Yvonne Klug, who

---

[204] Republique Francaise, *Summary of the Work by the Study Mission*, pp. 31–32; see also Annette Wieviorka, *Les Biens des Internés des Camps de Drancy, Pithiviers et Beaune-la-Rolande* (Paris: La Documentation française, 2000).

[205] Nicolas Reymes, "Le pillage des bibliothèques apartenant à des juifs pendant l'occupation," *Revue d'Histoire de la Shoah*, no. 168 (Jan. – Avril 2000): 31–56, here p. 40.

[206] For further details, see Jean-Marc Dreyfus and Sarah Gensburger, *Des camps dans Paris: Austerlitz, Lévitan, Bassano, juillet 1943 – août 1944* (Paris: Fayard, 2003); at least 795 persons are known to have passed through these camps, of whom 166 were subsequently deported, see p. 269.

among other tasks had the job of cleaning household goods, remembered that "often we had the impression that people had been arrested in the midst of a meal, for the saucepans were sticky and dirty and so were the plates."[207]

Confiscation in Western Europe in Comparative Perspective

The above case studies largely confirm the analysis of Jean-Marc Dreyfus that Aryanization in France was a comparatively bureaucratized procedure characterized by a proliferation of oversight bodies and the fragmentation of state authority, accounting in part for its slower pace and less comprehensive implementation than in the Netherlands.[208] Only 58 percent of Aryanization cases were ever concluded in the Occupied Zone.[209] Despite the aims of the Vichy government to exploit Aryanization to "rationalize" the economy, the percentage of Jewish businesses liquidated was also markedly lower (56 percent), than either in the Netherlands (90.5 percent) or Belgium (83 percent).[210] In France, it is notable also that the banks, which were usually suspicious of government interference in the private sector, let alone confiscation, went along quite willingly with most of the anti-Jewish measures. Notaries, however, were more wary, some warning their clients of the possible future legal difficulties entailed in purchasing former Jewish property, as by April 1941 the Gaullists had already announced on BBC radio that such sales would be annulled.[211]

The German authorities in the West were careful to avoid the appearance of a direct confiscation of Jewish property for their own benefit, paying lip service to the Hague Laws of War (1907), which forbade the seizure of private property other than to pay for legitimate "occupation costs."[212] As Joseph Billig notes, respect for international law was a prerequisite for

---

[207] Ibid., pp. 137, 156–60; Sarah Wildman, "Paris' Dirty Secret," *Jerusalem Report*, January 11, 2004.

[208] J.-M. Dreyfus, "Franco-German Rivalry," p. 86; on the slow pace of French Aryanization, see R. Hilberg, *Die Vernichtung*, vol. II, pp. 653–54.

[209] Republique Francaise, *Summary of the Work by the Study Mission*, p. 22.

[210] J.-M. Dreyfus, "Die Enteignung der Juden in Westeuropa," p. 53.

[211] M. O. Baruch, "Perpetrator Networks," pp. 201–202.

[212] The Hague Laws of War permitted the exaction of only limited requisitions and contributions by an occupying power, and these sums were to be proportionate to its own "occupation costs"; see Unabhängige Expertenkommission Schweiz – Zweiter Weltkrieg (ed.), *Die Schweiz, der Nationalsozialismus und das Recht, Band I, Öffentliches Recht* (Zürich: Chronos, 2001), p. 549.

collaboration with the French authorities.[213] Indeed, the "legal nature" of the confiscation process was quite marked in Western Europe; first, the process exploited means similar to those applied legitimately to "enemy property" by the Allies to concentrate and secure much Jewish property before moving stealthily toward confiscation in the wake of the deportations.

A comparison of the amount of Jewish property confiscated in the different countries, even given the extensive records of confiscation (and restitution) available, remains almost impossible. The overall total for the Netherlands appears to be in the region of 1 billion to 1.2 billion fl. (RM 750–900 million), although this remains a rough estimate. In the view of Rudi van Doorslaer, the wartime German figure of RM 225 million for Belgium is completely unreliable, as it includes assets that the Germans could not freely dispose of, although this sum appears to be well below the value of declared assets in the property census.[214] More reliable estimates are available for some types of property, such as bank accounts and real estate. In France, the Study Mission concluded that, in wartime values, more than seven billion francs in stocks and cash deposits were frozen and businesses and real estate worth some three billion francs were sold (making for all these types of assets a combined total of more than RM 500 million).[215] But even these "hard" figures are distorted by artificial price freezes, fixed exchange rates, and variable rates of wartime inflation. Therefore, the attempt to convert such rough estimates into modern-day values has been eschewed as an unprofitable exercise. It is perhaps more useful to assess and compare the extent of the confiscation conducted in each country, and especially who benefited and where the property ended up.

In terms of categories of assets, the attempt was made to secure almost all forms of Jewish property in the Netherlands, whereas in other countries specific types of assets were excluded or slipped through the net. In Belgium and France, for example, no comprehensive attempt was made to confiscate Jewish life insurance policies, whereas in the Netherlands a special law was passed in 1943 to overcome the practical and legal difficulties raised by the insurance companies.[216] The sale and conversion of Dutch Jewish shares into government bonds, ordered at the end of 1941 and implemented on a large scale in early 1942 (that is, before the deportations), were also not matched in other countries. In the Netherlands, 80 percent of shares were

---

[213] J. Billig, Le Commissariat, vol. I, p. 25; see also Richard H. Weisberg, Vichy Law and the Holocaust in France (New York: New York University Press, 1996), p. 255.

[214] R. van Doorslaer, "Raub und Rückerstattung," p. 140.

[215] Republique Francaise, Summary of the Work by the Study Mission, p. 10.

[216] J.-M. Dreyfus, "Die Enteignung der Juden in Westeuropa," p. 51; see also G. Aalders, Nazi Looting, pp. 180–83.

sold, whereas in France the rate was only 32 percent and in Belgium much less even than that.[217]

As with explanations for the widely differing deportation rates in the different countries, it would be a mistake to place too much emphasis on one contributory element alone. It seems that several variables played a role, including chronology, administrative structure, levels of collaboration, and even characteristics of the Jewish population. Although in no way exonerating the German military administration in Belgium and northern France, which administered both confiscation and deportation policies against the Jews, it does appear that the German military administration had a somewhat more tactical relationship to the Jewish Question as opposed to the ideological view predominant among the SS and police authorities.[218] The more comprehensive policy of confiscation pursued openly by the German civil authorities in Luxembourg even prior to the deportations appears to confirm this view, although in Norway the legal basis for confiscation was more of an afterthought decreed once the deportations were already under way. The role of the Vichy government, however, is more complex, as its concerns about sovereignty and control of both the process and the proceeds resulted in the widespread adoption of most of the German-inspired Aryanization and confiscation system, although bureaucratic mis-administration by French officials ameliorated some of the practical effects.[219]

In Luxembourg and the Netherlands, the main beneficiaries from Jewish property were the German administration authorities, along with German companies and individuals; German officials and the inhabitants of bombed German cities received most of the items from the Furniture Action as the ERR cleared the apartments of emigrant and then deported Jews. Local collaborators also benefited in all countries as profiteers, administrators, and investors, if to varying degrees. In Norway the Norwegian Nazi Party took a large portion of the spoils. Examples from Belgium and the Netherlands reveal that local officials and businessmen could have an impact by their attitude, although the Germans took measures to overcome passive resistance employing "legal" means. It should be stressed that in Western Europe there was considerably less reluctance by the local population to buy former Jewish businesses and other property at the start of the occupation, in the

---

[217] J.-M. Dreyfus, "Die Enteignung der Juden in Westeuropa," p. 53.

[218] W. Seibel (ed.), *Holocaust und 'Polykratie' in Westeuropa, 1940–1944: Nationale Berichte*, p. xxi.

[219] See, for example, Jacques Adler, *The Jews of Paris and the Final Solution: Communal Response and Internal Conflicts, 1940–44* (Oxford: Oxford University Press, 1985), p. 83.

immediate wake of German triumphs, than later when Germany's prospects of victory seemed less rosy. Local individuals and businesses profited also from the administration, transport, evaluation, and sale of Jewish property, although these perks probably did little to bind the local population to the Germans, as the bulk of the proceeds were generally paid into blocked accounts administered by the state.

From the perspective of the victims, Aryanization and confiscation came in a series of escalating stages intended to deceive, but some Jews took early counter-measures to try to save their property and themselves. These included attempts to smuggle valuables out of the country, the signing of creative investment and insurance contracts, the use of "straw men" to conceal ownership of enterprises, and the payment of bribes or submission to German blackmail, the latter not always honored. Nevertheless, the majority of Jews complied due to the gradual and "legal" nature of the measures, which also threatened stiff penalties for disobedience. Even the few wealthy Jews soon began to suffer economic hardship and humiliations through the blocking of accounts and the seizure of assets prior to the deportations. In Western Europe, many Jews managed to flee in time, and large numbers survived in hiding or avoided deportation from France, but all were victims of the extensive spoliation campaign. Only in Denmark, whose modus vivendi with Germany granted considerable autonomy, were the Jews spared from state measures directed against their property.

8

SOVEREIGN IMITATIONS: CONFISCATIONS CONDUCTED BY STATES ALLIED TO NAZI GERMANY

Figure 8.1. Romanian Jews are forced to surrender their household belongings in place of taxes. *Source:* Federation of the Romanian Jewish Communities, Neg # 04214. USHMM, WS # 20493.

Economic Antisemitism: Local Initiatives and German Models

A strong brand of economic antisemitism existed throughout Eastern Europe in the 1930s; it was influenced not only by German models and propaganda, for it also had deep indigenous roots. In Romania, for example, right-wing nationalist organizations could draw on a history of antisemitic pronouncements by prominent Romanian politicians and cultural figures reaching back into the nineteenth century.[1] In Hungary, the so-called *Numerus Clausus* Act of 1920 limited the number of Jewish students studying at the universities. This measure represented the acceptance of antisemitism by the political class, even if it remained in effect only for a short period of time. The mood was reflected in the aggressive antisemitic rhetoric that was part of Hungary's political discourse throughout the 1930s.[2] Nationalist politicians in Slovakia, as did those in Hungary and Romania, and radical Ukrainian nationalists viewed strong Jewish representation in certain trades and professions as an "obstacle" to the achievement of homogeneous "ethnic national" states. In Poland, the 1930s saw economic boycotts against Jewish businesses and the introduction of state regulations intended to affect Jewish traders adversely. Extreme right-wing parties in Poland also demanded the expulsion of the Jews, perhaps to Madagascar, with the expropriation of Jewish property to reduce the cost to the Polish nation.[3] Common to all Eastern European states that sought to encourage Jewish emigration in the 1930s was the notion that Jews should be permitted to take only a fraction of their assets with them.

It is of considerable significance that states such as Bulgaria and Romania, which were closely aligned to the Axis powers but ultimately did not comply with German demands to hand over the Jews from their core territories,

---

[1] *Final Report of the International Commission on the Holocaust in Romania*, eds. Tuvia Friling, Radu Ioanid, and Mihail E. Ionescu (Iasi: Polirom, 2005), pp. 19–29; see also Paul Shapiro, "Romanian Jews, Romanian Antisemitism, Romanian Holocaust," Conference on "Minorities, Cultural Heritage, Contemporary Romanian Civilization," co-sponsored by the Romanian Ministry of Foreign Affairs, B'nai B'rith International, and the Federation of Jewish Communities in Romania, Bucharest, October 21–22, 2003.

[2] Ivan T. Berend, "The Road toward the Holocaust: The Ideological and Political Background," in Randolph L. Braham and Bela Vago (eds.), *The Holocaust in Hungary: Forty Years Later* (New York: Social Science Monographs, Columbia University Press, 1985), p. 34; Zsuzsanna Ozsváth, "Can Words Kill? Anti-Semitic Texts and their Impact on the Hungarian Jewish Catastrophe," in Randolph L. Braham and Attila Pók (eds.), *The Holocaust in Hungary: Fifty Years Later* (Boulder, CO: Rosenthal Institute for Holocaust Studies, Social Science Monographs, 1997), pp. 97–98.

[3] Carla Tonini, *Operazione Madagascar: La questione ebraica in Polonia, 1918–1968* (Bologna: CLUEB, 1999), pp. 66–68, 77–80.

nonetheless implemented extensive anti-Jewish confiscation measures prior to the onset of the Holocaust. The Law for the Defense of the Nation ratified in Bulgaria in January 1941 included numerous provisions aimed at removing Jewish influence from the economy and depriving the Jews of property rights, but its full implementation was delayed pending more detailed legislation.[4] Bulgaria's measures were modeled partly on bureaucratic structures developed in Vichy France, as well as on methods perfected by Nazi Germany. In Hungary, limited confiscatory legislation enacted before April 1944 was rapidly overtaken by comprehensive spoliation under German occupation, implemented largely by the Hungarian administration. In Slovakia, the exclusion of the Jews from agricultural trades and small businesses was conducted very rapidly in 1941, even if some factories were initially exempted for fear of German penetration of the industrial sector.

The actual methods of Aryanization and expropriation in these states closely reflected those developed in Germany and Austria and applied comprehensively in the occupied territories. Common to almost all states allied to Nazi Germany were the registration of Jewish property; the application of special taxes and levies; the blocking of bank accounts to prevent capital flight and to secure the proceeds of Aryanization; and the seizure, administration, liquidation, or sale of businesses, real estate, securities, precious metals, valuables, furniture, and other personal possessions. There was also a large degree of personal enrichment, corruption, and theft in the handling of Jewish property in these countries. Yet, as with the German/Austrian experience, a dynamic tension existed between the popular "rush to enrichment" and government attempts to confine the process within a strict legal framework that would ensure that the bulk of the proceeds benefited hard-pressed state finances. The question of how far German advisors were able to steer the process is central to assessing the degree of sovereignty that these countries retained. Here the detailed analysis of Tatjana Tönsmeyer of the general role of German advisors in Slovakia is instructive: Tönsmeyer argues that Slovak politicians were very interested in the transfer of know-how, but proved surprisingly resistant to direct German interference in internal Slovak affairs.[5]

---

[4] An abbreviated version of the Law for the Protection of the Nation decreed by King Boris III on January 23, 1941, can be found in David Cohen, "King Boris III and the 'Final Solution' of the Jewish Problem in Bulgaria," *Annual of the Central Board of the Social, Cultural and Educational Association of the Jews in the People's Republic of Bulgaria,* Vol. XX (Sofia, 1985): 270–75.

[5] Tatjana Tönsmeyer, *Das Dritte Reich und die Slowakei, 1939–1945: Politischer Alltag zwischen Kooperation und Eigensinn* (Paderborn: Ferdinand Schöningh, 2003), pp. 320–34.

The development of Aryanization and confiscation policies in Fascist Italy is also outlined briefly in this chapter. In Italy there was an inherent tension between the importation of German models and more "pragmatic" Italian approaches. Although Benito Mussolini took a largely opportunistic line toward the ideology underlying the fascist racial laws, their application had real consequences for Italy's Jews, despite a number of exemptions and loopholes that remained. In Italy, complete confiscation was decreed only under German occupation of the North and after the deportations had started in the fall of 1943.

Nazi Germany was only able to implement its destruction and confiscation policies throughout Europe with the aid of considerable local cooperation. The comparative perspective offered in this chapter helps highlight the degree of choice involved in local complicity by several of Hitler's allies that all closely guarded their own sovereignty. The proceeds from the confiscation of Jewish property flowed mainly to the benefit of these states, although, as Götz Aly argues, the distribution of Jewish property among the population served both as "social policy" and as a means temporarily to contain inflation. German war finances profited indirectly by being able to extract more in war contributions or occupation costs from their allies, but in all of these countries, vital precepts of national sovereignty would not have permitted the direct exploitation of Jewish property by the Germans in any case.

The application of anti-Jewish economic measures by states allied to the Third Reich was not generally as comprehensive or complete as in the territories directly occupied by the Germans. In all of the countries examined here, pragmatic calculations caused the economic measures taken against the Jews to fall short of the full Nazi program. In Bulgaria, Jewish quotas were set for specific professions, in Italy many Jews were granted special exemptions, and in Hungary comprehensive measures were initially deferred out of a fear of damaging the economy. However, it is precisely such local divergences from the patterns established by the Germans in the Reich and the occupied territories that confirm the autonomy and independent responsibility of the collaborating states in the confiscation of Jewish property.

Slovakia

Tatjana Tönsmeyer makes a cogent case against characterizing President Jozef Tiso's clerical-nationalist regime as merely a German "satellite." Her study of the activities of the German advisors sent to Bratislava to steer the course of the new Slovak state reveals that Slovak officials retained a considerable degree of genuine sovereignty, even over anti-Jewish policy.[6] Although German and Austrian models clearly played an important role in Aryanization there – or rather "Slovakization" – drew also on strong indigenous antisemitism and was implemented with an eye to limiting German economic penetration. Other confiscation policies, if they applied German models, also aimed at securing Jewish wealth for the Slovak state. The German share of the "booty," so to speak, came in the form of payments to cover the "cost" of the deportations, but even these were paid only partially by the Slovak government.

Anti-Jewish propaganda formed an important element of the political platform of Hlinka's Slovak People's Party (SPP) before 1938; it was linked also to anti-capitalist slogans because of the comparatively important role played by Jews within the Slovak economy. Jews were well represented as traders and craftsmen, as well as in the free professions.[7] As well as Jewish capital, SPP propaganda also targeted "Judeo-Bolshevism." In addition, after 1939 the SPP cast the Jews as a disloyal element within the newly founded Slovak state, as many Jews spoke Hungarian and had previously looked to Budapest or Prague, rather than supporting Slovak aspirations for national independence.[8] There was even a largely unsuccessful attempt by the autonomous Slovak authorities to deport a number of Jews into the area occupied by Hungary at the time of the First Vienna Award in November 1938.[9]

[6] Ibid.; Tatjana Tönsmeyer, "Der Raub des jüdischen Eigentums in Ungarn, Rumänien und der Slowakei," in Constantin Goschler and Philipp Ther (eds.), *Raub und Restitution: "Arisierung" und Rückerstattung des jüdischen Eigentums in Europa* (Frankfurt am Main: Fischer Taschenbuch, 2003), p. 82. This chapter is also available in English; see Martin Dean et al. (eds.), *Robbery and Restitution: The Conflict over Jewish Property in Europe* (New York: Berghahn Books in association with the United States Holocaust Memorial Museum, 2007).

[7] According to the December 1940 census, there were 88,951 Jews in Slovakia. Of these, about 12,300 were owners of businesses, 22,000 were private employees, and a few thousand were officials or professionals.

[8] Ladislav Lipscher, *Die Juden im Slowakischen Staat 1939–1945* (Munich: Oldenbourg, 1980), pp. 11–15; James Ramon Felak, *At the Price of the Republic: Hlinka's Slovak People's Party, 1929–1938* (Pittsburgh: University of Pittsburgh Press, 1994), p. 186.

[9] Ivan Kamenec, "The Deportation of Jewish Citizens from Slovakia in 1942," in Dezider Tóth (ed.), *The Tragedy of Slovak Jews 1938–1945: Slovakia and the "Final Solution of the Jewish Question"* (Banská Bystrica, Slovakia: Ministry of Culture of Slovak Republic and Museum of Slovak National Uprising, 1992), p. 114. I am grateful to James Ward for bringing this source to my attention and for his helpful comments with regard to this section on the Holocaust in Slovakia.

Exclusion of Jews from the Slovak Economy

On June 1, 1940, the new law on "Jewish businesses and Jewish employees" came into force. It enabled the regional authorities to withdraw the licenses of Jewish businesses and subject them either to liquidation or Aryanization. Initially, Aryanizations could be undertaken either on a voluntary or a compulsory basis, although the latter was the more usual case. Prices were officially set low, leaving the Jewish former owner to pay off remaining debts from private assets. Factories were initially excluded from Aryanization to forestall Czech and German economic penetration. The law also restricted the proportion of Jewish employees in companies to one-quarter, with plans to reduce it to 10 percent over the following years.[10]

The government established the Central Economic Office (CEO) in August 1940 under the leadership of Augustín Morávek to implement the anti-Jewish economic measures. The CEO was modeled on the Property Processing Office (VVS) in Vienna and was responsible both for implementing Aryanization and issuing work permits to Jews. Like its Austrian precursor, the CEO had the right to conclude sale contracts with Jewish owners and to set the sale price. The proceeds were paid into blocked Jewish bank accounts, and part of this money was diverted into a fund for Jewish emigration that also covered the CEO's operational costs.[11]

The Slovak Interior Ministry dealt with certain other "Jewish" matters, especially those related to forced labor and the subsequent deportations. Interior Minister Alexander Mach announced in August 1940 that, once the financial preconditions had been established, "the Aryanization of the Slovak economy would be implemented without compromise."[12] Behind the scenes, the German Embassy played a role in the development of Slovak Jewish policy. Dieter Wisliceny was appointed as an "advisor on Jewish matters" by the RSHA, arriving in Bratislava on September 1, 1940.[13] In addition to giving advice on how to conduct Aryanization, Wisliceny exerted pressure to support the claims of the ethnic German minority to a share of the Jewish booty.[14]

[10] L. Lipscher, *Die Juden im Slowakischen Staat*, pp. 40–43.
[11] Hans Safrian, "'Head Money' for Destruction? Deportations and Jewish Assets in Satellite Slovakia," unpublished paper presented at the Annual Conference of the German Studies Association in 2004; see also his *Eichmann und seine Gehilfen* (Frankfurt am Main: Fischer, 1995), p. 210.
[12] *Warschauer Zeitung*, August 27, 1940. I am grateful to Dr. Joseph White for bringing this article to my attention.
[13] Raul Hilberg, *Die Vernichtung der europäischen Juden* (Frankfurt am Main: Fischer, 1982), vol. 2, p. 767; T. Tönsmeyer, *Das Dritte Reich und die Slowakei*, p. 140.
[14] T. Tönsmeyer, "Der Raub des jüdischen Eigentums," p. 77.

During the course of 1941, the Slovak authorities forced most Jews out of business as they kept their promise to proceed rapidly with Aryanization. The intention of the Slovak government was that the main beneficiaries from the sale or liquidation of Jewish businesses would be the Jews' Slovak competitors. For example, in Jacovce in 1941, the local authorities closed down ten Jewish businesses and transferred several stores into Slovak ownership.[15] In some cases, Jews continued to run their former businesses behind the scenes as "administrators," as their expertise remained essential. A major problem was the lack both of relevant business experience and available capital among potential Slovak entrepreneurs. German observers noted that some "lazy" Slovak Aryanizers simply extracted the capital from companies for personal benefit and allowed them to go bankrupt, leaving taxes unpaid. (Other critics noted that employees of the CEO had bought twenty Aryanized firms and run up excessive "business expenses.") By the end of 1941, 9,935 Jewish companies had been liquidated (84 percent), and 1,888 (16 percent) had been transferred into non-Jewish ownership, while some more complicated cases remained to be decided.[16]

On September 9, 1941, the Slovak government introduced the so-called Jewish Codex, which defined Jews along racial lines, similar to the Nuremberg Laws.[17] This measure was rapidly followed by widespread discriminatory and confiscatory measures. On September 22, 1941, Jews were compelled to wear the Star of David. A renewed wave of dismissals of Jews from government service and the army began, and the quota for Jewish lawyers and other professionals was reduced to 4 percent. In practice, doctors proved to be harder to replace than lawyers, and more of them retained their positions. Jews were also subjected to a low maximum wage of 1,500 Slovak kronen (RM 129) per month. In December 1941, the Slovak authorities ordered Jews to surrender their typewriters, and the Hlinka Guard collected all fur coats owned by Jews. In imitation of the German authorities, in early 1942 the CEO even demanded the surrender of spare clothes and fabrics that Jews were supposedly "hoarding."[18]

[15] Shmuel Spector and Geoffrey Wigoder (eds.), *The Encyclopedia of Jewish Life before and during the Holocaust* (Jerusalem: Yad Vashem, 2001), p. 557, see also the entry for Giraltovce on pp. 431–32.

[16] T. Tönsmeyer, "Der Raub des jüdischen Eigentums," p. 78; L. Lipscher, *Die Juden im Slowakischen Staat*, pp. 67–69.

[17] T. Tönsmeyer, "Der Raub des jüdischen Eigentums," p. 74

[18] L. Lipscher, *Die Juden im Slowakischen Staat*, p. 63; R. Hilberg, *Die Vernichtung*, pp. 769–72.

Confiscation of Private Property

In September 1940, the Slovak Jews were required to register their property if they owned more than 5,000 kronen (RM 430). At this time, 52,310 Jews acknowledged possession of at least this amount. The net sum registered (after subtracting debts) was 2.9 billion kronen.[19] Of this total, more than one-quarter was in agricultural land or other real estate, all of which subsequently was confiscated by the state. Part of the agricultural property was auctioned – some being sold to large estate owners – and a small part was even rented back to Jewish former owners. The government encountered more difficulties with disposing of urban real estate, very little of which had been sold by fall 1943. Therefore, the boost to the Slovak state's ailing finances from this source was limited, as real estate still had to be rented or sold to realize any revenue.[20]

As in the Reich, soon after the registration of Jewish property the Slovak government imposed on the Jews a property tax of 20 percent, to be paid in five installments. The tax was intended to reap a total of 600–700 million kronen (RM 50–60 million) for the Slovak treasury. In late 1940, a Central Jewish Organization (CJO) was established. As in areas under direct German control, the Slovak authorities forced the CJO to assist in collecting the special tax. To finance itself and conduct welfare work, the CJO was also directed to collect an income tax of 20 percent from Jews.

Forced Labor

From 1940, male Jews were subjected to forced labor in military labor battalions, as they were excluded from military service; the CEO granted several thousand Jews exemptions so they could continue working in the free economy. Because the economic measures against the Jews resulted in increasing pauperization, the Slovak authorities planned to isolate them in forced labor camps in 1941, partly to prevent them from garnering any sympathy among the Slovak population. Slovak officials even visited Jewish forced labor camps in nearby Eastern Upper Silesia to learn from the German experience, noting also the inhuman conditions there. Slovak plans to isolate the Jews were soon overtaken by the German request for the deportation of 20,000 Slovak Jews capable of work in early 1942. Some young Jews were temporarily protected from deportation by their deployment on

---

[19] L. Lipscher, *Die Juden im Slowakischen Staat*, p. 65.
[20] R. Hilberg, *Die Vernichtung*, p. 771.

particular forced labor projects. In May 1943, the military labor camps for Jews were dissolved.[21]

Confiscations and Slovak Payments Linked to the Deportations

From October 1941 on, the CEO in Slovakia could assign Jews to new residential areas. With the CJO's assistance, the CEO had resettled more than 6,700 Jews from Bratislava to nearby towns by March 1, 1942. Those being resettled had to fill out forms describing their property. The CJO then sent officials to the homes to be vacated and made an inventory of the property, which was split into two categories: things that the Jews could take with them and items that would be confiscated by the state. The property left behind was secured in warehouses and then auctioned; the proceeds were used to pay the costs of the resettlement action. Among the reasons cited for the action was the acute shortage of housing in Bratislava.[22]

In early 1942, the German Foreign Office, acting on behalf of the RSHA, requested the deportation of 20,000 young Slovak Jews to "the East." As the Slovak authorities now viewed the Jews mainly as a social burden, they agreed to this proposal.[23] CEO Chairman A. Morávek even argued that, since Aryanization was economically and legally completed, its best conclusion would be the emigration of the original Jewish owners.[24] Just as the deportations were starting in March 1942, the Germans demanded a payment of RM 500 for each Slovak Jew, as well as an additional sum to cover the transport costs. The figure of RM 500 was based loosely on the assumed share of each Jew in the total amount of Slovak Jewish property registered and was supposedly to cover Germany's costs for their training, housing, and upkeep. This meant that the deportation of all Slovak Jews would cost some RM 45 million (just short of the RM 55 million to be raised by the special tax). Eventually, after lengthy negotiations, the Slovak authorities agreed to this demand in September 1942. Nevertheless, they encountered serious difficulties in raising the money; according to the calculations of Hans Safrian, the Slovak state ultimately paid only about one-third of the amount owed for those deported in 1942.[25]

---

[21] Ibid., p. 773–74; L. Lipscher, *Die Juden im Slowakischen Staat*, pp. 89–93; T. Tönsmeyer, *Das Dritte Reich und die Slowakei*, p. 143.

[22] L. Lipscher, *Die Juden im Slowakischen Staat*, pp. 85–86; R. Hilberg, *Die Vernichtung*, p. 775.

[23] NARA, RG-238, T-1139, NG-182; H. Safrian, "'Head Money' for Destruction?"

[24] I. Kamenec, "The Deportation of Jewish Citizens from Slovakia," pp. 121–22.

[25] H. Safrian, "'Head Money' for Destruction?"; NARA, RG-238, T-1139, NG-2586-J; R. Hilberg, *Die Vernichtung*, p. 776.

In the fall of 1941, the German Foreign Office had asked the Slovak government for permission to deport Slovak Jews located in the Reich. The Slovak government acquiesced only after the Germans confirmed that Slovak claims to their property would be fully guaranteed.[26] In the course of these lengthy negotiations on the property of Slovak Jews in Germany, the Germans also considered reducing the price for the Slovak deportees from RM 500 to RM 300, in order to get the Slovaks to accept the territorial principle with regard to Jewish property, as German officials considered Slovak Jewish wealth in Germany to be worth more than that of German Jews in Slovakia.[27]

During the round-ups of Slovak Jews beginning in March 1942, members of the Hlinka Guard took some Jewish property "to prevent it falling into German hands."[28] German reports also complained of widespread corruption by the authorities and the police, who sometimes released Jews in exchange for bribes.[29] On May 15, 1942, the Slovak parliament passed a law authorizing the confiscation of "ownerless" Jewish property; in effect, this law was the Slovakian equivalent of the Eleventh Decree because so much Jewish property had become ownerless as a result of the deportations.[30]

As the round-ups of Slovak Jews progressed during 1942, about 7,000 fled to Hungary, and several thousand others converted to Christianity. The Catholic Church remained reluctant to receive a large number of new converts as it doubted their sincerity, so most converts became Protestants or joined the Greek Orthodox faith. The law protected only those who had converted to Christianity prior to March 14, 1939, but this protection also extended to family members. Previous exceptions granted on economic grounds also remained valid, as did those given to persons in mixed marriages. The Judencodex also permitted leading politicians to grant exemptions from deportation, which occurred on a large scale. By 1943, the Catholic Church was taking a strong stand to protect those who had converted to Catholicism. The Slovak economy was suffering from the loss of qualified personnel; accountants and clerks, for example, were in short supply after the deportations in 1942, so a considerable number of

---

[26] R. Hilberg, *Die Vernichtung*, p. 776; Peter Longerich, *Politik der Vernichtung: Eine Gesamtdarstellung der nationalsozialistischen Judenverfolgung* (Munich: Piper, 1998), p. 447.

[27] R. Hilberg, *Die Vernichtung*, p. 786.

[28] Ibid., p. 779; H. Safrian, *Eichmann und seine Gehilfen*, p. 212.

[29] See Eduard Niznanský (ed.), *Dokumenty nemeckej proveniencie (1939–1945)* (Bratislava: Nadácia Milana Simecku: Zidovská nábozenská obec Bratislava; Zvolen: Vydal Klemo, 2003), pp. 184–87.

[30] R. Hilberg, *Die Vernichtung*, p. 782.

Jews had to be allowed to remain active within the economy for pragmatic reasons.[31]

As a result of the large number of exemptions and a gradual shift in the popular mood, after June 1942, the rate of deportation slowed dramatically – after some 52,000 Jews had already been deported. Despite German pressure, only 57,500 had been deported by the end of March 1943. More than ten thousand Slovak Jews, many of them converts, received exemptions.[32]

Clearly, Jewish responses – fleeing, converting, and petitioning for exemptions – contributed to this slowdown in the rate of deportation. The ability of the Slovak regime to halt the deportations to a trickle also speaks to their autonomy in the area of Jewish policy. Unfortunately, the reprieve proved to be only temporary. In September 1944, as German forces put down the Slovak uprising, Alois Brunner arrived in Bratislava to coordinate the deportation of 13,000 Jews captured by Einsatzgruppe H. These unfortunates were deported mostly to Auschwitz, Sachsenhausen, or Theresienstadt (Terezin).[33] The German and Slovak authorities were still arguing about the financial aspects of the deportations in March 1945, as the Slovaks had not paid the fees in full. In total, the Germans deported about 70,000 Jews from Slovakia, of whom at least 65,000 did not return.[34]

In the view of Ladislav Lipscher, the Slovak authorities slowed the deportations partly in response to a change of mood within the population, partly due to the brutal way in which the Jews were deported, and partly because of Germany's declining fortunes in the war. Despite German efforts to secure its share of Slovak Jewish property "to cover the costs of the deportations," the bulk was confiscated by the Slovak state or fell into the hands of Slovak businessmen, families, and officials, who sought to profit from what were widely perceived as Jewish "ill-gotten gains" being returned into Slovak hands. In the summer of 2005, the names of those who bought Jewish property in Slovakia were published, sparking a heated debate on the extent of Slovak complicity in the economic exploitation of the Jews, although a few of the individuals named actually may have acted legitimately as "fronts" to help the original Jewish owners.

[31] Ibid., pp. 781–82.
[32] Ibid., pp. 784–85.
[33] Einsatzgruppe H was commanded by *Obersturmbannführer* Josef Witiska, who was also the Supreme Commander of the Security Police and the SD in Slovakia (Befehlshaber der Sicherheitspolizei und des SD in der Slowakei).
[34] R. Hilberg, *Die Vernichtung*, pp. 792–93; H. Safrian, *Eichmann und seine Gehilfen*, pp. 308–11.

Romania

Antecedents

In Romania, successive governments introduced their own antisemitic legislation and plundered Jewish property without much German prompting.
Many of the mechanisms applied were clearly influenced by similar measures taken in Germany, but certain aspects of "Romanianization" were
unique to the country.

The history of Romanian antisemitism dates back centuries, but it was
during the nineteenth century that a growing number of anti-Jewish laws
and decrees demonstrated that it had become firmly rooted in state policy.
The establishment of an independent state in 1878 saw an improvement
in the legal status of Jews due to international guarantees, but influen-
tial Romanian politicians repeatedly denounced the Jews as "enemies of
Romania" and very few were approved for "naturalization" by the parliament before World War I. The legal position of Jews improved thereafter,
again due to the international guarantees in the post-World War I peace
settlements, but this improvement did not lead to any decline in Romanian antisemitism, as it came about only in response to external pressure. In
1926, to take only one example, Alexandru Cuza, the founder of the Christian National Defense League (*Liga Apararii National Crestine*), demanded,
among other antisemitic prescriptions, that all land held by Jews should
be expropriated and that all Jewish residential properties in the towns be
confiscated.[35]

In the 1930s, a succession of Romanian governments implemented new
anti-Jewish laws. In 1934, the government introduced a Law for the Use of
Romanian Personnel in Enterprises, which required that at least 80 percent
of employees in all enterprises be Romanian, severely affecting the job
and professional prospects of many Jews.[36] Under the brief government
of Alexandru Cuza and Octavian Goga (from the end of December 1937
to February 10, 1938), a decree for the review of the citizenship status
of all Jews was proclaimed, and Goga even proposed the deportation of
"half a million recent Jewish immigrants" (supposedly arrived since 1913)
to Madagascar. In response, many Jews withdrew their money from the

[35] Radu Ioanid, *The Holocaust in Romania: The Destruction of Jews and Gypsies under the
Antonescu Regime, 1940–44* (Chicago: Ivan R. Dee in association with the United States
Holocaust Memorial Museum, 2000), pp. 5–8, 16–17; R. Hilberg, *Die Vernichtung*,
p. 814.

[36] "Background and Precursors to the Holocaust," in Tuvia Friling et al. (eds.), *Final Report
of the International Commission on the Holocaust in Romania*, p. 20.

banks in preparation for emigration, and the stock market had to be closed because of a dramatic fall in prices. France and Great Britain, the country's two largest creditors, demanded that the citizenship decree be rescinded. The outcome of the crisis was that the government had to resign, but the decree remained in force. It stripped citizenship from about 200,000 of Romania's Jews, especially in Bukovina and Bessarabia, and barred them from various categories of employment.[37]

Antisemitic Measures of the Iron Guard Regime

During the second half of 1940, the National Legionary (Iron Guard) regime conducted an extensive and violent campaign, robbing the Jews of their property, largely without any direct German input.[38] In September 1940, Ion Antonescu explained the underlying conception behind Romania's anti-Jewish economic legislation. He claimed that Jews formed the greatest obstacle to the expansion of the Romanian economy, and he promised to solve this problem by "replacing Jews with Romanians – in the first place Legionnaires" – promising disingenuously that "most Jewish property will be expropriated in return for compensation." He added that Jews who had arrived after 1913 would be removed from the economy as soon as possible, but that the rest would be replaced more gradually.[39]

At this time, many professional organizations expelled their Jewish members; among these associations were the Bucharest Bar, the Journalists' Union, the Society of Architects, and the General Assembly of University Fellows.[40] On August 8, 1940, the government enacted a law prohibiting Jews from purchasing landed or industrial property. In Ineu in southern Transylvania, for example, Iron Guard Legionnaires confiscated all Jewish businesses in November 1940.[41] A series of decrees issued in October and November 1940 authorized the Ministry for National Economy to appoint "commissars" for Jewish factories, effectively dismissed Jewish employees

---

[37] Mariana Hausleitner, "Auf dem Weg zur 'Ethnokratie': Rumänien in den Jahren des Zweiten Weltkrieges," in *Beiträge zur Geschichte des Nationalsozialismus 19, Kooperation und Verbrechen: Formen der "Kollaboration" im östlichen Europa 1939–1945* (Göttingen: Wallstein, 2003), p. 84; R. Ioanid, *The Holocaust in Romania*, pp. 17–18.

[38] See Jean Ancel, "Seizure of Jewish Property in Romania," in *Confiscation of Jewish Property in Europe, 1933–1945: New Sources and Perspectives*, Symposium Proceedings (Washington, DC: United States Holocaust Memorial Museum, 2003), pp. 44–46.

[39] R. Ioanid, *The Holocaust in Romania*, p. 24, quoting from an interview Ion Antonescu gave to the Italian newspaper *La Stampa* on September 28, 1940.

[40] Radu Ioanid, "The Antonescu Era," in Randolph L. Braham (ed.), *The Tragedy of Romanian Jewry* (Boulder, CO: Rosenthal Institute for Holocaust Studies; Social Science Monographs, 1994), pp. 119–20.

[41] S. Spector and G. Wigoder (eds.), *The Encyclopedia of Jewish Life*, p. 547.

from many businesses, and paved the way for the confiscation of Jewish agrarian and rural property.[42]

Under the guise of "Romanianization," the Legionnaires exploited the state apparatus for the purpose of simply robbing Jews. Many of the businesses taken over by Legionnaires quickly went bankrupt, and Ion Antonescu became concerned about the widespread disruption to the economy arising from this phase of "wild Romanianizations," reminiscent in some respects of the initial months of the Nazi takeover in Austria. In light of these developments, Antonescu decided to achieve the exclusion of Jews from the Romanian economy more gradually and through strictly legal means.[43]

Antonescu's conflict with the Iron Guard in January 1941 was closely linked to the excesses involved in Romanianization, and on January 18, Antonescu abolished the position of Romanianization Commissar, striking a blow against the Legionnaires. After the assassination in Bucharest of a German air force commander, Doering (probably by an agent of the British Intelligence Service), both sides opened hostilities on January 21, 1941. With the support of the Romanian army and also of Hitler and the German Foreign Ministry (but not the SS and the SD, who helped a number of Legionnaires escape), Antonescu managed to suppress the Iron Guard rebellion in a couple of weeks. During the rebellion, more than 120 Jews were brutally massacred in Bucharest, the excesses being accompanied by heinous plundering.[44]

After excluding the Legionary element from power, the Antonescu government nevertheless continued to implement its anti-Jewish measures, which aimed primarily at the confiscation of Jewish property and the elimination of Jews from the labor market.[45] However, Antonescu stressed now (in order to avoid economic collapse) that Romanianization would be a

[42] J. Ancel, "Seizure of Jewish Property in Romania," p. 45; "The Exclusion of Jews from Romanian Society during the Antonescu Governments with and without the Iron Guard: Antisemitic Legislation, Romanianization, and Expropriation," p. 7, in Tuvia Friling et al. (eds.), *Final Report of the International Commission on the Holocaust in Romania*; T. Tönsmeyer, "Der Raub des jüdischen Eigentums," p. 75. By 1943, these laws resulted in the nationalization of more than 519,000 hectares of agricultural land and forests, three quarters of which lay in Bessarabia and Bukovina.

[43] R. Ioanid, *The Holocaust in Romania*, pp. 52–53. On the use of the term "Romanianization," which was directed in part against other minorities, see R. Hilberg, *Die Vernichtung*, p. 816.

[44] R. Ioanid, *The Holocaust in Romania*, pp. 53–59; on the rebellion of the Iron Guard; see also Jean Ancel, "The German-Romanian Relationship and the Final Solution," *Holocaust and Genocide Studies*, vol. 19, no. 2 (Fall 2005): 253–54.

[45] Jean Ancel, "German-Romanian Relations During the Second World War," in R. L. Braham (ed.), *The Tragedy of Romanian Jewry*, p. 61.

steady process in planned stages, in contrast to the Iron Guard's brutal – and corrupt – approach. In particular, time was needed to prepare the "Romanian element" to occupy the spaces that would open up in the economy and for the accumulation of the required capital.[46]

Adoption of German Models and Resistance to German Economic Penetration

The extent of direct German influence on the anti-Jewish measures in Romania is hard to assess precisely. After the ousting of the Legionnaires from government, a number of German "advisors" were active in Bucharest; these included Dr. Hermann Neubacher, German Minister Plenipotentiary for Economic Affairs in the Balkans; SS-Brigadeführer Karl Pflaumer, who advised the Romanians on "administrative matters"; and, from May 1941, SS-Hauptsturmführer Gustav Richter, who was responsible for "Jewish issues" within the German Embassy. The German advisors made several proposals aimed at streamlining anti-Jewish measures in accordance with the German experience in Vienna and elsewhere.[47] For example, owners of Jewish real estate expropriated according to the March 27 decree received compensation equivalent to eight years' rent, but paid in the form of government bonds bearing only 3 percent interest – clearly adapted from Göring's model of "pensioning the Jews off" to the benefit of state finances.[48] Shortly after his arrival, Richter recommended the centralization of Romanian authorities dealing with the Jews and also of Jewish organizations. These two aims were realized in the creation of the Central Office of Romanian Jews before the end of 1941. Other recommendations included registration of all Jewish property and establishment of an "evacuation fund" to cover the costs of expelling the Jews. Richter received assurances that he would be permitted to see all future pieces of anti-Jewish legislation before they were passed into law.[49]

---

[46] "The Exclusion of Jews from Romanian Society," pp. 3, 8.

[47] Jean Ancel (ed.), *Documents Concerning the Fate of Romanian Jewry during the Holocaust* 12 vols. (New York: Beate Klarsfeld Foundation, 1986), vol. II, pp. 259–60, doc. no. 81.

[48] R. Hilberg, *Die Vernichtung*, pp. 820 and 836. The Romanian purchasers in turn were granted favorable credit rates, also in imitation of earlier Austrian practices. In the Regat (the core territories of Romania), some 75,000 Jewish apartments were expropriated.

[49] J. Ancel (ed.), *Documents Concerning the Fate of Romanian Jewry*, vol. II, pp. 401–404, doc. no. 129, activity report of Richter on his first two meetings with General Eugen Zwidenek, in charge of the Central Office for Romanianization in May 1941; M. Hausleitner, "Auf dem Weg zur 'Ethnokratie,'" p. 97. See also LAB, B Rep. 039–01/300 (Rumänien – Hausrat u. Fabrikeinrichtungen), Beschluss KG Bremen 1.6.65,

Among other German instruments adapted by Romania after May 1941 were special taxes on the Jewish population. On July 30, 1941, the Romanian Finance Minister informed the heads of the Jewish community in Bucharest (some already having been declared "hostages" subject to arrest) that the Jewish population of Romania was required to provide a "war loan" of ten billion lei.[50] In May 1943, Antonescu imposed a further "war contribution" of four billion lei on the Jews, alleging that the latter were "enjoying life" while Romanian soldiers were being killed at the front. This levy took the form of a property tax on Romania's 40,000 wealthiest Jews, similar to the Reich's punitive tax (see Figure 8.1). The Central Office of Romanian Jews was responsible for collecting this tax.[51] Other innovations included the creation of a Central Office for Romanianization in May 1941, directly answerable to Ion Antonescu, which took over the administration, rental, and sale of Jewish real estate in the interest of the state; it also reflected German technical input. However, under the new regulations, ethnic Germans were largely excluded from buying former Jewish property, and only after strong protests by Richter on their behalf were they permitted a maximum quota of 5 percent of Romanianized businesses.[52]

Properties in the Public Domain

Further economic measures followed throughout 1941 and 1942, and the Romanian military and civilian authorities began to seize Jewish communal property.[53] In September 1941, the Romanian army demanded large quantities of beds and clothing from the Central Office of Romanian Jews, threatening the Jewish population if it did not comply.[54] On October 10, the Jews were requested to surrender gold, silver, jewelry, and other valuables to the government. This was followed in November by a decree ordering

and NARA, RG-238, T-1139, NG-4962; and Jean Ancel, "The German-Romanian Relationship and the Final Solution," p. 260.

[50] See J. Ancel, "Seizure of Jewish Property," p. 47.

[51] Ibid., p. 48; see J. Ancel (ed.), *Documents Concerning the Fate of Romanian Jewry*, vol. IV, p. 566, doc. no. 307. It should be noted that not all of the 4 billion lei was actually collected; R. Hilberg, *Die Vernichtung*, pp. 839–41.

[52] J. Ancel (ed.), *Documents Concerning the Fate of Romanian Jewry*, vol. IV, pp. 2–8, doc. no. 2. The quota for real estate and land was only 3–4 percent; see also Osobyi (Special) Archive, Moscow, 1458-14-41, pp. 1–7, Volksdeutsche Mittelstelle an RWM, June 6, 1941. I am grateful to Gerald Feldman for drawing my attention to this reference.

[53] J. Ancel (ed.), *Documents Concerning the Fate of Romanian Jewry*, vol. II, pp. 493–94, doc. no. 198.

[54] J. Ancel, "Seizure of Jewish Property," p. 48.

the confiscation of cinemas and travel agencies. At the beginning of January 1942, Jews were also obliged to surrender clothing and linen items.

In Romania, the Jews were sorted into two categories; those deemed economically useful and those not. The latter were assigned to labor battalions as a substitute for military service. Those considered useful were permitted to remain in their jobs, but instead of performing military service, they had to pay a hefty tax, adjusted according to income. The long-term plan was to supplant all Jews by training Romanian replacements. By December 1942, after rejecting German requests to deport the Jews of the Regat (Romania's old core territories), Antonescu's regime still anticipated an income of several billion lei to be extracted from the Jews on their emigration to Palestine.[55]

An early 1943 report sent by the Zionist leadership in Bucharest to Geneva stated that Jews were subjected to four times the normal level of taxes and to other special levies. Jewish businesses were subjected to forced sales to Romanians at a fraction of their peacetime values, and Jews continued to be dismissed from their jobs and forced out of their apartments and houses. The same report estimated that since Romania's entry into the war the Jews had been forced to pay a "war loan" of 2.5 billion lei and clothing "donations" equivalent to 1.8 billion lei, and the diversion to the state of rental payments owed to them was valued at another 3 billion lei. Even the permission given by the Romanian government to send help to the Jews in Transnistria proved a double-edged sword. Much of the money sent was consumed by high currency conversion charges, material supplies were subjected to customs fees, and both experienced considerable delays.[56]

Pogroms, Plunder, and Genocide: The Romanian Experience

In the summer of 1940, army officers organized a pogrom in the town of Dorohoi; it resulted in the deaths of more than fifty Jews and widespread attacks on Jewish property.[57] This pattern was repeated on a much larger scale during the Jassy (Iasi) pogrom on the night of June 28/29, 1941. First,

[55] NARA, RG-242, T-120, reel 1205, Auswärtiges Amt (AA), Deutsche Gesandtschaft Bukarest, memorandum of the Romanian government concerning measures taken by the Romanian state for the solution of the Jewish problem in Romania, Bucharest, March 26, 1943 (478312–14); R. Hilberg, Die Vernichtung, p. 850.

[56] J. Ancel (ed.), Documents Concerning the Fate of Romanian Jewry, vol. IV, pp. 386–91, doc. no. 197, Report of the Zionist leadership in Bucharest, January 1943.

[57] Tuvia Friling et al. (eds.), Final Report of the International Commission on the Holocaust in Romania, p. 85; Armin Heinen, "Gewalt – Kultur," in Mariana Hausleitner, Brigitte Mihok, and Julianne Wetzel (eds.), Rumänien und der Holocaust: Zu den Massenverbrechen

agents provocateurs staged phony attacks on Romanian troops and spread rumors blaming the Jews. Then the local Jassy police, backed by the Bessarabian police, the gendarmerie, soldiers, and also many local civilians, especially youths, indulged in a night of looting, rape, and murder against the Jews of the city. Christians had marked their houses with crosses in advance to prevent the looting of non-Jewish property. The pogrom and subsequent murderous deportations by train of thousands of Jews from Jassy were carried out with the knowledge of and on the orders of the highest officials in the government. In this dramatic escalation toward genocide, the looting of Jewish property played a key role. As Jean Ancel notes, local women and men "initiated arrests, informed on Jews, directed the authorities to their homes, and always – without fail – looted the empty homes, sometimes even before the Jewish families had been forced out."[58]

As Romanian forces moved into Bessarabia and Northern Bukovina in July 1941, the army engaged in the looting of Jewish property and the massacre of Jews, sometimes assisted by the local population. The Antonescu regime blamed Jews for having sympathized with the Soviet forces during their occupation of the area from the end of June 1940 and for allegedly firing on retreating Romanian troops. It issued instructions to "cleanse" the countryside of Jews and concentrate them into camps and ghettos in the towns.[59] In the assessment of Radu Ioanid, "Most [of the Jewish victims] were killed by Romanian and German military units acting on superior orders. Others, however, fell victim to Romanian and Ukrainian peasants who wanted (or even felt it their duty) to murder (and, of course, rob) their Jewish neighbors." Ioanid describes how government provocation interacted with mob violence to make the murder and plunder of Jews a joint enterprise. Ultimately, such excesses led to more decisive state intervention to maintain control over the policy and the plunder.[60] The powerful evidence in Romanian sources demonstrates how at key junctures economic antisemitism contributed directly to the dynamics of the Holocaust.

---

in *Transnistrien 1941–1944* (Berlin: Metropol, 2001), pp. 34–35. Heinen's figures for the number of victims of the pogrom are almost certainly too high.

[58] Jean Ancel, "The Jassy Pogrom – June 29, 1941," in M. Hausleitner, B. Mihok, and J. Wetzel (eds.), *Rumänien und der Holocaust*, p. 64; R. Hilberg, *Die Vernichtung*, p. 821.

[59] R. Ioanid, *The Holocaust in Romania*, pp. 90–109; Marcu Rozen, *The Holocaust under the Antonescu Government: Historical and Statistical Data about Jews in Romania, 1940–44* (Bucharest: Association of Romanian Jews, Victims of the Holocaust, 2004), pp. 34–38. Estimates of the number of victims of these massacres vary from 10,000 to more than 50,000 (Rozen).

[60] R. Ioanid, *The Holocaust in Romania*, pp. 108–109.

The main element of the Romanian Holocaust was the deportation of the Jews from Bessarabia and Northern Bukovina into Transnistria, where a large proportion met their deaths. This deportation was accompanied by successive waves of state and private plundering. The Romanian authorities ordered the confiscation of the property of these Jews "without any notice or any other formalities."[61] They permitted Jews deported from the Chernovits area in October 1941 to take with them only a knapsack and some money. On arrival in Transnistria, the deportees had to exchange their remaining Romanian currency for nearly worthless rubles or German occupation currency at unfavorable rates, which represented a further act of confiscation.[62]

Extensive records from the Kishinev ghetto indicate that Jews were successively robbed as they entered the ghetto, when they were deported, and again as they crossed the River Dniestr. They were compelled to surrender valuables in exchange for only 20 percent of their value in worthless currency. The absence of records invited widespread corruption, leading to a subsequent government inquiry. Jews often sold their last possessions just prior to deportation, but received little in return as they were in a very weak bargaining position. The State Property Administration in Kishinev issued 3,514 permits to private citizens and 1,868 to public offices to take away furniture formerly owned by Jews.[63]

In the makeshift ghettos of Transnistria, the Romanian administration confiscated all movable Jewish assets (furniture and personal property) for its own use, and those items deemed not suitable for state purposes were auctioned locally. In addition, a tax was levied on the Jews, which the communities themselves had to collect. The levy was to be regarded as a contribution by the Jews "to saving their own lives and as a donation – but not as a one-time measure."[64] Among the beneficiaries of Jewish property in Transnistria were also local ethnic Germans who received former Jewish

---

[61] NARA, RG-242, T-120, reel 1205, AA, Deutsche Gesandtschaft Bukarest, memorandum of the Romanian government concerning measures taken by the Romanian state for the solution of the Jewish problem in Romania, Bucharest, March 26, 1943 (478312–14); "The Exclusion of Jews from Romanian Society," p. 7.

[62] LAB, B Rep. 039–01/300 (Rumänien – Hausrat u. Fabrikeinrichtungen); Jean Ancel, "The Romanian Campaigns of Mass Murder in Transnistria, 1941–1942," in Randolph L. Braham (ed.), *The Destruction of Romanian and Ukrainian Jews during the Antonescu Era* (Boulder, CO: Social Science Monographs, 1997), p. 91.

[63] Paul A. Shapiro, "The Jews of Chisinau (Kishinev): Romanian Reoccupation, Ghettoization, Deportation," in Randolph L. Braham (ed.), *The Destruction of Romanian and Ukrainian Jews during the Antonescu Era*, pp. 173–75.

[64] Jean Ancel (ed.), *Transnistria, 1941–1942* (Tel Aviv: Goldstein-Goren Diaspora Research Center, 2003), vol. 1, *History and Document Summaries*, p. 560, doc. 65, Legal Opinion of

apartments in some towns, as well as Ukrainian policemen who took bribes or simply helped themselves.[65] In the terrible conditions in Transnistria, the cumulative effects of the robbery campaign were tantamount to a death sentence. As one survivor recalled, "Those who owned nothing, or were not suited for begging, died of starvation."[66]

Assessment of "Romanianization" and Confiscation

What were the most significant characteristics of Romanianization and the confiscation of Jewish property by the Antonescu regime? The main impulse for the seizure of Jewish property clearly came from the Iron Guard and Antonescu's government, which shared a common antisemitic ideology. There is no doubt that Antonescu strove for the creation of a homogeneous nation-state, which meant the exclusion of Jews from the economy and society and ultimately from Romanian soil. Exclusion measures were applied most radically in the regained provinces of Northern Bukovina and Bessarabia, without any apparent German prompting, although German practices in "cleansing the economy" and the ethnic cleansing of annexed territories provided obvious models. Especially in the key period of time around the invasion of the Soviet Union, a clear transfer of know-how can be documented, but Antonescu's regime also took care to limit German economic penetration and not to destabilize the economy by moving too fast.

During the course of the war, most Jewish businesses were confiscated, and all shares in Jewish possession were registered by the state. Nevertheless, the gradual pace of "Romanianization" in certain branches still caused a group of former Legionnaires and supporters of Cuza to demand in fall 1943 that "all the assets" of the Jews should be confiscated so that they could "be placed in the hands of pure-blooded Romanians."[67] However, even in the "model" provinces of Bessarabia and Bukovina, the authorities had to employ some Jewish economic specialists to keep key industries functioning.[68]

The Jews of Romania did not remain passive spectators of their progressive expropriation. Widespread corruption offered the opportunity to

the Administration's Research Bureau on the Handling of Jewish Property, October 6, 1941.

[65] See NARA, RG-238, NO-5561.

[66] R. Hilberg, *Die Vernichtung*, pp. 834–35.

[67] R. Ioanid, *The Holocaust in Romania*, pp. 292–93.

[68] I am grateful to Vladimir Solonari for this information; he is currently conducting a study of the Romanian administration of these two provinces.

buy exemptions from forced labor or travel restrictions.[69] On several occasions, Dr. Wilhelm Filderman, president of the Union of Romanian Jewish Communities, and other Jewish leaders actively lobbied the Romanian government, and at times they were able to ameliorate their people's fate. In Timișoara, for example, the SS "specialist for Jewish affairs" Richter had strong evidence that Franz von Neumann, a Catholic of Jewish extraction, had offered a large bribe to the army to forestall the evacuation of Jews from the region.[70]

At his postwar trial, Ion Antonescu boasted that during most of the war he had maintained a strong economy and paid for the war without increasing the national debt. This in part reflected Romania's ability to obtain at least some payments in gold from the Reich in return for oil deliveries and other services to Germany.[71] Antonescu claimed that thirty billion lei had come from public "contributions." According to Ancel, however, between one-quarter and one-third of this sum was actually extorted from the Jews against "receipts," and much more was taken without receipts.[72]

Just as precise figures of Jewish deaths at Romanian hands are difficult to establish,[73] reliable figures on the value of the confiscations are not available for all types of assets. Ancel estimates that for the territories of the Regat and southern Transylvania alone the value of confiscated and nationalized property, combined with the spoils of the direct, officially sanctioned theft, was roughly 100 billion lei.[74] The significance of the Romanian example lies, however, not so much in the scale and wide variety of expropriation measures, as ultimately the economic exclusion of the Jews here was not completed. Rather, the close connections among private plunder, systematic state exploitation, and the onset of genocide in Romania are surprisingly well documented. As in Austria and Germany, along with racial ideology, economic antisemitism pursued from below and government attempts to channel this energy from above contributed to the unleashing of mass killing and murderous deportations by Romanian forces on the ground.

---

[69] R. Hilberg, *Die Vernichtung*, pp. 812 and 837–38.

[70] J. Ancel (ed.), *Documents Concerning the Fate of Romanian Jewry*, vol. IV, p. 283, doc. no. 141, note of Gustav Richter, October 3, 1942; R. Hilberg, *Die Vernichtung*, p. 847.

[71] G. Aly, *Hitlers Volksstaat*, pp. 265–73.

[72] J. Ancel, "Seizure of Jewish Property," p. 49.

[73] T. Friling et al. (eds.), *Final Report of the International Commission on the Holocaust in Romania*, p. 381, concludes that "between 280,000 and 380,000 Romanian and Ukrainian Jews were murdered or died during the Holocaust in Romania and the territories under its control."

[74] J. Ancel, "Seizure of Jewish Property," pp. 49–52. Here Ancel gives a detailed breakdown of the sums received from a wide variety of confiscation measures.

Bulgaria

In Bulgaria, there was no government-directed anti-Jewish program before the war, but antisemitic rhetoric was not absent from political debate either. Yet, antisemitism did not go unchallenged. In 1937, a Jewish journalist, Buko Piti, published a book of statements by 150 prominent Bulgarians denouncing antisemitism, perhaps unintentionally laying one of the foundations for the "myth" that there was no Bulgarian antisemitism. The need for such a book would seem to belie this claim. Indeed, there were a number of right-wing antisemitic groups and organizations, such as the Bulgarian National Socialist Party and the Association of Bulgarian National Legions, that spread racist propaganda in the 1930s, although their division into various small factions probably weakened their impact.[75]

The Law for the Defense of the Nation

Nationalist sentiment in Bulgaria intensified along with respect for Nazi Germany's growing power after the start of the war. In particular, Bulgaria's own revisionist ambitions drew her into the Axis orbit in return for regaining southern Dobruja from Romania in September 1940. In the summer of 1940, a young lawyer in the Bulgarian government, Aleksandur Belev, visited Germany to study the Nuremberg Laws. Together with the Minister for Internal Affairs, Petar Gabrovski, he helped prepare Bulgaria's antisemitic legislation, the Law for the Defense of the Nation, which was submitted to Parliament in the fall of 1940.[76]

The extent to which this law was the direct result of German pressure is difficult to determine. David Fraser points out that it was drafted, introduced, and enforced by a sovereign Bulgarian government as domestic legislation, using a religious rather than a racial definition of who was a Jew.[77]

---

[75] Guy H. Haskell, *From Sofia to Jaffa: The Jews of Bulgaria and Israel* (Detroit: Wayne State University Press, 1994), pp. 111–12; Frederick B. Chary, *The Bulgarian Jews and the Final Solution, 1940–1944* (Pittsburgh: University of Pittsburgh Press, 1972), pp. 32–34.

[76] Thomas M. Bohn, "Bulgariens Rolle im 'wirtschaftlichen Ergänzungsraum' Südosteuropa: Hintergründe für den Beitritt zum Dreimächtepakt am 1. März 1941," in *Besatzung und Bündnis: Deutsche Herrschaftsstrategien in Ost- und Südosteuropa (Beiträge zur nationalsozialistischen Gesundheits- und Sozialpolitik: 12)* (Berlin: Verlag der Buchläden, 1995), pp. 115–17.

[77] David Fraser, "National Constitutions, Liberal State, Fascist State and the Holocaust in Belgium and Bulgaria," *German Law Journal*, no. 2 (February 1, 2005); one of the advisors to King Boris noted in his diary that the king preferred that Bulgarians should initiate their own law first, rather than let the Germans dictate a harsher one; see F. B. Chary, *The Bulgarian Jews*, p. 37; R. Hilberg, *Die Vernichtung*, p. 798.

The German Foreign Office had only limited means to influence Bulgaria's domestic politics, and despite the appointment of a "Germanophile" prime minister, Bogdan Filov in 1940, the country demonstrated its continuing sovereignty by refusing to join Hitler's war against the Soviet Union in 1941.[78] Nevertheless, both sides viewed the anti-Jewish law as a concession to Hitler's "New Order," even if this did not prevent Bulgarian politicians from pursuing their own agendas and interests through its implementation.

The law's extensive provisions barred Jews from citizenship, public office, army service, activity in the media, intermarriage, and the employment of non-Jewish domestic servants. These provisions imposed severe restrictions on property ownership; Jewish participation in commerce, industry, the professions, and education was officially limited to their ratio within the general population (Bulgaria's 50,000 or so Jews represented only 1 percent of the total population). Forced labor was introduced for Jewish men, and Jews were required to register their property. All Jewish assets and the proceeds from liquidations were to be deposited with the Bulgarian National Bank, and Jews who did not comply and wished to leave the country would be refused the necessary travel documents.[79]

Once the terms of the law became known, protests were registered from the Holy Synod of the Bulgarian Church, the Executive Council of Bulgarian Doctors, and also the Union of Bulgarian Lawyers, which claimed that it would undermine the constitution. Yet, right-wing organizations and some business groups were among those who supported the bill, which became law on January 21, 1941.[80] The Law for the Defense of the Nation set the initial framework for Bulgarian anti-Jewish policy, but the government still had to pass a series of subsequent decrees to specify how it would be implemented.

In practice, a number of exceptions were permitted. About 1,000 Jews (along with their families) were granted exemptions as decorated war veterans, military volunteers, or war orphans. The effect of the Numerus Clausus regulations was weakened as they were applied according to the percentage of Jews living in a particular town and exempted Jews did not count against the quotas. Of more than 4,000 Jews active in commerce in the 1920s, only 505 were permitted to continue in business under the initial law. However, this quota was then increased to 761 by a revised law in 1942, only to be

---

[78] T. M. Bohn, "Bulgariens Rolle," p. 117.

[79] G. H. Haskell, *From Sofia to Jaffa*, p. 112; the "Law for the Protection of the Nation," in David Cohen, "King Boris III and the 'Final Solution,'" pp. 270–75.

[80] G. H. Haskell, *From Sofia to Jaffa*, p. 112–13; F. B. Chary, *The Bulgarian Jews*, p. 37.

reduced again in February 1943. Antisemites such as Deni Kostov accused judges and officials of profiting personally from the sale of exemptions.[81]

Taxes, Confiscations, and Imitations

In imitation of the punitive tax in the Reich after Kristallnacht, the Bulgarian government imposed a heavy tax on Jewish property in July 1941. Finance Minister Dobri Bozhilov justified the tax by claiming that it was the debt the Jews owed Bulgaria for "over sixty years of exploitation." All Jews owning more than 200,000 lewa were subject to the tax, which started at 20 percent and was increased to 25 percent for property worth more than 3 million lewa. The tax had to be paid within six months, and there were heavy penalties for noncompliance. Jews were forbidden to emigrate until the tax was paid.[82] During the 1941 fiscal year, the special tax produced state revenue of 574 million lewa, and ultimately 1.4 billion lewa were received from this source.[83]

Another law that affected Jews severely was the ban in early 1942 on owning more than one piece of real estate. Except for those defined as privileged, Jews were forbidden to own any real estate except for their home or business. The government was to reimburse Jews for property liquidated under this law, but repayment was to be spread over a long period – another version of Göring's concept of "pensioning off" the Jews to remove their influence within the economy.[84]

Commissariat for Jewish Questions (KEV)

After another visit to Berlin at the beginning of 1942, Belev proposed additional anti-Jewish measures and the centralization of authority for Jewish matters within a new government department to complete confiscation and prepare Bulgaria's Jews for deportation. The Bulgarian Commissariat for Jewish Questions (Komisarstvo za Evreiskite Vuprosi, or KEV) was established in accordance with Ministerial Decision no. 4,567 published on August 29, 1942. This granted the new commissar authority to coordinate all matters

---

[81] R. Hilberg, Die Vernichtung, p. 799; F. B. Chary, The Bulgarian Jews, pp. 42–43, 63.

[82] F. B. Chary, The Bulgarian Jews, pp. 43–44.

[83] Oberfinanzdirektion, Berlin (OFDB), Div. Ordner II (RFM Handakte Scheerans), Ref. Mädel, report on the Bulgarian state budget, January 16, 1943; Michael Bar-Zohar, Beyond Hitler's Grasp: The Heroic Rescue of Bulgaria's Jews (Holbrook, MA: Adams Media, 1998), p. 49. In light of the property confiscations and forced labor in Bulgaria, the term "rescue" has been questioned in critical scholarship.

[84] F. B. Chary, The Bulgarian Jews, p. 44.

concerning the Jews in consultation with other ministries. The same measure also altered Bulgaria's anti-Jewish laws from a religious to a racial basis, in line with German standards.[85]

A system similar to the German policy of blocking Jewish bank accounts was then introduced in Bulgaria. Jews first had to register their property with the Bulgarian National Bank, which then supervised their local accounts. In general, the Bank permitted Jews to withdraw only up to 6,000 lewa per month, with special permission required for anything more; usually, permission was granted only for the payment of taxes, necessary business transactions, or the settling of debts. According to the decree of August 1942, people who were owed money by Jews were given a deadline of two months to report this to the KEV.[86] The proceeds from the compulsory sale of shares and liquidated properties were also paid into blocked accounts. After August 1942, part of the contents of these blocked accounts (between 5 and 12 percent, depending on the amount in the account) was transferred to a "Jewish Communal Fund" intended to support needy Jews, but much disappeared into the salaries and expenses of the KEV. Decision no. 4,567 also required that Jews liquidate all insurance policies with a value in excess of 700 lewa, with the money to be paid into blocked accounts at the National Bank.[87]

Deportation of the Jews from Macedonia, Thrace, and Pirot

In July 1942, when Nazi Germany was at the zenith of its power, the Bulgarian government agreed to German demands to deport Bulgarian Jews from areas under German control, and their property was also subjected to confiscation. Then in the fall of 1942, the German Foreign Office began to pressure Bulgaria to deport all of its Jews, despite signs of local reluctance, as some members of the Bulgarian administration preferred to retain the Jews as forced laborers. At this time, the Germans also requested a fee of RM 250 per head for each Jew deported, but in November 1942, the Bulgarians replied that this price was too high, as part of the Jews' wealth was needed to

---

[85] LAB, B Rep. 039–01/318, German translation of Ministerial Decision no. 4,567 (establishing the Commissariat for Jewish Affairs) issued by the Interior Ministry and published in the *Bulgarian Official Journal* no. 192, August 29, 1942. I am grateful to Götz Aly for bringing this document to my attention; ibid., pp. 52–53.

[86] LAB, B Rep. 039–01/318, German translation of Ministerial Decision no. 4,567; OFDB, Div. Ordner II (RFM Handakte Scheerans), Bericht des Auswärtigen Amtes aus Sofia, September 4, 1942; Vicki Tamir, *Bulgaria and Her Jews: The History of a Dubious Symbiosis* (New York: Yeshiva University Press, 1979), p. 173.

[87] LAB, B Rep. 039–01/318, Ministerial Decision No. 4,567.

aid Bulgaria's economy.[88] At the beginning of 1943, SS-Hauptsturmführer Theodor Dannecker of the RSHA arrived in Sofia with the intention of deporting as many Jews as possible from the country. He received the assent of Commissar Belev for the deportation of 20,000 Jews from Macedonia, Thrace, and Pirot on February 22, 1943.[89]

In April 1941, Bulgaria had been rewarded by Germany with the annexation of Macedonia and Thrace from Yugoslavia and Greece, for having granted the Wehrmacht access for its military operations there one month earlier.[90] In these territories, the same anti-Jewish measures were then applied as in the rest of Bulgaria. Before their deportation, the Jews of the newly annexed territories were ghettoized, and the Bulgarian authorities confiscated most of their remaining possessions. The Jews were permitted to take only 45 kilograms of personal property each into the local concentration camps. The deportees were carefully searched for any valuables before departure, and their abandoned homes were sealed.[91] In March 1943, 11,235 Jews were deported to Nazi death camps in occupied Poland from Macedonia and Thrace.[92]

One estimate of Jewish property in Thrace and Macedonia puts its value at about 1.5 billion lewa,[93] all now subject to confiscation. First, government agencies received the opportunity to buy movable property at fixed prices, with the remainder then to be auctioned to the public. Dr. Ivan Popov, who visited Macedonia and Thrace after the deportations to investigate the liquidation of Jewish property, reported a variety of abuses. For example, military and police officials sometimes acted as middlemen, skimming off a personal profit. Government offices were buying items such as pianos or sewing machines for "official use." Many items were simply looted, and Popov criticized the lack of proper inventories and the slow progress of liquidations. The sums realized were well below expectations, even allowing for the reduced prices of most sales. According to Frederick

---

[88] LAB, B Rep. 039–01/319, Note of L. R. Wagner on the Jewish Question in Bulgaria, April 3, 1943; F. B. Chary, *The Bulgarian Jews*, pp. 69–76. This issue was unresolved at the time of the deportations, and it appears that subsequently no payments were made; see also *Akten zur Deutschen Auswärtigen Politik, Serie E: 1941–45* (Göttingen: Vandenhoeck & Ruprecht, 1975), vol. IV, pp. 329–31.

[89] R. Hilberg, *Die Vernichtung*, pp. 806–807.

[90] Ibid., p. 794.

[91] LAB, B Rep. 039–01/319, Report of German General Consulate in Skopje, March 18, 1943.

[92] F. B. Chary, *The Bulgarian Jews*, p. 127. These figures do not include 158 Jews deported from the region of Pirot that was also annexed from Serbia in 1941.

[93] F. B. Chary, *The Bulgarian Jews*, pp. 62–63.

Chary, the liquidations produced only 56.5 million lewa, a small fraction of the estimated total value, although this does not include valuables removed from the deportees' persons.[94]

Forced Labor, Ghettoization, and the Cessation of the Deportations

Following the enactment of the Law for the Defense of the Nation in early 1941, Bulgarian Jewish men were conscripted into labor battalions under the Ministry of Public Works and engaged mainly in road and railway construction projects.[95] In August 1941 – partly due to German pressure – they were separated into a special Jewish Labor Service, and by February 1943 the number of Jews performing forced labor in these units had risen to about 10,000.[96] From August 1942 on, Jews were compelled to wear the yellow star, and Jewish homes and businesses were marked. Jews were permitted to shop for only one hour each day, after most products had usually sold out. Ministerial Decision no. 4,567 even regulated precisely how much living space Jews were allowed, with at least two persons to share each room.[97]

Shortly after the establishment of the KEV, on October 20, 1942, the creation of a ghetto for Sofia was decreed, and preparations were made for establishing ghettos in at least ten other cities, including Varna, Ruse, Dupnitsa, Pleven, Plovdiv, and Vratsa.[98] As in occupied Poland and the Soviet Union, Jews living outside the designated ghetto area had to abandon their homes and most of their furniture on moving into the Sofia ghetto. As these displacements were intended to be only temporary, in preparation for subsequent deportation, conditions in the Bulgarian ghettos were poor. Jews suffered from overcrowding and shortages of food so that many relied on support provided by communal soup kitchens. The KEV remained reluctant to release money from the Jewish Communal Fund for their relief.[99]

---

[94] Ibid., pp. 112–14, 124–28.

[95] I am grateful to Steven Sage for sharing with me his unpublished paper "Jewish Ghettos in Axis Bulgaria, 1942–44," arising mainly from his work for the Conference on Jewish Material Claims against Germany and as a fellow at the United States Holocaust Memorial Museum's Center for Advanced Holocaust Studies.

[96] Vladimir Paounovski and Yosef Ilel, *The Jews in Bulgaria between the Holocaust and the Rescue* (Sofia: Adas, 2000), p. 99; R. Hilberg, *Die Vernichtung*, pp. 800–801.

[97] G. H. Haskell, *From Sofia to Jaffa*, p. 113; LAB, B Rep. 039–01/318, Ministerial Decision No. 4.567; R. Hilberg, *Die Vernichtung*, p. 803.

[98] According to Steven Sage's unpublished work "Jewish Ghettos," p. 2, the archival reference for this information is USHMM, RG-46, Acc.1997.A.0333, reel 299.

[99] S. Sage, "Jewish Ghettos," pp. 3–6.

German plans to deport the Jews from Bulgaria's core territories had advanced to the point of implementation by early 1943. The story of how the deportations were stopped on two separate occasions is well known and demonstrates Bulgarian sovereignty in its Jewish policy and reflects positively on the consciences of some Bulgarian individuals. However, the recent German defeats in the Soviet Union and growing Allied pressure on Bulgaria should also be kept in mind. Although the Bulgarian Jews were spared from deportation to German death camps in spring 1943, they nonetheless suffered severe persecution and considerable disruption to their lives.[100]

In May 1943, despite public protests involving non-Jews, most of the Jews were expelled from Sofia to other towns. On learning of their imminent expulsion, Jews tried to sell their possessions or gave them to friends for safekeeping to avoid confiscation. Peasants from the surrounding villages returned from the Jewish quarter with carts loaded with furniture, clothes, and kitchen utensils they had purchased for pennies.[101] In the wake of these successive displacements, the KEV confiscated remaining Jewish property. It liquidated all prohibited Jewish enterprises as well as some permitted businesses belonging to Jews who had also been expelled. The KEV admonished its officials to maintain the value of the properties it administered, but as Chary notes there was widespread graft, including within the Commissariat: Belev himself was allegedly involved in the misappropriation of funds from the expropriation of Jewish banks, according to testimony in postwar legal proceedings.[102]

Restitution Legislation, Jewish Emigration, and Renewed Expropriation

In November 1943, a new cabinet was formed under Dobri Bozhilov, and it started to repeal some of Bulgaria's anti-Jewish legislation. From this time, Jews no longer required official approval to sell items worth more than 10,000 lewa. In addition, the remaining Jewish property at the Commissariat for Jewish Affairs was to be sold off for the benefit of the Jewish community.[103] However, the Bulgarian government did not repeal its remaining anti-Jewish measures until the eve of Soviet occupation in

---

[100] F. B. Chary, *The Bulgarian Jews*, pp. 129–56.

[101] M. Bar-Zohar, *Beyond Hitler's Grasp*, p. 187; V. Paounovski and Y. Ilel, *The Jews in Bulgaria*, p. 193.

[102] F. B. Chary, *The Bulgarian Jews*, pp. 66–67.

[103] OFDB, Div. Ordner II (RFM Handakte Scheerans), pp. 409–19, report of German Foreign Office on Jewish measures in Bulgaria, November 18, 1943.

August 1944.[104] In early 1945, before the end of the war, the new communist Bulgarian authorities organized a major trial of Bulgarian wartime officials implicated in the main anti-Jewish measures. Of more than sixty people indicted, however, the majority were acquitted, wheras others received only lenient sentences, contrary to the practice in most Eastern European war crimes trials.[105]

On March 2, 1945, the government passed a Law of Restitution providing for the return of Jewish property. But because the new communist regime intended to abolish most private property, very little was actually restituted – perhaps 126 million of 4.5 billion lewa, a sum whose value was further undermined by inflation after the war. Their wartime experiences and postwar poverty encouraged almost 90 percent of Bulgarian Jews to migrate mainly to Israel by the end of 1949, leaving nearly all of their property behind to be nationalized by the communist regime. Bulgarian Jews who remained suffered from the slow and limited restitution of property, communist policies of nationalization, and difficulties exporting what they had, although there was nothing overtly anti-Jewish about the policies of the communists.[106]

Because Germany did not occupy Bulgaria, this country's experience is a clear example of a sovereign state adopting similar policies, albeit under considerable German pressure. Bulgaria not only confiscated Jewish property extensively but also prohibited emigration unless Jews had paid the special tax on all Jewish property.[107] Given the different ideological rationales and orientations, Bulgaria experienced a strange continuity between wartime expropriation under a right-wing regime and the de facto expropriation by the communists after the war.

Hungary

In view of the limited German manpower deployed in Hungary, the intact local Hungarian bureaucracy played a major role in the wholesale

---

[104] R. Hilberg, *Die Vernichtung*, pp. 800–10; F. B. Chary, *The Bulgarian Jews*, pp. 43–68.

[105] Presentation by Steven Sage entitled "HC VII: The Sofia Trials of March 1945," given at the United States Holocaust Memorial Museum's Center for Advanced Holocaust Studies Summer Workshop, "War Crimes Trials in the Soviet Union and Eastern Europe," June 2005.

[106] Congressional Research Service, draft papers prepared in 1999 on confiscation and restitution in European countries, here Bulgaria; G. H. Haskell, *From Sofia to Jaffa*, pp. 118–25.

[107] B. Chary, *The Bulgarian Jews*, p. 44.

expropriation of Jewish property in the summer of 1944. Götz Aly and Christian Gerlach draw attention to the Hungarian government's exploitation of Jewish property to mobilize support for the war and to reward specific groups within society through redistribution of the loot. These policies were also beneficial to German economic aims by helping contain Hungarian inflation and thereby enabling the Hungarian government to continue financing the war and meet the heavy burden of occupation costs demanded by the Reich.[108] However, these outcomes should be seen less as a carefully engineered result sought by German financial bureaucrats than the product of conflicting interests, as the Hungarians considered Jewish property an integral part of the national patrimony.

Antisemitic Legislation and Confiscation Policies before 1944

The seizure of Jewish property in Hungary was of considerable economic significance to the country. Jews comprised about 5 percent of the population, and 20 percent in Budapest. They were well represented in commerce and the liberal professions, although there were many impoverished Jews and poor Jewish artisans as well.[109] The total amount of Jewish wealth as of 1941 has been estimated in the range of seven to twelve billion pengős. According to one estimate, Jewish income in 1930–31 comprised about one-quarter of the nation's total income.[110]

In the 1930s, there was bureaucratic antisemitism in Hungary, exhibited in the stringent enforcement of regulations against Jewish shops. The chambers of commerce and professional organizations demanded the imposition of Jewish quotas in the economy.[111] In May 1938, Prime Minister Kálmán Darányi introduced legislation aimed at reducing the proportion of Jews in

---

[108] Christian Gerlach and Götz Aly, *Das letzte Kapitel: Der Mord an den ungarischen Juden* (Stuttgart: DVA, 2002), p. 188.

[109] Fifty percent of doctors and lawyers were Jewish, and more than 40 percent of businesses were owned by Jews, although most were small family businesses. Some of Hungary's most successful Jews in manufacturing and banking were well assimilated, and the Jewish community included many converts. See Randolph L. Braham, *The Politics of Genocide: The Holocaust in Hungary* 2 vols. (New York: Columbia University Press, 1993), vol. I, pp. 80–81. See also the figures published in Gábor Kádár and Zoltán Vági, *Self-Financing Genocide: The Gold Train, the Becher Case and the Wealth of Hungarian Jews* (Budapest: Central European University Press, 2004), pp. 10–22.

[110] G. Kádár and Z. Vági, *Self-Financing Genocide*, p. 25; Ronald W. Zweig, *The Gold Train: The Destruction of the Jews and the Looting of Hungary* (New York: Morrow, 2002), p. 60.

[111] G. Kádár and Z. Vági, *Self-Financing Genocide*, pp. 42–44.

the professions and industry to 20 percent. This law received endorsements from Hungarian church leaders.[112]

Prewar Hungarian measures were clearly influenced by anti-Jewish legislation in Nazi Germany and Fascist Italy. In January 1939, the Hungarian government agreed to assist Germany with the emigration of about 10,000 Hungarian Jews from the Reich, provided that their wealth was secured in a trustee account. The Germans were quite interested in Hungarian cooperation, as it would provide international legitimization for their antisemitic measures.[113] Under Prime Minister Béla Imrédy (1938–39), the liquor industry was nationalized, which mostly affected Jewish-owned factories. Compensation was paid partly in government bonds set to mature in twenty-five years and offering only 3.5 percent interest,[114] setting a precedent for subsequent anti-Jewish expropriations.[115]

The Second Anti-Jewish Law, passed by the government of Prime Minister Count Pál Teleki in May 1939, sought to reduce the number of Jewish businesses in each branch of industry to 6 percent and in commerce to 12 percent by progressively withdrawing their licenses. Other provisions restored the Numerus Clausus of 6 percent for institutions of higher learning, established a legal definition of who was Jewish based on religious grounds, and excluded Jews from working in government positions or leading positions in the media.[116] It has been estimated that approximately 40,000 Jews lost their employment as a result of this law. The Second Anti-Jewish Law also restricted the ability of Jews to take their property with them on emigration.[117]

---

[112] R. L. Braham, *The Politics of Genocide*, vol. I, pp. 121–30; Yehuda Don, "Economic Implications of the Anti-Jewish Legislation in Hungary" in David Cesarani (ed.), *Genocide and Rescue: The Holocaust in Hungary 1944* (Oxford: Berg, 1997), pp. 49–54. Don estimates that about 16 percent of economically active Jews in Budapest would have been laid off if the law had been fully implemented, which, however, was not the case.

[113] Nbg. Doc., NG-1533, Woermann note, January 5, 1939.

[114] G. Kádár and Z. Vági, *Self-Financing Genocide*, pp. 42–44.

[115] Albert Turvölgyi, in charge of Aryanization in the liquor industry, was subsequently appointed as government commissioner concerning the material and financial affairs of the Jews in the summer of 1944; see Gábor Kádár and Zoltán Vági, "The Economic Annihilation of the Hungarian Jews, 1944–1945," in Randolph L. Braham and Brewster S. Chamberlin (eds.), *The Holocaust in Hungary: Sixty Years Later* (Boulder, CO: Rosenthal Institute for Holocaust Studies, Graduate Center of City University of New York Social Science Monographs, published in association with the United States Holocaust Memorial Museum, 2006), pp. 77–88.

[116] R. L. Braham, *The Politics of Genocide*, vol. I, pp. 144–60.

[117] G. Kádár and Z. Vági, *Self-Financing Genocide*, pp. 59–61.

Because the Jews in Hungary constituted a considerable part of the middle class, the various governments of Regent Miklós Horthy were careful not to move too quickly against Jewish property. In October 1940, Horthy wrote to Prime Minister Teleki that he had been an antisemite all his life and that the sight of each and every factory, bank, or business in Jewish hands was "unbearable" to him, but he feared that handing them over quickly to "incompetent boasters" would only bankrupt the country.[118] Nonetheless, by January 1943, Jews had been completely excluded from many branches of Hungarian industry, including the cattle trade, the export of fruit, wholesale dealing in leather, sugar, cattle feed, and Christian religious items, as well as restaurants and the cement trade.[119] Some Jews attempted to get around the regulations by transferring companies nominally to "frontmen" (*Aladár,* in Hungarian), but often such transactions were denounced to the authorities.[120]

By fall 1941, many male Hungarian Jews were being forced to serve in Labor Battalions on the Eastern Front, where their status as Jews was distinguished by special armbands. By 1942, more than 50,000 Jews were serving in these units behind the German frontline. They suffered from inadequate supplies and clothing, as well as arbitrary abuse by their Christian commanders, which sometimes resulted in death by shooting, beatings, or other cruelties. After the defeat of Hungarian forces on the River Don in early 1943, about 10,000 Jews were captured by the Red Army, and about 15,000 others are believed to have lost their lives while serving in the occupied Soviet Union.[121]

In 1942, the ongoing expropriation of Jewish agricultural land was accelerated by a new law, promulgated in September, that provided for compensation in the form only of government bonds (paying 3.5 percent interest) that could not be sold on the open market. Up to 1942, some 450,000 hectares of farmland and forest had been expropriated, and a further 150,000 were confiscated by the Ministry of Agriculture and Food Supplies in early summer 1944. Some of the smaller agricultural plots were held back for men fighting at the front.[122] During 1941–42, antisemitic propagandists such as Zoltán Bosnyák advocated the expropriation of all "Jewish" businesses

---

[118] R. Hilberg, *Die Vernichtung*, p. 866.

[119] Ibid., pp. 868–69.

[120] G. Kádár and Z. Vági, *Self-Financing Genocide*, p. 63.

[121] H. Safrian, *Eichmann*, p. 294; C. Gerlach and G. Aly, *Das letzte Kapitel*, pp. 77–78.

[122] G. Kádár and Z. Vági, *Self-Financing Genocide*, pp. 64–65; T. Tönsmeyer, "Der Raub des jüdischen Eigentums," pp. 75–76; C. Gerlach and G. Aly, *Das letzte Kapitel*, p. 69; R. W. Zweig, *The Gold Train*, pp. 35–36, argues that Prime Minister Miklós Kállay supported this law as part of a deal to protect the Jews from deportation in return for expropriation

employing more than one hundred persons. This initiative was to be part of the surgical removal of the Jews from the economy in preparation for their anticipated forced emigration and as part of a Europe-wide solution to the "Jewish Problem." Finance Minster Lajos Reményi-Schneller stated during this period that he would prepare a detailed plan for the "liquidation of Jewish capital" before the departure of the Jews from Hungary, which he expected to follow shortly.[123]

Property Registration and Confiscation in Summer 1944

Comprehensive measures against Jewish property were, nonetheless, not taken in Hungary until the German occupation starting on March 19, 1944. The newly installed pro-German government of Döme Sztójay soon embraced plans for the rapid "solution of the Jewish problem." The German army and SS special units under Adolf Eichmann's supervision entered Budapest and immediately began requisitioning apartments and houses belonging to Jews. The Germans rushed to secure certain key prizes from among Jewish assets, and Eichmann's subordinates Dieter Wisliceny and Hermann Krumey presented many demands directly to the newly formed Jewish Council. In the second half of March, SS special units arrested more than 3,300 Jews in Hungary, including Ferenc Chorin, one of the joint owners of the Manfred Weiss armaments company, and exploited them for blackmail purposes; the Germans released about forty members of the owners' families to neutral countries in return for a controlling interest in the Manfred Weiss Corporation.[124] Subsequently, the SS extorted additional sums in local currency, foreign exchange, jewelry, and diamonds from Jewish leaders in various "rescue" schemes.[125]

At the end of March, the Sztójay government began issuing a series of anti-Jewish decrees; the previous anti-Jewish laws were now enforced more rigorously, and initiatives proposing additional restrictive measures came from the regional authorities and the general public.[126] A new law on

---

of part of their property as "a contribution to the national war effort." This would be reminiscent of policies pursued in Bulgaria and Romania.

[123] G. Kádár and Z. Vági, *Self-Financing Genocide*, pp. 66–69.

[124] H. Safrian, *Eichmann*, p. 297–98; R. W. Zweig, *The Gold Train*, p. 49; R. Hilberg, *Die Vernichtung*, pp. 892–93.

[125] R. L. Braham, *The Politics of Genocide*, vol. I, pp. 544–45; see also Yehuda Bauer, *Jews for Sale? Nazi-Jewish Negotiations, 1933–1945* (New Haven: Yale University Press, 1994), p. 163.

[126] Tim Cole, "Hungary, the Holocaust, and Hungarians: Remembering Whose History?" in *Hungary and the Holocaust: Confrontation with the Past: Symposium Proceedings* (Washington, DC: United States Holocaust Memorial Museum, 2001), pp. 1–10.

April 1, 1944, forbade Jews from selling real estate. On April 5, compulsory wearing of the Jewish star was introduced.[127]

These new regulations accompanied the blocking of all bank accounts in Hungary (similar to German measures in the Protectorate of Bohemia and Moravia) as a temporary measure "to stabilize the currency." However, in accordance with Decree no. 1600 of April 16, 1944, requiring the registration of Jewish property, Jewish bank accounts and safe-deposit boxes remained blocked, whereas the restrictions for non-Jews were lifted. For their personal use, Jews were permitted to withdraw only 1,000 pengös per month. Sums over this amount could be released only to cover outstanding utility bills, taxes, and rent. The same decree ordered all precious metals, jewelry, valuable artworks, and foreign currency to be surrendered to the authorities. To prevent Jews from giving property to friends for safekeeping, all transfers of money, securities, or valuables after March 22, 1944, were deemed invalid. A property tax in the form of a "war contribution" was applied to all Hungarian Jews owning more than 10,000 pengös in property. During April, Jews waited in long lines outside offices of the Royal Hungarian Postal Savings Bank to surrender their possessions. The Postal Savings Bank even issued detailed receipts, fostering the illusion that one day the Jews might receive their property back.[128]

The effects of these measures are described in an unnamed author's report given to Jean de Bavier representing the International Committee of the Red Cross in Budapest: "Jewish assets have been sequestrated: out of their bank accounts or deposits – if they have any – Jews are allowed to draw only 1,000 pengös per head per month; any income they may have, any they may recover, must be paid into their blocked accounts. No Jew is allowed to have more than 3,000 pengös in cash."[129]

On April 21, the government ordered the dismissal of Jewish employees from the economy and the immediate closing of all Jewish businesses and shops. This decree created considerable chaos in Budapest, where 18,000 Jewish-owned shops of 30,000 in total were required to close. The authorities appointed trustees to run those businesses considered essential for maintaining supplies to the population. These enterprises were eventually to be "Magyarized," with some reserved for soldiers returning from the front. The government portrayed the measure as necessary to reduce the "excessive" number of shops in the economy. In many areas, numerous applicants

---

[127] C. Gerlach and G. Aly, *Das letzte Kapitel*, p. 191.

[128] Ibid.; G. Kádár and Z. Vági, *Self-Financing Genocide*, p. 79.

[129] Quoted in Arieh Ben-Tov, *Facing the Holocaust in Budapest: The International Committee of the Red Cross and the Jews in Hungary, 1943–1945* (Boston: M. Nijhoff, 1988), p. 127, unsigned report dated Budapest, May 13, 1944.

competed to take over Jewish shops and businesses. For example, in Koloszvár (Cluj) there were 1,500 potential buyers for 400 businesses. The government ordered that the stock market be cleared of all Jewish traders by May 31, 1944; only 440 of the original 1,345 members of the stock exchange remained. As a result of these measures, the value of more than half of the 100 companies listed in Hungary fell by nearly 50 percent.[130]

The improvised ghettoization of the Jews in Hungary during April and May 1944 – in practice, only a temporary interlude prior to deportation – was primarily a socioeconomic measure. Tim Cole argues that the intent to deport most of Hungary's Jews cannot be read into the Hungarian ghettoization order drafted on April 7, 1944, which speaks only of putting Jews into "pre-arranged assembly centers." Rather, the aim in early April was to establish "Jewish" buildings or ghettos within towns, but first the Jews had to be moved into temporary camps to free up accommodations so that the Hungarians displaced by ghettoization had a place into which they could move. This process provided the opportunity for a general appropriation of household property, as Jews were permitted to take only 50 kilograms of luggage with them. The authorities sealed Jewish homes and businesses and seized any food or livestock, ostensibly to meet the needs of the army, the security organs, and the local population. During a similar displacement of Jews in Budapest in early April to make way for Hungarian victims of Allied bombing, the authorities planned for the furniture to be left behind for the new tenants.[131]

On May 17, Interior Minister Andor Jaross exalted in the fact that "all assets, wealth, and valuables that Jewish greed was able to amass during the liberal era no longer belong to them – it is now the property of the Hungarian nation."[132] A bill proposed in May by Minister of Justice István Antal envisaged the use of Jewish assets "to cover military expenditures and to revitalize the Hungarian economy by issuing long-term government bonds," with any remaining funds to provide Jews with a minimal subsistence before "financing their eventual expatriation."[133] The Hungarians imitated many of the methods developed by the Germans, but implemented them solely to advance their own view of the Hungarian national interest.

---

[130] C. Gerlach and G. Aly, *Das letzte Kapitel*, pp. 191–93.

[131] Tim Cole, *Holocaust City: The Making of a Jewish Ghetto* (New York: Routledge, 2003), pp. 76–83.

[132] G. Kádár and Z. Vági, "The Economic Annihilation of the Hungarian Jews, 1944–1945," pp. 77–88.

[133] Ibid.

Seizure of Jewish Property during the Deportations and the Division of the Spoils

Assisted by the Hungarian gendarmerie and local administration, the Germans deported about 437,000 Jews from Hungarian territory between the end of April and July 9, 1944.[134] As the Hungarian security forces rapidly concentrated the Jews in the regions prior to deportation, they also robbed them of any remaining valuables. In many places, the Jewish community was forced to cover the costs of ghettoization.[135] The deserted homes of the Jews were often plundered, even after they had been sealed. At the same time as the Jews were concentrated into makeshift ghettos, the Hungarian gendarmerie conducted brutal interrogations in an effort to reveal suspected hidden valuables. They also searched the deportees before their departure, not wanting any property to fall into German hands.[136]

The official sale of confiscated Jewish property in Hungary was not initiated until June 1944. Significantly, the pastoral letter drafted by Jusytinián Györg Cardinal Seredi and other clerics at the end of June protesting the deportations stated explicitly that it had no objection to the measures of state financial policy taken, which would lead to a legal and just resolution of the "Jewish Question."[137] On July 19, 1944, in response to widespread allegations of corruption and misappropriation, Finance Minister Lajos Reményi-Schneller insisted that "Jewish property is to be secured in the interest of the public. Its sale should be directed toward helping the needy and strengthening economic production."[138] One German commander, reporting on conditions close to the approaching front, noted that "after the deportation of the Jews the people are interested only in the distribution of their property.... but, often the high expectations are disappointed; not rare, however, are decisions that cannot stand close examination with regard to social fairness."[139] These comments reflect the concerns of the Hungarian authorities to meet popular expectations for a "fair" distribution of Jewish property in the face of considerable opportunities for self-enrichment and corruption. However, the rapid pace of the deportations in Hungary left little time for the establishment of careful oversight mechanisms, such as those in France, designed to reduce corruption and wastage in the treatment of Jewish property.

---

[134] R. Hilberg, *Die Vernichtung*, pp. 901, 914–15.
[135] G. Kádár and Z. Vági, *Self-Financing Genocide*, p. 137.
[136] H. Safrian, *Eichmann*, pp. 299–300; R. L. Braham, *The Politics of Genocide*, vol. I, p. 545; R. W. Zweig, *The Gold Train*, pp. 57–59.
[137] R. Hilberg, *Die Vernichtung*, p. 903.
[138] C. Gerlach and G. Aly, *Das letzte Kapitel*, p. 232.
[139] Ibid., p. 197.

The return of some Jews granted exemptions from deportation alarmed the beneficiaries, as these people then tried to reclaim their property. Furniture and clothing confiscated from the empty apartments were generally sold off cheaply to the local population.[140] Subsequently, the bulk of Jewish property was centralized under the supervision of the Ministry of Finance. Income from the sale of Jewish property and the collection of debts owed to Jews was concentrated in an account at the Royal Hungarian Postal Savings Bank, and part of it was used to cover the costs of deportation.

On October 16, 1944, a new and more extremist Arrow Cross regime under Ferenc Szálasi came to power. According to a decree issued on November 3, Jewish property was "to be regarded as national wealth transferred to the state. This wealth shall be used to cover the costs of war, war damages, and the implementation of the laws concerning the Jews."[141]

As the Red Army's advance continued in the fall of 1944, the Szálasi government supported German plans to strip Hungary of its remaining resources, in an effort to deny them to the Soviets and to support the German war effort. Every day, several trains loaded with goods departed Hungary for the Reich. Szálasi appointed Árpád Toldy as "Commissar for Jewish Affairs," and Toldy ordered most of the surrendered or confiscated Jewish valuables to be concentrated at several collection points in western Hungary. There, officials sorted the booty into different categories, ranging from cameras and Persian carpets to used silverware and stamp collections. The bulk of the property was then put on trains that crossed the border in the direction of Austria at the end of March 1945, where it ultimately fell into American hands. Some of the property was ultimately sold in New York for the benefit of Jewish displaced persons. However, Ronald Zweig's detailed research in French archives reveals that up to two tons of the most valuable items were taken by Toldy in trucks toward Switzerland. Part of this loot was buried in Austria or paid to Nazi functionaries during the last days of the war, but a large amount came into the possession of the French occupation authorities in Austria. Subsequently the French government returned more than 1,750 kilograms of gold, diamonds, and jewelry to the Hungarian authorities in 1948, with the stipulation that it be returned to the Jewish community in Hungary.[142]

---

[140] Ibid., p. 198.

[141] G. Kádár and Z. Vági, *Self-Financing Genocide*, p. 136; C. Gerlach and G. Aly, *Das letzte Kapitel*, pp. 232–34. At the time of the occupation of Hungary by the Red Army, there were 205 million pengös in account no. 157,880 at the Royal Hungarian Postal Savings Bank.

[142] Ronald W. Zweig, "Der ungarische Goldzug oder Der Mythos vom jüdischen Reichtum," in Constantin Goschler and Philipp Ther (eds.), *Raub und Restitution: "Arisierung"*

Assessment of the Confiscation of Jewish Property in Hungary

In Hungary, national decrees and bureaucratic measures progressed rapidly from the blocking of bank accounts to outright confiscation in lockstep with the deportations. There was a greater degree of direct German supervision than in Bulgaria or Romania, but the comprehensive confiscation measures were implemented by an existing Hungarian administration that easily could have sabotaged German plans had they wanted to do so. The active participation of the Hungarian administration in the expropriation of the Jews displayed considerable autonomy even under German occupation, a fact confirmed by Regent Horthy's July 1944 decision to stop the deportations, preserving much of Budapest's large Jewish community.[143]

The Germans did not benefit much directly from Jewish property confiscated in Hungary; its processing was left almost exclusively to the Hungarians. However, the Reich benefited indirectly from the net effects of meeting the demand for consumer goods, dampening inflation, and improving Hungarian revenues. The corresponding boost to the ailing Hungarian currency facilitated the continued payment of massive German "occupation costs." Broad sectors of Hungarian society were able at low prices to acquire Jewish property, very little of which was ever restituted.[144]

The recent research of Gábor Kádár and others reveals that in practice confiscation in Hungary was not a straightforward administrative process. Initiated in a rather haphazard fashion, it soon became a competition among private looters, various state agencies, and also the Germans to secure what they could under the chaotic conditions of rapid ghettoization. Central directives on how to administer and sell off Jewish property were issued only after ghettoization had already begun in the provinces. Many Jews were unable to comply with regulations on the registration and surrender

---

und Rückerstattung des jüdischen Eigentums in Europa (Frankfurt am Main: Fischer Taschenbuch, 2003), pp. 171–75. Zweig gives the value of items from the Hungarian Jews sold in New York at roughly U.S. $2 million. In a somewhat conflicting account, Kádár and Vági give a figure roughly twice this for the items sold in New York (although not all were from the so-called Gold Train) and draw attention to a variety of items misappropriated or sent to other destinations by U.S. officials rather than being restituted to Hungary. They estimate the value of the contents of the train in 1945 U.S. dollars at $6,508,336, but this is based on estimates of the weight of items packed in Hungary, rather than on records of what was placed into U.S. hands. In 2005 a U.S. court made a settlement of $25.5 million in favor of Jewish Hungarian victims of Nazism and their heirs, to be provided mainly in the form of social benefits rather than payments for specific property lost; G. Kádár and Z. Vági, *Self-Financing Genocide*, pp. 302–70.

[143] T. Tönsmeyer, "Der Raub des jüdischen Eigentums," p. 82.

[144] C. Gerlach and G. Aly, *Das letzte Kapitel*, pp. 229–30, 238–39.

of property for this reason.[145] This experience contrasts with the more careful preparation and better camouflaged measures, for instance, in the Netherlands. In Hungary, pressure from below interacted with and served to accelerate government intervention and regulation, partly to ensure a fair distribution, and partly to safeguard the interests of the state.

Italy: The Fascist Racial Laws and the Confiscations under German Occupation

The Racial Laws enacted by Mussolini's Fascist government on November 17, 1938, banned Jews from employment in the public sector and the military and ordered their dismissal from positions in banks of "national interest," private insurance companies, and the Fascist Party.[146] They were prohibited from owning land, factories, or businesses above a certain value, as well as enterprises related to national defense. The immediate effect was the loss of employment by hundreds of Jews. The expropriation regulations were enforced quite rigorously by the courts, with some regional exceptions. Subsequent decrees issued over the following months banned Jews (except within their own community) from work as architects, lawyers, judges, physicians, and mathematicians. In 1939, the Fascist government established a new Authority for the Management and Liquidation of Real Estate (*Ente di Gestione e Liquidazione Immobiliare*), which up until September 1943 seized and managed more than 400 properties.[147] However, in a number of categories it was possible to obtain exemptions, including for war veterans or Jews who had been members of the Fascist Party. In the insurance industry, for example, several Jews continued to play a significant role during the war.[148] In October 1942, the German Foreign Office

---

[145] G. Kádár and Z. Vági, "The Economic Annihilation of the Hungarian Jews, 1944–1945," pp. 77–88.

[146] See Decree Law no. 1,728 of November 17, 1938.

[147] Ilaria Pavan, "Indifferenz und Vergessen: Juden in Italien in der Kriegs- und Nachkriegszeit (1938–1970)," in Constantin Goschler and Philipp Ther (eds.), *Raub und Restitution*, pp. 155–56.

[148] Susan Zuccotti, *Under His Very Windows: The Vatican and the Holocaust in Italy* (New Haven: Yale University Press, 2000), pp. 43–44; Gerald D. Feldman, "Competition and Collaboration among the Axis Multinational Insurers: Munich Re, Generali, and Riunione Adriatica, 1933–1945," in Chris Kobrak and Per Hansen (eds.), *European Business, Dictatorship and Political Risk: 1920–1945* (New York: Berghahn, 2004), pp. 43–45.

complained that Jews remained in many key positions within the Italian economy.[149]

Following the Italian armistice with the Allies on September 8, 1943, German forces occupied the northern and central part of Italy (including Rome) and began the concentration and deportation of Jews to the death camps. In total, with the support of local Fascist organs, the Germans deported some 10,000 Italian Jews, of whom more than 8,000 perished. The round-up of Jews in Rome was preceded by the demand for fifty kilograms of gold, which was raised by the Jewish community within thirty-six hours.[150] The reconstituted Fascist regime in northern Italy (the so-called Republic of Salò) ordered, on November 30, 1943, the arrest of all Jews and the seizure of their property for the benefit of those who had suffered losses to enemy air raids.[151] This decree was superseded in January 1944 by Legislative Decree no. 2/1944, which ordered the confiscation of all Jewish property, including that previously subject to exemptions.[152] Regional offices were set up to organize the confiscations. As in other countries, there were widespread corruption, mismanagement, and theft of confiscated Jewish assets. In the period from September 1943 to the end of the war, the collaborationist Italian regime seized the property of more than 7,500 Jews.[153]

In the area around Trieste, administered directly by the Germans beginning in September 1943, SS forces under Odilo Globocnik carried out the arrest and deportation of the Jews, which was accompanied by the ruthless seizure of all Jewish property according to methods Globocnik had developed previously in the occupied East.[154] German reports from early 1945 indicate that some of the property seized from Jewish emigrants, which had become trapped in the port of Trieste by the war, was to be sent back to Vienna for sale at the Dorotheum, whereas items of jewelry with an estimated value of RM 2 million had been placed in the safe of

---

[149] *Akten zur Deutschen Auswärtigen Politik, Serie E: 1941–45* (Göttingen: Vandenhoeck & Ruprecht, 1975), vol. IV, p. 143.

[150] S. Zuccotti, *Under His Very Windows*, pp. 153–54; R. Hilberg, *Die Vernichtung*, p. 713.

[151] R. Hilberg, *Die Vernichtung*, p. 717; Presidenzia del Consiglio dei Ministri (ed.), *Rapporto Generale Allegati: Commissione per la ricostruzione delle vicende che hanno caratterizzato in Italia le attività di acquisizione dei bene cittadini ebrei dap arte di organismi pubblici e provati* (Dipartimento per l'Informazione e l'Editoria, Aprile 2001), p. 94.

[152] Liliana Picciotto Fargion, "The Anti-Jewish Policy of the Italian Social Republic (1943–1945)," *Yad Vashem Studies*, XVII (1986): 28–29.

[153] I. Pavan, "Indifferenz und Vergessen," p. 158.

[154] S. Zuccotti, *Under His Very Windows*, pp. 278–79.

the Kärntnerbank (Bank of Carinthia).[155] Even after the deportations had ceased, the systematic search for Jewish property continued until the end of the war.

Summary: Confiscation Policies of States Allied to Nazi Germany

Indigenous Roots of Economic Antisemitism

Clearly in Eastern Europe, the Nazis were not alone in seeking to exclude Jews from the economy and seize their property. Radical right-wing parties and also conservative authoritarian governments in Slovakia, Romania, Bulgaria, and Hungary (as also in Croatia) shared much of Hitler's agenda in the 1930s and early 1940s. Their confiscation of Jewish property was linked explicitly with plans for the expulsion of the Jews as part of a drive for the creation of homogeneous ethnic national states.[156] Even in countries such as Romania and Bulgaria, where the governments ultimately refused to comply with German pressure to deport the Jews from their core territories, the extensive nature of expropriation measures directed against the Jews indicates that these decisions probably were based more on timing and diplomatic calculation, rather than a sudden conversion to philosemitism.

In Hungary, anti-Jewish measures were intensified following the beginning of the German occupation in 1944, despite Germany's declining prospects in the war. Elek Karsai argues that the local authorities implemented central government decrees ahead of schedule or took even more drastic measures than required. Tim Cole supports this argument with additional evidence from May and June 1944, noting that some local initiatives actually presaged and may have prompted the central directives. In particular, Cole stresses the need to study prewar Hungarian antisemitism and public opinion during the war to better assess the significance of Hungarian initiatives "from the bottom up."[157] The eagerness and energy of the Hungarian administration in seizing Jewish property reflect in part continuity with prior independent measures to seize Jewish land in Hungary and to restrict the economic influence of the Jews.

Ladislav Lipscher demonstrates that in Slovakia nationalist calls for the expropriation of Jewish property predated the Munich agreement and any

---

[155] BAL, R 83 (Adriatisches Küstenland)/2.
[156] C. Gerlach and G. Aly, *Das letzte Kapitel*, pp. 425–29; M. Hausleitner, "Auf dem Weg zur 'Ethnokratie,'" p. 78.
[157] T. Cole, "Hungary, the Holocaust, and Hungarians," 1–7 to 1–12.

realistic prospects for establishing a Slovak state. The rapid application of Aryanization measures in Slovakia during 1941 was combined, moreover, with attempts to limit German economic penetration. A similar pattern of initiating economic measures against the Jews even before the start of the war can be found in Romania, where deep-rooted antisemitism had strong economic elements. The Antonescu regime also sought to limit the benefits flowing to indigenous ethnic Germans or to German investment while at the same time making use of German expertise and methods.

Application of German Methods

The comparison of measures applied in the states allied to Nazi Germany reveals a number of similarities but also key differences. For example, the blocking of bank accounts in order to secure Jewish property, especially proceeds from the liquidation of businesses and real estate, was common to all these Nazi allies. In Hungary and Romania, Jewish property owners were initially compensated with long-term low-interest government bonds, in imitation of Göring's original schemes for mobilizing Jewish wealth from 1938. Once secured in blocked accounts or in the form of government bonds, Jewish assets could be raided more easily by punitive taxation and ultimately subjected to outright confiscation. Confiscation usually followed the deportations, as occurred in the Reich and the Netherlands. In Slovakia and Hungary, the assets of deportees were simply declared state property. In Bulgaria and Romania, the treatment of property belonging to Jews deported from the annexed territories of Macedonia and Thrace, and the reoccupied provinces of Northern Bukovina and Bessarabia, suggests the intention to expropriate all Jewish property, had German plans for the deportation of the remaining Bulgarian and Romanian Jews not been halted.

In all four of the Eastern European countries surveyed in this chapter, the exclusion of the Jews from the economy and the confiscation of their property produced rapid impoverishment. This in turn created a serious social problem, as welfare support was cut at the same time. The German answer to this situation was forced labor and deportation. Therefore, the expropriations acted as a catalyst, transforming what had been mainly an ideological issue into the concrete problem of what to do with a Jewish minority no longer able to support itself in a period of wartime shortages.[158] Other German practices adopted by states allied to Nazi Germany included the use of Jewish property to pay the costs of administering anti-Jewish measures, the exploitation of Jewish communal leadership to assist in their

---

[158] T. Tönsmeyer, "Der Raub des jüdischen Eigentums," p. 75.

implementation, and the centralization of policies in regard to the Jews within a single coordinating authority.

A major deviation from German practices, however, was the tendency among Germany's allies to grant exemptions to the economic legislation for specific categories of Jews or to permit quotas of Jewish businesses or professions, at least until replacements could be trained. These exemptions reflected not only a pragmatic concern not to proceed too quickly with measures that might damage the economy but also reflected a weaker ideological basis than Nazi Germany's "scientific" racial *Weltanschauung*. In Italy too, numerous exemptions did not create any serious cognitive dissonance for Mussolini's regime.

The transfer of Jewish businesses into non-Jewish hands has been examined here in some detail as it demonstrates well the combination of national initiative and German know-how that characterized the treatment of Jewish property by Germany's allies. As the term "Romanianization" clearly illustrates, the aim was not only to eliminate Jewish influence from the economy but also to strengthen the Romanian element within the middle class to the exclusion of other minorities, including ethnic Germans. These aims of course, are comparable with German policies in Poland that strongly favored Reich Germans and indigenous ethnic Germans over Poles in taking over Jewish businesses. As the work of Tatjana Tönsmeyer stresses, the presence of German advisors in these Nazi-allied states represents more the transfer of know-how than any concession of national sovereignty; Germany's allies exploited its technical means in pursuit of their own self-defined national interests.

Sovereignty, Social Policy, and Postwar Continuities

Eastern Europe demonstrates vividly that legal measures for the economic exclusion and the expropriation of the Jews should not be seen only as a top-down process of government decrees aimed at restructuring the economy. The political context within which they were initiated was one of widespread anti-Jewish propaganda. Nationalist regimes denounced the Jews as a disloyal element; they accused Jews both of capitalist exploitation and sympathy for communist plans to undermine the nation from within. Popular support for the expropriation of Jewish property was mobilized under the banner of returning "ill-gotten" gains to the national patrimony as a matter of social justice.[159]

---

[159] Ibid., p. 73.

The confiscation of Jewish property in this region should be seen in part as an assertion of national sovereignty in resistance to German interference and also (as in areas under direct German control) as a reassertion of state authority in response to private looting, exploitation, and corruption. In Romania and Hungary especially, the flood of central directives and the establishment of new bureaucratic authorities came in large part as responses to the excesses and "wild looting" that accompanied rather chaotic ghettoization and deportation measures. Corruption and abuse accompanied the seizure of Jewish businesses and the administration of Jewish property in Slovakia and Bulgaria as well. Inevitably, a concern to secure the bulk of the profits for the state and to control the distribution of the benefits among specifically favored groups accompanied these large-scale transfers of wealth in wartime. Inflation and rapidly mounting state debt also provided an added incentive to seize Jewish property as a prop to ailing state finances. In addition, Jewish property created a political opportunity to shore up popular support by its redistribution at favorable prices to the majority population.

Several historians connect the expropriation of the Jews in this region to the development of "social policy." The plunder and resale of Jewish property were organized primarily by the state and produced widespread "complicity" in the anti-Jewish measures, as tens of thousands of citizens benefited.[160] As in Germany, special consideration was usually given to war veterans, the victims of bomb damage, loyal supporters of the regime, and other favored or needy groups. Under conditions of wartime shortages, there was an unseemly scramble to grab the spoils, which had both immediate and long-lasting effects on property ownership.

The seizure of Jewish property had a devastating impact on those who fled the country as well as the deportees. In Bulgaria and Romania, the antisemitic measures remained in force even after the deportations had been stopped. Despite the reversal of most anti-Jewish legislation by the end of the war, the question of Jewish property rights remained largely unresolved, as postwar communist expropriations served to consolidate the theft of Jewish property conducted during the war. Little was returned and those who left after the war could take almost nothing with them. Even in the 1990s, fears about the economic consequences of large-scale restitution blocked most efforts beyond the symbolic return of some Jewish communal property.

[160] Ibid., p. 83; C. Gerlach and G. Aly, *Das letzte Kapitel*, p. 418.

9

RECEIVING STOLEN PROPERTY: NEUTRAL STATES
AND PRIVATE COMPANIES

Which countries and companies were among the beneficiaries from the plunder of the Jews that accompanied their expulsion, deportation, and murder?[1] Cast in stark moral terms, in the late 1990s, a public debate raged about the belated compensation and restitution to victims of Nazi persecution. Swiss banks and other large international companies were denounced as having profited unscrupulously from Jewish suffering and were asked to pay their share of compensation. The focus was initially on Swiss bank accounts and the German sale of looted gold, including some stolen from Holocaust victims. It was subsequently expanded to include artworks, forced labor, insurance, and other property rights that had not been compensated or restored.

The results of this campaign have included not only a series of legal settlements and compensation funds designed to meet many of the grievances but also a considerable body of new historical research. In Nazi Germany, many businesses and individuals took advantage of the persecution of the Jews in the 1930s to acquire property for low prices. From 1939 onward, the state confiscated the bulk of remaining Jewish wealth throughout German-dominated Europe, permitting companies and individuals to buy up cheaply much of what could be resold. In addition to the high levels of corruption and outright theft involved, as Frank Bajohr notes,[2] considerable "profits from the Holocaust" were also to be made by acting as an agent for the state in implementing the confiscations, by employing forced laborers, and

---

[1] The initial draft for this chapter was presented at the German Studies Association conference in San Diego, in October 2002, and dealt primarily with the role of Switzerland.

[2] See Frank Bajohr, *Parvenüs und Profiteure: Korruption in der NS-Zeit* (Frankfurt am Main: S. Fischer, 2001).

by trading in "stolen goods." Not only Nazis reaped the benefits but also individuals and companies in all continental European countries, even many in the neutral states.

The aims of this chapter are to examine a few examples of how neutral states and private companies reaped those benefits and to reflect on how recent research has added a new perspective on the Holocaust. One key effect has been to dispel the myth that few people were aware of the fate of the Jews. The removal of the Jews from economic life required the tacit cooperation of many strata of society and directly involved bank clerks, realtors, auctioneers, lawyers, and stockbrokers, as well as policemen and tax officials. German housewives and refugees, second-hand booksellers, Bulgarian or Belorussian villagers, and the numerous victims of Allied bombing all competed for their share of the spoils at the bottom of the food chain.[3] Public auctions of former Jewish property in countries such as Norway or Belorussia, as well as the Reich, left little to the imagination concerning the origins of the items.

Switzerland and Other Neutrals

The Nazis usually selected only the most valuable items of Jewish and other looted property, such as diamonds, gold, securities, or fur coats, for sale in the neutral states. Germany needed all the foreign currency it could get to pay for strategic war materials, such as wolfram (tungsten) from the Iberian Peninsula or ball bearings from Sweden. Allied warnings about the consequences of trading with the Germans, especially in looted goods, served to reduce such trade, especially after the landings in France in June 1944. The clarity and frequency of such warnings negate the self-justifications of those who continued to deal with the Axis and clung to their ill-gotten gains after the war.

Swiss Gold Transactions

Despite the best efforts of hundreds of researchers around the world, it has not been possible to place a precise figure on the amount of "persecutee

[3] See, for example, Frank Bajohr, *"Aryanisation" in Hamburg: The Economic Exclusion of the Jews and the Confiscation of their Property in Nazi Germany* (New York: Berghahn, 2002), pp. 277–82; Martin Dean, "Die Enteignung 'jüdischen Eigentums' im Reichskommissariat Ostland 1941–1944," in Irmtrud Wojak and Peter Hayes (eds.), *"Arisierung" im National-sozialismus: Volksgemeinschaft, Raub und Gedächtnis* (Frankfurt am Main: Campus, 2000), pp. 201–18.

gold" that made its way to the vaults of the Swiss National Bank or banks in other neutral states.[4] The research of Jonathan Steinberg and others demonstrates that private banks such as the Deutsche and Dresdner Banks received victim gold from the Reichsbank and were involved in its profitable resale in neutral Turkey.[5] The proportion of "victim gold" traded internationally remained comparatively small within overall wartime gold transactions, as much of it was used domestically within the Reich.[6] However, the large-scale trading in gold looted from Europe's central banks made the handling of stolen property a major blemish on the record of the neutrals, one that has remained the subject of intense diplomatic haggling for many years after the war.[7]

Bank Accounts

The outcome of the highly expensive auditing of Swiss bank accounts, conducted in the late 1990s, has also remained somewhat unsatisfactory. Of 53,886 dormant accounts identified and publicized, only about half

[4] For a detailed summary of what we know about the transmission of gold in the Melmer shipments to the Swiss National Bank, see Independent Commission of Experts: Switzerland – Second World War (ed.), *Switzerland and Gold Transactions in the Second World War* (Bern: EDMZ, 1998), pp. 48–49; see also Commission on Jewish Assets in Sweden at the Time of the Second World War, *The Nazigold and the Swedish Riksbank: Interim Report* (Stockholm, 1998), p. 49, which is cautious with regard to putting a figure on the proportion of German Reichsbank gold plundered from individuals. Independent Commission of Experts (ICE): Switzerland – Second World War (ed.), *Switzerland, National Socialism and the Second World War: Final Report* (Zürich: Pendo, 2002), pp. 249–50, concludes that it is "impossible to determine what happened to the physical atoms of gold extracted from the victims of Nazi genocide."

[5] See Jonathan Steinberg, *The Deutsche Bank and its Gold Transactions during the Second World War* (Munich: C. H. Beck, 1999); Johannes Bähr, *Der Goldhandel der Dresdner Bank im Zweiten Weltkrieg* (Leipzig: Kiepenheuer, 1999).

[6] For example, according to the second Eizenstat report, the value of gold delivered into the Melmer account was estimated at some $4.6 million in contemporary values, whereas the Swiss Bergier Commission estimated the total amount of gold transferred through Switzerland at around $444 million: *U.S. and Allied Wartime and Postwar Relations and Negotiations with Argentina, Portugal, Spain, Sweden, and Turkey on Looted Gold and German External Assets and U.S. Concerns about the Fate of the Wartime Ustasha Treasury*, coordinated by Stuart E. Eizenstat, Under Secretary of State for Economic, Business and Agricultural Affairs (Washington, DC: Department of State, 1998), pp. iv–v. I am grateful also to Ralf Banken for his insights into the destination of much "victim gold."

[7] Ibid., p. xvi; ICE: Switzerland (ed.), *Final Report*, pp. 252–53; see also, for example, Tom Bower, *Blood Money: The Swiss, the Nazis and the Looted Billions* (London: Macmillan, 1997).

were deemed likely to be Holocaust-related.[8] Payments to claimants from the $800 million set aside for bank account holders in the Swiss bank settlement were made only slowly, and once the Swiss banks agreed to the settlement, public attention soon shifted to the U.S. court and the complex mechanism for the settlement's disbursement.[9] Evidence collected by the Volcker Commission (established to investigate the Swiss banks' role) indicates that in some four hundred documented cases Swiss banks had transferred money to the Nazi authorities (against their clients' wishes or interests). For example, in one case a Swiss bank followed instructions given by the account holder under duress while imprisoned in Germany to transfer funds to the Nazis, despite the client's previous orders to pay out only to him personally once he reached Switzerland.[10] In such cases, the Swiss financial institutions did not profit from the transfers, but nevertheless they assisted Nazi looting of Jewish property.

The Swiss banks took some comfort from the finding of the Volcker Commission's final report that there was "no evidence of...organized discrimination against the accounts of victims of Nazi persecution, or concerted efforts to divert the funds of victims of Nazi persecution to improper purposes." But the commission did claim to have found evidence of "questionable and deceitful actions" by the Swiss banks.[11] In the 1960s, for example, the Swiss government attempted to register all victims' assets, but many banks still failed to contact heirs if they were "uncertain" whether the heirs were entitled to the assets in question.[12]

Switzerland's Trade Relations with Germany

Did the Swiss willingly assist the German war economy for profit and thereby prolong the war, as the first report compiled for U.S. Under-Secretary of State Stuart Eizenstat implied?[13] Or did they have little choice

---

[8] John Authers and Richard Wolffe, *The Victim's Fortune: Inside the Epic Battle over the Debts of the Holocaust* (New York: HarperCollins, 2002), pp. 356–57.

[9] Ibid., p. 361.

[10] Independent Committee of Eminent Persons (ICEP) (ed.), *Report on Dormant Accounts of Victims of Nazi Persecution in Swiss Banks* (Bern: Staempfli, 1999), Annex 5, pp. 86–87.

[11] J. Authers and R. Wolffe, *The Victim's Fortune*, pp. 357–58.

[12] Barbara Bonhage, Hanspeter Lussy, and Marc Perrenoud, *Nachrichtenlose Vermögen bei Schweizer Banken: Depots, Konten und Safes von Opfern des nationalsozialistischen Regimes und Restitutionsprobleme in der Nachkriegszeit* (Zürich: Chronos, 2001–2), p. 3 (English summary).

[13] *U.S. and Allied Efforts to Recover and Restore Gold and Other Assets Stolen or Hidden by Germany During World War II*, Preliminary Study, coordinated by Stuart E. Eizenstat, (Washington, DC: Department of State, 1997), p. v.

but to continue trading, given the threat of German invasion and Swiss dependence on Germany as a market for exports and for vital imports? The extensive research of the Swiss Independent Commission of Experts certainly confirmed the high degree of German-Swiss cooperation in many economic fields. This cooperation must be seen, however, within the context of German encirclement up to 1944 and of longstanding German-Swiss interdependence that was likely to continue after the war. The Swiss acceptance of looted gold from Germany can be viewed as an extension of the policy granting massive wartime credits to Germany, pursued to enable trade to continue. Inevitably, such pacts with the devil have their darker sides. The question of looted gold can be understood fully only as part of the overall picture of German-Swiss trade.[14]

In response to the German threat of a trade embargo in the summer of 1940, the Swiss government agreed to deliver considerable amounts of war material to Germany – according to one telegram from the German delegation in Bern, "as much as Switzerland is able to provide." Among the items supplied were rifle ammunition and tank shells.[15] It does not appear that there was much protest on the Swiss side about this contribution to the German war effort: even the trade unions at munitions plants in Schaffhausen do not appear to have protested.[16] Historians estimate the total value of war material provided to Germany at more than one billion Swiss francs.[17]

Much of this material was paid for in credits guaranteed by the Swiss government. Eventually, all wartime Swiss credits to Germany also exceeded one billion francs or four times that provided by all other neutrals together. This large amount of credit, however, was also a lever the Swiss employed to extract trade concessions in return; for instance, obtaining strategic raw materials from Germany.[18]

Following the Allies' London Declaration of January 1943 warning against property transactions with Nazi Germany, the Swiss considerably

---

[14] See Stefan Frech, *Clearing: Der Zahlungsverkehr der Schweiz mit den Achsenmächten* (Zürich: Chronos, 2001–2).

[15] Werner Rings, *Raubgold aus Deutschland: Die "Golddrehscheibe" Schweiz im Zweiten Weltkrieg* (Munich: R. Piper, 1996), pp. 131–33.

[16] Hans Ulrich Wipf, *Georg Fischer AG 193–1945: Ein Schweizer Industrieunternehmen im Spannungsfeld Europas* (Zürich: Chronos, 2001), pp. 110–12.

[17] Werner Rings, *Raubgold aus Deutschland*, p. 135; ICE: Switzerland (ed.), *Final Report*, p. 189, estimates, however, that the Swiss contribution amounted to "just one percent of German armament end products."

[18] W. Rings, *Raubgold*, pp. 136–39; see also ICE: Switzerland (ed.), *Final Report*, pp. 184–85.

reduced their export of war material.[19] Nevertheless, they granted further credits to Germany for coal deliveries, among other items. This relationship greatly assisted Germany's purchases from other neutrals: in the period up to the end of 1942, the credits issued by Switzerland were considerably greater than the value of gold transferred from Germany.[20]

The Swiss Market for Stolen and Confiscated Art

The trade in confiscated artworks via Switzerland began before the war with the sale of so-called degenerate works that had been removed primarily from German public galleries. At an auction held at the Galerie Fischer in Lucerne in June 1939, 125 pieces were put up for sale. In total the Nazis received more than a half-million Swiss francs, although forty-three lots remained unsold. Goebbels and Göring exchanged other "degenerate" artworks for classical masterpieces via the neutral countries.[21]

The significance of the art trade via Switzerland should not be overemphasized, and after 1939 it declined from prewar levels. Nevertheless, several art dealers, such as Theodor Fischer, took advantage of the situation by dealing in pieces of dubious origin. Among Fischer's dealings was the sale of looted objects to the collector Emil G. Bührle, a rich industrialist living in Zürich.[22] Ribbentrop helped arrange the sale of art confiscated by the Einsatzstab Reichsleiter Rosenberg in France to dealers in Switzerland.[23] At the same time, Switzerland served as a refuge for what the Independent Commission of Experts called "flight assets" (attempting to escape Nazi seizure) and provided a base for many art dealers, including some of Jewish origin, who sought refuge there.[24]

The detailed study of the Swiss art market by Thomas Buomberger used the records of the *Schweizerische Verrechnungsstelle* (Swiss Clearing Office, SVST) to reconstruct these transactions.[25] Describing the illegal Swiss

---

[19] ICE: Switzerland (ed.), *Final Report*, pp. 423–25.

[20] W. Rings, *Raubgold*, pp. 142–48.

[21] Jonathan Petropoulos, *Art as Politics in the Third Reich* (Chapel Hill: University of North Carolina Press, 1996), pp. 76–83; Esther Tisa Francini, Anja Heuss, and Georg Kreis, eds., *Fluchtgut – Raubgut: Der Transfer von Kulturgütern in und über die Schweiz 1933–1945 und die Frage der Restitution* (Zürich: Chronos, 2002), pp. 208–14.

[22] "Switzerland's Role in the Trade of Art Works Stolen by the Nazis," in J. D. Bindenagel (ed.), *Washington Conference on Holocaust-Era Assets, November 30-December 3, 1998 Proceedings* (Washington, DC: U.S. Government Printing Office, 1999), pp. 355–59.

[23] J. Petropoulos, *Art as Politics*, p. 211.

[24] E. T. Francini, A. Heuss, G. Kreis, *Fluchtgut – Raubgut*, p. 1 (English summary).

[25] Among the many functions of the SVST was the search for stolen art after World War II. On this topic, see Thomas Buomberger, *Raubkunst – Kunstraub: Die Schweiz und der*

market as composed of "opportunists, profiteers, small crooks, and collaborators who seized the chance to enrich themselves," Buomberger notes that, although the SVST often manifested a strong suspicion of illegal activity, nobody was charged with theft, blackmail, or receiving stolen goods.[26] He concludes that the Swiss transport companies that moved the art around must have been aware of the shady nature of the business. These included firms such as Baumeler (Luzern) and Bronner (Basel), both of which worked for Fischer, and especially Schenker, based in Zürich, which transported for the Nazis cultural goods stolen from France.[27]

Fate of Confiscated Jewish Property

Diamonds and Other Valuables

As German rearmament accelerated in the 1930s, the shortage of foreign exchange became increasingly critical. In response, the Nazi economic leadership, under Göring's direction, sought to exploit all available stocks of foreign currency, precious metals, and international securities to serve the state's economic needs. The large-scale processing of gold, silver, and jewelry surrendered by Jews to the municipal pawnshops set a precedent for the handling of subsequent confiscations. The most valuable items were concentrated at the Municipal Pawnshop in Berlin, where they were sorted and applied in accordance with the needs of the war economy. Diamonds and jewelry were marked for export to raise foreign currency. Most precious metals were melted down for use in war production. For example, silver was used extensively for war-related photography. Less valuable items were sold to German jewelers for domestic resale, as the cost of selling them abroad was too great.[28]

Items confiscated from political opponents, denaturalized Jewish emigrants, or by the courts were dealt with in the same fashion. Once the German offensives in the West and East opened the way for large-scale looting of state, Jewish, and other property from the occupied territories,

---

Handel mit gestohlenen Kulturgütern zur Zeit des Zweiten Weltkriegs (Zürich: Orel Füssli, 1998), pp. 21–23.

[26] Ibid., pp. 23–25.

[27] Ibid., pp. 185–86.

[28] On the collection of silver items and other valuables in Germany, see for example Wolf Gruner, "The German Council of Municipalities (*Deutscher Gemeindetag*) and the Coordination of Anti-Jewish Local Politics in the Nazi State," *Holocaust and Genocide Studies*, vol. 13, no. 2 (Fall 1999): 171–99.

a similar system was adopted. Again, the most valuable items were usually sent to Berlin to be sold for foreign exchange or otherwise exploited for the war economy. Less valuable items were sold locally or reserved for particular groups of the population.[29]

A few examples help illustrate the pattern. In Belgium and the Netherlands, the Nazi authorities went to considerable lengths to try to recover stocks held by the local diamond industry, much of which had been in Jewish hands. Industrial diamonds were used directly for the German war economy, whereas the Nazi authorities exported polished diamonds abroad, probably to be exchanged for hard currency, industrial diamonds, or raw diamonds to be cut for industrial use.[30]

In Prague, a company named HADEGA processed much of the confiscated property from Czech Jews, especially precious metals and jewelry. Most of the metals were resmelted and used for the war economy, although some of the gold may have been delivered to the Reichsbank. Jewelry and diamonds were sorted, with the most valuable going directly for export abroad. After 1945, a former employee of HADEGA recalled preparing packages of precious stones during the war to be sent to jewelers in Switzerland. Other jewelry went to German and Czech jewelers. The same former employee also remembers "two Swiss businessmen" who came to Prague personally in connection with the deals.[31]

The research of Michael MacQueen confirms that other diamonds confiscated from Jews were regularly exported to Switzerland, using the diplomatic pouch, for sale by the dealer Ernst Färber. Färber made more than nineteen visits to Switzerland, mostly between 1940 and 1942. His special arrangements with the German authorities provoked the envy of other

---

[29] See, for example, V. Adamushko, G. Knat'ko, and N. Redkozubova (eds.), *"Nazi Gold" from Belarus: Documents and Materials* (Minsk: National Archives of the Republic of Belarus, 1998), pp. 110–13; Reichsministerium für die besetzten Ostgebiete an RK Ostland u. Ukraine, September 7, 1942.

[30] On the German exploitation of the Antwerp diamond industry, see *Les biens des victimes des persécutions anti-juives en Belgique: Spoliation – Rétablissement des droits. Résultats de la Commission d'étude. Rapport Final de la Commission d'étude sur le sort des biens des members de la Communauté juive de Belgique spoliés ou délaissés pendant la guerre 1940–45* (Brussels: Services du Premier Ministre, July 2001), pp. 94–118, based on the research of Eric Laureys; on the Aryanization of the Dutch diamond industry, see Gerard Aalders, *Geraubt! Die Enteignung jüdischen Besitzes im Zweiten Weltkrieg* (Cologne: Dittrich, 2000), pp. 205–209.

[31] LAB, B Rep. 039-01/307 Information from Annemarie Wolfram on May 19 and June 16, 1961. "Sendungen an die ich mich erinnern kann waren lediglich die Wertpäckchen an die Juweliere in der Schweiz, die anderen Edelsteine wurden den Käufern/Juweliere direkt ausgehändigt."

diamond traders, who wanted a piece of this lucrative business. In February 1942, the German Foreign Office even considered appointing and stationing at the German Legation in Switzerland a permanent specialist for the diamond trade. Ernst Rademacher, a Jewish Affairs Specialist at the German Foreign Office, urged strongly that "since the supply of industrial diamonds is a matter of life and death for the German war economy, I do not see how the Foreign Office can ignore the wishes of the Reich Economics Ministry and the Four-Year Plan."[32]

As with gold, major sources of diamonds and jewelry were the ghettos, extermination camps, and killing fields in the East. From the beginning of 1942, a large amount of jewelry and precious metals was received by the War Booty Office of the Reichsbank from the Einsatzgruppen and other killing units in the occupied Soviet Union.[33] The infamous Melmer deliveries to the Reichsbank from the death camps included large amounts of precious metals and jewelry. Documentation from the SS and the Finance Ministry in 1944 confirms that jewelry from the concentration camps was also sent to the Berlin Municipal Pawnshop for expeditious sale. It also mentions that a commission of 3 percent was to be paid to agents selling diamonds and jewelry in Switzerland and other neutral states.[34]

Fur Coats

Another surprising example of how trading with Nazi Germany might entail the risk of receiving stolen Jewish property in payment is the case of fur coats and pelts. During the first few weeks of the German occupation of Poland, the Nazi authorities confiscated large stocks from the warehouses of Jewish furriers.[35] Much was sent to the Reich, mainly to Leipzig, the

---

[32] Letter from Legationsrat Rademacher to Undersecretary Martin Luther, February 1, 1943, NARA, RG-242, T-120, reel 1003, fr. 394154-15. For further details of this story, see Michael MacQueen, "The Conversion of Looted Jewish Assets to Run the German War Machine," *Holocaust and Genocide Studies*, vol. 18, no. 1 (Spring 2004): 27–45.

[33] See Martin Dean, "Jewish Property Seized in the Occupied Soviet Union in 1941 and 1942: The Records of the *Reichshauptkasse Beutestelle*," *Holocaust and Genocide Studies*, vol. 14, no. 1 (Spring 2000): 83–101.

[34] See NARA, RG-238, T-1139, NG-4096 and NG-5248.

[35] LAB, B Rep. 039-01/274 (Polen-Fabrikeinrichtungen 5), Verbindungsoffizier OKW Wi Rue. Amt zur HTO, report of June 10, 1940, mentions that the military transported RM 2.75 million of leather and furs as part of raw materials worth RM 73 million sent from Poland to the Reich in the fall of 1939. On the confiscations, see also the statement of Fritz Schultz on May 28, 1964, and those of other witnesses, to be found in file B Rep. 039-01/251 (Polen-Pelze).

center of the German fur industry.[36] According to one Leipzig furrier, the international trade in furs continued during the war. Germany bought pelts from Scandinavia, Yugoslavia, and Iran and sold finished fur products to Switzerland, Italy, Romania, and Scandinavia. State control over the distribution of furs meant that German furriers were keen to export as much of their production as possible, as only in this way were they able to buy more pelts overseas.[37] According to a former official of the Four-Year Plan, the furs stolen in Poland were intended for export to Sweden to pay for the import of vital iron ore.[38]

Securities

A large part of Jewish assets, especially in Western Europe, was invested in securities. Initially Jews used this fairly liquid form of capital to help finance their emigration. After Kristallnacht, however, most Jewish share capital in Germany was transferred to the Reich, either in payment of discriminatory taxes or through outright confiscation, and implemented with the assistance of the banks, which then sold many of these shares to their own clients. In December 1938, new laws forced Jews to deposit all securities with the banks and forbade them from making further purchases.

In the occupied territories, many shares were seized by mobile Currency Protection Squads (*Devisenschutzkommandos*) together with other valuables from bank safe-deposit boxes, or they were confiscated with the remaining property of the Jewish deportees.[39] In part, the occupation authorities exploited these reserves of confiscated Jewish shares to assist German firms in penetrating local markets by gaining a controlling interest in established companies.[40] However, some stolen shares of international origin were used to raise foreign currency for the Reich by sale in neutral states.

In the Netherlands the "Robbery Bank" – Lipmann, Rosenthal & Co. – became the depository for nearly all Jewish-owned securities in accordance with decrees issued by the German civil administration under

---

[36] On the Leipzig fur industry and its Aryanization, see also Harold James, *The Deutsche Bank and the Nazi Economic War against the Jews* (Cambridge: Cambridge University Press, 2001), pp. 124–25.

[37] LAB, B Rep. 039-01/251 (Polen-Pelze), statement of Karl Walter März on November 10, 1965.

[38] Ibid., (148 WGK) 81 WGA 6707.59(42.64), Beschluss Landgericht (LG) Berlin April 1, 1965, summary of the statement of former official Hildebrandt.

[39] See, for example, NARA, RG-165, Box 643, PW Paper 73.

[40] See, for example, Raul Hilberg, *Die Vernichtung der europäischen Juden* 3 vols. (Frankfurt am Main: Fischer, 1982), vol. 2, p. 601.

Reichskommissar Seyss-Inquart. In November 1941, Seyss-Inquart issued instructions to begin the sale of Jewish-owned shares. This meant that international shares and securities formerly belonging to Jews were sold openly on the Dutch stock exchange, whose head was aware of their origins and did not object, despite warnings by the Dutch government-in-exile and the Allies.[41]

Gerard Aalders and others demonstrate how confiscated Jewish shares from Western Europe found their way onto the markets of Switzerland, Sweden, and other countries with the aid of the German firm, Otto Wolff, acting on behalf of the Four-Year Plan. The Otto Wolff Corporation was selected for its excellent foreign connections and because it was considered undesirable for an official German body to appear as the vendor overseas. This well-documented case reveals how the trade in foreign currency and looted securities was organized centrally by the Four-Year Plan.[42]

This large-scale international trade in securities by the Otto Wolff concern began in 1940 as part of an attempt by the Reich Economics Ministry to buy up German investments in foreign hands, thereby pre-empting the anticipated rise in the Reichsmark that would follow a general peace settlement. This policy was abandoned once the chances of a general peace faded and the practice threatened instead to become a drain on Germany's foreign currency reserves. Nevertheless, it served as a model for subsequent transactions in the other direction using the same overseas contacts.[43]

In the fall of 1941, Rudolf Siedersleben of the Otto Wolff concern negotiated a contract with the Economics Ministry to buy up shares in occupied countries and sell them in the neutrals to gain vital foreign currency. The Economics Ministry granted a commission of 3 percent on each transaction to be paid to the Otto Wolff concern in Reichsmark. The majority of shares were purchased on the Dutch stock exchange, although Otto Wolff agents purchased some shares directly in France and Belgium, including large amounts of Swiss securities from blocked accounts at confiscated British

---

[41] G. Aalders, *Geraubt!*, pp. 273–78.

[42] Gerard Aalders and Cees Wiebes, *The Art of Cloaking Ownership: The Secret Collaboration and Protection of the German War Industry by the Neutrals – The Case of Sweden* (Amsterdam: Amsterdam University Press, 1996), p. 99.

[43] NARA, RG-260, Box 612 (Kurt Eichel): Seidersleben (Otto Wolff Geschäftsleitung), letter to Joint Special Financial Detachment, U.S. Group Control Council dated November 15, 1945; see also Barbara Bonhage, Hanspeter Lussy, and Christian Horn, *Schweizerische Wertpapiergeschäfte mit dem "Dritten Reich": Handel, Raub, Restitution* (Zürich: Chronos, 2001), pp. 132–33.

and American banks in Paris.[44] The Eidgenössische Bank in Switzerland and the Enskilda Bank in Sweden helped sell the shares in their home markets. A common pattern was for overseas securities to be sold back to buyers in the countries that had issued them, which included Sweden, Switzerland, Turkey, and Portugal. According to one source, about RM 6.3 million in foreign currency was brought in by the sales of shares, although a much larger sum in Reichsmark was expended by the Reich to achieve this result.

After the war, Seidersleben was at pains to stress that the Otto Wolf Company had not been seeking to profit from the trade in stolen property. He even claimed to have recalled some Dutch Shell shares back from the Swiss purchasers after it was realized that they had originated from confiscated shares traded on the Dutch stock exchange. As the Otto Wolff Company remained liable for any losses made on these transactions, one can understand his caution. Yet, this example confirms that confiscated shares were sold in Switzerland, which had escaped the checks supposedly undertaken by both buyers and sellers.[45]

In reality, the security measures referred to were introduced only in response to Allied counter-measures. This is suggested by the comments of Kurt Eichel, who conducted purchases for Otto Wolff in Belgium and France:

> Late in 1943, Siedersleben . . . [said] that it was getting increasingly difficult to dispose of the securities on the above-mentioned [Zürich, Stockholm, and Lisbon] stock exchanges. The local banks were becoming suspicious at the quantity of securities offered, and began to ask for declarations of origin. There was a rumor that Allied pressure was behind this move. After that the transactions almost ceased, and by the beginning of 1944, business was done only on a very small scale.[46]

Aalders and Wiebes point out that, in the case of some securities that had certificates of voluntary sale, it subsequently became clear that the Nazi authorities had obtained them by extortion.[47]

---

[44] NARA, RG-84, Box 116, Office of Military Government for Germany (U.S.), report regarding the Four-Year Plan in connection with the investigation of the Otto Wolff firm, by G. A. J. M. Rotherham (1946).

[45] NARA, RG-260, Box 612 (Kurt Eichel): Seidersleben (Otto-Wolff Geschäftsleitung), letter to Joint Special Financial Detachment, U.S. Group Control Council dated November 15, 1945.

[46] NARA, RG-260, Box 612, Kurt Eichel statement on June 18, 1947.

[47] G. Aalders and C. Wiebes, *The Art of Cloaking,* pp. 98–102.

Research by members of the Swiss Independent Commission of Experts (ICE, also known as the Bergier Commission) demonstrates that the Swiss quietly effected partial compensation for looted securities after the war. A group settlement worth 635,000 Swiss francs was negotiated for several hundred Dutch claimants; it was partially paid for by the Swiss banks. Still, only the Eidegnössische Bank publicly admitted to having traded in looted securities.[48] Government intervention in the immediate postwar period helped limit the damage to the banking industry by cloaking the extent of Swiss bank involvement. Dutch claims against the Enskilda Bank in Sweden were less successful, partly due to the failure of the Americans to follow through on wartime threats of sanctions.[49]

Businesses Acting as Middlemen and Facilitators

A number of large and small businesses came into contact with the process of destruction and exploitation, doing so by delivering specific products or services to the SS or, more commonly, by receiving, handling, and selling former Jewish property. Among the most notorious examples of a direct contribution to Nazi mass murder were supplying the SS with Zyklon B and constructing crematoria for the death camps by such companies as the subsidiary of Degussa (Degesch) and Topf & Söhne. According to Peter Hayes, there is little doubt that Bruno Tesch, the head of Tesch & Stabenow GmbH (itself a subsidiary of Degesch), which sold Zyklon B to the SS, was aware by mid-June 1942 that his product was being used to kill people. However, although some suspicions clearly arose among employees, company bosses squelched curiosity by warning subordinates not to ask awkward questions.[50]

There is also ample evidence that German banks and insurance companies wrote contracts financing and insuring business activities in particular ghettos, concentration camps, and death camps. Jewish forced laborers were initially employed mainly by German communal authorities in 1939–40, but soon after that, many private and state-owned companies came to employ Jewish forced and slave laborers. In assessing the culpability of third parties in the financial aspects of genocide, very difficult questions emerge about the knowledge such actors had and also their freedom of action. In most cases,

[48] B. Bonhage, H. Lussy, and C. Horn, *Schweizerische Wertpapiergeschäfte*, pp. 351–58.

[49] G. Aalders and C. Wiebes, *The Art of Cloaking,* pp. 100–104.

[50] Peter Hayes, *From Cooperation to Complicity: Degussa in the Third Reich* (Cambridge: Cambridge University Press, 2004), pp. 284–85.

independent economic agencies were not coerced into cooperating with Nazi policies of robbery, exploitation, and murder; yet, in a state-directed war economy, there were considerable financial incentives for working with the regime and even fierce competition for contracts.

Awareness of Complicity: Banks and Insurance and Industrial Companies

German banks profited in a number of ways from the expropriation measures taken against the Jewish population, even if these financial institutions were not always pleased by the loss of reliable customers. Profits came, for example, in the form of commissions from mediating Aryanizations or from the resale of shares acquired by the Reich from confiscations or payment of discriminatory taxes. The cost of administering blocked accounts was passed on directly to their Jewish "clients."[51] The drastic reduction of credit ratings for Jewish businesses and individuals due to the changed "political climate" in the late 1930s demonstrates how effectively "economic forces" served to accelerate the pauperization and expropriation of the Jews. Loss of credit facilities rapidly pushed many Jewish businesses and much Jewish-owned real estate into forced sales at knock-down prices, as Jews could obtain credit only at very unfavorable rates or, after Kristallnacht, scarcely at all.[52]

It has been demonstrated that the directors of the Dresdner Bank were well aware of the looting of gold reserves from the national banks of occupied countries; it is less easy to prove the extent to which they were informed about the origins of "persecutee gold" they handled.[53] Nonetheless, with regard to the large-scale resmelting operations of Degussa, which included the melting down of dental gold, a former employee of Degussa in Berlin commented that sometimes deliveries arrived in a condition that made drawing conclusions hard to avoid. Further evidence of conscious complicity in the regime's crimes can be deduced from the extensive destruction of records by German companies in 1945. Peter Hayes argues that, for

---

[51] Hannah Ahlheim, "Die Commerzbank und die Einziehung jüdischen Vermögens," in Ludolf Herbst and Thomas Wiehe (eds.), *Die Commerzbank und die Juden 1933–1945* (Munich: C. H. Beck, 2004), p. 153.

[52] Susanne Meinl and Jutta Zwilling, *Legalisierter Raub: Die Ausplünderung der Juden im Nationalsozialismus durch die Reichsfinanzverwaltung in Hessen* (Frankfurt: Campus, 2004), p. 61; Ludolf Herbst, "Banker in einem prekären Geschäft: Die Beteiligung der Commerzbank an der Vernichtung der jüdischen Gewerbetätigkeit," in L. Herbst and T. Wiehe (eds.), *Die Commerzbank und die Juden*, p. 106.

[53] Ralf Banken, "Kurzfristiger Boom oder langfristiger Forschungsschwerpunkt? Die neuere deutsche Unternehmensgeschichte und die Zeit des Nationalsozialismus," *Geschichte in Wissenschaft und Unterricht* 3 (2005): 183–96.

corporations such as Degussa, the aim of cooperation (and thereby also complicity) was not so much to obtain large immediate profits from trading in former Jewish possessions, but rather to secure future rewards and to avoid the costly economic penalties that noncooperation in government measures might have entailed.[54]

Banks and insurance companies were extensively involved in the liquidation of assets belonging to tens of thousands of German and Austrian Jews. In most instances, this involvement brought relatively little direct benefit to the companies, as they acted more or less as agents of the state, assisting with the implementation of "legal" confiscation measures.[55] German banks and other firms were certainly well informed about the scale of the deportations and their financial implications. The Deutsche Bank, for one, received copies of the relevant deportation lists from the Senior Finance President (OFP) in Hamburg so that it could compare the names with those of its customers and inform the OFP of additional accounts to be confiscated. In a letter dated May 6, 1942, the Hamburg branch of the Deutsche Bank even noted that one person on the first deportation list could not have been evacuated, as he had recently been seen at one of the bank's branches.[56]

Attempts to contact deported Jews to resolve outstanding financial issues usually only confirmed the widely received impression that they would not be returning. For example, a notary, who had the exact address of the deportee Salli Levi in the Łódź ghetto, received the reply that postal deliveries could not be made to that address. The notary received that reply when he attempted to obtain authorization for the return of an overpaid amount from Levy's still blocked account.[57] An insurance company in Cologne decided not even to try to contact a Jewish customer who had been deported to the Warsaw ghetto in May 1942, as "in view of the given circumstances, such a step would be pointless."[58] In August 1943, AEG

---

[54] Peter Hayes, "The Degussa AG and the Holocaust," in Ronald Smelser (ed.), *Lessons and Legacies*, vol. 5, *The Holocaust and Justice* (Evanston, IL: Northwestern University Press, 2002), p. 156.

[55] H. Ahlheim, "Die Commerzbank," p. 170.

[56] Deutsche Bank, Filiale Hamburg an den Herrn Oberfinanzpräsidenten Hamburg – Dienststelle für die Verwertung eingezogenen Vermögens, May 6, 1942, doc. 4 published in Karl-Heinz Roth, "Hehler des Holocaust: Degussa und Deutsche Bank," in *1999*, no. 13 (1998), p. 144.

[57] Wolfgang Dreßen (ed.), *Betrifft: "Aktion 3". Deutsche verwerten jüdische Nachbarn. Dokumente zur Arisierung* (Berlin: Aufbau Verlag, 1998), pp. 107–109.

[58] Britta Bopf, *"Arisierung in Köln": Die wirtschaftliche Existenzvernichtung der Juden 1933–1945* (Köln: Emons, 2004), p. 297.

in Berlin, the former employer of the husband of the elderly deportee F. E., gave the following reply to the Senior Finance President for Berlin-Brandenburg when requested to pay the capitalized value of her pension to the state: "whether these demands are still valid or whether they have in the meantime become invalidated by her death is not known to us in detail. Heil Hitler, AEG."[59]

Allianz and other insurance companies even insured facilities such as the Łódź ghetto against fire damage and other possible losses to production, or to goods being transported into and out of the ghetto. Other insured facilities included the forced labor camp at Kraków-Plaszów and concentration camps, including those at Auschwitz, Lublin, Stutthof, Sachsenhausen, and Dachau.[60] The contracts usually involved visits by company staff to the sites, although in the case of Auschwitz the SS did not permit an inspection.[61] However, an inkling of what was going on there might still have been gained from "routine" correspondence: in February 1943, the Dresdner Bank asked the State Police in Litzmannstadt (Łódź) when it would receive the money it was owed for the use of a bone-grinding machine that had recently been returned from Auschwitz (the machine had been ceded to the Dresdner Bank in lieu of payment by its manufacturer, Schriever & Co. in Hanover).[62]

Many German companies followed the Wehrmacht into the occupied territories with the aim of exploiting wartime business opportunities. In this respect, they were following the same opportunistic line that had determined prior responses to Nazi policies. However, in view of the ill-concealed crimes of the Nazis in Eastern Europe and the extensive reliance of German industry on forced and slave labor, the managers of German firms inevitably became aware of the compromising nature of their relationship with the German state. Ironically, the fear of embarrassing legal cases abroad, which might threaten German overseas assets with retaliation,

---

[59] LAB, Rep. 092/8498, file concerning F. E. born 1884, AEG an OFP Vermögensverwertungsstelle, August 20, 1943: "Ob diese Forderungen noch bestehen oder ob nicht durch den Tod inzwischen die Forderungen erloschen sind, ist uns im Einzelnen nicht bekannt."

[60] Gerald Feldman, *Die Allianz und die deutsche Versicherungswirtschaft 1933–1945* (Munich: C. H. Beck, 2001), pp. 473–81.

[61] Ibid., p. 484.

[62] Ingo Loose, "Die Kommerzbank und das Konzentrations- und Vernichtungslager Auschwitz-Birkenau," in L. Herbst and T. Wiehe (eds.), *Die Commerzbank und die Juden*, p. 305.

rather than any moral scruples, was the main argument deployed by German business to delay or limit the anti-Jewish confiscations.[63]

Auctions, Auditors, and Assessors

For auction houses, court bailiffs (*Gerichtsvollzieher*), and other private and official property assessors, forced Jewish emigration and the sale of items left by the deportees provided a lucrative source of income. For example, in December 1939, the public prosecutor (*Generalstaatsanwalt*) offered for sale 700 paintings (modern classics including one by P. P. Rubens) through the antique house of Mathias Lampertz in Cologne, as advertised in the *Westdeutschen Beobachter*.[64] In summer 1942, the Nazi corporatist organization for the city's main auction houses approached the Senior Finance President (OFP) to try to win the concession for the sale of "abandoned" Jewish items. In support of their bid, the auctioneers cited their previous work for the Gestapo in selling off Jewish removal items promptly, which had reaped such high profits that the four auction houses involved had paid more than RM 320,000 in taxes.[65] The profits were limited somewhat by the application of state price controls on some items, but the middlemen could sometimes influence the outcome for some items, as they were often entrusted with estimating the value before sale, with their commission representing a fixed percentage of the price. On average, the sales prices paid at the auctions were roughly one-third below those estimated by the assessors. In Cologne alone, hundreds of public auctions took place, in which tens of thousands of people participated.[66]

Many business auditors (*Wirtschaftsprüfer*) were employed either directly within the German bureaucracy or as outside contractors to assess the value of companies and to prepare the paperwork necessary for Aryanization, confiscation, and subsequent sale. The Deutsche Revisions- und Treuhand-anstalt AG, which provided auditing services, opened up new branches in Prague and Amsterdam, as well as becoming very active in Vienna.[67] In many regions, the court assessors employed by the financial and legal authorities for processing confiscated items were extremely busy evaluating the mass of Jewish items, which had suddenly come into the Reich's possession in one fell swoop.

---

[63] BAL, R 2/9172b, pp. 26–35, Deutsche Bank an OFP Berlin-Brandenburg, March 10, 1942; L. Herbst and T. Wiehe (eds.), *Die Commerzbank und die Juden*, pp. 166–67.

[64] Britta Bopf, *"Arisierung in Köln,"* p. 300.

[65] Susanne Meinl and Jutta Zwilling, *Legalisierter Raub*, pp. 196–98.

[66] Britta Bopf, *"Arisierung in Köln,"* p. 302.

[67] See BAL, R 8135.

When used furniture dealers emptied the Berlin apartments of deported Jews, they would contact Herr Niederlechner, the secretary of the bookstore Lange & Springer in Steglitz, if they found a large collection of books, so that he could estimate their value for resale through the second-hand book trade.[68] The names of the previous Jewish owners were recorded on preprinted forms, so that the amount received could be booked to the correct individual account to pay off remaining debts.[69] In Mainz, employees of the auction houses collected household items directly from the evacuated apartments under an agreement concluded with the Senior Finance President in Darmstadt shortly after the start of the deportations there.[70]

The employees of moving companies, traders in second-hand goods, auction houses, and even bookstores must, therefore, have received a clear impression of the nature of the deportations that forced the Jews to abandon almost all their worldly goods. In Paris, nearly all moving vans in the city were mobilized to clear Jewish apartments, spreading awareness of the deportations. The huge amount of former Jewish property brought into the Reich from Belgium, France, and the Netherlands also must have conveyed to many German citizens the Europe-wide scale of the anti-Jewish measures.[71] Some advertisements for the auctions did not neglect to mention that the "merchandise" came from "non-Aryan possession," to make it clear that bargains would be on offer.[72]

Prisms for Viewing Degrees of Awareness and Complicity in the Holocaust

It may appear optimistic to claim that much can be learned about the Holocaust from the largely peripheral involvement of individuals and companies that traded in stolen property, especially if we focus on neutral Switzerland.

---

[68] LAB, A Rep. 092, Generalia, OFP B-B Vv, circular of June 12, 1942, Betr.: Verwertung der dem Reich mit dem Judenvermögen verfallenen Bücher.

[69] Ibid., OFP B-B Vv, circular April 7, 1942. The date of the Jewish owner's deportation and the destination were to be recorded secretly in pencil on the back of the form (for internal use only).

[70] Walter Rummel and Jochen Rath (eds.), *"Dem Reich verfallen" – "den Berechtigten zurückzuerstatten": Enteignung und Rückerstattung jüdischen Vermögens im Gebiet des heutigen Rheinland-Pfalz, 1938–1953* (Koblenz: Verlag der Landesarchivverwaltung Rheinland-Pfalz, 2001), pp. 181–82.

[71] W. Dreßen (ed.), *Betrifft: "Aktion 3,"* pp. 45–53.

[72] B. Bopf, *"Arisierung in Köln,"* pp. 302–303.

However, looking through the wrong end of the telescope in this fashion can sometimes help clarify things that are right in front of our noses. If a wealth of detail can be pieced together by the Bergier Commission and others on the many ways people in Switzerland interacted economically with the Nazi government and the Holocaust, despite their physical separation from events, how much greater must have been the interaction in the occupied territories and Germany itself.

The Nazis skimmed off only the most valuable items for sale in neutral countries. Nevertheless, in cases such as securities or artwork, as well as gold and diamonds, there were reasonable grounds for suspecting these were stolen goods. As items in limited supply, the Germans plundered them systematically to gain foreign currency and raw materials.

The Swiss experience can serve as a microcosm of the pattern throughout Europe. The widespread participation of the local population as beneficiaries spread complicity and, therefore, acceptance of German measures against the Jews. In particular, the public auctions of Jewish property serve as a powerful symbol of how "normal" the economic destruction of the Jews became. The sale of "modern art" in Switzerland was a harbinger of things to come. Many auction houses, such as the renowned Dorotheum in Vienna or Leo Spik in Berlin, sold confiscated Jewish property for a tidy commission. Many German transport companies outdid their Swiss counterparts in assisting massive Nazi looting.

The recent work of national commissions in Norway, France, Belgium, Austria, and elsewhere confirms the participation of many individuals and organizations in the spoliation of the Jews. Extensive financial records from German archives reveal the participation of officials, bank clerks, and private companies. Often, profits were concealed within the generous commissions and high salaries paid to trustees and officials. Many thousands of individuals wrote hopeful letters of application for the opportunity to purchase Jewish real estate cheaply, stressing their loyalty to and sacrifices on behalf of the Nazi regime, and handling such requests even became a serious disruption for the offices that dealt with former Jewish property. As soon as the Jews were deported, an unseemly scramble for their possessions ensued, confirming that most people shared the view that they would not be returning.[73]

---

[73] See, for example, Bernward Dörner, *"Heimtücke": Das Gesetz als Waffe: Kontrolle, Abschreckung und Verfolgung in Deutschland 1933–1945* (Paderborn: Schöningh, 1998), p. 238.

In many respects, the recent research that has focused mainly on the neutrals, German companies, and the financial administration still represents only the tip of the iceberg. Much work remains to be done on the intimate relationship between racist persecution and financial exploitation in the Holocaust. Ripples of complicity spread throughout Europe propelled by the universality of human greed.

10

SEIZURE OF PROPERTY AND THE SOCIAL DYNAMICS
OF THE HOLOCAUST

Was the seizure of Jewish property a precondition, a contributory cause, or a consequence of the Holocaust? What insights can a comparative study of the confiscation process across Europe reveal about its nature and the social dynamics involved?

Almost everywhere, economic persecution measures and confiscations preceded the deportations and killings. Even in the German-occupied territories of eastern Poland (Soviet-occupied in 1939–41), many of the first anti-Jewish operations took the form of looting Jewish property (often before the Germans arrived), prohibitions on trade, and hefty "contributions"; these occurred before the mass shootings.[1] In Western Europe too, the aim was to secure Jewish assets before the deportations, especially in the form of businesses, bank accounts, and securities, using a complex structure of pseudo-legal measures.[2] The prospect of obtaining Jewish

---

[1] Shmuel Spector has identified more than twenty places in the former Polish province of Volhynia, where the Ukrainian population carried out pogroms against the Jews at this time. In some cases the persecution began even before the Germans arrived. The most common motive seems to have been the acquisition of Jewish property: see Shmuel Spector, *The Holocaust of Volhynian Jews, 1941–44* (Jerusalem: Yad Vashem, 1990), pp. 64–67. For a similar if less widespread pattern in Belorussia, see Shalom Cholawsky, *The Jews of Bielorussia during World War II* (Amsterdam: Harwood, 1998), pp. 272–73. On the events in Korelicze, for example, see Hasya Turtl-Glukovitsh, "The History of the Jews of Korelicze" (Hebrew), in Michael Walzer-Fass (ed.), *Korelits-Korelitsh: Hayeha ve-hurbanah shel kehilah Yehudit* (Tel Aviv: Korelicze Society in Israel and the USA, 1973), pp. 19–34.

[2] Wolfgang Seibel (ed.), *Holocaust und 'Polykratie' in Westeuropa, 1940–1944: Nationale Berichte* (December, 2001), p. lxiv, notes that the state-organized theft of Jewish property was closely coordinated with the plans for the mass deportation of the Jews in France; Gerard Aalders, "Die Arisierung der niederländischen Wirtschaft: Raub per Verordnung," in Alfons Kenkmann and Bernd-A. Rusinek (eds.), *Verfolgung und Verwaltung:*

property provided an additional motive for many perpetrators or bought more widespread complicity, whereas the effect on the victims of that property loss was stigmatizing, demoralizing, and debilitating. In a variety of ways, the plunder of Jewish property acted as a catalyst for genocide, as individuals, organizations, and governments competed over the spoils.

Before the Nazis seized power, they exploited economic envy and exaggerated claims about Jewish influence to stir up antisemitic sentiments; in particular, they depicted Jewish wealth as "ill-gotten gains," to be reclaimed for the benefit of the German people. Similar tropes of economic antisemitism were widespread throughout Eastern Europe, espoused by populist or fascist parties. In Germany, and especially in Austria, Jewish property was claimed as a reward by Party "Old Fighters," who sought compensation for their own alleged past sufferings.[3]

Development of Nazi Aryanization and Confiscation Measures

The Nazis did not possess a blueprint for the spoliation of Jewish wealth when they seized power. Their initial measures in the summer of 1933 were directed mainly at their political opponents, including some Jews. They directed the key 1933 Law for the Denaturalization of Emigrants, which included provisions for the confiscation of property, against only a few hundred prominent political exiles. Only in 1937 did Heinrich Himmler and Reinhard Heydrich issue new instructions for the denaturalization of Jewish emigrants, singling out those suspected of "racial" or "economic crimes." This paved the way for the subsequent exploitation of denaturalization to seize almost all Jewish property after the start of the war.[4]

The boycotts against Jews' businesses, the laws excluding them from the civil service and other professions, and the program of Aryanization reflected a combination of pressure from the lower ranks and legal measures steered from above that steadily drove the Jews out of the German economy.[5] The

Die wirtschaftliche Ausplünderung der Juden und die westfälischen Finanzbehörden (Münster: Oberfinanzdirektion Münster, 1999), pp. 122–37.

[3] See Gerhard Botz, *Wohnungspolitik und Judendeportation in Wien 1938 bis 1945* (Vienna: Geyer, 1975), p. 120.

[4] See also Martin Dean, "The Development and Implementation of Nazi Denaturalization and Confiscation Policy up to the Eleventh Decree to the Reich Citizenship Law," *Holocaust and Genocide Studies,* vol. 16, no. 2 (Fall 2002): 217–42.

[5] See for example *Plunder and Restitution: The U.S. and Holocaust Victims' Assets: Findings and Recommendations of the Presidential Advisory Commission on Holocaust Assets in the United States and Staff Report* (Washington, DC: U.S. Government Printing Office, 2000), pp. SR–14–16.

spoliation of the Jews in the Reich evolved in a series of intensifying steps using a wide variety of mechanisms. Nevertheless, before 1938, the Reich government stopped short of comprehensive legislation on Aryanization and confiscation, partly out of concern for possible economic and political costs.

Aryanization – the transfer of Jewish businesses into "Aryan" hands – remained largely a private matter up to 1938. Nevertheless, the chicanery of Party and state organs, exploited by opportunistic businessmen, increased the economic and psychological pressure on Jews to sell out and leave. Even "market forces," such as the effect of lowered credit ratings, served only to accelerate the run on Jewish businesses, more than 50 percent of which had been liquidated or sold by early 1938, representing a considerable erosion of Jewish wealth. As unemployment among Jews rose and savings rapidly dwindled, their progressive exclusion from the economy compelled almost all to consider emigration. Even before Kristallnacht, a form of "ethnic cleansing" driven primarily by discrimination and economic pressure was taking place.

Emigration and Expropriation

From the start, expropriation was closely linked to the emigration process. The Nazi state sharpened the provisions of the Reich flight tax, introduced in 1931 to limit capital flight, and converted it primarily into a tax on Jewish emigration, as in more than 90 percent of cases it was applied to Jews. Foreign currency restrictions were progressively tightened during the 1930s, until by 1939 only 4 percent of sums legally transferred abroad arrived at their destination. Additional difficulties in obtaining visas and other paperwork rendered emigration an obstacle course that many Jews could not complete in time. The frustration of legitimate efforts to export capital explains why some Jews sought to circumvent the law to rescue a small part of their property.

A key instrument that the financial authorities employed against Jews was the Currency Law of December 1936, permitting the blocking of bank accounts and other property on the mere suspicion of Jews' emigration plans. Because withdrawals from blocked accounts, other than a small amount for subsistence, were permitted only in support of emigration preparations or for certain extraordinary expenditures such as medical emergencies, in practice this law coerced Jews toward emigration. Jews preparing to leave also had to pay an extra tax on any recently acquired possessions. Already by the mid-1930s, the SD and others in the German bureaucracy began to envisage the "problems" that would occur as the active and propertied sections of the Jewish population departed, leaving behind the elderly, sick, and indigent.

Austrian Models of Aryanization

The "wild Aryanizations" in Austria immediately following the Anschluss gave new impetus to Nazi legal and institutional measures by forcing the authorities to respond. Both the registration of Jewish property and the decrees regulating the compulsory Aryanization of businesses reflected the efforts of Hermann Göring and others to reassert state control.[6] The widespread private Aryanization in Germany prior to 1938 had already created some spectacular private profits. Therefore, during the course of 1938, Göring authorized the creation of a network of laws and supervisory institutions to ensure that henceforth the German state would pocket much of the difference between the low price paid to Jewish owners (into blocked accounts) and the actual market price. In Austria, Josef Bürckel, the Commissioner for the Integration of Austria into the Reich, "saw no alternative to legalizing the commissar system as a 'necessary evil' that had developed spontaneously, in order to limit the worst excesses and gradually introduce a more orderly 'Aryanization' process."[7]

Many of the institutions and mechanisms established in 1938 to complete Aryanization in Austria and the Reich, such as the use of independent trustees and institutions ensuring state and Party oversight, were later employed in the occupied territories. Based on the practices of the Austrian Property Transfer Office (*Vermögensverkehrstelle*) and the enforcement of compulsory Aryanization in Germany, the model for the Aryanization of Jewish businesses had proven itself, by the spring of 1939, ready for application in most of Western Europe in 1940 and 1941. The technique of securing part of Jewish assets by controlling the Jewish communal organizations, developed by the Central Office for Jewish Emigration (*Zentralstelle für jüdische Auswanderung*), was the SD's alternative "Vienna model," which it soon applied in Prague.

In April 1938, Hermann Göring developed another mechanism to mobilize Jewish assets for state purposes. He envisaged the conversion of remaining Jewish property into low-interest government bonds (as a form of

---

[6] Helmut Genschel, *Die Verdrängung der Juden aus der Wirtschaft im Dritten Reich* (Göttingen: Musterschmidt Verlag, 1966), p. 172.

[7] Gerhard Botz, *Nationalsozialismus in Wien: Machtübernahme und Herrschaftssicherung 1938/39* (Buchloe: Obermayer, 1988), pp. 330–31, refering to Bürckel's report to Göring dated April 29, 1938.

pension) to eliminate Jewish influence from the economy. This mechanism would also have the advantage of boosting government credit at a time of budget crisis. Although for a variety of reasons this plan was implemented only partially and belatedly in the Reich, it was applied more agressively elsewhere, especially in the Netherlands, as a means for tapping into Jewish wealth without openly declaring its confiscation.

Kristallnacht and Its Consequences

After the violence of Kristallnacht in November 1938, Göring complained about the looting and wanton destruction of property. Nevertheless, he exploited the situation to proclaim the "punitive tax" and secure 20 percent (later raised to 25 percent) of Jewish property directly for the Reich using the tax system: forcing the victims to pay a much greater sum than all the damages they suffered. This was the first and most spectacular of many special taxes imposed on Jewish communities throughout Europe.[8] The regional Tax Offices were assigned to collect more than one billion RM from the Jews; some RM 300 million came in the form of shares, enabling the state to manipulate financial markets through their gradual sale via the Prussian State Bank (*Seehandlung*).

During and in the aftermath of the pogrom, many Jews were arrested and much property seized by state and Party organs. Arrested Jews were released only in return for a commitment to surrender their property and emigrate. This intensification of persecution compelled the remaining Jews to contemplate emigration. In December 1938, Göring ordered the compulsory Aryanization of remaining Jewish businesses, under state supervision, and in February 1939, Jews were obliged to surrender all precious metal items. Such excesses as the personal enrichment of regional Party bosses, the activities of "wild Aryanizers" in Austria, and private looting during Kristallnacht encouraged Göring to secure as much Jewish property for the state as possible through state intervention in Aryanization and other "legal" measures.

Blocked Accounts and the Eleventh Decree

The full-scale blocking of Jewish bank accounts was ordered in August 1939, just before Hitler's attack on Poland. It was motivated by the authorities'

---

[8] On the extortion of gold from the Jews in Rome, see Susan Zuccotti, *Under His Very Windows: The Vatican and the Holocaust in Italy* (New Haven: Yale University Press, 2000), pp. 153–55; for Minsk, see Bernhard Chiari, *Alltag hinter der Front: Besatzung, Kollaboration und Widerstand in Weissrussland, 1941–1944* (Düsseldorf: Droste, 1998), pp. 261–62.

concern to prevent Jews from smuggling any assets abroad, and it resulted in considerable hardship. Jews were permitted only a small allowance each month from their own savings and had to obtain permission from the Currency Offices for any extraordinary expenditure. Combined with the introduction of forced labor and the withdrawal of social benefits, the block-ing of bank accounts contributed to the rapid pauperization of the Jews. The Gestapo used the *Reichsvereinigung* to maintain some welfare support, but this was paid for by the liquidation of remaining communal property and the extortion of compulsory contributions from its members. The impoverishment and isolation of the Jews prompted some regional Nazi leaders to call upon Hitler to bring forward plans to deport them to the East (once emigration became impossible), so that Jewish apartments could go to needy Aryans. Ultimately, the blocking of bank accounts secured remaining Jewish assets, so the state could seize them in the wake of mass deportations beginning in October 1941.

The Reich Security Main Office also targeted the wealth of emigrant Jews, recommending in September 1940 the denaturalization of those who possessed more than RM 5,000 inside Germany. However, issuing individual denaturalization orders proved cumbersome, so the bureaucracy proposed new legislation to simplify the confiscation of Jewish property. The Eleventh Decree to the Reich Citizenship Law, issued in November 1941, ordered the confiscation of all remaining property of German Jewish emigrants; by stripping the remaining Jews in Germany of their citizenship and property the moment they crossed the Reich's border, it inextricably linked confis-cation to the deportation of Germany's Jews. As in most of Europe, the removal of the Jews to death camps and ghettos in the East proved decisive in separating them from their property, because it was clear that they were not meant to return.

The "East"

In the Occupied Eastern Territories, the Nazi seizure of Jewish property was linked directly to the process of destruction. In contrast to Western Europe, little regard was paid to preserving and exploiting the existing financial infrastructure. Instead, robbery was conducted quite openly, with legal means coming into play mainly during jurisdictional disputes within the administration. There were three basic stages in the plundering of the Jews there: initial military operations, ghettoization, and mass murder.

In the wake of the advancing Wehrmacht, a host of new economic regulations were imposed on the Jews, accompanied by forced contribu-tions, the requisitioning of raw materials and private property, and violence directed against the Jewish leadership. In occupied Soviet territory, Himmler's security forces quickly broadened the shooting of the Jewish "intelligentsia" (along with other "suspected enemies") into the wiping out of entire Jewish communities. Much of the property secured by the Einsatzgruppen and other units during the first wave of mass killings in the summer and fall of 1941 was initially handled as "war booty" and sent back to the Reichsbank through regular channels in the absence of other instructions.

The creation of ghettos (in Poland from the end of 1939 and in occupied Soviet territory from July 1941) exacerbated the rapidly declining material situation of the Jews. Much property was seized during ghettoization, and the little that remained was soon used up for Jewish subsistence. In the Warsaw ghetto, tens of thousands died of starvation.[9] The widespread illegal trade across the boundaries of most ghettos quickly drained Jewish resources, the terms of that trade being highly unfavorable. Jewish forced labor was booked as a financial asset by the German administration. Economic isolation, the extraction of "contributions," and overcrowding in the ghettos led to disease and starvation, accelerating the destruction process.

During the mass shootings, Jewish property served as an important incentive for local collaborators who eagerly hoped to inherit Jewish possessions. The liquidation of the ghettos was accompanied by widespread looting as local policemen searched both for hidden Jews and for hidden valuables. At the mass graves, the perpetrators collected wedding rings and even clothing from the victims, with the more precious objects tallied and sent to Berlin. A few reports explicitly stated that items had been obtained from Jews who had been shot. The German authorities made considerable efforts in the ghettos and camps to exploit economically even those who had been murdered: hair was cut from the victims and shoes piled up by the thousands. The German overseers temporarily spared a few Jews to continue working until these tasks were completed. In some instances, Jewish workers recognized a friend's or a relative's clothing that now was being recycled.

In the occupied Soviet territories, the German civil administration officially confiscated all Jewish property. It undertook considerable efforts to register and reclaim it from locals who had stolen it in the wake of the massacres. However, as we have seen, the bureaucratic effort involved was scarcely justified by the financial results. The state administration of real estate, for instance, produced little if any profit due to wartime rent controls

---

[9] Itamar Levine, *Walls Around: The Plunder of Warsaw Jewry during World War II and Its Aftermath* (Westport, CT: Praeger, 2004), p. 139, gives official figures of 43,329 recorded deaths in 1941 and 22,760 in the period from January to May 1942. He comments that the actual death toll was almost certainly much higher.

and the high costs of administration and repairs. The net proceeds, including income from Jewish valuables sent to Berlin, were to be paid back into the budget of the civil administration.[10] Yet, the SS also secured much property during its operations and handed this over only reluctantly, diverting some to cover its expenses. Throughout the East, the handling of Jewish property was accompanied by rampant corruption and theft, which were punished only sporadically.

Settling Accounts after the Deportations

In October 1941, the Nazi leadership began the mass deportation of German Jews from the Reich. Based on earlier experience, the bureaucracy made detailed preparations for handling the remaining property. The regional financial administrations liquidated bank accounts, confiscated securities and real estate, and saw to the payment and collection of outstanding debts. The empty apartments sealed by the Gestapo had to be cleared quickly to avoid claims for unpaid rent.

Before deportation, each Jewish family was obliged to prepare a property inventory to assist with the liquidation of their assets. Surviving forms present a touching snapshot of the meager resources remaining to German Jews on the eve of their destruction. From those with some means left, the Security Police diverted considerable amounts, particularly by extortion just prior to their departure. The Security Police, arguing that anti-Jewish measures were to be self-financing, confronted the Finance Ministry with a *fait accompli*.

Tax officials instructed banks and life insurance companies to dissolve accounts and transfer capitalized values directly to the government. The settling of outstanding obligations and loans demanded a considerable bureaucratic effort, requiring separate files for each victim, and in thousands of cases this work had not been completed by 1945. The deportations left a very large economic footprint. Many contractors and private individuals became involved; among these were property assessors, auction houses, trustees, estate agents, notaries, and transport companies. Hundreds of thousands of individuals benefited from the sale of cheap household items or the availability of apartments.[11] The Nazis attempted to maintain a hierarchy

---

[10] See Vladimir Adamushko, Galina Knat'ko, and Natalia Redkozubova (eds.), *"Nazi Gold" from Belarus: Documents and Materials* (Minsk: National Archive of the Republic of Belarus, 1998), pp. 110–13.

[11] Frank Bajohr, *"Aryanisation" in Hamburg: The Economic Exclusion of the Jews and the Confiscation of their Property in Nazi Germany* (New York: Berghahn, 2002), p. 279, estimates at least 100,000 beneficiaries for the Hamburg region alone.

of beneficiaries ranked according to the Party's racial and social priorities. However, rampant corruption ensured that Nazi potentates and hangers on, as well as police and finance personnel, secured the best items for themselves. The processing of property became a pivotal act in the destruction process, involving hundreds of thousands of ordinary Germans who thereby became complicit in the destruction of their Jewish neighbors.

Western Europe

In Western Europe the economic persecution of the Jews from 1940 on resulted primarily from legal decrees and administrative measures.[12] A clear legal framework was necessary to provide purchasers and middlemen with secure legal title. Several exile regimes outlawed all cooperation in German confiscation measures, which served to undermine the salability and value of property, especially once Germany's military fortunes began to wane.

Considerable differences from country to country arose depending on the nature of the German occupation (civilian or military) and the degree of local participation in the process.[13] In almost all the Western countries, the securing of Jewish private property was initiated prior to the deportations using methods developed in the Reich: registration of property, blocking accounts, special taxes, and restrictions on transfers. Measures were directed first against persons who had fled before the German advance or who had been arrested.

In the Netherlands, the German civil administration effectively applied many lessons learned inside the Reich. Reichskommissar Arthur Seyss-Inquart had a choice between two alternative models borrowed from Austria, which indeed supplied much of his personnel. Whereas Dr. Hans Fischböck urged the comprehensive confiscation of Jewish wealth based on the pseudo-legal "confiscation by decree" developed in Austria and the "Old Reich," the Security Police also pushed its own plans based on an adaptation of Eichmann's Central Office for Jewish Emigration, as applied in Vienna and also Prague.[14] During 1941–42, Seyss-Inquart chose Fischböck's model of "technocratic" plunder, as it proved better suited to

---

[12] W. Seibel (ed.), *"Holocaust und 'Polykratie'" in Westeuropa, 1940–1944*, p. iv.

[13] See especially, Jean-Marc Dreyfus, "Die Enteignung der Juden in Westeuropa," in Constantin Goschler and Philipp Ther (eds.), *Raub und Restitution: "Arisierung" und Rückerstattung des jüdischen Eigentums in Europa* (Frankfurt am Main: Fischer Taschenbuch, 2003), pp. 41–57.

[14] Joseph Michman, "Planning for the Final Solution Against the Background of Developments in Holland in 1941," *Yad Vashem Studies* XVII (1986): 148–53.

the need for concealment and use of the existing financial infrastructure. Despite German complaints, Dutch financial institutions and stockbrokers largely cooperated in the measures, reasoning that it was better to keep the business in Dutch hands.[15] The large-scale forced exchange of Jewish shares for government bonds in the Netherlands put a sizable part of Jewish assets at the disposal of the Reich even before the deportations.

Comparisons with neighboring states, such as Luxembourg, Belgium, Norway, and France, are instructive, as there were certain key differences. Clearly, the form of German occupation administration influenced the manner and extent of Jewish property confiscation. Vichy France's attempts to defend its sovereignty played a considerable role in the spoliation of the Jews there. French concerns to limit German interference in its internal affairs and retain control over the process led Vichy to seize the initiative, passing its own legislation for the whole of France, but incorporating much of Germany's program of Aryanization and confiscation.[16]

In Luxembourg, initial confiscation measures taken against the property of the Jews who fled were simply extended later to all remaining Jews, well in advance of the deportations.[17] The small Jewish community in Norway was fully expropriated in connection with the deportations, although the bulk of the money was paid into a communal fund, part of which was still in existence at the liberation.[18] In Belgium, the local administrators and notaries displayed some resistance to confiscation; there too, the military administration assigned confiscation a lower priority than in the Netherlands, not enforcing blocked accounts until September 1942.[19]

The general pattern of confiscation in the West was one of carefully calculated legal measures coordinated with the deportations. Some care was taken not to provoke adverse public opinion, but local participation was quite widespread, if by no means universal. Many benefited as purchasers,

---

[15] Gerard Aalders, *Geraubt! Die Enteignung jüdischen Besitzes im Zweiten Weltkrieg* (Cologne: Dittrich, 2000), pp. 278–82.

[16] See, for example, Jean-Marc Dreyfus, "Franco-German Rivalry and 'Aryanization' as the Creation of a New Policy in France, 1940–44," in *Confiscation of Jewish Property in Europe, 1933–1945: New Sources and Perspectives*, Symposium Proceedings (Washington, DC: United States Holocaust Memorial Museum, 2003), pp. 75–92.

[17] LAB, B Rep. 039-01/327, Luxembourg 26, *Die Judenfrage* (newspaper), May 31, 1941.

[18] *The Reisel/Bruland Report on the Confiscation of Jewish Property in Norway* (Part of Official Norwegian Report 1997: 22) (Oslo, 1997), pp. 17–23.

[19] W. Seibel (ed.), *Holocaust und 'Polykratie' in Westeuropa, 1940–1944*, p. lviii; and in the same volume Maxime Steinberg, "Belgien: Polizeiliche und wirtschaftliche Verfolgung," pp. 237–38; Rudi van Doorslaer, "Raub und Rückerstattung jüdischen Eigentums in Belgien," in C. Goschler and P. Ther (eds.), *Raub und Restitution*, pp. 135–53.

trustees, notaries, administrators, and even "*Bewahrier,*" false friends who kept property in trust but did not return it at the end of the war.

In comparing Aryanization in France to that in Belgium and the Netherlands, Jean-Marc Dreyfus argues that the French applied more bureaucratic resources, with the aim of increasing oversight and reducing corruption. Nonetheless, the French model was closely adapted from German practices, although the measures were not as comprehensive or complete as in the Netherlands.[20]

In Western Europe, the Germans also extracted vast sums from local budgets through "occupation costs" and also unfavorable clearing agreements.[21] These amounts dwarfed the proceeds they took from Jewish property, which the Germans used mainly for the purposes of economic penetration or obtaining foreign currency (through the sale of diamonds and shares), rather than contributing directly to the Reich budget. Considerable amounts of seized Jewish artwork and furniture were exported to Germany for Nazi potentates, museums, and those whose residences had been bombed.

Overall, however, the "legal" character of confiscation throughout Western Europe meant that much Jewish wealth remained in state hands, still in blocked accounts or under trusteeship, at the end of the occupation.[22] Local initiative and greed smoothed the path to widespread confiscation, but both the Germans and local governments preferred a bureaucratic, albeit slow, approach that was more restrained than the rampant looting more prevalent in the East.

Sovereign Imitations

In Eastern Europe, the Nazis were not the only nationalist party to espouse a virulently antisemitic economic rhetoric. Radical right-wing parties and

---

[20] J.-M. Dreyfus, "Die Enteignung der Juden in Westeuropa," pp. 41–57.

[21] According to estimates from the archive of the former RFM, income from these "occupation costs" exceeded RM 47 billion during the war; see BAL, R2 Anh./51, p. 103; Götz Aly, *Hitlers Volksstaat: Raub, Rassenkrieg und nationaler Sozialismus* (Frankfurt am Main: S. Fischer, 2005), p. 320, details occupation costs in excess of RM 50 billion for Western Europe, whereas unpaid clearing debts account for roughly another RM 20 billion from this region.

[22] For Belgium, see *Les biens des victimes des persécutions anti-juives en Belgique: Spoliation – Rétablissement des droits. Résultats de la Commission d'étude. Rapport Final de la Commission d'étude sur le sort des biens des membres de la Communauté juive de Belgique spoliés ou délaissés pendant la guerre 1940–45* (Brussels: Services du Premier Ministre, July 2001).

conservative authoritarian governments in Slovakia, Romania, Bulgaria, Croatia, and Hungary adopted much of the Nazi program for excluding Jews from the economy and seizing their property. This program was also linked explicitly with preparations for the physical removal of the Jews, a process itself part of the drive to create homogeneous ethnic nation-states.

It is important to recognize that even states that ultimately did not consign most of their long-resident or prewar citizen Jews to death still implemented extensive confiscation. Bulgaria created a Commissariat for the Jewish Question similar to that in France, imposed a stiff property tax, and collected in blocked accounts at the National Bank the proceeds from the compulsory sale of Jewish businesses and securities.[23] In Hungary, the limited confiscation prior to 1944 was overtaken by comprehensive spoliation under the German occupation, which was implemented, however, by the Hungarian authorities.

A comparative perspective underlines the degree of choice involved in local complicity: the Germans could not implement their destruction and confiscation policies on their own. Götz Aly argues that much of the proceeds from Jewish property, even from Germany's allies, ultimately supported the German war economy: it did so in a roundabout way, by propping up ailing local currencies and state revenues, thereby enabling those states to continue paying onerous German war contributions, requisitions, and even soldiers' pay.[24] However, by relying on the local administrations as their instruments and by including local populations among the beneficiaries, the Nazis spread complicity with both immediate and long-lasting effects.

To what extent were collaborating regimes actually sovereign, and to what degree did they implement confiscation measures on their own initiative? It can be argued that stopping the deportations in Slovakia, Romania, and even occupied Hungary demonstrates that these states exercised some freedom of action in Jewish affairs. All three states pursued their own confiscation measures, based on indigenous antisemitic policies, with only limited German input. Indeed, many measures were specifically designed to prevent the Germans from exploiting the removal of the Jews as a means to further economic penetration. Thus, in Slovakia, Romania, and Hungary,

---

[23] LAB, B Rep. 039-01/318, German translation of Ministerial Decision no. 4,567 (anti-Jewish legislation establishing the Commissariat for Jewish Affairs) issued by the Interior Ministry and published in the Bulgarian *Official Journal* no. 192, August 29, 1942. I am grateful to Götz Aly for bringing this document to my attention.

[24] G. Aly, *Hitlers Volksstaat*, pp. 253–73, 315–17.

the governments implemented "Slovakization," "Romanianization," and "Magyarization" – not Aryanization.[25]

Jean Ancel draws attention to the fact that mob violence and widespread looting in Romania acted as a catalyst for state intervention to establish control over the ongoing "expropriation."[26] In Hungary full-scale confiscation began in May 1944 – concurrent with the start of the deportations – with a government declaration that all Jewish assets were deemed to be Hungarian national property. However, new research demonstrates that, in practice, confiscation in Hungary became a fierce competition among private looters, state agencies, and the Germans to grab what they could under the chaotic conditions of sudden ghettoization.[27] In all of these countries, confiscated Jewish property also become a tool of wartime "social policy," providing a useful reserve of goods and property that could be distributed strategically to bolster support for the regime. Businesses, housing, furniture, and clothing were rented, sold, or given away according to a specific hierarchy of ethnic, social, and political groups, but the administration of these programs inevitably boosted the inherent corruption and cronyism in these authoritarian regimes.

Neutral States, Knowledge of Events, and the Spread of Complicity

In the 1990s, the role of Switzerland as a recipient of Nazi looted assets and especially its failure to repay dormant accounts to the rightful heirs attracted considerable public attention. This in turn prompted detailed new research into the part played by the neutrals in World War II. Documents reveal a wide variety of economic contacts between Switzerland and Nazi Germany, ranging from the provision of wartime credits and the sale of munitions to

[25] See Tatjana Tönsmeyer, "Der Raub des jüdischen Eigentums in Ungarn, Rumänien und der Slowakei," in C. Goschler and P. Ther (eds.), *Raub und Restitution*, pp. 73–91.

[26] Jean Ancel, "Seizure of Jewish Property in Romania," in *Confiscation of Jewish Property in Europe*, pp. 43–55; on pages 46–47, for example, the author notes the violent looting in January 1941.

[27] Gábor Kádár and Zoltán Vági, "The Economic Annihilation of the Hungarian Jews, 1944–1945," in Randolph L. Braham and Brewster S. Chamberlin (eds.), *The Holocaust in Hungary: Sixty Years Later* (Boulder, CO: Rosenthal Institute for Holocaust Studies, Graduate Center of City University of New York and Social Science Monographs, published in association with the United States Holocaust Memorial Museum, 2006), pp. 77–88.

the laundering of looted gold (including a small proportion from Holocaust victims). Generally, the Nazis selected only the most valuable items of Jewish property for sale in neutral countries: diamonds, gold, securities, and so on. The advantages for Nazi Germany from using the neutrals as a key marketplace were considerable, as Germany desperately needed foreign currency to help pay for strategic materials, such as wolfram (tungsten) from the Iberian Peninsula.

One important consequence of recent research on Holocaust-era assets has been to dispel the myth that few people in Europe were aware of the disappearance of the Jews and their likely fate. The vast number of institutions, organizations, companies, and individuals mentioned in this book makes this point abundantly clear. Viewing the Holocaust through the prism of Swiss complicity as receivers of stolen goods only reinforces this impression. Swiss companies were involved in the dismissal of Jewish employees in Germany and the transport of goods looted from the apartments of Holocaust victims. German companies that smelted victims' dental gold, manufactured crematoria, or insured concentration camps could not remain unaware of the unspeakable activities in which they were involved.

The exclusion of the Jews from economic life required the tacit cooperation of many strata of society. It directly involved bank clerks, realtors, auctioneers, lawyers, stockbrokers, policemen, and tax officials. German housewives, refugees, and second-hand booksellers all competed for their share of the spoils. When banks received copies of deportation lists and insurance companies declined to pursue inquiries concerning the fate of deportees, the level of knowledge was clearly greater than many Germans later wanted to admit. The transport companies and auction houses that cleared the apartments, as well as those vying to move in, did not expect that the Jews would ever return.

In addition to the widespread corruption, much of the "profits from the Holocaust" were made by companies and individuals acting as agents of the state in implementing confiscations, managing properties, assessing their worth, employing forced laborers, and trading in stolen goods. Not only Nazis reaped the benefits but also individuals and companies throughout Europe (including the neutral states).

How Much Was Stolen and Where Did It Go?

It is not possible to put a figure on the value of Jewish property stolen, confiscated, and destroyed during the Nazi era. Estimates for the value of

Jewish property in Germany in 1933 range from ten to sixteen billion RM,[28] of which only RM 7.1 billion remained to be officially registered by the Reich in the summer of 1938 (including Austria). An amount exceeding 40 percent of this figure (more than RM 3 billion) was confiscated directly by the Reich before the end of the war (mainly using the punitive tax, the flight tax, and the Eleventh Decree and including prior denaturalizations). Considerable amounts of Jewish wealth were extracted for the Reich by transfer and export fees paid to the German Gold Discount Bank (Dego), the Main Trustee Office East (HTO), payments extorted by the SS for the Reichsvereinigung, and other special taxes and confiscations.

Nonetheless, in the overall context of the Reich's wartime income of more than RM 250 billion (against expenditure probably in excess of RM 500 billion),[29] the income from German Jewish property contributed less than 2 percent, and that from all the Jews of Europe probably not more than 5 percent.[30] "Occupation costs" collected from France – estimated at RM 31.6 billion – were of considerably greater significance.[31] Nonetheless, the imposition of the punitive tax against the Jews in the autumn of 1938 was spurred by Göring's urgent need to find new sources of revenue.[32] Göring in particular sought to combine Nazi ideological grounds for "reclaiming" Jewish property with the material interests of the Nazi state.

After 1938, the German state was the main beneficiary of Jewish property. However, hundreds of thousands of individuals also gained by obtaining former Jewish property from the state well below market prices. No detailed analysis has yet compared the scale of private versus state profits; in any case, the value of private gains is particularly difficult to assess. However, a rough indication of the relationship can be gleaned from available figures

---

[28] Helen B. Junz, "Report on the Pre-War Wealth Position of the Jewish Population in Nazi-Occupied Countries, Germany and Austria," prepared for the Independent Committee of Eminent Persons and included as Appendix S in their *Report on Dormant Accounts of Victims of Nazi Persecution in Swiss Banks* (December 1999), p. A-168; Sidney Zabludoff, *"And It All But Disappeared": The Nazi Seizure of Jewish Assets* (Policy Forum No. 13) (Jerusalem: Institute of the World Jewish Congress, 1998), p. 14, explains the rationale behind Hilberg's estimate of German Jewish wealth at RM 10 to 12 billion in 1933.

[29] G. Aly, *Hitlers Volksstaat*, pp. 323–25 estimates war income in excess of RM 250 billion from domestic and external sources; BAL, R 2 Anh./27, Archive of the former Reich Finance Ministry, report on the development of the Reich indebtedness from 1932 to 1945 gives a figure of RM 376 billion in debt by war's end.

[30] G. Aly, *Hitlers Volksstaat*, p. 313.

[31] Stefan Mehl, *Das Reichsfinanzministerium und die Verfolgung der deutschen Juden 1933–1943* (Berlin, 1990), p. 89; this is the figure reproduced in G. Aly, *Hitlers Volksstaat*, p. 320.

[32] G. Aly, *Hitlers Volksstaat*, pp. 58–63.

for postwar restitution. According to calculations of the West German government in 1986, compensation under the Allied and subsequent Federal German restitution laws for state confiscations and taxes amounted to some DM 5.16 billion. In comparison, the available estimate of Walter Schwarz for the amount of property restituted by private persons lies between DM 3 and 3.5 billion. These figures can provide only one rough marker, but they suggest that probably about 60 percent of recoverable property had been confiscated by the state.[33]

Reliable figures for other countries, both for the prewar value of Jewish property and the amounts confiscated or stolen, are even harder to obtain. For the Netherlands it appears that some 1 to 1.2 billion fl. (RM 750–900 million) were confiscated, representing more than 90 percent of Jewish domestic assets, whereas in France the amount frozen or sold was certainly in excess of RM 500 million (in converted values). Ancel's estimate for the value of Jewish property confiscated, stolen, or destroyed in Romania at 100 billion lei is perhaps on the high side, as converted it would be equivalent to more than RM 1.5 billion. In any case, it is certainly several times higher than the total from official receipts in Romania and also reflects the favorable exchange rate of the lei against the Reichsmark (because of Romanian oil). In Bulgaria, the value of all Jewish property registered was probably not much more than RM 200 million.[34] In the occupied East, the sums officially recorded are small indeed. If only RM 10 million from Jewish property went into the budget in Reichskommissariat Ostland, as Christian Gerlach estimates, that made only a small contribution to the civil administration, even if this figure omits various additional amounts that disappeared into other channels.[35] Yet, official figures are generally low estimates of the values seized. In most cases, there was no single centralized account, much money was lost to corruption and administrative costs, and a good deal remained in blocked accounts or in storage, where it made no contribution to the German war effort.

In Western Europe, the survival of blocked accounts in some countries facilitated partial restitution, reflecting the fact that confiscation was not

---

[33] Jürgen Lillteicher, "Rechtsstaatlichkeit und Verfolgungserfahrung: 'Arisierung' und fiskalische Ausplünderung vor Gericht," in Constantin Goschler and Jürgen Lillteicher (eds.), *Die Rückerstattung jüdischen Eigentums in Deutschland und Österreich nach 1945 und 1989* (Göttingen: Wallstein, 2002), p. 129.

[34] For the basis of these calculations, see the sources cited in Chapter 8. Conversion rates are based on those given by G. Aly, *Hitlers Volksstaat*, p. 365, reflecting the "artificial" fixed exchange rates set by the Germans.

[35] Christian Gerlach, *Kalkulierte Morde: Die deutsche Wirtschafts- und Vernichtungspolitik in Weissrussland 1941 bis 1944* (Hamburg: HIS, 1999), pp. 681–83.

always completed. The experiences of the few survivors who came back to reclaim their property, however, was generally negative, as they often faced many bureaucratic obstacles and delays. In Germany, restitution or compensation could be achieved only where proof of title was available, and the sums received were often much reduced due to inflation and the currency reform. The issue of heirless property was a thorny one, as it was politically unacceptable for the German state to benefit from it, so that Jewish "successor organizations" had to be established to distribute these assets.

The lengthy correspondence on restitution preserved in the archives reflects the frustrations of the victims and their heirs, who were sometimes pitted against the same bureaucrats who had originally confiscated their property. These men continued to defend the material interests of the state, believing they had acted "in accordance with the law."[36] Obtaining compensation from the Austrian government was particularly frustrating, as survivors faced a combination of bureaucratic delay and studied denial of responsibility.[37] In Eastern Europe, Jews returning to reclaim housing and other property faced particular hostility from those who had moved in during the war, eliciting occasional violent attacks and fueling local antisemitism that postwar communist governments did little to suppress.[38]

In practice, much of the property that had belonged to Jews was simply wiped out as profitable businesses withered and stocks were sold off at discounted prices. The Aryanization and confiscation programs resulted in much destruction of value, as profiteers interested only in short-term gain replaced careful owners, leading to the loss of valued customers and business expertise. As the Reisel-Bruland minority report on Norway stressed, it is very problematic to try to evaluate "in economic terms the annihilation of a minority with its religious, cultural, and social centres."[39] These values quite clearly cannot be measured or replaced. As Ronald Zweig argues,

> The material possessions of the Jews, which could be seized and redis-
> tributed ... [were not the same] ... as their prosperity and economic well-
> being, which was based on intangibles such as education, expectations, moti-
> vation, professional standing, and experience, as much as it was based on the
> ownership of property. These are cultural attributes, which cannot be seized

[36] Wolfgang Dreßen (ed.), *Betrifft: "Aktion 3." Deutsche verwerten jüdische Nachbarn. Doku-mente zur Arisierung* (Berlin: Aufbau Verlag, 1998), pp. 129–30.

[37] For an example of Austrian handling of compensation claims from the perspective of the victims, see USHMM RG-10.135, Weinmann family papers.

[38] See especially Jan T. Gross, *Fear: Anti-Semitism in Poland after Auschwitz* (New York: Random House, 2006).

[39] *The Reisel/Bruland Report*, pp. 2, 23.

and redistributed. They can only be destroyed, together with the society that created them and gave them meaning.[40]

Property Seizure as a Catalyst for Genocide

What role did Jewish property play in the development of the Holocaust? The murder of Europe's Jews was carried out primarily to achieve racial-ideological goals and not for financial reasons. Nevertheless, an important financial subtext helped shape the course of events. At certain key stages, both private and state greed acted as a catalyst in the development of violent "solutions" – a fact that has to be integrated into the narrative of the Holocaust. The unfolding of events in Ottoman Turkey (against the Armenians), in Rwanda, or in the former Yugoslavia demonstrates that "ethnic cleansing" and genocide usually have a powerful materialist component: seizure of property, looting of the victims, and their economic displacement are intertwined with other motives for racial and interethnic violence and intensify their devastating effects.

The radicalization of state measures against the Jewish population from 1938 onward was closely linked to a full-scale assault on their property. Economic discrimination and plunder contributed directly to the Nazi process of destruction in a variety of ways. The steady diminution of their means reduced the opportunities for Jews to flee, wore down their physical ability to resist, and eliminated their hope of buying material support in hiding.

Who were the main beneficiaries? Despite the widespread incidence of private plunder and corruption, overall the seizure of Jewish property in Europe was primarily a state-directed process linked closely to the development of the Holocaust. However, the widespread participation of the local population as beneficiaries from Jewish property spread complicity and therefore also acceptance of German-inspired measures against the Jews. In this way, economic motives contributed to the mobilization of European populations in support of radical antisemitic policies. "Economic antisemitism" and sheer opportunism must therefore be incorporated into interpretations of the Holocaust – interpretations that once focused mainly on racist ideology. Negative stereotypes of Jews, after all, were usually based on a wildly exaggerated estimate of their economic influence that stressed their allegedly detrimental effect on the "national" economy.

[40] Ronald W. Zweig, *The Gold Train: The Destruction of the Jews and the Looting of Hungary* (New York: Morrow, 2002), pp. 217–18.

Ultimately, the "Austrian model" of rampant self-enrichment constrained by pseudo-legal measures to protect the interests of the state, which
evolved during 1938, demonstrates the dual quality of the confiscation policies practiced throughout Europe. At first glance, there could be no greater
contrast than that between the highly bureaucratic confiscation using financial instruments practiced in the West and the gold seized directly from the
mouths of victims in the ghettos and death camps in the East. However,
these two extremes were in fact closely related.

The transactions in stolen Jewish shares conducted by stockbrokers in
the Netherlands were as intimately connected to the Holocaust as the
theft of rickety furniture from desolated ghettos by former neighbors. The
motive of greed, applied by states and individuals, fed off and contributed to
widespread indifference to the victims. A similar bureaucratic thoroughness
was attempted with the registration of Jewish property in the East, even
if the extent of personal opportunism and corruption was much greater
there. Examples from states allied to the Reich also demonstrate how the
competition between personal and state enrichment gave added impetus
to the development of indigenous antisemitic measures. The last personal
possessions of Jews deported from Slovakia or Hungary were robbed by
policemen in the transit camps "to prevent it falling into German hands."[41]

The radicalization of confiscation evolved from the dynamic interaction of local initiatives and bureaucratized state control, designed to steer
the process toward specific beneficiaries. On several occasions, such as the
"wild Aryanizations" in Austria, "the night of the long fingers" during
Kristallnacht, the spontaneous plunder of Jewish property in the East, or
even the clamor for Jewish possessions in Hungary, an almost revolutionary situation emerged, offering opportunities for great changes in property
relations, which contributed to the radicalization of antisemitic policy. The
aim of the state was generally to bureaucratize and channel these violent
impulses, but essentially the popular outbursts of racist-inspired greed and
its more bureaucratic state manifestations were two sides of the same coin,
both intrinsically linked to the dynamics of the Holocaust.

---

[41] R. Hilberg, *Die Vernichtung*, vol. II, p. 779; Hans Safrian, *Eichmann und seine Gehilfen*
(Frankfurt am Main: Fischer, 1995), pp. 212 and 300.

ARCHIVAL SOURCES AND BIBLIOGRAPHY

ARCHIVAL COLLECTIONS CITED

Brandenburgisches Landeshauptarchiv, Potsdam (BLHAP)

Pr. Br. Rep. 36A OFP Berlin-Brandenburg

Brest Oblast' KGB Archive, Belarus

File no. 42, Trial of Stanislav D. Shepel (1944)

Bundesarchiv, Berlin-Lichterfelde (BAL)

NS 6 Partei-Kanzlei (Party Chancellory)
NS 19 Persönlicher Stab Reichsführer SS (Personal Staff Office of the Reich
  Leader SS (Himmler))
R 2 Reich Finance Ministry (RFM)
R 2 Anh. RFM (post-war records)
R 7 Reich Economics Ministry (RWM)
R 18 Reichsministerium des Innern (Reich Interior Ministry, RMdI)
R 29 Reischkreditkasse (Reich Credit Bank, RKK)
R 38 Deutsche Golddiskontbank (German Gold Discount Bank, DeGo)
R 43 II Reichskanzlei (Reich Chancellory)
R 58 Reichssicherheitshauptamt (Reich Security Main Office, RSHA)
R 83 Adriatisches Küstenland (Adriatic Coast)
R 87 Reichskommissar für die Behandlung des feindlichen Vermögens (Reich
  Commissar for the Treatment of Enemy Property)
R 92 Generalkommissar Riga
R 104 F Reichskommissar für die Wiedervereinigung Österreichs mit dem
  Deutschen Reich (Reich Commissar for the Reuniting of Austria with the
  German Reich)

R 139 II OFP Thüringen (Senior Finance President Thüringia)
R 177 Reichskommissariat Niederlanden (Reich Commissar's Office, Netherlands)
R 182 Deutsche Golddiskontbank (Dego); payments made by Jews for relocation goods
R 8135 Deutsche Revisions- und Treuhand AG (German Oversight and Trustee Co.)
R 1500 Anh. Reichsfeststellungsbehörde (Reich Investigative Authority)
R 2104 Reichshauptkasse Beutestelle (Reich Main Treasury War Booty Office)
R 2301 Rechnungshof des Deutschen Reiches (Reich Audit Office)
R 2501 Deutsche Reichsbank (German National Bank)

Bundesarchiv-Militärarchiv, Freiburg (BA-MA)

RH 26 Infanteriedivisionen

Centre de documentation juive contemporaine (Center for Contemporary Jewish Documentation, Paris, CDJC)

CL-1 (Nuremberg Document)

Geheimes Staatsarchiv Preussischer Kulturbesitz, Berlin-Dahlem (GSPK)

Rep. 151, Reg. II G, HA IA, Prussian Finance Ministry
I Rep. 109, Preussischer Staatsbank (Seehandlung) (Prussian State Bank)

Historisches Archiv der Deutschen Bank, Frankfurt am Main (HADB)

F 28 Mannheim Collection (Jewish clients, Filiale Mannheim, 1930s)

Landesarchiv, Berlin (LAB)

A Rep. 092 OFP Berlin-Brandenburg (now transferred to BLHAP)
B Rep. 039-01 Archiv für Wiedergutmachung (Compensation Archive)

Landesarchiv Magdeburg, Landeshauptarchiv (LMLHA)

Rep. G 11 Devisenstelle (Currency Office)

Minsk Oblast' KGB Archive, Belarus

Archive File no. 902, Criminal Case no. 35930

National Archives and Records Administration (NARA), College Park, MD

RG-59 State Department Records
RG-84 Records of the Foreign Service Posts of the Department of State
RG-165 Records of the War Department General and Special Staffs
RG-238 National Archives Collection of World War II War Crimes Records
    T-1139, NG series
    T-301, NI series
    NO series
RG-242 National Archives Collection of Foreign Records Seized
    T-75 Records of the Plenipotentiary for the Serbian Economy
    T-120 German Foreign Office
    T-175 Persönlicher Stab Reichsführer SS (Personal Staff Office of the Reich Leader SS (Himmler))
    T-459 Reichskommissar für das Ostland
    T-580 Captured German Records Filmed at Berlin
    A 3343 BDC collection, SS Officer files
RG-260 U.S. Occupation Headquarters, WWII (OMGUS)

Oberfinanzdirektion, Berlin (OFDB)

Haupttreuhandstelle Ost (Sonderabteilung Altreich)
Judenvermögensabgabe (JuVa) Punitive Tax Files
Patzer Akten (Securities)
Reichsfluchtsteuer (Flight Tax)
Restitutionsakten (Restitution Files)
Div. Ordner I–IV (RFM Handakte Scheerans)
Leitz Ordner 49–50, Preuss. Staatsbank (Seehandlung), Verwertungslisten 1942–1945

Politisches Archiv des Auswärtigen Amtes (PAAA), Berlin

Inl. II Abteilung Deutschland (Germany Section)
    Inl. II A/B
    Inl. IIg (Geheim (secret))

Russian State Military Archive, Moscow (former Special (*Osobyi*) Archive, now RGVA)

Fond 1458 Reichswirtschaftsministerium (Reich Economics Ministry, RWM)

United States Holocaust Memorial Museum Archives (USHMM)

RG-02.208M Pamietniki Żydów (Memoirs of Jews, 1939–1945, Jewish Historical Institute Warsaw, syg. 302)

RG-02.061*01 Testimony of Harry Richard Loewenberg

RG-6.005.02 Office of the U.S. Chief of Counsel for War Crimes, Nuremberg Preliminary Briefs of Economics Division, vol. 1

RG-7.0008M Oberfinanzdirektion: Property Seized from Roma and Sinti

RG-10.135 Weinmann family papers

RG-10.141 # 03 Diary of Erich Frey

RG-11.001M.01 RGVA (former Osobyi), Moscow (Fond 500, Gestapo records)

RG-11.001M.04 RGVA (former Osobyi), Moscow (Fond 503, Gestapo Stettin records)

RG-11.001M.31 RGVA (former Osobyi), Moscow, Centralverein der Juden in Deutschland

RG-14.001M Gestapo Düsseldorf

RG-14.003M Reichsvereinigung der Juden (Reich Union of Jews)

RG-14, Acc. 2000.10 Deutsche Bank Archive (HADB), P 276 and P10563

RG-14.011M Sächsisches Hauptstaatsarchiv Dresden, reels 2 and 13

RG-18.002M*30 Latvian State Historical Archive, Riga (LSHA)

RG-30, Acc.1996.A.0342 Deportation Lists of Jews from the Reich

RG-31.002M Central State Archives, Kiev

RG-41, Acc. 1997.A.1007, Netherlands Institute for War Documentation (NIOD)

RG-43.023M France: Commissariat général aux questions juives (AJ 38, 1940–47)

RG-46, Acc.1997.A.0333 Bulgarian Commissariat for Jewish Affairs

RG-48.005M Czech State Archive, Prague

RG-50.030 Oral Histories

RG-53.002M National Archive of the Republic of Belarus (NARB)

RG-53.004M State Archives of the Grodno Oblast'

RG-68, Acc.1996.A.0169 (copies from former Soviet archives, received from Yad Vashem Archives)

RG-68, Central Archive for the History of the Jewish People (CAHJP), reel Alpha 01

Eichmann Trial Documents, T-37 (300), T-112, T-130, T-135, T-147, T-536, and T-571

Villa ten Hompel, Geschichtsort, Münster

Miscellaneous Files of Oberfinanzdirektion (OFD) Münster

Zollamt Münster (Customs Office Münster, ZAM)

Devisenakten (Currency Office Files)

PUBLISHED SOURCES, OFFICIAL PUBLICATIONS, MEMORIAL
BOOKS, MEMOIRS, AND UNPUBLISHED DISSERTATIONS

Abrahamsen, Samuel, *Norway's Response to the Holocaust* (New York: Holocaust Library, 1991).

Adamushko, Vladmir, Knat'ko, Galina, and Redkozubova, Natalia, eds., *"Nazi Gold" from Belarus: Documents and Materials* (Minsk: National Archive of the Republic of Belarus, 1998).

Ahlheim, Hannah, "Die Commerzbank und die Einziehung jüdischen Vermögens," in Ludolf Herbst and Thomas Wiehe, eds. *Die Commerzbank und die Juden 1933–1945* (Munich: C. H. Beck, 2004): 138–172.

Akten zur Deutschen Auswärtigen Politik, Serie E: 1941–45 (Göttingen: Vandenhoeck & Ruprecht, 1975).

Ancel, Jean, ed., *Documents Concerning the Fate of Romanian Jewry during the Holocaust* (New York: Beate Klarsfeld Foundation, 1986), 12 vols.

Ancel, Jean (ed.), *Transnistria, 1941–1942* (Tel Aviv: Goldstein-Goren Diaspora Research Center, 2003), vol. 1, *History and Document Summaries*.

Andrieu, Claire, et al., eds., *Mission d'étude sur la Spoliation des Juifs de France, Vol. 1 La spoliation financière* (Paris: Documentation française, 2000).

Anderl, Gabriele, Rupnow, Dirk, and Wenck, Alexandra-Eileen, eds., *Die Zentralstelle für jüdische Auswanderung als Beraubungsinstitution* (Vienna: Historikerkommission, 2002).

Benz, Wolfgang, Kwiet, Konrad, and Matthäus, Jürgen, eds., *Einsatz im "Reichskommissariat Ostland": Dokumente zum Völkermord im Baltikum und in Weißrußland 1941–44* (Berlin: Metropol, 1998).

Berliner Börsen Zeitung.

Biber, Jacob, *Survivors: A Personal Story of the Holocaust* (San Bernadino, CA: Borgo Press, 1986).

Les biens des victimes des persécutions anti-juives en Belgique: Spoliation – Rétablissement des droits. Résultats de la Commission d'étude. Rapport Final de la Commission d'étude sur le sort des biens des membres de la Communauté juive de Belgique spoliés ou délaissés pendant la guerre 1940–45 (Brussels: Services du Premier Ministre, 2001).

Bindenagel, J. D., ed., *Washington Conference on Holocaust-Era Assets, November 30-December 3, 1998 Proceedings* (Washington, DC: U.S. Government Printing Office, 1999).

Blodig, Vojtech, *Terezín in the "Final Solution of the Jewish Question" 1941–1945: Guide to the Permanent Exhibition of the Ghetto Museum in Terezín* (Prague: Oswald, 2003).

Böhme, Rolf and Haumann, Heiko, eds., *Das Schicksal der Freiburger Juden am Beispiel des Kaufmanns Max Mayer und die Ereignisse des 9./10. November 1938* (Freiburg im Breisgau: Schillinger, 1989).

Bonhage, Barbara, Lussy, Hanspeter, and Horn, Christian, *Schweizerische Wertpapiergeschäfte mit dem "Dritten Reich": Handel, Raub, Restitution* (Zürich: Chronos, 2001).

Bonhage, Barbara, Lussy, Hanspeter, and Perrenoud, Marc, *Nachrichtenlose Vermögen bei Schweizer Banken: Depots, Konten und Safes von Opfern des nationalsozialistischen Regimes und Restitutionsprobleme in der Nachkriegszeit* (Zürich: Chronos, 2001–02).

Boriak, Hennadii, Dubyk, Maryna, and Makovs'ka, Natalia, eds., *"Natsysts'ke zoloto" z Ukraïny: u poshukakh arkhivnykh svidchen'*, 2 vols. (Kiev: Ukraïns'kyi natsional'nyi fond "Vzaiemorozuminnia i prymyrennia", 1998).

Bradsher, Greg, ed., *Holocaust-Era Assets: A Finding Aid to Records at the National Archives at College Park, Maryland* (Washington, DC: Published for the National Archives and Records Administration by the National Archives Trust Fund Board, 1999).

Brechtken, Magnus, "Zwischen Rassenideologie und Machtpragmatismus – 'zerstreuende' Auswanderung, Palästinafrage, und die Entwicklung des 'Endlösungs'-Begriffs (1933–1940)," unpublished conference paper given in Gainesville, Florida.

Bundesarchiv, *The Whereabouts of the Records of the Deutsche Reichsbank: A Research Report* (Koblenz: Bundesarchiv, 1998).

Caplan, Hannah and Rosenblatt, Belinda, eds., *International Biographical Dictionary of Central European Émigrés 1933–1945* (Munich: K.G. Saur, 1983).

Cohen, David, "King Boris III and the 'Final Solution' of the Jewish Problem in Bulgaria," in *Annual of the Central Board of the Social, Cultural and Educational Association of the Jews in the People's Republic of Bulgaria, Vol. XX* (Sofia, 1985).

Commission on Jewish Assets in Sweden at the Time of the Second World War, ed., *The Nazigold and the Swedish Riksbank: Interim Report* (Stockholm, 1998).

Deutschland-Berichte der Sozialdemokratischen Partei Deutschlands (Sopade) 1934–1940, 5. Jahrgang, 1938 (Frankfurt am Main: P. Nettelbeck, 1980).

Diment, Michael, *The Lone Survivor: A Diary of the Lukacze Ghetto and Svyniukhy, Ukraine* (New York: Holocaust Library, 1991).

Documents on German Foreign Policy, Series D (Washington, DC: U.S. Government Printing Office, 1953), vol. V.

Dokumenty i materiały do dziejów okupacji niemieckiej w Polsce, vol. 3 (*Ghetto Łódzkie*) (Łódź, 1946).

Domarus, Max, ed., *Hitler: Speeches and Proclamations 1932–1945. The Chronicle of a Dictatorship* (Würzburg: Henninger, 1990), 3 vols.

Dreyfus, Jean-Marc, "L'aryanisation economique aux Pays-Bas (et sa comparison avec le cas français), 1940–1945," unpublished paper presented at the United States Holocaust Memorial Museum in summer 2001.

Ehrenburg, Ilya and Grossman, Vasily, eds., *The Black Book: The Ruthless Murder of Jews by German-Fascist Invaders Throughout the Temporarily-Occupied Regions of the Soviet Union and in the Death Camps of Poland During the War of 1941–1945* [Translated from Russian by John Glad and James S. Levine] (New York: Holocaust Library, 1981).

Elazar, Daniel J., et al. eds., *The Jewish Communities of Scandinavia–Sweden, Denmark, Norway, and Finland* (Lanham, MD: University Press of America, 1984).

Encyclopaedia Judaica (Jerusalem: Keter, 1972).

Francini, Esther Tisa, Heuss, Anja, and Kreis, Georg, eds., *Fluchtgut – Raubgut. Der Transfer von Kulturgütern in und über die Schweiz 1933–1945 und die Frage der Restitution* (Zürich: Chronos, 2002).

Frech, Stefan, *Clearing: Der Zahlungsverkehr der Schweiz mit den Achsenmächten* (Zürich: Chronos, 2001–2002).

Friedenberger, Martin, Gössel, Klaus-Dieter, and Schönknecht, Eberhard, eds., *Die Reichsfinanzverwaltung im Nationalsozialismus: Darstellung und Dokumente* (Bremen: Edition Temmen, 2002).

Friedlander, Henry and Milton, Sybil, eds., *Archives of the Holocaust: Volume 10 American Jewish Joint Distribution Committee, New York* (New York: Garland, 1991).

Friedlander, Henry, and Milton, Sybil, eds., *Archives of the Holocaust, Volume 20, Bundesarchiv of the Federal Republic of Germany, Koblenz and Freiburg* (New York: Garland, 1993).

Friedlander, Henry, and Milton, Sybil, eds., *Archives of the Holocaust, Volume 22, Zentrale Stelle der Landesjustizverwaltungen, Ludwigsburg* (New York: Garland, 1993).

Freie Universität Berlin, Zentralinstitut für sozialwissenschaftliche Forschung, ed., *Gedenkbuch Berlins: Der jüdischen Opfer des Nationalsozialismus* (Berlin: Hentrich, 1995).

Friling, Tuvia, Ioanid, Radu, and Ionescu, Mihail E., eds., *Final Report of the International Commission on the Holocaust in Romania* (Presented to Romanian President Ion Iliescu in November 2004) (Iasi: Polirom, 2005).

Fritz Bauer Institut, ed., *Legalisierter Raub: Der Fiskus und die Ausplünderung der Juden in Hessen 1933–1945* (Ausstellungskatalog: Frankfurt am Main, 2003).

Fröhlich, Elke, ed., *Die Tagebücher von Joseph Goebbels: Sämtliche Fragmente. Teil I, Aufzeichnungen 1924–1941* (Munich: K. G. Saur, 1987).

Fuchs, Gertrud, "Die Vermögensverkehrsstelle als Arisierungsbehörde Jüdischer Betriebe," (Diplomarbeit eingereicht an der Wirtschaftsuniversität Wien, Oktober 5, 1989).

Gall, Lothar, Feldman, Gerald D., James, Harold, Holtfrerich, Carl-Ludwig, and Büschgen, Hans E., *Die Deutsche Bank 1870–1995* (Munich: C. H. Beck, 1995).

Gedenkbuch: Opfer der Verfolgung der Juden unter der nationalsozialistischen Gewaltherrschaft in Deutschland, 1933–1945 (Frankfurt am Main: J. Weisbecker, 1986), 2 vols.

Goebbels, Joseph, *Der Angriff: Aufsätze aus der Kampfzeit* (Munich: Franz Eher Nachf., 1936).

Goodman, Myrna, "Resistance and Rescue: German-Occupied Denmark, 1940–1943 – Ideology, Politics, and Culture" (Ph.D. Diss., University of California, Davis, 2002).

Har El, Moshe, *"Ich habe nicht gewusst, dass wir noch eine schlimmere Zeit vor uns hatten": Von Mährisch-Ostrau in die Berge der Tatra und nach Israel (herausgegeben von Jolanda Rothfuss; bearbeitet von Olaf Schulze)* (Konstanz: Labhard, 2001).

Herbst, Ludolf, "Banker in einem prekären Geschäft: Die Beteiligung der Commerzbank an der Vernichtung der jüdischen Gewerbetätigkeit," in Ludolf Herbst and Thomas Wiehe (eds.), *Die Commerzbank und die Juden 1933–1945* (Munich: C. H. Beck, 2004): 74–137.

Herbst, Ludolf and Wiehe, Thomas, eds., *Die Commerzbank und die Juden 1933–1945* (Munich: C. H. Beck, 2004).

Heusler, Andreas and Weger, Tobias, eds., *"Kristallnacht": Gewalt gegen die Münchner Juden im November 1938* (Munich: Buchendorfer, 1998).

Hindemith, Bettina and Meinl, Susanne, eds., *Legalisierter Raub: Der Fiskus und die Ausplünderung der Juden in Hessen 1933–1945* (Frankfurt am Main: Sparkassen-Kulturstiftungen Hessen-Thüringen, 2002).

Historikerkommission, ed., *Vermögensentzug während der NS-Zeit sowie Rückstellungen und Entschädigungen seit 1945 in Österreich: Schlussbericht* (Vienna: Historikerkommission, 2003).

Honikel, Karl, ed., *Geschichte der Jüdischen Gemeinde Schenklengsfeld* (Schenklengsfeld: Christlich-Jüdischer Arbeitskreis Schenklengsfeld, 1988).

Independent Committee of Eminent Persons (ICEP), ed., *Report on Dormant Accounts of Victims of Nazi Persecution in Swiss Banks* (Bern: Staempfli, 1999).

Independent Commission of Experts: Switzerland – Second World War, ed., *Switzerland and Gold Transactions in the Second World War* (Bern: EDMZ, 1998).

Independent Commission of Experts: Switzerland – Second World War, ed., *Switzerland, National Socialism and the Second World War: Final Report* (Zürich: Pendo, 2002).

International Military Trials: Nazi Conspiracy and Aggression [Red Series] (Buffalo, NY: William S. Hein, 1996).

International Military Tribunal, ed., *The Trial of the Major War Criminals before the International Military Tribunal (IMT)* [Blue Series] (Nuremberg, 1947–1949).

Joods Historisch Museum Amsterdam, ed., *Documents of the Persecution of the Dutch Jewry* (Amsterdam: Polak and Van Genneo, 1979).

Junz, Helen B., "Report on the Pre-War Wealth Position of the Jewish Population in Nazi-Occupied Countries, Germany and Austria," prepared for the Independent Committee of Eminent Persons and included as Appendix S in their *Report on Dormant Accounts of Victims of Nazi Persecution in Swiss Banks* (December 1999).

Junz, Helen B., *Where Did All The Money Go?: The Pre-Nazi Era Wealth of European Jewry* (Bern: Staempfli, 2002).

Kingreen, Monica, "Wie sich Museen Kunst aus jüdischem Besitz aneigneten," in *Frankfurter Rundschau*, May 9, 2000.

Klein, Peter, ed., *Die Einsatzgruppen in der besetzten Sowjetunion 1941/42* (Berlin: Hentrich, 1997).

Kleine, Fritz, *Konzentrationslager: Ein Appell an das Gewissen der Welt: Ein Buch der Greuel; die Opfer klagen an* (Karlsbad: Graphia, 1934).

Klemperer, Victor, *Ich will Zeugnis ablegen bis zum letzten: Tagebücher 1933–1941* (Berlin: Aufbau, 1996); also in English translation: *I Will Bear Witness: A Diary of the Nazi Years*; translated by Martin Chalmers (New York: Random House, 1998).

Kommission zur Erforschung der Geschichte der Frankfurter Juden, ed., *Dokumente zur Geschichte der Frankfurter Juden 1933–1945* (Frankfurt am Main: Waldemar Kramer, 1963).

Kuperhand, Miriam, and Kuperhand, Saul, *Shadows of Treblinka* (Urbana, IL: University of Illinois Press, 1998).

Lichter, Matthias, *Das Staatsangehörigkeitsrecht im Grossdeutschen Reich* (Berlin: Heymanns, 1943).

Loose, Ingo, "Die Kommerzbank und das Konzentrations- und Vernichtungslager Auschwitz-Birkenau," in Herbst, Ludolf and Wiehe, Thomas, eds. *Die Commerzbank und die Juden 1933–1945* (Munich: C. H. Beck, 2004): 272–309.

Meinl, Susanne, and Zwilling, Jutta, *Legalisierter Raub: Die Ausplünderung der Juden im Nationalsozialismus durch die Reichsfinanzverwaltung in Hessen* (Frankfurt am Main: Campus, 2004).

Memorial Book of Glebokie [a translation into English of *Khurbn Glubok* by M. and Z. Rajak] (Buenos Aires: [Glebokie] Former Residents' Association in Argentina, 1994).

Meyerowitz, A., *Sefer Vladimerets, galed lezekher iranu* [*The Vladimirets Book, Testimony to the Memory of Our City*] (Tel Aviv: [Vladimirets] Former Residents in Israel, 1963).

Möllenhoff, Gisela, and Schlautmann-Overmeyer, Rita, eds., *Jüdische Familien in Münster 1918 bis 1945, Teil 1: Biographisches Lexikon* (Münster: Westfälisches Dampfboot, 1995).

Möllenhoff, Gisela, and Schlautmann-Overmeyer, Rita, eds., *Jüdische Familien in Münster, Teil 2,1: Abhandlungen und Dokumente 1918–1935* (Münster: Westfälisches Dampfboot, 1998).

Möllenhoff, Gisela, and Schlautmann-Overmeyer, Rita, eds., *Jüdische Familien in Münster, Teil 2,2: Abhandlungen und Dokumente 1935–45* (Münster: Westfälisches Dampfboot, 2001).

Nathan, Otto, "Nazi War Finance and Banking," in *National Bureau of Economic Research: Our Economy in War* (Occasional Paper 20: April 1944).

Niznanský, Eduard, ed., *Dokumenty nemeckej proveniencie (1939–1945)* (Bratislava: Nadácia Milana Simecku: Zidovská nábozenská obec Bratislava; Zvolen: Vydal Klemo, 2003).

Offenburg, Mario, ed., *Adass Jisroel: Die Jüdische Gemeinde in Berlin (1869–1942): Vernichtet und Vergessen* (Berlin: Museumspädagogischer Dienst, 1986).

Pfeifer, Monika Ilona, "Entrechtung und Verfolgung," in Evangelischer Arbeitskreis "Christen – Juden" Hanau in Zusammenarbeit mit dem Magistrat der Stadt Hanau, eds. *Hanauer Juden 1933 –1945* (Hanau: CoCon, 1998).

Plunder and Restitution: The U.S. and Holocaust Victims' Assets: Findings and Recommendations of the Presidential Advisory Commission on Holocaust Assets in the United States and Staff Report (Washington, DC: U.S. Government Printing Office, 2000).

Präg, Werner, and Jacobmeyer, Hans, eds., *Das Diensttagebuch des deutschen Generalgouverneurs in Polen 1939–1945* (Stuttgart: Deutsche Verlags-Anstalt, 1975).

Presidenzia del Consiglio dei Ministri, ed., *Rapporto Generale Allegati: Commissione per la ricostruzione delle vicende che hanno caratterizzato in Italia le attività di acquisizione dei bene cittadini ebrei dap arte di organismi pubblici e provati* (Dipartimento per l'Informazione e l'Editoria, 2001).

Reichsgesetzblatt (RGBl.) I (1938–1941).

Reimann, Guenter, *The Vampire Economy: Doing Business under Fascism* (New York: Vanguard, 1939).

The Reisel/Bruland Report on the Confiscation of Jewish Property in Norway (Part of Official Norwegian Report 1997: 22) (Oslo, 1997).

Republique Française, *Summary of the Work by the Study Mission on the spoliation of the Jews in France* (Paris: Documentation française, 2000).

Robinson, Jacob, and Sachs, Henry eds., *The Holocaust: The Nuremberg Evidence. Part One: Documents* (Jerusalem: Yad Vashem and YIVO, 1976).

Rummel, Walter, and Rath, Jochen, eds., *"Dem Reich verfallen" – "den Berechtigten zurückzuerstatten": Enteignung und Rückerstattung jüdischen Vermögens im Gebiet des heutigen Rheinland-Pfalz, 1938–1953* (Koblenz: Verlag der Landesarchivverwaltung Rheinland-Pfalz, 2001).

Rupnow, Dirk, "'Zur Förderung und beschleunigten Regelung der Auswanderung. . .' Die Wiener Zentralstelle für jüdische Auswanderung als Modell," unpublished paper presented at the conference "'Arisierung' und Restitution: Die Rückerstattung jüdischen Eigentums in Deutschland und Österreich nach 1945 und 1989," held at Freiburg in Breisgau in October 2000.

Safrian, Hans, "'Head Money' for Destruction? Deportations and Jewish Assets in Satellite Slovakia," unpublished paper presented at the Annual Conference of the German Studies Association in 2004.

Sage, Steven, "HC VII: The Sofia Trials of March 1945," unpublished paper first presented at the United States Holocaust Memorial Museum's Center for Advanced Holocaust Studies Summer Workshop, "War Crimes Trials in the Soviet Union and Eastern Europe" in June 2005.

Sage, Steven, "Jewish Ghettos in Axis Bulgaria, 1942–1944," unpublished paper prepared for the Conference on Jewish Material Claims against Germany.

Sauer, Paul, *Die Schicksale der jüdischen Bürger Baden-Württembergs während der nationalsozialistischen Verfolgungszeit 1933–1945: Statistische Ergebnisse der Erhebungen der Dokumentationsstelle bei der Archivdirektion Stuttgart und zusammenfassende Darstellung* (Stuttgart: W. Kohlhammer, 1969).

Schelvis, Jules, *Vernichtungslager Sobibor* (Münster: Unrast, 2003), available in English as *Sobibor: A History of a Nazi Death Camp* (Oxford: Berg Publishers in association with the United States Holocaust Memorial Museum, 2007).

Second World War Assets Contact Group, ed., *Second World War: Theft and Restoration of Rights. Final Report of the Second World War Assets Contact Group* (Amsterdam, 2000).

Seibel, Wolfgang, "Perpetrator Networks and the Holocaust: Resuming the 'Functionalism' versus 'Intentionalism' Debate," paper prepared for delivery at the 2000 Annual Meeting of the American Political Science Association.

Silberklang, David, "The Holocaust in the Lublin District" (Unpublished English version of his PhD Dissertation submitted to Hebrew University in Jerusalem in February 2003).

Simmert, Johannes, and Herrmann, Hans-Walter, eds., *Die nationalsozialistische Judenverfolgung in Rheinland-Pfalz 1933 bis 1945: Das Schicksal der Juden im Saarland 1920 bis 1945* (Koblenz: Landesarchivverwaltung Rheinland-Pfalz, 1974).

Smilovitsky, Leonid, *Katastrofa evreev v Belorussii 1941–1944 gg.* [The Holocaust in Belorussia, 1941–1944] (Tel Aviv: Biblioteka Matveia Chernogo, 2000).

Spector, Shmuel, and Wigoder, Geoffrey, eds., *The Encyclopedia of Jewish Life before and during the Holocaust* (Jerusalem: Yad Vashem, 2001).

Steen, Jürgen, and von Wolzogen, Wolf, eds., *"Die Synagogen brennen . . . !" Die Zerstörung Frankfurts als jüdische Lebenswelt* (Frankfurt am Main: Historisches Museum Frankfurt am Main, 1988).

Steiner, Hubert, and Kucsera, Christian, eds., *Recht als Unrecht: Quellen zur wirtschaftlichen Entrechtung der Wiener Juden durch die NS-Vermögensverkehrsstelle. Teil I: Privatvermögen, Personenverzeichnis.* (Vienna: Österreichisches Staatsarchiv, 1991).

Stenge, Margrit Rosenberg, *Margrit's Story: Narrow Escape to and from Norway* (Montreal: Concordia University Chair in Canadian Jewish Studies: Montreal Institute for Genocide and Human Rights Studies, 2004).

Strauss, Herbert A., ed., *Jewish Immigrants of the Nazi Period in the USA, vol. 6, Essays on the History, Persecution, and Emigration of German Jews* (New York: K. G. Saur, 1987).

Strauss, Herbert A., ed., *Jewish Immigrants of the Nazi Period in the USA, vol. 4, Jewish Emigration from Germany 1933–1942* (New York: K. G. Saur, 1992).

Trials of War Criminals before the Nuernberg Military Tribunals under Control Council Law No. 10, Nuernberg, October 1946-April 1949 [Green Series] (Washington, DC: U.S. Government Printing Office, 1949–1953) (Reprinted in Buffalo, NY: William S. Hein, 1997), 15 vols.

Unabhängige Expertenkommission Schweiz – Zweiter Weltkrieg, ed., *Die Schweiz, der Nationalsozialismus und das Recht, Band I Öffentliches Recht* (Zürich: Chronos, 2001).

U.S. and Allied Efforts to Recover and Restore Gold and Other Assets Stolen or Hidden by Germany During World War II, Preliminary Study, coordinated by Stuart E. Eizenstat (Washington, DC: Department of State, 1997).

U.S. and Allied Wartime and Postwar Relations and Negotiations with Argentina, Portugal, Spain, Sweden, and Turkey on Looted Gold and German External Assets and U.S. Concerns about the Fate of the Wartime Ustasha Treasury, coordinated by Stuart E. Eizenstat, Under Secretary of State for Economic, Business and Agricultural Affairs (Washington, DC: Department of State, 1998).

Ütermöhle, Walther, and Schmerling, Herbert, *Die Rechtsstellung der Juden im Protektorat Böhmen und Mähren: Eine systematische Darstellung der gesamten Judengesetzgebung* (Prague: Böhmisch-Mährische Verlags- Druckerei-Gesellschaft, 1940).

Walk, J., ed., *Das Sonderrecht für die Juden im NS-Staat*, Second edition (Heidelberg: C.F. Müller, 1996).

Walzer-Fass, Michael, ed., *Korelits-Korelitsh: Hayeha ve-hurbanah shel kehilah Yehudit* (Tel Aviv: Korelicze Society in Israel and the USA, 1973).

Warschauer Zeitung, August 27, 1940.

Watts, David, "German Forced-Labor Policy in Belgium, 1916–1917 and 1942–1944," unpublished paper presented at the Research Workshop on "Forced and Slave Labor" at the United States Holocaust Memorial Museum in summer 2003.

Weiss, George, ed., *Einige Dokumente zur Rechtsstellung der Juden und zur Entziehung ihres Vermögens 1933–1945: Schriftenreihe zum Berliner Rückerstattungsrecht VII* (Germany: G. Weiss, 1950).

Weissman, Mordechai, "My Escape from the Ditches of Slaughter," in Meyerowitz (ed.), *Sefer Vladimirets, galed lezekher iranu* (The Vladimirets Book, Testimony to the Memory of Our City) (Tel Aviv: Former Residents of Vladimirets in Israel, 1963).

Widerstand und Verfolgung in Wien 1934–1945, vol. 3 (Vienna: Österreichischer Bundesverlag für Unterricht, Wissenschaft und Kunst Jugend und Volk Verlagsges. MbH, 1975).

Wiehn, Erhard R., ed., *Oktoberdeportation 1940: Die sogenannte "Abschiebung" der badischen und saarpfälzischen Juden in das französische Internierungslager Gurs und andere Vorstationen von Auschwitz: 50 Jahre danach zum Gedenken* (Konstanz: Hartung-Gore, 1990).

Wieviorka, Annette, *Les Biens des Internés des Camps de Drancy, Pithiviers et Beaune-la-Rolande* (Paris: Documentation française, 2000).

Wildman, Sarah, "Paris' Dirty Secret," in *Jerusalem Report*, January 11, 2004.

Wildt, Michael, ed., *Die Judenpolitik des SD 1935 bis 1938: Eine Dokumentation* (Munich: Oldenbourg, 1995).

Wolf, Kerstin and Frank, eds., *Reichsfluchtsteuer und Steuersteckbriefe 1932–42* (Berlin: Biographische Forschungen und Sozialgeschichte, 1997).

Zabludoff, Sidney, *"And It All But Disappeared": The Nazi Seizure of Jewish Assets* (Policy Forum No. 13) (Jerusalem: Institute of the World Jewish Congress, 1998).

Zeugin, Bettina, and Sandkühler, Thomas, eds., *Die Schweiz und die deutschen Lösegelderpressungen in den besetzten Niederlanden: Vermögensentziehung, Freikauf, Austausch 1940–1945: Beiheft zum Bericht Die Schweiz und die Flüchtlinge zur Zeit des Nationalsozialismus* (Bern: Unabhängige Expertenkommission Schweiz, Zweiter Weltkrieg, 1999).

Ziegler, Dieter, *Die Dresdner Bank und die deutschen Juden* (Munich: R. Oldenbourg, 2006).

BOOKS AND ARTICLES

Aalders, Gerard, "Die Arisierung der niederländischen Wirtschaft: Raub per Verordnung," in Alfons Kenkmann and Bernd-A. Rusinek (eds.), *Verfolgung und Verwaltung: Die wirtschaftliche Ausplünderung der Juden und die westfälischen Finanzbehörden* (Münster: Oberfinanzdirektion Münster, 1999): 122–137.

Aalders, Gerard, *Geraubt! Die Enteignung jüdischen Besitzes im Zweiten Weltkrieg* (Cologne: Dittrich, 2000).

Aalders, Gerard, *Nazi Looting: The Plunder of Dutch Jewry during the Second World War* (Oxford: Berg, 2004).

Aalders, Gerard and Wiebes, Cees, *The Art of Cloaking Ownership: The Secret Collaboration and Protection of the German War Industry by the Neutrals – The Case of Sweden* (Amsterdam: Amsterdam University Press, 1996).

Abitbol, Michael, *The Jews of North Africa during the Second World War* (Detroit: Wayne State University Press, 1989).

Adler, H. G., *Der verwaltete Mensch: Studien zur Deportation der Juden aus Deutschland* (Tübingen: J. C. B. Mohr, 1974).

Adler, Jacques, *The Jews of Paris and the Final Solution: Communal Response and Internal Conflicts, 1940–44* (Oxford: Oxford University Press, 1985).

Aly, Götz, *"Endlösung": Völkerverschiebung und der Mord an den europäischen Juden* (Frankfurt am Main: S. Fischer, 1995).

Aly, Götz, *Hitlers Volksstaat: Raub, Rassenkrieg und nationaler Sozialismus* (Frankfurt am Main: S. Fischer, 2005); also available in English as *Hitler's Beneficiaries* (New York: Metropolitan Books, 2007).

Aly, Götz, and Heim, Susanne, *Vordenker der Vernichtung. Auschwitz und die deutschen Pläne für eine europäischer Neuordnung* (Hamburg: Hofmann und Campe, 1991).

Ancel, Jean, "German-Romanian Relations during the Second World War," in Randolph L. Braham (ed.), *The Tragedy of Romanian Jewry* (New York: Rosenthal Institute for Holocaust Studies, Graduate Center City University of New York; Boulder: Social Science Monographs; New York: Distributed by Columbia University Press, 1994): 57–76.

Ancel, Jean, "The Jassy Pogrom – June 29, 1941," in M. Hausleitner, B. Mihok, and J. Wetzel (eds.), *Rumänien und der Holocaust: Zu den Massenverbrechen in Transnistrien 1941–1944* (Berlin: Metropol, 2001): 53–68.

Ancel, Jean, "Seizure of Jewish Property in Romania," in *Confiscation of Jewish Property in Europe, 1933–1945: New Sources and Perspectives*, Symposium Proceedings (Washington, DC: United States Holocaust Memorial Museum, 2003).

Ancel, Jean, *Transnistria, 1941–1942* (Tel Aviv: Goldstein-Goren Diaspora Research Center, 2003), 3 vols.

Ancel, Jean, "The German-Romanian Relationship and the Final Solution," *Holocaust and Genocide Studies*, vol. 19, no. 2 (Fall 2005): 252–75.

Arad, Yitzhak, "Plunder of Jewish Property in the Nazi-Occupied Areas of the Soviet Union," *Yad Vashem Studies*, XXI (2000): 109–48.

Authers, John, and Wolffe, Richard, *The Victim's Fortune: Inside the Epic Battle over the Debts of the Holocaust* (New York: HarperCollins, 2002).

Bähr, Johannes, *Der Goldhandel der Dresdner Bank im Zweiten Weltkrieg* (Leipzig: Kiepenheuer, 1999).

Bajohr, Frank, "The Beneficiaries of 'Aryanization': Hamburg as a Case Study," *Yad Vashem Studies* XXVI (Jerusalem, 1998): 173–201.

Bajohr, Frank, "'Arisierung' als gesellschaftlicher Prozess: Verhalten, Strategien und Handlungsspielräume jüdischer Eigentümer und 'arischer' Erwerber," in Irmtrud Wojak and Peter Hayes (eds.), *"Arisierung" im Nationalsozialismus: Volksgemeinschaft, Raub und Gedächtnis. Jahrbuch 2000 zur Geschichte und Wirkung des Holocaust* (Frankfurt am Main: Campus, 2000).

Bajohr, Frank, *Parvenüs und Profiteure: Korruption in der NS-Zeit* (Frankfurt am Main: S. Fischer, 2001).

Bajohr, Frank, *"Arisierung" in Hamburg*, 2nd ed (Hamburg: Hans Christians, 1997). Available in translation as: *"Aryanisation" in Hamburg: The Economic Exclusion of the Jews and the Confiscation of their Property in Nazi Germany* (New York: Berghahn, 2002).

Banken, Ralf, "Die nationalsozialistische Goldreserven und Devisenpolitik 1933–1939," *Jahrbuch für Wirtschaftsgeschichte* 1 (2003): 49–78.

Banken, Ralf, "Kurzfristiger Boom oder langfristiger Forschungsschwerpunkt? Die neuere deutsche Unternehmensgeschichte und die Zeit des Nationalsozialismus," *Geschichte in Wissenschaft und Unterricht* 3 (2005): 183–96.

Barendregt, Jaap, *Securities at Risk: The Restitution of Jewish Securities Stolen in the Netherlands during World War II* (Amsterdam: Aksant, 2004).

Barkai, Avraham, *Vom Boykott zur "Entjudung": Der wirtschaftliche Existenzkampf der Juden im Dritten Reich 1933–1943* (Frankfurt am Main: Fischer, 1987).

Bartoszewski, Władysław, *Warsaw Death Ring, 1939–1944* (Warsaw: Interpress Publishers, 1968).

Baruch, Marc-Olivier, "Perpetrator Networks and the Holocaust: The Spoliation of Jewish Property in France, 1940–44," in Wolfgang Seibel and Gerald Feldman (eds.), *Networks of Nazi Persecution: Division-of-Labor in the Holocaust* (New York: Berghahn, 2005): 189–212.

Bar-Zohar, Michael, *Beyond Hitler's Grasp: The Heroic Rescue of Bulgaria's Jews* (Holbrook, MA: Adams Media, 1998).

Bauer, Yehuda, *Jews for Sale? Nazi-Jewish Negotiations, 1933–1945* (New Haven: Yale University Press, 1994)

Ben-Tov, Arieh, *Facing the Holocaust in Budapest: The International Committee of the Red Cross and the Jews in Hungary, 1943–1945* (Boston: M. Nijhoff, 1988).

Berend, Ivan T., "The Road toward the Holocaust: The Ideological and Political Background," in Randolph L. Braham and Bela Vago (eds.), *The Holocaust in Hungary: Forty Years Later* (New York: Social Science Monographs, Columbia University Press, 1985): 31–51.

Berschel, Holger, *Bürokratie und Terror: Das Judenreferat der Gestapo Düsseldorf 1933–1945* (Essen: Klartext, 2001).

Bertz, Inka, "Ein Karteiblatt für jeden abgeschobenen Juden erleichtert die Übersicht," in Dorothea Kolland (ed.), *Zehn Brüder waren wir gewesen . . . : Spuren jüdischen Lebens in Berlin-Neukölln* (Berlin: Edition Hentrich, 1988): 372–86.

Billig, Joseph, *Le Commissariat Général aux Questions Juives, 1941–1944* (Paris: Editions du Centre, 1953–60), 3 vols.

Birkwald, Ilse, "Die Steuerverwaltung im Dritten Reich," in Wolfgang Leesch et al. (eds.), *Geschichte der Finanzverfassung- und verwaltung in Westfalen seit 1815* (Münster: OFD, 1998): 239–86.

Blumberg, Gerd, "Die Zollverwaltung," in Wolfgang Leesch et al. (eds.), *Geschichte der Finanzverfassung- und verwaltung in Westfalen seit 1815* (Münster: Oberfinanzdirektion Münster, 1998).

Blumberg, Gerd, "Etappen der Verfolgung und Ausraubung und ihre bürokratische Apparatur," in Alfons Kenkmann and Bernd-A. Rusinek (eds.), *Verfolgung und Verwaltung: Die wirtschaftliche Ausplünderung der Juden und die westfälischen Finanzbehörden* (Münster: Oberfinanzdirektion Münster, 1999): 15–40.

Bohn, Thomas M., "Bulgariens Rolle im 'wirtschaftlichen Ergänzungsraum' Südosteuropa: Hintergründe für den Beitritt zum Dreimächtepakt am 1. März 1941," in *Besatzung und Bündnis: Deutsche Herrschaftsstrategien in Ost- und Südosteuropa (Beiträge zur nationalsozialistischen Gesundheits- und Sozialpolitik: 12)* (Göttingen: Verlag der Buchläden, 1995).

Bopf, Britta, *"Arisierung in Köln": Die wirtschaftliche Existenzvernichtung der Juden 1933–1945* (Cologne: Emons, 2004).

Botz, Gerhard, *Wohnungspolitik und Judendeportation in Wien 1938 bis 1945* (Vienna: Geyer, 1975).

Botz, Gerhard, *Nationalsozialismus in Wien: Machtübernahme und Herrschaftssicherung 1938/39* (Buchloe: Obermayer, 1988).

Bower, Tom, *Blood Money: The Swiss, the Nazis and the Looted Billions* (London: Macmillan, 1997).

Bracher, Karl Dietrich, *The German Dictatorship: The Origins, Structure and Consequences of National Socialism* (New York: Praeger, 1970).

Braham, Randolph L., *The Politics of Genocide: The Holocaust in Hungary* 2 vols. (New York: Columbia University Press, 1993).

Brechtken, Magnus, *"Madagaskar für die Juden": Antisemitische Idee und politische Praxis 1885–1945* (Munich: Oldenbourg, 1997).

Browning, Christopher R., *The Path to Genocide: Essays on Launching the Final Solution* (Cambridge: Cambridge University Press, 1992).

Browning, Christopher R., *Initiating the Final Solution: The Fateful Months of September-October 1941* (Washington, DC: United States Holocaust Memorial Museum, 2003).

Browning, Christopher R., and Matthäus, Jürgen, *Die Entfesselung der 'Endlösung': Nationalsozialistische Judenpolitik 1939–1942* (Berlin: Propyläen, 2003).

Brüns-Wüstefeld, Alex, *Lohnende Geschäfte: Die "Entjudung" der Wirtschaft am Beispiel Göttingens* (Hanover: Fackelträger, 1997).

Buchholz, Marlis, *Die hannoverschen Judenhäuser: Zur Situation der Juden in der Zeit der Ghettoisierung und Verfolgung 1941 bis 1945* (Hildesheim: A. Lax, 1987).

Buomberger, Thomas, *Raubkunst – Kunstraub: Die Schweiz und der Handel mit gestohlenen Kulturgütern zur Zeit des Zweiten Weltkriegs* (Zürich: Orel Füssli, 1998).

Chary, Frederick B., *The Bulgarian Jews and the Final Solution, 1940–1944* (Pittsburgh: University of Pittsburgh Press, 1972).

Chiari, Bernhard, *Alltag hinter der Front: Besatzung, Kollaboration und Widerstand in Weissrussland, 1941–1944* (Düsseldorf: Droste, 1998).

Cholawsky, Shalom, *The Jews of Bielorussia during World War II* (Amsterdam: Harwood, 1998).

Cole, Tim, "Hungary, the Holocaust, and Hungarians: Remembering Whose History?" in *Hungary and the Holocaust: Confrontation with the Past: Symposium Proceedings* (Washington, DC: United States Holocaust Memorial Museum, 2001).

Cole, Tim, *Holocaust City: The Making of a Jewish Ghetto* (New York: Routledge, 2003).

Confiscation of Jewish Property in Europe, 1933–1945: New Sources and Perspectives (Washington, DC: United States Holocaust Memorial Museum, 2003).

Curtis, Michael, *Verdict on Vichy: Power and Prejudice in the Vichy France Regime* (New York: Arcade, 2002).

Dean, Martin, *Collaboration in the Holocaust: Crimes of the Local Police in Belorussia and Ukraine, 1941–44* (London: Macmillan in association with the United States Holocaust Memorial Museum, 1999).

Dean, Martin, "Die Enteignung 'jüdischen Eigentums' im Reichskommissariat Ostland 1941–1944," in Irmtrud Wojak and Peter Hayes (eds.), *"Arisierung" im Nationalsozialismus: Volksgemeinschaft, Raub und Gedächtnis* (Frankfurt am Main: Campus, 2000): 201–18.

Dean, Martin, "Jewish Property Seized in the Occupied Soviet Union in 1941 and 1942: The Records of the *Reichshauptkasse Beutestelle*," *Holocaust and Genocide Studies*, vol. 14, no. 1 (Spring 2000): 83–101.

Dean, Martin, "Seizure, Registration, Rental and Sale: the Strange Case of the German Administration of Moveable Property in Latvia (1941–1944)," in *Latvia in World War II: Materials of an International Conference, 14–15 June 1999, Riga* (Riga: Latvijas vestures institute apgads, 2000): 372–78.

Dean, Martin, "The Development and Implementation of Nazi Denaturalization and Confiscation Policy up to the Eleventh Decree to the Reich Citizenship Law," *Holocaust and Genocide Studies*, vol. 16, no. 2 (Fall 2002): 217–42.

Dean, Martin, "Microcosm: Collaboration and Resistance during the Holocaust in the Mir Rayon of Belarus, 1941–1944," in D. Gaunt, P. A. Levine, and L. Palosuo (eds.), *Collaboration and Resistance during the Holocaust: Belarus, Estonia, Latvia, Lithuania* (Bern: Peter Lang, 2004): 223–60.

Dean, Martin "Multinational Jewish Businesses and the Transfer of Capital Abroad in the Face of 'Aryanization', 1933–39," in Chris Kobrak and Per Hansen (eds.), *European Business, Dictatorship and Political Risk: 1920–1945* (New York: Berghahn, 2004): 103–21.

Dean, Martin, "The Role of Law in the Seizure of Property in Nazi-Occupied Eastern Europe," in Johannes Bähr and Ralf Banken (eds.), *Das Europa des "Dritten Reichs": Recht Wirtschaft, Besatzung, Das Europa der Diktatur* vol. 5 (Frankfurt am Main: Klostermann, 2005): 81–104.

Dean, Martin, "Seizure of Jewish Property and Inter-Agency Rivalry in the Reich and in the Occupied Soviet Territories," in W. Seibel and G. Feldman (eds.), *Networks of Nazi Persecution: Division-of-Labor in the Holocaust* (New York: Berghahn, 2005): 88–102.

Dean, Martin, Goschler, Constantin, and Ther, Philipp, eds., *Robbery and Restitution: The Conflict over Jewish Property in Europe* (New York: Berghahn in association with the United States Holocaust Memorial Museum, 2007).

Dehnel, Regine (ed.), "Jüdischer Buchbesitz als Raubgut," *Zeitschrift für Bibliothekswesen und Bibliographie Sonderheft* 88 (2005).

Dingell, Jeanne, "Property Seizures from Poles and Jews: The Activities of the Haupttreuhandstelle Ost," in *Confiscation of Jewish Property in Europe, 1933–1945: New Sources and Perspectives* (Washington, DC: United States Holocaust Memorial Museum, 2003): 33–41.

Döring, Martin, *"Parlamentarischer Arm der Bewegung": Die Nationalsozialisten im Reichstag der Weimarer Republik* (Düsseldorf: Droste, 2001).

Dörner, Bernward, *"Heimtücke": Das Gesetz als Waffe: Kontrolle, Abschreckung und Verfolgung in Deutschland 1933–1945* (Paderborn: Schöningh, 1998).

Don, Yehuda, "Economic Implications of the Anti-Jewish Legislation in Hungary," in David Cesarani (ed.), *Genocide and Rescue: The Holocaust in Hungary 1944* (Oxford: Berg, 1997): 47–76.

van Doorslaer, Rudi, "Raub und Rückerstattung jüdischen Eigentums in Belgien," in Constantin Goschler and Philipp Ther (eds.), *Raub und Restitution: "Arisierung" und Rückerstattung des jüdischen Eigentums in Europa* (Frankfurt am Main: Fischer Taschenbuch, 2003): 134–53.

Doulut, Alexandre, "La spoliation des biens juifs dans le Lot-et-Garonne," in *Revue d'histoire de la Shoah*, no. 186, *Spoliations en Europe* (Janvier-Juin 2007): 291–328.

Dreßen, Wolfgang, (ed.), *Betrifft: "Aktion 3." Deutsche verwerten jüdische Nachbarn. Dokumente zur Arisierung* (Berlin: Aufbau Verlag, 1998).

Dreyfus, Jean-Marc, "French Banks and Aryanization 1940–1944," in Oliver Rathkolb (ed.), *Revisiting the National Socialist Legacy: Coming to Terms with Forced Labor, Expropriation, Compensation, and Restitution* (Innsbruck: Studien Verlag, 2002): 145–53.

Dreyfus, Jean-Marc, "Die Enteignung der Juden in Westeuropa," in Constantin Goschler and Philipp Ther (eds.), *Raub und Restitution: "Arisierung" und Rückerstattung des jüdischen Eigentums in Europa* (Frankfurt am Main: Fischer Taschenbuch, 2003): 41–57.

Dreyfus, Jean-Marc, and Gensburger, Sarah, *Des camps dans Paris: Austerlitz, Lévitan, Bassano, juillet 1943 – août 1944* (Paris: Fayard, 2003).

Dreyfus, Jean-Marc, "Franco-German Rivalry and 'Aryanization' as the Creation of a New Policy in France, 1940–44," in *Confiscation of Jewish Property in Europe, 1933–1945: New Sources and Perspectives*, Symposium Proceedings (Washington, DC: United States Holocaust Memorial Museum, 2003): 75–92.

Eichwede, Wolfgang, and Hartung, Ulrike (eds.), *"Betr.: Sicherstellung" – NS-Kunstraub in der Sowjetunion* (Bremen: Temmen, 1998).

Eizenstat, Stuart, *Imperfect Justice: Looted Assets, Slave Labor, and the Unfinished Business of World War II* (New York: PublicAffairs, 2003).

Endler, Renate, and Schwarze, Elisabeth (eds.), *Die Freimaurerbestände im Geheimen Staatsarchiv Preussischer Kulturbesitz Bd. 1 Grosslogen und Protektor Freimaurerische Stiftungen und Vereinigungen* (Frankfurt am Main: Peter Lang, 1994).

Essner, Cornelia, *Die "Nürnberger Gesetze" oder die Verwaltung des Rassenwahns 1933–1945* (Paderborn: Schöningh, 2002).

Fargion, Liliana Picciotto, "The Anti-Jewish Policy of the Italian Social Republic (1943–1945)," *Yad Vashem Studies*, XVII (1986): 17–49.

Feilchenfeld, Werner, Michaelis, Dolf, and Pinner, Ludwig, *Haavara-Transfer nach Palästina und Einwanderung Deutscher Juden 1933–1939* (Tübingen: J. C. B. Mohr, 1972).

Felak, James Ramon, *At the Price of the Republic: Hlinka's Slovak People's Party, 1929–1938* (Pittsburgh: University of Pittsburgh Press, 1994).

Feldman, Gerald, *Die Allianz und die deutsche Versicherungswirtschaft 1933–1945* (Munich: C. H. Beck, 2001); also available in English as *Allianz and the German Insurance Business, 1933–1945* (New York: Cambridge University Press, 2001).

Feldman, Gerald D., "Competition and Collaboration among the Axis Multi-national Insurers: Munich Re, Generali, and Riunione Adriatica, 1933–1945," in Chris Kobrak and Per Hansen (eds.), *European Business, Dictatorship and Political Risk: 1920–1945* (New York: Berghahn, 2004).

Feliciano, Hector, *The Lost Museum: The Nazi Conspiracy to Steal the World's Greatest Works of Art* (New York: Basic Books, 1997).

Fichtl, Franz, Link, Stephan, May, Herbert, and Schaible, Sylvia, *"Bambergs Wirtschaft Judenfrei": Die Verdrängung der jüdischen Geschäftsleute in den Jahren 1933 bis 1939* (Bamberg: Collibri, 1998).

Fraser, David, "National Constitutions, Liberal State, Fascist State and the Holocaust in Belgium and Bulgaria," *German Law Journal*, no. 2 (February 2005).

Freitag, Gabriele, and Grenzer, Andreas, "Der nationalsozialistische Kunstraub in der Sowjetunion," in Wolfgang Eichwede and Ulrike Hartung (eds.), *"Betr.: Sicherstellung": NS-Kunstraub in der Sowjetunion* (Bremen: Edition Temmen, 1998): 20–66.

Friedenberger, Martin, "Das Berliner Finanzamt Moabit-West und die Enteignung der Emigranten des Dritten Reichs 1933–1942," *Zeitschrift für Geschichtswissenschaft* 49:8 (2001): 677–94.

Friedenberger, Martin, "Die Rolle der Finanzverwaltung bei der Vertreibung, Verfolgung und Vernichtung der deutschen Juden," in Martin Friedenberger, Klaus Dieter Gössel, and Eberhard Schönknecht (eds.), *Die Reichsfinanzverwaltung im Nationalsozialismus: Darstellung und Dokumente* (Bremen: Edition Temmen, 2002): 10–94.

Genschel, Helmut, *Die Verdrängung der Juden aus der Wirtschaft im Dritten Reich* (Göttingen: Musterschmidt Verlag, 1966).

Gerlach, Christian, *Kalkulierte Morde: Die deutsche Wirtschafts- und Vernichtungspolitik in Weissrussland 1941 bis 1944* (Hamburg: HIS, 1999).

Gerlach, Christian, and Aly, Götz, *Das letzte Kapitel: Der Mord an den ungarischen Juden* (Stuttgart: DVA, 2002).

Goschler, Constantin, and Ther, Philipp (eds.), *Raub und Restitution: "Arisierung" und Rückerstattung des jüdischen Eigentums in Europa* (Frankfurt am Main: Fischer Taschenbuch, 2003).

Grahn, Gerlinde, "Die Enteignung des Vermögens der Arbeiterbewegung und der politischen Emigration 1933 bis 1945," *1999* (Heft 3/97): 13–38.

Grimsted, Patricia Kennedy, "Twice Plundered or 'Twice Saved'? Identifying Russia's 'Trophy' Archives and the Loot of the Reichssicherheitshauptamt," *Holocaust and Genocide Studies*, vol. 15, no. 2 (Fall 2001): 191–244.

Grimsted, Patricia Kennedy, "The Postwar Fate of Einsatzstab Reichsleiter Rosenberg Archival and Library Plunder, and the Dispersal of ERR Records," *Holocaust and Genocide Studies*, vol. 20, no. 2 (Fall 2006): 278–308.

Gross, Jan T., *Fear: Anti-Semitism in Poland after Auschwitz* (New York: Random House, 2006).

Grossmann, Kurt R., *Emigration: Geschichte der Hitler-Flüchtlinge, 1933–1945* (Frankfurt am Main: Europäische Verlagsanstalt, 1969).

Gruner, Wolf, "Die Reichshauptstadt und die Verfolgung der Berliner Juden 1933–1945," in Reinhard Rürup (ed.), *Jüdische Geschichte in Berlin* (Berlin: Hentrich, 1995): 229–66.

Gruner, Wolf, *Der geschlossene Arbeitseinsatz deutscher Juden: Zur Zwangsarbeit als Element der Verfolgung 1938–1943* (Berlin: Metropol, 1997).

Gruner, Wolf, "The German Council of Municipalities (*Deutscher Gemeindetag*) and the Coordination of Anti-Jewish Local Politics in the Nazi State," in *Holocaust and Genocide Studies*, vol. 13, no. 2 (Fall 1999): 171–99.

Gruner, Wolf, "Die Grundstücke der 'Reichsfeinde': Zur 'Arisierung' von Immobilien durch Städte und Gemeinden 1938–1945," in Irmtrud Wojak and Peter Hayes (eds.), *"Arisierung" im Nationalsozialismus: Volksgemeinschaft, Raub und Gedächtnis. Jahrbuch 2000 zur Geschichte und Wirkung des Holocaust* (Frankfurt am Main: Campus, 2000): 125–56.

Gruner, Wolf, "Poverty and Persecution: The Reichsvereinigung, the Jewish Population, and Anti-Jewish Policy in the Nazi State, 1939–1945," *Yad Vashem Studies* XXVII (1999): 23–60.

Gruner, Wolf, "Das Protektorat Böhmen und Mähren und die antijüdische Politik 1939–1941," in *Theresienstädter Studien und Dokumente* (2005): 27–62.

Gruner, Wolf, *Zwangsarbeit und Verfolgung: Österreichische Juden im NS-Staat 1938–45* (Innsbruck: Studien, 2000).

Gruner, Wolf, "Von der Kollektivausweisung zur Deportation der Juden aus Deutschland (1938–1945) – Neue Perspektiven und Dokumente," *Beiträge zur Geschichte des Nationalsozialismus 20, Die Deportation der Juden aus Deutschland: Pläne – Praxis – Reaktionen 1938–1945* (Göttingen: Wallstein, 2004): 21–62.

Gruner, Wolf, *Jewish Forced Labor under the Nazis: Economic Needs and Racial Aims, 1938–1944* (New York: Cambridge University Press, published in association with the United States Holocaust Memorial Museum, 2006).

Händler-Lachmann, Barbara, and Werther, Thomas, *Vergessene Geschäfte – verlorene Geschichte: Jüdisches Wirtschaftsleben in Marburg und seine Vernichtung im Nationalsozialismus* (Marburg: Hitzeroth, 1992).

Haskell, Guy H., *From Sofia to Jaffa: The Jews of Bulgaria and Israel* (Detroit: Wayne State University Press, 1994).

Hausleitner, Mariana, "Auf dem Weg zur 'Ethnokratie': Rumänien in den Jahren des Zweiten Weltkrieges," in *Beiträge zur Geschichte des Nationalsozialismus 19, Kooperation und Verbrechen: Formen der "Kollaboration" im östlichen Europa 1939–1945* (Göttingen: Wallstein, 2003): 78–112.

Hayes, Peter, "Big Business and 'Aryanization' in Germany," *Jahrbuch für Antisemitismusforschung*, Jg. 3 (1994): 254–81.

Hayes, Peter, "Profits and Persecution: German Big Business and the Holocaust," J. B. and Maurice C. Shapiro Annual Lecture given at the United States Holocaust Memorial Museum on February 17, 1998 (Washington, DC: United States Holocaust Memorial Museum, 1998).

Hayes, Peter, "The Degussa AG and the Holocaust," in Ronald Smelser (ed.), *Lessons and Legacies*, Vol. 5, *The Holocaust and Justice* (Evanston, IL: Northwestern University Press, 2002): 140–77.

Hayes, Peter, *From Cooperation to Complicity: Degussa in the Third Reich* (Cambridge: Cambridge University Press, 2004).

Heim, Susanne, "'Deutschland muss ihnen ein Land ohne Zukunft sein.' Die Zwangsemigration der Juden 1933 bis 1938," *Beiträge zur Nationalsozialistischen Gesundheits- und Sozialpolitik* 11: 48–81.

Heim, Susanne, "Vertreibung, Raub und Umverteilung: Die jüdischen Flüchtlinge aus Deutschland und die Vermehrung des 'Volksvermögens,'" *Beiträge zur Nationalsozialistschen Gesundheits- und Sozialpolitik* 15: 107–38.

Heinen, Armin, "Gewalt – Kultur," in Mariana Hausleitner, Brigitte Mihok, and Julianne Wetzel (eds.), *Rumänien und der Holocaust: Zu den Massenverbrechen in Transnistrien 1941–1944* (Berlin: Metropol, 2001): 33–51.

Hepp, Michael (ed.), *Die Ausbürgerung deutscher Staatsangehöriger 1933–45 nach den im Reichsanzeiger veröffentlichten Listen* (Munich: K. G. Saur, 1985), 3 vols.

Heuss, Anja, *Kunst- und Kulturgutraub: Eine vergleichende Studie zur Besatzungspolitik der Nationalsozialisten in Frankreich und der Sowjetunion* (Heidelberg: Winter, 2000).

Hilberg, Raul, *Die Vernichtung der europäischen Juden* (Frankfurt am Main: Fischer, 1982), 3 vols.; also available in English in an updated form as *The Destruction of the European Jews*, 3rd ed. (New Haven, CT: Yale University Press, 2003).

Holzbauer, Robert, "Einziehung volks- und staatsfeindlichen Vermögens im Lande Österreich: Die 'VUGESTA' – die 'Verwertungsstelle für jüdisches Umzugsgut der Gestapo,'" *Spurensuche*, 1–2 (2000): 38–50.

Ioanid, Radu, "The Antonescu Era," in Randolph L. Braham (ed.), *The Tragedy of Romanian Jewry* (Boulder, CO: Rosenthal Institute for Holocaust Studies; Social Science Monographs, 1994): 117–71.

Ioanid, Radu, *The Holocaust in Romania: The Destruction of Jews and Gypsies under the Antonescu Regime, 1940–44* (Chicago: Ivan R. Dee in association with the United States Holocaust Memorial Museum, 2000).

James, Harold, "Die Deutsche Bank 1933–45," in Lothar Gall et al., *Die Deutsche Bank 1870–1995* (Munich: C. H. Beck, 1995): 277–356.

James, Harold, *The Deutsche Bank and the Nazi Economic War against the Jews* (Cambridge: Cambridge University Press, 2001).

Jonca, Karol, "The Expulsion of Polish Jews from the Third Reich in 1938," *Polin*, vol. 8 (1994): 255–81.

Kádár, Gábor, and Vági, Zoltán *Self-Financing Genocide: The Gold Train, the Becher Case and the Wealth of Hungarian Jews* (Budapest: Central European University Press, 2004).

Kádár, Gábor, and Vági, Zoltán, "The Economic Annihilation of the Hungarian Jews, 1944–1945," in Randolph L. Braham and Brewster S. Chamberlin (eds.), *The Holocaust in Hungary: Sixty Years Later* (Boulder, CO: Rosenthal Institute for Holocaust Studies, Graduate Center of City University of New York Social Science Monographs, published in association with the United States Holocaust Memorial Museum, distributed by Columbia University Press, 2006): 77–88.

Kamenec, Ivan, "The Deportation of Jewish Citizens from Slovakia in 1942," in Dezider Tóth (ed.), *The Tragedy of Slovak Jews 1938–1945: Slovakia and the "Final Solution of the Jewish Question"* (Banská Bystrica, Slovakia: Ministry of Culture of Slovak Republic and Museum of Slovak National Uprising, 1992): 111–40.

Kaplan, Marion A., *Between Dignity and Despair: Jewish Life in Nazi Germany* (New York: Oxford University Press, 1998),

Kenkmann, Alfons, and Rusinek, Bernd-A. (eds.), *Verfolgung und Verwaltung: Die wirtschaftliche Ausplünderung der Juden und die westfälischen Finanzbehörden* (Münster: Oberfinanzdirektion Münster, 1999).

Kershaw, Ian, *Hitler 1889–1936: Hubris* (London: Penguin, 1998).

Kershaw, Ian, *Hitler 1936–45: Nemesis* (New York: W. W. Norton, 2002).

Kingreen, Monica, "Gewaltsam verschleppt aus Frankfurt: Die Deportationen der Juden in den Jahren 1941–45," in Monica Kingreen (ed.), *"Nach der Kristallnacht:" Jüdisches Leben und antijüdische Politik in Frankfurt am Main 1938–1945* (Frankfurt am Main: Campus, 1999).

Kingreen, Monica, "'Wir werden darüber hinweg kommen': Letzte Lebenszeichen deportierter hessischer Juden. Eine dokumentarische Annäherung," *Beiträge zur Geschichte des Nationalsozialismus 20, Die Deportation der Juden aus Deutschland: Pläne – Praxis – Reaktionen 1938–1945* (Göttingen: Wallstein, 2004): 86–111.

Knight, Robert (ed.), *"Ich bin dafür, die Sache in die Länge zu ziehen": Wortprotokolle der österreichischen Bundesregierung von 1945–1952 über die Entschädigung der Juden* (Frankfurt am Main: Athenäum, 1988).

Kolbe, Christian, and Wirtz, Stephan (eds.), *Enteignung der jüdischen Bevölkerung in Deutschland und nationalsozialistische Wirtschaftspolitik 1933–1945: Annotierte Bibliographie* (Frankfurt am Main: Fritz Bauer Institut, 2000).

Konieczny, Alfred, *Tormersdorf, Grüssau, Riebnig: Obozy przej'sciowe dla Zydów Dolnego 'Slaska z lat 1941–1943* (Wroclaw: Wydawn. Uniwersytetu Wroclawskiego, 1997).

Kratzsch, Gerhard, *Der Gauwirtschaftsapparat der NSDAP: Menschenführung – "Arisierung" – Wehrwirtschaft im Gau Westfalen-Süd* (Münster: Aschendorffsche Verlag, 1989).

Kropat, Wolf-Arno, *"Reichskristallnacht": Der Judenpogrom vom 7. bis 10. November 1938– Urheber, Täter, Hintergründe* (Wiesbaden: Kommission für die Geschichte der Juden in Hessen, 1997).

Kuller, Christiane, "'Erster Grundsatz: Horten für die Reichsfinanzverwaltung': Die Verwertung des Eigentums der deportierten Nürnberger Juden," *Beiträge zur Geschichte des Nationalsozialismus 20, Die Deportation der Juden aus Deutschland: Pläne – Praxis – Reaktionen 1938–1945* (Göttingen: Wallstein, 2004): 160–79.

Kwiet, Konrad, "Nach dem Pogrom: Stufen der Ausgrenzung," in Wolfgang Benz (ed.), *Die Juden in Deutschland 1933–1945: Leben unter nationalsozialistischer Herrschaft* (Munich: C. H. Beck, 1993): 545–659.

van Laak, Dirk, "Die Mitwirkenden bei der 'Arisierung.' Dargestellt am Beispiel der rheinisch-westfälischen Industrieregion 1933–1940," in Ursula Büttner (ed.), *Die Deutschen und die Judenverfolgung im Dritten Reich* (Hamburg: Christians, 1992): 231–58.

Laureys, Eric, "The Plundering of Antwerp's Jewish Diamond Dealers," in *Confiscation of Jewish Property in Europe, 1933–1945: New Sources and Perspectives* (Washington, DC: United States Holocaust Memorial Museum, 2003): 57–74.

van der Leeuw, A. J., "Zur Vorgeschichte der Enteignung jüdischen Vermögens durch die Elfte VO-RbuergerG," in *Rechtsprechung zum Wiedergutmachungsrecht*, vol. 1 (January 1962): 1–4.

van der Leeuw, A. J., "Die Aktion Bozenhardt und Co.," in A. H. Paape (ed.), *Studies over Nederland in oorlogstijd* ('s-Gravenhage: Martinus Nijhoff, 1972): 257–77.

van der Leeuw, A. J., "Der Griff des Reiches nach dem Judenvermögen," in A. H. Paape (ed.), *Studies over Nederland in oorlogstijd* ('s-Gravenhage: Martinus Nijhoff, 1972): 211–36, first published in *Rechtsprechung zum Wiedergutmachungsrecht* (1970): 383–92.

van der Leeuw, A. J., "Die Käufe des Generalkommissars z.b.V. Fritz Schmidt," in A. H. Paape (ed.), *Studies over Nederland in oorlogstijd* ('s-Gravenhage: Martinus Nijhoff, 1972): 278–82.

van der Leeuw, A. J., "Reichskommissariat und Judenvermögen in den Niederlanden," in A. H. Paape (ed.), *Studies over Nederland in oorlogstijd* ('s-Gravenhage: Martinus Nijhoff, 1972): 237–49.

Levin, Itamar, *The Last Chapter of the Holocaust?* (Israel: Jewish Agency for Israel in co-operation with The World Jewish Restitution Organization, 2nd ed. 1998).

Levin, Itamar, *Walls Around: The Plunder of Warsaw Jewry during World War II and Its Aftermath* (Westport, CT: Praeger, 2004).

van Liempt, Ad, *Kopgeld: Nederlandse premiejagers op zoek naar joden 1943* (Amsterdam: Balans, 2002).

Lillteicher, Jürgen, "Rechtsstaatlichkeit und Verfolgungserfahrung: 'Arisierung' und fiskalische Ausplünderung vor Gericht," in Constantin Goschler and

Jürgen Lillteicher (eds.), *Die Rückerstattung jüdischen Eigentums in Deutschland und Österreich nach 1945 und 1989* (Göttingen: Wallstein, 2002).

Lindner, Stephan H., *Das Reichskommissariat für die Behandlung feindlichen Vermögens im Zweiten Weltkrieg: Eine Studie zur Verwaltungs-, Rechts- und Wirtschaftsgeschichte des nationalsozialistischen Deutschlands* (Stuttgart: Franz Steinert, 1991).

Lindner, Stephan H., *Hoechst: Ein I.G. Farben Werk im Dritten Reich* (Munich: C. H. Beck, 2005).

Lipscher, Ladislav, *Die Juden im Slowakischen Staat 1939–1945* (Munich: Oldenbourg, 1980).

Longerich, Peter, *Politik der Vernichtung. Eine Gesamtdarstellung der nationalsozialistischen Judenverfolgung* (Munich: Piper, 1998).

Loose, Ingo, "Die Enteignung der Juden im besetzten Polen, 1939–1945," in Katharina Stengel (ed.), *Vor der Vernichtung: Die staatliche Enteignung der Juden im Nationalsozialismus* (Frankfurt am Main: Campus, 2007).

Lorentz, Bernhard, "Die Commerzbank und die 'Arisierung' im Altreich: Ein Vergleich der Netzwerkstrukturen und Handlungsspielräume von Grossbanken in der NS-Zeit," *Vierteljahrshefte für Zeitgeschichte* 50. Jg., Heft 2 (April 2002): 237–68.

Lower, Wendy, *Nazi Empire-Building and the Holocaust in Ukraine* (Chapel Hill: University of North Carolina Press in association with the United States Holocaust Memorial Museum, 2005).

Ludwig, Johannes, *Boykott – Enteignung – Mord. Die "Entjudung" der deutschen Wirtschaft* (Munich: Facta, 1989).

MacQueen, Michael, "The Conversion of Looted Assets to Run the German War Machine," *Holocaust and Genocide Studies*, vol. 18, no. 1 (Spring 2004): 27–45.

Maierhof, Gudrun, "Selbsthilfe nach dem Novemberpogrom: Die jüdische Gemeinde in Frankfurt am Main 1938 bis 1942," in Monica Kingreen (ed.), *"Nach der Kristallnacht": Jüdisches Leben und antijüdische Politik in Frankfurt am Main 1938–1945* (Frankfurt am Main: Campus, 1999): 157–86.

Majer, Diemut, *"Fremdvölkische" im Dritten Reich* (Boppard am Rhein: Harald Boldt Verlag, 1981, 2nd edition, 1993); also available in English as *"Non-Germans" under the Third Reich: The Nazi Judicial and Administrative System in Germany and Occupied Eastern Europe, with Special Regard to Occupied Poland, 1939–1945* (Baltimore: Johns Hopkins University Press, in association with the United States Holocaust Memorial Museum, 2003).

Manoschek, Walter, *"Serbien ist judenfrei": Militärische Besatzungspolitik und Judenvernichtung in Serbien 1941/42* (Munich: R. Oldenbourg, 1995).

Marrus, Michael R., and Paxton, Robert O. *Vichy France and the Jews* (New York: Basic Books, 1981).

Mehl, Stefan, *Das Reichsfinanzministerium und die Verfolgung der deutschen Juden 1933–1943, Berliner Arbeitshefte und Berichte zur Sozialwissenschaftlicher Forschung*, no. 38 (Berlin, 1990).

Melzer, Ralf, *Konflikt und Anpassung: Freimaurerei in der Weimar Republik und im "Dritten Reich"* (Vienna: Bramüller, 1999).

Mendelsohn, Oskar, *The Persecution of the Norwegian Jews in World War II* (Oslo: Norges Hjemmefrontmuseum, 1991).

Metzger, Karl-Heinz et al. (eds.), *Kommunalverwaltung unterm Hakenkreuz: Berlin-Wilmersdorf 1933–1945* (Berlin: Hentrich, 1992).

Meyer, Beate, "Handlungsspielräume regionaler jüdischer Repräsentanten (1941–1945) – Die Reichsvereinigung der Juden in Deutschland und die Deportationen," in *Beiträge zur Geschichte des Nationalsozialismus 20, Die Deportation der Juden aus Deutschland: Pläne – Praxis – Reaktionen 1938–1945* (Göttingen: Wallstein, 2004): 63–83.

Michman, Joseph, "Planning for the Final Solution Against the Background of Developments in Holland in 1941," *Yad Vashem Studies* XVII (1986): 145–80.

Młynarczyk, Jacek A., "Organisation und Durchführung der 'Aktion Reinhard' im Distrikt Radom," in Bogdan Musial (ed.), *"Aktion Reinhardt": Der Völkermord an den Juden im Generalgouvernement 1941–1944* (Osnabrück: Fibre, 2004): 165–95.

Moore, Bob, *Victims and Survivors: The Nazi Persecution of the Jews in the Netherlands 1940–1945* (London: Arnold, 1997).

Musial, Bogdan, *Deutsche Zivilverwaltung und Judenverfolgung im Generalgouvernement: Eine Fallstudie zum Distrikt Lublin 1939–1944* (Wiesbaden: Harrassowitz, 1999).

Mussgnug, Dorothee, *Die Reichsfluchtsteuer* (Berlin: Duncker & Humblot, 1993).

Neliba, Günter, *Der Legalist des Unrechtsstaates: Wilhelm Frick. Eine politische Biographie* (Paderborn: Schönigh, 1992).

Neuberger, Helmut, *Winkelmass und Hakenkreuz: Die Freimaurer und das Dritte Reich* (Munich: Herbig, 2001).

Nicholas, Lynn, *The Rape of Europa: The Fate of Europe's Treasures in the Third Reich and the Second World War* (London: Macmillan, 1994).

Niewyk, Donald L., *Jews in Weimar Germany* (New Brunswick, NJ: Transaction, 2001).

Opfermann, Ulrich Friedrich, "Zigeunerverfolgung, Enteignung, Umverteilung: Das Beispiel der Wittgensteiner Kreisstadt Berleburg," in Alfons Kenkmann and Bernd-A. Rusinek (eds.), *Verfolgung und Verwaltung: Die wirtschaftliche Ausplünderung der Juden und die westfälischen Finanzbehörden* (Münster: Oberfinanzdirektion Münster, 1999): 67–86.

Overy, Richard, *Russia's War: Blood upon the Snow* (New York: TV Books, 1997).

Ozsváth, Zsuzsanna, "Can Words Kill? Anti-Semitic Texts and their Impact on the Hungarian Jewish Catastrophe," in Randolph L. Braham and Attila Pók (eds.), *The Holocaust in Hungary: Fifty Years Later* (Boulder, CO: Rosenthal Institute for Holocaust Studies, Social Science Monographs, 1997): 79–116.

Paounovski, Vladimir, and Ilel, Yosef, *The Jews in Bulgaria between the Holocaust and the Rescue* (Sofia: Adas, 2000).

Pavan, Ilaria, "Indifferenz und Vergessen: Juden in Italien in der Kriegs- und Nachkriegszeit (1938–1970)," in Constantin Goschler and Philipp Ther (eds.), *Raub und Restitution: "Arisierung" und Rückerstattung des jüdischen Eigentums in Europa* (Frankfurt am Main: Fischer Taschenbuch, 2003): 154–68.

Perz, Bertrand, and Sandkühler, Thomas, "Auschwitz und die 'Aktion Reinhard' 1942–1945: Judenmord und Raubpraxis aus neuer Sicht," *Zeitgeschichte* 26. Jg., Heft 5 (Sept./Okt. 1999): 283–316.

Petropoulos, Jonathan, *Art as Politics in the Third Reich* (Chapel Hill: University of North Carolina Press, 1996).

Petropoulos, Jonathan, "The Polycratic Nature of Art Looting: The Dynamic Balance of the Third Reich," in Wolfgang Seibel and Gerald Feldman (eds.), *Networks of Nazi Persecution: Division-of-Labor in the Holocaust* (New York: Berghahn, 2005): 103–17.

Pohl, Dieter, *Von der "Judenpolitik" zum Judenmord: Der Distrikt Lublin des Generalgouvernements 1939–1944* (Frankfurt am Main: Peter Lang, 1993).

Pohl, Dieter, *Nationalsozialistische Judenverfolgung in Ostgalizien 1941–1944* (Munich: Oldenbourg, 1996).

Pohl, Dieter, "Schauplatz Ukraine: Der Massenmord an den Juden im Militärverwaltungsgebiet und im Reichskommissariat 1941–1943," in Norbert Frei, Sybille Steinbacher, and Bernd C. Wagner (eds.), *Ausbeutung, Vernichtung, Öffentlichkeit: Neue Studien zur nationalsozialistischen Lagerpolitik* (Munich: K. G. Saur, 2000): 135–74.

Pohl, Dieter, "Ukrainische Hilfskräfte beim Mord an den Juden," in Gerhard von Paul (ed.), *Die Täter der Shoah: Fanatische Nationalsozialisten oder ganz normale Deutsche?* (Göttingen: Wallstein, 2002): 205–34.

Pohl, Dieter, "Der Raub an den Juden im besetzten Osteuropa 1939–1942," in Constantin Goschler and Philipp Ther (eds.), *Raub und Restitution: "Arisierung" und Rückerstattung des jüdischen Eigentums in Europa* (Frankfurt am Main: Fischer Taschenbuch, 2003): 58–72.

Potthast, Jan Björn, "Antijüdische Massnahmen im Protektorat Böhmen und Mähren und das 'Jüdische Zentralmuseum' in Prag," in Irmtrud Wojak and Peter Hayes (eds.), *"Arisierung" im Nationalsozialismus: Volksgemeinschaft, Raub und Gedächtnis* (Frankfurt am Main: Campus, 2000): 157–201.

Potthast, Jan Björn, *Das jüdische Zentralmuseum der SS in Prag: Gegnerforschung und Völkermord im Nationalsozialismus* (Frankfurt am Main: Campus, 2002).

Presser, Jacob, *The Destruction of the Dutch Jews* (New York: E. P. Dutton, 1969).

Reichelt, Katrin, "Der Anteil von Letten an der Enteignung der Juden Ihres Landes," *Beiträge zur Geschichte des Nationalsozialismus 19, Kooperation und Verbrechen: Formen der "Kollaboration" im östlichen Europa 1939–1945* (Göttingen: Wallstein, 2003): 224–42.

Reschwamm, D., "Die Vertreibung und Vernichtung der Juden im Spiegel der Akten des Finanzamtes Nordhausen," *Geschichte, Erziehung, Politik* 7, 7/8 (1996): 404–13.

Reymes, Nicolas, "Le pillage des bibliothèques apartenant à des juifs pendant l'occupation," *Revue d'Histoire de la Shoah*, no. 168 (Jan. – Avril 2000): 31–56.

Rings, Werner, *Raubgold aus Deutschland: Die "Golddrehscheibe" Schweiz im Zweiten Weltkrieg* (Munich: R. Piper, 1996).

Robinson, Nehemiah, *Spoliation and Remedial Action: The Material Damage Suffered by Jews under Persecution, Reparations, Restitution, and Compensation* (New York: Institute of Jewish Affairs, World Jewish Congress, 1962).

Rosenkötter, Bernhard, *Treuhandpolitik: Die "Haupttreuhandstelle Ost" und der Raub polnischer Vermögen 1939–1945* (Essen: Klartext, 2003).

Rosenkranz, Herbert, *Verfolgung und Selbstbehauptung: Die Juden in Österreich 1938–1945* (Vienna: Herold, 1978).

Roth, Karl Heinz, "Hehler des Holocaust: Degussa und Deutsche Bank," *1999*, 13 (1998): 137–44.

Rozen, Marcu, *The Holocaust under the Antonescu Government: Historical and Statistical Data about Jews in Romania, 1940–44* (Bucharest: Association of Romanian Jews, Victims of the Holocaust, 2004).

Ryan, Donna F., *The Holocaust and the Jews of Marseille: The Enforcement of Anti-Semitic Policies in Vichy France* (Urbana: University of Illinois Press, 1996).

Saerens, Lieven, "Antwerp's Attitude toward the Jews from 1918 to 1940 and its Implications for the Period of Occupation," in Dan Michman (ed.), *Belgium and the Holocaust: Jews, Belgians, Germans* (Jerusalem: Yad Vashem, 1998): 159–94.

Safrian, Hans, "Beschleunigung der Beraubung und Vertreibung: Zur Bedeutung des 'Wiener Modells' für die antijüdische Politik des 'Dritten Reiches' im Jahr 1938," in Constantin Goschler and Jürgen Lillteicher (eds.), *"Arisierung" und Restitution: Die Rückerstattung jüdischen Eigentums in Deutschland und Österreich nach 1945 und 1989* (Göttingen: Wallstein, 2002): 61–89.

Safrian, Hans, *Eichmann und seine Gehilfen* (Frankfurt am Main: Fischer, 1995).

Safrian, Hans, "Expediting Expropriation and Expulsion: The Impact of the 'Vienna Model' on Anti-Jewish Policies in Nazi Germany, 1938," *Holocaust and Genocide Studies*, vol. 14, no. 3 (Winter 2000): 390–414.

Safrian, Hans, and Witek, Hans, *Und keiner war dabei: Dokumente des alltäglichen Antisemitismus in Wien 1938* (Vienna: Picus, 1988).

Scheiger, Brigitte, "Juden in Berlin," in Stefi Jersch-Wenzel und Barbara John (eds.), *Von Einwanderern zu Einheimischen: Hugenotten, Juden, Böhmen, Polen in Berlin* (Berlin: Nicolai, 1990): 153–488.

Scheren, Jos, "Aryanization, Market Vendors, and Peddlers in Amsterdam," *Holocaust and Genocide Studies*, vol. 14, no. 3 (Winter 2000): 415–29.

Schilde, Kurt, *Bürokratie des Todes: Lebensgeschichten jüdischer Opfer des NS-Regimes im Spiegel von Finanzamtsakten* (Berlin: Metropol, 2002).

Schlarp, Karl-Heinz, *Wirtschaft und Besatzung in Serbien, 1941–1944: Ein Beitrag zur Nationalsozialistischen Wirtschaftspolitik in Südosteuropa* (Wiesbaden: Franz Steiner, 1986).

Schmidt, Monika, "'*Arisierungspolitik*' *des Bezirksamtes*," in Karl-Heinz Metzger et al. (eds.), *Kommunalverwaltung unterm Hakenkreuz: Berlin-Wilmersdorf 1933–1945* (Berlin: Hentrich, 1992): 169–228.

Schulze, Hagen, *Weimar Deutschland 1917–1933* (Berlin: Severin and Siedler, 1982).

Schwarz, Angela, "Von den Wohnstiften zu den 'Judenhäusern,'" in Angelika Ebbinghaus and Karsten Linne (eds.), *Kein abgeschlossenes Kapitel: Hamburg im "Dritten Reich"* (Hamburg: Europäische Verlagsanstalt, 1997): 232–47.

Seibel, Wolfgang (ed.), *Holocaust und 'Polykratie' in Westeuropa, 1940–1944: Nationale Berichte* (December, 2001).

Seibel, Wolfgang, "A Market for Mass Crime? Inter-institutional Competition and the Initiation of the Holocaust in France, 1940–42," *International Journal of Organization Theory and Behavior*, vol. 5, nos. 3 and 4 (2002): 219–57.

Shapiro, Paul A., "The Jews of Chisinau (Kishinev): Romanian Reoccupation, Ghettoization, Deportation," in Randolph L. Braham (ed.), *The Destruction of Romanian and Ukrainian Jews During the Antonescu Era* (Boulder, CO: Social Science Monographs, 1997): 135–93.

Shapiro, Paul A., "Romanian Jews, Romanian Antisemitism, Romanian Holocaust," Remarks presented at the Conference on "Minorities, Cultural Heritage, Contemporary Romanian Civilization," co-sponsored by the Romanian Ministry of Foreign Affairs, B'nai B'rith International and the Federation of Jewish Communities in Romania, Bucharest, October 21–22, 2003.

Spector, Shmuel, *The Holocaust of Volhynian Jews, 1941–44* (Jerusalem: Yad Vashem, 1990).

Stallbaumer, L. M., "Big Business and the Persecution of the Jews: The Flick Concern and the 'Aryanisation' of Jewish Property before the War," *Holocaust and Genocide Studies*, vol. 13, no. 1 (Spring 1999): 1–27.

Steck, Anatol, "The Archives of the Jewish Community of Vienna: A Cooperative Microfilming Project to Preserve Holocaust-Relevant Records," in *Stammbaum: The Journal of German-Jewish Genealogical Research*, no. 24 (Winter 2004): 4–9.

Steinberg, Jonathan, "The Third Reich Reflected: German Civil Administration in the Occupied Soviet Union, 1941–4," *English Historical Review*, CX, no. 437 (June 1995): 620–51.

Steinberg, Jonathan, *The Deutsche Bank and its Gold Transactions during the Second World War* (Munich: C. H. Beck, 1999).

Steinberg, Maxime, "Belgien: Polizeiliche und wirtschaftliche Verfolgung," in Wolfgang Seibel (ed.), *"Holocaust und 'Polykratie'" in Westeuropa, 1940–1944: Nationale Berichte* (December, 2001): 194–373.

Steinberg, Maxime, *L'etoile et le fusil: La Question Juive 1940–42* (Brussels: Vie ouvrière, 1983–86), 3 vols.

Steinberg, Maxime, "The Judenpolitik in Belgium within the West European Context: Comparative Observations," in Dan Michman (ed.), *Belgium and the Holocaust: Jews, Belgians, Germans* (Jerusalem: Yad Vashem, 1998): 199–224.

Stengel, Katharina (ed.), *Vor der Vernichtung: Die staatliche Enteignung der Juden im Nationalsozialismus* (Wissenschaftliche Reihe des Fritz Bauer Instituts, Bd. 15) (Frankfurt am Main: Campus, 2007).

Surminski, Arno, *Versicherung unterm Hakenkreuz* (Berlin: Ullstein, 1999).

Tamir, Vicki, *Bulgaria and Her Jews: The History of a Dubious Symbiosis* (New York: Yeshiva University Press, 1979).

Teitelbaum-Hirsch, Viviane, *Comptes d'une mort annoncée* (Brussels: Edition Labor, 1997).

Tönsmeyer, Tatjana, *Das Dritte Reich und die Slowakei, 1939–1945: Politischer Alltag zwischen Kooperation und Eigensinn* (Paderborn: Ferdinand Schöningh, 2003).

Tönsmeyer, Tatjana, "Der Raub des jüdischen Eigentums in Ungarn, Rumänien und der Slowakei," in Constantin Goschler and Philipp Ther (eds.), *Raub und Restitution: "Arisierung" und Rückerstattung des jüdischen Eigentums in Europa* (Frankfurt am Main: Fischer Taschenbuch, 2003): 73–91.

Tonini, Carla, *Operazione Madagascar: La questione ebraica in Polonia, 1918–1968* (Bologna: CLUEB, 1999).

Trunk, Isaiah, *Judenrat: The Jewish Councils in Eastern Europe under Nazi Occupation* (Lincoln: University of Nebraska Press, 1996 (first published 1972).

Verhoeyen, Etienne, *La Belgique Occupée: de l'an 40 a la libération* (Brussels: De Boeck Université, 1940).

Verse-Herrmann, A., *Die Arisierungen in der Land und Forstwirtschaft 1938–42* (Stuttgart: Steiner, 1997).

Weinert, Rainer, *"Die Sauberkeit der Verwaltung im Kriege": Der Rechnungshof des Deutschen Reiches 1938–1946* (Opladen: Westdeutscher Verlag, 1993).

Weissberg-Bob Nea and Irmer, Thomas, *Heinrich Richard Brinn (1874–1944) Fabrikant-Kunstsammler-Frontkämpfer: Dokumentation einer "Arisierung"* (Berlin: Lichtig, 2002).

Wetzel, Julianne, "Frankreich und Belgien," in Wolfgang Benz (ed.), *Dimension des Völkermords: Die Zahl der jüdischen Opfer des Nationalsozialismus* (Munich: Oldenbourg, 1991).

Wilhelm, Hans-Heinrich, *Die Einsatzgruppe A der Sicherheitspolizei und des SD 1941/42* (Frankfurt am Main: Peter Lang, 1996).

Willems, Susanne, *Der entsiedelte Jude: Albert Speers Wohnungsmarktpolitik für den Berliner Hauptstadtbau* (Berlin: Hentrich, 2000).

Wipf, Hans Ulrich, *Georg Fischer AG 1930–1945: Ein Schweizer Industrieunternehmen im Spannungsfeld Europas* (Zürich: Chronos, 2001).

Witte, Peter, "Two Decisions Concerning the 'Final Solution of the Jewish Question': Deportations to Łódź and Mass Murder in Chelmno," in *Holocaust and Genocide Studies*, vol. 9, no. 3 (Winter 1995); 318–45.

Wolf, Herbert, "Zur Kontrolle und Enteignung jüdischen Vermögens in der NS-Zeit: Das Schicksal des Rohtabakhändlers Arthur Spanier," *Bankhistorisches Archiv*, Jg. 16, Heft 1 (1990): 55–62.

Yahil, Leni, *The Rescue of Danish Jewry: Test of a Democracy* (Philadelphia: Jewish Publication Society of America, 1983).

Ziegler, Dieter, "Die Verdrängung der Juden aus der Dresdner Bank 1933–1938," *Vierteljahrshefte für Zeitgeschichte* Jg. 47, Heft 2 (1999): 187–216.

Zuccotti, Susan, *Under His Very Windows: The Vatican and the Holocaust in Italy* (New Haven: Yale University Press, 2000).

Zweig, Ronald W., *German Reparations and the Jewish World: A History of the Claims Conference* (Boulder: Westview Press, 1987; republished London: Frank Cass, 2001).

Zweig, Ronald W., *The Gold Train: The Destruction of the Jews and the Looting of Hungary* (New York: Morrow, 2002).

Zweig, Ronald W., "Der ungarische Goldzug oder Der Mythos vom jüdischen Reichtum," in Constantin Goschler and Philipp Ther (eds.), *Raub und Restitution: "Arisierung" und Rückerstattung des jüdischen Eigentums in Europa* (Frankfurt am Main: Fischer Taschenbuch, 2003): 169–83.